Roger Ebert's
Book of
Film

ROGER EBERT'S
BOOK OF
FILM

Edited by

ROGER EBERT

W · W · NORTON & COMPANY · NEW YORK · LONDON

First Edition

The text of this book is composed in 11.5/13 Adobe Perpetua
with the display set in Monotype Felix Titling and typositor Nadall from Solotype.
Composition and Manufacturing by The Haddon Craftsmen, Inc.

Library of Congress Cataloging-in-Publication Data
Roger Ebert's book of film / edited by Roger Ebert.
p. cm.
ISBN 0-393-04000-3
1. Motion pictures.
PN1994.R5625 1996
791.43—dc20   96-14271
                                          CIP

W. W. Norton & Company, Inc., 500 Fifth Avenue, New York, N.Y. 10110
http://web.wwnorton.com

W. W. Norton & Company Ltd., 10 Coptic Street, London WC1A 1PU

1 2 3 4 5 6 7 8 9 0

For Aunt Martha,
Who took me to the movies

CONTENTS

The Business

SEX AND SCANDAL

EARLY DAYS

GENRES

DIRECTORS

WRITERS

CRITICS

TECHNIQUE

HOLLYWOOD

Introduction

Roger Ebert

The way to criticize a movie, Godard said, is to make one yourself. If he is right, then the way to assemble a book of the movies would be to fill it with films, a different one on every page—sideways for wide-screen. I'd like to have a book like that, but I wouldn't want to give up reading and writing about movies, because the best of such writing is not about the movies anyway: It's about the author.

Movies strike us in intensely personal ways. Good ones get inside our skins. I received a letter the other day from a man who said he broke down during the last ten minutes of *Dead Man Walking.* There aren't many movies that can inspire such a powerful reaction, but anyone who loves movies can remember once or twice when that has happened. For me, it was with *Do the Right Thing.* And, many years before that, the first time I saw Kurosawa's *Ikiru.*

This anthology begins with the first-person memories of moviegoers. Terry McMillan, as a young girl in Michigan, wondered why Dorothy would even consider leaving the Emerald City to go back to Kansas, which, to her, looked all too much like Michigan. Pauline Kael famously told us, "I lost it at the movies." Walker Percy, in my favorite single passage about the movies, wrote: "Other people, so I have read, treasure memorable moments in their lives: the time one climbed the Parthenon at sunrise, the summer night one met a lonely girl in Central Park and achieved with her a sweet and natural relationship, as they say in books. I too once met a girl in Central Park, but it is not much to remember. What I remember is the time John Wayne killed three men with a carbine as he was falling to the dusty street in *Stagecoach,* and the time the kitten found Orson Welles in the doorway in *The Third Man.*"

I remember the kitten in the doorway too. It was a rainy day in Paris in 1962, and I was visiting Europe for the first time. A little cinema on the Left Bank was showing *The Third Man,* and I went, into the humid cave of Gauloise smoke and perspiration, and saw the movie for the first time. When Welles made his entrance, I was lost to the movies. In my childhood and adolescence I'd liked the movies, to be sure, but they were like other forms of entertainment, like books or the radio, and I didn't view them as an art form—maybe because I wasn't seeing very good ones. In 1958, in high school, I saw *Citizen Kane* for the first time and understood two things: that a movie could suggest the truth about a human life and that movies were the expression of the vision of those who made them. I went back again and again to the cozy little Art Theater in Champaign–Urbana, Illinois, to see Bergman and Fellini, Cassavetes, and the Angry Young Men. Those experiences gave me a background in good movies, and then, when the kitten rubbed against the big black shoe, I understood the whole story. For me, no other art form touches life the way the movies do.

Gathering the pieces for this book took place over a couple of years. I determined at the outset not to make any rules, not to try for some sort of "survey" suitable for a classroom. I was simply looking for good writing about the movies. With five or six exceptions, every selection comes from a book I found on my own shelves. I put in what I enjoyed and admired. I'm particularly pleased with some of the more obscure choices. When Joe Bonomo describes a stunt going horribly wrong, you can see an injured man hanging from a rope ladder, swinging to his doom. I am amazed that Maxim Gorky, Leo Tolstoy, and Vachel Lindsay knew so much, so early, about what the movies really were. Donald Ritchie's piece about Setsuko Hara expresses how we feel that we possess movie stars, who are not allowed to break free from our love. Ben Hecht is wonderfully brazen as he explains to Capone's henchmen why *Scarface* is not about Scarface.

I am grateful to Gerald Howard, my editor at Norton, for guidance and inspiration. And to Jonathan Rosenbaum, film critic of the *Chicago Reader,* for several suggestions, including Delmore Schwartz and Maxim Gorky. Many thanks to my assistant, Carol Iwata, for help in assembling the materials. And great love to my wife, Chaz, who likes the movies as much as I do—which is just as well, considering how many we see.

GOING TO THE MOVIES

JAMES AGEE

James Agee was a generalist whose writings often seemed to circle back to the movies. He was a film critic for Time *and the* Nation, *he wrote screenplays (*The African Queen *and four others), he wrote essays for* Life *(John Huston, silent comedians), and not surprisingly his only novel,* A Death in the Family, *opens with a boy and his father going to the movies.*

from *A Death in the Family*

At supper that night, as many times before, his father said, "Well, spose we go to the picture show."

"Oh, Jay!" his mother said. "That horrid little man!"

"What's wrong with him?" his father asked, not because he didn't know what she would say; but so she would say it.

"He's so *nasty*!" she said, as she always did. "So *vulgar*! With his nasty little cane; hooking up skirts and things, and that nasty little walk!"

His father laughed, as he always did, and Rufus felt that it had become rather an empty joke; but as always the laughter also cheered him; he felt that the laughter enclosed him with his father.

They walked downtown in the light of mother-of-pearl, to the Majestic, and found their way to seats by the light of the screen, in the exhilarating smell of stale tobacco, rank sweat, perfume and dirty drawers, while the piano played fast music and galloping horses raised a grandiose flag of dust. And there was William S. Hart with both guns blazing and his long, horse face and his long, hard lip, and the great country rode away behind him as wide as the world. Then he made a bashful face at a girl and his horse raised its upper lip and everybody laughed, and then the screen was filled with a city and with the sidewalk of a side street of a city, a long line of palms and there was Charlie; everyone laughed the minute they saw him squattily walking with his toes out and his knees wide apart, as if he were chafed; Rufus' father laughed, and Rufus laughed too. This time Charlie stole a whole bag of eggs and when a cop came along he hid them in the seat of his pants. Then he caught sight of a pretty woman and he began to squat and twirl his cane and make silly faces. She tossed her head and walked away with her chin up high and her dark mouth as small as she could make it and he followed her very busily, doing all sorts of things with his cane that made everybody laugh, but she paid no attention. Finally she stopped at a corner to wait for a streetcar, turning her back to him, and pretending he wasn't even there, and after trying to get her attention for a while, and not succeeding, he looked out at the audience, shrugged his shoulders, and acted as if *she* wasn't there. But after tapping his foot for a little, pretending he didn't care, he became interested again, and with a charming smile, tipped his derby; but she only stiffened, and tossed her head again, and everybody laughed. Then he walked back and forth behind her, looking at her and squatting a little while he walked very quietly, and everybody laughed again; then he flicked hold of the straight end of his cane and, with the crooked end, hooked up her skirt to the knee, in exactly the way that disgusted Mama, looking very eagerly at her legs, and everybody laughed very loudly; but she pretended she had not noticed. Then he twirled his cane and suddenly squatted, bending the cane and hitching up his pants, and again hooked up her skirt so that you could see the panties she wore, ruffled almost like the edges of curtains, and everybody whooped with laughter, and she suddenly turned in rage and gave him a shove in the chest, and he sat down straight-legged, hard enough to hurt, and everybody whooped again; and she walked haughtily away up the street, forgetting about the streetcar, "mad as a hornet!" as his father exclaimed in delight; and there was Charlie, flat on his bottom on the sidewalk, and the way he looked, kind of sickly and disgusted, you could see that he suddenly remembered those eggs, and suddenly you remembered them too. The way his face looked, with the lip wrinkled off the teeth and the sickly little smile, it made you feel just the way those broken eggs must feel against your seat, as queer and awful as that time in the white pekay suit, when it ran down out of the pants-legs and showed all over your stockings and you had to walk home that way with people looking; and Rufus' father nearly tore his head off laughing and so did everybody else, and Rufus was sorry for Charlie, having been so recently in a similar predicament, but the contagion of laughter was too much for him, and he laughed too. And then it was even funnier when Charlie very carefully got himself up from the sidewalk, with that sickly look even worse on his face, and put his cane under one arm, and began to pick at his pants, front and back, very carefully, with his little fingers crooked, as if it were too dirty to touch, picking the sticky cloth away from his skin. Then he reached behind him and took out the wet bag of broken eggs and opened it and peered in; and took out a broken egg and pulled the shell disgustedly apart, letting the elastic yolk slump from one half shell into the other, and dropped it, shuddering. Then he peered in again and fished out a whole egg, all slimy with broken yolk, and polished it off carefully on his sleeve, and looked at it, and wrapped it in his dirty handkerchief, and put it carefully into the vest pocket of his little coat. Then he whipped out his cane from under his armpit and took command of it again, and with a final look at everybody, still sickly but at the same time cheerful, shrugged his shoulders and turned his back and scraped backward with his big shoes at the broken shells and the slimy bag, just like a dog, and looked back at the mess (everybody laughed again at that) and started to walk away, bending his cane deep with every shuffle, and squatting deeper, with his knees wider apart, than ever before, constantly picking at the seat of his pants with his left hand, and shaking one foot, then the other, and once gouging deep into his seat and then pausing and shaking his whole body, like a wet dog, and then walking on; while the screen shut over his small image a sudden circle of darkness: then the player-piano changed its tune, and the ads came in motionless color. They sat on into the William S. Hart feature to make sure why he had killed the man with the fancy vest—it was as they had expected by her frightened, pleased face after the killing; he had insulted a girl and cheated her father as well—and Rufus' father said, "Well, reckon this is where we came in," but they watched him kill the man all over again; then they walked out.

It was full dark now, but still early; Gay Street was full of absorbed faces; many of the store windows were still alight. Plaster people, in ennobled postures, stiffly wore untouchably new clothes; there was even a little boy, with short, straight pants, bare knees and high socks, obviously a sissy: but he wore a cap, all the same, not a hat like a baby. Rufus' whole insides lifted and sank as he looked at the cap and he looked up at his father; but his father did not notice; his face was wrapped in good humor, the memory of Charlie. Remembering his rebuff of a year ago, even though it had been his mother, Rufus was afraid to speak of it. His father wouldn't mind, but she wouldn't want him to have a cap, yet. If he asked his father now, his father would say no, Charlie Chaplin was enough.

DELMORE SCHWARTZ

The narrator imagines himself inside a movie theater, watching a film of his parents' courtship and being moved to tears and alarm by his knowledge of the way their story turns out. He sees them as in a silent film; they talk, but in no more words than could be car-

ried on title cards, and the individual images—a young man's call on his sweetheart's family, a visit to Coney Island—are familiar from countless films. Yet these are his parents, and so he cannot enjoy the film in the simple way urged by those seated around him. This story by Delmore Schwartz (1913–1966) appeared as the first item of fiction in the first issue of Partisan Review *in 1937, and here is James Atlas, writing about the great impact it had at the time: "But what can the audience do about it? The past revived must obey its own unfolding, true to the law of mistakes. The reel must run its course; it cannot be cut; it cannot be edited."*

"In Dreams Begin Responsibilities"

I

I think it is the year 1909. I feel as if I were in a motion picture theatre, the long arm of light crossing the darkness and spinning, my eyes fixed on the screen. This is a silent picture as if an old Biograph one, in which the actors are dressed in ridiculously old-fashioned clothes, and one flash succeeds another with sudden jumps. The actors too seem to jump about and walk too fast. The shots themselves are full of dots and rays, as if it were raining when the picture was photographed. The light is bad.

It is Sunday afternoon, June 12th, 1909, and my father is walking down the quiet streets of Brooklyn on his way to visit my mother. His clothes are newly pressed and his tie is too tight in his high collar. He jingles the coins in his pockets, thinking of the witty things he will say. I feel as if I had by now relaxed entirely in the soft darkness of the theatre; the organist peals out the obvious and approximate emotions on which the audience rocks unknowingly. I am anonymous, and I have forgotten myself. It is always so when one goes to the movies, it is, as they say, a drug.

My father walks from street to street of trees, lawns and houses, once in a while coming to an avenue on which a street-car skates and gnaws, slowly progressing. The conductor, who has a handle-bar mustache, helps a young lady wearing a hat like a bowl with feathers on to the car. She lifts her long skirts slightly as she mounts the steps. He leisurely makes change and rings his bell. It is obviously Sunday, for everyone is wearing Sunday clothes, and the street-car's noises emphasize the quiet of the holiday. Is not Brooklyn the City of Churches? The shops are closed and their shades drawn, but for an occasional stationery store or drug-store with great green balls in the window.

My father has chosen to take this long walk because he likes to walk and think. He thinks about himself in the future and so arrives at the place he is to visit in a state of mild exaltation. He pays no attention to the houses he is passing, in which the Sunday dinner is being eaten, nor to the many trees which patrol each street, now coming to their full leafage and the time when they will room the whole street in cool shadow. An occasional carriage passes, the horse's hooves falling like stones in the quiet afternoon, and once in a while an automobile, looking like an enormous upholstered sofa, puffs and passes.

My father thinks of my mother, of how nice it will be to introduce her to his family. But he is not yet sure that he wants to marry her, and once in a while he becomes panicky about the bond already established. He reassures himself by thinking of the big men he admires who are married: William Randolph Hearst, and William Howard Taft, who has just become President of the United States.

My father arrives at my mother's house. He has come too early and so is suddenly embarrassed. My aunt, my mother's sister, answers the loud bell with her napkin in her hand, for the family is still at dinner. As my father enters, my grandfather rises from the table and shakes hands with him. My mother has run upstairs to tidy herself. My grandmother asks my father if he has had dinner, and tells him that Rose will be downstairs soon. My grandfather opens the conversation by remarking on the mild June weather. My father sits uncomfortably near the table, holding his hat in his hand. My grandmother tells my aunt to take my father's hat. My uncle, twelve years old, runs into the house, his hair tousled. He shouts a greeting to my father, who has often given him a nickel, and then runs upstairs. It is evident that the respect in which my father is held in this household is tempered by a good deal of mirth. He is impressive, yet he is very awkward.

II

Finally my mother comes downstairs, all dressed up, and my father being engaged in conversation with my grandfather becomes uneasy, not knowing whether to greet my mother or continue the conversation. He gets up from the chair clumsily and says "hello" gruffly. My grandfather watches, examining their congruence, such as it is, with a critical eye, and meanwhile rubbing his bearded cheek roughly, as he always does when he reflects. He is worried; he is afraid that my father will not make a good husband for his oldest daughter. At this point something happens to the film, just as my father is saying something funny to my mother; I am awakened to myself and my unhappiness just as my interest was rising. The audience begins to clap impatiently. Then the trouble is cared for but the film has been returned to a portion just shown, and once more I see my grandfather rubbing his bearded cheek and pondering my father's character. It is difficult to get back into the picture once more and forget myself, but as my mother giggles at my father's words, the darkness drowns me.

My father and mother depart from the house, my father shaking hands with my mother once more, out of some unknown uneasiness. I stir uneasily also, slouched in the hard chair of the theatre. Where is the older uncle, my mother's older brother? He is studying in his bedroom upstairs, studying for his final examination at the College of the City of New York, having been dead of rapid pneumonia for the last twenty-one years. My mother and father walk down the same quiet streets once more. My mother is holding my father's arm and telling him of the novel which she has been reading; and my father utters judgments of the characters as the plot is made clear to him. This is a habit which he very much enjoys, for he feels the utmost superiority and confidence when he approves and condemns the behavior of other people. At times he feels moved to utter a brief "Ugh"—whenever the story becomes what he would call sugary. This tribute is paid to his manliness. My mother feels satisfied by the interest which she has awakened; she is showing my father how intelligent she is, and how interesting.

They reach the avenue, and the street-car leisurely arrives. They are going to Coney Island this afternoon, although my mother considers that such pleasures are inferior. She has made up her mind to indulge only in a walk on the boardwalk and a pleasant dinner, avoiding the riotous amusements as being beneath the dignity of so dignified a couple.

My father tells my mother how much money he has made in the past week, exaggerating an amount which need not have been exaggerated. But my father has always felt that actualities somehow fall short. Suddenly I begin to weep. The determined old lady who sits next to me in the theatre is annoyed and looks at me with an angry face, and being intimidated, I stop. I drag out my handkerchief and dry my face, licking the drop which has fallen near my lips. Meanwhile I have missed something, for here are my mother and father alighting at the last stop, Coney Island.

III

They walk toward the boardwalk, and my father commands my mother to inhale the pungent air from the sea. They both breathe in deeply, both of them laughing as they do so. They have in common a great interest in health, although my father is strong and husky, my mother frail. Their minds are full of theories of what is good to eat and not good to eat, and sometimes they engage in heated discussions of the subject, the whole matter ending in my father's announcement, made with a scornful bluster, that you have to die sooner or later anyway. On the boardwalk's flagpole, the American flag is pulsing in an intermittent wind from the sea.

My father and mother go to the rail of the boardwalk and look down on the beach where a good many bathers are casually walking about. A few are in the surf. A peanut whistle pierces the air with its pleasant and active whine, and my father goes to buy peanuts. My mother remains at the rail and stares at the ocean. The ocean seems merry to her; it pointedly sparkles and again and again the pony waves are released. She notices the children digging in the wet sand, and the bathing costumes of the girls who are her own age. My father returns with the peanuts. Overhead the sun's lightning strikes and strikes, but neither of them are at all aware of it. The boardwalk is full of people dressed in their Sunday clothes and idly strolling. The tide does not reach as far as the boardwalk, and the strollers would feel no danger if it did. My mother and father lean on the rail of the boardwalk and absently stare at the ocean. The ocean is becoming rough; the waves come in slowly, tugging strength from far back. The moment before they somersault, the moment when they arch their backs so beautifully, showing green and white veins amid the black, that moment is intolerable. They finally crack, dashing fiercely upon the sand, actually driving, full force downward, against the sand, bouncing upward and forward, and at last petering out into a small stream which races up the beach and then is recalled. My parents gaze absentmindedly at the ocean, scarcely interested in its harshness. The sun overhead does not disturb them. But I stare at the terrible sun which breaks up sight, and the fatal, merciless, passionate ocean, I forget my parents. I stare fascinated and finally, shocked by the indifference of my father and mother, I burst out weeping once more. The old lady next to me pats me on the shoulder and says: "There, there, all of this is only a movie, young man, only a movie," but I look up once more at the terrifying sun and the terrifying ocean, and being unable to control my tears, I get up and go to the men's room, stumbling over the feet of the other people seated in my row.

IV

When I return, feeling as if I had awakened in the morning sick for lack of sleep, several hours have apparently passed and my parents are riding on the merry-go-round. My father is on a black horse, my mother on a white one, and they seem to be making an eternal circuit for the single purpose of snatching the nickel rings which are attached to the arm of one of the posts. A hand-organ is playing; it is one with the ceaseless circling of the merry-go-round.

For a moment it seems that they will never get off the merry-go-round because it will never stop. I feel like one who looks down on the avenue from the 50th story of a building. But at length they do get off; even the music of the hand-organ has ceased for a moment. My father has acquired ten rings, my mother only two, although it was my mother who really wanted them.

They walk on along the boardwalk as the afternoon descends by imperceptible degrees into the incredible violet of dusk. Everything fades into a relaxed glow, even the ceaseless murmuring from the beach, and the revolutions of the merry-go-round. They look for a place to have dinner. My father suggests the best one on the boardwalk and my mother demurs, in accordance with her principles.

However, they do go to the best place, asking for a table near the window, so that they can look out on the boardwalk and the mobile ocean. My father feels omnipotent as he places a quarter in the waiter's hand as he asks for a table. The place is crowded and here too there is music, this time from a kind of string trio. My father orders dinner with a fine confidence.

As the dinner is eaten, my father tells of his plans for the future, and my mother shows with expressive face how interested she is, and how impressed. My father becomes exultant. He is lifted up by the waltz that is being played, and his own future begins to intoxicate him. My father tells my mother that he is going to expand his business, for there is a great deal of money to be made. He wants to settle down. After all, he is twenty-nine, he has lived by himself since he was thirteen, he is making more and more money, and he is envious of his married friends when he visits them in the cozy security of their homes, surrounded, it seems, by the calm domestic pleasures, and by delightful children, and then, as the waltz reaches the moment when all the dancers swing madly, then, then with awful daring, then he asks my mother to marry him, although awkwardly enough and puzzled, even in his excitement, at how he had arrived at the proposal, and she, to make the whole business worse, begins to cry, and my father looks nervously about, not knowing at all what to do now, and my mother says: "It's all I've wanted from the moment I saw you," sobbing, and he finds all of this very difficult, scarcely to his taste, scarcely as he had thought it would be, on his long walks over Brooklyn Bridge in the revery of a fine cigar, and it was then that I stood up in the theatre and shouted: "Don't do it. It's not too late to change your minds, both of you. Nothing good will come of it, only remorse, hatred, scandal, and two children whose characters are monstrous." The whole audience turned to look at me, annoyed, the usher came hurrying down the aisle flashing his searchlight, and the old lady next to me tugged me down into my seat, saying: "Be quiet. You'll be put out, and you paid thirty-five cents to come in." And so I shut my eyes because I could not bear to see what was happening. I sat there quietly.

V

But after awhile I begin to take brief glimpses, and at length I watch again with thirsty interest, like a child who wants to maintain his sulk although offered the bribe of candy. My parents are now having their picture taken in a photographer's booth along the boardwalk. The place is shadowed in the mauve light which is apparently necessary. The camera is set to the side on its tripod and looks like a Martian man. The photographer is instructing my parents in how to pose. My father has his arm over my mother's shoulder, and both of them smile emphatically. The photographer brings my mother a bouquet of flowers to hold in her hand but she holds it at the wrong angle. Then the photographer covers himself with the black cloth which drapes the camera and all that one sees of him is one protruding arm and his hand which clutches the rubber ball which he will squeeze when the picture is finally taken. But he is not satisfied with their appearance. He feels with certainty that somehow there is something wrong in their pose. Again and again he issues from his hidden place with new directions. Each suggestion merely makes matters worse. My father is becoming impatient. They try a seated pose. The photographer explains that he has pride, he is not interested in all of this for the money, he wants to make beautiful pictures. My father says: "Hurry up, will you? We haven't got all night." But the photographer only scurries about apologetically, and issues new directions. The photographer charms me. I approve of him with all my heart, for I know just how he feels, and as he criticizes each revised pose according to some unknown idea of rightness, I become quite hopeful. But then my father says angrily: "Come on, you've had enough time, we're not going to wait any longer." And the photographer, sighing unhappily, goes back under his black covering, holds out his hand, says: "One, two, three, Now!", and the picture is taken, with my father's smile turned to a grimace and my mother's bright and false. It takes a few minutes for the picture to be developed and as my parents sit in the curious light they become quite depressed.

VI

They have passed a fortune-teller's booth, and my mother wishes to go in, but my father does not. They begin to argue about it. My mother becomes stubborn, my father once more impatient, and then they begin to quarrel, and what my father would like to do is walk off and leave my mother there, but he knows that that would never do. My mother refuses to budge. She is near to tears, but she feels an uncontrollable desire to hear what the palm-reader will say. My father consents angrily, and they both go into a booth which is in a way like the photographer's, since it is draped in black cloth and its light is shadowed. The place is too warm, and my father keeps saying this is all nonsense, pointing to the crystal ball on the table. The fortune-teller, a fat, short woman, garbed in what is supposed to be Oriental robes, comes into the room from the back and greets them, speaking with an accent. But suddenly my father feels that the whole thing is intolerable; he tugs at my mother's arm, but my mother refuses to budge. And then, in terrible anger, my father lets go of my mother's arm and strides out, leaving my mother stunned. She moves to go after my father, but the fortune-teller holds her arm tightly and begs her not to do so, and I in my seat am shocked more than can ever be said, for I feel as if I were walking a tight-rope a hundred feet over a circus-audience and suddenly the rope is showing signs of breaking, and I get up from my seat and begin to shout once more the first words I can think of to communicate my terrible fear and once more the usher comes hurrying down the aisle flashing his searchlight, and the old lady pleads with me, and the shocked audience has turned to stare at me, and I keep shouting: "What are they doing? Don't they know what they are doing? Why doesn't my mother go after my father? If she does not do that, what will she do? Doesn't my father know what he is doing?"—But the usher has seized my arm and is dragging me away, and as he does so, he says: "What are you doing? Don't you know that you can't do whatever you want to do? Why should a young man like you, with your whole life before you, get hysterical like this? Why don't you *think* of what you're doing? You can't act like this even if other people aren't around! You will be sorry if you do not do what you should do, you can't carry on like this, it is not right, you will find that out soon enough, everything you do matters too much," and he said that dragging me through the lobby of the theatre into the cold light, and I woke up into the bleak winter morning of my 21st birthday, the windowsill shining with its lip of snow, and the morning already begun.

R. K. NARAYAN

R. K. Narayan (1906–), who was one of Graham Greene's favorite novelists, has never received the popularity he deserves. He writes about the daily lives of small shopkeepers, professionals, educators, and civil servants in an India where circumspection is a way of life. Here is an ordinary enough scene, about two friends going to the movies, that suggests not only why they are going but what they are escaping.

from *The Bachelor of Arts*

They walked to the cinema. Chandran stopped at a shop to buy some betel leaves and a packet of cigarettes. Attending a night show was not an ordinary affair. Chandran was none of your business-like automatons who go to the cinema, sit there, and return home. It was an æsthetic experience to be approached with due preparation. You must chew the betel leaves and nut, chew gently, until the heart was stimulated and threw out delicate beads of perspiration and caused a fine tingling sensation behind the ears; on top of that you must light a cigarette, inhale the fumes, and with the night breeze blowing on your perspiring forehead, go to the cinema, smoke more cigarettes there, see the picture, and from there go to an hotel nearby for hot coffee at midnight, take some more betel leaves and cigarettes, and go home and sleep. This was the ideal way to set about a night show. Chandran squeezed the maximum æsthetic delight out of the experience, and Ramu's company was most important to him. It was his presence that gave a sense of completion to things. He too smoked, chewed, drank coffee, laughed (he was the greatest laugher in the world), admired Chandran, ragged him, quarrelled with him, breathed delicious scandal over the names of his professors and friends and unknown people.

The show seemed to have already started, because there was no crowd outside the Select Picture House. It was the only theatre that the town possessed, a long hall roofed with corrugated iron sheets. At the small ticket-window Chandran inquired, "Has the show begun?"

"Yes, just," said the ticket man, giving the stock reply.

You might be three-quarters of an hour late, yet the man at the ticket window would always say, "Yes, just."

"Hurry up, Ramu," Chandran cried as Ramu slackened his pace to admire a giant poster in the narrow passage leading to the four-annas entrance.

The hall was dark; the ticket collector at the entrance took their tickets and held apart the curtains. Ramu and Chandran looked in, seeking by the glare of the picture on the screen for vacant seats. There were two seats at the farthest end. They pushed their way across the knees of the people already seated. "Head down!" somebody shouted from a back seat, as two heads obstructed the screen. Ramu and Chandran stooped into their seats.

It was the last five minutes of a comic in which Jas Jim was featured. That fat genius, wearing a ridiculous cap, was just struggling out of a paint barrel.

Chandran clicked his tongue in despair: "What a pity. I didn't know there was a Jas two-reeler with the picture. We ought to have come earlier."

Ramu sat rapt. He exploded with laughter. "What a genius he is!" Chandran murmured as Jas got on his feet, wearing the barrel around his waist like a kilt. He walked away from Chandran, but turned once to throw a wink at the spectators, and, taking a step back, stumbled and fell, and rolled off, and the picture ended. A central light was switched on. Chandran and Ramu raised themselves in their seats, craned their necks, and surveyed the hall.

The light went out again, the projector whirred. Scores of voices read aloud in a chorus, "Godfrey T. Memel presents Vivian Troilet and Georgia Lomb in *Lightguns of Lauro . . .*" and then came much unwanted information about the people who wrote the story, adapted it, designed the dresses, cut the film to its proper length, and so on. Then the lyrical opening: "Nestling in the heart of the Mid-West, Lauro city owed its tranquillity to the eagle-eyed sheriff———"; then a scene showing a country girl (Vivian Troilet) wearing a check skirt, going up a country lane. Thus started, though with a deceptive quietness, it moved at a breathless pace, supplying love, valour, villainy, intrigue, and battle in enormous quantities for a whole hour. The notice "Interval" on the screen, and the lights going up, brought Chandran and Ramu down to the ordinary plane. The air was thick with tobacco smoke. Ramu yawned, stood up, and gazed at the people occupying the more expensive seats behind them. "Chandar, Brown is here with some girl in the First Class."

"May be his wife," Chandran commented without turning.

"It is not his wife."

"Must be some other girl, then. The white fellows are born to enjoy life. Our people really don't know how to live. If a person is seen with a girl by his side, a hundred eyes stare at him and a hundred tongues comment, whereas no European ever goes out without taking a girl with him."

"This is a wretched country," Ramu said with feeling.

At this point Chandran had a fit of politeness. He pulled Ramu down, saying that it was very bad manners to stand up and stare at the people in the back seats.

Lights out again. Some slide advertisements, each lasting a second.

"Good fellow, he gets through these inflictions quickly," said Chandran.

"For each advertisement he gets twenty rupees a month."

"No, it is only fifteen."

"But somebody said that it was twenty."

"It is fifteen rupees. You can take it from me," Chandran said.

"Even then, what a fraud! Not one stays long enough. I hardly take in the full name of that baby's nourishing food, when they tell me what I ought to smoke. Idiots. I hate advertisements."

The advertisements ended and the story started again from where it had been left off. The hero smelt the ambush ten yards ahead. He took a short cut, climbed a rock, and scared the ruffians from behind. And so on and on it went, through fire and water, and in the end the good man Lomb always came out triumphant;

he was an upright man, a courageous man, a handsome man, and a strong man, and he had to win in the end. Who could not foresee it? And yet every day at every show the happy end was awaited with breathless suspense. Even the old sheriff (all along opposed to the union of Vivian with Georgie) was suddenly transformed, and with tears in his eyes he placed her hands on his. There was a happy moment before the end, when the lovers' heads were shown on an immense scale, their lips welded in a kiss. Good-night.

Lights on. People poured out of the exits, sleepy, yawning, rubbing their smarting eyes. This was the worst part of the evening, this trudge back home, all the way from the Select Picture House to Lawley Extension. Two or three cars sounded their horns and started from the theatre.

"Lucky rascals. They will be in their beds in five minutes. When I start earning I shall buy a car first of all. Nothing like it. You can just see the picture and go straight to bed."

"Coffee?" Chandran asked, when they passed a brightly lit coffee hotel.

"I don't much care."

"Nor do I."

They walked in silence for the most part, occasionally exchanging some very dull, languid jokes.

As soon as his house was reached, Ramu muttered, "Good-night. See you tomorrow," and slipped through his gate.

Chandran walked on alone, opened the gate silently, woke up his younger brother sleeping in the hall, had the hall door opened, and fumbled his way to his room. He removed his coat in the dark, flung it on a chair, kicked a roll of bedding on the floor, and dropped down on it and closed his eyes even before the bed had spread out.

TERRY McMILLAN

This memoir is a reminder of how intensely children experience films. Most movies probably slide right past, but when one really touches a child, it becomes part of its life and interacts with the other parts. McMillan interweaves her daily existence in a small Michigan town with Dorothy's adventures in Oz, finding that lessons can be applied in both directions. Is there a hint of the story line of Waiting to Exhale *in her observation that Dorothy should have chosen the Emerald City over Kansas? "She could make new city friends and get a hobby and a boyfriend and free rent and never have to do chores. . . ."*

"The Wizard of Oz"

I grew up in a small industrial town in the thumb of Michigan: Port Huron. We had barely gotten used to the idea of color TV. I can guess how old I was when I first saw *The Wizard of Oz* on TV because I remember the house we lived in when I was still in elementary school. It was a huge, drafty house that had a fireplace we never once lit. We lived on two acres of land, and at the edge of the backyard was the woods, which I always thought of as a forest. We had weeping willow trees, plum and pear trees, and blackberry bushes. We could not see into our neighbors' homes. Railroad tracks were part of our front yard, and the house shook when a train passed—twice, sometimes three times a day. You couldn't hear the TV at all when it zoomed by, and I was often afraid that if it ever flew off the tracks, it would land on the sun porch, where we all watched TV. I often left the room during this time, but my younger sisters and brother thought I was just scared. I think I was in the third grade around this time.

It was a raggedy house which really should've been condemned, but we fixed it up and kept it clean. We had our German shepherd, Prince, who slept under the rickety steps to the side porch that were on the verge of collapsing but never did. I remember performing a ritual whenever *Oz* was coming on. I either baked cookies or cinnamon rolls or popped popcorn while all five of us waited for Dorothy to spin from black and white on that dreary farm in Kansas to the luminous land of color of Oz.

My house was chaotic, especially with four sisters and brothers and a mother who worked at a factory, and if I'm remembering correctly, my father was there for the first few years of the *Oz* (until he got tuberculosis and had to live in a sanitarium for a year). I do recall the noise and the fighting of my parents (not to mention my other relatives and neighbors). Violence was plentiful, and I wanted to go wherever Dorothy was going where she would not find trouble. To put it bluntly, I wanted to escape because I needed an escape.

I didn't know any happy people. Everyone I knew was either angry or not satisfied. The only time they seemed to laugh was when they were drunk, and even that was short-lived. Most of the grown-ups I was in contact with lived their lives as if it had all been a mistake, an accident, and they were paying dearly for it. It seemed as if they were always at someone else's mercy—women at the mercy of men (this prevailed in my hometown) and children at the mercy of frustrated parents. All I knew was that most of the grown-ups felt trapped, as if they were stuck in this town and no road would lead out. So many of them felt a sense of accomplishment just getting up in the morning and making it through another day. I overheard many a grown-up conversation, and they were never life-affirming: "Chile, if the Lord'll just give me the strength to make it through another week . . ."; "I just don't know how I'ma handle this, I can't take no more. . . ." I rarely knew what they were talking about, but even a fool could hear that it was some kind of drudgery. When I was a child, it became apparent to me that these grown-ups had no power over their lives, or, if they did, they were always at a loss as to how to exercise it. I did not want to grow up and have to depend on someone else for my happiness or be miserable or have to settle for whatever I was dished out—if I could help it. That much I knew already.

I remember being confused a lot. I could never understand why no one had any energy to do anything that would make them feel good, besides drinking. Being happy was a transient and very temporary thing which was almost always offset by some kind of bullshit. I would, of course, learn much later in my own adult life that these things are called obstacles, barriers—or again, bullshit. When I started writing, I began referring to them as "knots." But life wasn't one long knot. It seemed to me it just required stamina and common sense and the wherewithal to know when a knot was before you and you had to dig deeper than you had in order to figure out how to untie it. It could be hard, but it was simple.

.   .   .   .

The initial thing I remember striking me about *Oz* was how nasty Dorothy's Auntie Em talked to her and everybody on the farm. I was used to that authoritative tone of voice because my mother talked to us the same way. She never asked you to do anything; she gave you a command and never said "please," and, once you finished it, rarely said "thank you." The tone of her voice was always hostile, and Auntie Em sounded just like my mother—bossy and domineering. They both ran the show, it seemed, and I think that because my mother was raising five children almost single-handedly, I must have had some inkling that being a woman didn't mean you had to be helpless. Auntie Em's husband was a wimp, and for once the tables were turned: he took orders from her! My mother and Auntie Em were proof to me that if you wanted to get things done you had to delegate authority and keep everyone apprised of the rules of the game as well as the consequences. In my house it was punishment—you were severely grounded. What little freedom we had was snatched away. As a child, I often felt helpless, powerless, because I had no control over my situation and couldn't

tell my mother when I thought (or knew) she was wrong or being totally unfair, or when her behavior was inappropriate. I hated this feeling to no end, but
what was worse was not being able to do anything about it except keep my mouth
shut.

So I completely identified when no one had time to listen to Dorothy. That
dog's safety was important to her, but no one seemed to think that what Dorothy
was saying could possibly be as urgent as the situation at hand. The bottom line
was, it was urgent to her. When I was younger, I rarely had the opportunity to
finish a sentence before my mother would cut me off or complete it for me, or,
worse, give me something to do. She used to piss me off, and nowadays I catch
myself—stop myself—from doing the same thing to my seven-year-old. Back
then, it was as if what I had to say wasn't important or didn't warrant her undivided attention. So when Dorothy's Auntie Em dismisses her and tells her to
find somewhere where she'll stay out of trouble, and little Dorothy starts thinking about if there in fact is such a place—one that is trouble free—I was right
there with her, because I wanted to know, too.

I also didn't know or care that Judy Garland was supposed to have been a child
star, but when she sang "Somewhere over the Rainbow," I *was* impressed. Impressed more by the song than by who was singing it. I mean, she wasn't exactly Aretha Franklin or the Marvelettes or the Supremes, which was the only
vocal music I was used to. As kids, we often laughed at white people singing on
TV because their songs were always so corny and they just didn't sound anything like the soulful music we had in our house. Sometimes we would mimic
people like Doris Day and Fred Astaire and laugh like crazy because they were
always so damn happy while they sang and danced. We would also watch square-
dancing when we wanted a real laugh and try to look under the women's dresses.
What I hated more than anything was when in the middle of a movie the white
people always had to start singing and dancing to get their point across. Later,
I would hate it when black people would do the same thing—even though it was
obvious to us that at least they had more rhythm and, most of the time, more
range vocally.

We did skip through the house singing "We're off to see the Wizard," but
other than that, most of the songs in this movie are a blank, probably because I
blanked them out. Where I lived, when you had something to say to someone,
you didn't sing it, you told them, so the cumulative effect of the songs wore
thin.

I was afraid for Dorothy when she decided to run away, but at the same time
I was glad. I couldn't much blame her—I mean, what kind of life did she have,
from what I'd seen so far? She lived on an ugly farm out in the middle of nowhere
with all these old people who did nothing but chores, chores, and more chores.
Who did she have to play with besides that dog? And even though I lived in a

house full of people, I knew how lonely Dorothy felt, or at least how isolated she must have felt. First of all, I was the oldest, and my sisters and brother were ignorant and silly creatures who often bored me because they couldn't hold a decent conversation. I couldn't ask them questions, like: Why are we living in this dump? When is Mama going to get some more money? Why can't we go on vacations like other people? Like white people? Why does our car always break down? Why are we poor? Why doesn't Mama ever laugh? Why do we have to live in Port Huron? Isn't there someplace better than this we can go live? I remember thinking this kind of stuff in kindergarten, to be honest, because times were hard, but I'd saved twenty-five cents in my piggy bank for hot-dog-and-chocolate-milk day at school, and on the morning I went to get it, my piggy bank was empty. My mother gave me some lame excuse as to why she had to spend it, but all I was thinking was that I would have to sit there (again) and watch the other children slurp their chocolate milk, and I could see the ketchup and mustard oozing out of the hot-dog bun that I wouldn't get to taste. I walked to school, and with the exception of walking to my father's funeral when I was sixteen, this was the longest walk of my entire life. My plaid dress was starched and my socks were white, my hair was braided and not a strand out of place; but I wanted to know why I had to feel this kind of humiliation when in fact I had saved the money for this very purpose. Why? By the time I got to school, I'd wiped my nose and dried my eyes and vowed not to let anyone know that I was even moved by this. It was no one's business why I couldn't eat my hot dog and chocolate milk, but the irony of it was that my teacher, Mrs. Johnson, must have sensed what had happened, and she bought my hot dog and chocolate milk for me that day. I can still remember feeling how unfair things can be, but how they somehow always turn out good. I guess seeing so much negativity had already started to turn me into an optimist.

I was a very busy child, because I was the oldest and had to see to it that my sisters and brother had their baths and did their homework; I combed my sisters' hair, and by fourth grade I had cooked my first Thanksgiving dinner. It was my responsibility to keep the house spotless so that when my mother came home from work it would pass her inspection, so I spent many an afternoon and Saturday morning mopping and waxing floors, cleaning ovens and refrigerators, grocery shopping, and by the time I was thirteen, I was paying bills for my mother and felt like an adult. I was also tired of it, sick of all the responsibility. So yes, I rooted for Dorothy when she and Toto were vamoosing, only I wanted to know: Where in the hell was she going? Where would I go if I were to run away? I had no idea because there was nowhere to go. What I did know was that one day I would go somewhere—which is why I think I watched so much TV. I was always on the lookout for Paradise, and I think I found it a few years later on "Adventures in Paradise," with Gardner McKay, and on "77 Sunset Strip." Palm trees and blue water and islands made quite an impression on a little girl from a flat, dull little depressing town in Michigan.

Professor Marvel really pissed me off, and I didn't believe for a minute that that crystal ball was real, even before he started asking Dorothy all those questions, but I knew this man was going to be important, I just couldn't figure out how. Dorothy was so gullible, I thought, and I knew this word because my mother used to always drill it in us that you should "never believe everything somebody tells you." So after Professor Marvel convinced Dorothy that her Auntie Em might be in trouble, and Dorothy scoops up Toto and runs back home, I was totally disappointed, because now I wasn't going to have an adventure. I was thinking I might actually learn how to escape drudgery by watching Dorothy do it successfully, but before she even gave herself the chance to discover for herself that she could make it, she was on her way back home. "Dummy!" we all yelled on the sun porch. "Dodo brain!"

The storm. The tornado. Of course, now the entire set of this film looks so phony it's ridiculous, but back then I knew the wind was a tornado because in Michigan we had the same kind of trapdoor underground shelter that Auntie Em had on the farm. I knew Dorothy was going to be locked out once Auntie Em and the workers locked the door, and I also knew she wasn't going to be heard when she knocked on it. This was drama at its best, even though I didn't know what drama was at the time.

In the house she goes, and I was frightened for her. I knew that house was going to blow away, so when little Dorothy gets banged in the head by a window that flew out of its casement, I remember all of us screaming. We watched everybody fly by the window, including the wicked neighbor who turns out to be the Wicked Witch of the West, and I'm sure I probably substituted my mother for Auntie Em and fantasized that all of my siblings would fly away, too. They all got on my nerves because I could never find a quiet place in my house— no such thing as peace—and I was always being disturbed.

It wasn't so much that I had so much I wanted to do by myself, but I already knew that silence was a rare commodity, and when I managed to snatch a few minutes of it, I could daydream, pretend to be someone else somewhere else— and this was fun. But I couldn't do it if someone was bugging me. On days when my mother was at work, I would often send the kids outside to play and lock them out, just so I could have the house to myself for at least fifteen minutes. I loved pretending that none of them existed for a while, although after I finished with my fantasy world, it was reassuring to see them all there. I think I was grounded.

When Dorothy's house began to spin and spin and spin, I was curious as to where it was going to land. And to be honest, I didn't know little Dorothy was actually dreaming until she woke up and opened the door and everything was in color! It looked like Paradise to me. The foliage was almost an iridescent green, the water bluer than I'd ever seen in any of the lakes in Michigan. Of course, once I realized she was in fact dreaming, it occurred to me that this very well might be the only way to escape. To dream up another world. Create your own.

I had no clue that Dorothy was going to find trouble, though, even in her dreams. Hell, if I had dreamed up something like another world, it would've been a perfect one. I wouldn't have put myself in such a precarious situation. I'd have been able to go straight to the Wizard, no strings attached. First of all, that she walked was stupid to me; I would've asked one of those Munchkins for a ride. And I never bought into the idea of those slippers, but once I bought the whole idea, I accepted the fact that the girl was definitely lost and just wanted to get home. Personally, all I kept thinking was, if she could get rid of that Wicked Witch of the West, the Land of Oz wasn't such a bad place to be stuck in. It beat the farm in Kansas.

At the time, I truly wished I could spin away from my family and home and land someplace as beautiful and surreal as Oz—if only for a little while. All I wanted was to get a chance to see another side of the world, to be able to make comparisons, and then decide if it was worth coming back home.

What was really strange to me, after the Good Witch of the North tells Dorothy to just stay on the Yellow Brick Road to get to the Emerald City and find the Wizard so she can get home, was when Dorothy meets the Scarecrow, the Tin Man, and the Lion—all of whom were missing something I'd never even given any thought to. A brain? What did having one really mean? What would not having one mean? I had one, didn't I, because I did well in school. But because the Scarecrow couldn't make up his mind, thought of himself as a failure, it dawned on me that having a brain meant you had choices, you could make decisions and, as a result, make things happen. Yes, I thought, I had one, and I was going to use it. One day. And the Tin Man, who didn't have a heart. Not having one meant you were literally dead to me, and I never once thought of it as being the house of emotions (didn't know what emotions were), where feelings of jealousy, devotion, and sentiment lived. I'd never thought of what else a heart was good for except keeping you alive. But I did have feelings, because they were often hurt, and I was envious of the white girls at my school who wore mohair sweaters and box-pleat skirts, who went skiing and tobogganing and yachting and spent summers in Quebec. Why didn't white girls have to straighten their hair? Why didn't their parents beat each other up? Why were they always so goddamn happy?

And courage. Oh, that was a big one. What did having it and not having it mean? I found out that it meant having guts and being afraid but doing whatever it was you set out to do anyway. Without courage, you couldn't do much of anything. I liked courage and assumed I would acquire it somehow. As a matter of fact, one day my mother *told* me to get her a cup of coffee, and even though my heart was pounding and I was afraid, I said to her pointblank, "Could you please say please?" She looked up at me out of the corner of her eye and said, "What?" So I repeated myself, feeling more powerful because she hadn't slapped me across the room already, and then something came over her and she looked at me and said, "Please." I smiled all the way to the kitchen, and from that point forward, I managed to get away with this kind of behavior until I left home when I was seventeen. My sisters and brother—to this day—don't know how I stand up to my mother, but I know. I decided not to be afraid or intimidated by her, and I wanted her to treat me like a friend, like a human being, instead of her slave.

I do believe that *Oz* also taught me much about friendship. I mean, the Tin Man, the Lion, and the Scarecrow hung in there for Dorothy, stuck their "necks" out and made sure she was protected, even risked their own "lives" for her. They told each other the truth. They trusted each other. All four of them had each other's best interests in mind. I believe it may have been a while before I actually felt this kind of sincerity in a friend, but really good friends aren't easy to come by, and when you find one, you hold on to them.

Okay. So Dorothy goes through hell before she gets back to Kansas. But the bottom line was, she made it. And what I remember feeling when she clicked those heels was that you have to have faith and be a believer, for real, or nothing will ever materialize. Simple as that. And not only in life but even in your dreams there's always going to be adversity, obstacles, knots, or some kind of bullshit you're going to have to deal with in order to get on with your life. Dorothy had a good heart and it was in the right place, which is why I supposed she won out over the evil witch. I've learned that one, too. That good *always* overcomes evil; maybe not immediately, but in the long run, it does. So I think I vowed when I was little to try to be a good person. An honest person. To care about others and not just myself. Not to be a selfish person, because my heart would be of no service if I used it only for myself. And I had to have the courage to see other people and myself as not being perfect (yes, I had a heart and a brain, but some other things would turn up missing, later), and I would have to learn to untie every knot that I encountered—some self-imposed, some not—in my life, and to believe that if I did the right things, I would never stray too far from my Yellow Brick Road.

. . . .

I'm almost certain that I saw *Oz* annually for at least five or six years, but I don't remember how old I was when I stopped watching it. I do know that by the time my parents were divorced (I was thirteen), I couldn't sit through it again. I was a mature teen-ager and had finally reached the point where Dorothy got on my nerves. Singing, dancing, and skipping damn near everywhere was so corny and utterly sentimental that even the Yellow Brick Road became sickening. I already knew what she was in for, and sometimes I rewrote the story in my head. I kept asking myself, what if she had just run away and kept going, maybe she would've ended up in Los Angeles with a promising singing career. What if it had turned out that she hadn't been dreaming, and the Wizard had given her an offer she couldn't refuse—say, for instance, he had asked her to stay on in the Emerald City, that she could visit the farm whenever she wanted to, but, get a clue, Dorothy, the Emerald City is what's happening; she could make new city friends and get a hobby and a boyfriend and free rent and never have to do chores . . .

I had to watch *The Wizard of Oz* again in order to write this, and my six-and-a-half-year-old son, Solomon, joined me. At first he kept asking me if something was wrong with the TV because it wasn't in color, but as he watched, he became mesmerized by the story. He usually squirms or slides to the floor and under a table or just leaves the room if something on TV bores him, which it usually does, except if he's watching Nickelodeon, a high-quality cable kiddie channel. His favorite shows, which he watches with real consistency, and, I think, actually goes through withdrawal if he can't see them for whatever reason, are "Inspector Gadget," "Looney Tunes," and "Mr. Ed." "Make the Grade," which is sort of a junior-high version of "Jeopardy," gives him some kind of thrill, even though he rarely knows any of the answers. And "Garfield" is a must on Saturday morning. There is hardly anything on TV that he watches that has any real, or at least plausible, drama to it, but you can't miss what you've never had.

The Wicked Witch intimidated the boy no end, and he was afraid of her. The Wizard was also a problem. So I explained—no, I just told him pointblank—"Don't worry, she'll get it in the end, Solomon, because she's bad. And the Wizard's a fake, and he's trying to sound like a tough guy, but he's a wus." That offered him some consolation, and even when the Witch melted he kind of looked at me with those *Home Alone* eyes and asked, "But where did she go, Mommy?" "She's history," I said. "Melted. Gone. Into the ground. Remember, this is pretend. It's not real. Real people don't melt. This is only TV," I said. And then he got that look in his eyes as if he'd remembered something.

Of course he had a nightmare that night and of course there was a witch in it, because I had actually left the sofa a few times during this last viewing to smoke a few cigarettes (the memory bank is a powerful place—I still remembered many details), put the dishes in the dishwasher, make a few phone calls, water the plants. Solomon sang "We're off to see the Wizard" for the next few days because he said that was his favorite part, next to the Munchkins (who also showed up in his nightmare).

So, to tell the truth, I really didn't watch the whole movie again. I just couldn't. Probably because about thirty or so years ago little Dorothy had made a lasting impression on me, and this viewing felt like overkill. You only have to tell me, show me, once in order for me to get it. But even still, the movie itself taught me a few things that I still find challenging. That it's okay to be an idealist, that you have to imagine something better and go for it. That you have to believe in *something,* and it's best to start with yourself and take it from there. At least give it a try. As corny as it may sound, sometimes I am afraid of what's around the corner, or what's not around the corner. But I look anyway. I believe that writing is one of my "corners"—an intersection, really; and when I'm confused or reluctant to look back, deeper, or ahead, I create my own Emerald Cities and force myself to take longer looks, because it is one sure way that I'm able to see.

Of course, I've fallen, tumbled, and been thrown over all kinds of bumps on my road, but it still looks yellow, although every once in a while there's still a loose brick. For the most part, though, it seems paved. Perhaps because that's the way I want to see it.

RYSZARD KAPUŚCIŃSKI

Whenever people are where they wish not to be, or feel ill at ease, or are lonely or far from home, a movie theater can provide an escape not just because of the images on the screen but also because of the reassuring ritual of simply buying a ticket and going in and sitting down and knowing that for an hour or two decisions can be deferred.

from *Another Day of Life*

And in Luanda? What can you do on Sunday in our abandoned city, upon which—as it turns out—sentence has already been passed? You can sleep until noon.

You can turn on the faucet to check—ha!—just in case there is water.

You can stand before the mirror, thinking: so many gray hairs in my beard already.

You can sit in front of a plate on which lies a piece of disgusting fish and a spoonful of cold rice.

You can walk, sweating from weakness and effort, up the Rua de Luis de Camões, toward the airport or down toward the bay.

And yet that's not all—you can go to the movies, too! That's right, because we still have a movie theater, only one in fact, but it is panoramic and in the open air and, to top it off, free. The theater lies in the northern part of town, near the front. The owner fled to Lisbon but the projectionist remained behind, and so did a print of the famous porno film *Emmanuelle*. The projectionist shows it uninterrupted, over and over, gratis, free for everyone, and crowds of kids rush in, and soldiers who have got away from the front, and there's always a full house, a crush, and an uproar and indescribable bellowing. To enhance the effect, the projectionist stops the action at the hottest moments. The girl is naked—stop. He has her in the airplane—stop. She has her by the river—stop. The old man has her—stop. The boxer has her—stop. If he has her in an absurd position—laughter and bravos from the audience. If he has her in a position of exaggerated sophistication, the audience falls silent and analyzes. There's so much merriment and hubbub that it is hard to hear the distant, heavy echoes of artillery on the nearby front. And of course there is no way—not because of *Emmanuelle*, but the great distance—to hear the roaring motors of the armored column moving along the road.

WALKER PERCY

What Walker Percy's famous novel captures above all is the way some people live so completely through the movies that they come not only to prefer them to real life but to make them into a higher reality. His passage beginning "Other people, so I have read . . ." is subtle in the way it sneaks in the words "so I have read," informing us that the narrator is comparing two forms of vicarious entertainment and has few actual experiences of his own to measure up against either of them. That is his plight. It is revealing that when he meets the real William Holden, he has no desire to approach him. It is enough to look.

from *The Moviegoer*

Life in Gentilly is very peaceful. I manage a small branch office of my uncle's brokerage firm. My home is the basement apartment of a raised bungalow belonging to Mrs. Schexnaydre, the widow of a fireman. I am a model tenant and a model citizen and take pleasure in doing all that is expected of me. My wallet is full of identity cards, library cards, credit cards. Last year I purchased a flat olive-drab strongbox, very smooth and heavily built with double walls for fire protection, in which I placed my birth certificate, college diploma, honorable discharge, G.I. insurance, a few stock certificates, and my inheritance: a deed to ten acres of a defunct duck club down in St. Bernard Parish, the only relic of my father's many enthusiasms. It is a pleasure to carry out the duties of a citizen and to receive in return a receipt or a neat styrene card with one's name on it certifying, so to speak, one's right to exist. What satisfaction I take in appearing the first day to get my auto tag and brake sticker! I subscribe to *Consumer Reports* and as a consequence I own a first-class television set, an all but silent air conditioner and a very long lasting deodorant. My armpits never stink. I pay attention to all spot announcements on the radio about mental health, the seven signs of cancer, and safe driving—though, as I say, I usually prefer to ride the bus. Yesterday a favorite of mine, William Holden, delivered a radio announcement on litterbugs. "Let's face it," said Holden, "Nobody can do anything about it—but you and me." This is true. I have been careful ever since.

In the evenings I usually watch television or go to the movies. Week-ends I often spend on the Gulf Coast. Our neighborhood theater in Gentilly has permanent lettering on the front of the marquee reading: Where Happiness Costs So Little. The fact is I am quite happy in a movie, even a bad movie. Other people, so I have read, treasure memorable moments in their lives: the time one climbed the Parthenon at sunrise, the summer night one met a lonely girl in Central Park and achieved with her a sweet and natural relationship, as they say in books. I too once met a girl in Central Park, but it is not much to remember. What I remember is the time John Wayne killed three men with a carbine as he was falling to the dusty street in *Stagecoach,* and the time the kitten found Orson Welles in the doorway in *The Third Man. . . .*

.   .   .   .

I alight at Esplanade in a smell of roasting coffee and creosote and walk up Royal Street. The lower Quarter is the best part. The ironwork on the balconies sags like rotten lace. Little French cottages hide behind high walls. Through deep sweating carriageways one catches glimpses of courtyards gone to jungle.

Today I am in luck. Who should come out of Pirate's Alley half a block ahead of me but William Holden!

Holden crosses Royal and turns toward Canal. As yet he is unnoticed. The tourists are either browsing along antique shops or snapping pictures of balconies. No doubt he is on his way to Galatoire's for lunch. He is an attractive fellow with his ordinary good looks, very suntanned, walking along hands in pockets, raincoat slung over one shoulder. Presently he passes a young couple, who are now between me and him. Now we go along, the four of us, not twenty feet apart. It takes two seconds to size up the couple. They are twenty, twenty-one, and on their honeymoon. Not Southern. Probably Northeast. He wears a jacket with leather elbow patches, pipestem pants, dirty white shoes, and affects the kind of rolling seafaring gait you see in Northern college boys. Both are plain. He has thick lips, cropped reddish hair and skin to match. She is mousy. They are not really happy. He is afraid their honeymoon is too conventional, that they are just another honeymoon couple. No doubt he figured it would be fun to drive down the Shenandoah Valley to New Orleans and escape the honeymooners at Niagara Falls and Saratoga. Now fifteen hundred miles from home they find themselves surrounded by couples from Memphis and Chicago. He is anxious; he is threatened from every side. Each stranger he passes is a reproach to him, every doorway a threat. What is wrong? he wonders. She is unhappy but for a different reason, because he is unhappy and she knows it but doesn't know why.

Now they spot Holden. The girl nudges her companion. The boy perks up for a second, but seeing Holden doesn't really help him. On the contrary. He can only contrast Holden's resplendent reality with his own shadowy and precarious existence. Obviously he is more miserable than ever. What a deal, he must be thinking, trailing along behind a movie star—we might just as well be rubbernecking in Hollywood.

Holden slaps his pockets for a match. He has stopped behind some ladies looking at iron furniture on the sidewalk. They look like housewives from Hattiesburg come down for a day of shopping. He asks for a match; they shake their heads and then recognize him. There follows much blushing and confusion. But nobody can find a match for Holden. By now the couple have caught up with him. The boy holds out a light, nods briefly to Holden's thanks, then passes on without a flicker of recognition. Holden walks along between them for a second; he and the boy talk briefly, look up at the sky, shake their heads. Holden gives them a pat on the shoulder and moves on ahead.

The boy has done it! He has won title to his own existence, as plenary an existence now as Holden's, by refusing to be stampeded like the ladies from Hattiesburg. He is a citizen like Holden; two men of the world they are. All at once the world is open to him. Nobody threatens from patio and alley. His girl is open to him too. He puts his arm around her neck, noodles her head. She feels the difference too. She had not known what was wrong nor how it was righted but she knows now that all is well.

Holden has turned down Toulouse shedding light as he goes. An aura of heightened reality moves with him and all who fall within it feel it. Now everyone is aware of him. He creates a regular eddy among the tourists and barkeeps and B-girls who come running to the doors of the joints.

I am attracted to movie stars but not for the usual reasons. I have no desire to speak to Holden or get his autograph. It is their peculiar reality which astounds me. The Yankee boy is well aware of it, even though he pretends to ignore Holden. Clearly he would like nothing better than to take Holden over to his fraternity house in the most casual way. "Bill, I want you to meet Phil. Phil, Bill Holden," he would say and go sauntering off in the best seafaring style.

JONATHAN ROSENBAUM

Jonathan Rosenbaum, who is one of America's most important film critics, has for some years written for the Chicago Reader. *Before that he lived a nomadic life, viewing movies and writing about them in Paris, London, and many other places. And before that, we learn with a certain surprise, he grew up in Florence, Alabama, where his grandfather once owned movie theaters probably not much different from those attended by the hero of Walker Percy's* The Moviegoer. *These words, written for the Venice Biennale in 1979 as both home video and the multiplex were first appearing on the American scene, are a poignant look at how we used to go to the movies and how our habits were about to change.*

from *Moving Places*

Rocky Horror Playtime vs. Shopping Mall Home

Seven weeks ago, when I received a call from Adriano Aprà in Rome inviting me to speak at this conference, I was in my hometown, Florence, Alabama, where my parents live today. I have moved with all my belongings seventeen times in the past twenty years, and I will have to find and move to yet another place in New York as soon as I return from this conference. Nevertheless, I consider myself unusually fortunate, fortunate not only in being here—in this city and this country for the first time in my life—but in having a hometown to return to year after year: a fixed reference point. And fortunate in being the grandson of the man who ran most of the local movie theaters when I was growing up, which meant that I had virtually unlimited access to most of what was shown.

Moving Places is an attempt at a narrative exposition of myself through movies and of movies through me, and Florence has been providing me with a sort of personal and historical measuring stick in this process. So when Adriano told me that I was to speak about audiences in the 1980s, I naturally thought first about the audiences in Florence, what they were and what they are, which is my most reliable guide to what they will be.

I have to admit that Florence has undergone radical social changes since I left in 1959. The town is now racially integrated, which wasn't the case when I was growing up. Today black people in Florence don't have to attend separate schools, use separate bathrooms (in the nearest train station one facility was labeled "colored women," the other "white ladies"), or drink from separate drinking fountains. State law no longer requires them to sit in the back of a bus or in a special section of a movie theater.

Another drastic change is that downtown Florence is dying, perhaps almost dead. The center of town, where three of my grandfather's theaters once stood—each of them only a block or so from where the courthouse used to be—now seems deserted. Despite lots of brand new parking lots, the place feels haunted, like a ghost town. The largest of the three theaters, the Shoals—built when I was five and originally seating 1300 people—is the only one standing today. It still shows movies; I saw *Meatballs* there three days after Adriano phoned. But it no longer functions as anything like the place of worship or the community gathering-place that it was twenty and thirty years ago.

The cashier's booth at the Shoals used to have two windows, one around the corner from the other, in order to conform to the Jim Crow laws. The window directly in front of the cashier was for selling tickets to white folks; the one on her left was for black customers, who had already come into the building through a special side entrance. At the side window they would purchase "colored" tickets, which were ten or fifteen cents cheaper than "white" tickets, and climb their own set of stairs to their own special section of the balcony.

After the Civil Rights Act of 1964 was passed, making Jim Crow laws illegal, some of the old habits were allowed to linger for a period. Both windows in the cashier's booth at the Shoals remained open, and for a while she continued to sell cheaper tickets at the side window. In theory, any black person could pay more and sit downstairs, and any white person could pay less and sit upstairs. Today the balcony is closed and has been for years; everyone sits downstairs, in fewer and wider seats, generally watching worse movies for more money.

In fact a theater like the Shoals is little more than a relic now, and everyone knows this, including the subsequent owners, who have tried to bring some aspects of the building "up to date" and in doing so have eliminated whatever inclinations toward beauty, monumentality, or eccentricity that may once have been in the design. The only movies the Shoals shows now are bland items such as *Meatballs* and Disney comedies, and a lot of the older kids wouldn't be caught dead there. Their turf is the strip on the outskirts of town where all the shopping centers and one enormous shopping mall are located.

And that is where the other movie theaters are, the brand new ones whose auditoriums have the feel of the insides of cheap jewelry boxes, where I saw *Moonraker,* a couple of sex films, *Dracula,* and *The Muppet Movie* in late July. As a rule, the people I know in Florence who see movies today watch them either out there, in those frigid space stations that are as strictly utilitarian as circus tents and offer even less of an invitation to linger after the show, or on their TV sets at home. (Cable TV, I should add, is very popular.)

.   .   .   .

I suspect that most American audiences in the 1980s will be watching films either in homes or in shopping malls. What's particularly disturbing about this is that homes and shopping malls are beginning to resemble one another, along with the movies and the audiences inside them. The separate forms of social behavior that we associate with film and television are also starting to break down as the two media become increasingly difficult to differentiate, thanks in part to such expensive toys as Betamaxes and Advent screens. The arsenals of new communications equipment, which are currently being paraded before us like sophisticated armaments, indirectly yet unmistakably testify to the poverty of what we have to communicate. By trusting ourselves less, we wind up trusting the machines more. And because of these machines, word-of-mouth news trav-

els more slowly these days, as though it were creeping from one petulant medieval stronghold to another—in striking contrast to the sixties, when certain
kinds of news traveled like wildfire.

It is estimated that nearly half of all the retail business in the United States
today is transacted in approximately 18,000 strip and enclosed shopping com-
plexes known variously as plazas, centers, and malls. They occupy over two bil-
lion square feet, employ more than 4.5 million people, represent $60 billion in
investments, and their rate of failure over the past twenty-five years is said to
be less than one percent.

A study conducted at Temple University indicates that malls are the most popular gathering places for teenagers in the United States. In a controversial paper
presented to the Popular Culture Association, Richard Francaviglia compared
malls to amusement parks such as Disneyland. William Severini Kowinski expands on this notion by describing malls as "the feudal castles of contemporary
America."

> By keeping weather out and keeping itself always in the present—if not in the
> future—a mall aspires to create timeless space. Removed from everything else
> and existing in a world of its own, a mall is also placeless space.

An article in the socialist magazine *Dollars & Sense* points out that in recent
years the U.S. Supreme Court has twice ruled in separate cases that malls are
not public places where citizens can express their views, distribute leaflets, or
congregate freely—unlike the old town squares.

> To keep people inside the mall and encourage them to see shopping as enter-
> tainment, designers attempt to create a "carnival" atmosphere! Once inside a cen-
> ter, shoppers have few decisions to make. Corners are kept to a minimum so the
> customers will flow along from store to store, propelled, as the developers say,
> by "retail energy." Said one observer of mall design. "The mirrors, the music and
> the sound of rushing water create a sense of distortion. There is never a clock to
> remind one of the world outside the mall."

I think this is a pretty fair description of most of the cinema today. Both films
and shopping malls function as media that aim at producing and controlling their
own notions and measurements of space and time, designed to supersede all others. They offer themselves to us like self-contained planets, not tools to assist
us anywhere else in the universe. Which suggests that we may be losing our mar-
bles.

In these terms, *Apocalypse Now*—which I saw twice last month in New York—
is a $30 million shopping mall, offering Michael Herr's *Dispatches* as well as Con-

rad's *Heart of Darkness* in the bookstore, The Doors and Wagner in the record and tape shop, Marlon Brando and Dennis Hopper in the snazzy nightclub, *Playboy, Time, Rolling Stone,* and *Reader's Digest* at the newsstand, fancy roast beef and plain rice at the fast-food restaurant. To make sure that all of this goes down well, a clever pattern of continuous percussion and exotic jungle noise is pumped seductively into our ears like Muzak, controlling our inner rhythms and emotional temperatures while helping to screen out all vestiges of the outside world, including Vietnam.

To refer to such an all-purpose marketing and environmental complex as a personal form of self-expression, and to try to reduce *or* elevate this expression to a political statement of any sort, is merely to become a blind man in relation to Francis Coppola's elephant—and perhaps part of the film's promotional campaign in the bargain. In order to confront anything like the whole package (which is so much bigger than we are) one first has to acknowledge the presence of a complex pleasure machine, loads of fun, programmed to stimulate and then gratify as many opposing viewpoints as possible. This machine has nothing to do with Vietnam. It is designed to appeal to good ole boys who kill gooks for the fun of it as well as to pacifists, liberals, blacks, whites, moderates, fascists, conservatives, humanitarians, racists, misanthropes, novelists, avant-garde filmmakers, rock and drug enthusiasts, and literature professors—all of whom are designed, in turn, to feel that it's a movie made just for them.

In the same context, what about homes, which are the only spaces we have left once we've rejected public life for a private boat ride through Coppolaland? Writer-director George Romero his on a parodic relationship of home to shopping mall in the first two parts of his horror trilogy, *Night of the Living Dead* and *Dawn of the Dead,* by passing directly from the home as fortress to the shopping mall fortress as home. An alternative version of this interchange—the home as shopping mall—can easily be imagined if one starts with either of Hugh Hefner's Playboy Mansions as a model.

.   .   .   .

Having outlined such a deprived and limited future, I would like to cite a couple of things that still make me hopeful, in spite of everything. Both of these things signal the potential return of the *active* audience, in contrast to the passive, refrigerated, cut-off, narcissistic sensibilities that so many recent movies and movie theaters take (or ask) us to be. And both imply (albeit somewhat subversively in the present context) a community of common interests inside a theater, rather than a set of separate, elegantly upholstered masturbation stalls.

Decentered, nonprivileged space and a crowd of people contriving to reclaim what is rightfully theirs is what both these things are about. One of them is my favorite film, *Playtime,* made by Jacques Tati in the sixties, which I saw first in 1968 as an American tourist in Paris. The other is an event created by an audience *around* a film called *The Rocky Horror Picture Show,* an event that has been occurring and evolving in the United States over the past three years.

Playtime was made twelve years ago, although as a practical tool for learning how to cope with the hideous world that we're building it is only beginning to be understood. When I screened it for 150 college students in San Diego two years ago, I was pleased to discover that many of them had less trouble understanding its basic principles than most film critics did when the movie first appeared—perhaps because they had fewer preconceptions about film comedy. Turning us all into tourists as it charts the movements of a group of Americans through a studio approximation of Paris, *Playtime* implies that empty space becomes alive (*and* curved) once it assumes a social function—and that the shortest distance between any two supposedly unrelated individuals within the same public space is comedy.

The film's strategy, lesson, and advice are the same: It directs us to look around at the world we live in (the one we keep building), then at each other, and to see how funny that relationship is and how many brilliant possibilities we still have in a shopping-mall world that perpetually suggests otherwise; to look and see that there are *many* possibilities and that the *play* between them, activated by the dance of our gaze, can become a kind of comic ballet, one that we both observe and perform as we navigate our way through Paris's imprisoning patterns, reflections, and deceptions.

By connecting our observations with our performances *as* observers, Tati returns us to the real world, as he does again in *Parade.* He doesn't pretend, like Disney or Coppola, to give us anything better. Instead he helps us to become a better audience by presenting us precisely with our social predicament as spectators, and then trying to show us how we might become partners in and through that experience.

Much the same could be said for the event generated by a mainly teenage audience around showings of *The Rocky Horror Picture Show* in more than two hundred cities across the United States. (I'm told that the fad has even passed through Florence, though not, alas, when I was there.) As an amateur of this curious phenomenon, one who has witnessed only three performances at the 8th Street Playhouse in New York, I cannot claim to be qualified to discuss the movement as a whole. But I can't deny, either, that my three visits were all exhilarating experiences.

Both the film and the stage musical on which the film is based (I first encountered them while living in London four and five years ago, respectively) describe the initiation of an ingenuous American couple into the bisexual joys practiced in a haunted house by English denizens of Grade B horror and science fiction films. (The crossovers between England and America are possibly as intricate here as those between female and male.) A distanced theatrical narrative that is interrupted repeatedly by a narrator and bracketed by self-conscious film references, the movie began to be appropriated spontaneously about three years ago by isolated members of an audience that attended regularly the midnight screenings of the film in Greenwich Village.

Their appropriation can be seen as an unconscious yet authentic act of film criticism, one that returns in-the-flesh theatricality and confrontation to a flashy work that needs them. Some fans fill the pauses in the film's dialogue with wisecracks, many of them retained from one show to the next and recited in unison. Other habitués get themselves up, often in drag, to resemble the main characters and then mimic the onscreen performers' gestures, standing beneath the screen and in the aisles, while friends spotlight their actions with flashlight beams. Props are used; rice is thrown during the wedding sequence, and water pistols and umbrellas are sometimes brandished to accompany the subsequent rainstorm. These rituals and others have gradually developed into a richly elaborated, multifaceted "text" in which the film itself is only the ostensible centerpiece; it is not always the precise center of attention.

At a *Rocky Horror* midnight show about a week ago I met a couple of proud veterans, each of whom had seen the film nearly three hundred times. Two women were present to play the Tim Curry part of Dr. Frank N. Furter (the leading transsexual character, who appears in drag), along with more than a dozen other performers, many of whom went through several elaborate costume changes to match their screen counterparts. One of the women playing Frank was a New York regular who told me she had seen the film fifty times; the other, a young black woman from Chicago, took over the role for a few guest appearances toward the end.

Despite some competitive divisions and hierarchies within this cult, the spirit of the shows I have attended has been markedly democratic and nonelitist. No one is treated like an outsider; anyone, theoretically, can make her or his own contribution to the "text," which is in a state of continual change and refinement.

What is it about these shows that is so energetic and exciting? Above all, I think it is the experience of a film's being used by people as a means of communicating with one another—not after the film has ended, but while it is still in progress. I think we could learn a great deal about our own favorite movies if we knew how to use them that way.

Some commentators have found the implications of this practice to be fascistic and mindless. The adoption of such a movie (or any movie) as a sacred text to be memorized, recited as a catechism, or elaborated upon as in a religious commentary offends their sense of propriety and aesthetics. Without wishing to idealize this ritual, I would like to point out that it is much more appealing to experience it than to hear or read about it. (As a group activity, the closest parallels that spring to mind are jam sessions among jazz musicians and responses from congregations to sermons at black revival meetings.) With its characteristic open-mindedness, *Newsweek* reports that "Some middle-aged viewers are disgusted by the film's blatant transsexuality; others merely dislike it." Still others, less self-defensive, have simply enjoyed the show, recognizing at once how fundamentally innocent it is. Or perhaps I should say innocently perverse, like the rest of filmgoing.

What most of the objections fail to acknowledge is that the meaning of any work of art is in part bound up in its social function. The *Rocky Horror* phenomenon—not, I should stress, the film—is a work of art whose audience and creators are essentially one, grouped around a shared irony about sexual roles and social taboos that remains as a legacy of the sixties, and whose social function is largely to bring together strangers and open up new channels of communication between them. I like it because it resurrects moviegoing as a communal event, making one proud, not embarrassed, to be sitting next to other people in the dark.

LARRY MCMURTRY

At first I went to the movies to see the movies: the Saturday matinees with Hopalong Cassidy and the Bowery Boys. Then, with a suddenness so swift I can still remember it, I became aware of girls, and instantly the local movie theaters became transformed from places where you watched the screen to places where you were acutely, painfully aware that twelve- and thirteen-year-old girls were watching it also—not with you but nearby. And these girls, whom I had known since the first grade, now turned into little clusters of giggles and intrigue, and every sexual reference in a film, no matter how subtle and nuanced, caused them to dissolve. At last I took a girl to a movie. It was The Bridge over the River Kwai. *I had asked her to attend the graduation dance at Thelma Leah Rose's Dance Studio, upstairs over the Princess Theater on Main Street in Urbana, Illinois, but I had the wrong night, and there was no dance, and so we went to the movies instead. Slowly, with excruciating care, I put my arm around her, until my hand at last rested on her sa-*

cred shoulder, and there it stayed, the arm growing numb, for the next two hours. When Pauline Kael writes "I lost it at the movies," what she is reflecting is the truth that for many decades in America, a movie theater was about the only place where teenage boys and girls could be alone and unsupervised. And from those moments in the dark arose a whole matrix of eroticism, so that to this day, for all of us, there is always something sexy about going to the movies. Here Larry McMurtry, in the novel that Peter Bogdanovich made into the wonderful 1971 film, recalls just such a moment and where it led. The selections are from Chapters 2, 25, and 26.

from *The Last Picture Show*

Sonny . . . took his week's wages and walked across the dark courthouse lawn to the picture show. Jacy's white Ford convertible was parked out front, where it always was on Saturday night. The movie that night was called *Storm Warning,* and the posterboards held pictures of Doris Day, Ronald Reagan, Steve Cochran, and Ginger Rogers. It was past 10 P.M., and Miss Mosey, who sold tickets, had already closed the window; Sonny found her in the lobby, cleaning out the popcorn machine. She was a thin little old lady with such bad eyesight and hearing that she sometimes had to walk halfway down the aisle to tell whether the comedy or the newsreel was on.

"My goodness, Frank oughtn't to work you so late on weekends," she said. "You done missed the comedy so you don't need to give me but thirty cents."

Sonny thanked her and bought a package of Doublemint gum before he went into the show. Very few people ever came to the late feature; there were not more than twenty in the whole theater. As soon as his eyes adjusted Sonny determined that Jacy and Duane were still out parking; Charlene Duggs was sitting about halfway down the aisle with her little sister Marlene. Sonny walked down the aisle and tapped her on the shoulder, and the two girls scooted over a seat.

"I decided you had a wreck," Charlene said, not bothering to whisper. She smelled like powder and toilet water.

"You two want some chewin' gum?" Sonny offered, holding out the package. The girls each instantly took a stick and popped the gum into their mouths almost simultaneously. They never had any gum money themselves and were both great moochers. Their father, Royce Duggs, ran a dinky little one-man garage out on the highway; most of his work was done on pickups and tractors, and money was tight. The girls would not have been able to afford the toilet water either, but their mother, Beulah Duggs, had a secret passion for it and bought it with money that Royce Duggs thought was going for the girls' school lunches. The three of them could only get away with using it on Saturday night when Royce was customarily too drunk to be able to smell.

After the feature had been playing for a few minutes Sonny and Charlene got up and moved back into one of the corners. It made Sonny nervous to sit with Charlene and Marlene both. Even though Charlene was a senior and Marlene just a sophomore, the two looked so much alike that he was afraid he might accidentally start holding hands with the wrong one. Back in the corner, he held Charlene's hand and they smooched a little, but not much. Sonny really wanted to see the movie, and it was easy for him to hold his passion down. Charlene had not got all the sweetness out of the stick of Doublemint and didn't want to take it out of her mouth just to kiss Sonny, but after a few minutes she changed her mind, took it out, and stuck it under the arm of her seat. It seemed to her that Sonny looked a little bit like Steve Cochran, and she began to kiss him energetically, squirming and pressing herself against his knee. Sonny returned the kiss, but with somewhat muted interest. He wanted to keep at least one eye on the screen, so if Ginger Rogers decided to take her clothes off he wouldn't miss it. The posters outside indicated she at least got down to her slip at one point. Besides, Charlene was always getting worked up in picture shows; at first Sonny had thought her fits of cinematic passion very encouraging, until he discovered it was practically impossible to get her worked up *except* in picture shows.

The movies were Charlene's life, as she was fond of saying. She spent most of her afternoons hanging around the little beauty shop where her mother worked, reading movie magazines, and she always referred to movie stars by their first names. Once when an aunt gave her a dollar for her birthday she went down to the variety store and bought two fifty-cent portraits to sit on her dresser: one was of June Allyson and the other Van Johnson. Marlene copied Charlene's passions as exactly as possible, but when the same aunt gave *her* a dollar the variety store's stock of portraits was low and she had to make do with Esther Williams and Mickey Rooney. Charlene kidded her mercilessly about the latter, and took to sleeping with Van Johnson under her pillow because she was afraid Marlene might mutilate him out of envy.

After a few minutes of squirming alternately against the seat arm and Sonny's knee, lost in visions of Steve Cochran, Charlene abruptly relaxed and sat back. She languidly returned the chewing gum to her mouth, and for a while they watched the movie in silence. Then she remembered a matter she had been intending to bring up.

"Guess what?" she said. "We been going steady a year tonight. You should have got me something for an anniversary present."

Sonny had been contentedly watching Ginger Rogers, waiting for the slip scene. Charlene's remark took him by surprise.

"Well, you can have another stick of gum," he said. "That's all I've got on me."

"Okay, and I'll take a dollar, too," Charlene said. "It cost that much for me and Marlene to come to the show, and I don't want to pay my own way on my anniversary."

Sonny handed her the package of chewing gum, but not the dollar. Normally he expected to pay Charlene's way to the show, but he saw no reason at all why he should spend fifty cents on Marlene. While he was thinking out the ethics of the matter the exit door opened down to the right of the screen and Duane and Jacy slipped in, their arms around one another. They came back and sat down by Sonny and Charlene.

"Hi you all, what are you doin' back here in the dark?" Jacy whispered gaily. Her pretty mouth was a little numb from two hours of virtually uninterrupted kissing. As soon as it seemed polite, she and Duane started kissing again and settled into an osculatory doze that lasted through the final reel of the movie. Charlene began nervously popping her finger joints, something she did whenever Jacy came around. Sonny tried to concentrate on the screen, but it was hard. Jacy and Duane kept right on kissing, even when the movie ended and the lights came on. They didn't break their clinch until Billy came down from the balcony with his broom and began to sweep.

"Sure was a short show," Jacy said, turning to grin at Sonny. Her nose wrinkled delightfully when she grinned. She shook her head so that her straight blond hair would hang more smoothly against her neck. Duane's hair was tousled, but when Jacy playfully tried to comb it he yawned and shook her off. She put on fresh lipstick and they all got up and went outside.

Miss Mosey had taken the *Storm Warning* posters down and was gallantly trying to tack up the posters for Sunday's show, which was *Francis Goes to the Army*. The wind whipped around the corners of the old building, making the posters flop. Miss Mosey's fingers were so cold she could barely hold the tacks, so the boys helped her finish while the girls shivered on the curb. Marlene was shivering on the curb too, waiting for Sonny to drop her off at the Duggses. Duane walked Jacy to her convertible and kissed her goodnight a time or two, then came gloomily to the pickup, depressed at the thought of how long it was until Saturday night came again.

When they had taken Marlene home and dropped Duane at the rooming house, Sonny and Charlene drove back to town so they could find out what time it was from the clock in the jewelry store window. As usual, it was almost time for Charlene to go home.

"Oh, let's go on to the lake," she said. "I guess I can be a few minutes late tonight, since it's my anniversary.

"I never saw anything like that Jacy and Duane," she said. "Kissing in the picture show after the lights go on. That's pretty bad if you ask me. One of these days Mrs. Farrow's gonna catch 'em an' that'll be the end of that romance."

Sonny drove on to the city lake without saying anything, but the remark depressed him. So far as he was concerned Jacy and Duane knew true love and would surely manage to get married and be happy. What depressed him was that it had just become clear to him that Charlene really wanted to go with Duane, just as he himself really wanted to go with Jacy.

As soon as the pickup stopped Charlene moved over against him. "Crack your window and leave the heater on," she said. "It's still too cold in here for me."

Sonny tried to shrug off his depression by beginning the little routine they always went through when they parked: first he would kiss Charlene for about ten minutes; then she would let him take off her brassiere and play with her breasts; finally, when he tried to move on to other things she would quickly scoot back across the seat, put the bra back on, and make him take her home. Sometimes she indulged in an engulfing kiss or two on the doorstep, knowing that she could fling herself inside the house if a perilously high wave of passion threatened to sweep over her.

After the proper amount of kissing Sonny deftly unhooked her bra. This was the signal for Charlene to draw her arms from the sleeves of her sweater and slip out of the straps. Sonny hung the bra on the rear-view mirror. So long as the proprieties were observed, Charlene liked being felt; she obligingly slipped her sweater up around her neck.

"Eeh, your hands are like ice," she said, sucking in her breath. Despite the heater the cab was cold enough to make her nipples crinkle. The wind had blown all the clouds away, but the moon was thin and dim and the choppy lake lay in darkness. When Sonny moved his hand the little dash-light threw patches of shadow over Charlene's stocky torso.

In a few minutes it became apparent that the cab was warming up faster than either Sonny or Charlene. He idly held one of her breasts in his hand, but it might have been an apple someone had given him just when he was least hungry.

"Hey," Charlene said suddenly, noticing. "What's the matter with you? You act half asleep."

Sonny was disconcerted. He was not sure what was wrong. It did not occur to him that he was bored. After all, he had Charlene's breast in his hand, and in Thalia it was generally agreed that the one thing that was never boring was feeling a girl's breasts. Grasping for straws, Sonny tried moving his hand downward, but it soon got entangled in Charlene's pudgy fingers.

"Quit, quit," she said, leaning her head back in expectation of a passionate kiss.

"But this is our anniversary," Sonny said. "Let's do something different."

Charlene grimly kept his hand at navel level, infuriated that he should think he really had license to go lower. That was plainly unfair, because he hadn't even given her a present. She scooted back toward her side of the cab and snatched her brassiere off the mirror.

"What are you trying to do, Sonny, get me pregnant?" she asked indignantly.

Sonny was stunned by the thought. "My lord," he said. "It was just my hand."

"Yeah, and one thing leads to another," she complained, struggling to catch the top hook of her bra. "Momma told me how that old stuff works."

Sonny reached over and hooked the hook for her, but he was more depressed than ever. It was obvious to him that it was a disgrace not to be going with someone prettier than Charlene, or if not prettier, at least someone more likable. The problem was how to break up with her and get his football jacket back.

"Well, you needn't to get mad," he said finally. "After so long a time I get tired of doing the same thing, and you do too. You wasn't no livelier than me."

"That's because you ain't good lookin' enough," she said coldly. "You ain't even got a ducktail. Why should I let you fiddle around and get me pregnant. We'll have plenty of time for that old stuff when we decide to get engaged."

Sonny twirled the knob on his steering wheel and looked out at the cold scudding water. He kept wanting to say something really nasty to Charlene, but he restrained himself. Charlene tucked her sweater back into her skirt and combed angrily at her brownish blond hair. Her mother had given her a permanent the day before and her hair was as stiff as wire.

"Let's go home," she said. "I'm done late anyway. Some anniversary."

Sonny backed the pickup around and started for the little cluster of yellow lights that was Thalia. The lake was only a couple of miles out.

"Charlene, if you feel that way I'd just as soon break up," he said. "I don't want to spoil no more anniversaries for you."

Charlene was surprised, but she recovered quickly. "That's the way nice girls get treated in this town," she said, proud to be a martyr to virtue.

"I knew you wasn't dependable," she added, taking the football jacket and laying it in the seat between them. "Boys that act like you do never are. That jacket's got a hole in the pocket, but you needn't ask me to sew it up. And you can give me back my pictures. I don't want you showin' 'em to a lot of other boys and tellin' them how hot I am."

Sonny stopped the pickup in front of her house and fished in his billfold for the three or four snapshots Charlene had given him. One of them, taken at a swimming pool in Wichita Falls, had been taken the summer before. Charlene was in a bathing suit. When she gave Sonny the picture she had taken a ballpoint pen and written on the back of the snapshot, "Look What Legs," hoping he would show it to Duane. The photograph showed clearly that her legs were short and fat, but in spite of it she managed to think of herself as possessing gazellelike slimness. Sonny laid the pictures on top of the football jacket, and Charlene scooped them up.

"Well, good-night," Sonny said. "I ain't got no hard feelings if you don't."

Charlene got out, but then she bethought herself of something and held the pickup door open a moment. "Don't you try to go with Marlene," she said. "Marlene's young, and she's a good Christian girl. If you try to go with her I'll tell my Daddy what a wolf you was with me and he'll stomp the you-know-what out of you."

"You was pretty glad to let me do what little I did," Sonny said, angered. "You just mind your own business and let Marlene mind hers."

Charlene gave him a last ill-tempered look. "If you've given me one of those diseases you'll be sorry," she said.

She could cheerfully have stabbed Sonny with an ice pick, but instead, to impress Marlene, she went in the house, woke her up, and cried for half the night about her blighted romance. She told Marlene Sonny had forced her to fondle him indecently.

"What in the world did it look like?" Marlene asked, bug-eyed with startled envy.

"Oh, the awfulest thing you ever saw," Charlene assured her, smearing a thick coating of beauty cream on her face. "Ouuee, he was nasty. I hope you don't ever get involved with a man like that, honey—they make you old before your time. I bet I've aged a year, just tonight."

Later, when the lights were out, Marlene tried to figure on her fingers what month it would be when Charlene would be sent away in disgrace to Kizer, Arkansas to have her baby. They had an aunt who lived in Kizer. Marlene was not exactly clear in her mind about how one went about getting pregnant, but she assumed that with such goings on Charlene must have. It was conceivable that her mother would make Charlene leave the picture of Van Johnson behind when she was sent away, and that thought cheered Marlene very much. In any case, it would be nice to have the bedroom to herself.

. . . .

A week before the picture show closed down Duane came home from boot camp. He drove in on Sunday morning and word soon got around that he was leaving for Korea in a week's time. Sonny learned that he was home Sunday night, when he and Billy were having a cheeseburger in the café.

"Wonder where he is?" he asked. "He hasn't been to the poolhall."

"I kinda doubt he'll come," Genevieve said, frowning. "His conscience is hurting him too much about your eye. I think he's gonna stay at the rooming house this week."

"Well, maybe he'll come in," Sonny said. "There ain't much to do in this town. I couldn't live in it a week without going to the poolhall, I know that."

"I think it's all silly," Genevieve said. "Why don't you go see him? Be a shame if he goes to Korea without you all seein' one another."

Sonny thought so too, but he was nervous about going to see Duane. He kept hoping Duane would show up at the poolhall and save him having to make a decision; but Duane didn't. So far as anyone knew, he spent the whole week watching television at his mother's house. A couple of boys saw him out washing his Mercury one afternoon, but he never came to town.

As the week went by, Sonny got more and more nervous. Several times he was on the verge of picking up the phone and calling—once he did pick it up, but his nerve failed him and he put it back down. If Duane didn't want to be bothered there was no point in bothering.

Friday night there was a football game in Henrietta, but Sonny didn't go. He heard the next morning that Duane had been there drunk. All day he considered the problem and finally decided that he would go see Duane at the rooming house and let the chips fall where they may—it couldn't hurt much to try. If Duane didn't want to see him all he had to do was say so.

About five-thirty, as it was beginning to grow dark, Sonny got in the pickup and drove to the rooming house. Duane's red Mercury was parked out front. A norther had struck that afternoon and sheets of cold air rushed through the town, shaking the leafless mesquite and rattling the dry stems of Old Lady Malone's flowers. Sonny rang the doorbell and then stuffed his hands in his pockets to keep them warm.

"H'lo, Mrs. Malone," he said, when the old lady opened the inside door. The screen door was latched, as always. "Duane here?"

"That's his car, ain't it?" she said, edging behind the door so the wind wouldn't hit anything but her nose and her forehead. "He's here if he ain't walked off."

She shut the door and went to get Duane. Sonny shuffled nervously on the porch. In a minute, Duane opened the door and stepped outside.

"Hi," Sonny said, finding it hard to get his breath because of the wind. "Thought I'd better come by and see you before you got off."

"Glad you did," Duane said. He was nervous, but he did look sort of glad. He was wearing Levi's and a western shirt.

"Want to go eat a bite?" Sonny suggested.

"Yeah, let me get my jacket."

He got his football jacket, the one from the year when the two of them had been cocaptains, they got in the warm pickup, and drove to the café. Conversation was slow in coming until Sonny thought to ask about the army, but then Duane loosened up and told one army story after another while they ate their hamburger steaks. It was pretty much like old times. Penny waited on them— she had had twin girls during the winter, put on twenty-five pounds, and was experimenting that night with purple lipstick. Old Marston had died in February of pneumonia—he had gone to sleep in a bar ditch in the wrong season. Genevieve had hired a friendly young widow woman to do the cooking.

"Guess we ought to take in the picture show," Sonny said. "Tonight's the last night."

"A good thing, too," Penny said, overhearing him. "Picture shows been gettin' more sinful all the time, if you ask me. Them movie stars lettin' their titties hang out—I never seen the like. The last time I went I told my old man he could just take me home, I wasn't sittin' still for that kind of goings on."

"Yeah, we might as well go," Duane said, ignoring her. "Hate to miss the last night."

They went to the poolhall and Sonny got his football jacket too. Then they angled across the square to the picture show and bought their tickets. A few grade-school kids were going in. The picture was an Audie Murphy movie called *The Kid from Texas,* with Gale Storm.

"Why hello, Duane," Miss Mosey said. "I thought you was done overseas. Hope you all like the show."

The boys planned to, but somehow the occasion just didn't work out. Audie Murphy was a scrapper as usual, but it didn't help. It would have taken *Winchester '73* or *Red River* or some big movie like that to have crowded out the memories the boys kept having. They had been at the picture show so often with Jacy that it was hard to keep from thinking of her, lithely stretching herself in the back row after an hour of kissing and cuddling. Such thoughts were dangerous to both of them.

"Hell, this here's a dog," Duane said.

Sonny agreed. "Why don't we run down to Fort Worth, drink a little beer?" he asked.

"My bus leaves at six-thirty in the mornin'," Duane said. "Reckon we could make it to Fort Worth and back by six-thirty?"

"Easy."

Miss Mosey was distressed to see them leaving so soon. She tried to give them their money back, but they wouldn't take it. She was scraping out the popcorn machine, almost in tears. "If Sam had lived, I believe we could have kept it goin'," she said, "but me and Jimmy just didn't have the know-how. Duane, you watch out now, overseas." Outside the wind was so cold it made their eyes water.

.   .   .   .

Of all the people in Thalia, Billy missed the picture show most. He couldn't understand that it was permanently closed. Every night he kept thinking it would open again. For seven years he had gone to the show every single night, always sitting in the balcony, always sweeping out once the show was over; he just couldn't stop expecting it. Every night he took his broom and went over to the picture show, hoping it would be open. When it wasn't, he sat on the curb in front of the courthouse, watching the theater, hoping it would open a little later; then, after a while, in puzzlement, he would sweep listlessly off down the highway toward Wichita Falls. Sonny watched him as closely as he could, but it still worried him. He was afraid Billy might get through a fence or over a cattleguard and sweep right off into the mesquite. He might sweep away down the creeks and gullies and never be found.

Once, on a Friday afternoon, Miss Mosey had to go into the theater to get something she had left and she let Billy in for a minute. The screen was disappointingly dead, but Billy figured that at least he was in, so he went up into the balcony and sat waiting. Miss Mosey thought he had gone back outside and locked him in. It was not until late that night, when Sonny got worried and began asking around, that Miss Mosey thought of the balcony. When they got there, Billy was sitting quietly in the dark with his broom, waiting, perfectly sure that the show would come on sometime.

All through October, then through November, Billy missed the show. Sonny didn't know what to do about it, but it was a bad time in general and he didn't know what to do about himself either. He had taken another lease to pump. He wanted to work harder and tire himself out, so he wouldn't have to lie awake at night and feel alone. Nothing much was happening, and he didn't think much was going to. One day he went to Wichita and bought a television set, thinking it might help Billy, but it didn't at all. Billy would watch it as long as Sonny was around, but the minute Sonny left he left too. He didn't trust the television. He kept going over to the picture show night after night, norther or no norther— he sat on the sidewalk and waited, cold and puzzled. He knew it would open sooner or later, and Sonny could think of no way to make him understand that it wouldn't.

One cold, sandstormy morning in late November Sonny woke up early and went downstairs to light the poolhall fires. Billy was not around, but that was not unusual. Sonny sneezed two or three times, the air was so dry. One of the gas stoves was old and he had to blow on it to get all the burners to light. While he was blowing on the burners he heard a big cattle truck roar past the poolhall, coming in from the south. Suddenly there was a loud shriek, as the driver hit the brakes for all he was worth—the stoplight was always turning red at the wrong time and catching trucks that thought they had it made.

Sonny went back upstairs and dressed to go eat breakfast. He couldn't find either one of his eye patches and supposed Billy must have them. It was the kind of morning when a welding helmet would have been a nice sort of thing to wear. The sky was cloudy and gritty, and the wind cut. When he stepped outside Sonny noticed that the big cattle truck was stopped by the square, with a little knot of men gathered around it. The doctor's car had just pulled up to the knot of men and the old doctor got out, his hair uncombed, his pajamas showing under his bathrobe. Someone had been run over. Sonny started to turn away, but then he saw Billy's broom laying in the street. By the time he got to the men the doctor had returned to his car and was driving away.

Billy was lying face up on the street, near the curb. For some reason he had put both eye patches on—his eyes were completely covered. There were just four or five men there—the sheriff and his deputy, a couple of men from the filling stations, one cowboy, and a pumper who was going out early. They were not paying attention to Billy, but were trying to keep the truck driver from feeling bad. He was a big, square-faced man from Waurika, Oklahoma, who didn't look like he felt too bad. The truck was loaded with Hereford yearlings and they were bumping one another around and shitting, the bright green cowshit dripping off the sideboards and splatting onto the street.

"This sand was blowin'," the trucker said. His name was Hurley. "I never noticed him, never figured nobody would be in the street. Why he had them damn blinders on his eyes, he couldn't even see. What was he doin' out there anyway, carryin' that broom?"

"Aw, nothing', Hurley," the sheriff said. "He was just an ol' simpleminded kid, sort of retarded—never had no sense. Wasn't your fault, I can see that. He was just there—he wasn't doin' nothing."

Sonny couldn't stand the way the men looked at the truck driver and had already forgotten Billy.

"He was sweeping, you sons of bitches!" he yelled suddenly, surprising the men and himself. They all looked at him as if he were crazy, and indeed, he didn't know himself why he had yelled. He walked over on the courthouse lawn, not knowing what to do. In a minute he bent over and vomited by one of the dusty, stunted little cedar trees that the Amity club had planted. His father had come by that time.

"Son, it's a bad blow," he said. "You let me take care of things, okay? You don't want to be bothered with any funeral-home stuff, do you?"

Sonny didn't; he was glad to let his father take care of it. He walked out in the street and got Billy's broom and took it over to him.

"Reckon I better go try to sell a little gas," one of the filling-station men said. "Look's like this here's about wound up."

Sonny didn't want to yell at the men again, but he couldn't stand to walk away and leave Billy there by the truck, with the circle of men spitting and farting and shuffling all around him. Before any of them knew what he was up to he got Billy under the arms and started off with him, dragging him and trying to run. The men were so amazed they didn't even try to stop him. The heels of Billy's brogans scraped on the pavement, but Sonny kept on, dragged him across the windy street to the curb in front of the picture show. That was as far as he went. He laid Billy on the sidewalk where at least he would be out of the street, and covered him with his Levi jacket. He just left the eye patches on.

The men slowly came over. They looked at Sonny as if he were someone very strange. Hurley and the sheriff came together and stood back a little way from the crowd.

"You all got some crazy kids in this town," Hurley said, spitting his tobacco juice carefully down wind.

Geoffrey O'Brien

What O'Brien remembers here is something I had almost forgotten: how, when you are young, the savor of a movie title itself suggests exciting and forbidden worlds. For weeks before I saw The Blackboard Jungle, *the title obsessed me. And every Sunday in church, I turned to the page of* Our Sunday Visitor *on which a critic named Dale Francis sniffed at the latest immorality from Hollywood. Beneath his column was the list of the Legion of Decency ratings, and under "C (for Condemned)" I read eagerly about* One Summer with Monica, The Naked Night, *and* The Moon Is Blue. *Such innocent words to inspire inflamed fantasies!*

from *The Phantom Empire*

The kids in the neighborhood had seen many movies by now, and had even learned almost all there was to know about endangered caravans, men half-mad with thirst, eyes peering through underbrush, alligators breaking the surfaces of rivers, lost explorers starting at the rumble of distant drums, burning arrows flying over the walls of stockades, cavalry troops riding into canyons.

Once the model had been established they could find movies everywhere. Only a slight variation in intensity distinguished the real movies on the screen from the numberless movielike artifacts and experiences: the expedition through the crazy house at the seashore park, the skeletons of dinosaurs rearing up in the natural history museum, the comic-book adventures of ghosts and ducks and Stone Age hunters, the episodes of drama or history isolated on bubble-gum cards, the three-dimensional plays staged with metal-and-rubber figurines, the movie stars proffering cigarettes or facial cream in the pages of *Look* and *The Saturday Evening Post,* the fragmentary violence of the drugstore book covers with their brawling mobsters and strangled blondes. In yard and playground and parking lot the children enacted poses copied from production stills.

Through the bush telegraph of the electric world the children got word of the movies that were coming. Some hadn't even been filmed yet. Some had opened in a far-off city and had not yet come to town, or might never come; and some they might in any event be forbidden to see. Advance messages arrived in comic-book versions, in paperbacks of the novels the movies were based on, in lobby posters glimpsed as they exited from the matinee showing of *The African Lion* or *The Lone Ranger and the Lost City of Gold.*

From the posters and the newspaper ads they learned many phrases: "Frank and revealing!" "Shattering power!" "The emotional experience of a lifetime!" "All the human depth and electrifying drama of the tremendous best-seller!" The concepts were still vague: they did not yet, for instance, know precisely what "human depth" meant. It suggested an intimate but still foreign space, a network of hallways inside an adult body.

They were haunted by the titles of all the movies they had missed. Each title stood for a story that might have been different from all the other stories, if only they could have experienced it. Each was a door, and there were thousands of doors they had not entered. They imagined themselves in the dark watching whatever such a title might denote, a place with different-colored vegetation, exotic legal codes, novel varieties of emotion and behavior. There was no telling how deep the space concealed by the name might be. Each was like a planet hidden under cloud cover.

It might be simply a name: *Rebecca* or *Diane, Hondo* or *Jubal, Moonfleet* or *Dragonwyck.* Was it the name of a woman, a house, a ship, a dynasty, a treasure, a crime? And why would any one name be so overwhelmingly powerful that a movie had be named after it?

It might be plainly in another language, a sound of imminent unknown danger: *Odongo, Jivaro, Mogambo, Simba, Hukl, Bwana Devil, Macumba Love.* It might simply specify the place where the strange erupted into the real—*Istanbul,*

Malaya, Tanganyika, Timbuktu, Beyond Mombasa, East of Sumatra—or add some no-
tation of the action that took place there: *Flight to Hong Kong, Flight to Tangier,
Escape to Burma, Storm over the Nile.*

It might suggest a world of infinite choreographic frivolity, where adults
wore bright clothes and laughed wildly, a drunkenly exuberant picnic: *You Can't
Run Away from It, It Happens Every Spring, Everybody Does It, The More the Merrier,
It Should Happen to You, It Happened to Jane, It Had to Happen, It started with a Kiss,
You're Never Too Young, It's Never Too Late.*

It might assume a riddling form. It referred to an event but provided no clues
to its real nature. *The Man Who Died Twice.* How? *The Woman They Almost Lynched.*
Why? *The Ship That Died of Shame.* Why? How? It spoke of fantastic and cata-
strophic events in the past tense, as if they had already occurred: *It Came from
Outer Space, It Conquered the World, From Hell It Came, The Day the World Ended,
The Day the Sky Exploded, The Night the World Exploded.* What? When?

It might, by contrast, conjure up an outpouring of vast cyclonic emotion, a
potentially annihilating tumult urged on by violin ensembles: *All This and Heaven
Too, All That Heaven Allows, Now and Forever, Goodbye Again, Never Say Goodbye,
Heaven Can Wait, There's Always Tomorrow, Tomorrow Is Forever.* Time was to be
overwhelmed by feeling. How would anyone make a photograph of that?

Those domains of large feeling were inhabited by companies of equally enormous humans, who could be defined only by broad sweeps of adjectives: *The
Proud and Profane, The Bold and the Brave, The Tall Men, The Violent Men, The High
and the Mighty.* What would such people look like? What kind of heightened language and monumental gestures would that race of giants use?

Emotion could be tuned to an even shriller, more ominous pitch: *Too Much,
Too Soon, They Dare Not Love, To the Ends of the Earth, None Shall Escape, The Damned
Don't Cry, No Way Out.* It was something that somebody might scrawl on a win-
dow or a wall in a moment of ultimate panic.

It sketched an emotional landscape of conflagration—*Foxfire, Fire Down Below,
Flame of the Islands*—or meteorological upheaval—*Written on the Wind, Blowing
Wild, Wild Is the Wind, Storm Fear, Storm Warning*—or simply promised to strip
the world bare: *Naked Alibi, Naked Earth, The Naked Edge, The Naked Dawn, The
Naked Street, The Naked Hills, The Naked Jungle.*

It was a voice, perhaps, trying (against a background noise of breaking glass,
someone having just hurled a bottle at a mirror) to scream out a confession: *I'll
Cry Tomorrow, I Died a Thousand Times, I Want to Live!*

A good title was something to be recited again and again, an empowering
chant. The strongest evoked the worst that could befall and warded it off through
the sheer power of their syllabic configuration—*Bad Day at Black Rock, Pickup on
South Street, Stakeout on Dope Street*—or through an arcane sort of number magic:
*Riot in Cell Block 1 1, Seven Men from Now, Five against the House, Ten Seconds to Hell,
One Minute to Zero.*

The most endlessly mysterious were those that packed into a single word a world of undefined possibilities—*Illicit, Notorious, Ruthless, Shockproof, Dangerous, Caught, Caged, Cornered, Branded, Desperate, Forbidden*—as if the fullness of a life could be represented by one undifferentiated sign.

Those children occasionally wondered—looking across at the marquee and noticing how it filled the street and put a label on it, how it turned the street into a frame around a name—what would be the right name for the movie to be made of their lives.

. . . .

To be made into a movie was salvation, because the picture could not die: it was life itself. The saturated hues of Technicolor constituted all by themselves a tropical garden, a warm bath at the end of the mind. It required only swimming-pool logic to wade out into the sarongs and geometries of South Seas movies and Esther Williams vehicles, *Pagan Love Song* and *Pearl of the South Pacific,* the gaudy recurrent dance parties of heathens and pirates and jungle princesses.

There was another aspect to this extended game of dress-up: it was called history. In that enchanted world, John Wayne conquered Central Asia (while making eyes at Debra Paget), Jack Hawkins built the pyramids (while having troubles with Joan Collins), Gary Cooper spoke Seminole (while flirting somewhat coyly with Mari Aldon), and (in *Yankee Pasha*) the American adventurer (Jeff Chandler) seeking to rescue his fiancée (Rhonda Fleming) from Barbary pirates stumbled into a Vegas-style harem populated by the Miss Universe finalists of 1952 and presided over by Lee J. Cobb.

Across the screen's shimmering surface floated a circus of elements—gauze and feathers, chain mail and drawbridges, Arabs and Indians, forests, pools, fires—among which the eye moved like a swimmer. They appeared, they shifted, they reassembled in different shapes and colors. At every instant they gratified. An arcane vocabulary categorized varieties of pleasure: CinemaScope, Technicolor, Eastmancolor, Trucolor, Cinerama.

The cowboy movies in particular existed to give prominence to certain colors: blue sky, green fir, ocher rockface, a Crayola landscape. In *The Naked Spur* or *The Man from Laramie* the spectator's function was to appreciate the solidity of the landscape and the force and velocity with which the actors moved through it. Some ultimate reassurance about the thereness of things was implicit in the arroyos and salt flats of the desolate territories where grizzled old scouts—Arthur Hunnicutt, Walter Brennan, Millard Mitchell—cooked bacon and read signs. At the end the producers expressed their gratitude to Montana or Utah for existing. But where had there ever been such places outside of a movie?

Technicolor made scant distinction between the actual lakes and mountains of the westerns and the man-made costumes and furnishings appropriate to

Knights of the Round Table or *The Band Wagon*. It was all equally and ravishingly unreal. The lens converted even sky and sea into artificial constructions. The air was different in those bright outdoor scenes that could be observed only in a darkened interior: it was sustenance.

The deep hunger that it fed defined itself most vividly through trappings, frivolities, backdrops. Bric-a-brac was essence. The ribbons and packaging were busy enough in themselves that you barely needed to follow the plot or notice the new faces of 1957: Taina Elg, Diane Varsi, Miyoshi Umeki, Russ Tamblyn, John Gavin. The actors were there to provide a support system for the props and costumes, to give the camera something to encircle or swoop down on.

The screen was a second sky, where what you saw was nothing compared to the anticipation of what you might at any moment witness: a shooting star, a spaceship, an apocalypse. Going to the movies involved, always, a religious sense of hope. An incipient sense of worshipful attention was ready for the unimagined, the barely imaginable, God or world war or Martians. You wanted visible proof.

.   .   .   .

In Sunday school, reference was made repeatedly to certain uncanny and world-shaping events, but that was hearsay. Church amounted to little more than an anteroom to actual experience, a place where things were spoken of at a distance. Listening to Bible stories was at best like listening to tantalizing synopses of forthcoming releases. It wasn't quite enough, any more than leafing through back issues of *Photoplay* was enough. The thirst was to *see* the truth, to be overwhelmed by it.

That was what movie theaters were for: they were the places where something real was going on, where plagues and floods really happened. A verbal account of the Red Sea parting or the Angel of Death gliding over the rooftops of Egypt couldn't compare to witnessing it in *The Ten Commandments*. It couldn't even compare to the trailer for *The Ten Commandments*. Why settle for words when you could go see photographs of God? And if He couldn't quite (considering the buildup) measure up—if the burning bush was, after all, not sufficiently different from the brushfires of *Flaming Feather* and *The Flame and the Arrow* and *Fire over Africa,* and if (to one's secret disappointment) they didn't even *show* God—that was surely not the fault of the movies.

God was not interesting if He only occurred in the remote past and was incapable of being played by a movie star. If the most important thing in the world was invisible, how important could it be? It was fitting that there *should* be a movie of God, a movie that would live up to what the promotional kit for *The Big Fisherman* promised: "the stirring physical action, the massive spectacle, and the exalted spiritual theme." He belonged in that atmosphere, and would ultimately be judged by its standards, in the same way it was said of certain famous stage actors that they just couldn't make it in the movies.

It was when your world blacked out and the other radiant world imposed itself that you understood the word "awe." The kingdom of heaven consisted of robed Saracens, half-naked princesses, ululating high priests, dust-covered troupes of elephants and camels, earthquakes and cobras, thousands of bits of metal clanking in unison, an ensemble sustained by the rumbling of a gigantic orchestra. It was the authentic noise and texture of an ancient alien planet.

Wasn't this like the effect of prayer, to have such things realized? To be enabled to see those hosts of armed warriors assembled? To travel those enormous distances—soaring into the air and crossing over plains and mountains—and in the midst of it to hear the voice of God in all its thunderous sonority? The voice alone would not have meant so much. The manifold glory lay not in the voice but in the thousands of extras and horses and terraced palaces assembled at its command.

Whereas the empty church was just empty. You and your friends crept in one afternoon as if expecting to find God relaxing at home. There was nothing. That is, there was nothing *playing* there. Some awkward posters of Jesus at table, by a lake, on a hill, patting children on the head, smiling at lepers: coming attractions. But those illustrations were drained images, not remotely as gritty or turbulent as the lobby cards for *Demetrius and the Gladiators* or *The Big Fisherman*. If God was anywhere He was across town working wide-screen miracles.

. . . .

Not that all the movies had His stamp on them. It was a gradual education to scout the borders of the diabolical territories in which scenes, subplots, and whole movies might be located. There was a curse on some movies, so that you could never undo the fact of having seen them. The loop would run again and again. You enter the steamy little movie theater in the tropical port and find a movie about a steamy little tropical port. The white men, in white jackets, penetrate a clearing. They have to bend their heads to get into the hut. There is a fire on the screen. Voodoo drums. Piles of skulls. An amulet made of twisted roots. The dancers move in a circle. The eyes move toward the center of the screen where the center of the ritual is happening. Ceremonial cooch dance.

Americans break a taboo and are cursed. Having violated the sanctuary of the cobra goddess, they will each be seduced in turn by the beautiful woman (Faith Domergue) who deep down is cobra. The bedroom scenes elide into slithers and hisses. "You ready for me, baby?" Scream and darkness. It's never what is shown, it's what is about to be shown: the threatening music, the camera inching toward the unspeakable. But in the end you remember best the act of entering the theater, as if the theater were itself the forbidden tropical clearing given over to the power of cobras and skulls and amulets.

It was the source of the talk. You talked your way out of what the images had made you feel. Limit their power by tagging them—or get rid of the curse by passing it on to someone else. For every frightening and forbidden image you had seen, there were thousands more of which you had only heard. A daily seminar filled in the blanks. From the beginning movies were incorporated indissolubly into a system of orally transmitted folklore.

Older brothers came home late from the movies and could be overheard talking on the phone, or sitting up late in the kitchen telling what happened in the last reel of *Try and Get Me*—how the lynch mob set the jail on fire, how the terror was visible on the face of the trapped kidnapper as they lifted him from his cell and passed him like a doll over the heads of the crowd—or how Gene Krupa was a junkie—or how Kim Novak saw a black-robed nun emerge from the darkness and was so surprised she fell backward off the belltower to her death—or how the aliens in *The Mysterians* abducted earth women to mate with them and repopulate their dying planet.

Retelling a movie was an art in itself. Children grew up telling each other plots. There would be sessions where the most frightening or disgusting episodes would be elicited from a circle of people. "The sickest thing I ever saw was when the giant ants invaded the communications room on board the ship in *Them!* and wrapped their pincers around the sailors' bodies." "The worst thing was the mark the aliens made on people's necks in *Invaders from Mars*." "They staked him out in the desert and coated him with honey and let the ants devour him." "The mask had nails inside it." "The man sent her a pair of binoculars that poked her eyes out." You didn't have to have seen it, hearing about it was bad enough. Years were spent trying to define the precise point where pleasure became disturbance, the border between too upsetting and not upsetting enough.

The folklore had to do with aliens in sunglasses who drank blood and whose language had to be translated by subtitles, baby monsters spawned by radiation, husbands who devised clever methods of murdering their wives or driving them insane and detectives who laid equally clever traps to catch them, exotic tortures practiced by Apaches and medieval warlords, children abducted by desert marauders, bombing raids in the big war against Germany and Japan and Russia and Korea, madmen whose urge to kill was unleashed by particular melodies or colors, people haunted by dreams that told them they had lived another life before this one, archaic chants that brought mummies to life. Stories of miracles, all of them, like Lazarus clambering groggily from his tomb in the stiffly uncoordinated manner of a resurrected Boris Karloff.

The real miracle was simply that those creatures lived and moved. Once set in motion, the legions of walking ghosts never stopped. The thousands of celluloid beings who inhabited movies were like windup toys that would run for eternity, or like the proliferating animate mops unwittingly activated by the sorcerer's apprentice in *Fantasia,* or like the irradiated insects who in *Them!* and *Tarantula* and *The Deadly Mantis* seemed on the verge of sweeping over the earth's surface. At night, in the dark, the disembodied creatures swarmed in the mind, indestructible.

MOVIE STARS

H. L. MENCKEN

H. L. Mencken meets Rudolph Valentino (1895–1926) shortly before the actor's final illness and is startled to find what he least expected: a gentleman, recoiling at "the whole grotesque futility of his life." Mencken (1880–1956) was not known as a show business writer; politics, philosophy, and human nature were his subjects. Yet here he produces a poignant examination of celebrity and sees Valentino with eyes not blinded by his stardom.

Rudolph Valentino

By one of the chances that relieve the dullness of life and make it instructive, I had the honor of dining with this celebrated gentleman in New York, a week or so before his fatal illness. I had never met him before, nor seen him on the screen; the meeting was at his instance, and, when it was proposed, vaguely puzzled me. But soon its purpose became clear enough. Valentino was in trouble and wanted advice. More, he wanted advice from an elder and disinterested man, wholly removed from the movies and all their works. Something that I had written, falling under his eye, had given him the notion that I was a judicious fellow. So he requested one of his colleagues, a lady of the films, to ask me to dinner at her hotel.

The night being infernally warm, we stripped off our coats, and came to terms at once. I recall that he wore suspenders of extraordinary width and thickness. On so slim a young man they seemed somehow absurd, especially on a hot Summer night. We perspired horribly for an hour, mopping our faces with our handkerchiefs, the table napkins, the corners of the tablecloth, and a couple of towels brought in by the humane waiter. Then there came a thunderstorm, and we began to breathe. The hostess, a woman as tactful as she is charming, disappeared mysteriously and left us to commune.

The trouble that was agitating Valentino turned out to be very simple. The ribald New York papers were full of it, and that was what was agitating him. Some time before, out in Chicago, a wandering reporter had discovered, in the men's wash-room of a gaudy hotel, a slot-machine selling talcum-powder. That, of course, was not unusual, but the color of the talcum-powder was. It was pink. The news made the town giggle for a day, and inspired an editorial writer on the Chicago *Tribune* to compose a hot weather editorial. In it he protested humorously against the effeminization of the American man, and laid it lightheartedly to the influence of Valentino and his sheik movies. Well, it so happened that Valentino, passing through Chicago that day on his way east from the Coast, ran full tilt into the editorial, and into a gang of reporters who wanted to know what he had to say about it. What he had to say was full of fire. Throwing off his 100% Americanism and reverting to the *mores* of his father-land, he challenged the editorial writer to a duel, and, when no answer came, to a fist fight. His masculine honor, it appeared, had been outraged. To the hint that he was less than he, even to the extent of one half of one per cent, there could be no answer save a bath of blood.

Unluckily, all this took place in the United States, where the word honor, save when it is applied to the structural integrity of women, has only a comic significance. When one hears of the honor of politicians, of bankers, of lawyers, of the United States itself, everyone naturally laughs. So New York laughed at Valentino. More, it ascribed his high dudgeon to mere publicity-seeking: he seemed a vulgar movie ham seeking space. The poor fellow, thus doubly beset, rose to dudgeons higher still. His Italian mind was simply unequal to the situation. So he sought counsel from the neutral, aloof and seasoned. Unluckily, I could only name the disease, and confess frankly that there was no remedy— none, that is, known to any therapeutics within my ken. He should have passed over the gibe of the Chicago journalist, I suggested, with a lofty snort—perhaps, better still, with a counter gibe. He should have kept away from the reporters in New York. But now, alas, the mischief was done. He was both insulted and ridiculous, but there was nothing to do about it. I advised him to let the dread-ful farce roll along to exhaustion. He protested that it was infamous. Infamous? Nothing, I argued, is infamous that is not true. A man still has his inner integrity. Can he still look into the shaving-glass of a morning? Then he is still on his two legs in this world, and ready even for the Devil. We sweated a great deal, dis-cussing these lofty matters. We seemed to get nowhere.

Suddenly it dawned upon me—I was too dull or it was too hot for me to see it sooner—that what we were talking about was really not what we were talk-ing about at all. I began to observe Valentino more closely. A curiously naïve and boyish young fellow, certainly not much beyond thirty, and with a disarm-ing air of inexperience. To my eye, at least, not handsome, but nevertheless rather attractive. There was some obvious fineness in him; even his clothes were not precisely those of his horrible trade. He began talking of his home, his people, his early youth. His words were simple and yet somehow very eloquent. I could still see the mime before me, but now and then, briefly and darkly, there was a flash of something else. That something else, I concluded, was what is commonly called, for want of a better name, a gentleman. In brief, Valentino's agony was the agony of a man of relatively civilized feelings thrown into a situation of intolerable vulgarity, destructive alike to his peace and to his dignity—nay, into a whole series of such situations.

It was not that trifling Chicago episode that was riding him; it was the whole grotesque futility of his life. Had he achieved, out of nothing, a vast and dizzy success? Then that success was hollow as well as vast—a colossal and preposterous nothing. Was he acclaimed by yelling multitudes? Then every time the multitudes yelled he felt himself blushing inside. The old story of Diego Valdez once more, but with a new poignancy in it. Valdez, at all events, was High Admiral of Spain. But Valentino, with his touch of fineness in him—he had his commonness, too, but there was that touch of fineness—Valentino was only the hero of the rabble. Imbeciles surrounded him in a dense herd. He was pursued by women—but what women! (Consider the sordid comedy of his two marriages—the brummagem, star-spangled passion that invaded his very deathbed!) The thing, at the start, must have only bewildered him. But in those last days, unless I am a worse psychologist than even the professors of psychology, it was revolting him. Worse, it was making him afraid.

I incline to think that the inscrutable gods, in taking him off so soon and at a moment of fiery revolt, were very kind to him. Living, he would have tried inevitably to change his fame—if such it is to be called—into something closer to his heart's desire. That is to say, he would have gone the way of many another actor—the way of increasing pretension, of solemn artiness, of hollow hocuspocus, deceptive only to himself. I believe he would have failed, for there was little sign of the genuine artist in him. He was essentially a highly respectable young man, which is the sort that never metamorphoses into an artist. But suppose he had succeeded? Then his tragedy, I believe, would have only become the more acrid and intolerable. For he would have discovered, after vast heavings and yearnings, that what he had come to was indistinguishable from what he had left. Was the fame of Beethoven any more caressing and splendid than the fame of Valentino? To you and me, of course, the question seems to answer itself. But what of Beethoven? He was heard upon the subject, *viva voce,* while he lived, and his answer survives, in all the freshness of its profane eloquence, in his music. Beethoven, too, knew what it meant to be applauded. Walking with Goethe, he heard something that was not unlike the murmur that reached Valentino through his hospital window. Beethoven walked away briskly. Valentino turned his face to the wall.

Here was a young man who was living daily the dream of millions of other young men. Here was one who was catnip to women. Here was one who had wealth and fame. And here was one who was very unhappy.

STARK YOUNG

By "wanting to be alone," by refusing interviews, by avoiding the star-making game, Greta Garbo (1905–1990) was successful more than most movie stars in existing only on the screen. She wanted to seem to have no other existence than as the characters she played. This quality was apparent right from the start of her career, when she positioned herself apart from all other actresses and invented her own style of personal publicity, which was nonpublicity. Stark Young, the film critic of the New Republic, *analyzed her strategy early in her career, in 1932.*

Greta Garbo

Since Miss Greta Garbo came to America some years ago, her fame has grown and grown. In her last picture, a Hollywood and rather nursery version of Pirandello's *As You Desire Me,* she has come to the end of her contract and to her highest success; the piece has passed from one end of the country to the other in triumph, and Miss Garbo has gone back to Sweden, to return or not to return as the case may be. During all this time her position has steadily advanced. As to her drawing capacity I know very little, these are delicate and falsified matters on the whole, and what drawing power means, crowded box offices, I am still uncertain. I remember once, coming back from Italy, half an hour after Gibraltar, and just as we were passing the coast of Spain, with a vista magnificent and everchanging, how most of the passenger list had hastened below decks to see Jackie Coogan. There is no proverb about the ears and eyes of people being the ears and eyes of God. Miss Garbo's box office realities, nevertheless, are very great and, I feel sure, have steadily increased, or there would not be so many pictures of her promulgated or efforts at spreading news, such news, that is, as can be snappily concocted, about her, all of which costs the producers money.

Certainly it can be said that Miss Garbo is unique among Hollywood ladies and curiously untouched by its vulgar silliness of report and its obvious and intimate Kodak and journalism. Meantime she supplies an odd comment on our public, with regard to its popular philosophy, its esthetic theory, and its soul. Both satire and poetry and common dream are involved.

By Miss Garbo's being a comment on the popular philosophy of a great people and a great democratic legend I mean two things. The first is in a lighter vein. The managerial publicity for Miss Garbo, based soundly enough on facts, has created unceasingly the theme of her solitude. She does not make a part of crowds; she has moments when she likes to be alone; she flees publicity; she likes to live privately. In general this is a thought that almost strangles our average citizen. What, not go to a committee, not ride forth, not take a part in the community; if you can sing, not do it on the radio; if you are blessed with a motor, not speed somewhere; if you have a house, not create a swarming for it; if you have emotions, not carry them and tell! At any rate, conceive of someone who stays in when he could go out, who could see people but thinks it a kind of communion, peace, rest, or right to be alone sometimes! This has made Miss Garbo almost a national puzzle. It could have been explained away by making her a freak or a high-hat. But she is neither. She is not even sick; Swedish people are athletic. We must swallow it, then, as a cosmic mystery, this successful star really likes at times to be alone.

In the course of democratic thought another point, much more serious, has arisen. What are artists? Are they any different from anybody else? To this challenge many of our artists of the theater have arisen. They are as everyday as everybody. I was told in Grand Rapids once of a singer from the Metropolitan who, at a Rotarian dinner in his honor, told the diners that he was just like the rest of them, no different, singing was his business just as bonding, banking, running a laundry, was theirs. This was no doubt true, but it does not affect the question. One of the things to ponder in the theater now, in the opera especially, is the vast melee of fallen stars. They are not fallen from fiscal stardom, they are fallen from glamor. As stars they are known for their hits, their successes, their salaries and contracts, sometimes for their personalities, real or created by their agents and managers; they remain just folks like the rest of us. That is the great balm. But they are not the glamor and wonder of the heart, not any longer. As the dramatist tells us in *The Swan,* royalty, like swans, should stay well away from the bank; seen close at hand they are apt to be at best but waddling animals. So it is in the theater ultimately, but not in democratic theory.

The sarcasm of all this is that Miss Garbo contradicts the whole business. We know very little of her, not really. Visitors to Hollywood do not see her. Junior

League conventions, given a dinner by the producers, with all the screen stars lined up as *hors d'oeuvres* and flashlights as souvenirs, miss this one relish in the lot; they see everybody but Greta Garbo, and though they like the haircut of some great artist, they depart with a certain awe about this refusing Swedish player. A little actress, renting Miss Garbo's house, may get a picture published of Garbo's bed, renting publicity. Nor do we see photographs of Greta Garbo meeting someone at the train or drinking Swedish punch with a millionaire, or buried in the midst of a pile of books (wooden movie properties), or any other blessed fiddledeedee for the popular heart. There were tricks in plenty among the old stars. Patti was not without her special coaches and her parrots and imperial gems, nor did the Barnum method leave untouched the great figure of Bernhardt, who carried in her his soul's epic. But when all was said and done, their splendor and ability shone at the proper shining time. These ancient tricks are tired now, overworked, and most stars are starry in long-runs, incomes, romances, and scandals. It can be said that to Miss Garbo some of the glamor, old-style, baffling, full of dreams, imaginings, and wonder, has returned. If nothing else, in many instances, she is a blessed rebuff to the back-slapping and personal-friend-of-mine citizens that appropriate the artists of the theater, who in their turn are too scared of their positions, too greedy, or too mediocre themselves to do anything different. It would be a sad day in our midst if our great ticket-buying public should learn one chief and simple fact about art, which is that a great artist is like everybody else but is not like anybody else. Alas, equality and the folks!

Esthetically, the case of Miss Greta Garbo is a kind of joke on the whole theater public. The realism-democracy theory that the great public holds concerning the theater tells us that acting is just being natural, being the character, things as they are, none of the spouting and artificiality of the old fellows. Down deep, this prose-nature business is the last thing wanted; most people, however flat, want art to be art, without offending them by being anything different from anything else. The lurking dream is there, nevertheless, the desire for creation anew, the fresh world of fiction, flux, or ideality. What they think they want would be best found in the zoo, since nothing so acts like an elephant as an elephant. What they really want is the difference between the moon in the sky and the moon in the water; they want a new birth with a nameless difference; they want resemblance with escape. What they declare and actually seek is what they won't like when they get it. The public arrives by things outside of its declarations, and obeys constantly forces it could never understand. In whatever style, what people want in acting is acting. Miss Garbo solves this problem without seeming to, and, for that matter, even when she is not acting at all. At the very start her foreign accent gives her a certain removal. It is not necessarily a style, a treatment, a definite elevation, or distillation; it is primarily a physical fact that removes her from the ordinary and makes possible the illumination, unreality, and remoteness that we thirst after. That remote entity of her spirit, a certain noble poignancy in her presence, a certain solitary fairness, a sense of mood that is giving and resisting at the same time: these defeat and break down the poor little common theory of naturalness and prose method. This player is not hoity-toity or highbrow or any of that, the public feels; she is not unnatural; she is like somebody, they don't know just who, but still—Her mere physical factual distance from the audience parallels the distance that style in art assures and that instinct expects, so that what they would deny in theory they now run after in fact.

This is leaving out of account the side of the public's relation to Miss Garbo that is so much to its credit. People's souls sense in her some concentration of magnetism that they value. There is a muteness, inaccessibility, and beauty that attracts both men and women. She presents an instance of the natural and right progress of the poetic: from the concrete toward ideality. There is in her work no cheapness of attack, it is clear that her services could not be obtained for such effects. Her mind is not patently technical, her spirit not easily flexible, so that it is mainly a larger something that comes off to the audience, and in the future there will be a fuller development and radiance of her natural resources according to her own study, training, and the influences to which she is subjected.

As to Miss Garbo's performances, her creations of the roles assigned her, they have been variable. Such a role as Mata Hari, in a silly play, with a cast made up largely of lollipops and a brindling, venal atmosphere of Hollywood danger and war, was not for her, though the piece could have been written for her particular qualities. *Romance* was a cruel venture to subject her to, not because she could not have played some Nordic artist, beautiful, absorbed, passionate, and changing, but because she was burdened with creating a child of the sun, rich, impish, swanlike, and typical, cosmic as legend, and this had no relation either to her realm of feeling and beauty or her external technique. In Pirandello's *As You Desire Me,* Miss Garbo for the first time came, in my opinion, into her own, so far forward indeed that this discussion of her must remain inadequate. For the first time she seemed to me to show in her playing an inner delight and happy dedication to the love and joy of it. Her stage movement has grown lighter and more varied; the line of her hands has taken on a new and vivid life; and the diversity in technical attack and in the player's vitality seemed to me much greater. The secret luminous center of such playing cannot be conveyed, of course, any more than its shining fluency can be forgotten. Something is given in this playing of Miss Garbo's that I have not seen given before, and from the moments of her playing it seemed to me something radiant returned to her; she seemed to me not another person but a new artist in her art.

Marcelle Clements

Gregory Nava, the film director, once told me, "Whenever any question of style or taste in dress comes up, I simply ask myself: What would Fred Astaire have done?"

"They Can't Take That Away from Me"

Fred Astaire is my hero, and I don't care who knows it. "Gimme a break!" sneer the technocrats, the pseudodandies with the punk haircuts, all those who favor business lunches and open relationships. Yes, they will mock, but I don't care. Indeed, my sentiments regarding Fred Astaire are almost of a missionary nature. After all, everyone's got his prescription for improving the world: these days, social critics beg for less narcissism, environmentalists for conservation, and Republicans for lower taxes. I say Fred is our ticket. I say: Bring back moonlight!

Naturally, I speak of Fred Astaire as metaphor. Consider how certain concepts evoke, beyond themselves, the pinnacles of Western culture. The Acropolis. The sonata-allegro form. The British Museum. The Theory of Relativity. Fred Astaire. But whereas in the history of our civilization there are many landmarks of power, money, and, more seldom, beauty and wisdom, only Astaire consummately exemplifies casual elegance. I speak not merely of the now venerable dancer, but of the concept of the icon of finesse, the embodiment of grace, the paragon of romance. Fred Astaire is the *summum bonum* of debonair charm, a quality that, alas, is disappearing from our cultural shores.

I happen to believe that the public TV stations in this country should run Fred Astaire movies all night, every night. It would indeed be a public service. We could all go to sleep with the sets on and, just as we are subliminally influenced by commercials we thought we hadn't noticed, we might unconsciously absorb some of the glorious Astaire allure that we who are stranded in the eighties so desperately need. Think of all we'd learn: how to walk, how to dress, how to banter, how to dance "The Piccolino."

But no, we enthusiasts are left to peruse local listings for the sporadic appearance of our idol. He's always worth the wait for the "Late, Late, Late Show." The more I see of these films, however, the more a bizarre and compelling urge overtakes me. I want to find Fred Astaire. Not in *Top Hat,* not in *Carefree,* not in *Swing Time,* but, you know, in Real Life. Not the literal Astaire, of course. What I'm looking for is the Fred Astaire attitude, the mood, the subtle certain something that made life seem, how shall I say, worthwhile, in 1935. . . .

Needless to say, my search so far has been perfectly futile. Otherwise I wouldn't be writing this. I'd be dancing on some parquet floor wearing a dress made of ostrich feathers. (And I'd be blond, but that's beside the point.)

Why can't I find Fred Astaire? Is his persona a total fiction? It's odd, but the Astaire character as I imagine it seems so plausible, so likely, that I simply can't understand why he's only to be found on celluloid. Why, there must be hundreds, maybe even thousands of Fred Astaires out there. You know, guys who can strike a jaunty pose next to a candelabra without getting their hair singed; guys who assure you that not only are they in heaven but they can hardly speak when they're dancing with you cheek to cheek. Most guys I know won't even dance cheek to cheek except as a joke, and it's usually with one another. But so far I'm not discouraged. I'm keeping my hopes up and staying on the lookout. One thing I'm convinced of: I'll know the real thing when I see it.

I'm sure Fred Astaire doesn't read paperbacks. (Whether he reads at all is another matter, but never mind, you know what I mean.) And he wouldn't own a digital clock. He'd never wake up angry in the morning. You couldn't pay him to be rude to a waiter. And he would never, *never* have a recording machine answer his telephone.

Speaking as a woman, I pine for Fred on numerous occasions. I pine, for example, when the man who walks into the restaurant ahead of me allows the door to slam neatly in my face. I pine when my lover comes to breakfast in his Jockey shorts. I pine when my editor rudely insults me without subsequently tearing off my glasses and falling in love with me. (Actually, I believe it's Humphrey Bogart who tears off girls' glasses and falls in love with them, but you get the general idea. In fact, as it happens, I don't wear glasses.) I even pine for Fred Astaire seasonally. In the spring and summer, I pine for the tender hand-in-hand walks in appropriately bucolic surroundings. And in the fall and winter, I pine on schedule once a week, in splendid solitude, for the entire duration of "Monday Night Football."

I think the trouble with young men today is that they don't have any romantic ideals. And it's no wonder: all of their role models are hicks, schlepps, stiffs, or studs. After all, who is there? Richard Gere? Robert De Niro? Bill Murray? Please. I mean, in your heart, you *know* these people have terrible table manners. And as for their wardrobes, it's strickly heartbreak city.

I'm not saying they should bring back white tie and tails—though that would be lovely at crucial points in a relationship, the first time a man spends the night in one's apartment, for example. But let's be realistic; what with the frequency of one-night stands these days, the dry-cleaning bills would be astronomical. Certainly, the very least men could do, in memory of the great silhouette, would be to try and develop some Attitude about what they wear, instead of contenting themselves with whipping out their MasterCard as soon as they've found their size. Think of how great Astaire always managed to look, though he may in fact have been wearing a business suit, a sailor's outfit, or even one of those ridiculous ascots.

And if you think dress is not all that important except on nights out, you are sadly mistaken. "It is only the shallow people who do not judge by appearances," said Oscar Wilde, who knew a thing or two about such matters. Why, Fred Astaire looks impeccable in pajamas! His dress, his carriage, his manners all evoke that sexiest of attributes, breeding. And that's why, whether he was cast as a millionaire, a psychiatrist, or a struggling vaudevillian, Astaire always managed to convey an ambience of affluence and glamour. The Attitude, so well illustrated by his wardrobe and, of course, his dancing, was also marvelously epitomized by the tilt of his hat, the way he descended a staircase, the way he phrased a song, the way he made Ginger Rogers feel, the rose in the bud vase. No, no, they can't take that away from me.

Glamour, after all, is a state of mind. Granted, Astaire is a superb dancer. And granted, he got plenty of help in his films by way of props, sets, the costumes of his partners, to say nothing of some great scores. But for the truly ardent Astaire enthusiasts, for the hardcore, guts-to-the-wall fans, the most splendid moments in the Astaire films are the simplest ones, those in which he subtly turns the merely pedestrian gesture into the natural expression of exquisite grace: his gait when he crosses the street, the way he enters a room, how he holds his cane, the instant in a dance when he pauses and looks into his partner's eyes. Now, next time you're spending the evening in a disco, look around. Need I say more?

But my hero isn't only charming, glamorous, refined, and elegant. He is also honorable, brave, and audacious if need be, and this despite his obvious (and so endearing!) natural timidity. Fred Astaire dared! He dared to go after the girl, he dared to wear spats, he dared to call Audrey Hepburn "Funny Face," he dared to dance. He was somewhat homely, not particularly tall, much too skinny, yet he dared, dared to be a movie star. But even when he was bold, he had grace— none of this brassy vulgarity so evident in the behavior of the contemporary go-for-it set. After all, would anyone ever accuse Fred Astaire of being coarse or pushy? Certainly not. He remained modest and restrained and he still got the girl or the job. Even when he had a temporary setback, he did not throw a nasty tantrum. If Joan Fontaine was (for the moment) unresponsive, he did not turn on her like a Doberman pinscher and inform her that she was a repressed lesbian and a disgusting ballbreaker. No, not once in any of his numerous films did Astaire ever exhibit the urge to utter a primal scream. I guess no therapist had ever told Fred to Look Out for Number One. He may have sulked every once in a while, but he always remained civilized. At worst, he'd go out in the London fog and sing a little.

In fact, Astaire's boyish cheer is part of his appeal. It seems impossible not to be fond of Fred Astaire. He is inexhaustibly good-natured. (Who else could put up with Edward Everett Horton?) Even in these cynical times, his perennially winsome mien seems pleasant rather than irritating. And I speak as one who is ready to kill when a waiter says "Enjoy" as he places a plate in the vicinity of my seething bosom and clenched jaw. . . . The Astaire genius consists in never dancing over the line. And this is the magic one looks for, in vain, among the business-lunch/open-relationship types: good cheer without doltism, warmth without mawkishness, elegance without archness, nonchalance without indifference, and excellence devoid of arrogance. He embodied that uniquely American combination of energy and looseness, but he added to it a Continental gloss, the result being an irresistible mélange of chic and good humor. He's perfect.

All right, I know. I know the Astaire films are hokey. I know people watch them as camp artifacts, as frivolous confections filled with air. But let them eat hot dogs. As for me, I'm hooked on soufflés. I'll take it: the candelabra, the carnation in the lapel, the bashful smile, the top hat, and even "The Yam." I can't help it. Try as I might to maintain the proper contemporary disdain for sexist film themes, and as much as I may attempt to regard with mere contemptuous amusement the absurd plots with their chestnut devices of mistaken identities and the inevitability of the wedded-bliss conclusions, I can't help it, I'm sold. As far as I'm concerned, the worst part of watching Fred Astaire movies is the bilious aftermath of two solid hours of being jealous of Ginger Rogers.

Just think how much better the world would be if more people felt as I do: All personal problems would be resolved as soon as boy got girl, which would invariably occur. There'd be champagne parties every night, and all the men would be clever and wonderful dancers, and all the women would be beautiful blondes wearing dresses made of ostrich feathers. Why, there'd even be moonlight again.

ROBERT LEWIS TAYLOR

Has the death of repertory theaters finally killed the fashion for W. C. Fields (1879–1946)? In the 1960s Fields enjoyed a huge revival on college campuses, where students recited his dialogue along with him. There was even a feature film based on his life, with Fields impersonated eerily by Rod Steiger. Then Fields drifted out of favor, and in the age of home video young viewers program their own revivals and seem not to have stumbled on him; his name is relatively unknown on campuses today. Fields's anarchic misogynism is, however, timeless, and no doubt he will drift back into view. The best book about his life is by Robert Lewis Taylor, who makes little attempt to separate the Fields of fact and legend, perhaps because for Fields himself the line was blurred. Fields was known for dialogue that seemed to drift perilously close to obscenity while always remaining apparently innocent, and for his drinking, which in his movies was presented as the permanent preoccupation of his characters, even while they were engrossed in other activities. Groucho Marx, who was a friend of Fields's, told me in 1972: "He had a ladder leading up to his attic. Without exaggeration, there was fifty thousand dollars of liquor up there. Crated up like a wharf. I'm standing there and Fields is standing there, and nobody says anything. The silence is oppressive. Finally, he speaks: 'This will carry me twenty-five years.'"

from *W. C. Fields: His Follies and Fortunes*

Fields' favorite exclamations—"Godfrey Daniel," "Mother of Pearl," "Drat!" and others—always had a peculiar standing at the Hays office. Just as many comedians have been able, on the legitimate stage, to utter the fiercest oaths and make them sound innocent, Fields could voice tea-party pleasantries and make them sound profane. An audience, seeing the wicked leer and sensing the unfathomable mischief behind his frosty, belligerent stare, realized that, whatever he might say, he meant considerable more, so that "Godfrey Daniel!" always came out "Goddamn," not only to the Hays office but to the general public. In spite of this, the essential fraudulence of his established character removed the sting from all hints of the grossest immorality.

The censors were obliged to keep an especially alert eye on Fields' educational efforts for children, both in the script and on the set. There can be no question that Fields disliked children, in a persecuted, un-angry sort of way. His encounters with the infant thespian, Baby LeRoy, with whom he played in several films, were well known to Hollywood. He considered that the child was deliberately trying to wreck his career, and he stalked him remorselessly. "When he stole entire scenes from Baby LeRoy in *Tillie and Gus* a year and a half ago, his greatness was acknowledged," a reporter said of Fields in 1935. The comedian realized that, whatever else might be going on in a scene, people would watch the antics of a baby. His competitive treatment of LeRoy was, therefore, exactly the same as he would have accorded an adult. Between takes he sat in a corner, eyed the child, and muttered vague, injured threats.

In one Fields-LeRoy picture directed by Norman Taurog, action was suspended so that the infant could have his orange juice. When the others busied themselves with scripts, Fields approached the child's nurse and said, "Why don't you take a breather? I'll give the little nipper his juice." She nodded gratefully, and left the set.

With a solicitous nursery air, Fields shook the bottle and removed its nipple, then he drew a flask from his pocket and strengthened the citrus with a generous noggin of gin.

Baby LeRoy, a popular, warm-hearted youngster, showed his appreciation by gulping down the dynamite with a minimum of the caterwauling that distinguishes the orange-juice hour in so many homes. But when the shooting was ready to recommence, he was in a state of inoperative bliss.

Taurog and others, including the returned nurse, inspected the tot with real concern. "I don't believe he's just sleepy," said the nurse. "He had a good night's rest."

"Jiggle him some more," suggested Taurog. "We're running a little behind schedule."

Several assistants broke into cries of "Hold it!" "Stand by with Number Seven!" and "Make-up—LeRoy's lost his color!"

"Walk him around, walk him around," was Fields' hoarse and baffling comment from a secluded corner.

The child was more or less restored to consciousness, but in the scene that followed, Taurog complained of his lack of animation. Despite the most urgent measures to revive him he remained glassy-eyed and in a partial coma. For some inexplicable reason Fields seemed jubilant.

"He's no trouper," he kept yelling. "The kid's no trouper. Send him home."

Several years later, when Baby LeRoy was grown to boyhood, Fields heard he was re-entering films. "The kid's no trouper," the comedian told several people. "He'll never make a comeback." LeRoy did come back, however, and continued to perform successfully.

Fields always thought that one of the most agreeable events in his movie career took place in *The Old-Fashioned Way,* during a scene with the troublesome LeRoy. In the course of a boarding-house meal, the infant dropped Fields' watch in the molasses, turned over his soup, and hit him in the face with a spoonful of cream. After dinner, by chance, Fields found himself in a room alone with his tormentor, who was in the all-fours stance on the carpet. Tiptoeing up softly, his face filled with benevolence, he took a full leg swing and kicked the happy youngster about six feet. The comedian threw himself into this scene, as he tried to do with all his pictures, and wrapped up some splendid footage for Paramount.

But his conscience must have bothered him, for the next day he appeared on the set with presents for Baby LeRoy. It taxes the historian's ingenuity to explain the many paradoxes of Fields. While he was authentically jealous of the child, he made sheepish and comradely gestures on the sly. One time when Baby LeRoy's option was due, Fields needlessly wrote a part for him into one of his pictures, to emphasize the child's importance to the studio. In his home the comedian once had a photograph, prominently displayed, of himself and the child star riding kiddie cars. And yet, asked in interviews how he liked children, or child actors, he always replied with a sincere growl, "Fried," or "Parboiled," or something equally unaffectionate.

.   .   .   .

Of Fields' several peculiarities, his drinking aroused the widest interest and misinformation. By the middle of his movie period his need for alcohol had crystallized into a habit pattern from which he deviated only slightly until the end of his life. On the radio, in interviews, often in the movies, he was pictured as a frequent drunk, a rip who enjoyed wild excesses and spent a lot of time under tables. It would be difficult to imagine a more erroneous conception.

Fields drank steadily, but he abhorred drunks. Drunken visitors in his home seldom came back a second time. The signs of drunkenness—thick speech, unsteady gait, rowdiness, overemotional confidences—filled him with unease and disgust. Of one of the best-known figures of the American stage, after a party at Fields' house, Fields said to his secretary, "Never let that fellow come through these doors again." The comedian once sulked for weeks at John Barrymore, of whom he was particularly fond, because the great lover, in elevating his feet to relax, scratched up Fields' favorite sofa. "All that Romeo stuff's gone to his head," Fields told his secretary as he telephoned some inexpensive upholsterers.

In his later years, he started a day off with two double martinis before breakfast. He arose about nine o'clock, took a shower, came downstairs, and drank the martinis slowly, on a porch or terrace if the day was fine. His breakfast was modest, by the most austere standards. A small glass of pineapple juice generally sufficed, but if he was especially ravenous, he added a piece of toast and another martini to the menu. The liquor had no apparent effect save to sharpen, ever so slightly, his usual morning good humor and enhance his appreciation of the California weather, which he loved. After breakfast, before going to work, whether he was employed at the studios or occupied with scripts at home, he walked over his grounds for an hour. He inspected his flowers, an exercise that became a guiding passion in his life. Fields was one of the great nature men of his generation. His cultivation of flowers and his pride at exhibiting them to guests were not affected; he was happiest, some of his friends believed, when he was submerged in horticulture and removed from the strain of society. He had a tendency, however, to personalize his flowers, which occasionally plagued him as people did. He once called up Gregory La Cava, who devoted many hours, in the California manner, to watering plants, and said, "I want you to come right over here—I've got some Jack roses that are blooming as big as cabbages."

"Oh, nonsense," La Cava replied. "There isn't any such thing. I'm busy."

Fields insisted, with angry trumpetings, and La Cava left his house at Malibu Beach and drove over, a trip of several miles. The day was warm, the traffic brisk, and it was some time before he arrived. Fields growled at the delay, but ushered him swiftly down a lane toward the waiting exhibit. The roses had apparently made their bow for the morning; when their sponsor arrived with his guest they had retreated into small, tight buds. Fields was enraged. He ran up and down the lane, lashing at the offenders with a cane, and crying, "Bloom! Bloom, damn you! Bloom for my friend!"

BOB HOPE AND BOB THOMAS

Bob Hope has become such an American icon in his later years that it's easy to forget how brash and irreverent he was as a young performer. When someone like Woody Allen seriously holds him up as an idol, it helps us to brush aside the Christmas specials and the

golf classics and Hope entertaining the troops and to remember his first-rate movie come-
dies and his long-running Road *series with Bing Crosby and Dorothy Lamour. Here Hope*
remembers, mostly in inevitable one-liners and no doubt with the truth greatly gilded, his
adventures on the Roads.

from *The Road to Hollywood*

Like Webster's dictionary,
We're Morocco-bound . . .

Ah yes, in 1942, Bing, Dotty, and I were off on our merry adventures again. As
in the first *Road,* Tony Quinn was the heavy—this was long before Zorba the
Greek had opened up his first restaurant. Directing *The Road to Morocco*—the
three Bs. No, not Bach, Beethoven, and Brahms, but Blubberbutt Butler.

Dave was a cagey character. He knew that Bing and I spent half our studio
time on the phone, talking about our radio shows, our investments, and other
minor matters. Dave wanted our full attention. In those days there was only one
telephone on a movie set; not even the biggest star had a phone in his dressing
room. So Dave ordered the assistant director to station the phone for *The Road
to Morocco* a block and a half away from the set where we were working.

Not only that. The telephone was installed under a pile of lumber, so that
anyone answering it would have to slide in horizontally to pick up the receiver.

Dave's answer to AT&T worked well until the day that Sam Goldwyn called.
It came at a time when Dave was directing a crowd scene that involved a couple of hundred mules and twice that many people.

"Mr. Goldwyn is calling you, Mr. Butler," the assistant director said.

Dave told Bing and me and the entire company to wait, then he trudged across
the sound stage and into the next one and slid under the lumber pile. "Hello,
Sam. What is it?" Dave said.

Goldwyn was working on the script that Dave was going to direct next—for
me, as it turned out. For fifteen minutes, Goldwyn expounded on the intrica-
cies of the story while the *Road to Morocco* company waited. Finally Goldwyn said,
"Thanks very much for calling me," and hung up.

We had a lot of adventures on *The Road to Morocco,* and some of them were
in the script. The real ones were lots of fun—it says here.

Like the time Bing and I were washed up on the North African coast. A camel
sneaks up behind us and licks us on the cheeks. We begin to think it's love at
second sight until we see that it was a camel doing the kissing, not each other.

I don't know if you've ever been kissed by a camel, but I've got to tell you that it's not like being kissed by Raquel Welch. This particular camel may have been listening to my radio show, because after he kissed me, he spat right in my face.

You wouldn't believe what a camel stores up in his chaw. I thought I had been hit by the Casbah Garbage Department.

When you see *The Road to Morocco* on the late show, you'll notice that I stagger out of the scene when the camel spits at me. Bing broke up, and I was gasping for breath, but Dave kept the camera rolling.

"Great scene," he said afterward.

"But don't you want another take?" I said, wiping the muck out of my eyes. "The whole crew was laughing, and I disappeared out of the frame."

"No, that's it," Dave replied. For years afterward, people asked him, "How did you get that camel to spit at Hope on cue?" Dave replied, "I worked with that beast for weeks until it responded to my direction."

Dave was full of tricks. During one scene in *The Road to Morocco,* Bing and I were to be chased through the Casbah by Arabian horsemen. Dave had hired an old pal to lead the stunt riders—Ken Maynard, the cowboy star.

I guess Ken was trying to make a show of it. Because when Dave gave the cue, Ken led his horsemen through the Casbah like the first furlong of the Kentucky Derby.

"My God, Paramount wants to get rid of us!" I yelled as I saw the horses charging at me.

"We never should have asked for a raise," Bing agreed. He made a flying dive, and I jumped off the set, landing on the concrete floor.

"Cut!" Dave yelled. "Great shot!"

"Great shot!" Bing replied. "You almost killed Bob and me!"

"Oh, I wouldn't do that," Dave said. "Not until the final scene, anyway."

That wasn't the first time that I learned movies could be a risky business. In my first picture, *The Big Broadcast of 1938,* there was a running gag that Martha Raye would break mirrors every time she looked into them. For one shipboard scene, she was supposed to look into a room-length mirror and the thing would crack.

A funny scene, but it almost turned into a tragedy. The special-effects men put too much air pressure behind the mirror. When Martha looked into it, the huge mirror shattered with the noise of a cannon, and thousands of glass fragments were blasted toward us. It was a miracle that no one was seriously hurt.

Several years later, Bing and I were making *The Road to Utopia.* One of the scenes called for Bing and me to bed down in our Klondike cabin and be joined by a bear. A real bear. They told us it was a very tame bear, but Bing and I had our doubts.

We climbed under a rug and feigned sleep. The bear came sniffing up to us. Then we heard a growl. Right then I had laundry problems.

"Did you hear what I heard?" Bing asked.

"I sure did," I said. "Lead the way, Dad."

We set an Olympic record for leaping out of bed—Errol Flynn couldn't have done it faster.

"That's it with the bear," Bing announced, and I heartily agreed. The next day, the same bear tore an arm off his trainer.

One day on *Utopia,* we were shooting a glacier scene on the De Mille stage—named after Cecil B. because he shot many of his epics there. Bing and I were supposed to be climbing a wall of ice, and we were doing it many feet above the stage floor. Ordinarily there were mattresses beneath us, but somebody moved them.

Right in the middle of the scene the rope broke, and Bing and I went tumbling down. I looked for a soft spot to land and found it: Crosby. His back hasn't been the same since.

Over the years, I have been subjected to many more indignities, all for the sake of Art. If I ever catch him, I'm going to kill the guy.

LAUREN BACALL

Bacall's memoir of her early days in Hollywood is one of the best movie star autobiographies because she remembers so vividly. Reading her description of how she held her head low to conceal its trembling, I went back to look at that scene in Howard Hawks's To Have and Have Not *again and saw it through different eyes. Once you have the clue, Bacall turns from a sultry woman into a scared kid. Then you blink, and she's the woman again—for the rest of her career.*

from *By Myself*

I went onto the set the first day of shooting to see Howard and Bogart—I would not be working until the second day. Bogart's wife, Mayo Methot, was there—

he introduced us. I talked to Howard, watched for a while, and went home to prepare for my own first day.

It came and I was ready for a straitjacket. Howard had planned to do a single scene that day—my first in the picture. I walked to the door of Bogart's room, said, "Anybody got a match?," leaned against the door, and Bogart threw me a small box of matches. I lit my cigarette, looking at him, said "Thanks," threw the matches back to him, and left. Well—we rehearsed it. My hand was shaking—my head was shaking—the cigarette was shaking. I was mortified. The harder I tried to stop, the more I shook. What must Howard be thinking? What must Bogart be thinking? What must the crew be thinking? Oh God, make it stop! I was in such pain.

Bogart tried to joke me out of it—he was quite aware that I was a new young thing who knew from nothing and was scared to death. Finally Howard thought we could try a take. Silence on the set. The bell rang. "Quiet—we're rolling," said the sound man. "Action," said Howard. This was for posterity, I thought—for real theatres, for real people to see. I came around the corner, said my first line, and Howard said, "Cut." He had broken the scene up—the first shot ended after the first line. The second set-up was the rest of it—then he'd move in for close-ups. By the end of the third or fourth take, I realized that one way to hold my trembling head still was to keep it down, chin low, almost to my chest, and eyes up at Bogart. It worked, and turned out to be the beginning of "The Look."

I found out very quickly that day what a terrific man Bogart was. He did everything possible to put me at ease. He was on my side. I felt safe—I still shook, but I shook less. He was not even remotely a flirt. I was, but I didn't flirt with him. There was much kidding around—our senses of humor went well together. Bogie's idea, of course, was that to make me laugh would relax me. He was right to a point, but nothing on earth would have relaxed me completely!

The crew were wonderful—fun and easy. It was a very happy atmosphere. I would often go to lunch with Howard. One day he told me he was very happy with the way I was working, but that I must remain somewhat aloof from the crew. Barbara Stanwyck, whom he thought very highly of—he'd made *Ball of Fire* with her, a terrific movie—was always fooling around with the crew, and he thought it a bad idea. "They don't like you any better for it. When you finish a scene, go back to your dressing room. Don't hang around the set—don't give it all away—save it for the scenes." He wanted me in a cocoon, only to emerge for work. Bogart could fool around to his heart's content—he was a star and a man—"though you notice he doesn't do too much of it."

One day at lunch when Howard was mesmerizing me with himself and his plans for me, he said, "Do you notice how noisy it is in here suddenly? That's because Leo Forbstein just walked in—Jews always make more noise." I felt that

I was turning white, but I said nothing. I was afraid to—a side of myself I have never liked or been proud of—a side that was always there. Howard didn't dwell on it ever, but clearly he had very definite ideas about Jews—none too favorable, though he did business with them. They paid him—they were good for that. I would have to tell him about myself eventually or he'd find out through someone else. When the time came, what would happen would happen, but I had no intention of pushing it.

Howard started to line up special interviews for me. Nothing big would be released until just before the picture, and everything would be chosen with the greatest care. *Life, Look,* Kyle Crichton for *Collier's, Pic, Saturday Evening Post.* Only very special fan magazines. Newspapers. I probably had more concentrated coverage than any beginning young actress had ever had—due to Hawks, not me.

Hoagy Carmichael had written a song called "Baltimore Oriole." Howard was going to use it as my theme music in the movie—every time I appeared on screen there were to be strains of that song. He thought it would be marvelous if I could be always identified with it—appear on Bing Crosby's or Bob Hope's radio show, have the melody played, have me sing it, finally have me known as the "Baltimore Oriole." What a fantastic fantasy life Howard must have had! His was a glamorous, mysterious, tantalizing vision—but it wasn't me.

On days I didn't have lunch with Howard, I would eat with another actor or the publicity man or have a sandwich in my room or in the music department during a voice lesson. I could not sit at a table alone. Bogie used to lunch at the Lakeside Golf Club, which was directly across the road from the studio.

One afternoon I walked into Howard's bungalow and found a small, gray-haired, mustached, and attractive man stretched out on the couch with a book in his hand and a pipe in his mouth. That man was William Faulkner. He was contributing to the screenplay. Howard loved Faulkner—they had known each other a long time, had hunted together. Faulkner never had much money and Howard would always hire him for a movie when he could. He seldom came to the set—he was very shy—he liked it better in Howard's office.

Howard had a brilliantly creative work method. Each morning when we got to the set, he, Bogie, and I and whoever else might be in the scene, and the script girl would sit in a circle in canvas chairs with our names on them and read the scene. Almost unfailingly Howard would bring in additional dialogue for the scenes of sex and innuendo between Bogie and me. After we'd gone over the words several times and changed whatever Bogie or Howard thought should be changed, Howard would ask an electrician for a work light—one light on the set—and we'd go through the scene on the set to see how it felt. Howard said, "Move around—see where it feels most comfortable." Only after all that had been worked out did he call Sid Hickox and talk about camera set-ups. It is the perfect way for movie actors to work, but of course it takes time.

After about two weeks of shooting I wrote to my mother—she'd read one or two things in newspapers about my not having the first lead opposite Bogart—

> Please, darling, don't worry about what is written in the newspapers concerning first and second leads. You make me so goddamn mad—what the hell difference does it make? As long as when the public sees the picture they know that I'm the one who is playing opposite Bogart. Everything is working out beautifully for me. Howard told Charlie the rushes were sensational. He's really very thrilled with them. I'm still not used to my face, however. Bogie has been a dream man. We have the most wonderful times together. I'm insane about him. We kid around—he's always gagging—trying to break me up and is very, very fond of me. So if I were you, I'd thank my lucky stars, as I am doing and not worry about those unimportant things. The only thing that's important is that I am good in the picture and the public likes me.

I don't know how it happened—it was almost imperceptible. It was about three weeks into the picture—the end of the day—I had one more shot, was sitting at the dressing table in the portable dressing room combing my hair. Bogie came in to bid me good night. He was standing behind me—we were joking as usual—when suddenly he leaned over, put his hand under my chin, and kissed me. It was impulsive—he was a bit shy—no lunging wolf tactics. He took a worn package of matches out of his pocket and asked me to put my phone number on the back. I did. I don't know why I did, except it was kind of part of our game. Bogie was meticulous about not being too personal, was known for never fooling around with women at work or anywhere else. He was not that kind of man, and also he was married to a woman who was a notorious drinker and fighter. A tough lady who would hit you with an ashtray, lamp, anything, as soon as not.

I analyzed nothing then—I was much too happy—I was having the time of my life. All that mattered to me was getting to the studio and working—my hours of sleep just got in the way! From the start of the movie, as Bogie and I got to know each other better—as the joking got more so—as we had more fun together—so the scenes changed little by little, our relationship strengthened on screen and involved us without our even knowing it. *I* certainly didn't know it. Gradually my focus began to shift away from Howard, more toward Bogie. Oh, I still paid full attention to Howard, but I think I depended more on Bogie. The construction of the scenes made that easy. I'm sure Howard became aware fairly early on that there was something between us and used it in the film.

At the end of the day of the phone number, I went home as usual to my routine: after eating something, I looked at my lines for the next day and got into bed. Around eleven o'clock the phone rang. It was Bogie. He'd had a few drinks, was away from his house, just wanted to see how I was. He called me Slim—I called him Steve, as in the movie. We joked back and forth—he finally said good night, he'd see me on the set. That was all, but from that moment on our relationship changed. He invited me to lunch at Lakeside a few times—or we'd sit in my dressing room or his with the door open, finding out more about one another. If he had a chess game going on the set—he was a first-rate chess player—I'd stand and watch, stand close to him. Physical proximity became more and more important. But still we joked.

Hedda Hopper came on the set one day and said, "Better be careful. You might have a lamp dropped on you one day."

PETER BOGDANOVICH

Humphrey Bogart (1899–1957) somehow succeeded in being an everyman and a movie star at the same time. In Treasure of the Sierra Madre, *his baffled dismay in the face of his own greed is shown with an actor's humility that other stars might have resisted. And notice how in* Casablanca *he becomes a self-sacrificing patriot without ever once seeming to go for that effect. In the 1960s, before he began directing, Peter Bogdanovich was part of the group of writers who created the New Journalism, often in articles written for the great editor Harold Hayes at* Esquire *magazine. This article from the September 1964* Esquire *does as good a job as anything I've read of explaining the Bogart mystique.*

"Bogie in Excelsis"

Usually he wore the trench coat unbuttoned, just tied with the belt, and a slouch hat, rarely tilted. Sometimes it was a captain's cap and a yachting jacket. Almost always his trousers were held up by a cowboy belt. You know the kind: one an Easterner, waiting for a plane out of Phoenix, buys just as a joke and then takes a liking to. Occasionally, he'd hitch up his slacks with it, and he often jabbed his thumbs behind it, his hands ready for a fight or a dame.

Whether it was Sirocco or Casablanca, Martinique or Sahara, he was the only American around (except maybe for the girl) and you didn't ask him how he got there, and he always worked alone—except for the fellow who thought he took care of him, the rummy, the piano player, the one *he* took care of, the one you didn't mess with. There was very little he couldn't do, and in a jam he could do anything: remove a slug from a guy's arm, fix a truck that wouldn't start. He was an excellent driver, knowing precisely how to take those curves or how to lose a guy that was tailing him. He could smell a piece of a broken glass and tell you right away if there'd been poison in it, or he could walk into a room and know just where the button was that opened the secret door. At the wheel of a boat, he was beautiful.

His expression was usually sour and when he smiled only the lower lip moved. There was a scar on his upper lip, maybe that's what gave him the faint lisp. He would tug meditatively at his earlobe when he was trying to figure something out and every so often he had a strange little twitch—a kind of backward jerk of the sides of his mouth coupled with a slight squinting of the eyes. He held his cigarette (a Chesterfield) cupped in his hand. He looked right holding a gun.

Unsentimental was a good word for him. "Leave 'im where he is," he might say to a woman whose husband has just been wounded. "I don't want 'im bleeding all over my cushions." And blunt: "I don't like you. I don't like your friends and I don't like the idea of her bein' married to you." And straight: "When a man's partner is killed he's supposed to do something about it. It doesn't make any difference what you thought of him. He was your partner and you're supposed to do something about it."

He was tough; he could stop you with a look or a line. "Go ahead, slap me," he'd say, or, "That's right, go for it," and there was in the way he said it just the right blend of malice, gleeful anticipation and the promise of certain doom. He didn't like taking orders. Or favors. It was smart not to fool around with him too much.

As far as the ladies were concerned, he didn't have too much trouble with them, except maybe keeping them away. It was the girl who said if he needed anything, all he had to do was whistle: he never said that to the girl. Most of the time he'd call her "angel," and if he liked her he'd tell her she was "good, awful good."

Whatever he was engaged in, whether it was being a reporter, a saloon-keeper, a gangster, a detective, a fishing-boat owner, a D.A., or a lawyer, he was impeccably, if casually, a complete professional. "You take chances," someone would say. "I get paid to," was his answer. But he never took himself too seriously. What was his job, a girl would ask. Conspiratorially, he'd lean in and say with the slightest flicker of a grin, "I'm a private dick on a case." He wasn't going to be taken in by Art either; he'd been to college, but he was a bit suspicious of the intellectuals. If someone mentioned Proust, he'd ask, "Who's he?," even though he knew.

Finally, he was wary of Causes. He liked to get paid for taking chances. He was a man who tried very hard to be Bad because he knew it was easier to get along in the world that way. He always failed because of an innate goodness which surely nauseated him. Almost always he went from belligerent neutrality to reluctant commitment. From: "I stick my neck out for nobody." To: "I'm no good at being noble, but it doesn't take much to see that the problems of three little people don't amount to a hill o' beans in this crazy world." At the start, if the question was, "What are your sympathies?," the answer was invariably, "Minding my own business." But by the end, if asked why he was helping, risking his life, he might say, "Maybe 'cause I like you. Maybe 'cause I don't like them." Of course it was always "maybe" because he wasn't going to be that much of a sap, wasn't making any speeches, wasn't going to be a Good guy. Probably he rationalized it: "I'm just doing my job." But we felt good inside. We knew better.

.   .   .   .

Several months ago, the New Yorker Theatre in Manhattan ran a cycle of thirty Humphrey Bogart movies. A one-day double bill of *The Big Sleep* and *To Have and Have Not* broke all their attendance records. "I had two hundred people sitting on the floor," said Daniel Talbot, owner of the 830-seat revival house and one of the two producers of *Point of Order*. "It was wild. I had to turn away a couple of hundred people. And that audience! First time Bogie appeared they applauded, and that was just the beginning. Any number of scenes got hands. And the laughs! Bogart is very hot right now," Talbot explained. "It's more than a cult, it's something else too. He's not consciously hip, but hip by default. You get the feeling that he lives up to the Code. Anyone who screws up deserves the fate of being rubbed out by Bogart. He's also very American, and his popularity, I think, is a reaction to this currently chic craze for foreign films and things foreign in general. With Bogart you get a portrait of a patriot, a man interested in the landscape of America. I think he's an authentic American hero—more existential than, say, Cooper, but as much in the American vein, and more able to cope with the present." Talbot paused and grinned. "Frankly, I just like to watch him at work. He hits people beautifully."

The French have a more intellectual, if nonetheless affectionate, approach to Bogart and the legend he has left behind. As Belmondo stares mystically at a photo of Bogart in Godard's *Breathless,* slowly exhaling cigarette smoke and rubbing his lip with his thumb, he murmurs wistfully, "Bogie . . ." and you can almost hear his director's thoughts, echoed, for instance, in the words of the late André Bazin, probably France's finest film critic. "Bogart is the man with a past," he wrote in *Cahiers du Cinéma* in 1957, a month after Bogart died. "When he comes into a film, it is already 'the morning after'; sardonically victorious in his macabre combat with the angel, his face scared by what he has seen, and his step heavy from all he has learned, having ten times triumphed over his death, he will surely survive for us this one more time. . . . The Bogartian man is not defined by his contempt for bourgeois virtues, by his courage or cowardice, but first of all by his existential maturity which little by little transforms life into a tenacious irony at the expense of death." Of course, the French too can have a more basic approach. "Finally in full color," wrote Robert Lachenay in the same magazine, "we see Bogie as he was in real life—as he was to Betty Bacall every night on his pillow. . . . I loved Bogart even better then. . . ."

The Bogart cult has been perpetuated for the last several years in colleges all over the United States. "I met a Harvard fellow recently," said writer Nathaniel Benchley, "who believed in only two things: the superiority of Harvard and the immortality of Humphrey Bogart." During every exam period in Cambridge, it has become customary for the Brattle Theatre to run a Bogart film festival. Some-times they don't even list the pictures: they just put a large photograph of him outside the theatre. It seems to be enough. Walk into the Club Casablanca (in the same building) and ask one of the undergraduates. "Bogart has a coolness you can't get away from," he might tell you. "It's a wryness, a freedom," he'll say, at the same time denying that there is a real cult and that he's just so refreshing, so pleasantly removed from their academic world. "There's no crap about Bo-gart," another student may observe. "He's also kind of anti-European and pro-American. Like he dumps on the European, you know what I mean?" By this time his date won't be able to control herself any longer. "He's so masculine!" she'll blurt out. "He's so fantastically tough!" Was he? "He satirized himself a great deal," said writer Betty Comden. Raymond Massey recalled an incident during the shooting of *Action in the North Atlantic* (1943): "The scene called for our doubles to jump from the bridge of a burning tanker into the water below, which was aflame with oil. Bogie turned to me and said, '*My* double is braver than yours.' I said that wasn't so, that *my* double was the bravest man. Then Bogie looked at me and he said, 'The fact is I'm braver than you are.' I said that was nonsense. And the next thing I knew we did the doggone stunt ourselves." Massey chuckled. "I burned my pants off and Bogie singed his eyebrows."

To Joseph L. Mankiewicz, who'd directed him in *The Barefoot Contessa* (1954), Bogart's toughness was a façade. "You'd be having dinner with him," he said, "and someone would come over and you could just see the tough guy coming on." And to Chester Morris: "He had a protective shell of seeming indifference. He wasn't, but he did a lotta acting offstage. He liked to act tough, liked to talk out of the side of his mouth." Writer Nunnally Johnson said Bogart was con-vinced that people would have been disappointed if he didn't act tough with them. "A fan came over during dinner one time," said Johnson, "and Bogie told him to beat it. When the guy got back to his table I heard his companion say, quite happily, 'See, I told ya he'd insult you.' " Johnson reflected a moment. "But he was a lot tougher than I would be and a lot tougher than most people I know. I remember one time Judy Garland and her husband, Sid Luft, were at his home. Now Luft was a big alley fighter and a good deal broader than Bogart. But Bogie got annoyed about something or other and he walked right over to Luft, who also was a good head taller, and nodded at Judy. 'Would you take that dame out of this house,' he said, 'and never come back.' Luft kind of looked at him a moment and then he took her out." Johnson smiled. "Bogie took big risks."

Adlai Stevenson didn't find him that way. "He wasn't tough, not really," said the Ambassador. "He was, to me, a nonconformist. He had a cynicism without being unhealthy. He had great curiosity and an arch kind of skepticism." And still another opinion: "He was a pushover," said Lauren Bacall.

.   .   .   .

"I never broke through his barrier," said critic John McLain. "I don't think anyone really got underneath. Bogart didn't unburden himself to men. He loved to be in love and with a woman. I think he came closer to leveling with them than with anybody." Bogart married four women during his fifty-seven years, each of them an actress: Helen Mencken (1926), Mary Phillips (1928), the late Mayo Methot (1938), and in 1945, Lauren Bacall. "I think once a person was out, they were really out," said Truman Capote, discussing the divorces. "He had emotional attachments."

The Bogart-Methot marriage was a stormy one. "Their neighbors were lulled to sleep," Dorothy Parker once said, "by the sounds of breaking china and crashing glass." Johnson recalled that Methot once had Bogart followed. "She was very jealous and positive that he was playing around. But Bogie never had a weakness for dames. The only weakness he ever had was for a drink and a talk." Johnson smiled. "Bogie soon found out a guy was tailing him, and he called up the fellow's agency. 'Hello, this is Humphrey Bogart,' he said. 'You got a man on my tail. Would you check with him and find out where I am.' "

The first time Bogart met Betty Bacall was coming out of director Howard Hawks's office. She had made a test for Hawks, who had discovered her and first teamed the couple in *To Have and Have Not* (1945). "I saw your test," Bogart said to her. "We're gonna have a lotta fun together." It was with Bacall that he had his only children, a boy named Steve, which is what she called Bogart in that first movie, and a girl named Leslie Howard, after the actor who had insisted that Bogart be cast in the film version of *The Petrified Forest* (1936), the movie that really began his picture career. "He missed her when they were apart," Capote said. "He loved her. He used to talk a terrific line, but he was monogamous. Although that isn't entirely true—he fell in love with Bacall while he was still married to Mayo."

Bogart put it this way: "I'm a one-woman man and I always have been. I guess I'm old-fashioned. Maybe that's why I like old-fashioned women, the kind who stay in the house playing *Roamin' in the Gloamin'*. They make a man think he's a man and they're glad of it." The stories go that Bogart was a heavy drinker, but Johnson thinks otherwise. "I don't think Bogie drank as much as he pretended to," he said. "Many's a time I was with him, the doorbell would ring, and he'd pick up his glass just to go answer the door. He couldn't have been as good at his job if he drank as much as he was supposed to have."

But Bogart did drink. "I think the world is three drinks behind," he used to say, "and it's high time it caught up." On one occasion he and a friend bought two enormous stuffed panda bears and took them as their dates to El Morocco. They sat them in chairs at a table for four and when an ambitious young lady came over and touched Bogart's bear, he shoved her away. "I'm a happily married man," he said, "and don't touch my panda." The woman brought assault charges against him, and when asked if he was drunk at four o'clock in the morning, he replied, "Sure, isn't everybody?" (The judge ruled that since the panda was Mr. Bogart's personal property, he could defend it.)

But Bogart didn't have to drink to start trouble. "He was an arrogant bastard," said Johnson, grinning. "It's kinda funny, this cult and everything. When he was alive, as many people hated him as loved him. I always thought of him as somewhat like Scaramouche." Johnson chuckled. "What was it? 'Born with the gift of laughter and the sense that the world was mad. . . .' He'd start a skirmish and then sit back and watch the consequences. Of course, there was nearly always something phony about the guy he was needling. Needle is the wrong word—howitzer would be more like it. The other fellow could use deflating, but it didn't take all that artillery."

The Holmby Hills Rat Pack, which Bogart initiated and which died with him, sprang from this distaste for pretense. "What is a rat?" he once explained. "We have no constitution, charter or bylaws, yet, but we know a rat when we see one. There are very few rats in this town. You might say that rats are for staying up late and drinking lots of booze. We're against squares and being bored and for lots of fun and being real rats, which very few people are, but if you're a real rat, boy! Our slogan is, 'Never rat on a rat.' A first principle is that we don't care who likes us as long as we like each other. We like each other very much."

John McClain tells of the yacht club Bogart belonged to and of the people who rented the large house next door for a summer. They were the Earls and they Dressed for Dinner. The members of the club (who were never invited) used to peer over their fence, watching the lush festivities. McClain had been invited to a Sunday dinner and had asked if he might bring Bogart along as they would be together on his yacht over the weekend. As they docked, McClain reminded Bogart to dress for the occasion and went off to get ready himself. Bogart went into the club for a drink or two. "After a while," McClain recalled, "Bogie announced to everyone in the club, 'My dear friends, the Earls,' he said, 'are having an open house and they want you all to come.' And into the Earl house comes Bogie followed by about thirty people, all wearing shorts and sport shirts and sneakers." McClain laughed. "It was pretty funny, actually, but I was furious at the time."

"He could be very wrong too," said Benchley. "One time at '21' I was standing at the bar with a couple of friends and Bogie got up from his table and came over. 'Are you a homosexual?' he said to one of them, just like that. The fellow looked rather taken aback and said he didn't see that it was any of his business. 'Well are you?' said Bogie. 'Come on, we got a bet going at the table.' The fellow said, 'Since you ask, no.' I think Bogie could feel he'd been wrong and he turned to the other guy with us and asked him if *he* was a homosexual. The guy said no. He asked me and I said no and then he said, 'Well, I am,' and kinda minced away. He knew he'd been wrong."

A few weeks after Bogart's death, Peter Ustinov said, in a speech: "Humphrey Bogart was an exceptional character in a sphere where characters are not usually exceptional. To a visitor hot from the cold shores of England, he would put on an exaggerated Oxford accent and discuss the future of the 'British Empah' as though he wrongheadedly cared for nothing else in the wide world. His aim was to shake the newcomer out of his assumed complacency by insults which were as shrewdly observed as they were malicious. . . . The way into his heart was an immediate counterattack in a broad American accent, during which one assumed a complicity between him and his *bête noire,* Senator McCarthy, in some dark scheme. . . . It was in the character of the man that he smiled with real pleasure only when he had been amply repaid in kind."

Capote would go along with that: "The turning point in our friendship—the beginning really—was during *Beat the Devil* (1954). Bogie and John Huston and some others, they were playing that game—you know the one, what d'ya call it—you take each other's hand across a table and try to push the other's arm down. Well, it just happens that I've very good at that game. So, anyway, Bogie called over, 'Hey, Caposy.' That's what he called me, 'Caposy.' He said, 'C'mon, Caposy, let's see you try this.' And I went over and I pushed his arm down. Well, he looked at me. . . . He had such a suspicious mind, he was sure that Huston had cut off my head and sewed it onto someone else's body. 'Let's see you do that again,' he said. And again I pushed his arm down. So he said once more, and I said I would only if we bet a hundred dollars, which we did. I won again and he paid me, but then he came over and he started sort of semi-wrestling with me. It was something they did. He was crushing me and I said, 'Cut that *owat,*' and he said, 'Cut that *owat.*' I said. 'Well, do,' and he said, 'Why?' I said, 'Because you're hurting me.' But he kept right on squeezing, so I got my leg around behind him and pushed and over he went. He was flat on his can looking up at me. And from then on we were very good friends."

"Bogie's needling tactics were quite calculated," Johnson explained. "I had lunch with him and Betty at Romanoff's one time and she was giving him hell about some row at a party. He'd provoked it, of course. 'Someday somebody's gonna belt you,' she said, and he said, 'No, that's the art of it—taking things up to that point and then escaping.' "

· ·

In 1947, Bogart led a march to Washington to protest the investigations of the Un-American Activities Committee. Some people labeled him a pinko. He didn't like that. 'I am an American," he said. Bogart's political freethinking was considered dangerous in Hollywood. In 1952, however, he campaigned most actively for Stevenson for President. "He never seemed to give a damn what people thought or said," Mr. Stevenson recalled. "And it was quite perilous in those days to be a Democrat, especially one partisan to me. He was disdainful about anybody trying to muscle about in a free country."

"He wasn't an extremist in anything," said Miss Bacall, "except telling the truth. You had to admire Bogie. He always said what he thought. 'Goddammit,' he used to say, 'if you don't want to hear the truth, don't ask me.' "

"That's true," Johnson agreed. "Everything he did was honest. He used to say, 'What's everybody whispering about? I've got cancer!' He'd say, 'For Christ's sake, it's not a venereal disease.' "

Bogart also said that the only point in making money is "so you can tell some big shot to go to hell." And: "I have politeness and manners. I was brought up that way. But in this goldfish-bowl life, it is sometimes hard to use them."

His widow thinks it was more than just good manners Bogart had. Finally, she'll tell you, "He was an old-fashioned man, a great romantic. And very emotional. He would cry when a dog died. You should have seen him at our wedding, tears streaming down his face. He told me that he started thinking about the meaning of the words. He was tough about life and totally uncompromising, but I remember he went to see Steve at nursery school and when he saw him sitting at his little desk, he cried."

Alistair Cooke met the Bogarts on the Stevenson campaign train and he remembered sitting with them one afternoon and saying that, of course, Stevenson wouldn't win. " 'What!' said Bogie, astounded. 'Not a prayer, I'm afraid,' I said. 'Why you son of a bitch,' Betty said, 'that's a fine thing to say.' 'Look,' I said, 'I'm a reporter. You're the lieutenants.' We bet ten dollars on it and when Stevenson lost he paid it to me. But he didn't really think I'd take it. You know what he said? 'It's a hell of a guy who bets against his own principles.' "

Cooke commented on this Bogart trait in an article he wrote for *The Atlantic*

Monthly (May, 1957). "A touchy man who found the world more corrupt than he had hoped . . . he invented the Bogart character and imposed it on a world impatient of men more obviously good. And it fitted his deceptive purpose like a glove. . . . From all . . . he was determined to keep his secret: the rather shameful secret, in the realistic world we inhabit, of being a gallant man and an idealist."

Other friends detected a similar quality in Bogart. Mankiewicz called it, "A sadness about the human condition. He had a kind of eighteenth-century, Alexander Pope nature. I think he would have made a superb Gatsby. His life reflected Gatsby's sense of being an outsider." Stevenson found "a wistful note in him, as there often is in thinking people. He was much more profound than one might think." And Capote called him lost. "It was his outstanding single characteristic—that something almost pathetic. Not that he would ever ask for sympathy, far from it. It just always seemed to me as though he were permanently lonely. It gave him a rather poetic quality, don't you think?"

That secret inner world of Humphrey Bogart was reflected in his passion for sailing and his love for the *Santana,* his boat, on which he went off whenever he could, accompanied by a few friends. They used to drink Drambuies and play dominoes or just sail. He had learned early about the sea, having left school (at their request) at seventeen and joined the Navy. It was on the troopship *Leviathan* that he received the injury that permanently scarred his upper lip. "Sailing. That was the part of him no one could get at," Capote said. "It wasn't anything materialistic. It was some kind of inner soul, an almost mystical hideaway."

.   .   .   .

If the *Motion Picture Herald*'s annual Fame Poll of the Top Ten movie stars can be trusted, it appears that Bogart's peak years of popularity were 1943–1949, during and just after World War II. Cooke explained it this way: "He was . . . a romantic hero inconceivable in any time but ours. . . . When Hitler was acting out scripts more brutal and obscene than anything dreamed of by Chicago's North Side or the Warner Brothers, Bogart was the only possible antagonist likely to outwit him and survive. What was needed was no Ronald Colman, Leslie Howard or other knight of the boudoir, but a conniver as subtle as Goebbels. Bogart was the very tough gent required, and to his glory he was always, in the end, on our side."

He didn't get his Oscar, however, until 1952 (for *The African Queen*), and popped up on the top ten again in 1955, a little more than a year before he died. Betty Comden: "I don't think this cult is anything new. . . ." Adolph Green: "No. . . ." Comden: "Bogart never stopped being popular. . . ." Green: "There are so few originals around. . . ." Comden: "Bogart's style had an innate sophistication. . . ." Green: "He was less an actor . . .", Comden: ". . . than a

personality." Bogart agreed. "Sure I am. It took fifteen years to make us personalities. Gable and Cooper can do anything in a picture, and people would
say, 'Oh, that's just good old Clark.' "

"His great basic quality," said Ustinov, "was a splendid roughness. Even when
perfectly groomed, I felt I could have lit a match on his jaw. . . . He knew his
job inside out, and yet it was impossible not to feel that his real soul was elsewhere, a mysterious searching instrument knocking at doors unknown even to
himself. . . ."

Perhaps this is what Bogart's admirers sense. "There was something about him
that came through in every part he played," said Miss Bacall. "I think he'll always be fascinating—to this generation and every succeeding one. There was
something that made him able to be a man of his own and it showed through his
work. There was also a purity, which is amazing considering the parts he played.
Something solid too. I think as time goes by we all believe less and less. Here
was someone who believed in something."

"Like all really great stars," said director George Cukor, "he had a secret. You
never really know him altogether. He also had boldness of mind, freedom of
thought—a buccaneer. I think these young people haven't seen him," he went
on, trying to explain the cult. "They're simply rediscovering him. After all, Bogie
had class."

"The average college student would sooner identify with Bogart than, say,
Sinatra, don't you think?" said Mankiewicz. "He had that rather intellectual dis-
respect for authority. Also I don't think anyone ever really believed that Bogart
was a gangster—that's what fascinated people. Bogart never frightened them."

"It's angry youth," Chester Morris said. "They're cheering for the heavy
today. Everything must be nonconformist. They'd also like to do the kind of
things he did. He was a forerunner of James Bond." Benchley: "He's a hero without being a pretty boy."

"Could it be anything as simple as sex appeal?" Capote wondered. "He had
an image of sophisticated virility and he projected it remarkably well. And with
such humor. At last, he had such style that it doesn't wither, it doesn't age, it
doesn't date. Like Billie Holiday."

"I think Robin Hood has always been attractive," said Adlai Stevenson.

.   .   .   .

Before the adulation, there must be something to adulate. And this must be created. "If a face like Ingrid Bergman's looks at you as though you're adorable,"
Bogart once said, "everyone does. You don't have to act very much." The late
Raymond Chandler thought otherwise: "All Bogart has to do to dominate a scene
is to enter it." Evidently it wasn't always that way. In 1922, playing one of his
first stage roles, he was reviewed by Alexander Woollcott: "His performance

could be mercifully described as inadequate." But two years later, of another performance, Woollcott again: "Mr. Bogart is a young actor whose last appearance was recorded by your correspondent in words so disparaging that it is surprising to find him still acting. Those words are hereby eaten." It would figure that Bogart often used to quote the first review but never the second.

" 'Why, I'm a National Institution,' he used to say," Capote recalled. "He was very proud of his success and fame. But he was most serious about his acting. He thought of it as a profession, one that he was curious about, knew something about. After all, it was almost the sum total of his life. In the end, Bogart really was an artist. And a very selective one. All the gestures and expressions were pruned down and pruned down. One time I watched *The Maltese Falcon* with him and he sat there, muttering in that hoarse way, criticizing himself in the third person. 'Now he's gonna come in,' he'd say. 'Then he's gonna do this and that's where he does the wrong thing.' I gathered during the silences that he liked it. It was braggadocio through silence."

Howard Hawks directed Bogart in his two most archetypal roles, as Harry (Steve) Morgan in *To Have and Have Not* and Philip Marlow in *The Big Sleep* (1946). "He was extremely easy to work with," Hawks said. "Really underrated as an actor. Without his help I couldn't have done what I did with Bacall. Not many actors would sit around and wait while a girl steals a scene. But he fell in love with the girl and the girl with him, and that made it easy."

Bogart used to say that an audience was always a little ahead of the actor. "If a guy points a gun at you," he explained, "the audience knows you're afraid. You don't have to make faces. You just have to believe that you are the person you're playing and that what is happening is happening to you."

Ustinov acted with Bogart once, in a comedy called *We're No Angels* (1955). "Bogart had an enormous presence," he said, "and he carried the light of battle in his eye. He wished to be matched, to be challenged, to be teased. I could see a jocular and quarrelsome eye staring out of the character he was playing into the character I was playing—rather as an experienced bullfighter might stare a hotheaded bull into precipitate action."

"When the heavy, full of crime and bitterness," said Bogart, "grabs his wounds and talks about death and taxes in a husky voice, the audience is his and his alone."

.   .   .   .

This emotion, elicited so consciously from his movie audiences, ironically became a reality. His death was horribly, heartbreakingly in character. He died on January 14, 1957, of a cancer of the esophagus, and it had taken well over a year to kill him. "These days," he said, "I just sit around and talk to my friends, the people I like." Which is what he did.

"I went to see him toward the end," said Ambassador Stevenson. "He was very ill and very weak, but he made a most gallant effort to keep gay. He had an intolerance for weakness, an impatience with illness."

"I went a few times," Capote said. "Most of his friends went, some almost every day, like Sinatra. Some were very loyal. He seemed to bring out the best in them all. He looked so awful, so terribly thin. His eyes were huge and they looked so frightened. They got bigger and bigger. It was real fear and yet there was always that gay, brave self. He'd have to be brought downstairs on the dumbwaiter and he'd sit and wait and wait for his Martini. He was only allowed one, I think, or two. And that's how we used to find him, smoking and sipping that Martini."

During that time, his wife rarely left the house, though her friends and even Bogart urged her to go out more often. When someone asked why she had only been out six or seven times in ten months, Bogart replied: "She's my wife and my nurse. So she stays home. Maybe that's the way you tell the ladies from the broads in this town."

"He went through the worst and most agonizing pain any human can take," said Dr. Maynard Brandsma. "I knew this and when I'd see him I'd ask, 'How is it?' Bogie would always answer simply, 'Pretty rough.' He never complained and he never whimpered. I knew he was dying and during the last weeks I knew he knew it too."

"I saw him twenty-three days before he died," said Cukor. "He couldn't come downstairs anymore and he was heavily sedated. He kept closing his eyes. Still he'd be telling jokes and asking to hear the gossip. But his voice was the wonder. That marvelous voice. It was absolutely alive. It was the last thing that died."

His death came in the early morning and that day the papers carried the news to the world. Most of the reports were similar. Quite a few of them told it this way: "Usually he kissed his wife Lauren Bacall and said, 'Good night.' But according to Dr. Michael Flynn, this time he put his hand on her arm and murmured in his familiar brusque fashion, 'Good-bye, kid.' "

Whether it really happened that way or not is beside the point. Bogart the man and Bogart the hero had merged until now one couldn't tell the difference between the two, if indeed there ever had been any. He had walked through seventy-five movie nights for his public and it was too late now to change the image, too late to alter a legend that had really just begun.

DAVID THOMSON

David Thomson is a San Francisco–based Englishman whose Biographical Dictionary
of Film *is one of the key reference works: quirky, personal, opinionated, infuriating, and
quite often right on the money. He has written a lot of fiction incorporating the real-life
personas of movie stars, and in* Suspects *he does the reverse: He takes famous movie characters, writes as if they were real people, and places them in the times and experiences he
imagines they would have encountered. He is of course committing a folly forbidden by
serious criticism, which teaches us that as characters are fictional, they have no reality
other than that invented by their creators. But because many movie characters do live on
in our imaginations, it is seductive to read their "real" stories.*

from *Suspects*

NORMA DESMOND

Gloria Swanson in Sunset Boulevard, *1950,
directed by Billy Wilder*

You can look at movie magazines from the early 1920s, amazed at the faces of
beautiful young actresses, stars then, but so little known now that their eupho-
nious names sound concocted—Barbara La Marr, Lupe Velez, Agnes Ayres,
Alexandra Laguna, Leatrice Joy, Norma Desmond, and so on. All brunettes, with
black lips, curls stuck on their brows and eyes like bulletholes: they seem to cherish the pain of sexual exploitation by men. There is implacability in the faces,
like a ship's figurehead battling into the elements. It comes from signaling feelings; those silent women are stranded in the impossibility of utterance. A few
years later, after sound, women's faces softened. The loveliness grew quiet and
intriguing. Words were put out, like bait on the threshold of their being. They
smiled, where silent faces had had trumpeting frowns.

It must have been maddening. Not many of them lasted more than a few years; the business was exhausting, and that kind of beauty is our endless American resource. It was only will that made any of them famous, or put forbidding strength in their faces. Somehow, they all seemed overdone; no matter how hard they tried, they must have known the shame of feeling coarse or clumsy. You can imagine them killing even, at the end of their tether, laughing if the gun went off and there was only a small puff of light to show explosion. But the man aimed at was staggering, stupefied, his hands clutched to the hole where life was leaking out. The ladies could make you believe.

So many of their names were false. Norma Desmond was born May Svensson in Milwaukee in 1899. She was the daughter of Swedish immigrants, the youngest of five children. Years later, some version of Miss Desmond told *Photoplay:* "I had picked a good time and place to be born. The automobile was not much older than I was, so there weren't many of them. Trolleys and wagons were pulled by horses, and none of them went too fast. It was a safe, clean time. When you were thirsty in the summer, your mother made a pitcher of lemonade. And everyone did the family wash on Monday and hung it out in the fresh air to dry."

Charming, don't you think? But actresses are in love with such crystal-clear happiness. May Svensson's early life was not a pitcher of homemade lemonade or the bouquet of fresh laundry. Instead, she was taken by her father on his tours of Wisconsin and Minnesota, selling Bibles and being driven by penury into increasingly reckless confidence tricks in which the daughter was often the decoy. They lived in cheap hotels, or on the run: there were a few nights in town jails, the child in a cot next to the sheriff's desk waiting for her father to be released.

And so it was, in 1911, that May saw her father shot down by a man named Gregson, the victim of a small enough fraud, a God-fearing but choleric man who had pursued Svensson for seven months. May was holding her father's hand, and talking to him, coming out of a diner in Kenosha, when a pistol blast met them. She felt the pressure in the air and was dragged sideways by her father's fall, his dead grip on her growing tighter.

She had her picture in the Chicago papers, wide-eyed, floridly becurled and stricken. A manager at the Essanay studios noticed it, and his flabby head was so touched by her plight that he saw a way of making money. He found her and devised a series of one-reelers about a waif, "Sweedie" she was called, an orphan and an outcast who got into sentimental scrapes and comic adventures. The films were poorly made, but the child bloomed in them. The camera breathed in time with the rising beat of puberty; in a year of those short movies she became an object of furtive lust, her picture pinned in lockers. The movies learned early how to fashion an arousing innocence that inspires its own spoiling.

"Norma Desmond," as Essanay had called her, was married at fifteen to Wallace Beery, twice her age and the robust exponent of his own ugliness. It was like a virgin princess being taken by a barbarian. The public was thrilled with alarm. In reality, Norma scolded him incessantly, until he left her with the beach house, all but one of their cars and the vases filled with his cash. This was 1917.

She had an extraordinary career in silent pictures, earning as much as $15,000 a week, to say nothing of bonuses. She worked for Marshall Neilan, Cecil B. De Mille, Harry D'Abbadie D'Arrast and Allan Dwan. Her burning gaze played on audiences like the light of the screen. The industry romanticized her and her "enchanted" life. Perhaps she believed those stories herself—her image was overpowering. She had gone so swiftly from the sordid to the luxurious, from being abused to being worshipped. She was a Cinderella who became a tyrant queen, without time to clean the coal dust from her fingernails. An aura of transformation surrounded her. There was a famous portrait of her face staring through an embroidered veil, a celebration of beauty as a fatal delusion. She met the tycoon Noah Cross and he mounted a play with her as Salome, discarding hundreds of veils, while he sat on a stool in the wings to see her body emerge through the misty gauze.

Perhaps her conviction was too intense for the naturalism of sound pictures? Or were her demands for money more than the industry could endure? *Princess of the Micks,* her film for Max von Mayerling, her husband, was a disaster in which she sank one million dollars of her own money. And so she went to France, marrying a marquis whose name she never learned to spell. She made a film there, *Une Jeune Fille de campagne,* about Charlotte Corday, in which the character will not speak—to protect her excessive expressiveness or the actress's lack of French.

While in Europe, she married the German Baron von Rauffenstein. Mayerling had never really been given up during these other marriages. He simply went from being husband to personal manager; it meant he dressed earlier in the day. There was consternation in the press, but the three figures handled the "ménage" without dismay. Moreover, in 1931–32, Norma Desmond had an affair with Serge Alexandre, also known as Stavisky. To this day there is a rumor in France that she had a child by the swindler, a daughter, who was passed on to a simple farming couple on the estate of Baron Raoul, a friend of Alexandre's. (An unexpectedly striking face in an out-of-the-way place will often inspire such fancies. But suppose real foundlings are not especially pretty, what then?)

In 1934, she returned to the mansion on Sunset Boulevard (bought for her by Noah Cross), where she would remain until her removal, at the hands of the police, in 1950. Mayerling came back to America in 1939 and became her butler. Norma Desmond slipped from glory to oblivion, unaware in her retreat of any change in her power or her looks. She was so removed from public contact now, she may have thought herself divine.

She had only a monkey as an intimate until Joe Gillis strayed into her life. He seemed to offer the means of a comeback, but he was also a lover and a slave. When he thought to leave her, she shot him, in the belly, as yet unaware that her own body nurtured his child. In the asylum hospital, she never deigned to notice her swelling or the birth of the boy. She was officially insane, lecturing the other inmates and shooting them with imaginary guns when they ignored her. She died in 1959, still firing.

RICHARD BLAINE

Humphrey Bogart in Casablanca, *1942, directed by Michael Curtiz*

We used to tell stories about Rick. He was only ten or so years older than this writer, but can't you remember the luster that ten years has for a kid? Growing up near Omaha, I used to see him around the city. He seemed tall and unshaven, a wild fellow. But I find now that he never grew above five feet eight. In the few pictures I have of him later in life he seems to be making an effort to look dapper and impressive. In those early days, you heard stories about Rick "borrowing" someone's car for a night drive and outrunning the cops. He had girls hanging around him a lot of the time. He looked bored with them, but he'd let them kiss him sometimes. It was a privilege to catch the dime he tossed through the sunlight and hear the "Hey, kid, get me a Nehi, will you?" I did that twice, and the second time he grinned at me. I thought I felt the sun beaming. Yet I saw Rick's crooked teeth when his mouth bared.

He had been born in Omaha in 1900, the son of a pharmacist. (Later, I know, he said he was younger, and from big tough New York; forgive him—no one in this book has managed without a few lies.) If I remember him as a kid out of school, the figure in the best adventures, older-seeming than his peers, a boy's man, it wasn't that he neglected his studies. It surprised me, on going into it, that his grades were steady and high. He had an A— average, and he kept on working, trying to be better. The more I look at his record now, the more clearly I see a short, diligent man, whose amiability and natural bravery must have furnished his legend. Or was the legend just something I and others like me required? Was he only the conscientious boy who had to act up to it? When you think about how he turned out, you have to wonder whether his disillusion had something to do with that early feeling of inadequacy. Maybe I helped urge heroism on him and it became his curse. But was I supposed to look at the world and not use my imagination?

Richard Blaine went to Lincoln, to the university, in 1918. He majored in history, and he was especially interested in economics. He was one of the group that owed so much to Professor Wilson Keyes, though he and Keyes had heated arguments in class. Rick was already affected by radical ideas, and Keyes was a tough conservative who could never see past the sacrifices imposed in Russia in the name of communism. But that's how Rick grew in our eyes. He was quarterback on the football team his junior and senior years—which was a big thing in Nebraska then and now. But he had a reputation, too, as a red-hot debater and a guy who tried to read Lenin in Russian.

All the same, in those days he still helped out in his dad's pharmacy on Ames. He was generally ready to do a good turn for the old folks. He was best friends with Ralph Hunt, and he was godfather to Ralph's second daughter, Laura, born in 1920. Here's a picture of him outside the church, holding the baby. And Ralph's next to him, holding Mary Frances's hand. She's gazing up at her younger sister with that fretful look on her face. So young, so worried. Rick looks as proud as can be.

It surprised everyone when he went to Detroit to work in the Ford factory. Rick could have been in management, I'm sure, but he stayed on the assembly line because he said he wanted to get to know the working man. He was there for three years, and he came back a lot harder and a sight less cheerful.

He lived in a room in Omaha then, full of books and Mitzi Glass. They had gone together a little at Lincoln, and she was the best-known radical in town. Because of her great red hair, and her severe looks, people used to call her "Red Mitzi." Now, I'm sure there were some who hated what she believed in, or were afraid of it, but I think a lot of people were fond of her really. Rick loved her. They never got married because they said it was an irrelevance, and that made for a gulf between Rick and Ralph. But Omaha could take him then, without spitting him out. There was never any of the outrage that got talked up later.

Anyway, in those years, Mitzi was organizing farm labor and Rick helped her; he was writing his novel about the automobile industry—*Drums of Steel*—and he was drinking. No one ever denied that. I know some people who'd admired him once gave up on him. They called him a layabout and a lush, and no one much liked his book: it's awkward and high-minded, but the stuff in the factories is good, I think. It was what happened to Mitzi that moved Rick on. In 1930, there was a strike up near Bassett. Strikebreakers came in and Mitzi got hit on the head with a fence post. It took her five months to die but she never regained consciousness. The word was that Rick went into the hospital one night and smothered her. If so, it was merciful.

He went out to California then and he did a lot of organizing with fruit workers. That was hard. The labor was poor, Spanish most of it, and itinerant, and the bosses were rough on union men. Rick stuck to it and that's the period when he joined the Party. But he got pneumonia in 'thirty-three, a bad case. He was always weaker afterward, and drinking still. Then in 1935 he went on a trip to Moscow. It was for students mainly, but Rick managed to go on it and he was there two months. From all I can gather, he came back redder than ever. But he returned by way of Africa, having gone on from Moscow to Abyssinia on some sort of mission.

It was no surprise in 1936 that he started speaking for Spain and the Republic and early the following year he was over there with the Abraham Lincoln Brigade. He fought all through the war, at Madrid and then in Barcelona. He was a captain, and his health was finally shot by the experience. Worse than that, I think, he was disenchanted. That war, he thought, could have been won. He despaired not so much at the free countries staying neutral, but at the dissension in Spain itself among the various branches of the anarchists and the Communists. In addition, he didn't like anything he heard about the trials going on in Moscow. By the end of the war, he had given up the Party and he was looking for a different life.

Rick was in Paris for a time doing not much, except trading on the black market and carrying on with Ilsa Lund. He was regarded as a cynic by then. The drinking was constant, and not even Sam, a guy who had come out of Spain with him, could keep him cheerful. The affair with Ilsa was hopeless; she had all these causes, perhaps Rick used her to remind himself of all he'd lost. He wanted it to fail, he was dependent now on self-pity. So when the Germans came in, Rick got out. As I heard it from Sam, Rick was going anyway but later he persuaded himself that Ilsa had let him down.

He got to Casablanca and he opened the Café Americain, where anything was possible. You could buy or sell whatever you wanted—jewels, drugs, papers, lives—it was a rat-race of a market. There were people of all nationalities and persuasions. The war was held down by money, greed and fear. It was an ugly place, and the movie they made romanticized it and Rick. He was as vicious as he had to be by then, just taking his cut on whatever happened, OK-ing every kind of deal and arrangement.

The big new thing in his life was Louis Renault (1891–1964), the head of the Vichy police in Casablanca. Apparently he took one long look at Rick and knew he was homosexual underneath all the brooding and the sneers about women. He could see Rick was dying too, and he was decent enough to do what he could for him. After Strasser was killed and the weird but wonderful Victor Laszlo got away, Rick and Louis slipped off into the fog together. They went south, to Marrakech, and they lived there after the war, until Rick died in 1949. I can see him sitting out in the sun, slipping a coin in an Arab boy's hand in return for one of those sweet cordials. Louis took the best care of him, and at the very end they were laughing together over reports of the red scare in America.

NICHOLAS RAY

I first saw Nicholas Ray during the tumultuous days of the 1968 Chicago Democratic Convention. A tall, gaunt man with unruly hair and an eye patch, he came striding out of a crowd of demonstrating students. He was living in a shabby apartment in Old Town and preparing a movie about what he saw as a developing revolutionary situation in America; drinking through a long night, he explained how he wanted to raise money to shoot a film in the streets as "the kids" attacked the establishment. (Oddly, Haskell Wexler's Medium Cool *was filming in Chicago with much the same vision at about the same time.) This was the same Nicholas Ray who had made some of the great noir classics* (They Live by Night, In a Lonely Place), *and whose* Rebel without a Cause *(1955) defined James Dean and added a phrase to the language. In his memoir,* I Was Interrupted, *Ray remembered his Hollywood days with a frankness assisted by his knowledge that he would never work there again. Here he remembers Dean with the tenderness of a lover—or a father.*

James Dean

First there was the revolver.

Jimmy kept a Colt .45 in his dressing room, where he also slept. He had come back to Hollywood at the age of 22 for *East of Eden,* but everything that he did suggested he had no intention of belonging to the place. He had come to work; but he would remain himself. He found in the Warners studio a sanctuary of steel and concrete. At night he could be alone in this closed, empty kingdom. Perhaps the revolver was a symbol, of self-protection, of warning to others.

He rode a motorcycle. He dressed casually, untidily, which invariably was interpreted as a gesture of revolt. Not entirely true. For one thing, it saved time, and Jim detested waste. It also saved money. (This is a simple consideration, often ignored. Most young actors are poor: T-shirt and jeans for work, later to become a mannerism, was originally a quick and comfortable way to cut down the laundry bill.) Some days he would forego shaving if there was something more important to do. And what's wrong with that?

Like the revolver these habits were self-protective. Riding a motorcycle, he traveled by himself. Sleeping in a studio dressing room, he had complete solitude. He could leave, but nobody else could come in. He shied away from manners and social convention because they suggested disguise. He wanted his self to be naked. "Being a nice guy," he once said, "is detrimental to actors. When I first came to Hollywood, everyone was nice to me, everyone thought I was a nice guy. I went to the commissary to eat, and people were friendly, and I thought it was wonderful. But I decided not to continue to be a nice guy. Then people would have to respect me for my work."

Soon after shooting on *East of Eden* was finished, he went to his dressing room and found the gun had disappeared. He was furious, but this was only the beginning. A few days later the studio authorities told him he could no longer sleep in the dressing room. (It came close to violating safety regulations, and Warners had had a couple of disastrous fires.) He refused to believe them until he was refused admittance at the gate that night.

There were name and number plates on each office door at Warners. Next morning Jimmy took them all down, changed some around, and hung others from ceilings and fountains, causing widespread confusion. Then he rode away on his motorcycle, vowing never to make a film there again.

Cat-like he had prowled around and found his own preferred corner. Then it was forbidden him. A wound to the pride of a cat is serious. Ask any of us cats.

Not long after I had written the first outline of *Rebel,* Kazan invited me to see a rough cut of *East of Eden* in the music room at Warners. The composer, Leonard Rosenman, was there, improvising at the piano. And Jimmy was there, aloof and solitary; we hardly exchanged a word. That he had talent was obvious, but I respected Kazan's skills too much to give full marks to any actor who worked with him.

My office at Warners adjoined Kazan's. One day Jimmy dropped by. He asked me what I was working on. I told him the idea and approach. He seemed warily interested, but didn't say very much. A day or two later he brought in a tough, dark-haired young man named Perry Lopez, whom he had met in New York. He told me that Perry came from the Lexington Avenue district: "You should talk to him," he said.

A few more such encounters and I decided to get Dean to play Jim Stark.

But he had to decide, too. It was not a simple question of whether or not he liked the part. Neither he nor Warners were sure he would ever work there again. And after the smell of success began to surround *East of Eden,* agents and well-wishers were eager to advise him. It would be foolish, they told him, to appear in any film not based on a best-seller, not adapted by a $3,000-a-week writer, and not directed by Elia Kazan, George Stevens, John Huston, or William Wyler. He was not the kind of person to take such advice very seriously, but intensely self-aware as he was, he could not fail to be troubled by "success." If there were aspects of it he enjoyed, it also played on his doubts.

One evening we had a long passionate discussion with Shelley Winters about acting and show business. "I better know how to take care of myself," he said. This attitude lay behind his choice of work. He had quarreled with Kazan during *East of Eden,* but retained a respect for him, and would have been flattered to work for him again.

There were probably few other directors with whom Jimmy could have worked. To work with Jimmy meant exploring his nature; without this his powers of expression were frozen. He wanted to make films in which he could personally believe, but it was never easy for him. Between belief and action lay the obstacle of his own deep, obscure uncertainty. Disappointed, unsatisfied, he was the child who skulks off to his private corner and refuses to speak. Eager and hopeful, he was the child exhilarated with new pleasure, wanting more, wanting everything, and often unconsciously subtle in his pursuit of it.

Late one evening he arrived at my house with Jack Simmons, at that time an unemployed actor, and Vampira, the television personality. (Jack was to become a close friend of Jim's and appear with him in a TV play. Jimmy often extended sudden affection to lonely and struggling people, several of whom he'd adopt. He had few permanent relationships, so his companion of the moment was most likely to be an adoption of the moment, or a new object of curiosity. He told me later he had wanted to meet Vampira because he was studying magic. Was she really possessed by satanic forces, as her TV program suggested? "She didn't know anything!" he exclaimed sadly.) On entering the room he turned a back somersault, then from the floor looked keenly at me.

"Are you middle-aged?"

I admitted it.

"Did you live in a bungalow on Sunset Boulevard, by the old Clover Club?"

"Yes," I said.

"Was there a fire there in the middle of the night?"

"Yes."

"Did you carry a boxer puppy out of the house in your bare feet across the street and cut your feet?"

I had.

He seemed to approve. He had heard the story from Vampira and came to find out if it were true.

On Sunday afternoons I used to invite a few people in to play music, sing, and talk. Jimmy always came to these gatherings and enjoyed them. We were exploring on both sides. Was he going to like my friends? Both of us had to know.

One afternoon he stayed on after the others had gone. Clifford Odets came by, and I introduced them. Jimmy was peculiarly silent and retreated to a corner. I went out to the kitchen to mix some drinks. Clifford later told me what had happened:

There had been a long silence. The distance of the room lay between them. At last, in a grave voice, Jimmy spoke:

"I'm a sonofabitch."

Clifford asked why.

"Well," he explained, "here I am, you know, in this room. With you. It's fantastic. Like meeting Ibsen or Shaw."

Clifford remembered this as one of the most flattering remarks ever so sincerely addressed to him.

. . . .

Jimmy approached all human beings with the same urgent, probing curiosity: *"Here I am. Here are you."* At encountering a new presence, invisible antennae seemed to reach out, grow tense, transmit a series of impressions.

Sometimes there'd be an extraordinary, unbearable tenderness. Michael and Connie Bessie, a couple I'd known for many years, arrived one day from New York. After I'd introduced them to Jimmy, Connie sat down on the couch. Without thinking she picked up the cushion beside her and cradled it in her lap.

Jimmy watched and, after a moment, very intent and quiet, he asked her, "Can't you have a child of your own?"

Connie was dumbstruck and left the room. I went after her. We had once wanted to marry. She and her husband had just adopted a baby.

Just before Christmas I went to New York to interview actors. Jimmy was already there, and I visited his apartment, for there were things I had to know, too. It was on the fifth floor of an old 68th Street building without an elevator. A fairly large furnished room with two porthole windows, a studio couch, a table, some unmatching chairs and stools. On the walls, a bullfighting poster, capes, and horns. Everywhere piles of books and records, some neatly stacked, some spilling over. A door led to the kitchen and bath, another to a flight upstairs to the roof. It was evening. The only light came from the scrap wood and fruit boxes burning in the fireplace.

He played record after record on the phonograph. Where did he first hear all those sounds? African tribal music, Afro-Cuban songs and dances, classical jazz, Jack Teagarten, Dave Brubeck, Haydn, Berlioz. Many of the books were about bullfighting. I remember *Matador* and *Death in the Afternoon*.

I introduced Jimmy to my son Tony, a Plato of sorts, to see if they'd get along and to see him through the eyes of his own generation. Tony stayed in New York and I went back to Hollywood. Later he told me he saw Jimmy several times, mainly at parties at the 68th Street apartment or in rooms of one of the half-dozen young actors and actresses he made his most frequent companions. It was always the same group, and no one ever wanted to go home. Jimmy played bongo drums, while another guy danced calypso and imitations of Gene Kelly. Conversation ranged from new plays and movies to (as dawn broke) Plato and Aristotle. They read stories and plays, going right through *Twenty-Seven Wagon Loads of Cotton*.

Jimmy also went to more orthodox parties. These were larger, given by people he knew less well. But he didn't like crowds, they made him insecure. Ignoring the talk and games, he would find his own melancholy corner.

He swerved easily from morbidity to elation. The depression could lift as completely and unexpectedly as it had settled in. Once it was cured by going to see Jacques Tati in *The Big Day*. Unshaven, tousled, wrapped in a dyed black trench coat, glasses on the end of his nose, Jim's mood was dark as he entered the theatre. But after ten minutes he was laughing so wildly, the nearby audience complained. He ignored them, there was nothing else he could do, the spell of delight had got him. Before the film was over he had to leave, which he did in a series of leaps and hurdles through the aisle. Back on the street, he stopped at a pastry shop. Then down the sidewalk, eclair in hand, with the Grouchian walk and the inquiring, bulbous-eyed face, he turned into Tati's postman.

Another sad, grey, rainy New York day he decided to buy an umbrella. Umbrellas were everywhere in the store, rack upon rack. But which one? Finally he let Tony choose one for him, an ordinary three-dollar model. Jimmy seized it as if it were the one he had been after his whole life. He played with it as a child with a new toy, exploring all its movements, flipping it open, pulling it shut, twirling it over his head. In the street as the rain poured down, suddenly brilliant and exhilarated, he became Charlie Chaplin.

It seemed that anything interested him. His gift for mime was uncanny. A friend wanted to audition for the Actor's Studio, and Jimmy offered to do the scene with him. They chose a fairy tale, a fight between a fox and the little prince. Immediately and with a ferocious longing Jimmy concentrated on the fox, and his imagination winged. He did not imitate; the stealth, the grace, the menace of the animal seemed to enter his body. He *became* a human fox.

He became other people with obvious passion and relief. "If I were he," he would say—and bless him for that, for it was a great part of his magic as an actor. It was the magic IF Stanislavsky had learned about from all the great actors he'd interviewed. But Jim hadn't learned it, not from Lee Strasberg, for chrissake. Nobody learns it, and nobody can breathe it into another.

Like the fox he was wary and hard to catch. For many, a relationship with Jimmy was complex, even obsessive. For him it was simple and probably much less important. He was intensely determined not to be loved or love. He could be absorbed, fascinated, attracted by things new or beautiful, but he would never surrender himself. There were girls convinced they were the only ones in his life (often at the same time, there were so many people and things in his life at the same time), when they were no more than occasions.

When he was poor and unknown in New York, he had reason to be grateful to several people for food and companionship, yet this was not enough for him to trust them. Returning to New York after *East of Eden,* he sometimes used his success to be cruel.

A young photographer he had known quite well in the struggling days wanted to buy a Rolliflex camera. He asked Jim to go halves with him: the price was $25. Jim was affronted: "Why should I get a second-hand camera with you when I can get all the new stuff I want now."

He complained of his companions: "They bum meals from me." One day in a restaurant he wondered out loud, "Where are my friends?" Four of his closest ones were with him at the table, but before they could answer he abruptly got up and walked out.

"I don't want anything seventy-thirty," he liked to say. "Fifty-fifty's enough for me." He came back to this idea often.

. . . .

Every day he threw himself upon the world like a starved animal after a scrap of food. The intensity of his fears and desires could make the search arrogant, egocentric, but behind it was such a desperate vulnerability that one could not but be moved by it, even frightened. Probably when he was faithless or cruel, he believed he was paying off an old score. The affection that he rejected was affection that once had been his but had found no answer.

The night before I went back to Hollywood we had dinner together, as we had done every night of my New York stay. We ate at an Italian restaurant, and Jim ordered the food with great ceremony, taking pride in his knowledge of obscure dishes. I felt he had come to trust me. And that he would like to do the film, though if this were so, other difficulties would lie ahead, including the situation with Warners and the objections of his agents and others who were beginning to hitch their wagons to the new star. And though I knew what I wanted in the story, I had only thirty pages of script.

I was mulling this over when he looked up at me. Something in his expression suggested he was about to impart a special confidence. He was restless, more so than usual.

"I got crabs," he said. "What do I do?"

I took him to a drugstore and introduced him to Cuprex. Outside in the street, we parted. He thanked me for the help, smiled, then said:

"I want to do your film, but don't tell those bastards at Warners."

I said I was glad, and that I wouldn't tell Warners anything except that I wanted him. We shook hands on it.

FRANÇOIS TRUFFAUT

More than most other directors, François Truffaut remained a film student and critic even after he began directing. It was the cinema, and particularly the guidance of the French critic André Bazin, that rescued him from an adolescence that seemed headed for nothing good, and as an adult he continued to devour films and write about them, even capturing Hitchcock for a book-length interview about all his films. Truffaut's Day for Night *was an autobiographical film about a movie director, and in it the director has a dream in which he recalls being a small boy and visiting the cinema in his town that was showing an Orson Welles film, and reaching in through the locked gates to steal a poster. Here he writes about Welles and James Dean, two of his great influences in the 1950s—Welles because of his direction and Dean because he so greatly increased the emotional freedom of actors on the screen ("He killed psychology the day he appeared on the set").*

from *The Films of My Life*

ORSON WELLES

Citizen Kane: The Fragile Giant

Though it was made in Hollywood in August–September 1940, and shown in the United States during 1941, because of the war *Citizen Kane* didn't make it to France until six years later. When it opened in Paris in July 1946, it was a great event for the film buffs of my generation. Since the Liberation we had been discovering American movies and were busily abandoning the French filmmakers we had admired during the war. We were even more emphatic about our disaffection with French actors and actresses as we rushed to the Americans. Out with Pierre Fresnay, Jean Marais, Edwige Feuillère, Raimu, Arletty; long live Cary Grant, Humphrey Bogart, James Stewart, Gary Cooper, Spencer Tracy, Lauren Bacall, Gene Tierney, Ingrid Bergman, Joan Bennett, et al.

We excused our radical shift on the grounds that French movie magazines, especially *L'Ecran Français,* were so devoted to corporate anti-Americanism that we were profoundly irritated. During the Occupation, because German films were so mediocre and English-language films were forbidden, the French movie industry prospered, our films were snatched up, the theaters were usually full. After the Liberation, the Blum-Byrnes accords authorized the release of a great many American films in France and the box-office receipts of French films went down. It was not unusual to see French stars and directors demonstrating in the streets of Paris for a reduction in the number of American films allowed to be imported.

Also, a taste for escaping one's own milieu, a thirst for novelty, romanticism, and also obviously a spirit of contrariness, but mostly a love of vitality, made us love anything that came from Hollywood. It was in this mood that we first heard the name Orson Welles in the summer of 1946. I rather think that his unusual first name contributed to our fascination: Orson sounded like *ourson,* a bear cub, and we heard that this cub was only thirty, that he'd made *Citizen Kane* at twenty-six, the same age at which Eisenstein had made *Potemkin*.

The French critics were full of praise—Jean-Paul Sartre, who had seen it in America, wrote an article preparing the ground. Still, a number of them were confused as they recounted the screenplay; they contradicted each other in the various journals over the meaning of the word "rosebud." Some critics said it was the name given to the glass filled with snowflakes that slips from Kane's hands as he dies. Denis Martin and André Bazin were the leaders in this journalistic inquiry and they persuaded the distributor, RKO, to add the subtitle "Rosebud" at the precise moment when a child's sled is going up in flames.

The confusion between the sled and the glass was exactly what Welles wished. The glass was filled with drops of snow falling on a little house, and twice Kane says the word in relation to the glass—first when he picks it up as his second wife, Susan Alexander, is leaving him, and then, as he is dying, drops it.

As magical for us as "rosebud" was the name "Xanadu." In France we didn't know Coleridge's poem about Kubla Khan. Even though it is explicitly quoted in the film, it was lost on our French ears in the text of "News on the March."

> In Xanadu did Kubla Khan
> A stately pleasure dome decree: . . .
> So twice five miles of fertile ground
> With walls and towers were girdled round.

It was thus reasonable to conclude that even the name Kane came from Khan, as that of Arkadin probably came from Irina Ardakina, the actress-heroine of Chekhov's *The Sea Gull*.

Citizen Kane, which was never dubbed, sobered us up from our Hollywood binge and made us more demanding film lovers. This film has inspired more vocations to cinema throughout the world than any other. This seems a little odd since Welles's work is always rightly described as inimitable, and also because the influence he exerted, if it is sometimes discernible as in Mankiewicz' *The Barefoot Contessa,* Astruc's *Les Mauvaises Rencontres,* Max Ophuls' *Lola Montès,* and Fellini's *8 1/2,* is most often indirect and under the surface. The Hollywood productions I spoke of earlier, which we had so loved, were seductive, but they seemed unattainable. You could go again and again to see films like *The Big Sleep, Notorious, The Lady Eve, Scarlet Street,* but these movies never hinted to us that we would become filmmakers one day. They served only to show that, if cinema was a country, Hollywood was clearly its capital.

So, it was no doubt the double pro-and-con-Hollywood aspect that made *Citizen Kane* stir us so, as well as Welles's impudent youth and a strong European element in his attitudes. Even more than his wide travels, I think that it was his intense and intimate knowledge of Shakespeare that gave Welles an anti-Manichaean world view and allowed him to mix good and bad heroes so gleefully. I will make a confession. I was fourteen in 1946 and had already dropped out of school. I discovered Shakespeare through Orson Welles, just as my taste for Bernard Hermann's music brought me to Stravinsky, who so often was its inspiration.

Because Welles was young and romantic, his genius seemed closer to us than the talents of the traditional American directors. When Everett Sloane, who plays the character of Bernstein in *Kane,* relates how, one day in 1896, his ferryboat crossed the path of another in Hudson Bay on which there was a young woman in a white dress holding a parasol, and that he'd only seen the girl for a second but had thought of her once a month all his life . . . ah, well, behind this Chekhovian scene, there was no big director to admire, but a friend to discover, an accomplice to love, a person we felt close to in heart and mind.

We loved this film absolutely because it was so complete—psychological, social, poetic, dramatic, comic, grotesque. *Kane* both demonstrates and mocks the will to power; it is a hymn to youth and a meditation on age, a study of the vanity of all human ambition and a poem about deterioration, and underneath it all a reflection on the solitude of exceptional beings, geniuses or monsters, monstrous geniuses.

Citizen Kane has both the look of a "first film," because of its grab bag of experiments, and a film of a director's highest maturity, because of its universal portrait of the world.

I didn't understand until long after that first great encounter in July 1946 why *Kane* is what it is and the ways in which it is unique; it's the only first film made by a man who was already famous. Chaplin was only a little emigrant clown when he made his debut in front of the camera. Renoir was, in the view of the profession, just a daddy's boy keeping himself busy with a camera and wasting his family's money when he shot *Nana;* Hitchcock was only a credits designer who was being promoted when he made *Blackmail.* But Orson Welles was already very well known in America—and not only because of the notorious radio play about Martians—when he started *Citizen Kane.* He was a famous man and the trade papers in Hollywood were laying for him. "Quiet," they ordered, "genius at work." The normal course of events is to become famous after having made a number of good films. It's rare to be famous at twenty-six, and even rarer to be given a film to make at that age. This is the reason that *Citizen Kane* is the only first film to have for its theme celebrity as such. In the long run, it is clearly Welles's legend and precocity which enabled him to lay before us plausibly and accurately the span of an entire lifetime—we follow Charles Foster Kane from childhood to death. As opposed to a timid beginner who might try to make a good film in order to win acceptance in the industry, Welles, with his considerable reputation already established, felt constrained to make a movie which would sum up everything that had come before in cinema, and would prefigure everything to come. His extravagant gamble paid off handsomely.

There has always been considerable talk about the technical aspect of Welles's work. Had he acquired all that technique in a few weeks before shooting *Kane,* or had he picked it up by watching a lot of movies? The question is beside the point. Hollywood is full of directors who have made forty films and still don't know how to fade two shots into each other harmoniously. To make a good film, you need intelligence, sensitivity, intuition, and a few ideas, that's all. Welles had all these to spare. When Thatcher challenges him, "So, that's really how you think a newspaper should be run?" the young Kane answers, "I have absolutely no experience in running a paper, Mr. Thatcher. I just try out all the ideas that come into my head."

When I see *Kane* today, I'm aware that I know it by heart, but in the way you know a recording rather than a movie. I'm not always as certain what image comes next as I am about what sound will burst forth, or the very timbre of the next voice that I'm going to hear, or the musical link to the next scene. (Before *Kane,* nobody in Hollywood knew how to set music properly in movies.) *Kane* was the first, in fact the only, great film that uses radio techniques. Behind each scene, there is a resonance which gives it its color: the rain on the windows of the cabaret, "El Rancho," when the investigator goes to visit the down-and-out female singer who can only "work" Atlantic City; the echoes in the marble-lined Thatcher library; the overlapping voices whenever there are several characters.

A lot of filmmakers know enough to follow Auguste Renoir's advice to fill the eyes with images at all cost, but only Orson Welles understood that the sound track had to be filled in the same way.

Before he had decided on *Citizen Kane,* Welles was preparing an adaptation of Joseph Conrad's *Heart of Darkness* in which the narrator would be replaced by a subjective camera. Something of the idea is retained in *Kane.* The investigator, Thomson, is shot from the back all through the film, which also discards the rules of classical cutting according to which one scene must be backed onto the next. The story is moved along as if it were a newspaper story. Visually the film is more aptly described as "page setting" rather than stage setting. A quarter of the shots are faked, the camera manipulates almost as if it were an animated film. So many of the shots in depth of focus—the glass of poison in Susan's bedroom, to begin with—were trick shots, a kind of "hide-and-don't-seek," the cinematic equivalent of the photomontage of sensational newspapers. One can also view *Citizen Kane* as a film of artful manipulation if you compare it to its successor, *The Magnificent Ambersons,* which is the opposite, a romantic film with drawn-out scenes, an emphasis on action over camera work, the stretching of real time.

In *The Magnificent Ambersons* Welles uses less than two-hundred shots to relate a story which spans twenty-five years (as opposed to 562 in *Citizen Kane*), as if the second movie had been shot in a fury by a different director who hated the first and wanted to give Welles a lesson in modesty. Because he's always very much the artist *and* the critic, Welles is a director who is very easily carried away but who later judges his flights of fancy on the cutting table with growing attention in his subsequent films. Many of Welles's recent films give the impression that they were shot by an exhibitionist and edited by a censor.

Let's return to *Citizen Kane,* in which everything happens as if Welles, with extraordinary arrogance, had rejected the rules of cinema, the limits of its powers of illusion and, with quick strokes and tricks—some more clever and successful than others—made his movie resemble the form of American comics in which fantasy allows the artist to draw one character close up, behind him at full length the person who's talking to him, and at the back ten characters with the designs on their ties as clear as the wart on the nose of the character in closeup. It's this singular marvel, never reedited, that is brought off fifty times in a row. It gives the film a stylization, an idealization of visual effects that had not been attempted since Murnau's films *The Last Laugh* and *Sunrise.* The great moviemakers who are conscious of form—Murnau, Lang, Eisenstein, Dreyer, Hitchcock—all got their start before the talkies, and it's no exaggeration to see in Welles the only great natural visual artist to arrive on the scene after the advent of sound.

If you see a superb scene from a Western, it could be John Ford, Raoul Walsh, William Wellman, or Michael Curtiz, whereas Welles's style, like Hitchcock's, is instantly recognizable. Welles's visual mode is his alone, and it is inimitable because, for one reason, like Chaplin's, it emanates from the physical presence of the author-actor at the center of the screen. It is Welles who comes slowly across the image; who creates a hubbub and then breaks it by suddenly speaking very softly; Welles who hurls his retorts over the heads of his characters as if he deigned to speak only to the gods (the Shakespearean influence); Welles, working against all custom, who breaks away from the flat horizon so that sometimes the whole scene spins haphazardly, the ground seeming to seesaw in front of the hero as he strides toward the lens.

Welles might well find all other films slack, flat, static, because his are so dynamic. They unroll before the eyes the way music moves in the ear.

Seeing *Citizen Kane* again today, we discover something else: this film, which had seemed extravagantly luxurious and expensive, is made up of fragments of stage tricks, actually put together out of odds and ends. There are very few extras and a lot of stock shots, lots of large pieces of furniture but a great many faked walls, and, above all, a lot of closeups of small bells, cymbals, "spliced-in" shots, newspapers, accessories, photographs, miniature portraits, a great many fade-ins and dissolves. The truth is that *Citizen Kane* is a film that if not cheap was at least modest, and was made to look sumptuous on the cutting-room table. This result was achieved by an enormous amount of work to enhance all the separate elements, and especially through the extraordinary strengthening of the visual track by the most ingenious sound in the history of movies.

.   .   .   .

When I saw *Citizen Kane* as an adolescent film buff, I was overcome with admiration for the film's main character. I thought he was marvelous, splendid, and I linked Orson Welles and Charles Foster Kane in the same idolatry. I thought the film was a panegyric to ambition and power. When I saw it again, after I'd become a *critic,* accustomed to analyzing my enjoyment, I discovered its true critical point of view: satire. I understood then that we're supposed to sympathize with the character of Jedediah Leland (played by Joseph Cotten). I saw that the film clearly demonstrates the absurdity of all worldly success. Today, now that I am a director, when I see *Kane* again for perhaps the thirtieth time, it is its twofold aspect as fairy tale and moral fable that strikes me most forcefully.

I can't say whether Welles's work is puritanical because I don't know the significance of the word in America, but I've always been struck by its chastity. Kane's downfall is brought about by a sexual scandal: "Candidate Kane found in bed with 'singer' "; and yet we've observed that Kane's and Susan's relationship was a father-daughter, protective bond. Their liaison, if one can call it that, is actually linked to Kane's childhood and to the idea of family. It's when he's coming back from a family pilgrimage (he had gone to see his parents' furniture, including probably the sled "Rosebud" stored in a shed) that he meets Susan on the street. She's coming out of a drugstore, holding her jaw because she has a toothache. He's just been splashed by a passing car. Notice that later Kane twice pronounces the word "rosebud"—when he's apparently dying and once before that, when Susan leaves him. He smashes all the furniture in his bedroom—it's a famous scene—but note that Kane's anger is only appeased when he takes the glass in his hand. At that point, it is quite clear that "rosebud," already connected to his separation from his mother, will henceforth be linked to Susan's abandoning him. There are partings which are like deaths.

What we already have found in *Citizen Kane,* and will find better expressed in other of Welles's works, is a world view which is personal, generous, and noble. There is no vulgarity, no meanness in this film, only the satirical, imbued by a fresh and imaginative antibourgeois morality, a lecture on how to behave: what to do, what not to do.

What all of Welles's films have in common is a liberalism, the assertion that belief in conservatism is an error. The fragile giants that are at the center of his cruel fables discover that you cannot conserve anything—not youth, not power, not love. Charles Foster Kane, George Minafer Amberson, Michael O'Hara, Gregory Arkadin come to understand that life is made up of terrible tears and wrenches.

JAMES DEAN IS DEAD

On the evening of September 30, 1955, against the wishes of the Warner Brothers studio executives, James Dean got behind the wheel of his sports car and was killed on a road in northern California.

The news, which we learned in Paris the next day, did not arouse much emotion at the time. A young actor, twenty-four years old, was dead. Six months have passed and two of his films have appeared, and now we realize what we have lost.

Dean had been noticed two years before on Broadway when he played the role of the young Arab in an adaptation of André Gide's *The Immoralist.* Following that, Elia Kazan starred him in *East of Eden*—Dean's movie debut. Then Nicholas Ray chose him for the hero of *Rebel Without a Cause,* and finally George Stevens picked him to play the principal role in *Giant,* the story of a man we follow from twenty to sixty. His next part was to have been the boxer Rocky Graziano in *Somebody Up There Likes Me.*

Dean worked very hard at *Giant*; he never took his eye off George Stevens or the camera. When the film was finished, he told his agent, Dick Clayton, "I think I could be a better director than an actor." He wanted to establish an independent company so he could shoot only properties he had chosen himself. Clayton promised to talk it over with the Warner Brothers executives. Then, Dean, who had been forbidden by contract to drive his car while the film was being shot, roared off to Salinas to compete in a race.

The accident: "I think I'll take a ride in the Spyder [the brand name of his Porsche]," he told George Stevens. Near Paso Robles that evening, he and his Spyder were cut off by another car coming onto the highway from a side road. Dean died from multiple fractures and internal contusions on the way to the hospital.

It was his fate to die before his time, as have so many artists.

.   .   .   .

James Dean's acting flies in the face of fifty years of filmmaking; each gesture, attitude, each mimicry is a slap at the psychological tradition. Dean does not "show off" the text by understatement like Edwige Feuillère; he does not evoke its poetry, like Gérard Philipe; he does not play with it mischievously like Pierre Fresnay. By contrast, he is anxious not to show that he understands perfectly what he is saying, but that he understands it better than the director did. He acts *something beyond* what he is saying; he plays alongside the scene; his expression doesn't follow the conversation. He *shifts* his expression from what is being expressed in the way that a consummately modest genius might express profound thoughts self-deprecatingly, as if to excuse himself for his genius, so as not to make a nuisance of himself.

There were special moments when Chaplin reached the ultimate in mime: he became a tree, a lamppost, an animal-skin rug next to a bed. Dean's acting is more animal than human, and that makes him unpredictable. What will his next gesture be? He may keep talking and turn his back to the camera as he finishes a scene; he may suddenly throw his head back or let it droop; he may raise his arms to heaven, stretch them forward, palms up to convince, down to reject. He may, in a single scene, appear to be the son of Frankenstein, a little squirrel, a cowering urchin or a broken old man. His nearsighted look adds to the feeling that he shifts between his acting and the text; there is a vague fixedness, almost a hypnotic half-slumber.

When you have the good luck to write for an actor of this sort, an actor who plays his part physically, carnally, instead of filtering everything through his brain, the easiest way to get good results is to think abstractly. Think of it this way: James Dean is a cat, a lion, or maybe a squirrel. What can cats, lions and squirrels do that is most unlike humans? A cat can fall from great heights and land on its paws; it can be run over without being injured; it arches its back and slips away easily. Lions creep and roar; squirrels jump from one branch to another. So, what one must write are scenes in which Dean creeps (amid the beanstalks), roars (in a police station), leaps from branch to branch, falls from a great height into an empty pool without getting hurt. I like to think this is how Elia Kazan, Nicholas Ray, and, I hope, George Stevens proceeded.

Dean's power of seduction was so intense that he could have killed his parents every night on the screen with the blessing of the snobs and the general public alike. One had to witness the indignation in the movie house when, in *East of Eden,* his father refuses to accept the money that Cal earned with the beans, the wages of love.

More than just an actor, James Dean, like Chaplin, became a personality in only three films: Jimmy and the beans and at the country fair, Jimmy on the grass, Jimmy in the abandoned house. Thanks to Elia Kazan's and Nicholas Ray's sensitivity to actors, James Dean played characters close to the Baudelairean hero he really was.

The underlying reasons for his success? With women, the reason is obvious and needs no explanation. With young men, it was because they could identify with him; this is the basis for the commercial success of his films in every country of the world. It is easier to identify with James Dean than with Humphrey Bogart, Cary Grant, or Marlon Brando. Dean's personality is truer. Leaving a Bogart movie, you may pull your hat brim down; this is no time for someone to hassle you. After a Cary Grant film, you may clown around on the street; after Brando, lower your eyes and feel tempted to bully the local girls. With Dean, the sense of identification is deeper and more complete, because he contains within himself all our ambiguity, our duality, our human weaknesses.

Once again, we have to go back to Chaplin, or rather Charlie. Charlie always starts at the bottom and aims higher. He is weak, despised, left out. He fails in all his efforts; he tries to sit down to relax and ends up on the ground, he's ridiculous in the eyes of the woman he courts or in the eyes of the brute he wants to tame. What happens at this point is a pure gift: Chaplin will avenge himself and win out. Suddenly he begins to dance, skate, spin better than anyone else, and now he eclipses everyone, he triumphs, he changes the mood and has all the jeerers on his side.

What started out as an inability to adapt becomes super-adeptness. The entire world, everybody and everything that had been against him, is now at his service. All this is true of Dean, too, but we must take into account a fundamental difference: never do we catch the slightest look of fear. James Dean is beside everything; in his acting neither courage nor cowardice has any place any more than heroism or fear. Something else is at work, a poetic game that lends authority to every liberty—even encourages it. Acting right or wrong has no meaning when we talk about Dean, because we expect a surprise a minute from him. He can laugh when another actor would cry—or the opposite. He killed psychology the day he appeared on the set.

With James Dean everything is grace, in every sense of the word. That's his secret. He isn't better than everybody else; he does *something else,* the opposite; he protects his glamour from the beginning to end of each film. No one has ever seen Dean walk; he ambles or runs like a mailman's faithful dog (think of the opening of *East of Eden*). Today's young people are represented completely in James Dean, less for the reasons that are usually given—violence, sadism, frenzy, gloom, pessimism, and cruelty—than for other reasons that are infinitely more simple and everyday: modesty, continual fantasizing, a moral purity not related to the prevailing morality but in fact stricter, the adolescent's eternal taste for experience, intoxication, pride, and the sorrow at feeling "outside," a simultaneous desire and refusal to be integrated into society, and finally acceptance and rejection of the world, such as it is.

No doubt Dean's acting, because of its contemporaneous quality, will start a new Hollywood style, but the loss of this young actor is irreparable; he was perhaps the most inventively gifted actor in films. Good cousin of Dargelos that he was, he met his death on the road, one cool September evening, like the young American described in Cocteau's *Enfants Terribles*: ". . . the car leapt, twisted, crashed against a tree and became a silent ruin, one wheel spinning slower and slower like a raffle wheel."

REX REED

Rex Reed was a gifted and innovative magazine writer in the 1960s, although his later fame dissipated that role; by becoming a celebrity himself, he got inside the system and could no longer see it in quite the same way. He started as irreverent and became protective. But he was certainly one of the most influential inventors of the new style of celebrity interview that began to flourish in Esquire and has since more or less defined how movie stars are described in print. He wrote about his interview experiences, seeing his subjects in the round, reporting everything he was allowed to see, or glimpse, or guess.

"Ava: Life in the Afternoon"

She stands there, without benefit of a filter lens, against a room melting under the heat of lemony sofas and lavender walls and cream-and-peppermint-striped movie-star chairs, lost in the middle of that gilt-edge birthday-cake hotel of cupids and cupolas called The Regency. There is no script. No Minnelli to adjust the CinemaScope lens. Ice-blue rain beats against the windows and peppers Park Avenue below as Ava Gardner stalks her pink malted-milk cage like an elegant cheetah. She wears a baby-blue cashmere turtleneck sweater pushed up to her Ava elbows and a little plaid mini-skirt and enormous black horn-rimmed glasses and she is gloriously, divinely barefoot.

Elbowing his way through the mob of autograph hunters and thrill seekers clustered in the lobby, all the way up in the gilt-encrusted elevator, the press agent Twentieth Century-Fox has sent along murmurs, "She doesn't see *any-body*, you know," and "You're very lucky, you're the only one she asked for." Remembering, perhaps, the last time she had come to New York from her hide-out in Spain to ballyhoo *The Night of the Iguana* and got so mad at the press she chucked the party and ended up at Birdland. And nervously, shifting feet under my Brooks Brothers polo coat, I remember too all the photographers at whom she allegedly threw champagne glasses (there is even a rumor that she shoved one Fourth Estater off a balcony!), and—who could forget, Charlie?—the holocaust she caused the time Joe Hyams showed up with a tape recorder hidden in his sleeve.

Now, inside the cheetah cage without a whip and trembling like a nervous bird, the press agent says something in Spanish to the Spanish maid. "Hell, I've been there ten years and I still can't speak the goddamn language," says Ava, dismissing him with a wave of the long porcelain Ava arms. "*Out!* I don't need press agents." The eyebrows angle under the glasses into two dazzling, sequined question marks. "Can I trust him?" she asks, grinning that smashing Ava grin, and pointing at me. The press agent nods, on his way to the door: "Is there anything else we can do for you while you're in town?"

"Just get me *out* of town, baby. Just get me *outta* here."

The press agent leaves softly, walking across the carpet as if treading on rose glass with tap shoes. The Spanish maid (Ava insists she is royalty, "She follows me around because she digs me") closes the door and shuffles off into another room.

"You *do* drink—right, baby? The last bugger who came to see me had the gout and wouldn't touch a drop." She roars a cheetah roar that sounds suspiciously like Geraldine Page playing Alexandra Del Lago and mixes drinks from her portable bar: Scotch and soda for me, and for herself a champagne glass full of cognac with another champagne glass full of Dom Perignon, which she drinks successively, refills and sips slowly like syrup through a straw. The Ava legs dangle limply from the arm of a lavender chair while the Ava neck, pale and tall as a milkwood vase, rises above the room like a Southern landowner inspecting a cotton field. At forty-four, she is still one of the most beautiful women in the world.

"Don't look at me. I was up until four A.M. at that goddam premiere of *The Bible*. Premieres! I will personally kill that John Huston if he ever drags me into another mess like that. There must have been ten thousand people clawing at me. I get claustrophobia in crowds and I couldn't breathe. Christ, they started off by shoving a TV camera at me and yelling, 'Talk, Ava!' At intermission I got lost and couldn't find my goddam seat after the lights went out and I kept telling those little girls with the bubble hairdos and the flashlights, 'I'm with John Huston,' and they kept saying, 'We don't know no Mr. Huston, is he from Fox?' There I was fumbling around the aisles in the dark and when I finally found my seat somebody was sitting in it and there was a big scene getting this guy to give me my seat back. Let me tell you, baby, Metro used to throw much better circuses than that. On top of it all, I lost my goddam mantilla in the limousine. Hell, it was no souvenir, that mantilla. I'll never find another one like it. Then Johnny Huston takes me to this party where we had to stand around and smile at Artie Shaw, who I was married to, baby, for Chrissake, and his wife Evelyn Keyes, who Johnny Huston was once married to, for Chrissake. And after it's all over, what have you got? The biggest headache in town. Nobody cares who the hell was there. Do you think for one minute the fact that Ava Gardner showed up at that circus will sell that picture? Christ, did you *see* it? I went through all that hell just so this morning Bosley Crowther could write I looked like I was posing for a monument. All the way through it I kept punching Johnny on the arm and saying, 'Christ, how could you let me do it?' Anyway, nobody cares what I wore or what I said. All they want to know anyway is was she drunk and did she stand up straight. This is the last circus. I am not a bitch! I am not temperamental! I am scared, baby. *Scared.* Can you possibly understand what it's like to feel scared?"

She rolls her sleeves higher than the elbows and pours two more champagne glasses full. There is nothing about the way she looks, up close, to suggest the life she has led: press conferences accompanied by dim lights and an orchestra; bullfighters writing poems about her in the press; rubbing Vaseline between her bosoms to emphasize the cleavage; roaming restlessly around Europe like a woman without a country, a Pandora with her suitcases full of cognac and Hershey bars ("for quick energy"). None of the ravaged, ruinous grape-colored lines to suggest the affairs or the brawls that bring the police in the middle of the night or the dancing on tabletops in Madrid cellars till dawn.

The doorbell rings and a pimply-faced boy with a Beatle hairdo delivers one dozen Nathan's hot dogs, rushed from Coney Island in a limousine. "Eat," says Ava, sitting crosslegged on the floor, biting into a raw onion.

"You're looking at me again!" she says shyly, pulling short girlish wisps of hair behind the lobes of her Ava ears. I mention the fact that she looks like a Vassar co-ed in her mini-skirt. "Vassar?" she asks suspiciously. "Aren't they the ones who get in all the trouble?"

"That's Radcliffe."

She roars. Alexandra Del Lago again. "I took one look at myself in *The Bible* and went out this morning and got all my hair cut off. This is the way I used to wear it at M-G-M. It takes years off. What's *that?*" Eyes narrow, axing her guest in half, burning holes in my notebook. "Don't tell me you're one of those people who always go around scribbling everything on little pieces of paper. Get rid of that. Don't take notes. Don't ask questions either because I probably won't answer any of them anyway. Just let Mama do all the talking. Mama knows best. You want to ask something, I can tell. Ask."

I ask if she hates all of her films as much as *The Bible.*

"Christ, what did I ever do worth talking about? Every time I tried to act, they stepped on me. That's why it's such a goddam shame, I've been a movie star for twenty-five years and I've got nothing, *nothing* to show for it. All I've got is three lousy ex-husbands, which reminds me. I've got to call Artie and ask him what his birthday is. I can't remember my own family's birthdays. Only reason I know my own is because I was born the same day as Christ. Well, almost. Christmas Eve. 1922. That's Capricorn, which means a lifetime of *hell,* baby. Anyway, I need Artie's birthday because I'm trying to get a new passport. I tramp around Europe, but I'm not giving up my citizenship, baby, for *any*body. Did you ever try living in Europe and renewing your passport? They treat you like you're a goddam Communist or something. Hell that's why I'm getting the hell out of Spain, because I hate Franco and I hate Communists. So now they want a list of all my divorces so I told them hell, call The New York *Times*—they know more about me than I do!"

But hadn't all those years at M-G-M been any fun at all? "Christ, after seventeen years of slavery, you can ask that question? I hated it, honey. I mean I'm not exactly stupid or without feeling, and they tried to sell me like a prize hog. They also tried to make me into something I was not then and never could be. They used to write in my studio bios that I was the daughter of a cotton farmer from Chapel Hill. Hell, baby, I was born on a tenant farm in Grabtown. How's that grab ya? Grabtown, North Carolina. And it looks exactly the way it sounds. I should have stayed there. The ones who never left home don't have a pot to pee in but they're happy. Me, look at me. What did it bring me?" She finishes off another round of cognac and pours a fresh one. "The only time I'm happy is when I'm doing absolutely nothing. When I work I vomit all the time. I know nothing about acting so I have one rule—trust the director and give him heart and soul. And nothing else." (Another cheetah roar.) "I get a lot of money so I can afford to loaf a lot. I don't trust many people, so I only work with Huston now. I used to trust Joe Mankiewicz, but one day on the set of *The Barefoot Contessa* he did the unforgivable thing. He insulted me. He said, 'You're the sittin'est goddam actress,' and I never liked him after that. What I really want to do is get married again. Go ahead and laugh, everybody laughs, but how great it must be to tromp around barefoot and cook for some great goddamn son of a bitch who loves you the rest of your life. I've never had a good man."

What about Mickey Rooney? (A glorious shriek.) "Love comes to Andy Hardy."

Sinatra? "No comment," she says to her glass.

A slow count to ten, while she sips her drink. Then, "And Mia Farrow?" The Ava eyes brighten to a soft clubhouse green. The answer comes like so many cats lapping so many saucers of cream. Unprintable.

Like a phonograph dropping a new LP, she changes the subject. "I only want to do the things that don't make me suffer. My friends are more important to me than anything. I know all kinds of people—bums, hangers-on, intellectuals, a few phonies. I'm going to see a college boy at Princeton tomorrow and we're going to a ball game. Writers. I love writers. Henry Miller sends me books to improve my mind. Hell, did you read *Plexus*? I couldn't get through it. I'm not an intellectual, although when I was married to Artie Shaw I took a lot of courses at U.C.L.A. and got A's and B's in psychology and literature. I have a mind, but I never got a chance to use it doing every goddam lousy part in every goddam lousy picture Metro turned out. I *feel* a lot, though. God, I'm sorry I wasted those twenty-five years. My sister Dee Dee can't understand why after all these years I can't bear to face a camera. But I never brought anything to this business and I have no respect for acting. Maybe if I had learned something it would be different. But I never did anything to be proud of. Out of all those movies, what can I claim to have done?"

"*Mogambo, The Hucksters*—"

"Hell, baby, after twenty-five years in this business, if all you've got to show for it is *Mogambo* and *The Hucksters* you might as well give up. Name me one actress who survived all that crap at M-G-M. Maybe Lana Turner. Certainly Liz Taylor. But they all hate acting as much as I do. All except for Elizabeth. She used to come up to me on the set and say, 'If only I could learn to be good,' and by God, she made it. I haven't seen *Virginia Woolf*—hell, I *never* go to movies—but I hear she is good. I never cared much about myself. I didn't have the emotional makeup for acting and I hate exhibitionists anyway. And who the hell was there to help me or teach me acting was anything else? I really tried in *Show Boat* but that was M-G-M crap. Typical of what they did to me there. I wanted to sing those songs—hell, I've still got a Southern accent—and I really thought Julie should sound a little like a Negro since she's supposed to have Negro blood. Christ, those songs like *Bill* shouldn't sound like an opera. So, what did they say? 'Ava, baby, you can't sing, you'll hit the wrong keys, you're up against real pros in this film, so don't make a fool of yourself.' *Pros!* Howard Keel? And Kathryn Grayson, who had the biggest boobs in Hollywood? I mean I like Graysie, she's a sweet girl, but with her they didn't even need 3-D! Lena Horne told me to go to Phil Moore, who was her pianist and had coached Dorothy Dandridge, and he'd teach me. I made a damn good track of the songs and they said, 'Ava, are you outta your head?' Then they got Eileen Wilson, this gal who used to do a lot of my singing on screen, and *she* recorded a track with the same background arrangement taken off *my* track. They substituted her voice for mine, and now in the movie my Southern twang stops talking and her soprano starts singing—hell what a mess. They wasted God knows how many thousands of dollars and ended up with crap. I still get royalties on the goddam records I did."

The doorbell rings and in bounces a little man named Larry. Larry has silver hair, silver eyebrows and smiles a lot. He works for a New York camera shop. "Larry used to be married to my sister Bea. If you think I'm something you ought to see Bea. When I was eighteen I came to New York to visit them and Larry took that picture of me that started this whole megilah. He's a sonuvabitch, but I love him."

"Ava, I sure loved you last night in *The Bible*. You were really terrific, darlin'."

"Crap!" Ava pours another cognac. "I don't want to hear another word about that goddam *Bible*. I didn't believe *it* and I didn't believe that Sarah bit I played for a minute. How could anybody stay married for a hundred years to *Abraham,* who was one of the biggest bastards who ever lived?"

"Oh, darlin', she was a wonderful woman, that Sarah."

"She was a jerk!"

"Oh, darlin', ya shouldn' talk like that. God will hear ya. Don'tcha believe in God?" Larry joins us on the floor and bites into a hot dog, spilling mustard on his tie.

"Hell, no." The Ava eyes flash.

"I pray to him every night, darlin'. Sometimes he answers, too."

"He never answered me, baby. He was never around when I needed him. He did nothing but screw up my whole life since the day I was born. Don't tell *me* about *God!* I know all about that bugger!"

The doorbell again. This time a cloak-and-dagger type comes in; he's wearing an ironed raincoat, has seventeen pounds of hair and looks like he has been living on plastic vegetables. He says he is a student at New York University Law School. He also says he is twenty-six years old. "*What?*" Ava takes off her glasses for a closer look. "Your father told me you were twenty-seven. Somebody's lying!" The Ava eyes narrow and the palms of her hands are wet.

"Let's get some air, fellas." Ava leaps into the bedroom and comes out wearing a Navy pea jacket with a Woolworth scarf around her head. Vassar again.

"I thought you were gonna cook tonight, darlin'," says Larry, throwing his fist into a coat sleeve.

"I want spaghetti. Let's go to the Supreme Macaroni Company. They let me in the back door there and nobody ever recognizes *any*body there. Spaghetti, baby. I'm starved."

Ava slams the door shut, leaving all the lights on. "Fox is paying, baby." We all link arms and follow the leader. Ava skips ahead of us like Dorothy on her way to Oz. *Lions and tigers and bears, oh my!* Moving like a tiger through Regency halls, melting with hot pink, like the inside of a womb.

"Are those creeps still downstairs?" she asks. "Follow me."

She knows all the exits. We go down on the service elevator. About twenty autograph hunters crowd the lobby. Celia, queen of the autograph bums, who leaves her post on the door at Sardi's only on special occasions, has deserted her station for this. *Ava's in town this week.* She sits behind a potted palm wearing a purple coat and green beret, arms full of self-addressed postcards.

Cool.

Ava gags, pushes the horn-rims flat against her nose, and pulls us through the lobby. Nobody recognizes her. "Drink time, baby!" she whispers, shoving me toward a side stairway that leads down to The Regency Bar.

"Do you know who *that* was?" asks an Iris Adrian type with a mink-dyed fox on her arm as Ava heads for the bar. We check coats and umbrellas and suddenly we hear that sound-track voice, hitting E-flat.

"You *sonuvabitch*! I could buy and sell you. How *dare* you insult my friends? Get me the manager!"

Larry is at her side. Two waiters are shushing Ava and leading us all to a corner booth. Hidden. Darker than the Polo Lounge. Hide the star. This is New York, not Beverly Hills.

"It's that turtleneck sweater you're wearing," whispers Larry to me as the waiter seats me with my back to the room.

"They don't like me here, the bastards. I never stay in this hotel, but Fox is paying, so what the hell? I wouldn't come otherwise. They don't even have a jukebox, for Chrissake." Ava flashed a smile in Metrocolor and orders a large ice-tea glass filled with straight tequila. "No salt on the side. Don't need it."

"Sorry about the sweater—" I begin.

"You're beautiful. Gr-r-r!" She laughs her Ava laugh and the head rolls back and the little blue vein bulges on her neck like a delicate pencil mark.

Two tequilas later ("I *said* no salt!") she is nodding grandly, surveying the bar like the Dowager Empress in the Recognition Scene. Talk buzzes around her like hummingbird wings and she hears nothing. Larry is telling about the time he got arrested in Madrid and Ava had to get him out of jail and the student is telling me about N.Y.U. Law School and Ava is telling *him* she doesn't believe he's only twenty-six years old and can he prove it, and suddenly he looks at his watch and says Sandy Koufax is playing in St. Louis.

"You're kidding!" Ava's eyes light up like cherries on a cake. "Let's go! God-damit we're going to St. Louis!"

"Ava, darlin', I gotta go to work tomorrow." Larry takes a heavy sip of his Grasshopper.

"Shut up, you bugger. If I pay for us all to go to St. Louis we go to St. Louis! Can I get a phone brought to this table? Someone call Kennedy airport and find out what time the next plane leaves. I *love* Sandy Koufax! I *love* Jews! God, sometimes I think I'm Jewish myself. A Spanish Jew from North Carolina. *Waiter!*"

The student convinces her that by the time we got to St. Louis they'd be halfway through the seventh inning. Ava's face falls and she goes back to her straight tequila.

"Look at 'em, Larry," she says. "They're such babies. Please don't go to Vietnam." Her face turns ashen. Julie leaving the showboat with William Warfield singing *Ol' Man River* in the fog on the levee. "We gotta do it. . . ."

"What are you talkin' about, darlin'?" Larry shoots a look at the law student who assures Ava he has no intention of going to Vietnam.

". . . didn't ask for this world, the buggers made us do it. . . ." A tiny bubble bath of sweat breaks out on her forehead and she leaps up from the table. "My God, I'm suffocating! Gotta get some air!" She turns over the glass of tequila and three waiters are flying at us like bats, dabbing and patting and making great breathing noises.

Action!

The N.Y.U. student, playing Chance Wayne to her Alexandra Del Lago, is all over the place like a trained nurse. Coats fly out of the checkroom. Bills and quarters roll across the wet tablecloth. Ava is on the other side of the bar and out the door. On cue, the other customers, who have been making elaborate excuses for passing our table on their way to the bathroom, suddenly give great breathy choruses of "Ava" and we are through the side door and out in the rain.

Then as quickly as it started it's over. Ava is in the middle of Park Avenue, the scarf falling around her neck and her hair blowing wildly around the Ava eyes. Lady Brett in the traffic, with a downtown bus as the bull. Three cars stop on a green light and every taxi driver on Park Avenue begins to honk. The autograph hunters leap through the polished doors of The Regency and begin to scream. Inside, still waiting coolly behind the potted palm, is Celia, oblivious to the noise, facing the elevators, firmly clutching her postcards. No need to risk missing Ava because of a minor commotion on the street. Probably Jack E. Leonard or Edie Adams. Catch them next week at Danny's.

Outside, Ava is inside the taxi flanked by the N.Y.U. student and Larry, blowing kisses to the new chum, who will never grow to be an old one. They are already turning the corner into Fifty-seventh Street, fading into the kind of night, the color of tomato juice in the headlights, that only exists in New York when it rains.

"Who was it?" asks a woman walking a poodle.

"Jackie Kennedy," answers a man from his bus window.

JOHN O'HARA

John O'Hara (1905–1970) knew Hollywood inside out. He sold books and stories to the movies, he wrote screenplays, and for a time in the 1940s he was the film critic for Newsweek *magazine. He was also a film fan, who judged actors and particularly actresses according to his own unforgiving subjective standards. That's clear in this brutally frank letter to the producer David Brown, assessing the qualities of various stars under discussion for starring roles in the movies of his novels.*

from *Selected Letters*

TO: David Brown

TLS, 3 pp. Wyoming
Princeton

6 April 59

Dear Dave:

Having made a clean sweep of the Academy awards—not even a set dressing nomination[1]—I can give an objective opinion of the ceremonies, and I would say that except for Jerry Lewis and Mort Sahl, it was the dullest exhibition I've ever seen in person or on TV. Luckily, however, Jerry Lewis and Mort Sahl were there to remind everybody that no matter how good the pictures may be, Hollywood can always be depended upon to make a horse's ass of itself. The great tradition of cheapness and vulgarity will be maintained, even if only by a few stalwarts like Lewis and Sahl. The selection of those two snipes was an inspired one, and if they can't be signed up for next year, the Academy ought to start right away to make a deal with Mickey Cohen[2] and Oscar Levant, the only two names that come to mind as I consider the field of worthy successors.

My personal interest in the proceedings began with Bergman, and I yield to your earlier judgment: for *From the Terrace* she won't do. But I also yield to you as the picker of Rock Hudson. He might do.[3] I know I have seen him in pictures, when I was writing the Collier's column, but I honestly don't remember him. However, he looked all right tonight. With sadness in my heart (for she was lovely in her day) I confess to the thought that in not too many years Bergman will be able to do the Life of Eleanor Roosevelt very convincingly (we explain the accent by planting early that she had a Swedish governess) but not all the skill of Shamroy, Ruttenberg, Barnes, Daniels[4] and Thomas A. Edison will make her a convincing Natalie. The only technician who could help her is Paul Weatherwax, who, as you know, is a cutter; unless we resurrect Joe von Sternberg,[5] who, long before you got in the business was famous for shooting through tennis racquets. But if we're going to shoot through tennis racquets we might as well sign Althea Gibson[6] and get a little action for our money. I can also see that signing Althea might have other advantages, such as presenting the American way of life favorably to the foreign market, which would make us real big at the Cannes Film Festival, the club theaters in London, and Loew's Nairobi. Let us think about it. She is probably handled by Doc Shurr,[7] who always liked tall ones.

My other personal interest tonight was in Susan Hayward, who may or may not do *A Rage to Live.* I couldn't tell much, because she appeared to be loaded with a tranquilizer. Nobody has *that* much dignity, unassisted. If she has, she'd certainly be perfect for Grace, since the one way to ruin Grace on screen will be to show her without dignity.

Elizabeth Taylor has been spoken of as the lead in *Butterfield 8* but since then she has announced she is quitting pictures, and strangely enough I believe her. A long time ago I used to hear that she hated pictures and was forced to work by her ever-lovin' family. By the look of Mr. Fisher[8] tonight she is still going to have to work, but I don't think all the returns are in yet on Miss Taylor. For years I have had a morbid hunch about that girl, and when Todd[9] was killed, you remember that the first reports had her on the plane. The Irish, of which I am one, do have these morbid hunches about certain people. True, we may have them so often that we kind of copper our bets, but when I've had them strongly, they often come true. Too often. If I were a serious young novelist I would make myself an authority on Elizabeth Taylor, because she has such stuff as great novels are made on. Thus, when I read that she was going to do *Butterfield 8* my immediate reaction was that Larry Weingarten and Pan Berman[10] had much more sense than I ever gave them credit for; and my secondary reaction was that if she ever read the book she would shy away from it because I invented her in the same sense that I invented Frank Sinatra. (When I invented Joey, Sinatra was about 18; when I created Gloria Wandrous, Elizabeth Taylor was 2.) But the big difference between Elizabeth Taylor and Gloria Wandrous is the difference between a local novel at a very specific time, and a novel about a world symbol in what many people (not I) think are the Final Fifties, which are anything but specific. It may be too big a theme for a novel, although Cleopatra and Catherine the Great have been cut down to size, centuries later.

In moments of humility and disappointment I sometimes think of my own contributions to literature *qua* history, and I feel better. Julian English. Gloria Wandrous (and Weston Liggett). Jimmy Malloy. Joey Evans. Grace Caldwell Tate. Joe Chapin. Alfred Eaton. It's quite a roster, but nobody's going to know it in our lifetime.

My new novel is coming into the stretch, a figure I use because it finishes in a gallop, not because I am racing against anything except, possibly, time. But then I can't seem to help that. I predict that it will sell about 40,000 copies in the trade edition, and that it is going to throw a lot of people. I will lose some admirers, but that figures anyway. I got some new ones with *From the Terrace;* I can tell that from the letters; especially many who had never read me before. That is a book that people take personally, men and women, more than any of my books except *Appointment in Samarra.* But I don't figure to gain substantially from now on, in circulation; and critically I can only expect what might be called a consolidation of respect while at the same time losing some of those who have gone along with me so far. With that knowledge I have written this novel under less tension than my last two big ones (this one will be about the size of TNF, or less). I foresee no picture sale, by the way, so you will have to read it on your own time, as a friend. There is a possible play in it, but I don't know who could dramatize it. Tennessee Williams has already redramatized Pal Joey under the title Sweet Bird of Youth, or I might have suggested him. But I guess this is one of those novels that should stay in its original form. When I've finished I am going to think up something that will make a good picture, specifically for the medium.

Come and see us soon. Sister joins me in affectionate regards,

JOHN

[1]For *Ten North Frederick*.
[2]Los Angeles gangster.
[3]*From the Terrace* starred Paul Newman and Joanne Woodward.
[4]Cameramen.
[5]Director Joseph von Sternberg.
[6]Negro tennis player.
[7]Louis Shurr, talent agent.
[8]Eddie Fisher, Elizabeth Taylor's third husband.
[9]Mike Todd, Miss Taylor's fourth husband.
[10]Laurence Weingarten and Pandro S. Berman, MGM producers.

JOAN DIDION

I know what Joan Didion means by her title because I could write an essay beginning in the same place. John Wayne, who may after all have been the greatest star of the first fifty years of the talkies, was not a perfect man, but he was an engaging one, with few of the airs and less of the touchiness of many of his contemporaries. What you saw was more or less what you got. He was never given much respect as a "serious actor," but he commanded the screen like few others, he found authority even in dialogue that would have sounded ridiculous coming from anyone else, and he was the dominant figure in the western. He was the first big star I interviewed, and I remember a day in 1967 at a southern military base where he was shooting The Green Berets. *Because helicopters were taking aerial shots, no one out of costume could venture onto the airfield. Wayne was told by walkie-talkie that his interviewer had arrived, and he came striding toward me in full combat gear: helmet, boots, camouflage uniform, rifle, grenades, canteen, sidearm. He was a long way away. I stood in the shade, out of sight of the helicopters, and watched him walking closer in the shimmering heat. Finally he was towering over me and sticking out a hand. "John Wayne," he said. "I know," I said.*

"John Wayne: A Love Song"

In the summer of 1943 I was eight, and my father and mother and small brother and I were at Peterson Field in Colorado Springs. A hot wind blew through that summer, blew until it seemed that before August broke, all the dust in Kansas would be in Colorado, would have drifted over the tar-paper barracks and the temporary strip and stopped only when it hit Pikes Peak. There was not much to do, a summer like that: there was the day they brought in the first B-29, an event to remember but scarcely a vacation program. There was an Officers' Club, but no swimming pool; all the Officers' Club had of interest was artificial blue rain behind the bar. The rain interested me a good deal, but I could not spend the summer watching it, and so we went, my brother and I, to the movies.

We went three and four afternoons a week, sat on folding chairs in the darkened Quonset hut which served as a theater, and it was there, that summer of 1943 while the hot wind blew outside, that I first saw John Wayne. Saw the walk, heard the voice. Heard him tell the girl in a picture called *War of the Wildcats* that he would build her a house, "at the bend in the river where the cottonwoods grow." As it happened I did not grow up to be the kind of woman who is the heroine in a Western, and although the men I have known have had many virtues and have taken me to live in many places I have come to love, they have never been John Wayne, and they have never taken me to that bend in the river where the cottonwoods grow. Deep in that part of my heart where the artificial rain forever falls, that is still the line I wait to hear.

I tell you this neither in a spirit of self-revelation nor as an exercise in total recall, but simply to demonstrate that when John Wayne rode through my childhood, and perhaps through yours, he determined forever the shape of certain of our dreams. It did not seem possible that such a man could fall ill, could carry within him that most inexplicable and ungovernable of diseases. The rumor struck some obscure anxiety, threw our very childhoods into question. In John Wayne's world, John Wayne was supposed to give the orders. "Let's ride," he said, and "Saddle up." "Forward *ho*," and "A man's gotta do what he's got to do." "Hello, there," he said when he first saw the girl, in a construction camp or on a train or just standing around on the front porch waiting for somebody to ride up through the tall grass. When John Wayne spoke, there was no mistaking his intentions; he had a sexual authority so strong that even a child could perceive it. And in a world we understood early to be characterized by venality and doubt and paralyzing ambiguities, he suggested another world, one which may or may not have existed ever but in any case existed no more: a place where a man could move free, could make his own code and live by it; a world in which, if a man did what he had to do, he could one day take the girl and go riding through the draw and find himself home free, not in a hospital with something going wrong inside, not in a high bed with the flowers and the drugs and the forced smiles, but there at the bend in the bright river, the cottonwoods shimmering in the early morning sun.

"Hello, there." Where did he come from, before the tall grass? Even his history seemed right, for it was no history at all, nothing to intrude upon the dream. Born Marion Morrison in Winterset, Iowa, the son of a druggist. Moved as a child to Lancaster, California, part of the migration to that promised land sometimes called "the west coast of Iowa." Not that Lancaster was the promise fulfilled; Lancaster was a town on the Mojave where the dust blew through. But Lancaster was still California, and it was only a year from there to Glendale, where desolation had a different flavor: antimacassars among the orange groves, a middle-class prelude to Forest Lawn. Imagine Marion Morrison in Glendale. A Boy Scout, then a student at Glendale High. A tackle for U.S.C., a Sigma Chi. Summer vacations, a job moving props on the old Fox lot. There, a meeting with John Ford, one of the several directors who were to sense that into this perfect mold might be poured the inarticulate longings of a nation wondering at just what pass the trail had been lost. "Dammit," said Raoul Walsh later, "the son of a bitch looked like a man." And so after a while the boy from Glendale became a star. He did not become an actor, as he has always been careful to point out to interviewers ("How many times do I gotta tell you, I don't act at all, I *re*-act"), but a star, and the star called John Wayne would spend most of the rest of his life with one or another of those directors, out on some forsaken location, in search of the dream.

> *Out where the skies are a trifle bluer*
> *Out where friendship's a little truer*
> *That's where the West begins.*

Nothing very bad could happen in the dream, nothing a man could not face down. But something did. There it was, the rumor, and after a while the headlines. "I licked the Big C," John Wayne announced, as John Wayne would, reducing those outlaw cells to the level of any other outlaws, but even so we all sensed that this would be the one unpredictable confrontation, the one shootout Wayne could lose. I have as much trouble as the next person with illusion and reality, and I did not much want to see John Wayne when he must be (or so I thought) having some trouble with it himself, but I did, and it was down in Mexico when he was making the picture his illness had so long delayed, down in the very country of the dream.

.   .   .   .

It was John Wayne's 165th picture. It was Henry Hathaway's 84th. It was number 34 for Dean Martin, who was working off an old contract to Hal Wallis, for whom it was independent production number 65. It was called *The Sons of Katie Elder,* and it was a Western, and after the three-month delay they had finally shot the exteriors up in Durango, and now they were in the waning days of interior shooting at Estudio Churubusco outside Mexico City, and the sun was hot and the air was clear and it was lunchtime. Out under the pepper trees the boys from the Mexican crew sat around sucking caramels, and down the road some of the technical men sat around a place which served a stuffed lobster and a glass of tequila for one dollar American, but it was inside the cavernous empty commissary where the talent sat around, the reasons for the exercise, all sitting around the big table picking at *huevos con queso* and Carta Blanca beer. Dean Martin, unshaven. Mack Gray, who goes where Martin goes. Bob Goodfried, who was in charge of Paramount publicity and who had flown down to arrange for a trailer and who had a delicate stomach. "Tea and toast," he warned repeatedly. "That's the ticket. You can't trust the lettuce." And Henry Hathaway, the director, who did not seem to be listening to Goodfried. And John Wayne, who did not seem to be listening to anyone.

"This week's gone slow," Dean Martin said, for the third time.

"How can you say that?" Mack Gray demanded.

"This . . . week's . . . gone . . . slow, that's how I can say it."

"You don't mean you want it to end."

"I'll say it right out, Mack, I want it to *end.* Tomorrow night I shave this beard, I head for the airport, I say *adiós amigos!* Bye-bye *muchachos!"*

Henry Hathaway lit a cigar and patted Martin's arm fondly. "Not tomorrow, Dino."

"Henry, what are you planning to add? A World War?"

Hathaway patted Martin's arm again and gazed into the middle distance. At the end of the table someone mentioned a man who, some years before, had tried unsuccessfully to blow up an airplane.

"He's still in jail," Hathaway said suddenly.

"In jail?" Martin was momentarily distracted from the question whether to send his golf clubs back with Bob Goodfried or consign them to Mack Gray. "What's he in jail for if nobody got killed?"

"Attempted murder, Dino," Hathaway said gently. "A felony."

"You mean some guy just *tried* to kill me he'd end up in jail?"

Hathaway removed the cigar from his mouth and looked across the table. "Some guy just tried to kill *me* he wouldn't end up in jail. How about you, Duke?"

Very slowly, the object of Hathaway's query wiped his mouth, pushed back his chair, and stood up. It was the real thing, the authentic article, the move which had climaxed a thousand scenes on 165 flickering frontiers and phantasmagoric battlefields before, and it was about to climax this one, in the commissary at Estudio Churubusco outside Mexico City. "Right," John Wayne drawled. "I'd kill him."

.   .   .   .

Almost all the cast of *Katie Elder* had gone home, that last week; only the principals were left, Wayne, and Martin, and Earl Holliman, and Michael Anderson, Jr., and Martha Hyer. Martha Hyer was not around much, but every now and then someone referred to her, usually as "the girl." They had all been together nine weeks, six of them in Durango. Mexico City was not quite Durango; wives like to come along to places like Mexico City, like to shop for handbags, go to parties at Merle Oberon Pagliai's, like to look at her paintings. But Durango. The very name hallucinates. Man's country. Out where the West begins. There had been ahuehuete trees in Durango; a waterfall, rattlesnakes. There had been weather, nights so cold that they had postponed one or two exteriors until they could shoot inside at Churubusco. "It was the girl," they explained. "You couldn't keep the girl out in cold like that." Henry Hathaway had cooked in Durango, *gazpacho* and ribs and the steaks that Dean Martin had ordered flown down from the Sands; he had wanted to cook in Mexico City, but the management of the Hotel Bamer refused to let him set up a brick barbecue in his room. "You really missed something, *Durango*," they would say, sometimes joking and sometimes not, until it became a refrain, Eden lost.

But if Mexico City was not Durango, neither was it Beverly Hills. No one else was using Churubusco that week, and there inside the big sound stage that said LOS HIJOS DE KATIE ELDER on the door, there with the pepper trees and the bright sun outside, they could still, for just so long as the picture lasted, maintain a world peculiar to men who like to make Westerns, a world of loyalties and fond raillery, of sentiment and shared cigars, of interminable desultory recollections; campfire talk, its only point to keep a human voice raised against the night, the wind, the rustlings in the brush.

"Stuntman got hit accidentally on a picture of mine once," Hathaway would say between takes of an elaborately choreographed fight scene. "What was his name; married Estelle Taylor, met her down in Arizona."

The circle would close around him, the cigars would be fingered. The delicate art of the staged fight was to be contemplated.

"I only hit one guy in my life," Wayne would say. "Accidentally, I mean. That was Mike Mazurki."

"Some guy. Hey, Duke says he only hit one guy in his life, Mike Mazurki."

"Some choice." Murmurings, assent.

"It wasn't a choice, it was an accident."

"I can believe it."

"You bet."

"Oh boy. Mike Mazurki."

And so it would go. There was Web Overlander, Wayne's makeup man for twenty years, hunched in a blue Windbreaker, passing out sticks of Juicy Fruit. "*Insect* spray," he would say. "Don't tell us about insect spray. We saw insect spray in Africa, all right. Remember Africa?" Or, "*Steamer* clams. Don't tell us about steamer clams. We got our fill of steamer clams all right, on the *Hatari!* appearance tour. Remember Bookbinder's?" There was Ralph Volkie, Wayne's trainer for eleven years, wearing a red baseball cap and carrying around a clipping from Hedda Hopper, a tribute to Wayne. "This Hopper's some lady," he would say again and again. "Not like some of these guys, all they write is sick, sick, sick, how can you call that guy *sick,* when he's got pains, coughs, works all day, *never complains.* That guy's got the best hook since Dempsey, not *sick.*"

And there was Wayne himself, fighting through number 165. There was Wayne, in his thirty-three-year-old spurs, his dusty neckerchief, his blue shirt. "You don't have too many worries about what to wear in these things," he said. "You can wear a blue shirt, or, if you're down in Monument Valley, you can wear a yellow shirt." There was Wayne, in a relatively new hat, a hat which made him look curiously like William S. Hart. "I had this old cavalry hat I loved, but I lent it to Sammy Davis. I got it back, it was unwearable. I think they all pushed it down on his head and said *O.K., John Wayne*—you know, a joke."

There was Wayne, working too soon, finishing the picture with a bad cold and a racking cough, so tired by late afternoon that he kept an oxygen inhalator on the set. And still nothing mattered but the Code. "That guy," he muttered of a reporter who had incurred his displeasure. "I admit I'm balding. I admit I got a tire around my middle. What man fifty-seven doesn't? Big news. Anyway, that guy."

He paused, about to expose the heart of the matter, the root of the distaste, the fracture of the rules that bothered him more than the alleged misquotations, more than the intimation that he was no longer the Ringo Kid. "He comes down, uninvited, but I ask him over anyway. So we're sitting around drinking mescal out of a water jug."

He paused again and looked meaningfully at Hathaway, readying him for the unthinkable denouement. "He had to be *assisted* to his room."

They argued about the virtues of various prizefighters, they argued about the price of J & B in pesos. They argued about dialogue.

"As rough a guy as he is, Henry, I still don't think he'd raffle off his mother's *Bible.*"

"I like a shocker, Duke."

They exchanged endless training-table jokes. "You know why they call this memory sauce?" Martin asked, holding up a bowl of chili.

"Why?"

"Because you *remember it in the morning.*"

"Hear that, Duke? Hear why they call this memory sauce?"

They delighted one another by blocking out minute variations in the free-for-all fight which is a set piece in Wayne pictures; motivated or totally gratuitous, the fight sequence has to be in the picture, because they so enjoy making it. "Listen—this'll really be funny. Duke picks up the kid, see, and then it takes both Dino and Earl to throw him out the door—*how's that?*"

They communicated by sharing old jokes; they sealed their camaraderie by making gentle, old-fashioned fun of wives, those civilizers, those tamers. "So Señora Wayne takes it into her head to stay up and have one brandy. So for the rest of the night it's 'Yes, Pilar, you're right, dear. I'm a bully, Pilar, you're right, I'm impossible.' "

"You hear that? Duke says Pilar threw a table at him."

"Hey, Duke, here's something funny. That finger you hurt today, get the Doc to bandage it up, go home tonight, show it to Pilar, tell her she did it when she threw the table. You know, make her think she was really cutting up."

They treated the oldest among them respectfully; they treated the youngest fondly. "You see that kid?" they said of Michael Anderson, Jr. "What a kid."

"He don't act, it's right from the heart," said Hathaway, patting his heart.

"Hey, kid," Martin said. "You're gonna be in my next picture. We'll have the whole thing, no beards. The striped shirts, the girls, the hi-fi, the eye lights."

They ordered Michael Anderson his own chair, with "BIG MIKE" tooled on the back. When it arrived on the set, Hathaway hugged him. "You see that?" Anderson asked Wayne, suddenly too shy to look him in the eye. Wayne gave him the smile, the nod, the final accolade. "I saw it, kid."

.   .   .   .

On the morning of the day they were to finish *Katie Elder,* Web Overlander showed up not in his Windbreaker but in a blue blazer. "Home, Mama," he said, passing out the last of his Juicy Fruit. "I got on my getaway clothes." But he was subdued. At noon, Henry Hathaway's wife dropped by the commissary to tell him that she might fly over to Acapulco. "Go ahead," he told her. "I get through here, all I'm gonna do is take Seconal to a point just this side of suicide." They were all subdued. After Mrs. Hathaway left, there was desultory attempts at reminiscing, but man's country was receding fast; they were already halfway home, and all they could call up was the 1961 Bel Air fire, during which Henry Hathaway had ordered the Los Angeles Fire Department off his property and saved the place himself by, among other measures, throwing everything flammable into the swimming pool. "Those fire guys might've just given it up," Wayne said. "Just let it burn." In fact this was a good story, and one incorporating several of their favorite themes, but a Bel Air story was still not a Durango story.

In the early afternoon they began the last scene, and although they spent as much time as possible setting it up, the moment finally came when there was nothing to do but shoot it. "Second team out, first team in, *doors closed*," the assistant director shouted one last time. The stand-ins walked off the set, John Wayne and Martha Hyer walked on. "All right, boys, *silencio*, this is a picture." They took it twice. Twice the girl offered John Wayne the tattered Bible. Twice John Wayne told her that "there's a lot of places I go where that wouldn't fit in." Everyone was very still. And at 2:30 that Friday afternoon Henry Hathaway turned away from the camera, and in the hush that followed he ground out his cigar in a sand bucket. "O.K.," he said. "That's it."

. . . .

Since that summer of 1943 I had thought of John Wayne in a number of ways. I had thought of him driving cattle up from Texas, and bringing airplanes in on a single engine, thought of him telling the girl at the Alamo that "Republic is a beautiful word." I had never thought of him having dinner with his family and with me and my husband in an expensive restaurant in Chapultepec Park, but time brings odd mutations, and there we were, one night that last week in Mexico. For a while it was only a nice evening, an evening anywhere. We had a lot of drinks and I lost the sense that the face across the table was in certain ways more familiar than my husband's.

And then something happened. Suddenly the room seemed suffused with the dream, and I could not think why. Three men appeared out of nowhere, playing guitars. Pilar Wayne leaned slightly forward, and John Wayne lifted his glass almost imperceptibly toward her. "We'll need some Pouilly-Fuissé for the rest of the table," he said, "and some red Bordeaux for the Duke." We all smiled, and drank the Pouilly-Fuissé for the rest of the table and the red Bordeaux for the Duke, and all the while the men with the guitars kept playing, until finally I realized what they were playing, what they had been playing all along: "The Red River Valley" and the theme from *The High and the Mighty*. They did not quite get the beat right, but even now I can hear them, in another country and a long time later, even as I tell you this.

Tom Wolfe

Tom Wolfe was the flag bearer for the New Journalism, the one who used the most italics and apostrophes yet was also a brilliant reporter. In this piece he handles the most basic yet most difficult assignment of the celebrity reporter: the dreaded Hotel Room Interview, although here the prey, Cary Grant, has at least moved downstairs to the dining room. One is given a little under an hour to commune with a star who is inevitably "opening a new picture" and who has come to town expressly to spend all day, or several days, talking about it. In the days before "sound bites" had entered the language, these assembly line PR ordeals had already perfected them. See here how, in the end, it is Wolfe who does most of the talking.

"Loverboy of the Bourgeoisie"

On their way into the Edwardian Room of the Plaza Hotel all they had was that sort of dutiful, forward-tilted gait that East Side dowagers get after twenty years of walking small dogs up and down Park Avenue. But on their way out the two of them discover that all this time, in the same room, there has been their dreamboat, Cary Grant, sitting in the corner. Actually, Grant had the logistics of the Edwardian Room figured out pretty well. In the first place, the people who come to the Plaza for lunch are not generally the kind who are going to rise up and run, skipping and screaming, over to some movie star's table. And in the second place, he is sitting up against the wall nearest the doorway. He is eating lunch, consisting of a single bowl of Vichyssoise, facing out the window towards three old boys in silk toppers moseying around their horses and hansoms on 59th Street on the edge of Central Park.

Well, so much for logistics. The two old girls work up all the courage they need in about one-fourth of a second.

"Cary Grant!" says the first one, coming right up and putting one hand on his shoulder. "Look at you! I just had to come over here and touch you!"

Cary Grant plays a wonderful Cary Grant. He cocks his head and gives her the Cary Grant mock-quizzical look—just like he does in the movies—the look that says, "I don't know what's happening, but we're not going to take it very seriously, are we? Or are we?"

"I have a son who's the spitting image of you," she is saying.

Cary Grant is staring at her hand on his shoulder and giving her the Cary Grant fey-bemused look and saying, "Are you trying to hold me down?"

"My son is forty-nine," she's saying. "How old are you?"

"I'm fifty-nine," says Cary Grant.

"*Fifty-nine!* Well, he's forty-nine and he's the spitting image of you, except that he looks *older* than you!"

By this time the other old girl is firmly planted, and she says: "I don't care if you hate me, I'm going to stand here and *look* at you."

"Why on earth should I hate you?" says Cary Grant.

"You can say things about me after I'm gone. I don't care, I'm going to stand here and look at you!"

"You poor dear!"

Which she does, all right. She takes it all in; the cleft chin; this great sun tan that looks like it was done on a rotisserie; this great head of steel-gray hair, of which his barber says: "It's real; I swear, I yanked it once"; and the Cary Grant clothes, all worsteds, broadcloths and silks, all rich and underplayed, like a viola ensemble.

"Poor baby," says Cary Grant, returning to the Vichyssoise. "She meets some one for the first time and already she's saying, 'I don't care if you hate me.' Can you imagine? Can you imagine what must have gone into making someone feel that way?"

Well, whatever it was, poor old baby knows that Cary Grant is one leading man who, at least, might give it a second thought. Somehow Cary Grant, they figure, is the one dreamboat that a lady can walk right up to and touch, pour soul over and commune with.

And by the time Grant's picture, "Charade," with Audrey Hepburn, had its première at the Radio City Music Hall, thousands turned out in lines along 50th Street and Sixth Avenue, many of them in the chill of 6 A.M., in order to get an early seat. This was Grant's 61st motion picture and his 26th to open at Radio City. He is, indeed, fifty-nine years old, but his drawing power as a leading man, perhaps the last of the genuine "matinee idols," keeps mounting toward some incredible, golden-aged crest. Radio City is like a Nielsen rating for motion pictures. It has a huge seating capacity and is attended by at least as many tourists, from all over the country, as New Yorkers. Grant's first 25 premières there played a total of 99 weeks. Each one seems to break the records all over again. Before "Charade," "That Touch of Mink," with Doris Day, played there for 10 weeks and grossed $1,886,427.

And the secret of it all is somehow tied up with the way he lit up two aging dolls in the Edwardian Room at the Plaza Hotel. In an era of Brandoism and the Mitchumism in movie heroes, Hollywood has left Cary Grant, by default, in sole possession of what has turned out to be a curiously potent device. Which is to say, to women he is Hollywood's lone example of the Sexy Gentleman. And to men and women, he is Hollywood's lone example of a figure America, like most of the West, has needed all along: a Romantic Bourgeois Hero.

One has only to think of what the rest of Hollywood and the international film industry, for that matter, have been up to since World War II. The key image in film heroes has certainly been that of Marlon Brando. One has only to list the male stars of the past 20 years—Brando, Rock Hudson, Kirk Douglas, John Wayne, Burt Lancaster, Robert Mitchum, Victor Mature, William Holden, Frank Sinatra—and already the mind is overpowered by an awesome montage of swung fists, bent teeth, curled lips, popping neck veins, and gurglings. As often as not the Brandoesque hero's love partner is some thyroid hoyden, as portrayed by Brigitte Bardot, Marilyn Monroe, Jayne Mansfield, Gina Lollobrigida or, more recently, Sue Lyons and Tuesday Weld. The upshot has been the era of Rake-a-Cheek Romance on the screen. Man meets woman. She rakes his cheek with her fingernails. He belts her in the chops. They fall in a wallow of passion.

The spirit of these romances, as in so many of the early Brando, James Dean and Rock Hudson pictures, has been borrowed from what Hollywood imagines to be the beer-and-guts verve of the guys-and-dolls lower classes. Undoubtedly, the rawness, the lubricity, the implicit sadism of it has excited moviegoers of all classes. Yet it should be clear even to Hollywood how many Americans, at rock bottom, can find no lasting identification with it. The number of American men who can really picture themselves coping with a little bleached hellion who is about to rake a cheek and draw blood with the first kiss is probably embarrassingly small. And there are probably not many more women who really wish to see Mister Right advancing toward them in a torn strap-style undershirt with his latissimae dorsae flexed.

After all, this is a nation that, except for a hard core of winos at the bottom and a hard crust of aristocrats at the top, has been going gloriously middle class for two decades, as far as the breezeways stretch. There is no telling how many millions of American women of the new era know exactly what Ingrid Bergman meant when she said she loved playing opposite Cary Grant in "Notorious" (1946): "I didn't have to take my shoes off in the love scenes."

Yet "Notorious," one will recall, was regarded as a highly sexy motion picture. The Grant plot formula—which he has repeated at intervals for 25 years—has established him as the consummate bourgeois lover: consummately romantic and yet consummately genteel. Grant's conduct during a screen romance is unfailingly of the sort that would inspire trust and delight, but first of all trust, in a middle-class woman of any age. Not only does Grant spare his heroines any frontal assault on their foundation garments, he seldom chases them at all at the outset. In fact, the Grant plot formula calls for a reverse chase. First the girl— Audrey Hepburn in "Charade," Grace Kelly in "To Catch a Thief," Betsy Drake in "Every Girl Should Be Married"—falls for Grant. He retreats, but always slowly and coyly, enough to make the outcome clear. Grant, the screen lover, and Grant, the man, were perfectly combined under the escutcheon of the middle-class American woman—"Every Girl Should Be Married"—when Grant married Betsy Drake in real life.

During the chase Grant inevitably scores still more heavily with the middle-class female psyche by treating the heroine not merely as an attractive woman but as a witty and intelligent woman. And, indeed, whether he is with Katharine Hepburn or Audrey Hepburn or Irene Dunne or Doris Day, both parties are batting incredibly bright lines back and forth, and halfway through the film they are already too maniacally witty not to click one way or another.

Because of the savoir faire, genial cynicism and Carlyle Hotel lounge accent with which he brings it all off, Grant is often thought of as an aristocratic motion picture figure. In fact, however, the typical Grant role is that of an exciting bourgeois. In "Charade" he is a foreign service officer in Paris; in "Bringing Up Baby" he was a research professor; in "Mr. Blandings Builds His Dream House" he was an enthusiastic suburbanite; and in countless pictures—among them "Crisis," "People Will Talk," "Kiss and Make Up"—he was in the most revered middle-class role of them all, exploited so successfully by television over the past three years: the doctor. Seldom is Grant portrayed as a lower-class figure—he did not make a good beatnik Cockney in "None But the Lonely Heart"— and rarely is he anything so formidable as the trucking tycoon he played in "Born to Be Bad" in 1934. The perfect Grant role is one in which he has a job that gives him enough free time so that he does not have to languish away at the office during the course of the movie; but he has the job and a visible means of support and highly visible bourgeois respectability all the same.

Grant, of course, has had no Hollywood monopoly on either savoir faire or gentility on the screen. Many suave, humorous gentlemen come to mind: Jimmy Stewart, David Niven, Fred Astaire, Ronald Colman, Franchot Tone. None of them, however, could approach Grant in that other part of being the world's best bourgeois romantic: viz., sex appeal. It was Cary Grant that Mae West was talking about when she launched the phrase "tall, dark and handsome" in "She Done Him Wrong" (1933), and it was Cary Grant who was invited up to see her sometime. Even at age fifty-nine, the man still has the flawless squared-off face of a comic strip hero, a large muscular neck and an athletic physique which he still exhibits in at least one scene in each picture. Every good American girl wants to marry a doctor. But a Dr. Dreamboat? Is it too much to hope for? Well, that is what Cary Grant is there for.

So Cary Grant keeps pouring it on, acting out what in the Age of Brando seems like the most unlikely role in the world: the loverboy of the bourgeoisie. The upshot has been intriguing. In 1948, at the age of forty-four he came in fourth in the box-office poll of male star popularity, behind Clark Gable, Gary Cooper and Bing Crosby. By 1958, when he was fifty-four, he had risen to No. 1. This fall—when he was fifty-nine—the motion picture Theater Owners Association named him as the No. 1 box-office attraction, male or female.

Well, the two old dolls had left, and the next crisis in the Edwardian Room was that an Italian starlet had walked in, a kind of tabescent bijou blonde. Old Cary Grant knows he has met her somewhere, but he will be damned if he can remember who she was. His only hope is that she won't see him, so he has his head tucked down to one side in his Cary Grant caught-out-on-a-limb look.

He can't keep that up forever, so he keeps his head turned by talking to the fellow next to him, who has on a wild solaro-cloth suit with a step-collared vest.

"Acting styles go in fads," Cary Grant is saying. "It's like girls at a dance. One night a fellow walks in wearing a motorcycle jacket and blue jeans and he takes the first girl he sees and embraces her and crushes her rib cage. 'What a man!' all the girls say, and pretty soon all the boys are coming to the dances in motorcycle jackets and blue jeans and taking direct action. That goes on for a while, and then one night in comes a fellow in a blue suit who can wear a necktie without strangling, carrying a bouquet of flowers. Do they still have bouquets of flowers? I'm sure they do. Well, anyway, now the girls say, 'What a charmer!' and they're off on another cycle. Or something like that.

"Well, as for me, I just keep going along the same old way," says Cary Grant with his Cary Grant let's-not-get-all-wrapped-up-in-it look.

But now that the secret is out, the prospects are almost forbidding. Think of all those Actors Studio people trussed up in worsted, strangling on Foulard silk, speaking through the mouth instead of the nose, talking nice to love-stricken old ladies in the Edwardian Room of the Plaza Hotel. The mind boggles, baby.

DONALD RITCHIE

*Donald Ritchie has lived in Japan for more than fifty years and knows more about the Japanese cinema than anyone outside Japan and probably anyone inside as well. It was he who first introduced Ozu to the West, after Japanese film executives argued he was "too Japanese" to be appreciated by Occidentals (in fact Ozu is the most universal of directors). Ritchie has been a free lance for most of his time in Japan, writing a travel memoir (*The Inland Sea*) that became a documentary film; writing the English subtitles for innumerable films; writing books on the Japanese cinema, Ozu, and Kurosawa; writing novels and short stories; and doing a regular column for the* Japan Times. *His book* Different People *contains an incredible essay that did not quite fit within the boundaries of this anthology; it tells the story of the woman who by cutting off her lover's penis in a death pact inspired Oshima's film* In the Realm of the Senses. *Ritchie finds her years later, employed to walk across a nightclub floor once every night, so that the patrons, almost all male, could simply look at her. In the following essay, also from* Different People, *he considers the strange case of Setsuko Hara, who became the most popular of Japanese film stars and then one day simply walked away from it all.*

"Setsuko Hara"

She must be in her sixties, Japan's "eternal virgin"—so billed, even now, in the continuing references to her in magazines, newspapers; even now, more than twenty years after her disappearance.

That 1963 disappearance was a scandal. She had been the most beloved of film stars, her handsome face, accepting smile, known to all. And then, suddenly, rudely, without a word of apology, she was going to disappear—to retire.

Here, where the stars hang on, voluntary retirement is unknown, particularly for one the caliber of Setsuko Hara. She had become an ideal: men wanted to marry someone like her; women wanted to be someone like her.

This was because on the screen she reconciled her life as real people cannot. Whatever her role in films—daughter, wife, or mother—she played a woman who at the same time, somehow, was herself. Her social roles did not eclipse that individual self, our Setsuko.

In Ozu's *Late Spring* she wanted to remain a daughter, did not want to become a wife. Staying on with her father was enough. But eventually she married and through it all she showed her real self. In *Late Autumn*, a 1960 version of the 1949 film, she played the parent rather than the daughter. She was now a mother, a widow, who realizes that it is best that her daughter get married, though it means that she herself will be lonely. And through it all she showed her real self.

This she did by transcending the limitations imposed on her. She won her freedom by realizing that it is only within limitations that the concept of freedom is relevant. She accepted.

At the conclusion of *Tokyo Story* she is talking with the younger daughter, who has been upset by her elder sister's behavior at the funeral. She would never want to be like that, she says: That would be just too cruel.

The daughter-in-law, Setsuko Hara, agrees, then says: It is, but children get that way . . . gradually.

—Then . . . you too? says the daughter.

—I may become like that. In spite of myself.

The daughter is surprised, then disturbed as she realizes the implications:

—But then . . . isn't life disappointing?

And Setsuko smiles, a full, warm, accepting smile:

—Yes, it is.

She welcomed life, accepted its terms. In the same way she welcomed her role, absorbed it into herself, left the precious social fabric intact. No matter that her words were written and her actions directed by Yasujiro Ozu. This screen persona became hers and, in any event, Ozu would not have created his character this way had it not been Setsuko Hara for whom he was writing.

Thus, on the screen, she did not disturb harmony, she created it. And in this harmony she found herself. It was for this that she was so loved.

Even her being an "eternal virgin" (never marrying, never having children in a country where fertile wedlock is almost mandatory) was never held against her. She was not, after all, an old maid. No, she was that positive thing, an eternal virgin.

And then this sudden retirement. And the way she did it. She simply announced it. This was no way for an Ozu character to behave.

Great was the outcry. Her studio, for which she was the major box-office attraction, tried every blandishment. She stood firm against them all. The critics, who had formerly adored her, were hurt, insulted—there was talk of her being *onna rashikunai,* un-womanlike. Them she ignored.

And then there was what she said, the reasons she gave. She implied that she had never enjoyed making films, that she had done so merely to make enough money to support her large family, that she hadn't thought well of anything she had done in the films, and now that the family was provided for she saw no reason to continue in something she didn't care for.

This was conveyed in the Setsuko Hara style, to be sure, with some show of hesitation, sudden smiles shining through the doubt, but this was one Hara performance, the only one, that was not appreciated.

For the first time since her 1935 debut she was severely criticized, not so much for wanting to retire as for the manner in which this desire was presented. There was no polite fiction about the cares of age—she was only forty-three—or about bad health or about a burning desire to take up charitable work, or a spiritual imperative that she enter a nunnery. Nothing of the sort—only a statement that sounded like the blunt truth.

She was never forgiven. But press and public were allowed no further opportunity to display their disappointment, for she never again appeared.

Where had she gone? It was as though she had walked from that final press conference straight into oblivion. But of course there is no such thing as oblivion in Japan. She was shortly discovered living by herself, under her own name—not the stage one chosen by studio officials—in a small house in Kamakura, where many of her films had been set. And there she remains, remote but still the most publicized of recluses, with readers of the daily or weekly press knowing what she buys when she shops, how often her laundry is visible each week, and which of her old school friends she sees.

Occasionally a photo is attempted, but her past experience has made her quick to sense intruders, and the picture is always taken from so far away and the high-speed film is so grainy that it could be one of any elderly woman airing the bedding or hanging out the wash.

Over the years since her retirement, public anger, pique, and disappointment have all faded. Only a hard-core curiosity has remained. This, and a new admiration.

It now seems, particularly to younger women, that this actress truly reconciled her life. Truly, in that though she played all the social roles—daughter, wife, and mother—she only played them in her films. They were inventions, these roles. They did not eclipse that individual self, our Setsuko. And in this way she exposed them for the fictions that they are.

She did not allow them to define her; rather, she defined herself. And she did this by setting up her own limitations, not those of her fictitious roles. Her real limitations are the self-determined ones of the little Kamakura house, the daily round, the visits with her women friends. Only within such chosen limits is the concept of any real self at all relevant.

And so Setsuko Hara/Masaé Aida continues as legend—to those of her own time and to the young women who came later. And a legend exerts a compulsive attraction for others, whether it wants to or not.

Thus, many times have photos been sought, many times have parts on screen or tube been offered, and only too often has the little house in Kamakura been approached. The answer is always the same—the door of the little house has been slammed in the intruders' faces.

Even when a group of former friends and co-workers appeared. A documentary was being made about the life and films of Yasujiro Ozu, Hara's mentor and the director who perhaps best captured, or created, this persona. Wouldn't she please appear in it? For the sake of her dead *sensei*? No door was slammed this time. It was politely closed. But the answer was still no.

JOHN UPDIKE

I was starting out as a film critic at just about the time Doris Day's movie career was ending, and I was not kind to her in several reviews. Perhaps movies like Where Were You When the Lights Went Out? *deserved to be mocked, but still—I was being a smartass and knocking Doris Day because, in the atmosphere of the late 1960s, she was a fashionable target. Had I forgotten how much I enjoyed her in* Young at Heart *or* Please Don't Eat the Daisies *or* Pillow Talk *or* Teacher's Pet? *Later, when I went back and looked at a lot of her other films, especially* Love Me or Leave Me, *I saw an enormous talent. I realized that with Day I had not followed Robert Warshow's advice ("A man goes to the movies. The critic must be honest enough to admit he is that man"). I had not acknowledged that I liked and admired a lot of what she had done. Here is John Updike, reviewing her autobiography and following Warshow's advice.*

"Suzie Creamcheese Speaks"

I have fallen in love with rather few public figures—with Errol Flynn, Ted Williams, Harry Truman, and Doris Day. The three men have a common denominator in cockiness; how cocky Miss Day also is did not strike me until the reading of *Doris Day: Her Own Story,* as orchestrated by A. E. Hotchner. "I must emphasize," she tells us in the autobiographical tapes that Hotchner has edited, "that I have never had any doubts about my ability in anything I have ever undertaken." Elsewhere, in describing her audition, at the age of sixteen, for the job of lead singer with Bob Crosby's Bobcats, she says, "But to be honest about it, despite my nervousness and reluctance to sing for these mighty professionals, it never occurred to me that I wouldn't get the job. I have never tried out for anything that I failed to get." And, it is true, her life shows a remarkably consistent pattern of professional success, alternating with personal tribulation. When she was eleven, her father, "Professor" William Kappelhoff, Cincinnati's "most sought-after conductor," left her mother for another woman; when Doris was twelve, the dance team of Doris & Jerry won the grand prize in a citywide amateur contest, and with the money they visited Hollywood, where people "were so enthusiastic about our ability that I had no doubt that we would do very well." But when she left a farewell party given on the eve of her moving to Hollywood, a locomotive struck the car in which she was riding. Her right leg was shattered and her dancing career with it (Jerry's, too; without Doris Kappelhoff as a partner, he became in time a Cincinnati milkman). During her nearly two years of convalescence, Doris listened to the radio, admiring especially the singing of Ella Fitzgerald, and before she was off crutches she was performing in a downtown Chinese restaurant and on local radio. A Cincinnati night-club job led to Chicago and the Bobcats, and from there to Les Brown and his Blue Devils—all this before her seventeenth birthday.

In one of the interviews that Hotchner usefully splices into his subject's account of her days, Les Brown remembers that he "listened to her for five minutes, immediately went backstage, and signed her for my band. She was every band leader's dream, a vocalist who had natural talent, a keen regard for the lyrics, and an attractive appearance. . . . The reason her salary rose so precipitously was that virtually every band in the business tried to hire her away from me." Yet at the age of seventeen she left the Blue Devils and married an obscure, surly trombonist named Al Jorden. "From the time I was a little girl," she says, "my only true ambition in life was to get married and tend house and have a family. Singing was just something to do until that time came, and now it was here." Though she had known Jorden back in Cincinnati, he surprised her, once married, with psychopathic behavior that bordered on the murderous. He was frantically jealous, beat her, begged forgiveness in fits of remorse that became as repellent as his rage, and demanded she abort the pregnancy that came along in the second month of the hasty match. Doris Day, as she was by then called, in rapid succession had the baby (her only child, Terry), divorced Al Jorden, went back to Les Brown, and recorded "Sentimental Journey," her first hit record and the point where I, among millions, began to love her. Unaware of my feelings, she married another bandman, George Weidler, who played alto sax; this marriage ended even sooner than the one to Al Jorden, though on a different note. Weidler, with whom she was contentedly living in a trailer camp in postwar Los Angeles, told her she was going to become a star and he didn't wish to become Mr. Doris Day. She protests even now, "I loved him, or at least I thought I did, and with all the hardship and struggle I was enjoying my trailer wifedom." Nor did Weidler seem to find her wanting. "I could not doubt his strong desire for me. But I guess his desire not to be Mr. Doris Day was even stronger, for in the morning we parted, and I knew it would be final." At this low ebb, then, homeless, husbandless, and penniless, she permitted herself to be dragged to a screen test, and was handed the lead in the first of her many successful movies, *Romance on the High Seas*. She and the cameras fell in love at first sight:

> I found I could enter a room and move easily to my floormark without actually looking for it. I felt a nice exhilaration at hearing the word "Action!" and then responding to the pressure of the rolling camera. It was effortless and thoroughly enjoyable. . . . From the first take onward, I never had any trepidation about what I was called on to do. Movie acting came to me with greater ease and naturalness than anything else I had ever done. . . . I never had a qualm. Water off a duck's back.

Two decades off her back found their high-water mark in the early Sixties, when she was No. 1 at the box office. In 1953, however, she had suffered an incapacitating nervous breakdown, and throughout her moviemaking prime her personal life was bounded by shyness, Christian Science, a slavish work schedule, and marriage to a man no one else liked—Marty Melcher. Les Brown is quoted as saying, "Marty Melcher was an awful man, pushy, grating on the nerves, crass, money-hungry. He lived off Patty Andrews; then, when Doris came along and looked like a better ticket, he glommed onto her." Sam Weiss, onetime head of Warner Brothers music, phrases it rather beautifully: "The fact was that the only thing Marty loved was money. He loved Patty's money until Doris's money came along and then, because there was more of it, he loved Doris's money more." "I put up with Marty," Weiss further avows, "and everybody else endured him, because of Doris. I don't know anybody who liked Marty. Not even his own family."

Her manager as well as her husband, Melcher kept the cameras churning out sugary Daydreams while the focus got softer and softer, and American audiences were moving on to skin and rock. In 1968, Doris Day made the last of her thirty-nine films and Marty Melcher suddenly died; the financial post mortem revealed that, like many a man in love with money, he could only lose it. Over the fat years, he had poured her fortune into the schemes of a swindler named Rosenthal, leaving her a half-million dollars in debt. She bailed herself out by going ahead, against her inclinations, with a television series Melcher had secretly signed her to, and put herself through five years of sit-com paces on the little box. As an additional trauma, her son, Terry, who had evolved into a young pop music entrepreneur, was peripherally involved in the Tate-Manson murders and retreated to a cave of pills and vodka; in an eerie rerun of her childhood accident, he broke *both* legs while carousing on a motorcycle. Now, on the far side of fifty, Doris Day has no visible career but has kept her celebrity status and her confidence. "I know that I can handle almost anything they throw at me, and to me that is real success," she concludes, cockily.

The particulars of her life surprise us, like graffiti scratched on a sacred statue. She appears sheer symbol—of a kind of beauty, of a kind of fresh and energetic innocence, of a kind of banality. Her very name seems to signify less a person than a product, wrapped in an alliterating aura. She herself, it turns out, doesn't like her name, which was given her because "Kappelhoff" didn't fit on a marquee. (Her first name, too, has to do with marquees; her mother named her after a movie star popular in 1924, Doris Kenyon. And in this tradition Doris named her own son, in 1942, after a favorite comic strip, "Terry and the Pirates.") Of her name Doris Day says:

> I never did like it. Still don't. I think it's a phony name. As a matter of fact, over the years many of my friends didn't feel that Doris Day suited me, and gave me names of their own invention. Billy De Wolfe christened me Clara Bixby . . . Rock Hudson calls me Eunice . . . and others call me Do-Do, and lately one of my friends has taken to calling me Suzie Creamcheese.

This shy goddess who avoids parties and live audiences fascinates us with the amount of space we imagine between her face and her mask. Among the co-actors and fellow-musicians who let their words be used in this book, only Kirk Douglas touches on the mystery: "I haven't a clue as to who Doris Day really is. That face that she shows the world—smiling, only talking good, happy, tuned into God—as far as I'm concerned, that's just a mask. I haven't a clue as to what's underneath. Doris is just about the remotest person I know." In a spunky footnote, she counterattacks—"But then Kirk never makes much of an effort toward anyone else. He's pretty much wrapped up in himself"—and the entire book is announced by her as an attack upon her own image as "Miss Chastity Belt," "America's la-di-da happy virgin!" True, her virginity seems to have been yielded before she married in her mid-teens, and her tough life shows in the tough advice she gives her readers. "You don't really know a person until you live with him, not just sleep with him. . . . I staunchly believe no two people should get married until they have lived together. The young people have it right." For all her love of marriage, she refused both her early husbands when they begged to reconcile, and at one point in her marriage to Melcher she kicked him out, observing simply, "There comes a time when a marriage must be terminated. Nothing is forever." She brushes aside Patty Andrews's belief that Doris had stolen her husband with the sentence "A person does not leave a good marriage for someone else," and of a post-Marty lover she says, "I didn't care whether he was married or not. I have no qualms about the other person's marital life."

How sexy is she, America's girl next door? Her son, who is full of opinions, claims, "She has her heart set on getting married again but she really doesn't have any idea how to react to a man's attention. . . . Sad to say, I don't think my mother's had much of a sex life." But she makes a point of telling us, of each husband, that their sex life was good, and James Garner, with whom she made two of the romantic comedies that followed the great success of *Pillow Talk,* confides,

> I've had to play love scenes with a lot of screen ladies . . . but of all the women I've had to be intimate with on the screen, I'd rate two as sexiest by far—Doris and Julie Andrews, both of them notorious girls next door. Playing a love scene with either of them is duck soup because they communicate something sexy which means I also let myself go somewhat and that really makes a love scene work. . . . The fact of the matter is that with Doris, one hundred grips or not, there *was* always something there and I must admit that if I had not been married I would have tried to carry forward, after hours, where we left off on the sound stage.

The fact of this matter is that star quality is an emanation of superabundant nervous energy and that sexiness, in another setting, would be another emanation.

At the outset of her screen career, the director Michael Curtiz told her (as she remembers his Hungarian locutions), "No matter what you do on the screen, no matter what kind of part you play, it will always be you. What I mean is, the Doris Day will always shine through the part. This will make you big important star. You listen to me. Is very rare thing. You look Gable acting, Gary Cooper, Carole Lombard, they are playing different parts but always is the same strong personality coming through." The same strong personality behind her professional success has no doubt contributed to her personal problems; Al Jorden's jealousy, George Weidler's walkout, and Marty Melcher's disastrous dealing can all be construed as attempts of a male ego to survive an overmatch with a queen bee. Of a recent lover, Miss Day, having sung his praises, rather chillingly confesses, "But as it turned out, he was a man who passed through my life without leaving a trace of himself." At about the same time, she passed her second husband on the street and didn't recognize him—"The most embarrassing part of it was that his appearance hadn't changed very much." Even at seventeen, she was the executioner:

> "I'm sorry, Al," I said, "but the feelings I once had for you are dead and gone. There's no way to resurrect them. I don't love you anymore, and without love it just wouldn't work. There's nothing to talk about—the good feelings are gone, and it's over. All over." . . .
> As I started to get out of the car, he put his hand on my arm. I looked at him. His face was full of pain and he was near tears. I thought to myself, No, I am through comforting you. I felt a curious kind of revulsion.

She longs for the marital paradise, but cannot bring to it that paradise's customary component of female dependence.

> "How will you get along?" my aunt asked.
> "Why I'll get a job," I said. All my life I have known that I could work at whatever I wanted whenever I wanted.

And worked she has. Thoroughly German in her ancestry, she is a dedicated technician in the industry of romantic illusion. Singing or acting, she manages to produce, in her face or in her voice, an "effect," a skip or a tremor, a feathery edge that touches us. In these spoken memoirs she seems most herself, least guarded and most exciting, talking shop—details such as how to avoid popping the "p"s when singing into a radio microphone (turn the head "slightly to the side") and the special difficulties of dancing before movie cameras ("A film dancer does not have the freedom of a stage dancer. She must dance precisely to a mark. Her turns must be exact. She must face precisely in the camera direction required while executing very difficult steps"). Her co-performers praise her technical mastery; Bob Hope marvels at the "great comedy timing" she brought to their radio shows, and Jack Lemmon explains why she is a "director's delight"—"Once she performs a scene, she locks it in, and no matter how many takes are required, she gives the same matched performance. In my book, this is the most difficult part of movie acting." She never watches rushes, and cannot sit through one of her old movies without wanting "to redo every shot." She not only dislikes performing before a live audience but often records to the prerecorded accompaniment of an absent band. "In the solitude of a room with perfect acoustics, I could record a song as many times as necessary to get it right." Melcher's long and steady betrayal of her evidently won no worse recrimination than this, after he had signed her up for a clunker called *Caprice*:

"You made a deal—you and Rosenthal, that it? Well, you and Rosenthal don't have to get in front of the camera and try to make something out of terrible stuff like this! I know that you and your friends are only interested in making money, but I'm interested in something more. I don't give a damn about money. I never see any of it and I don't have the time to use any of it even if I knew what to do with it—which I don't."

She is very much the modern artist in being happiest within her art, a haven from life:

I really like to sing; it gives me a sense of release, another dimension; it makes me happy; and I think the people who listen to me instinctively know that and feel it.

I felt very real in the make-believe parts I had to play. I felt what the script asked me to feel. I enjoyed playing and singing for the cameras and I guess that enjoyment came through on the screen. . . . When the camera turned . . . I easily and rather happily responded to whatever was demanded of me.

That Marty Melcher was pouring her earnings down the sewer of his own greed mattered less to her than the memory of Al Jorden's beatings, which she could conjure up whenever the camera asked her to cry.

.   .   .   .

The words "Doris Day" get a reaction, often adverse. They are an incantation, and people who have no reason to disdain her fine entertainer's gifts shy from her as a religious force. Her starriness has a challenging, irritating twinkle peculiar to her—Monroe's image lulled us like a moon seen from a motel bed, and there is nothing about Katharine Hepburn's "goodness" that asks us to examine our own. On the jacket of *Doris Day: Her Own Story* the sprightly photograph of the heroine uncomfortably reminds us of those tireless, elastic television ladies who exhort us to get up in the morning and do exercises; and the book ends with a set of exercises that Doris Day does, and that do sound exhausting. She *likes* the movie actor's Spartan regimen, which begins at five in the morning, and more than once she speaks with pleasure of "coming up to the mark" chalked on the floor of a movie set. For years, she was a professed Christian Scientist; but, then, so were Ginger Rogers and Charlotte Greenwood, and no one held it against them. Miss Day, religiously, is in fact an American Pelagian, an enemy of the despair-prone dualism that has been the intellectual pride of our Scots Protestants and our Irish Catholics alike. Doris Kappelhoff was raised as a Catholic, but "the Catholic side of me never took." She resented the obscurity of the Latin, and resented even more being asked, at the age of seven, to make up sins to confess. "I had my own built-in church. It allowed me to question a lot of Catholic dogma." She turned to the Church once, after the collapse of her first marriage, "desperate to find some way to restore the positive view I had always had toward life." When the priest told her she had never been really married and her son was illegitimate, she walked out. All three of her marriages have been casual civil ceremonies, and she makes a point of not going to funerals—not even her father's. After their divorce, George Weidler (the most phantasmal and, in a way, most appealing man in her life) interested her in the teachings of Mary Baker Eddy, and from the first line she read—"To those leaning on the sustaining infinite, today is big with blessings"—she met in "words of gleaming light" a prefiguration of her "own built-in church." Though in some of her crises she has consulted doctors, and after Melcher's death broke with the organized church, Christian Science's tenet that "All is infinite Mind" has remained a sustaining principle. She describes herself sitting outside her son's hospital room thinking, "I can't pray to a God to make him well, because there is no duality, no God outside of Terry. . . . There is but one power, and if that lovely son of mine is supposed to *live,* then nothing on this earth can take him." The fatalism that goes with monism suits both her toughness and her optimism. Almost brutally she enlists her misfortunes in the progress of her career: "And Marty's death—well, to be honest about it, had he lived I would have been totally wiped out." *Que sera, sera.* Unchastened, she sees her life as an irresistible blooming:

> It is not luck that one seed grows into a purple flower and another, identical seed grows up to be a yellow flower, nor is it luck that Doris Kappelhoff of Cincinnati grows up to be a sex symbol on the silver screen.

Her sense of natural goodness and universal order gets a little cloying when extended to her pet dogs, but by and large she speaks of her religious convictions uninsistently and reasonably, as something that has worked for her. Concerning others, she has scarcely a judgmental or complaining word. She is rather a purist but no puritan; her sexual ethics, like her Man-is-Spirit mysticism, are as Seventies as her image is Fifties. But, then, our movie queens have long been creating metaphysics for themselves on the frontier where bourgeois norms evaporate. Doris Day is naïve, I think, only about her own demon; it was not just by divine determination that peaceful obscure marriage eluded her and fame did not. When she had her nervous breakdown, her psychiatrist described her as "self-demanding." Her father before her failed as a domestic creature; his "whole life was music." She was driven to perform, and permitted life situations to keep forcing her back on the stage. Now she has felt compelled to give this account of herself. How much editorial magic A. E. Hotchner sprinkled upon her tapes there is no telling; but the sections of Doris Day ostensibly speaking are rather better written than Hotchner's own press-releasy prologue and epilogue. She can, if we take her words as truly hers, toss off the terms "sanctum sanctorum" and "reactive," recall patches of dialogue thirty years old, be quite funny about a hideous hotel built in her name, and evoke Bob Hope, "the way his teeth take over his face when he smiles. And the way he swaggers across the stage, kind of sideways, beaming at the audience, spreading good cheer." She became a successful comedienne, surely, in part because she is one of the few movie actresses of her generation whose bearing conveys intelligence.

Now, love must be clear-eyed, and Doris Day's accomplishment, resilient and versatile as she is, should not be exaggerated. Though she learned from Ella Fitzgerald "the subtle ways she shaded her voice, the casual yet clean way she sang the words," there are dark sweet places where Ella's voice goes that her disciple's doesn't. And it was not just Hollywood crassness that cast her in so many tame, lame vehicles; her Pelagianism makes it impossible for her to be evil, so the top of her emotional range is an innocent victim's hysteria. But, as Michael Curtiz foretold when he prepared her for her first motion picture, the actor's art in a case like hers functions as a mere halo of refinements around the "strong personality." Her third picture, strange to say, ended with her make-believe marriage to Errol Flynn. A heavenly match, in the realm where both are lovable. Both brought to the corniest screen moment a gallant and guileless delight in being themselves, a faint air of excess, a skillful insouciance that, in those giant dreams projected across our Saturday nights, hinted at how, if we were angels, we would behave.

Truman Capote

This is a deceptively simple piece, recording in some detail a few hours that Truman Capote (1924–1984) spent in the company of Marilyn Monroe. Capote famously claimed that the quotes in his In Cold Blood *were accurate because he had trained himself to remember exactly and write down each conversation as soon as possible after having it. Here the words seem to have the accuracy of a tape recording, yet at the same time they flow in such a smooth and particular manner that they seem ready to be performed in a one-act play.*

Capote's perfect little piece records not only Monroe's personality but also, with a certain objectivity, his own lifetime role of confidant and confessor to beautiful, insecure women.

"A Beautiful Child"

Time: 28 April 1955.

Scene: The chapel of the Universal Funeral Home at Lexington Avenue and Fifty-second Street, New York City. An interesting galaxy packs the pews: celebrities, for the most part, from an international arena of theatre, films, literature, all present in tribute to Constance Collier, the English-born actress who had died the previous day at the age of seventy-five.

Born in 1880, Miss Collier had begun her career as a music-hall Gaiety Girl, graduated from that to become one of England's principal Shakespearean actresses (and the longtime fiancée of Sir Max Beerbohm, whom she never married, and perhaps for that reason was the inspiration for the mischievously unobtainable heroine in Sir Max's novel *Zuleika Dobson*). Eventually she emigrated to the United States, where she established herself as a considerable figure on the New York stage as well as in Hollywood films. During the last decades of her life she lived in New York, where she practiced as a drama coach of unique caliber; she accepted only professionals as students, and usually only professionals who were already "stars"—Katharine Hepburn was a permanent pupil; another Hepburn, Audrey, was also a Collier protégée, as were Vivien Leigh and, for a few months prior to her death, a neophyte Miss Collier referred to as "my special problem," Marilyn Monroe.

Marilyn Monroe, whom I'd met through John Huston when he was directing her in her first speaking role in *The Asphalt Jungle,* had come under Miss Collier's wing at my suggestion. I had known Miss Collier perhaps a half-dozen years, and admired her as a woman of true stature, physically, emotionally, creatively; and, for all her commanding manner, her grand cathedral voice, as an adorable person, mildly wicked but exceedingly warm, dignified yet *Gemütlich*. I loved to go to the frequent small lunch parties she gave in her dark Victorian studio in mid-Manhattan; she had a barrel of yarns to tell about her adventures as a leading lady opposite Sir Beerbohm Tree and the great French actor Coquelin, her involvements with Oscar Wilde, the youthful Chaplin, and Garbo in the silent Swede's formative days. Indeed she was a delight, as was her devoted secretary and companion, Phyllis Wilbourn, a quietly twinkling maiden lady who, after her employer's demise, became, and has remained, the companion of Katharine Hepburn. Miss Collier introduced me to many people who became friends: the

Lunts, the Oliviers, and especially Aldous Huxley. But it was I who introduced her to Marilyn Monroe, and at first it was not an acquaintance she was too keen to acquire: her eyesight was faulty, she had seen none of Marilyn's movies, and really knew nothing about her except that she was some sort of platinum sex-explosion who had achieved global notoriety; in short, she seemed hardly suitable clay for Miss Collier's stern classic shaping. But I thought they might make a stimulating combination.

They did. "Oh yes," Miss Collier reported to me, "there is something there. She is a beautiful child. I don't mean that in the obvious way—the perhaps too obvious way. I don't think she's an actress at all, not in any traditional sense. What she has—this presence, this luminosity, this flickering intelligence—could never surface on the stage. It's so fragile and subtle, it can only be caught by the camera. It's like a hummingbird in flight: only a camera can freeze the poetry of it. But anyone who thinks this girl is simply another Harlow or harlot or whatever is *mad*. Speaking of mad, that's what we've been working on together: Ophelia. I suppose people would chuckle at the notion, but really, she could be the most exquisite Ophelia. I was talking to Greta last week, and I told her about Marilyn's Ophelia, and Greta said yes, she could believe that because she had seen two of her films, very bad and vulgar stuff, but nevertheless she had glimpsed Marilyn's possibilities. Actually, Greta has an amusing idea. You know that she wants to make a film of *Dorian Gray?* With her playing Dorian, of course. Well, she said she would like to have Marilyn opposite her as one of the girls Dorian seduces and destroys. Greta! So unused! Such a gift—and rather like Marilyn's, if you consider it. Of course, Greta is a consummate artist, an artist of the utmost control. This beautiful child is without any concept of discipline or sacrifice. Somehow I don't think she'll make old bones. Absurd of me to say, but somehow I feel she'll go young. I hope, I really pray, that she survives long enough to free the strange lovely talent that's wandering through her like a jailed spirit."

But now Miss Collier had died, and here I was loitering in the vestibule of the Universal Chapel waiting for Marilyn; we had talked on the telephone the evening before, and agreed to sit together at the services, which were scheduled to start at noon. She was now a half-hour late; she was *always* late, but I'd thought just for once! For God's sake, goddamnit! Then suddenly there she was, and I didn't recognize her until she said . . .

MARILYN: Oh, baby, I'm so sorry. But see, I got all made up, and then I decided maybe I shouldn't wear eyelashes or lipstick or anything, so then I had to wash all that off, and I couldn't imagine what to wear . . .

(What she had imagined to wear would have been appropriate for the abbess of a nunnery in private audience with the Pope. Her hair was entirely concealed by a black chiffon scarf;

her black dress was loose and long and looked somehow borrowed; black silk stockings dulled the blond sheen of her slender legs. An abbess, one can be certain, would not have donned the vaguely erotic black high-heeled shoes she had chosen, or the owlish black sunglasses that dramatized the vanilla-pallor of her dairy-fresh skin.)

TO: You look fine.

MARILYN (gnawing an already chewed-to-the-nub thumbnail): Are you sure? I mean, I'm so jumpy. Where's the john? If I could just pop in there for a minute—

TC: And pop a pill? No! Shhh. That's Cyril Ritchard's voice: he's started the eulogy.

(Tiptoeing, we entered the crowded chapel and wedged ourselves into a narrow space in the last row. Cyril Ritchard finished; he was followed by Cathleen Nesbitt, a lifelong colleague of Miss Collier's, and finally Brian Aherne addressed the mourners. Through it all, my date periodically removed her spectacles to scoop up tears bubbling from her blue-grey eyes. I'd sometimes seen her without makeup, but today she presented a new visual experience, a face I'd not observed before, and at first I couldn't perceive why this should be. Ah! It was because of the obscuring head scarf. With her tresses invisible, and her complexion cleared of all cosmetics, she looked twelve years old, a pubescent virgin who has just been admitted to an orphanage and is grieving over her plight. At last the ceremony ended, and the congregation began to disperse.)

MARILYN: Please, let's sit here. Let's wait till everyone's left.

TC: Why?

MARILYN: I don't want to have to talk to anybody. I never know what to say.

TC: Then you sit here, and I'll wait outside. I've got to have a cigarette.

MARILYN: You can't leave me alone! My God! Smoke here.

TC: *Here?* In the chapel?

MARILYN: Why not? What do you want to smoke? A reefer?

TC: Very funny. Come on, let's go.

MARILYN: Please. There's a lot of shutterbugs downstairs. And I certainly don't want them taking my picture looking like this.

TC: I can't blame you for that.

MARILYN: You said I looked fine.

TC: You do. Just perfect—if you were playing the Bride of Frankenstein.

MARILYN: Now you're laughing at me.

TC: Do I look like I'm laughing?

MARILYN: You're laughing inside. And that's the worst kind of laugh. (Frowning; nibbling thumbnail) Actually, I could've worn makeup. I see all these other people are wearing makeup.

TC: I am. Globs.

MARILYN: Seriously, though. It's my hair. I need color. And I didn't have time to get any. It was all so unexpected, Miss Collier dying and all. See?

(She lifted her kerchief slightly to display a fringe of darkness where her hair parted.)

TC: Poor innocent me. And all this time I thought you were a bona-fide blonde.

MARILYN: I am. But nobody's *that* natural. And incidentally, fuck you.

TC: Okay, everybody's cleared out. So up, up.

MARILYN: Those photographers are still down there. I know it.

TC: If they didn't recognize you coming in, they won't recognize you going out.

MARILYN: One of them did. But I'd slipped through the door before he started yelling.

TC: I'm sure there's a back entrance. We can go that way.

MARILYN: I don't want to see any corpses.

TC: Why would we?

MARILYN: This is a funeral parlor. They must keep them somewhere. That's all I need today, to wander into a room full of corpses. Be patient. I'll take us somewhere and treat us to a bottle of bubbly.

(So we sat and talked and Marilyn said: "I hate funerals. I'm glad I won't have to go to my own. Only, I don't want a funeral—just my ashes cast on waves by one of my kids, if I ever have any. I wouldn't have come today except Miss Collier cared about me, my welfare, and she was just like a granny, a tough old granny, but she taught me a lot. She taught me how to breathe. I've put it to good use, too, and I don't mean just acting. There are other times when breathing is a problem. But when I first heard about it, Miss Collier cooling, the first thing I thought was: Oh, gosh, what's going to happen to Phyllis?! Her whole life was Miss Collier. But I hear she's going to live with Miss Hepburn. Lucky Phyllis; she's going to have fun now. I'd change places with her pronto. Miss Hepburn is a terrific lady, no shit. I wish she was my friend. So I could call her up sometimes and . . . well, I don't know, just call her up."

We talked about how much we liked New York and loathed Los Angeles ("Even though I was born there, I still can't think of one good thing to say about it. If I close my eyes, and picture L.A., all I see is one big varicose vein"); we talked about actors and acting ("Everybody says I can't act. They said the same thing about Elizabeth Taylor. And they were wrong. She was great in A Place in the Sun. *I'll never get the right part, anything I really want. My looks are against me. They're too specific"); we talked some more about Elizabeth Taylor, and she wanted to know if I knew her, and I said yes, and she said well, what is she like, what is she* really *like, and I said well, she's a little bit like you, she wears her heart on her sleeve and talks salty, and Marilyn said fuck you and said well, if somebody asked me what Marilyn Monroe was like, what was Marilyn Monroe really like, what would I say, and I said I'd have to think about that.)*

TC: Now do you think we can get the hell out of here? You promised me champagne, remember?

MARILYN: I remember. But I don't have any money.

TC: You're always late and you never have any money. By any chance are you under the delusion that you're Queen Elizabeth?

MARILYN: Who?

TC: Queen Elizabeth. The Queen of England.

MARILYN (frowning): What's that cunt got to do with it?

TC: Queen Elizabeth never carries money either. She's not allowed to. Filthy lucre must not stain the royal palm. It's a law or something.

MARILYN: I wish they'd pass a law like that for me.

TC: Keep going the way you are and maybe they will.

MARILYN: Well, gosh. How does she pay for anything? Like when she goes shopping.

TC: Her lady-in-waiting trots along with a bag full of farthings.

MARILYN: You know what? I'll bet she gets everything free. In return for endorsements.

TC: Very possible. I wouldn't be a bit surprised. By Appointment to Her Majesty. Corgi dogs. All those Fortnum & Mason goodies. Pot. Condoms.

MARILYN: What would she want with condoms?

TC: Not her, dopey. For that chump who walks two steps behind. Prince Philip.

MARILYN: Him. Oh, yeah. He's cute. He looks like he might have a nice prick. Did I ever tell you about the time I saw Errol Flynn whip out his prick and play the piano with it? Oh well, it was a hundred years ago, I'd just got into modeling, and I went to this half-ass party, and Errol Flynn, so pleased with himself, he was there and he took out his prick and played the piano with it. Thumped the keys. He played *You Are My Sunshine.* Christ! Everybody says Milton Berle has the biggest schlong in Hollywood. But who *cares?* Look, don't you have *any* money?

TC: Maybe about fifty bucks.

MARILYN: Well, that ought to buy us some bubbly.

(Outside, Lexington Avenue was empty of all but harmless pedestrians. It was around two, and as nice an April afternoon as one could wish: ideal strolling weather. So we moseyed toward Third Avenue. A few gawkers spun their heads, not because they recognized Marilyn as the Marilyn, but because of her funereal finery; she giggled her special little gig-

gle, a sound as tempting as the jingling bells on a Good Humor wagon, and said: "Maybe I should always dress this way. Real anonymous."

As we neared P. J. Clarke's saloon, I suggested P.J.'s might be a good place to refresh ourselves, but she vetoed that: "It's full of those advertising creeps. And that bitch Dorothy Kilgallen, she's always in there getting bombed. What is it with these micks? The way they booze, they're worse than Indians."

I felt called upon to defend Kilgallen, who was a friend, somewhat, and I allowed as to how she could upon occasion be a clever funny woman. She said: "Be that as it may, she's written some bitchy stuff about me. But all those cunts hate me. Hedda. Louella. I know you're supposed to get used to it, but I just can't. It really hurts. What did I ever do to those hags? The only one who writes a decent word about me is Sidney Skolsky. But he's a guy. The guys treat me okay. Just like maybe I was a human person. At least they give me the benefit of the doubt. And Bob Thomas is a gentleman. And Jack O'Brian."

We looked in the windows of antique shops; one contained a tray of old rings, and Marilyn said: "That's pretty. The garnet with the seed pearls. I wish I could wear rings, but I hate people to notice my hands. They're too fat. Elizabeth Taylor has fat hands. But with those eyes, who's looking at her hands? I like to dance naked in front of mirrors and watch my titties jump around. There's nothing wrong with them. But I wish my hands weren't so fat."

Another window displayed a handsome grandfather clock, which prompted her to observe: "I've never had a home. Not a real one with all my own furniture. But if I ever get married again, and make a lot of money, I'm going to hire a couple of trucks and ride down Third Avenue buying every damn kind of crazy thing. I'm going to get a dozen grandfather clocks and line them all up in one room and have them all ticking away at the same time. That would be real homey, don't you think?")

MARILYN: Hey! Across the street!
TC: What?
MARILYN: See the sign with the palm? That must be a fortunetelling parlor.
TC: Are you in the mood for that?
MARILYN: Well, let's take a look.

(It was not an inviting establishment. Through a smeared window we could discern a barren room with a skinny, hairy gypsy lady seated in a canvas chair under a hellfire-red ceiling lamp that shed a torturous glow; she was knitting a pair of baby-booties, and did not return our stares. Nevertheless, Marilyn started to go in, then changed her mind.)

MARILYN: Sometimes I want to know what's going to happen. Then I think it's better not to. There's two things I'd like to know, though. One is whether I'm going to lose weight.
TC: And the other?

MARILYN: That's a secret.

TC: Now, now. We can't have secrets today. Today is a day of sorrow, and sorrowers share their innermost thoughts.

MARILYN: Well, it's a man. There's something I'd like to know. But that's all I'm going to tell. It really *is* a secret.

(And I thought: That's what you think; I'll get it out of you.)

TC: I'm ready to buy that champagne.

(We wound up on Second Avenue in a gaudily decorated deserted Chinese restaurant. But it did have a well-stocked bar, and we ordered a bottle of Mumm's; it arrived unchilled, and without a bucket, so we drank it out of tall glasses with ice cubes.)

MARILYN: This is fun. Kind of like being on location—if you like location. Which I most certainly don't. *Niagara*. That stinker. Yuk.

TC: So let's hear about your secret lover.

MARILYN: (Silence)

TC: (Silence)

MARILYN: (Giggles)

TC: (Silence)

MARILYN: You know so many women. Who's the most attractive woman you know?

TC: No contest. Barbara Paley. Hands down.

MARILYN (frowning): Is that the one they call "Babe"? She sure doesn't look like any Babe to me. I've seen her in *Vogue* and all. She's so elegant. Lovely. Just looking at her pictures makes me feel like pig-slop.

TC: She might be amused to hear that. She's very jealous of you.

MARILYN: Jealous of *me*? Now there you go again, laughing.

TC: Not at all. She *is* jealous.

MARILYN: But why?

TC: Because one of the columnists, Kilgallen I think, ran a blind item that said something like: "Rumor hath it that Mrs. DiMaggio rendezvoused with television's toppest tycoon and it wasn't to discuss business." Well, she read the item and she believes it.

MARILYN: Believes *what*?

TC: That her husband is having an affair with you. William S. Paley. TV's toppest tycoon. He's partial to shapely blondes. Brunettes, too.

MARILYN: But that's batty. I've never met the guy.

TC: Ah, come on. You can level with me. This secret lover of yours—it's William S. Paley, *n'est-ce pas?*

MARILYN: No! It's a writer. He's a writer.

TC: That's more like it. Now we're getting somewhere. So your lover is a writer. Must be a real hack, or you wouldn't be ashamed to tell me his name.

MARILYN (furious, frantic): What does the "S" stand for?

TC: "S." What "S"?

MARILYN: The "S" in William S. Paley.

TC: Oh, *that* "S." It doesn't stand for anything. He sort of tossed it in there for appearance sake.

MARILYN: It's just an initial with no name behind it? My goodness. Mr. Paley must be a little insecure.

TC: He twitches a lot. But let's get back to our mysterious scribe.

MARILYN: Stop it! You don't understand. I have so much to lose.

TC: Waiter, we'll have another Mumm's, please.

MARILYN: Are you trying to loosen my tongue?

TC: Yes. Tell you what. We'll make an exchange. I'll tell you a story, and if you think it's interesting, then perhaps we can discuss your writer friend.

MARILYN (tempted, but reluctant): What's your story about?

TC: Errol Flynn.

MARILYN: (Silence)

TC: (Silence)

MARILYN (hating herself): Well, go on.

TC: Remember what you were saying about Errol? How pleased he was with his prick? I can vouch for that. We once spent a cozy evening together. If you follow me.

MARILYN: You're making this up. You're trying to trick me.

TC: Scout's honor. I'm dealing from a clean deck. (Silence; but I can see that she's hooked, so after lighting a cigarette . . .) Well, this happened when I was eighteen. Nineteen. It was during the war. The winter of 1943. That night Carol Marcus or maybe she was already Carol Saroyan, was giving a party for her best friend, Gloria Vanderbilt. She gave it in her mother's apartment on Park Avenue. Big party. About fifty people. Around midnight Errol Flynn rolls in with his alter ego, a swashbuckling playboy named Freddie McEvoy. They were both pretty loaded. Anyway, Errol started yakking with me, and he was bright, we were making each other laugh, and suddenly he said he wanted to go to El Morocco, and did I want to go with him and his buddy McEvoy. I said okay, but then McEvoy didn't want to leave the party and all those debutantes, so in the end Errol and I left alone. Only we didn't go to El Morocco. We took a taxi down to Gramercy Park, where I had a little one-room apartment. He stayed until noon the next day.

MARILYN: And how would you rate it? On a scale of one to ten.

TC: Frankly, if it hadn't been Errol Flynn, I don't think I would have remembered it.

MARILYN: That's not much of a story. Not worth mine—not by a long shot.

TC: Waiter, where is our champagne? You've got two thirsty people here.

MARILYN: And it's not as if you'd told me anything new. I've always known Errol zigzagged. I have a masseur, he's practically my sister, and he was Tyrone Power's masseur, and he told me all about the thing Errol and Ty Power had going. No, you'll have to do better than that.

TC: You drive a hard bargain.

MARILYN: I'm listening. So let's hear your best experience. Along those lines.

TC: The best? The most memorable? Suppose you answer the question first.

MARILYN: And *I* drive hard bargains! Ha! (Swallowing champagne) Joe's not bad. He can hit home runs. If that's all it takes, we'd still be married. I still love him, though. He's genuine.

TC: Husbands don't count. Not in this game.

MARILYN (nibbling nail; really thinking): Well, I met a man, he's related to Gary Cooper somehow. A stockbroker, and nothing much to look at—sixty-five, and he wears those very thick glasses. Thick as jellyfish. I can't say what it was, but—

TC: You can stop right there. I've heard all about him from other girls. That old swordsman really scoots around. His name is Paul Shields. He's Rocky Cooper's stepfather. He's supposed to be sensational.

MARILYN: He is. Okay, smart-ass. Your turn.

TC: Forget it. I don't have to tell you damn nothing. Because I know who you masked marvel is: Arthur Miller. (She lowered her black glasses: Oh boy, if looks could kill, wow!) I guessed as soon as you said he was a writer.

MARILYN (stammering): But how? I mean, nobody . . . I mean, hardly anybody—

TC: At least three, maybe four years ago Irving Drutman—

MARILYN: Irving *who?*

TC: Drutman. He's a writer on the *Herald Tribune.* He told me you were fooling around with Arthur Miller. Had a hang-up on him. I was too much of a gentleman to mention it before.

MARILYN: Gentleman! You bastard. (Stammering again, but dark glasses in place) You don't understand. That was long ago. That ended. But this is new. It's all different now, and—

TC: Just don't forget to invite me to the wedding.

MARILYN: If you talk about this, I'll murder you. I'll have you bumped off. I know a couple of men who'd gladly do me the favor.

TC: I don't question that for an instant.

(At last the waiter returned with the second bottle.)

MARILYN: Tell him to take it back. I don't want any. I want to get the hell out of
    here.

TC: Sorry if I've upset you.

MARILYN: I'm not upset.

*(But she was. While I paid the check, she left for the powder room, and I wished I had a
book to read: her visits to powder rooms sometimes lasted as long as an elephant's pregnancy. Idly, as time ticked by, I wondered if she was popping uppers or downers. Downers, no doubt. There was a newspaper on the bar, and I picked it up; it was written in
Chinese. After twenty minutes had passed, I decided to investigate. Maybe she'd popped
a lethal dose, or even cut her wrists. I found the ladies' room, and knocked on the door.
She said: "Come in." Inside, she was confronting a dimly lit mirror. I said: "What are you
doing?" She said: "Looking at Her." In fact, she was coloring her lips with ruby lipstick.
Also, she had removed the somber head scarf and combed out her glossy fine-as-cotton-
candy hair.)*

MARILYN: I hope you have enough money left.

TC: That depends. Not enough to buy pearls, if that's your idea of making
    amends.

MARILYN (giggling, returned to good spirits. I decided I wouldn't mention Arthur
    Miller again): No. Only enough for a long taxi ride.

TC: Where are we going—Hollywood?

MARILYN: Hell, no. A place I like. You'll find out when we get there.

*(I didn't have to wait that long, for as soon as we had flagged a taxi, I heard her instruct
the cabby to drive to the South Street Pier, and I thought: Isn't that where one takes the
ferry to Staten Island? And my next conjecture was: She's swallowed pills on top of that
champagne and now she's off her rocker.)*

TC: I hope we're not going on any boat rides. I didn't pack my Dramamine.

MARILYN (happy, giggling): Just the pier.

TC: May I ask why?

MARILYN: I like it there. It smells foreign, and I can feed the seagulls.

TC: With what? You haven't anything to feed them.

MARILYN: Yes, I do. My purse is full of fortune cookies. I swiped them from that
    restaurant.

TC   (kidding her): Uh-huh. While you were in the john I cracked one open.
    The slip inside was a dirty joke.

MARILYN: Gosh. Dirty fortune cookies?

TC: I'm sure the gulls won't mind.

(Our route carried us through the Bowery. Tiny pawnshops and blood-donor stations and dormitories with fifty-cent cots and tiny grim hotels with dollar beds and bars for whites, bars for blacks, everywhere bums, bums, young, far from young, ancient, bums squatting curbside, squatting amid shattered glass and pukey debris, bums slanting in doorways and huddled like penguins at street corners. Once, when we paused for a red light, a purple-nosed scarecrow weaved toward us and began swabbing the taxi's windshield with a wet rag clutched in a shaking hand. Our protesting driver shouted Italian obscenities.)

MARILYN: What is it? What's happening?
TC: He wants a tip for cleaning the window.
MARILYN (shielding her face with her purse): How horrible! I can't stand it. Give
    him something. Hurry. Please!

(But the taxi had already zoomed ahead, damn near knocking down the old lush. Marilyn was crying.)

    I'm sick.
TC: You want to go home?
MARILYN: Everything's ruined.
TC: I'll take you home.
MARILYN: Give me a minute. I'll be okay.

(Thus we traveled on to South Street, and indeed the sight of a ferry moored there, with the Brooklyn skyline across the water and careening, cavorting seagulls white against a marine horizon streaked with thin fleecy clouds fragile as lace—this tableau soon soothed her soul.

    As we got out of the taxi we saw a man with a chow on a leash, a prospective passenger, walking toward the ferry, and as we passed them, my companion stopped to pat the dog's head.)

THE MAN (firm, but not unfriendly): You shouldn't touch strange dogs. Especially chows. They might bite you.
MARILYN: Dogs never bite me. Just humans. What's his name?
THE MAN: Fu Manchu.
MARILYN (giggling): Oh, just like the movie. That's cute.
THE MAN: What's yours?
MARILYN: My name? Marilyn.
THE MAN: That's what I thought. My wife will never believe me. Can I have your
    autograph?

(He produced a business card and a pen; using her purse to write on, she wrote: God Bless
You—Marilyn Monroe)

MARILYN: Thank you.

THE MAN: Thank *you*. Wait'll I show this back at the office.

(We continued to the edge of the pier, and listened to the water sloshing against it.)

MARILYN: I used to ask for autographs. Sometimes I still do. Last year Clark Gable was sitting next to me in Chasen's, and I asked him to sign my napkin.

(Leaning against a mooring stanchion, she presented a profile: Galatea surveying unconquered distances. Breezes fluffed her hair, and her head turned toward me with an ethereal ease, as though a breeze had swiveled it.)

TC: So when do we feed the birds? I'm hungry, too. It's late, and we never had lunch.

MARILYN: Remember, I said if anybody ever asked you what I was like, what Marilyn Monroe was *really* like—well, how would you answer them? (Her tone was teaseful, mocking, yet earnest, too: she wanted an honest reply) I bet you'd tell them I was a slob. A banana split.

TC: Of course. But I'd also say . . .

(The light was leaving. She seemed to fade with it, blend with the sky and clouds, recede beyond them. I wanted to lift my voice louder than the seagulls' cries and call her back: Marilyn! Marilyn, why did everything have to turn out the way it did? Why does life have to be so fucking rotten?)

TC: I'd say . . .

MARILYN: I can't hear you.

TC: I'd say you are a beautiful child.

ELEANOR COPPOLA

Eleanor Coppola made a journal, tape recordings and a 16 mm documentary film on the Philippines locations of her husband's Apocalypse Now, *one of the most legendary and beleaguered shoots in film history. Here she recalls her first meeting on the set with Marlon Brando, who had been brought in to anchor the final act as the shadowy Kurtz. Eleanor Coppola's video and tape record was also used in an extraordinary documentary,* Hearts of Darkness: A Filmmaker's Apocalypse, *by George Hickenlooper and Fax Bahr, in which you can hear Coppola despairing that he has no idea what to do next and the entire film seems to be coming apart. In the end it became one of the greatest films of the century.*

from *Notes*

SEPTEMBER 2, PAGSANJAN

I went to the French plantation set to see how Francis was doing and how the boys were holding up. The shot was down on the dock, so I walked down there and found Francis in the shade talking to a heavyset man with short gray hair. When I got closer, the man said, "Hi, Ellie." He looked familiar and then I realized that he was Marlon Brando. I was fascinated that he recognized me and knew my name after such brief meetings. He seemed to be looking at me in microscopic detail. As if he noticed my eyebrows move slightly, or could see the irregular stitching on the buttonhole of my shirt pocket. Not in a judgmental way, just in a complete absorption of all the details.

Later, Francis was telling me that is part of what makes him such a great actor. He develops a fix, a vision of a character, down to the most minute detail. Francis has a more conceptual vision. He has the overall idea of how he wants the film to be and he counts on Dean and Vittorio and the actors to fill in many of the details.

SEPTEMBER 4, PAGSANJAN

Marlon is very overweight. Francis and he are struggling with how to change the character in the script. Brando wants to camouflage his weight and Francis wants to play him as a man eating all the time and overindulging.

.   .   .   .

I heard there are some real cadavers in body bags at the Kurtz Compound set. I asked the propman about it; he said, "The script says 'a pile of burning bodies'; it doesn't say a pile of burning dummies."

This morning Francis was talking about the Kurtz set being so big that there seemed to be no way to get it all in the frame. The only way to get it was perhaps to come in close and look at specific portions to give a sense of the whole. In a way, that is the same problem he is facing in the script. The ideas of what Kurtz represents are so big that when you try to get a handle on them they are almost undefinable. He has to define the specifics to give a sense of the whole. The production reflects the same thing. It is so big it only seems to make sense in specific ways. Today I have been thinking that the only way that I can show the enormity of the making of *Apocalypse Now* is by showing the details and hoping they give a sense of the larger picture.

.   .   .   .

Francis came home tonight really excited after his long talk with Marlon. He said that Marlon was really incredible. The greatest actor he has ever met, extremely hardworking. Brando had improvised all day. Going one way, then going another, never quitting. They had toughed it out until they came up with a way to go with his character. Brando was going to do something he had never tried before. He was going to play a bigger-than-life character, a mythical figure, a theatrical personage. He is the master of the natural, realistic performance and he was going to go for a different style of acting for the first time in his career. They haven't quite worked out all the details. It will have to be refined over the next few days, but Francis is really excited and he says Marlon is, too.

SEPTEMBER 5, PAGSANJAN

Late in the afternoon I was standing on the main steps of the temple with Francis and Marlon. The two of them were talking about Kurtz. Francis had asked Marlon to reread *Heart of Darkness*. Now Marlon was saying how his character should be more like Kurtz was in the book. Francis said, "Yes, that's what I've been trying to tell you. Don't you remember, last spring, before you took the part, when you read *Heart of Darkness* and we talked?"

Marlon said, "I lied. I never read it."

SEPTEMBER 8, PAGSANJAN

Francis got up at four this morning and went down to his room to write. About six he came into the bedroom and woke me up. He had just figured out why he hasn't been able to resolve the ending of the script. He has been struggling for over a year now, with different drafts of the end, trying to get it right. He said he just realized that there was no simple solution to the script. Just as there was no simple right answer as to why we were in Vietnam. Every time he tried to take the script one direction or the other, he met up with a fundamental contradiction, because the war was a contradiction. A human being contains contradictions. Only if we admit the truth about ourselves, completely, can we find a balance point between the contradictions, the love and the hate, the peace and the violence which exist within us.

We were talking for a long time and it was getting late, so I got dressed. We had some coffee and rode out to the set. It was eight thirty and Marlon was supposed to be there at eight. The assistant director was saying, "What shall we do? We've never worked with Brando before, shall we send another car for him, or how shall we handle it?" Francis said that Marlon would probably be late the first few days.

It seemed to me that Francis thought Marlon was late because the part was still not clearly defined in his mind. Finally, Marlon came around ten and he and Francis went to sit in his houseboat dressing room to talk it out.

At one in the afternoon, the company wrapped for the day and the cast and crew were sent home. Francis is still talking in there and it's past seven in the evening now.

SEPTEMBER 14, PAGSANJAN

When I got to the set around nine in the evening, the whole crew was waiting. Francis, Marlon and Marty were down on the houseboat talking. The crew had been standing by for about four hours. The propman got a basket of chocolate candy from his truck and passed it around. It had come from the States. The candy kisses I had were sort of that light color chocolate gets when it is old. Sitting there in the damp temple set, that didn't seem to matter to anybody. Finally, at 11:00 P.M., the first assistant called a wrap and everybody went home.

Just as I was going to the car, there was a radio message that Francis wanted me to wait for him. I walked down the path near Marlon's houseboat dressing room. The bodyguards and drivers and the wardrobe and makeup people were waiting for Francis and Marlon and Marty. We stood around and talked for about an hour and then the wardrobe and makeup men went home. It was starting to rain again, so I decided to go down to the boat and interrupt them and see if I couldn't get them to finish up. I was really sleepy and my clothes were wet and soggy. When I got to the houseboat, I thought for a moment maybe they were asleep or gone. The light was low and I couldn't see anyone. They were down in the back, sitting by the table. When I went in, I felt like I was slicing into their conversation. The air was like a solid mass of words. I started to wake up immediately. I sat down next to Marlon on the couch, only I miscalculated and sat halfway on a tray of leftover dinner. I never do those kinds of things. Being in Marlon's presence is not natural. I do things or say things that I wouldn't ordinarily. What a burden it must be for him to hardly have anyone who feels completely natural around him.

September 16, Pagsanjan

Last night Francis climbed up a scaffolding onto a lighting platform and just lay there. It was raining lightly, and when I climbed up, it was wet with standing puddles on top. He was about as miserable as I have ever seen him. It was his ultimate nightmare. He was on this huge set of this huge production with every asset mortgaged against the outcome; hundreds of crew members were waiting. Brando was due on the set and he was delaying because he didn't like the scene, and Francis hadn't been able to write a scene that Marlon thought was really right. The ultimate actor on the ultimate set of the ultimate production with the ultimate cinematographer, and Francis with no scene to play. He kept saying, "Let me out of here, let me just quit and go home. I can't do it. I can't see it. If I can't see it, I can't do anything. This is like an opening night; the curtain goes up and there is no show."

Vittorio came out from the interior of the temple where he was lighting and said, "Look, Francis, I think we can do something. I have made some strange light and smoke and I think you can do something." Finally Francis dragged himself back inside. Marlon came and they began doing an improvisation and shooting that. After the third take, it was midnight and they wrapped.

Francis was starting to feel better. It seemed to me that what was getting him down was that his talent is the ability to discriminate, the ability to see a moment of truthful acting and distinguish it from all the others. Since Brando hadn't started to work, there was nothing for Francis to use to lead him to the next moment and the next. As soon as Brando started to improvise, Francis could begin to direct, that is, see the direction the scene should go. Today he wrote a scene based on the improvisation. He is starting to see it.

September 21, Pagsanjan

I am in the kitchen. Sofia is making a pizza out of play dough. She is painting chunks yellow for cheese, red for tomatoes and green for peppers. The flour has weevils in it. I guess it's been in the canister since Manila. Now and then a groggy weevil gets up out of one of the pieces and walks off across the tray.

Francis, Marlon and Marty are in the living room talking about today's scene. I just brought Marty some coffee. I thought about women's lib. Here I am in the kitchen with the kid, making coffee.

I can hear parts of the conversation coming from the other room. "Don't you see, Kurtz is caught in this conflict of . . ." A truck just passed by, the chickens are crowing next door and the landlord's radio is blaring, Glen Campbell is singing "I'm a Rhinestone Cowboy."

September 29, Pagsanjan

I am sitting on a rock on the set. It feels like a rock, it looks like a temple fragment, but I know it was made by the art department. The crew has been waiting since 8:00 A.M. to shoot. It is almost three in the afternoon now. Francis and Marlon have been down in his houseboat, working out his death scene today, and most of yesterday. The assistant director is saying that if they don't start shooting in the next thirty minutes, it will be too late to get a shot today: "Eighty thousand dollars down the drain."

October 8

This is the last day that Marlon works. The shot is outside by the CONEX container. This morning it was warm and sort of tropical and balmy, not miserably hot. Francis and Marlon were talking out the scene. I got a couple of shots of them at a distance, sitting outside an Ifugao house, deep in discussion. It started to rain and everybody began to cover equipment. Now it is pouring. Francis and Marlon and Marty are crouched under an Ifugao house. I am sitting under a lighting reflector, quite comfortably. Some of my equipment got wet before I could get it covered. The crew is all huddled in little bunches under things. Bill and Jimmy Keane are under here with me. We've been talking about the Metropolitan Museum of Art. Jimmy was an elevator operator at the hotel where we stay in New York. He is talking about all the famous people he met who came to the hotel while he worked there. He said his favorite was Frank Capra, the director. "A little fellow, well over four feet."

I can see some big hunks of clear sky across the river. I can imagine Francis's tension, sitting out the rain when this is the last day Marlon works and there is a scene left to get.

I am listening to the sound of the rain hitting the reflector and watching all the little dramas of the other groups of people huddled together. The Italians started a dice game under the umbrella with the arc light. The prop- and wardrobe men are pitching little rocks, trying to hit a metal container. They are making bets and running out into the rain to get fresh supplies of rocks. Mario is getting a back rub from one of the Filipino electricians. Jimmy is talking about Monte Cristo cigars. The bottom of my shelter is starting to run with mud.

ROGER EBERT

The whole architecture of the celebrity interview has collapsed since this was written in 1970. When I began as a journalist, it was possible to win small glimpses of the real lives of celebrity subjects; today publicists try to dictate every condition of a brief séance with a star, which typically takes place in a neutral hotel room with the publicist hovering by the door. The resulting bloodless interview is usually about "career choices" and "how nice it was to work" with the subject's director and costars. At the same time the most intimate details of the subject's life appear in the weekly tabloids. I wonder if the publicists realize they could serve their clients better by protecting them less. Is this, for example, a negative portrait of Lee Marvin? I think not, because Marvin (1924–1987) allows himself to be seen in completely unrehearsed human terms. (His publicist, Paul Bloch, remained serene.) It had been arranged that I would spend some time with Lee Marvin in his Malibu beach home, for a profile in Esquire, and that arrangement was not affected by the fact that he was hung over and drinking. Of all the celebrity interviews I've done over the years, this is my favorite. I was free to share those hours and whatever happened during them.

"Lee Marvin"

WHO TAKES THE PILL FOR US NOW?
MALIBU, 1970

The door flew open from inside, revealing Lee Marvin in a torrid embrace, bent over Michelle Triola, a fond hand on her rump. "Love!" he said. "It's all love in this house. Nothing but love. *All you need is love. . . .*"

Michelle smiled as if to say, well. . . .

"What's this?" Marvin cried. He snatched the *Los Angeles Times* from his doormat and threw it at the front gate. LaBoo went careening after it, barking crazily.

"You bring that paper back here and I'll kill you," Marvin told LaBoo. He snarled at LaBoo and walked down the hallway and into the living room. LaBoo charged past him and jumped onto a chair. "LaBoo, you son of a bitch, I'm gonna kill you," Marvin said.

"Hello, LaBoo," Michelle said tenderly.

LaBoo wagged his tail.

"I need a beer," Marvin said. "Who's gonna get me a beer? *I'm* gonna get me a beer? I feel like a beer. Hell, I *need* a beer. Where are my glasses?" He peered around him. "Ever read this book? I got it for Christmas or some goddamn thing. A history of the West. Look here. All these cowboys are wearing chaps. Workingmen, see. Look here. Bronco Billy dressed up in the East's conception of the Western hero. See. From a dime novel. That's how authentic a Western we made when we made *Monte Walsh*. Where's that beer? That author, he knows what it was *really* like. Get me a beer."

"Finish your coffee," Michelle said.

"I said get me a *beer.*" Marvin paged through the book of Western lore, stopping to inspect an occasional page. When he stopped, he would pause for a moment and then whistle, moving on. Then silence. Only the pages turning. Now and again, a whistle.

"Where's that fucking beer, baby?" He dropped the book on the rug. "Look, if I want to develop an image, I'll do it my own fucking way."

Michelle went into the kitchen to get a beer.

"Anne . . . she seemed to be a nice girl," Marvin said. "This was when I was in London for the Royal Command Performance of *Paint Your Wagon*. Nice-enough girl, Anne. Lord somebody or other kept pounding me on the back. I told him I'd already made other arrangements." Marvin whistled. "He kept poking me. Lord somebody or other, never did catch his name. I advised him to fuck off." A pause. A whistle. "If that's swinging, I'll bring them back to Malibu. Maybe to commit suicide . . ."

A record, *Victory at Sea,* dropped on the stereo changer. *"Victory at Sea,"* Marvin said. "Well, thousands of ships went under, right? Tells you something."

Michelle returned with a bottle of Heineken. Marvin drank from the bottle, a long, deep drink, and then he smiled at her. "You gonna take off your clothes and jump on him now? Or later?" He smiled again. "Michelle, she's a good sport."

"Lee!" Michelle said.

"Where the hell are my glasses?" Marvin said. He took another drink from the bottle and looked on the floor around his chair.

"He took the lenses out of his glasses," Michelle said. "Last night. He said he didn't want to read any more scripts."

"Not another single goddamned script," Marvin said.

"So he took the lenses out of his glasses."

"I want simply to be the real Lee. The *real* Lee. The real Kirk Lee."

"You left the real Lee in London."

"Now I'm Kirk Lee. Not Lee Lee. Kirk Lee. I flew back from London with Sir Cary. I told him, I said, *Sir Cary, that's a nice watch you have."* Marvin pointed his finger like a gun and made a noise that began with a whistle and ended with a pop. *"A real nice watch, Sir Cary,* I said." Whistle-pop. On the pop, his thumb came down.

"Cary has the same watch you have," Michelle said.

"No," Marvin said, *"he* has the same watch *I* have. If I saw his watch in a photograph, I could identify it anywhere. But, who gives a shit?" Whistle-pop. "Going back to the old neighborhood. This was London. What was it? Bulgaria? No, *Belgravia.* Well it was only seven-thirty in the morning. *Don't you want to stay up and watch the junkies jet in?"* Whistle. "Fuck you, pal, I'm getting some *sleep."*

A moment's silence for symbolic sleep. Marvin closed his eyes and threw his head back against his chair. There was a door at the other end of the living room, opening onto a porch that overlooked the beach. Through the door you could hear the waves hitting the beach, *crush, crush,* and at this moment, while Marvin pretended to sleep, the morning resolved itself as a melancholy foggy Saturday.

"Have another anchovy, sweetheart," Marvin said, rousing himself at last. He drained the Heineken.

"I love them," Michelle said.

"She's been eating nothing but anchovies for the past day and a half," Marvin said. "You know why you like anchovies so much all of a sudden? You're knocked up. You're gonna have a little Lee Marvin."

"Lee!" Michelle said. "You can't say that."

"Why not?" he said. "Put it down: Michelle's knocked up. If you make it good enough, they'll never print it. And if they *do* print it, and come around and ask me, *did you really say that?*, I'll say, *sure, I said it.* I need another beer."

Michelle got up and went into the kitchen.

"She's not *really* knocked up," Marvin said.

He threw a leg over the arm of the chair. "I got a haircut before I went to London," he said. "I mean, it got a little ridiculous there after a while. I didn't get my hair cut for two movies, and it got a little long. I'm going back to a . . . not a crew cut. Back to, oh, about a Presbyterian length. I'm tired of all this horseshit about hair."

Marvin sighed, got up, and walked out to the porch. The air was heavy with fog.

"That goddamn buoy," he said. Just down from his stretch of beach, a buoy stood in the sand. "It floated in one morning and they stuck it up there. It's on their property. Christ, I hate the sight of it, but I can't do anything about it. It looks like a phallic symbol. Hell, it *is* a phallic symbol. You get up in the morning and come out here and there's that goddamn *buoy* staring you in the face."

He yawned. Down on the beach, a setter ran howling at a flock of birds. There was a chill this Saturday morning, and sounds were curiously muffled. Marvin peered out to sea. "Is that Jennifer Jones coming in on the surf?" he said. "No? Good."

Michelle came up behind him with a Heineken. "Thanks, sweetheart." He walked back into the living room and sat down. "What was that we saw? Bob and Carol and Bill and Ted? What a piece of shit that was. Good performances, but what a piece of shit."

"I loved it," Michelle said.

"You go for all that touch-me-feel-me bullshit anyway," Marvin said. "Esalen. They take your money and teach you to put one hand on two nipples. Big fucking deal, baby."

"It's about *love*," Michelle said. "It's *looking* at people. Look at me with love, Lee."

"Take off your clothes, baby." Whistle. "Who takes the Pill for us now?" Pop! "LaBoo, come in here, you mean black prince." LaBoo came in from the porch and settled down on the rug with resignation and a sigh. "And *still* she wants to marry me," Marvin said. "It used to be, we'd check into a hotel, it was Mr. Marvin and Miss Triola. So she changed her name to Marvin, to save all that embarrassment. Now it's Mr. Marvin and Miss Marvin. . . ."

He yawned and took a pull of Heineken. Michelle excused herself and wandered down the hallway. Silence. The waves. "I never did read that interview in *Playboy*," Marvin said. "I read excerpts. It was all a lot of shit. They sent some guy to interview me. I sucked him in *so bad*. I even gave him the garbage-man story. *How do you feel about violence in films*, he says. *I'll throw you the fuck out of here if you ask me that again*, I say."

Michelle wandered back into the room. "You took some pills?" Marvin said. "How many did you take? Should I call the doctor?"

Michelle smiled. LaBoo, on the carpet, sighed deeply.

"LaBoo," Michelle said, "you're supposed to stand around and pose in a movie star's home. That's what a poodle is for."

"He stands around and shits, that's what kind of star I am," Marvin said. "It's not everybody gets a Jap lighter from Hugh Hefner. *Gee, thanks, Hef.*" Whistle. Pop. "Well, the royal family *seemed* to like the movie, anyway. Lord somebody said he liked Jean Seberg. That was something."

"Jean has good insides."

"What?"

"I said Jean Seberg has good insides," Michelle said.

"Jesus Christ, I'm living with a dyke!" Marvin said. Whistle! Pop! "My ex-wife had something about *Playboy* when I read it."

"*Playboy* exploits women," Michelle said. "Women's liberation is against *Playboy*."

"Against *Playboy*?" Marvin said. "Whyever more?"

"It exploits women," Michelle said. "It presents women as sex objects."

"Why not?" Marvin said. "Take a snatch away from a broad and what's she got left?" Marvin spread his legs and breathed deeply. *"Oh me oh my, why must I be a sex symbol? Why won't they let me act?"*

LaBoo snorted in his sleep, waking himself. He stood up, made a circle, lay down again and closed his eyes.

The telephone rang. LaBoo growled with his eyes closed. Michelle went to answer it.

"Who's calling?" Marvin said.

"Meyer Mishkin."

"Tell him nothing for you today, Meyer, but call back tomorrow." Marvin finished his Heineken, turned it upside down, watched a single drop fall out. "My agent," he said. "He keeps wanting to know if I've read any more scripts. Fuck scripts. You spend the first forty years of your life trying to get in this fucking business, and the next forty years trying to get out. And then when you're making the bread, who needs it?

"Newman has it all worked out. I get a million. He gets a million two, but that includes $200,000 expenses. So, if that's the game . . ." Marvin shrugged. "I never talked to Newman in my life. No, I talked to him on Park Avenue once.

Only to give him a piece of advice. This fifteen-year-old girl wanted his auto-graph. He told her he didn't give autographs, but he'd buy her a beer. *Paul,* I said, *she's only fifteen. I don't give a shit,* he said." Marvin whistled. "I think it shows," he said. "With Newman, it shows. Cut to an old broad in Miami Beach looking at his picture in *Life* magazine: *A Gary Cooper he ain't.*"

Marvin took another beer from Michelle. "'I'm waiting for some young guy to come along and knock me off so I can go to the old actor's home and talk about how great we were in nineteen-you-know. Am I waiting for him? I'd hire guys to knock *him* off. Something the other day really brought it home. . . ."

He rummaged in a stack of magazines and papers next to his chair.

"I lost it."

Michelle held up a book.

"No," he said, "the other one. Yeah, here it is. *The United States Marine Corps in World War II.* Wake Island. Let's see."

He produced a pair of glasses and put them on. "This cat in command. Let's see here . . ." He paged through the book, looking for something. "This cat—yeah, here it is. He was defending the island. When the brass asked the defender of the island if there was anything to be done for them, the cat wired back: *Yes. Send us more Japs.*"

Marvin whistled and squinted down at the page in wonder.

"*Send us more Japs.* Well, Japs were the last thing we needed at the time. Cut to John Wayne: *Yes, send us more Japs!* The bitch of it is, not until years later did it come out that it's the decoder's job to pad messages at the beginning and the end. So all the world was applauding this bastard's nerve, and what the world took as a gesture of defiant heroism was merely padding."

Marvin got up and went into the kitchen. "Something good about Duke, I gotta admit," he called back over his shoulder. "When he's on, he's on. *Send us more Japs.*"

There was a rattle of bottles from the kitchen. "You stole all the beer! Michelle? You drank it all?"

"We're out," Michelle said.

"Make the call," Marvin said, coming back into the living room.

"It'll take them two hours to get here," Michelle said.

"Make the call. Make the call, or I may have to switch to the big stuff."

"I have other plans for you this afternoon."

"No—not that!" Marvin fell back in his chair. "Anything but that!" Horrified.

"It's such a foggy, gray old day," Michelle said. "We ought to just sit in front of the fire and drink Pernod. I like foggy, gray days. . . ."

"Can the dog drink Pernod?" Marvin asked. "Now why the hell did I ask that? The dog gets no Pernod in this house." He stood up and looked through the win-dow at the surf, his hands in his pockets. "I mean she really could have hurt herself, Jennifer. Came floating in on a wave . . . What's the number of the liquor store, honey?"

"Oh, nine four six six something. *You* ought to know."

Marvin went into the kitchen to make the call. "Yeah, hi. Listen, this is Lee Marvin down at 21404." Pause. "Heh, heh. You did, huh? Yeah, well this is me again." Pause. "Heh, heh. Yeah, pal, get anything cold down here. Beer. Yeah. What? Whatdaya mean, light or dark? The green one." He hung up.

"Didn't you order any anchovies?" Michelle said. "It goes back to my Sicilian grandmother."

Another record dropped on the turntable: faint, ghostly harp music. Marvin whirled wildly, looking up into the shadows of the far corners of the room. "Jesus, mother," he said, "will you *please* stay out of the room? I asked you to come only at night." He hit the reject button. "I studied violin when I was very young," he said. "You think I'm a dummy, right? I'm only *in* dummies. *The Dirty Dozen* was a dummy money-maker, and baby, if you want a money-maker, get a dummy."

By now he was rummaging around in the bedroom.

"Lee," Michelle said, "you're not going to put it on and parade around in it again? Are you?"

"Where is it?" Marvin said.

"I think it's in your second drawer," Michelle said. "His cap and gown. He got an honorary degree."

Marvin came out of the bedroom with a pair of binoculars. "Look what I found," he said. He went out on the porch and peered into the mist at a thin line of birds floating beyond the surf. "What are they? Coots, or . . . are they ducks?"

Marvin's son, Chris, walked into the living room. "Hi, Chris," Marvin said. "Are these coots, or . . . ducks?" Chris went out onto the porch and had a look through the binoculars. "Hard to say," Chris said. He put a leash on LaBoo and took him down to the beach for a walk. Marvin fell back into his chair. The grayness of the day settled down again. On the stereo, Johnny Cash was singing "Greensleeves." The beautiful music of "Greensleeves."

"Do you realize," Marvin said, "that he gets three million a year for singing that shit? *I walk the line, I keep my eyes wide open all the time.* I met him in Nashville. He said, *You haven't heard my other stuff? No,* I said, *I haven't.* He sent us his complete twenty-seven fucking albums. Jesus, Johnny, I like your stuff, but for Christ's sake . . ."

Marvin got down on his knees and pulled twenty-seven Johnny Cash albums off a shelf.

"He's embarrassed," Marvin said, "I'm embarrassed. We have nothing to say, really. So he sends me all his albums. I tried to listen to all of them. It took me two weeks."

"How old is Cher?" Michelle said.

"Cher?"

"Yeah."

"We don't know yet," Marvin said. "These glasses are no goddamned good. Where are my glasses?"

"He went out on the porch and stepped on his other glasses," Michelle said. "They didn't break, and he said it was an act of God, telling him not to read any more scripts. So he took the lenses and scaled them into the ocean. Now he can't see."

"Why," Marvin said, "does it take sixty-seven percent of my income to pay the publicist? He says I should take some broad to lunch, right? It costs me thirty-seven dollars to get out of the joint, and then she knocks me. You know what I asked her? *I'll bet you've never had an orgasm, have you,* I asked her."

"Lee, you didn't say that? Really?"

"I never said anything like that in my life."

Another record dropped on the stereo. "When it comes to 'Clair de Lune,' " he said, "I have to go pass water. Tinkle, is the expression. Oh, sweetheart, do you think this day will soon be o'er? I have a hangover. We had fun last night. Went up to the corner, had a few drinks, told a few lies."

He disappeared down the hallway. Chris, a good-looking kid of sixteen or seventeen, came back with LaBoo, who was banished to the porch to dry out. LaBoo squinted in through the window, wet and forlorn. "Poor LaBoo," Michelle said. "It's the second time he's been rejected today."

Marvin returned. "So what have you decided on?" he asked Chris.

"I was looking at a four-door 1956 Mercedes," Chris said.

"Hitler's car?" Marvin said. Whistle. Pop! "Kid, you deserve the best because you're the son of a star. Why don't you get a job?"

"Chris is working at a record store," Michelle said. "He's working for free right now, until the owner of the store makes enough money to pay his employees."

"Jesus Christ," Marvin said.

"I was looking at a BMW," Chris said. "It's $2,100. New, it would be three thousand."

"Why not get new?" Marvin said.

"I don't have three thousand."

"But big daddy does."

"Let's order pizza," Michelle said. She picked up the phone and ordered three pizzas, one with anchovies.

"You're pregnant," Marvin said. "She's got to be. Christopher, you're going to be a grandfather."

LaBoo, who had edged into the house through a crack in the door, walked out of the bedroom now with a pair of women's panties in his mouth.

"Christ, LaBoo, keep those *pants* out of sight." Marvin said. "Last night, she says, *where'd you get these pants? I dunno,* I say. She says, *well they're not mine.* I say, *honey, I sure as hell didn't wear them home."* Marvin sighed and held his hands palms up in resignation. "The only way to solve a situation with a girl," he said, "is just jump on her and things will work out."

He took the pants from LaBoo and threw them back into the bedroom. "So what do you think?" he asked Chris.

"The BMW has fantastic cornering, Dad," Chris said. "It has really fantastic quality."

Marvin paused at the door to look out at the surf. "Don't be deceived by quality," he said. "Get something you like now, and trade it in later. The car may turn out to have such fantastic quality you'll puke seeing it around so long."

He sighed and sat down in his chair again.

LaBoo jumped into his lap.

"LaBoo, you mean black prince," Marvin said, rubbing the dog's head carelessly.

KLAUS KINSKI

The great German director Werner Herzog told me that he was a small boy when he first saw Klaus Kinski (1926–1991), striding through the courtyard of the building where he lived. "I knew at that moment that I would be a film director and that I would direct Kinski," he said. Years later, convincing Kinski to make Aguirre, the Wrath of God *(1972), he told the actor it was his "fate" to make the film. It became legend that Herzog at one point drew a gun on Kinski to require him to stay on the impossible location. Kinski remembers it otherwise. This excerpt is from his memoirs, long unpublished in the United States because of the real possibility of libel suits but finally being released this year. When you read Kinski's venomous attack on Herzog, it is incredible to reflect that he made two additional films with Herzog:* Nosferatu *(1979) and* Fitzcarraldo *(1982), the latter on South American locations similar to those described here.*

from *Kinski Uncut*

Herzog, who's producing the film, also wrote the script—and he wants to direct it, too. I promptly ask him how much money he's got.

When he visits me in my pad, he's so shy that he barely has the nerve to come in. Maybe it's just a ploy. In any case, he lingers at the threshold for such an idiotically long time that I practically have to drag him inside. Once he's here, he starts explaining the movie without even being asked. I tell him that I've read the script and I know the story. But he turns a deaf ear and just keeps talking and talking and talking. I start thinking that he'll never be able to stop talking even if he tries. Not that he talks quickly, "like a waterfall," as people say when someone talks fast and furious, pouring out the words. Quite the contrary: His speech is clumsy, with a toadlike indolence, long-winded, pedantic, choppy. The words tumble from his mouth in sentence fragments, which he holds back as much as possible, as if they were earning interest. It takes forever and a day for him to push out a clump of hardened brain snot. Then he writhes in painful ecstasy, as if he had sugar on his rotten teeth. A very slow blab machine. An obsolete model with a nonworking switch—it can't be turned off unless you cut off the electric power altogether. So I'd have to smash him in the kisser. No, I'd have to knock him unconscious. But even if he were unconscious, he'd keep talking. Even if his vocal cords were sliced through, he'd keep talking like a ventriloquist. Even if his throat were cut and his head were chopped off, speech balloons would still dangle from his mouth like gases emitted by internal decay.

I haven't the foggiest idea what he's talking about, except that he's high as a kite on himself for no visible reason, and he's enthralled by his own daring, which is nothing but dilettantish innocence. When he thinks I finally see what a great guy he is, he blurts out the bad news, explaining in a hardboiled tone about the shitty living and working conditions that lie ahead. He sounds like a judge handing down a well-deserved sentence. And, licking his lips as if he were talking about some culinary delicacy, he crudely and brazenly claims that all the participants are delighted to endure the unimaginable stress and deprivation in order to follow him, Herzog. Why, they would all risk their lives for him without batting an eyelash. He, in any case, will put all his eggs in one basket in order to attain his goal, no matter what it may cost, "do or die," as he puts it in his foolhardy way. And he tolerantly closes his eyes to the spawn of his megalomania, which he mistakes for genius. Granted, he sincerely confesses, he sometimes gets dizzy thinking about his own insane ideas—by which, however, he is simply carried away.

Then suddenly, out of a clear blue sky, he knocks me for a loop: He tries to make me believe that he's got a sense of humor. That is, he almost unintentionally, sort of carelessly hints at it—and, half in jest, he's embarrassed, as if caught with his pants down.

If he initially applied some cheap tricks to get me drunk, he now throws caution to the winds and starts lying through his teeth. He says he enjoys playing pranks; you can go and steal horses with him, and so forth. And since he's already confessed all that, he doesn't want to hide the fact that he can now laugh his head off at his own roguishness. While it's quite obvious that I've never in my life met anybody so dull, humorless, uptight, inhibited, unscrupulous, mindless, depressing, boring, and swaggering, he blithely basks in the glory of the most pointless and most uninteresting punch lines of his braggadocio. Eventually he kneels before himself like a worshipper in front of his idol, and he remains in that position until somebody bends down and raises him from his humble self-worship. After dumping these tons of garbage (which stinks so horribly that I felt like puking), he actually pretends to be a naive, innocent, almost rustic hick—a poetic dreamer, or so he emphasizes, as if he were living in his own little world and didn't have the slightest notion of the brutal material side of things. But I can very easily tell that he considers himself ever so cunning, that he's waiting in ambush, dogging my every step and desperately trying to read my mind. He's racking his brain, trying to determine how he can outfox me in every clause of the contract. In short, he has every intention of bamboozling me.

Still and all, I agree to do the movie—but only because of Peru. I don't even know where it is. Somewhere in South America, between the Pacific, the desert, and the glaciers, and in the most gigantic jungle on earth.

The script is illiterate and primitive. That's my big chance. The jungle smolders in it like something that infects you when you see it, a virus that invades you through your eyes and enters your bloodstream. I feel as if I knew this land with the magical name in some other lifetime. An imprisoned beast can never forget the reality of freedom. The caged bird cranes its neck through the bars to peer at the clouds racing by.

I tell Herzog that Aguirre has to be crippled because his power must not be contingent on his appearance. I'll have a hump. My right arm will be longer than my left, as long as an ape's. My left arm will be shortened so that since I'm a southpaw I have to carry my sword on the right side of my chest, and not in the normal way, on my hip. My left leg will be longer than my right, so that I have to drag it along. I'll advance sideways, like a crab. I'll have long hair—down to my shoulders by the time we start shooting. I won't need a phony hump, or a costumer or a makeup man smearing me up. I will *be* crippled because I *want* to be. I'll get my spine used to my crippling. Just as I'm beautiful when I want to be. Ugly. Strong. Feeble. Short or tall. Old or young. When I want to be. The way I hold myself will lift the cartilage from my joints and use up their gelatin.

I will be crippled—today, now, on the spot, this very instant. Henceforth everything will be geared to my condition: costumes, cuirasses, scabbards, weapons, helmets, boots, and so on.

I determine the costume: I tear a couple of pages out of books showing Old Master paintings. I explain the changes I want, and I fly to Madrid with Herzog to find armor and weapons. After days of rummaging through mountains of rusty scrap metal, I fish out a sword, a dagger, a helmet, and a cuirass, which has to be trimmed because I'm a cripple.

Traveling all the way to the jungle is the worst kind of agony. Penned up in old-fashioned trains, wrecks of trucks, and cagelike buses, we eat and camp out like pigs. Sometimes in Quonset huts or other torture chambers. We can't even think about getting any sleep. We can barely breathe. No toilets, no way to wash. Many days and nights. I stay dressed day and night; otherwise the mosquitoes would eat me alive. I feel as if I'm standing under a nonstop jet of boiling water. Indoors the heat is lethal. But outdoors it's just as venomously hot. Whole mountains of garbage, inundated by a cesspool of human piss and shit. The populace tosses the ripped-out eyes and innards of slaughtered animals into this sewage from hell. Huge carrion birds the size of great Danes strut and squat on this horror as if it were their private playground.

Wherever I go I see these disgusting Quonset huts. If only I didn't have to lay eyes on these half-finished cement barracks with corrugated-iron roofs. Nothing is completed. Everything is abandoned halfway through, as if it had been surprised by the decay. Iron window shades and fences jeer at you. Why?

Garbage heaps, sewage, eyes, innards, breeding grounds, carrion birds and— TV antennas. Just like in New York, Paris, London, Tokyo, or Hong Kong, but more loathsome.

The road into the wilderness is long and tortuous—but no abomination is too unbearable to escape this hell on earth.

And as if Minhoï and I were to be rewarded for our getaway, we feel that our hair is becoming silkier, our skin softer, like the fur of wild beasts that have been set free; our bodies are lither and suppler, our muscles are tensing for a leap, our senses are more alert and receptive. Minhoï has never been more beautiful since the tiger trap in Vietnam.

Swelling up from mosquito bites without having eaten or drunk anything, we reel toward the next leg of our journey.

A little Inca girl stands on the runway for military aircraft. She's got a small monkey on her arm and she wants to sell it. But the terrified monkey clings to the girl, afraid that the buyer might take it away.

Here we clamber into ancient, battered transport planes for paratroopers, and the propellers rage in my temples like pneumatic hammers. A pungent stench, the odor of gasoline, hunger, thirst, headaches, and stomach cramps, and no toilet here either. Pent up and huddling together on the hot steel floor of the windowless plane. Hour after hour. During the flight each passenger in turn can spend one moment climbing from the plane's tomblike rear into the cockpit and peering out through a tiny window. Far below, the green ocean, thousands of miles of jungle, with a yellow tangle of vipers winding through it—the biggest river network in the world.

Next, single-engine amphibians that have to nose-dive to avoid missing that slim chance when the jungle opens—and promptly closes again.

Then more trucks and bus cages. Indian canoes. And finally the rafts, on which we stand, chained to one another, to the cargo, and to the raft, as we shoot over raging rapids. Our fists clutching ropes, as if we were making a laughable effort to halt runaway horses by clasping their reins even though the horses have already plunged off a cliff. The raft is too heavily loaded; the Indians warned us. But blowhard Herzog, arrogant and ignorant as he is, mocked their warnings and called them ridiculous. We're all in costume and fully equipped, because we wanted to shoot while riding the rapids. Herzog misses out on the grandest and most incomprehensible things because he doesn't even notice them. I keep yelling at the stupid cameraman through the thunder of our nose-dive, telling him to at least roll the camera because we're risking our lives. But all he says is that Herzog ordered him not to press the button without his, Herzog's, say-so.

I'm disgusted by this whole movie mob—they act as if you're supposed to shoot a flick in a pigpen.

My heavy leather costume, my long boots, helmet, cuirass, sword, and dagger weigh over thirty pounds. If the raft were to capsize because of Herzog's delusions of grandeur, I'd be doomed. I'd be unable to get out of my cuirass and leather doublet, which are buckled in back. Besides, the rapids are cut through with a chain of jagged reefs, and their razorlike tips lurk under the spume like piranhas, sometimes even looming out of the lashed waters.

And so, like a fired missile, we hurtle downstream while the steep waves attack our raft like hysterical bulls and clap together way over our heads. The air is filled with foam like white drool.

Suddenly, as if the plunging water had furiously spat us out, we glide almost soundlessly along a calm and powerful branch of the river in the middle of the jungle and deeper and deeper into its interior. There it lies: the wilderness. It seizes me. Sucks me in—hot and naked like the sweaty, sticky, naked body of a lovesick woman with all her mysteries and wonders. I gape at the jungle and can't stop marveling and worshipping. . . .

Animals as graceful as in fairy tales . . . Plants strangling one another in their embraces . . . Orchids stretched on stumps of rotten trees like young girls on the laps of dirty old men . . . Radiant metallic-blue butterflies as big as my head . . . Pearly floods of butterflies alighting on my mouth and my hands—the panther's eye blending into the flowers . . . Frothy streams of flowers; green, red, and yellow clouds of birds . . . Silver suns . . . Violet fogs . . . The kissing lips of the fish . . . The golden song of the fish . . .

We're going to be living exclusively on rafts for the next two months. Drifting downstream toward the Amazon. Minhoï and I have a raft to ourselves. We either float way ahead of the other rafts or lag behind as far as possible. When night falls, we moor our raft to lianas. Then I lie awake, diving into the galaxies and starry archipelagoes, which hang down so low that I can reach out and feel them.

We have a small Indian canoe that we tie to the raft, towing it along. If I don't have to shoot, we sneak away in the canoe, searching for cracks in the jungle wall. Sometimes we penetrate a tight slit that may have never existed before and that will instantly close up again. The water inside the flooded forest is so still that it barely seems affected by our paddles, which we dip cautiously to avoid making any noise.

Perhaps no boat has ever glided across these waters, perhaps no man has set foot here in millions of years. Not even a native. We wait without speaking. For hours on end. I feel the jungle coming nearer, the animals, the plants, which have been watching us for a long while without showing themselves. For the first time in my life I have no past. The present is so powerful that it snuffs out all bygones. I know that I'm free, truly free. I am the bird that has managed to break out of its cage—that spreads its wings and soars into the sky. I take part in the universe.

Although I constantly try to keep out of his way, Herzog sticks to me like a shithouse fly. The mere thought of his existence here in the wilderness turns my stomach. When I see him approaching in the distance, I yell at him to halt. I shout that he stinks. That he disgusts me. That I don't want to listen to his bullshit. That I can't stand him!

I keep hoping he'll attack me. Then I'll shove him into a side branch of the river, where the still waters teem with murderous piranhas, and I'll watch them shred him to bits. But he doesn't do it; he doesn't attack me. He seems unfazed when I treat him like a piece of shit. Besides, he's too chicken. He attacks only when he thinks he'll keep the upper hand. Herzog pounces on a native, an Indian who's taken the job to keep his family from starving and puts up with anything for fear of being kicked out. Or else he assails a stupid, untalented actor or a helpless animal. Today he ties up a llama in a canoe and sends it tearing down the rapids—supposedly because this is required by the plot of the movie, which he wrote himself! I find out about the llama only when it's too late. The animal is already drifting toward the whirlpool, and no one can save it. I spot it rearing in its mortal fear and yanking at its fetters, struggling to escape its gruesome execution. Then it vanishes behind a bend of the river, shattering against the jagged reefs and dying a tortuous death by drowning.

Now I hate that killer's guts. I shriek into his face that I want to see him croak like the llama that he executed. He should be thrown alive to the crocodiles! An anaconda should strangle him slowly! A poisonous spider should sting him and paralyze his lungs! The most venomous serpent should bite him and make his brain explode! No panther claws should rip open his throat—that would be much too good for him! No! The huge red ants should piss into his lying eyes and gobble up his balls and his guts! He should catch the plague! Syphilis! Malaria! Yellow fever! Leprosy! It's no use; the more I wish him the most gruesome deaths, the more he haunts me.

We drift down the river all day long, shooting endlessly. Night falls. Nevertheless we all gather ashore, where a night scene is to be filmed. Herzog and his production morons haven't even supplied illumination—no flashlight, nothing. The night is pitch-black and we keep falling on our faces, one after another. We tumble into swampy holes, stumble over roots and tree trunks, run into the knives of thorny palms, get our feet caught in lianas, and almost drown. The area is teeming with snakes, which kill at night after storing up their reserves of poison throughout the day. We're completely exhausted, and once again it's been an eternity since we ate or drank anything, including water. No one has a clue as to what, where, and why we're supposed to shoot in this garbage dump, which stinks to high heaven.

Suddenly, in full armor, I plunge into a swamp hole. The harder I try to get my body out of the mud, the deeper I sink. Finally, in a blind fury, I yell, "I'm splitting! Even if I have to paddle all the way to the Atlantic!"

"If you split, I'll ruin you!" says that wimp Herzog, looking scared of the chance he's taking.

"Ruin me how, you bigmouth?" I ask him, hoping he'll attack me so I can kill him in self-defense.

"I'll shoot you," he babbles, like a paralytic whose brain has softened. "Eight bullets are for you, and the ninth is for me!"

Whoever heard of a pistol or a rifle with nine bullets? There's no such thing! Besides, he has no firearm; I know it for a fact. He's got no rifle or pistol, not even a machete. Not even a penknife. Not even a bottle opener. I'm the only one with a rifle: a Winchester. I have a special permit from the Peruvian government. To buy bullets I had to spend days on end running my legs off from one police station to the next for signatures, stamps, all that shit.

"I'm waiting, you vermin," I say, truly glad that things have reached this pass. "I'm going back to my raft now and I'll be waiting for you. If you come, I'll shoot you down."

Then I stride back to our raft, where Minhoï has fallen asleep in her hammock. I load my Winchester and I wait.

At around four A.M. Herzog comes paddling up to our raft and apologizes.

Herzog is a miserable, hateful, malevolent, avaricious, money-hungry, nasty, sadistic, treacherous, blackmailing, cowardly, thoroughly dishonest creep. His so-called "talent" consists of nothing but tormenting helpless creatures and, if necessary, torturing them to death or simply murdering them. He doesn't care about anyone or anything except his wretched career as a so-called filmmaker. Driven by a pathological addiction to sensationalism, he creates the most senseless difficulties and dangers, risking other people's safety and even their lives—just so he can eventually say that he, Herzog, has beaten seemingly unbeatable odds. For his movies he hires retards and amateurs whom he can push around (and allegedly hypnotize!), and he pays them starvation wages or zilch. He also uses freaks and cripples of every conceivable size and shape, merely to look interesting. He doesn't have the foggiest inkling of how to make movies. He doesn't even try to direct the actors anymore. Long ago, when I ordered him to keep his trap shut, he gave up asking me whether I'm willing to carry out his stupid and boring ideas.

If he wants to shoot another take because he, like most directors, is insecure, I tell him to go fuck himself. Usually the first take is okay, and I won't repeat anything—certainly not on his say-so. Every scene, every angle, every shot is determined by me, and I refuse to do anything unless I consider it right. So I can at least partly save the movie from being wrecked by Herzog's bungling.

After eight weeks most of the crew are still living like pigs. Penned together on rafts like cattle going to slaughter, they eat garbage fried in lard, and, most dangerous of all, they guzzle the river water, which can give them all kinds of diseases, even leprosy. None of them is vaccinated against any of these deadly scourges.

Minhoï and I cook alone on our raft. We dump soil on the wooden floor and start a fire. If either of us dives into the river to swim or wash, the other watches out for piranhas. Normally we have nothing to cook, and we feed on fantastic jungle fruits, which contain enough liquid. But these heavenly fruits are hard to get since we float downstream almost nonstop, and often there are long stretches when we can't go ashore to look for produce.

Eventually we start feeling our malnutrition. We grow weaker; my belly swells up, and I'm all skin and bones. The others are even worse off.

The wilderness isn't interested in arrogant bigmouth movie makers. It has no pity for those who flout its laws.

At three in the morning we're violently awakened on our rafts. We're told there's no time for breakfast, even coffee. We'll only be traveling for twenty minutes, up to the next Indian village on the river. There we'll get everything. The alleged twenty minutes turn into eighteen hours. Herzog has lied to us, as usual.

With our heads in heavy steel helmets that get so hot from the pounding sun that they burn us, we're exposed to the ruthless heat for days on end, without shelter, without the slightest shade, without food or drink. People drop like flies. First the girls, then the men, one after another. Almost everyone's legs are festering from mosquito bites and distorted by swelling.

Toward evening, we finally reach an Indian village, but it's blazing away. Herzog set it on fire, and even though we're starving and dying of thirst, reeling, exhausted after eighteen hours of infernal heat, we have to attack the village— just as it says in the mindless script.

We spend the night in the village, camping in the miserable barracks that haven't burned down. Giant rats insolently frolic about, circling closer and closer, drawing nearer and nearer to our bodies. They probably sense how feeble we are, and they're waiting for the right time to pounce on us. More and more of them appear.

Someone tells Herzog that his people can't continue if we don't get better food and especially water. Herzog answers that they can drink from the river. Besides, he goes on, they ought to collapse from exhaustion and starvation: That's what's called for in the script. Herzog and his head producer have their own secret cache of fresh vegetables, fruit, French camembert, olive oil, and beverages.

As we drift along, one of the Americans falls dangerously ill; he's got yellow fever and a high temperature, and he's writhing on the raft. Herzog claims that the American is malingering; he refuses to let him be brought ashore at Iquitos, which is getting closer and closer.

When we're near Iquitos and our rafts drift into the Amazon, we ignore Herzog and carry our patient ashore, to a hospital. We take the day off in order to buy the most necessary food, mineral water, bandages, medicines, and salves for mosquito bites.

Ten weeks later the final scene of the movie is shot: Aguirre, the sole survivor, his mind gone, is on his raft with several hundred monkeys, floating downstream toward the Atlantic. Most of the monkeys on the raft jump into the water and swim back to the jungle. A gang of trappers plans to sell them to American laboratories for experiments. Herzog has borrowed them. When only some hundred monkeys are left, waiting to dive into the waves and regain their freedom, I order Herzog to film right away. I know that this opportunity won't knock twice. When the take is done, the last monkeys spring into the river and swim toward the jungle, which receives them.

MIKE ROYKO

Mike Royko and John Belushi didn't look at all alike, but Belushi was the right choice to play a Royko-esque character in the movies because he came from the same Chicago neighborhood, spoke the same language, and had been studying Royko since he was a child; few actors are given such preparation. Continental Divide, *directed by Michael Apted, is a movie that's overlooked on Belushi's filmography—it wasn't one of his big hits, and it didn't permit the kind of over-the-top performance that made him famous—but it has a lot of heart to it. One might have wished for a story set entirely in the newspaper world of Chicago, where Royko is a modern reincarnation of the* Front Page *era, instead of all the silliness about the love affair with the bird-watcher, but in its own way the movie is charming. Like Royko, I knew Belushi; I remember late nights in the speakeasy he and Dan Aykroyd opened behind the Earl of Old Town, across the street from Second City. Like Royko, I miss him. There wasn't a mean bone in his body.*

John Belushi

BELUSHI'S OK, BUT . . .

September 27, 1981

At least a hundred people have asked me for my reaction to the movie *Continental Divide,* which recently opened.

Even radio and TV stations want to interview me on the subject.

It isn't that I'm a movie expert, because I'm not. I just like to look at them, especially ones with Bo Derek.

But the male star of *Continental Divide* plays a chain-smoking newspaper columnist who regularly appears on page two of the *Chicago Sun-Times.* And the movie's publicists have said that he is supposed to be a "Royko-like" character.

So, obviously, part of my reaction is that I feel flattered.

Of course, I'm not the first newspaperman to be portrayed in a movie.

In *All the President's Men,* Bob Woodward was played by Robert Redford, whom many women consider to be the world's handsomest man.

In the same movie, Carl Bernstein was played by Dustin Hoffman, who many women say has an intense, electric sexuality about him.

And in that same movie, editor Ben Bradlee was played by Jason Robards, who many women say has a craggy-faced, tough, worldly, mature sex appeal.

But me? My character was played by pudgy John Belushi, who became famous as Bluto, the gluttonous, disgusting fraternity slob in the movie *Animal House.* Many women say that he makes them want to throw up and dial 911.

So as much as I like Belushi personally, I think the producers might have made a mistake in casting my part.

I think Paul Newman would have been a better choice, although he's older than I am. And in appearance we're different because he has blue eyes and mine are brownish-green.

And I would have been satisfied with Clint Eastwood, although he's taller than I am. Or even Burt Reynolds or Alan Alda.

Some of my friends have said John Travolta would have been the perfect choice to play me. He's probably too young, but I suppose if they touched his sideburns with a bit of gray, he would have been believable in the part.

As to the plot of the movie itself, I had mixed reactions. Some of it was realistic, and some of it was ridiculous.

Some examples:

The movie began with the columnist picking on a dishonest Chicago alderman. That's realistic. I can no more ignore a Chicago alderman than a dog can ignore a fireplug.

However, the alderman soon has the columnist beaten to a pulp by two Chicago cops. That's unrealistic. Chicago cops haven't beaten up a newsman since the 1968 Democratic convention, and most of those newsmen were from New York and Washington, so they had it coming.

After the columnist is hospitalized by the beating, his editor is so concerned for his safety that he gets him out of town, sending him into a remote mountain wilderness to try to interview a female, hermit-like bird-expert who lives in the mountains and studies eagles.

That's unrealistic. For one thing, I'm afraid of heights. And I'd never climb a mountain to interview a bird-watcher. I'd ask her to come down the mountain for dinner so we could study such birds as coq au vin, or rock cornish hen and wild rice.

On the way up the mountain, the columnist loses his supply of liquor and cigarettes and is heartbroken. That's stunningly realistic. In fact, I wept during that part of the film.

But he goes on without them. That's unrealistic. I would have immediately gone back down the mountain to the nearest bar to get new supplies. Then I would have grabbed the next train back to Chicago.

When he finally finds the female bird-watcher, she turns out to be beautiful, self-reliant and brilliant, and she thinks the columnist is a jerk. That is so grimly realistic that I almost left the theater.

But later, she becomes fond of him, and they ended up more or less sharing the same sleeping bag, which wasn't very realistic, since a bird-watcher's vision couldn't be *that* bad.

Then he leaves her in the mountains and comes back to Chicago, where he just mopes around feeling miserable, low, blue, and filled with self-pity. That's realistic because I feel that way when things are going good.

But soon he pulls himself out of the dumps by chasing the crooked alderman again, and that's realistic. There's nothing like good, clean sport to make a person feel better.

Then the beautiful bird-watcher turns up in Chicago and they resume their romance, and he takes her to eat in the restaurant on the ninety-fifth floor of the John Hancock. That's unrealistic. At that joint's prices, she'd have to eat cheeseburgers in Billy Goat's.

I won't describe the finish of the movie, although it has a happy ending. And that's unrealistic, especially considering that once he got back from the mountain he had a chance to replenish his liquor supply, and when she came to Chicago, she had a chance to meet lean young men who wear gold chains and Gucci shoes.

There was one other thing that bothered me (and made my friends hoot and jeer and snicker at me): the sex scene, which wasn't at all explicit, except that the columnist didn't have any clothes on from the waist up.

As I bluntly told Belushi when he asked me about that scene: "John, I didn't like it because I don't have a hairy back."

And he answered: "Yeah? And you don't have a hairy head, either."

See? They should have cast Yul Brynner in my part.

MY BELUSHI PALS

March 7, 1982

Like so many Chicagoans, last Thursday night I was watching a rerun of the original "Saturday Night Live" show.

I was rewarded when John Belushi came on to do one of his outrageous skits.

As happened whenever I saw John perform, I felt a mix of emotions.

Amusement, of course. All he had to do was lift a brow and curl his lip and he could make me laugh.

But I also felt pride. As I wrote here once before, I go back a long way with the Belushi family. John's late Uncle Pete was one of my closest friends and was godfather to my first child. John's father and I were also friends. I first set eyes on John when he was about five years old, running around his uncle's back yard while I devoured his Aunt Marion's wonderful Greek cooking. I don't remember that he was very funny then. But he and the other Belushi kids were sure noisy.

So when John became successful, I suppose I felt something like a distant uncle and was proud for him.

But, as I watched him on my TV or in a movie theater, I always felt puzzled. Where had this incredible comic instinct come from? His parents were good people, but not visibly humorous. Yet they produced two sons, John and Jim, who have the rare gift of being able to make strangers laugh.

I remember when I first learned that John had become an entertainer. It had to be, oh, a dozen years ago and I was at an independent political rally at a big restaurant on the South Side. A young man came up to me and, in a shy way, said: "Uncle Mike?"

I guess I blinked for a moment because he said: "You don't remember me?"

I said: "I know you're one of the Belushi kids by your goofy face, but I'm not sure which one."

He laughed. "I'm John. Adam's son."

I asked him if he was there because he was interested in politics.

"I just joined Second City. We're going to be doing a few skits here tonight."

I was impressed. Second City was already a nationally known improvisational theater group. I wish I could say that after I saw him perform, I knew he would one day be a big star. But I didn't. I could see he had a flair, but I wouldn't have bet you money that by the time he was thirty, he'd have one of the most familiar faces in America. A lot of people are funny, but very few have a talent that might be called genius.

As I said, I always had a mix of feelings when I watched John. And last Thursday night, I also felt a twinge of sad nostalgia.

That's because he was playing Pete the Greek, the owner of the short-order diner. You know the one: "Chizbooga, chizbooga, cheeps, cheeps, cheeps."

Whenever I watched him do that character, it was like flipping back in time almost thirty years.

I'd be sitting in a short-order diner in Logan Square, waiting for my wife to finish work upstairs in a doctor's office. The diner was where Eddie's Barbeque now stands, just across the side street from where the old "L" terminal used to be.

John's Uncle Pete would be at the grill, slapping cheeseburgers on the grill, jiggling the fries. Marion would be serving the food and coffee and handling the cash register.

I don't remember if Pete said "chizbooga" and "cheeps" exactly the way John later did. His thick accent was Albanian, not Greek. But it was close.

And somewhere in another neighborhood, in another short-order joint, Adam Belushi was slapping cheeseburgers on another grill. Everybody in the family was chasing the American dream. And they were doing it the way immigrants have always done it. Whatever works—and never mind how many grease burns you get on your arms.

If it was a Friday, we'd probably wind up in Peter's third-floor flat or my attic flat, drinking Metaxa and talking about the things we might do some day. If I ever got off that weekly neighborhood newspaper and he and Adam could pyramid those short-order grills into the restaurant of his dreams.

We were all together the night a few years later that the dream restaurant opened. Adam, Pete, and me and our wives. The place had thick carpets and cloth wallpaper, oil paintings, a piano player in the bar and the best prime rib I've ever had. Maybe you remember it—Fair Oaks, on Dempster, in Morton Grove. It's now a big Mexican restaurant.

We toasted their success. It was a long way from tending sheep in Albania, and they had earned it. It didn't stop there, either. Before long there were other businesses. Peter figured he might as well go on and become an American tycoon.

But life has a way of giving you the gladhand. Then slamming you with a fist.

A few years ago, Pete, still in his forties, died. At the funeral, we talked about John and how he had gone to New York and was starting to make a name, and how proud everybody was.

And the last time I saw John, we talked about those times and my friend Pete. It might surprise those who saw him only on the TV or in movies, but he was still shy and often quiet. And he had not let his success and wealth turn him into a jerk. He was still a genuinely nice kid.

That was the night his movie *Continental Divide* opened in Chicago and there was a party after the show. A reporter for *Rolling Stone,* who covered the evening, later wrote that as the evening ended, John and I were hugging.

I guess we were. When you feel like a proud uncle, and see the kid up there on a movie screen, you ought to give him a hug.

This column seems to have rambled. I'm sorry, but I just heard about John a few hours ago, and I have difficulty writing when I feel the way I do right now.

He was only thirty-three. I learned a long time ago that life isn't always fair. But it shouldn't cheat that much.

THE BUSINESS

ALVA JOHNSTON

Philip French's biography of Darryl F. Zanuck was titled Don't Say Yes until I've Finished Talking, *and the title captured one side of Zanuck, but there were others. Of the
Golden Age moguls, he was one of the smartest, and if Orson Welles became a Boy Wonder by directing* Citizen Kane *at twenty-five, reflect that Zanuck was studio manager at
Warner's at twenty-six and had by then already spent eight years in the film industry.
This* New Yorker *profile was published in 1934, when Zanuck was engineering the hardboiled black-and-white social melodramas that became the Warner trademark; his entire
career at 20th Century-Fox, where he did his most important work, was still ahead. One
usually thinks of him in late middle age, graying, a big cigar in his hand. In 1934 he
was a kid, like the young Spielberg or Katzenberg, and had only just started to not finish talking.*

"The Wahoo Boy"

College men have not covered themselves with glory in Hollywood. Some have
been brilliant successes as directors and writers, but few are in places of power.
Generally speaking, the university alumni are working for the high-school alumni
and the high-school alumni are working for the grammar-school alumni. You
can roughly measure the importance of a man in the movie industry by the number of stories told about his ignorance.

A complete survey of Hollywood might explain what is wrong with American universities and why a lower education is better than a higher education in
the picture business. University training is an essential in the old, standard professions, but is apparently a handicap in a new, changing, experimental calling
in which imagination and judgment are more important than specialized knowledge. The semi-literates often seem to have a vehemence, decisiveness, and
single-mindedness which are commonly educated out of college men.

It is sometimes said that Hollywood does not appreciate educated men, which is like saying that the Olympic Games do not appreciate inferior athletes. University men go to Hollywood in droves and carry off many second and third prizes, but the first prizes go to men of no Latin, no Greek, and not much English. The advantage possessed by the uneducated man or half-educated man seems to be that he is forced at an early age to face his own problems, to accept responsibilities, to make decisions. Not every illiterate has the natural ability to use his advantages. Start a hundred Masters of Arts and a hundred non-academic men in a race in any pioneer field; the odds seem to be that most of the leaders and most of the tail-enders will be uneducated men, and that the fair-to-middling honors will be carried off by collegians.

Darryl Francis Zanuck has had a dazzling career in Hollywood. From the greatness of his achievements it would be inferred that he had stopped school in the sixth grade. He was a clever writer of scenarios at eighteen; at twenty-two, he had such prestige that he was trusted to create rôles for Rin-Tin-Tin; at twenty-four, he was an acknowledged master of the horselaugh, his masterpiece of low and broad comedy being "The Better 'Ole," based on Bairnsfather's cartoons; at twenty-six, he became the studio manager of Warner Brothers and was a leader in the transition of the film industry from the silent to the talking pictures; he put a new boldness and realism in the films in his Gangster Cycle, and was rewarded with great box-office successes. At thirty, when he was one of the biggest figures in Hollywood, Zanuck tore up his five-thousand-dollar-a-week contract with Warner Brothers. He did this because the Warners insisted on extending last year's fifty-per-cent pay cut for two weeks after the date on which Zanuck had promised Warner employees that the old salaries would be restored. He immediately formed Twentieth Century Pictures, Inc., in coöperation with Joseph Schenck, and claims to have broken all records in the last year with his high percentage of hits. These include "The House of Rothschild," "The Affairs of Cellini," "Bulldog Drummond Strikes Back," and "The Gallant Lady." From Zanuck's record, anyone would naturally guess that he must have stopped school in the sixth grade. The fact is, however, that he went on and on and reached the eighth grade before he quit the academic halls of Wahoo, Nebraska.

His present job is no sinecure. In addition to bossing his company's pictures, he undergoes a terrific reading grind in search of new material. Ten professional digesters digest every new Broadway drama and nearly every new novel in the English language for him. Thousands of works go through this mill for Zanuck's benefit. Short, medium, and long digests are made of each play or drama. The short digest is one paragraph. Ordinarily that is all that Zanuck reads. If, however, there is anything in the first digest which catches his attention, he reads the second digest, which is three paragraphs long. If he is still interested, he calls for the third digest, which consists of twenty paragraphs. If he thinks he has an idea for a picture, he calls for the book or the play. If it is historical or bio-graphical, he may send for all the available literature on the subject. When he boarded the train last May on his way to Africa for a hunting trip, he took with him a five foot shelf of books on Cardinal Richelieu because he planned to cast Arliss as the deft and domineering old prelate.

When he stopped a few days in New York on this trip, Zanuck was described by one interviewer as a Napoleon in a vermilion bathrobe with polo ponies painted on it. A bitter jest. Napoleons are an inferior caste in Hollywood. The place is so overrun with Little Corporals that no one pays any attention to them. Zanuck has accomplished too much to be dismissed with such a sneer. He is no cheap Corsican, but it might be fair to describe him as a bantamweight, dandi-fied Theodore Roosevelt. He has an odd resemblance to T.R. His teeth stick out. The lower part of his face is compressed by the weight of a massive fore-head. He has something of the Colonel's swagger, dash, and obstacle-smashing explosiveness.

Zanuck is primarily a great journalist using the screen instead of the printing press. His news instinct was manifested in the first story he wrote for the movies. State troopers were just beginning to be a factor in national life, and Zanuck's first tale was based on their pursuit of automobile thieves. The great journalist is not the man who tries to anticipate the whims of millions; he is the man who says, "This excites me, and I'll make it excite them." Zanuck has this power of getting excited and selling his excitement to the public. The Gangster Cycle did not enter its major phase until Zanuck read one day in the *Reader's Digest* that four hundred and eighty-six gangsters had been killed in Chicago in a year. "It's war!" exclaimed Zanuck. He went about the Warner Brothers studio exclaim-ing, "It's war! It's war!" He began devouring contemporary Chicago literature and sending for contemporary Chicago historians. He acquired a taste for undi-luted horror; then, with his own journalistic ability to force his own tastes on the public, he made undiluted horror a national dish.

Zanuck became the chief interpreter of the Hardboiled Era. He backed his own newly acquired hardboiled mood against all the canons of the American screen by producing "Doorway to Hell" a cold and gory picture, which had an unhappy ending, no hero, no major character that inspired sympathy. The Warn-ers regarded it as a reckless experiment and allowed Zanuck to spend only a small sum in making it, but it was a box-office hit. Zanuck's masterpiece of movie jour-nalism was "The Public Enemy," in which the star roughly handled his mother, hit one girl in the face with a grapefruit, punched another in the jaw, shot a horse for kicking and killing a man, slaughtered competing gangsters on a large scale, and wound up by being taken for a ride and delivered as a corpse at his mother's door. The picture was almost straight news-reporting, the horse-shooting inci-dent and nearly every other bit of action being based on real events which had appeared in the press. Zanuck's greatest pioneering feat was probably the lady-socking. Previously it had been allowable in the films to shoot a woman, to poison her, to rob her, to wrong her in almost every conceivable manner, but not to sock her. Zanuck had turned hardboiled enough to appreciate a hussy-slugging scene; so had the public. This novel touch was greeted with universal cheers, and wallops on the chins of America's sweethearts grossed millions for Hollywood before they became so monotonous that the fans became bored.

"The Public Enemy" was one of the greatest pieces of journalism of the decade. It was the kind of work that Joseph Pulitzer would have done, had he been born half a century later and been a movie magnate instead of a newspaper publisher. Earlier gangster pictures had portrayed the gangster as a demidevil or goblin damned, a supernatural being having no legitimate connection with the human race. Zanuck's Public Enemy, magnificently played by James Cagney, was a boy of decent family, a boy who had been overwhelmingly tempted by the enormous rewards of the nineteen-twenties, the decade when crime paid. Zanuck's gangster was a human being in a human environment, a victim of a corrupt time. It would be difficult to name one other thing that applied the lash to the public conscience as "The Public Enemy" did. The Gangster Cycle is probably the best social service performed by any agency in America in the last ten years. Showers of gangster books and daily sensations in the newspapers failed to rouse an apathetic public and government, but the gangster pictures stirred the public and even disturbed the fat slumbers of municipal and federal officials. One of President Hoover's few accomplishments, the flank attack on hoodlums through the income-tax gatherers, followed close upon Zanuck's cinematic-journalistic blast against the national disgrace. It is difficult to distribute the credit for repeal. The gold medal should undoubtedly be awarded to the idle dream of reduced income taxes; one of the various silver medals ought to be pinned on the chest of Zanuck. According to the custom of Hollywood, the motion-picture industry, instead of claiming credit for the Gangster Cycle, began to cringe and apologize and do public penance. Instead of being acclaimed for exposing and helping to end the gangster evil, the movies were roundly abused as the cause of the gangster evil. Public officials loathed the gangster pictures because they mirrored the incompetence and corruption of public officials. Politicians hated them because they indicated the harmony of politics and crime. Idealistic world-improvers and commercialized reformers hated them because they pictured, ten times more vividly than the printed word, the results of prohibition. Zanuck may suffer to some extent for his services to the nation. The reform hosts, shattered by repeal, are reorganizing and seeking something new to crusade about. They have made a determined effort to steal the crusade against Hollywood away from the Catholics.

This will probably not harm Zanuck greatly because he possesses the sovereign journalistic gift of getting bored in time and dropping a theme before it becomes a public nuisance. Long before the friars, parsons, and rabbis had begun to protest, Zanuck had announced that the hardboiled era was over. The great journalists are not men who worry about the public, but men who are fanatically interested in themselves. When Zanuck announced that the people were bored with lust and massacre in the films, it meant that he personally was bored with them. He asserts that the people want biographical films, which means that he is taking an interest in the lives of the great. Audiences desire romance, according to Zanuck, which means that he has turned soft and sentimental. He prophesies a trend toward Westerns, which means that he would like to see Bill Hart and Tom Mix cope once more with the caitiffs of the cow country. He adds that America is surfeited with comic-opera and musical films; that is, Zanuck is glutted with them.

Zanuck has another attribute of greatness, a turn for establishing his personal peculiarities as laws of nature. It takes a person of vast assurance and influence to raise his whims and weaknesses to the dignity of customs. Four-o'clock tea became a world-wide institution because a pace-setting British matron found that it agreed with her digestion to have a small meal between lunch and dinner. America was largely relieved of eyestrain because Adolph S. Ochs of the New York *Times* relieved himself of eyestrain. When the publisher's eyes were good enough to read fine print, he published his paper in fine print, paying no attention to the indignation of readers. When Ochs approached sixty, he began to have difficulty in deciphering his own microscopic characters, so he introduced larger type. A few years later his eyes began to bother him, and he enlarged the type again. This was a national blessing, because hundreds of publishers who took Ochs as a model began to print their newspapers in readable characters. Like Ochs and the British matron, Zanuck is trying to make the world adopt one of his peculiarities. He likes to take a vacation of six or eight weeks to hunt bear, moose, or lion. He started his propaganda for long vacations when he was with Warner Brothers. Through economic necessity, the Warners had to shut down for long periods, automatically treating Zanuck to hunting trips. Zanuck succeeded in convincing the Warners that pictures made immediately after a shut down were vastly superior to those made at other periods of the year. Others accepted Zanuck's logic. He has sold the long bear-hunting and lion-hunting furloughs widely in Hollywood. Thousands of others may, because of Zanuck's example, soon be chasing giraffes and okapis.

Zanuck was born at Wahoo, Nebraska, thirty-two years ago with the two qualities which earmarked him for greatness in Hollywood—an extraordinary inventiveness, and a hatred of school. His inventiveness first took the form of writing home letters full of lies about his hunting trips; his grandfather owned several large ranches, which were hunting grounds for the boy as soon as he was able to hold up a rifle. At eight, he went to Los Angeles with his mother, who had been sent there for her health. The boy was placed in the Page Military Academy. He began to play hooky as soon as he discovered that a dollar a day could be earned by acting as an extra at the old Essanay lot in Glendale. One day, when he was a little Indian girl supporting Bessie Barriscale, who was a big Indian girl, Bessie complained that her wig did not fit. Zanuck's wig was snatched from his head and placed on Bessie's. He was sent by streetcar to a costuming house to get a new wig. His mother happened to be on the streetcar, and that ended the first phase of his movie career. At eight, he had made his movie début. At nine, he made his literary début, a Zanuck letter of three columns appearing in the Norfolk, Nebraska, Sentinel. It was the story of his train trip from Los Angeles to Omaha, a travelogue about Indians, greasers, cowboys, wild animals, and fell deeds, as seen through a car window. The things that he saw, experienced, heard, read, or made up during his boyhood became raw materials for letters, of which he wrote enormous quantities. Relatives and friends of young Zanuck were furnished with voluminous minutes of all that passed in his mind. His favorite authors were Mark Twain and O. Henry. O. Henry is Zanuck's god. For mental nourishment, he reads an O. Henry story every night. Zanuck still has a passion for writing and regards himself primarily as a writer. He considers the writing corps in Hollywood more important than the actors or directors.

Zanuck's grandfather and the United States Army were about equally responsible for discovering him. In 1917 and 1918, the grandfather used to have Zanuck's letters from the Mexican border, and later from France, published in a Nebraska weekly. They were republished in Omaha and elsewhere. The letters in the Omaha papers attracted official attention, and Zanuck was appointed Thirty-seventh Division correspondent to the A.E.F. newspaper, *Stars and Stripes.* He had lied four years onto his age and joined the army when he was fourteen years old—one day before his fifteenth birthday.

It was on the advice of a major, an admirer of Zanuck's correspondence in the *Stars and Stripes,* that the boy decided to become an author. He was seventeen years old when he returned from France. He wrote short stories and serials for several months without getting much encouragement from publishers. Shortly after his eighteenth birthday, he received his first check—from Argosy. A little later, he landed "Mad Desire" in Physical Culture. Several others of his stories were accepted, and he was settling down to a literary career when he learned that the Fox Film Company had considered one of his stories as a vehicle for William Russell. Fox finally vetoed the story, but the fact that the company had shown an interest was enough for the young writer, and he went to Hollywood. The process of crashing the movies was simple in Zanuck's case. He sent in a card to William Russell, outlined an original story, and sold it for five hundred and twenty-five dollars. He later learned that the man who adapted his story for the screen got fourteen hundred dollars for the adaptation. The boy from Wahoo then and there became an adapter. He filled his next story with technical language such as "closeup," "medium shot," and "fade in" without knowing what they meant, and he collected an adapter's pay for his work. For the next three years he did a brisk business both in originals and adaptations.

II

Darryl Zanuck was a big man in Hollywood at the age of twenty. At twenty-one, he became a nonentity. The studios had been buying his stories in 1922. A year later they lost all interest in him.

Zanuck was a victim of the Big Name Corner of 1923. The Famous Players-Lasky Company had set out to gain a monopoly of the world's supply of Names. In self-defence the other companies began recruiting their own garrisons of celebrities. There was furious bidding for Sir Gilbert Parker, Harold Bell Wright, Mme. Glyn, Rex Beach, Rupert Hughes, Gouverneur Morris, and scores of others. Movie magnates were ready to cross the Mojave Desert on their hands and knees in order to be insulted by a Big Name.

Rupert Hughes and a few others made good, but the experiment on the whole was a failure. The scramble for Names had been too sudden and fierce for much discrimination. Fabulous sums were paid for literary reputations whose possessors had long outlived their productive capacity. It took Hollywood two years to discover that it had been importing large quantities of condescending arteriosclerosis. The experience was costly but valuable. It taught the movie industry that famous old gentlemen of letters seldom write satisfactory originals for the films and that the movie audiences care little for names of writers, with the exception of Zane Grey and a couple of others who belong to the ages.

In the meantime the everyday screenwriters who had no novels to their credit were starving. Poor Zanuck, who had not even written a book on Russia, was reduced to catching white-hot rivets in an iron bucket in a shipyard near Los Angeles. After months as a riveter's helper, he established the Darryl Poster & Window Display Service, which failed because he knew nothing about drawing posters or dressing windows. He became publicity man for a laundry and press-agent for a hair tonic. Now and then a magnificent cinematic idea would strike him, and he would rush to the studios with it, but would be received with sneers. He was an untouchable, a worm, one who had not written a book. "What shall I do?" Zanuck asked Raymond Griffith, the silk-hat comedian. Griffith, who was shaving at the time, stopped long enough to say, "Do a book."

Zanuck took the advice. "Habit," by Darryl F. Zanuck, issued from the press of a local job-printing house. Zanuck sent out engraved cards to all the studios announcing the book as a novel. The Los Angeles newspaper advertisements called it a novel. But it was not a novel. The frontispiece describes "Habit" as a collection of short stories, which is equally misleading. The book is what the honest publishers of the eighteenth century would call a "miscellany." It contained one short story, two rejected scenarios, and one hundred-page hair-tonic testimonial.

Zanuck had disguised the two scenarios as storiettes and given a veneer of fiction to the hundred-page hair-tonic ad. His literary mare's nest was described as a novel because there was a great demand for novelists, a small demand for short-story writers, and no demand for hair-tonic-testimonial writers. The hair-tonic ad was, nevertheless, the cornerstone of the book. Zanuck could not pay the printer's bill, and he had made an arrangement with A. F. Foster, the manufacturer of Yuccatone Hair Restorer, to defray the expense of publication in return for a hundred-page blurb for Yuccatone. Foster got his money's worth. The plot of Zanuck's hair-tonic testimonial started with a murder in a New York night club, moved on to the effort of a broken-hearted Wall Street broker to reform his gilded wastrel of a son, vaulted from there to a forgotten city of the Southwestern desert, worried its way through murders, kidnappings, conflagrations, bad men, greasers, and half-castes, and wound up with the arrival of the U.S. Cavalry and the discovery of Yuccatone.

It was a stroke of true Hollywood genius on Zanuck's part to send out engraved announcements of his "novel." That was pioneering in 1923; today it would be a routine Hollywood flourish. They open fish stores out there now with the splendor of an Elsa Maxwell party. Art Lasky, the heavyweight prize-fighter, sent out engraved invitations to the opening of his filling station in Hollywood last April, and concluded the invitation with "R.S.V.P." Zanuck is entitled to a share of the glory of putting Hollywood so far ahead in etiquette that the Old World will have to limp after it for decades.

Having a book to his credit, Zanuck now revisited the studios. "Habit" weighed as much as Sir Gilbert Parker's "The Right of Way," and was as bulky as Glyn's "Three Weeks." It could be tossed from hand to hand as nonchalantly as Zane Grey's "Riders of the Purple Sage" and brandished as impressively as Gertrude Atherton's "The Conqueror." Zanuck was undeniably an author. On his new round of the studios, he was welcomed. He sold the movie rights to the two warmed-over scenarios. He sold the movie rights to the short story. He sold the movie rights to the hair-tonic ad. Motion pictures were made of all four.

Zanuck got eleven thousand dollars from the movies for his Yuccatone ad and the three other trifles. The book was not a literary sensation, but it had a fair reception from critics. A reviewer in the New York *Times* said that "Habit" was "marked by ingenuity of plot and great variety of invention." It was also marked by the cloth-of-gold style and the unbending grand manner of a half-educated adolescent. Zanuck's characters never looked at things when they might as well rivet jet orbs on them. They never walked through doors when they might as well stride through portals. "Illuminating realization untangles the mass of conflicting thoughts that besieges the mind" of the hero. The hero tells his girl friend that he cannot fail with such a goal as her love for his pinnacle. He was a sensitive chap, and "thoughts of the man he had accidentally killed crept in like a chafing burr and ruffled his mind unpleasantly." His brow "corrugated in meditation," his "thoughts and emotions fumbled riotously and arrived at no definite decisions." In "Habit," Zanuck displayed his contempt for such pedantries as the distinction between transitive and intransitive verbs; his hero "functions" his mind; a sinister development "soars" his fears to a great height; slumber "ceases" his mental activity. He speaks of "ajar doors" and of "wayward strays from the beaten path." He describes the Chinatown of San Francisco as being "crowded to the lily-potted portals with throngs of heterogeneous denizens."

By quitting school in the eighth grade, Zanuck had escaped with his genius unscathed. He had saved his intellect from the confusion and bafflement of higher education. But he had to pay a price for his early advantages; he had to invent his education as he went along. He manufactures more verbal novelties in a year than Lewis Carroll, Mrs. Malaprop, and Shakespeare did in their lifetimes. Probably no man living gets more words recorded than Zanuck does. He has dictaphones all over his studio and home, and dictates nearly everything he thinks of. He has a dictaphone in a projection-room, where he sees the studio "rushes" of new photoplays; as the unedited film is run off, he dictates at high speed, ordering cuts, making criticisms, and finishing his work the minute the screening is over. He runs to a dictaphone on any pretext. Gene Fowler, who was writing the script for "The Great Barnum," had a two-hour conversation on Barnum with Zanuck. "I can't remember a word of this," complained Fowler. Zanuck went to the nearest dictaphone, dictated a thirty-thousand-word version of the conversation, and had it on Fowler's desk in typewritten form next morning. Zanuck has so much to utter in the course of a day that he has no time to pause and grope for expressions. If a standard English word fails to enter his mind, he invents an intelligible substitute. The substitute may be composed of the best parts of two or three other words, or it may be a wholly new creation; in any case, its meaning is always clear. As a rule, the new word fits smoothly into the stream of Zanuck's eloquence, and the listener does not suspect that it was coined on the spur of the moment. "It gives me more time for betterment and correctment," he said, for example, in speaking of his position with the newly organized Twentieth Century company.

Zanuck is at his greatest in motion-picture story conferences when his imagination runs away with his vocabulary. Things may triffle and blore and ruggle, but everybody knows exactly what Zanuck is saying. Sam Goldwyn is the world-renowned maestro of word-coinage. After conferring with Zanuck, Eddie Cantor said, "Zanuck is Goldwyn without the accent." Zanuck is never embarrassed by his own improvements on the English language. He is never rendered self-conscious by anything. It is not that he is nonchalant, but that his mental resources are focused on achievement. His brain is of the primary type, which is concerned with main issues only. He has no time or energy to squander on being self-conscious. A writer was once fired for laughing too much when Zanuck said "a milestone around the neck." Zanuck's feelings were not wounded; he simply did not want an employee who dissipated his talents on the distinction between "milestone" and "millstone." Zanuck's pronunciation is sometimes startling to Easterners, but he merely follows the Southern California trend, which is to disregard dictionaries and pronounce all words in a straightforward, reasonable way. When, for example, Zanuck desires to use the word "admirable," he says "admire" and tacks "able" onto it. One of the great institutions of Southern California is the "première," but neither Zanuck nor any other loyal Southern Californian gives it the affected, Frenchified pronunciation; he calls it "preemeer." Hollywood, the world capital, will probably in time impose its idiom on all the English-speaking provinces. The Hollywood dialect and the Hollywood angle of approach were summed up in a tribute which Zanuck paid to "Les Misérables," which he was planning to turn into a picture. He called it "Lee's Miserables," and added, "It's an 'I'm a Fugitive from a Chain Gang' in costume."

After the publication of "Habit" in 1923, Zanuck became thoroughly established in Hollywood. He has risen steadily ever since. He served for a while as scenario editor to Mack Sennett, but quit because that work bored him. He then had the good luck to become associated with the late H. C. Witwer, whose Leather Pusher and Telephone Girl tales and pictures were famous a decade ago. Witwer wrote the stories, and Zanuck adapted them for short screen plays. Witwer had an original method of composition. He carried small scratch pads and short pencils in his pockets. If a comic idea occurred to him on the sidewalk, at a party, in conference, in a taxicab, in a speakeasy, or anywhere else, he would thrust his hand in his side coat pocket, make a note on the pad, tear off the sheet, and leave the pad in readiness for the next idea. Whenever he heard a very bright remark or a very dumb remark, Witwer's right hand would dart into his coat pocket. From long practice he could scribble legibly and inconspicuously. After accumulating a hundred or two hundred of these notes, he would seat himself at his desk, cover the floor around him with the slips of paper, and start writing. When his invention lagged, he would lean over and pick up a slip of paper. If the paper failed to suggest anything useful at the moment, he would toss it back on the floor and pick up another. Sooner or later he would find a note which would inspire him. Once used, the slip would be crumpled and thrown into a waste-basket. Before Witwer had worked his way through all his notes, the script would be finished. Through association with Witwer, Zanuck became so expert in Leather Pusher and Telephone Girl psychology that he was able, when illness prevented Witwer from working, to write the pictures from start to finish. Without being highly original in the comic vein, Zanuck became one of the most successful writers of funny films.

Zanuck's greatest speed record was made in cooperation with Roy Del Ruth in a Warner Brothers picture called "Footloose Widows." They wrote the story and film adaptation in four days. Technically, it was an "original," but when Zanuck was asked where he got the idea for it, he said, "From some other film. I forget which." This masterpiece of speed-writing was good enough to be revived; it reappeared as "The Life of the Party," and later as "Havana Widows." One catastrophe of Zanuck's career was "Noah's Ark," which was made in 1927 shortly after he had become the head of Warners' studio. It was one of those idiotic super-spectacles with parallel Old Testament and Jazz Age sequences— Moses against Scott Fitzgerald. The Ark picture was further complicated by the coming of the talkies and had to be made as a combination of silent sequences and uproars. The director got sick in the middle of the shooting, and Zanuck had to take his place. "Noah's Ark" was widely conceded to be the worst picture ever made. However, it earned money in Europe, and Zanuck's standing was not hurt, especially as he made a high percentage of hits with all-talking pictures and musicals. His greatest success was the Gangster Cycle.

"I Am a Fugitive from a Chain Gang" is an example of Zanuck's motion-picture journalism. He read the book on a train eastbound from Hollywood and had started negotiations for it by wire before reaching Chicago. Southern prison camps were then being exposed in newspapers. The picture itself was a glorified newsreel. It was close enough to reality in its characterizations to bring some libel suits. It was a violation of box-office rules because the boy did not get the girl, because the fugitive remained a fugitive, and because the ending was tragic.

After experimenting successfully for three or four years with the translation of the front pages of the daily press into motion pictures, Zanuck, with his usual cocksureness, announced that news and contemporary sensations were extinct as sources of picture material. Nevertheless, in his biggest hit of this year, "The House of Rothschild," he cuts into news obliquely from two angles. The film is a romantic tale of events more than a century old, but it manages to be a joint exposure of anti-Semitism and international banking.

Like many other big Hollywood figures, Zanuck enjoys having a mob of retainers handy to argue with and agree with him. His retinue has included celebrities ranging from Aidan Roark, eight-goal polo-player, to Prince Mike Romanoff. Zanuck had the fake Prince under him for seven months at the Warner Brothers studio. Mike was employed as a technical director to assist Michael Curtiz, a Hungarian genius, who reported that Romanoff was the greatest technical director ever known. Zanuck, according to his own account, took two months to discover that Mike was a phony, but kept him around after that for amusement and instruction. The greatest amusement was that of watching the father of the Warner brothers trying to talk Russian to Mike. For six months the elder Warner tried to start a conversation in Russian with the impostor, but each time Romanoff bowed and slid swiftly away.

Zanuck has a keen sense of humor. His retinue includes a pal with a weak stomach, a stomach that particularly rebels at any kind of cheese. Nothing pleases Zanuck more than to sneak a bit of Roquefort or Limburger into the pal's ice cream. Anything else that makes his friend violently ill is equally acceptable to the sunnier side of Zanuck's nature. The producer gives full rein to his comedy gifts when on vacation. He never allows practical jokes to interfere with work, but on the contrary he sometimes uses practical jokes to speed up work. He perpetrated one on Gene Fowler in order to establish a pleasant understanding with him. Fowler, the author of "Timber Line" and other books, is a man of prejudices. One of his prejudices is a prejudice against any man who pays him a salary running into four figures a week. He works for people like that, but will not tolerate them personally. Anybody who hands Fowler big money and then tries to fraternize with him is likely to be thrown over a partition. Zanuck wanted Fowler to write a movie version of the life of Barnum and agreed to pay a huge salary. Fowler resented this. The deal had been arranged through an agent. Fowler had never met Zanuck, but he grew more indignant every time he thought of him. The day came when Fowler went to work on the Twentieth Century lot. He was ushered into Zanuck's office and introduced. At Zanuck's desk sat a man with his hat drawn down over his eyes and the first finger of his right hand at his forehead. The man didn't acknowledge the introduction. He didn't notice Fowler. He just went on thinking with his hat on. Fowler, accustomed to the bowing and scraping of magnates, was taken by surprise. He bore the snub for a few moments and then rose, bursting with indignation. The man at Zanuck's desk rose at the same time, pushed his hat back, and said, "Hello, Gene." It was Mark Kelly, a sportswriter and close friend of Fowler. The purpose of the gag was to put Fowler in good humor and to make him forgive Zanuck for paying him such a frightful amount of money. It effected its purpose. During their entire association, Fowler treated Zanuck kindly.

George Arliss has influenced the career of Zanuck. Formerly, Zanuck was strictly the newsman in pictures, his attention focused wholly on the present. He had a concentration on the present like that of the late Charles F. Murphy, boss of Tammany Hall, whose interviews consisted of one of two sentences: "That's past," or "We'll cross that bridge when we come to it." Zanuck discovered the past when he had to find historical pictures for Arliss; in the last year or two, he has gone wild about history and biography. When Zanuck split with

Warner Brothers and founded Twentieth Century, Arliss joined him. Arliss was told that he was making a great error; that Zanuck was good enough for gangster stuff, but not good enough for the quaint-old-gaffer pictures and the Beacon-Lights-of-History pictures in which Arliss is starred. "Zanuck is an artist," retorted Arliss. Zanuck's own answer to the charge of being a low-life special-ist was "The House of Rothschild." According to Arliss, Zanuck is a master of the difficult art of letting a man alone. Able writers and directors who have worked under Zanuck have echoed this. He can interfere violently when he sees fit, but he has a rare sense of when to let a man be.

Zanuck has not been infallible in forecasting the future of actors. He still smarts a little because he failed to see star possibilities in Charles Farrell when Farrell was supporting Rin-Tin-Tin in bowwow operas. Today he regards Myrna Loy as a brilliant actress. When she worked for him, he used her in slinky, Oriental-siren parts. He cannot understand today why he failed to discover the cleverness which she displayed in her later career. Zanuck discovered Clark Gable, but could not interest the Warners in him. One of the Warner brothers said, "His ears are too big;" another brother said. "He is a gangster type and gang-ster pictures are through." So Zanuck was forced to release Gable, who was in-stantly snapped up by M-G-M. Zanuck changed Cagney from an inexpensive hoofer into a star by one picture, "The Public Enemy." Among others who were boosted in their film careers by Zanuck are Warren William, Lee Tracy, and the Mad Hatter–faced comedian, Charles Butterworth.

Zanuck weighs a hundred and twenty-eight pounds. He has a two-goal rat-ing as a polo-player and is respected for his gameness. A two-goal rating is not bad for a man of small physique. Walt Disney, who is about Zanuck's size, has a zero rating. Zanuck does not believe in nepotism, the curse of Hollywood. His weakness is polo; he would, they say, gladly have none but International Cup men as filing clerks and let them name their own salaries. His national fame as a polo-player rests largely on Arthur Caesar's comment, "From Poland to polo in two generations." The fact, however, is that Zanuck, although a big man in Hollywood, is nothing but a plain, ordinary Aryan. He is of Swiss descent on his father's side. His mother's maiden name was Torpin, and he is related to a well-known Philadelphia family of that name. Some time after the Poland-to-polo crack by the witty Caesar (who, incidentally, is said to have, with deadly marksmanship, insulted every man in Hollywood who was in a position to do him any good), a genealogy of Zanuck appeared in various newspapers. It traced him on the Torpin side to a sixteenth-century British statesman named Turpin, whose descendants in the eighteenth century changed their name to Torpin in order to dissociate themselves from Dick Turpin, the highwayman. Zanuck says that he has never checked up on these historical delicacies, but they are tradi-tions in the family.

CAREY MCWILLIAMS

McWilliams, later and for many years editor of the Nation, *wrote this socio-financial-artistic dissection of Hollywood in 1946 in* Southern California Country, *a title in the* American Folkways *series of books on American regions, edited by Erskine Caldwell. It is a Marxist analysis, more interested in salaries and business methods than in the Hollywood product itself.*

"The Island of Hollywood"

"You can't explain Hollywood. There isn't any such place.
It's just the dream suburb of Los Angeles."

—RACHEL FIELD in *To See Ourselves*

Hollywood, as Katherine Fullerton Gerould pointed out years ago, exists only as a state of mind, not as a geographical entity. One of the most famous place-names in the world, Hollywood is neither a town nor a city; it is an integral part of Los Angeles. Despite its nebulous geographical status, however, Hollywood does exist as a community, but a community that must be defined in industrial rather than geographical terms. The concentration of the motion-picture industry in Los Angeles is what gives Hollywood its real identity. As Jerome Beatty once said, Hollywood exists as "a kingless kingdom within a kingdom," an island within an island.

The most highly publicized industry in the world, Hollywood has been reported, for many years, by a corps of some 400 newspapermen, columnists, and feature writers. "Only Washington," writes Leo Rosten, "the matrix of our political life, and New York, the nerve-center of our economic system, possess larger press corps." Every phase of the industry and every facet of Hollywood life has been thoroughly reported. In fact, there is only one aspect of Hollywood that is germane to the perspectives of this book, namely, the relation between Hollywood and Los Angeles. Is there an interacting influence between these communities? Where and how does the one community impinge upon the other?

1. THE COLONY PHASE

Originally the motion-picture colony was located in the Edendale district of Los Angeles, not in the suburb of Hollywood. The first motion-picture producers were attracted to Los Angeles, according to local tradition, by reports of the wide varieties of scenery to be found in the region. While producing motion pictures in New York, David Horsley is supposed to have read John Steven Mc-Groarty's roseate descriptions of scenic Southern California and to have concluded that there was the place to make pictures. In point of fact, however, the first producers who came to Los Angeles were fugitives—from process servers and the patent trust. Seeking to evade injunctions, they wanted to be as far from New York and as close to the Mexican border as possible. It is true that once located in Los Angeles they found the climate ideally adapted to the making of motion pictures. For within a two-hundred-mile radius of Los Angeles was to be found every variety of natural scenery from the Sahara Desert to the Khyber Pass. There was also available in Los Angeles an abundant supply of cheap labor. But these discoveries were accidental by-products of the main purpose which was to elude the patent trust.

Always looking over their shoulders for process servers, the first motion-picture "people" did not live in Los Angeles; they merely camped in the community, prepared, like Arabs, to fold their tents and steal away in the night. An impudent, troublesome, harum-scarum lot, they were regarded in Los Angeles as an unmitigated nuisance. In the period from 1908 to 1912, Los Angeles was still in its sedate and stuffy phase, a self-righteous and pious community. From the day that Colonel William N. Selig started shooting *The Count of Monte Cristo* in 1908, Los Angeles took an aggressively hostile attitude toward the new nickelodeon and peepshow industry. As Gene Fowler has pointed out, Colonel Selig's cowboys were hired on their ability to whoop as well as to ride. "The whooping put them in the proper mood. They also whooped while off the set and did some shooting at bar fixtures and in the palm-lined lanes. The citizens didn't like this racket and were sure the good Colonel Selig had cloven hooves and that his men wore tall sombreros to make room for horns." The churchgoing townspeople of Los Angeles spoke of the studios as "camps" and the motion-picture people as "the movie colony."

During the camp phase of the industry, cameramen shot scenes wherever and whenever they wished: in Westlake Park, on street corners, in residential districts. Never bothering to build sets, the producers improvised the background and setting, and made up the stories as they went along. Housewives were constantly infuriated by the ringing of doorbells and traffic was forever being snarled up by the shooting of street scenes. The curiously assorted characters who made up the colony were segregated like lepers in Los Angeles. "Over no decent threshold," writes Cedric Belfrage, "were they allowed to step. They were unfit to mingle with respectable citizens." Apartment houses and four-family flats soon carried signs reading: "No Dogs or Actors Allowed." Living in out-of-the-way rooming houses and hotels, they spent their leisure hours at the Vernon Night Club and other alcoholic oases in the outlying districts. When they began to invade Hollywood, "the most beautiful suburb of America," they were similarly ostracized.

From the Edendale section near Elysian Park, the colony moved to Hollywood in 1911, when Al Christie, and David and Bill Horsley rented the old Blondeau Tavern at Gower and Sunset one day and began shooting a film the next. Just why Hollywood should have been chosen remains something of a mystery. Founded by Horace W. Wilcox, a Kansas prohibitionist, Hollywood was incorporated in 1903 with an adult population of 166 residents. On the eve of its invasion by the motion-picture industry, Hollywood had surrendered its legal status, "but not its well-earned identity," by voting, in 1910, to join the City of Los Angeles. "An obscure and dusty suburb," it had a population of 4,000 in 1911 and a reputation as a center of piety and respectability. Resenting the motion-picture invasion, the residents of Hollywood finally succeeded, in 1919, in forcing the City of Los Angeles to enact zoning ordinances which restricted studios to seven prescribed areas. In fact, Hollywood was up in arms against the invading gypsy bands from 1911 until the opening of *The Birth of a Nation,* the first great premiere at Clune's Auditorium in Los Angeles on February 8, 1915.

After 1915 both Hollywood and Los Angeles began to experience a change of attitude toward the motion-picture industry. From a suburb of 4,000 population, Hollywood had grown to a community of 36,000 by 1920 (and to 235,000 by 1930). Mary Pickford was earning $1,000 a week in 1913; Jesse Lasky and Cecil B. De Mille had arrived the same year; and Charles Chaplin had gone to work at the Keystone lot for $150 a week, and, within two years, was earning $10,000 a week. With an annual payroll of $20,000,000 in 1915, the movies had arrived. Hollywood began to accept the colony and even to regard a few of its members, such as Cecil and William De Mille, Mary Pickford, Douglas Fairbanks, and Theodore Roberts, as among its leading citizens. The strenuous effort which the motion-picture people put forth in support of the war, in the years from 1916 to 1918, helped to bridge the gap between the industry and the community.

As the movies passed from their colony phase to their purple period, however, a series of events served to widen the breach. The Fatty Arbuckle case, the murder of William Desmond Taylor, the death of Wallace Reid, the murder (?) of Thomas Ince, and the shooting of Courtland Dines by the chauffeur of Mabel Normand (whose name had figured so prominently in the Taylor case), momentarily crystallized the earlier opposition and the movies were, once again, on the defensive. Forming the Motion Picture Producers Association, the producers retained Will ("Deacon") Hays to launch a clean-up campaign. A morals clause was written in all actors' contracts, detectives were hired to scrutinize the private lives of the stars, and the purple period came to an abrupt end.

The circus-and-carnival atmosphere completely vanished when sound was first introduced in 1925. Tourists and visitors were not welcome in the new double-walled, soundproof studios. Location trips were reduced to a minimum and the movies became an indoor industry. Before sound was introduced, well-known actors and actresses could be seen throughout the city, on the streets and on location. But after 1925 guides began to put up signs along the boulevards offering to take tourists on a tour of the studios and to point out the homes of the stars. The carnival atmosphere survived only in the gaudy premieres with their blazing klieg lights. At about the same time, the stars began to scatter to the Hollywood hills, to Bel-Air, to Beverly Hills, and, somewhat later, to San Fernando Valley. By 1930 there was not a single star or director of the first rank living in Hollywood. The exodus of the studios had begun even earlier, in 1922. Today there are only three studios in the Hollywood area. Acquiring social respectability with the introduction of sound, the movies proceeded to wall the industry off from the rest of the community. Once the retreat to the lots had been made, the earlier, tenuous, and always troubled relation between "Hollywood" and the rest of Los Angeles was terminated and a new relationship began to develop.

2. So Near and Yet So Far

The geographical area known as Hollywood extends from the summit of the Hollywood hills on the north to Beverly Boulevard on the south; from Hoover Street on the east, to Doheny Drive on the west. When other communities have threatened to appropriate the name Hollywood, the merchants and business men in this district have always raised an enormous rumpus and promptly threatened lawsuits. This is Hollywood, the suburb; Hollywood, the business and residential district. No longer the center of the motion-picture industry for any purpose, it is nevertheless a distinct community. A district of apartment houses and hotels, it has perhaps the highest occupancy turnover of any section of mobile Los Angeles. With relatively few old people and children, the population pyramid for the district is narrow at both extremes. According to the editor of *Dog*

World, Hollywood is the "doggiest area" in California, which, in turn, is "the doggiest state in the union." Here, as Rachel Field observed, the residents belong "to an unchartered free-masonry, whose badge is the leash and stick, and whose password is a word or look of mutual admiration." Here "dog status has been elevated to a high plane," with "a marked canine class distinction being everywhere apparent." Here live the hangers-on of the industry; its carpenters, painters, and machinists; its hordes of extras. Hollywood is, as Horace McCoy once said, perhaps the most "terrifying town" in America: lonely, insecure, full of marginal personalities, people just barely able to make ends meet; a place of opportunists and confidence men, petty chiselers and racketeers, bookies and race-track touts; of people desperately on the make. Once the main thoroughfare of the motion picture colony, Hollywood Boulevard is today a rather run-down tourist alley, lined with curio shops, used bookstores, hobby shops, motion-picture theaters, and mediocre stores. The center of the district is Hollywood and Vine, where, of course, you are almost sure to meet some one you know. When visiting British novelists, no longer on contract with the industry, denounce and revile Hollywood, it is this abandoned center of the industry—this geographical entity—that they usually have in mind. It is, indeed, as James Rorty once observed, a place of careerism and sycophancy, whose favorite word is phony, a place that suggests "the meretricious, derivative eloquence of the mocking birds" that haunt the ragged dusty palms of its bungalow courts.

But this district is not Hollywood. The community of Hollywood is made up of the people engaged in the production of motion pictures, few of whom live in this area. Where motion pictures are made, there is Hollywood. For undeniably there is a Hollywood community in the sense that the people engaged in the production of pictures have the center, the focus, of their lives in the industry and are bound together by the nature of the industry itself. Living over wide areas of Los Angeles, "picture people," and the phrase indicates their group-identity, constitute their own community, separate and distinct from the neighborhoods in which they reside and quite apart from Los Angeles proper. The relationship between this Hollywood and the rest of Los Angeles is, therefore, essentially symbiotic. When a resident of Los Angeles enters the motion-picture industry, he *disappears* almost as completely as though he had moved across the continent. "The world of movie stars," writes Frank Fenton, "was only across the hills and yet it was as far as the sun."

A world within a world, Hollywood-the-social-entity is a rigidly stratified community. The elite of the industry is made up of three strata: the two hundred or more individuals who make in excess of $75,000 a year, the junior elite who make from $25,000 to $50,000 a year, and the lesser elite who make from $10,000 to $15,000 a year. Beneath the elite are the "workers" of the industry: the craftsmen, the white-collar office workers, the skilled and unskilled laborers. The elite live outside Hollywood in Beverly Hills, Brentwood, Bel-Air, Santa Monica, the Hollywood Hills, and San Fernando Valley. Following the hierarchical structure of the industry itself, the communities in which picture people live have been perfectly zoned, as Scott Fitzgerald noted, "so you know exactly what kind of people economically live in each section, from executives and directors, through technicians in their bungalows, right down to the extras." Social rank in the industry is precisely graded in relation to income and fluctuates, as quickly and as sensitively as a barometer, with each change in earning capacity. The social barometer, however, only records changes within the industry. Once a person's relation with the industry is severed, he is automatically excluded from the Hollywood community, with rare exceptions, regardless of his income or the size of his fortune.

Highly stratified internally, Hollywood is nonetheless still a community. For the people who make up the industry, from the lowliest extra to Louis B. Mayer, all identify themselves with Hollywood and belong to a world of their own. However widely they may be separated on the social ladder of the industry, picture people still possess a strong sense of group-identity. Set apart from their fellow citizens of Los Angeles, even from those of a similar or comparable social rating, they think of themselves as a part of Hollywood. To be in pictures, in whatever capacity, denotes a vague and indefinable status, but one which is universally recognized.

This sense of community identification may be variously illustrated. The motion-picture industry has always had its own employer organizations, separate and apart from the Merchants and Manufacturers Association and Southern Californians, Incorporated. While most of the Hollywood trade unions are affiliated with the A.F. of L. and have representatives on the Los Angeles Central Labor Council, they have always felt more closely identified with Hollywood than with Los Angeles. The present-day Conference of Studio Unions is, in effect, a kind of Hollywood Central Labor Council. Such organizations as the Studio Club and the Motion Picture Relief Association also indicate the existence of a separate institutional life. Both the employers and the employees of the industry have their own separate political organizations. When Hollywood contributes to China Relief or Russian War Relief or to the Red Cross, it does so as Hollywood, that is, as the motion-picture industry.

The main studio lots are walled towns, each with its principal thoroughfares, sidestreets, and alleys. On the lot people work together, live together, eat together. With from two to three thousand employees, each lot is a community in itself. Occupying from thirty to forty acres of land, each lot has its own office buildings; its factories (the stages); its theaters and projection rooms; its laboratories, dressmaking shops, blacksmith shops, machine shops, wardrobes, restaurants, dressing rooms, lumber sheds; greenhouses; scene docks; electrical plant; garages; and planing mills. No one has ever precisely defined a motion-picture lot. It is neither a factory nor a business establishment nor yet a company town. Rather it is more in the nature of a community, a beehive, or, as Otis Ferguson said, "fairy-land on a production line." The analogy to a factory is destroyed by the bewildering variety of crafts and skills, the ever-changing personnel, and the fact that, while the production process is always the same, each "production" is separately organized and is, to some extent, a separate product. To call an industry which, in 1939, made only 376 major products, or feature pictures, a mass-production factory is to ignore a basic distinction. Each production involves a different cast, not merely of actors, but of directors, producers, and, to some extent, even of business executives and office and lot employees. Unlike the typical mass-production factory, production lacks continuity and employment lacks stability. People are constantly "in" and "out" of pictures. While personnel shifts from lot to lot and from studio to studio, picture people, however, continue to work in the same industry, in the same community.

On and off the lots, picture people associate with picture people: the elite with the elite, the junior elite with the junior elite, the craftsmen with the craftsmen, and even the office employees with other office employees in the same industry. It could even be shown that a surprisingly large number of picture people have married within the industry. Living in different sections of the city, the three elite categories, and, to some extent, even the lower-bracket employees, frequent the same shopping districts and seldom come to Los Angeles. A friend of mine, a writer, boasts that he has not been east of Western Avenue for fifteen years except to catch a train. The elite elements employ Hollywood business agents, retain Hollywood lawyers, and consult Hollywood physicians. They are protected, not merely by studio walls, but by a cordon of secretaries, managers, and agents from the rest of the community. They deal with Los Angeles, in fact, through these representatives, having few primary contacts with the outside world. Motion-picture people frequent the same mountain, beach, or desert resorts. Once a particular resort has been invaded by non-picture people, the movie folk promptly shift their patronage elsewhere. They are always just one step ahead of the Angelenos. When it becomes difficult to protect themselves from the rest of Southern California, they will even form their own corporations to acquire a particular mountain resort or desert hotel for their exclusive patronage. Some years ago, for example, the upper-bracket elite toyed with the idea of forming an Inner Circle Club as a means of segregating themselves from "the assistant directors and the $300-a-week writers." A special mezzanine was to have been provided where the elite, as the brochure announcing the project stated, "could be a part of, but still removed from, the crowd."

Motion-picture people even use, as Otis Ferguson reported, the same "clipped and extravagant speech." They patronize the same tailors and the same golf courses, attend the fights only on "movie night," and are always seen at the same cafes, night clubs, and restaurants. "The Trocadero was the place to be seen that season," observes a character in Budd Schulberg's novel, *What Makes Sammy Run?* and another character comments, "What always amazes me is that with all the turn-over in Hollywood from year to year, almost from month to month, the faces never seem to change." Picture people exhibit many similar affectations, use the same idioms, and, even in playing poker and betting on the races, show the same remarkable clannishness. While *Variety* and *The Reporter* are avidly read, the local press is ignored except for the gossip columns and the special Hollywood "society" sections. To some extent this clannishness is largely defensive, a means of protection against salesmen, bores, and bums seeking to make a touch. But it also indicates the centripetal force of the industry itself. "Everyone belonged to the films," observed Vicki Baum, "or was non-existent." "Out here," wrote Ward Morehouse in 1942, "you're sucked into a community life you have no feeling for."

In large part, the notorious cleavage between Hollywood and Los Angeles may be traced to the absorbing nature of employment in the motion-picture industry. A writer who is currently receiving $1,000 a week, who has made a down-payment on a $25,000 home, and whose option is about to expire, is about as engrossed with motion pictures as it is possible for a person to be with any single topic. He lives, breathes, and talks nothing but picture ideas. He may not like his work, he may loathe his particular assignment, but concentration on his work precludes the likelihood of his being interested in people who do not share a similar preoccupation. Instinctively, he turns in his leisure moments, such as they are, to people in the same or a similar predicament, who speak the same language, laugh at the same jokes, and appreciate the same personal anecdotes. Although his net earnings over a period of time may not be great, his scale of pay, while he is working, is such as to place him in a different category from those with whom he formerly associated. A man who is earning $750 or $1,000 a week, although he may only be employed for six or eight weeks in the year, lives a very different life from a man who regularly makes $6,000 a year. It should be noted, however, that to be in pictures can mean that one merely occupies a marginal relation to the industry, for example, the favorite bootlegger in prohibition days, a book salesman, or a well-known bookie or poker player. Referring to one of the characters in his novel, Scott Fitzgerald wrote that "she was *of* the movies but not *in* them." (Italics mine.)

The symbiotic relation between the two communities has been of great value to both. For Hollywood it has created a set of special prestige values long expertly exploited; for Los Angeles it has invested the proximity to Hollywood, the tantalizing "so near and yet so far" relationship, with a commercial value that can be weighed, measured, and capitalized. For example, if the motion-picture industry had merged with the rest of the community, it would long ago have become impossible to place a special premium on motion-picture patronage. But, under the existing relationship, Hollywood patronage of a particular shop or cafe or hotel or bar or art gallery can be made to pay dividends. Having the industry sequestered from the rest of the community has made possible the worldwide exploitation of the name Hollywood, which, in turn, has drawn thousands of people and vast sums of money to the region. To vulgarize the concept, it has made possible the distillation of a pure essence, Hollywood, used to sell clothes, real estate, ideas, books, jewelry, furniture, cold creams, deodorants, and perfume.

3. AN ISLAND INDUSTRY

God has always smiled on Southern California; a special halo has always encircled this island on the land. Consider, for example, the extraordinary good luck in having the motion-picture industry concentrated in Los Angeles. The leading industry of Los Angeles from 1920 to 1940, motion pictures were made to fit the economic requirements and physical limitations of the region like a glove. Here was *one* industry, perhaps the only industry in America, that required no raw materials, for which discriminatory freight rates were meaningless, and which, at the same time, possessed an enormous payroll. Employing from thirty to forty thousand workers, the industry in 1939 spent about $190,000,000 in the manufacture of films and of this total $89,884,841 represented salaries, $41,096,226, wages, and only $31,118,277 was spent on such supplies as film, fuel and energy, and miscellaneous items. Today Los Angeles is an industrial community, but it was only beginning to become industrialized when the movies appeared as a providential dispensation. To this island community of the West, motion pictures have attracted perhaps more people than they have ever employed and more capital than they have ever invested. They provided the community with precisely what it needed, payrolls, purchasing power—a simulated industrial base. Like the region itself, this key industry is premised upon improvisation, a matter of make-believe, a synthesis of air and wind and water. To J. B. Priestley, Southern California was "impermanent and brittle as a reel of film" and to Rupert Hughes the mountains rimming the region are "as unreal as flats of stage scenery, stage pieces." Approached from any point of view, there is an extraordinary affinity between the industry and its Southern California setting.

Not only was the industry precisely of the character that the community needed and made to meet its basic weaknesses, but it has always been essentially monopolistic in the twofold sense, first, that it is monopolistically controlled, and, second, that it is concentrated in the region. Just as the region itself is separated from the rest of the nation by a wall of mountains and desert, so the industry is barricaded against competition. Ninety per cent of all the films produced in the United States are made in Hollywood. While this circumstance has probably militated against a proper circulation of competitive ideas in the making of motion pictures, it has been a godsend to Southern California. For it has anchored in the region an industry partially protected against the ups and the downs of the business cycle. Movies are apparently a necessary luxury, slow to feel cuts in the family budget, for they continued to attract large patronage throughout the depression. The advertising value of the industry to the region simply cannot be estimated. It has certainly advertised Los Angeles more effectively than the All-Year Club of Southern California, an organization that has spent millions on exploitation. What could be more desirable than a monopolistic non-seasonal industry with 50,000,000 customers, an industry without soot or grime, without blast furnaces or dynamos, an industry whose production shows peaks but few valleys?

Motion pictures have also stimulated the development of literally hundreds of subsidiary, if minor, industries. According to Mae D. Huettig's study, Warner Brothers Pictures, Inc., lists 108 subsidiaries, including a film laboratory, Brunswick Radio Corporation, a lithographing concern, a concern that makes theater accessories, ten music publishing houses, real-estate companies, booking agencies, several broadcasting corporations, a cellulose products company, a television company, recording studios, and dozens of additional corporations. Not all of these subsidiary concerns, of course, are located in Southern California, but most of them are located here. Motion pictures have stimulated the expansion of service trades, the clerical categories, and the professions. If the figures were available, it could be easily demonstrated that a staggering amount of motion-picture money has been invested in a wide variety of enterprises in Southern California. The location of the film industry in Los Angeles has, in turn, resulted in a somewhat similar concentration of radio broadcasting. Today more than twenty-five national radio shows originate in Hollywood. In 1938 the six Hollywood radio stations spent more than $18,000,000 and paid out, to 600 film stars, more than $5,000,000. If ever an industry played the Fairy Prince to an impoverished Cinderella, it has been the motion-picture industry in relation to Los Angeles.

Here was an industry insulated against competition; requiring no raw materials other than film, a little lumber, a little grease paint, and a considerable amount of electrical energy; an industry whose product, a roll of film, could be shipped anywhere in the world for almost nothing; but which, at the same time, poured forth an enormous sum in payrolls and expenditures. In 1938 motion pictures ranked fourteenth among American industries by volume of business and eleventh in total assets. Ironically enough, it is the one industry that has not been lured to Los Angeles and that has had to fight for its right to exist in the community. No one can possibly appraise the value of this industry to Los Angeles. Only of recent years has Los Angeles become an important furniture and clothes-manufacturing center. In the manufacture of sportswear, it already occupies an unrivaled position. In both instances, the location of the film industry was an important accelerating factor. Hollywood is an all-important dateline and an equally important trademark.

4. SMOKED GLASSES AND FUR COATS

When the industry first came to Southern California, its camps or colonies were scattered about the region. Pictures were made in San Diego, Santa Barbara, Santa Monica, and Inceville, an abandoned colony located north of Santa Monica. While climatic considerations account for the location of the industry in Southern California, they do not account for its concentration in Los Angeles. Santa Barbara, for example, enjoys a slightly improved variety of the same climate as Los Angeles, while San Diego has more sunshine than any community in the region. How did it happen, therefore, that, within such a short time, all of the companies were concentrated in Los Angeles?

In part the explanation is functional; the manufacture of films is essentially the business of *an industry* rather than of any particular company. Unquestionably many conveniences result from the concentration of the industry within a fifteen-mile radius of Hollywood. But there is a more basic explanation, suggested by Ross Wills when he observed that Hollywood "is not America at all, but it is *all* America. It is Bangor, Maine, in intimate embrace with San Diego, California." An industry that must somehow reflect and appeal to *all* America must also be tied to its customers by some social and psychological nexus. Movies were drawn to "the enormous village" of Los Angeles as pieces of metal to a magnet. For here was the great domestic melting pot, a place which, as Morris Markey has said, "manifests in many ways a remarkable exaggeration of all those things which we are wont to call typically American." Here, in fact, was all America, America in flight from itself, America on an island. And here, of course, was the logical place to raise the big tent of the institutionalized circus which is the motion-picture industry.

Here, too, were to be found the variety of types, the loose social controls, the bigness of the city with the sucker-mindedness of the village; here in short was the kind of community in which a circus industry could take root. If one will momentarily forget climatic considerations, it becomes extremely difficult to imagine the growth of the motion-picture industry in Pittsburgh (too highly industrialized); or in New England (too much out of the main stream of American life); or in the South (too provincial, too backward). The industry required a location in which it could develop and function independently of community controls. In order to provide mass entertainment, the movies had to have social elbow-room, a factor best appraised in light of the strenuous opposition they encountered even in Los Angeles. What the industry required, in the way of mores, was a frontier town forever booming; a community kept currently typical-American by constant migration. The industry could easily have been stifled by a rigid social strait jacket. And, in this connection, it is quite beside the point to urge that the industry might have profited, in the long run, by being located in a half-dozen different cities, or to bewail the fact that it became concentrated in such a socially irresponsible community as Los Angeles.

By its partially self-imposed, partially externally coerced, isolation in Los Angeles, the motion-picture industry has profoundly influenced the culture of the region. Having said as much, however, I hasten to add that it is not always an easy task to trace this influence or to isolate the factors involved. One encounters the same difficulty here that others have faced in trying to define the influence of the movies on American culture. But there is this difference: Los Angeles is not only a moviegoing community, but a community in which movies are made. Outside Los Angeles, as Lillian Symes has pointed out, the influence of Hollywood "is diluted by the intenser realities of everyday experience. The rest of the world gets the shadow, not the essence of Hollywood."

In the field of manners and morals, Hollywood has certainly liberated Los Angeles from the sillier rituals of middle-class life. The Los Angeles that I first knew in 1922 has, in these respects, undergone a complete transformation. As late as 1922, Los Angeles was a center of Comstockism and Fundamentalism. During the 'twenties, the Rev. Robert P. Shuler, born in a log cabin in the Blue Ridge Mountains, a graduate of Elm Creek Academy, rose to great power in Southern California, the "boss" of its ethics, politics, and morals. At one time his radio audience was estimated to be the largest religious radio audience in the world. Zealot and fanatic, he unseated a mayor, a district attorney, and numerous police chiefs and was himself nearly elected to the United States Senate. Annoyed by the scientists at the California Institute of Technology, Reverend Shuler once organized a revival meeting in Pasadena, at which the Rev. Arthur I. Brown spoke on "Men, Monkeys, and Missing Links"; the Rev. Harry Rimmer on "Evolution Unmasked"; and Dr. Gerald B. Winrod, the native fascist of later years, "The Mark of the Beast." Three weeks after this meeting, the people of Southern California, by a vote of three to one, ordered the King James version of the Bible placed in the public schools of California (the measure was, however, defeated by the upstate vote). Today Shuler, now in the camp of Gerald L. K. Smith, is just another "preacher" and it would be utterly impossible to stampede the peo-

ple of the region in the direction of Comstockism. How much of this change can
be attributed to motion pictures, I do not know, but the movies have certainly
been a major influence.

The movies have unquestionably affected the appearance of the region. "They
may be blamed," writes Richard Neutra, "for many phenomena in this landscape
such as: half-timbered English peasant cottages, French provincial and 'mission-
bell' type adobes, Arabian minarets, Georgian mansions on 50 by 120 foot lots
with 'Mexican Ranchos' adjoining them on sites of the same size." The interiors reflect the same movie-inspired eclectic confusion: modernistically patterned wallpaper, adzed and exposed ceiling beams, Norman fireplaces,
machine-made Persian rugs, cheap Chippendale imitations, and an array of
"pickings and tidbits from all historical and geographical latitudes and longitudes."
These buildings are not constructed as they appear to be, but are built like sets,
with two by fours covered with black paper, chickenwire, and brittle plaster or
occasionally brick veneer, and are covered with "a multitude of synthetically colored roofing materials." Much of the construction resembles, or actually copies,
the type of construction used in the making of sets, that is, buildings are built
for a momentary effect and completely lack a sense of time or permanence.
Nearly every visitor to the region has commented on its resemblance to a
motion-picture set. "The city seems," writes Paul Schrecker, "not like a real city
resulting from natural growth, but like an agglomeration of many variegated
movie sets, which stand alongside one another but have no connection with one
another." "Hollywood," writes Aldous Huxley, "always seems like a movie set.
Everything is very pretty but the houses, which I think are charming, look impermanent, as though they might be torn down at any moment and something
else put up." "It is all made of papier-maché," complained Morris Markey,
"everything—the filling stations, the studios, the mansions, and even the
churches with their Neon signs gleaming among Gothic turrets. It's all just a
movie set."

To appreciate the influence of Hollywood on Los Angeles it is important to
note the timing: motion pictures arrived just when the community was beginning to assume the dimensions of a city. Had the movies arrived at an earlier,
or even at a later date, it is doubtful if their influence would have been so pronounced. Coming when they did, as Lillian Symes has pointed out, "the Hollywood sophistication was painlessly absorbed because it was, after all, little more
than Iowa-on-the-loose." Lacking socially prominent first families or deeply
rooted social traditions, Los Angeles quickly adopted the motion-picture elite
as its arbiters of taste and style. Although the movie elite moved in a world of
their own, this world was all the more conspicuous for having the spotlight riveted on its isolated, stage-like gyrations. Hence the movies came to set the tone
of opinion in style and taste, manner of living, and attitudes. In other words,
Los Angeles imitated Hollywood.

Elsewhere in America, the *nouveaux riches* have generally been under some mild restraint of settled custom, inherited wealth, or social tradition. But in the Los Angeles of the 'twenties, the extravagant, child-like tastes of the motion-picture elite were imitated at a dozen different socio-economic levels. The Cinderella attraction that the industry has exerted on all America has been greatly magnified in Los Angeles. To employ some dreadful terms, much of the "beauty consciousness" of the industry, its preoccupation with aesthetic effect (however hideous the result), its "glamour," its "slickness," have, to some extent, permeated the rest of the community. Motion-picture techniques of advertising have been widely copied; for example, produce markets are opened with a display of klieg lights and all the pomp and circumstance of a premiere. Attendants in drive-in restaurants dress like usherettes in movie theaters. The immodesty of the industry is reflected in a hundred different ways and nuances, impossible to document but easily recognizable. Los Angeles has imitated the speech mannerisms of Hollywood, its slapstick humor, its informality of existence, and its eccentricity of manner and speech, dress, and mode of living. Here, as Jerome Beatty pointed out, "the signs are bigger and redder, the shops look like moving picture sets, the automobiles run more to nickel trimmings and cream-colored bodies, the girls are more beautiful, and there are more goofy-looking men. Hollywood Boulevard blares at you, and nearly every other person seems to be trying to make himself conspicuous. Beauty shops ballyhoo a jar of cold cream as though it were a behemoth. The average grocer would rather be known as a 'showman' than as a man who knows his groceries." The "conscious factitiousness" of Hollywood has ever been imitated by the churches and temples of the region. Something of the same influence, of course, can be noticed across the nation, but in Los Angeles it stands forth in bold relief.

5. HOLLYWOOD CASE HISTORY

He lived in a fashionable apartment on Sunset Boulevard and over his boulevard shop appeared the caption "Paul Wharton, Couturier." No one knew much about him. He liked to propagate conflicting stories about his parentage. On occasion, he liked to imagine himself the son of fabulously wealthy Montana people, or again he would announce that his parents were Chinese, or, to others, he would say that his parents had gone down on the *Titanic*. He was born, however, in Billings, Montana, in 1909. Reporters described him, at the time of his death, as "a fragile, dark-haired youth, with dark, heavy-lidded, amative eyes, almost Oriental in quality." In 1926 this strange creature, so like a character out of Firbank or Van Vechten, began his Los Angeles career as a designer of pageants at Angelus Temple. Later, he moved westward along the boulevard and became a fashionable designer. At one time he was arrested for narcotic addiction and was released at the behest of Mrs. McPherson. The sharp cleavage in his mental life was revealed in his eccentric behavior. Once, while having tea in Beverly Hills, he casually slipped a diamond ring of his hostess on his finger, and, despite her protests, walked off with it. The next day he announced that the ring had been stolen. And for this affair he was again arrested. On an April night, in the year 1935, he was found murdered in his apartment. He had been reading, during the evening, two detective stories, *The Killing of Judge McFarland* and *The Second Shot*. At the time his murder was widely reported, no one seemed to notice that his career was thoroughly typical of the period, 1926–1935, and of the place, Hollywood. One could fill an encyclopedia with biographies of the Paul Whartons of Hollywood.

6. THE BREACH NARROWS

With the introduction of sound, the amount of capital invested in the motion-picture industry rapidly increased; between 1926 and 1933 the capital investment doubled. Hollywood became Big Business almost overnight. Eight major producing companies swiftly came to dominate the industry and five of these companies are today fully integrated, that is, they make, distribute, and exhibit motion pictures. Of the 92 companies engaged in the production of films in 1939, the eight "majors" released 396 or 82% of the 483 full-length feature films and received 53% of the gross income. The five integrated companies now own 2,600 theaters or 16% of the total. Through their control of these deluxe first-run theaters, they exercise a dominating influence in the distribution field. With more capital required, the major film companies became affiliated with or were financed by such concerns as the Western Electric Company, the American Telephone and Telegraph Company, the Chase National Bank, the House of Morgan, and the Radio Corporation of America.

The year sound was introduced, the Central Casting Corporation was formed to rationalize the employment of extras. Previously extras had applied for work at the rate of 4,000 an hour, but, by 1936, the extra work was divided among 22,937 employees and the number continued to decline: 15,936 in 1937; 8,887 in 1938; 7,007 in 1940. With the introduction of sound, a sharp wedge was driven between the actors and the extras. The average annual earnings of technicians, which was $2,463 in 1929, dropped to $1,767 in 1935, while in 1937 studio painters, carpenters, and plasterers were averaging $1,500 a year. With industrial maturity came internal division on class lines. At the same time, sections of the Hollywood labor movement began to identify themselves with the Los Angeles labor movement and the schism between the two communities began to narrow.

Efforts to organize the industry date from 1916, but it was not until November 29, 1926, that the first basic studio agreement was executed. With the New Deal program, the writers, actors, publicists, story analysts, directors, and the other crafts and skills, quickly organized. Today Hollywood is a union labor town, from the miscellaneous service employees to the highest paid writers, actors, and directors. Organization has not been achieved, however, without a long and bitter struggle. It took the Screen Writers Guild five years to secure a contract after they had organized. For the tycoons who rule the industry have "grown up" with motion pictures and, like similar industrialists in other fields, have a fixed notion that the industry is theirs to boss and to rule as they see fit. Resourceful strategists, they have fought the unionization of the industry by every trick and stratagem known to American employers. The Hollywood guilds and unions have long had to contend with more than the usual number of employer "stooges" and "yes men," the individuals who in 1935 formed the Hollywood Hussars (see my article in *The Nation*, May 29, 1935) and who today control the Motion Picture Alliance.

The beginning of a conscious rapprochement between Hollywood and Los Angeles dates from the formation of the Hollywood Anti-Nazi League in 1936 and the formation, in May, 1938, of the Studio Committee for Democratic Political Action. The impetus for the latter movement came from within the industry itself. At the time of the Epic campaign in 1934, the politically unorganized employees of the industry were caught off guard. Using undisguised compulsion, the tycoons of the industry forced these employees to contribute to the Republican Party campaign fund. But in 1938 the employees took the initiative, formed their own political organization, and were an important factor in the election of Governor Olson. Since 1938 the political importance of Hollywood has increased with every election.

Through their anti-fascist, trade-union, and political activities, the employees of the industry have now been brought into intimate collaboration with the people of Los Angeles. Nowadays no committee is complete which does not include representatives from the Hollywood arts and crafts, and Hollywood is included, as a matter of course, in all social and political projects of a liberal nature. This general leftward tendency of the Hollywoodians has been luridly reported by Martin Dies and John Rankin and clumsily satirized by professional informers, notorious renegades, and the usual witnesses who appeared before the Dies Committee. Much fun has been poked at high-salaried stars occupying "box seats at the barricades" and at the spectacle of "Stalin Over Hollywood." While the influx of liberal ideas has not been without its amusing sidelights, it would be a grave mistake, indeed, to write off this ferment as a mere fashion of the moment or as another manifestation of the exhibitionism of a community of actors. Hollywood will never again be a big happy family. The tensions which have developed in the industry, briefly noted in this section, were clearly outlined in Scott Fitzgerald's novel *The Last Tycoon,* which, if he had lived to finish it, would have shown that the Hollywood tycoons are really our last tycoons and that their control of this all-important medium for the communication of ideas is already on the wane. Fugitives and runaways, the early producers and their latter-day successors are no longer beyond the reach of democratic processes. Even Hollywood has repeated the quotation from John Donne made famous by Ernest Hemingway: "No man is an iland, intire of it selfe; every man is a peece of the Continent, a part of the maine."

SAM ARKOFF

Sam Arkoff and James Nicholson were the kings of Hollywood exploitation pictures from the 1950s until the 1970s; their American International Studios gave many big names (Coppola, Scorsese, Nicholson) their starts, in films that may have been good or may have been bad but were always underbudgeted. For many years a high point of the Cannes Film Festival was the annual luncheon given by Sam and Hilda Arkoff at the Hôtel du Cap d'Antibes. One year Arkoff premiered his new film, Q, about a flying lizard that nests in the Chrysler Building and swoops down on Wall Street to capture brokers to feed to its hatchlings. At the luncheon Rex Reed told Arkoff: "Sam! What a surprise! Right there in the middle of all that dreck—a great Method performance by Michael Moriarty." Arkoff beamed with pride. "The dreck was my idea," he said.

from *Flying through Hollywood by the Seat of My Pants*

In the wake of *Teenage Werewolf,* we began looking for ways to capitalize on the movie's success. Soon Jim came up with another classic title: *I Was a Teenage Frankenstein.*

We both looked at each other and nodded our heads.

"I think that's it," I said.

It didn't take us long to make decisions. By the end of the day, we had talked to Herman Cohen. He was interested in the title, hired Aben Kandel (using the pseudonym Kenneth Langtry) to write the screenplay, and *Teenage Frankenstein* was on the fast track toward production.

That fast track, however, accelerated into a frantic pace after a meeting Jim and I had with R. J. O'Donnell in Los Angeles just before Labor Day 1957. O'Donnell was from the Southwest, where he was the head of Texas Interstate, a large theater chain that was once part of the Paramount circuit before the consent decree. During our meeting, he was complaining about the studios.

"I spent all day yesterday arguing with them about percentages and grosses," O'Donnell said. "They want to squeeze every dollar out of us that they can. If we agreed to their terms, we'd almost be losing money with every ticket we sold."

Texas Interstate had booked *I Was a Teenage Werewolf*, but not in its largest and most prestigious theaters like the Majestic, its flagship house in Dallas. The Majestic had always been a single-bill theater that stuck with studio blockbusters like *The Bridge on the River Kwai* and *Around the World in 80 Days;* we had been relegated to the second tier of theaters, the so-called action houses.

During our conversation, Jim mentioned that *I Was a Teenage Frankenstein* was on AIP's drawing boards. And O'Donnell looked interested.

"When will it be ready?" he asked.

"The script will be done soon," I told him. "The picture should be ready for release in January."

O'Donnell thought for a few seconds, then said, "Here's what I have in mind. If you can get me the picture—and a second feature—by Thanksgiving, I'll put them into the Majestic. The majors just assume that I'm going to play their big Thanksgiving pictures without question. I want to show them that I don't need them as much as they think. Get me your pictures by Thanksgiving."

Of course, O'Donnell had no intention of paying us the same rental fees as the majors. The studios were getting 45 to 50 percent of the grosses; he offered us 35 percent. Even so, we jumped at the offer. It would have been a major coup for us to be booked into the Majestic, particularly on a big holiday like Thanksgiving, which was one of the most lucrative moviegoing weekends of the year.

"Are you sure you can do it?" O'Donnell asked. "Because if you can't, I'll book what the majors give me."

Jim and I looked at each other. "Yes," I said. "We'll have both movies ready for you by Thanksgiving." If we had had a rabbit's-foot handy, we would have been rubbing it furiously.

So between Labor Day and Thanksgiving, we set out to do the impossible.

As the script for *I Was a Teenage Frankenstein* was being finished, Herbert Strock (whose credits included *The Magnetic Monster* and *Gog* for United Artists) was hired to direct it. In October and November, the film was shot, edited, and mixed. At the same time, we also were feverishly working on a second feature, *Blood of Dracula.*

On Thanksgiving Day, the combination opened at the Majestic, much to the chagrin of the majors. It also opened doors for us, changing the attitude of many exhibitors, who finally recognized that AIP was making movies that could earn money for theater-owners in their prestige houses. And we had a *Teenage Frankenstein* to thank for it.

Almost everywhere it played, *Teenage Frankenstein* did nearly as much business as *Teenage Werewolf.* Whit Bissell, who played the sinister psychologist in *Teenage Werewolf* who catapults Michael Landon back into a "primitive state," returned for an equally evil role in *Teenage Frankenstein.* Bissell, portraying the grandson of the original Professor Frankenstein, is really a chip off the ol' mad scientist. A very demented forerunner to today's transplant surgeons, Bissell's character creates a facially deformed teenage monster (played by Gary Conway), using limbs and tissue from the cadavers of brawny teenagers who have, quite conveniently, died in car and plane crashes. "He's crying!" exclaims Bissell as he examines his ghoulish creation. "Even the tear ducts work!"

The monster, however, doesn't mingle well with people. He begins to terrorize the neighborhood, liquidating one innocent victim after another, finally disposing of the ultimate authoritarian parent, Professor Frankenstein himself, who will never again mutter, "I know what's best for you!" Eventually, as the police close in, the monster electrocutes himself as he stumbles into a control panel.

What would Mary Shelley have thought!? Who knows? But many of the reviews were kind. James Powers of *The Hollywood Reporter* said the movie was "intelligently and imaginatively done." Even so, some squeamish critics recoiled at the on-screen suggestions of body parts being prepared for grafting, with the sound of a buzz saw screeching in the background. Certain people just can't take a joke!

In creating the picture's advertising, we threw caution to the wind. The posters for *Teenage Frankenstein* read, "Body of a Boy! Mind of a Monster! Soul of an Unearthly Thing!" The artwork promised "the most gruesome horror ever shown! . . . Not for the squeamish! . . . Free first aid and smelling salts! . . . Don't come before dinner!"

We didn't leave a single cliché untouched.

I Was a Teenage Frankenstein rang the cash registers so often that we just couldn't give up on the teenage and horror themes. Herman Cohen and Herbert Strock teamed up again for *How to Make a Monster*—a horror film that was supposedly an insider's look at how monster movies are created, complete with reappearances by the teenage Frankenstein and werewolf. In *How to Make a Monster,* however, they ungratefully kill the movie studio executives (I presume that meant us!) who have nurtured their rebirth.

.   .   .   .

Meanwhile, Roger Corman was harder to sell on the value of teenage themes—and of titles that grabbed audiences and wouldn't let them go. He once approached us with a title that wouldn't end—*The Saga of the Viking Women and Their Voyage to the Waters of the Great Sea Serpent.* Jim and I found it unacceptable.

"Roger," I complained, *"no one's* ever going to be able to remember that title. Even if they did, they'd be out of breath after saying it just once!"

"But Sam," he countered, "it says exactly what I want it to."

"It would keep the marquees working overtime. Forget it!"

We finally agreed upon *Viking Women and the Sea Serpent*—but we should have also kept a closer watch on how the picture was doing in production. Roger had been approached by a team of special effects "experts" who made promises they couldn't keep. "We can create this great scene in which the monster rises from the sea to intimidate the Viking women in their ship," one of them told Roger. "We've got all the techniques to pull it off."

Roger could barely contain his enthusiasm. The scene looked great in the artist's rendition—but it lost something by the time it became the finished product. During the actual shooting, the model of the boat was positioned in front of a rear-projection screen, onto which Roger and his special-effects colleagues projected the image of the serpent emerging from the ocean. Unfortunately, they could never synchronize the elements quite right—and in the finished shot, the boat appears to be riding *above* the water! I was always proud of AIP's innovations, but even I couldn't justify defying the laws of gravity!

Roger realized he had gotten in over his head. "I'm still trying to pull the scene together," he said, as he reshot it again and again. "But this is not my area of expertise." He finally ended up lighting the scene very dimly to try to minimize its obvious shortcomings. If he really wanted to minimize them, I had a better idea—leave the film on the cutting-room floor!

After that picture, we began looking for a project for Roger whose title would take advantage of the word "teenage." Eventually, we settled on *Teenage Caveman,* although it was a choice with which Roger wasn't completely happy. He wanted to call the new picture *Prehistoric World,* which I abhorred.

"Roger," I argued, "there's nothing new or novel about it. Dozens of museums have exhibits called 'prehistoric world.' Also, take a look at the plot. Don't forget that near the end of the movie, the audience realizes that they're not watching a story about prehistoric men at all; it's about survivors of a modern-day atomic holocaust! A title like *Prehistoric World* is just going to confuse them. Besides, I'd like to get the word 'teenage' into the title, too." Roger was still a late convert to fully understanding the teenage market.

Teenage Caveman's story line depicts a different style of youthful rebellion, in which Robert Vaughn stars as a young caveman challenging the rules of his primitive clan, venturing out past the familiar, barren confines into the world beyond, exploring the postapocalyptic earth and looking for lusher pastures. There, moviegoers see evidence of the nuclear blast—in particular, a beast whose human ancestors were mutated into monsters by the bomb, and who carries a rather unlikely piece of evidence of the prenuclear era—a postcard from New York City.

Vaughn, then a twenty-five-year-old struggling actor, was still six years away from the TV hit *The Man From U.N.C.L.E.,* and he was delighted to get the starring role in *Teenage Caveman.* And he got used to the AIP way of making movies very quickly. At one point in the script, he was supposed to shoot a deer. And that presented some problems. First of all, we didn't have a deer. Even if we could find one, it was no longer deer season, particularly in the heart of Los Angeles. Also, the movie was so low-budget ($70,000) that we may not have even been able to afford a single bullet!

Nevertheless, Roger Corman wasn't easily deterred. He sent one of his assistants to either the Elks or the Moose Club, where he unofficially "borrowed" a stuffed deer. And that's what Robert Vaughn took aim at and "killed." In the movie, he beams with the pride of a big-game hunter as he parades the stuffed deer before the cameras. The picture would have played very well at a taxidermists' convention.

Roger, who often insisted that his movies contained subtle, social messages, must have loved the critical reaction to *Teenage Caveman.* For example, the reviewer for *Variety* called it "a plea for international cooperation in terms of the dangers of atomic radiation." That was music to Roger's socially conscious ears.

"Despite its ten-cent title, *Teenage Caveman* is a surprisingly good picture," the critic for the *Los Angeles Times* wrote.

WILLIAM CASTLE

John Waters, who wrote the introduction to William Castle's memoir, does a lecture in which he describes and even demonstrates some of Castle's exploitation techniques: insurance policies in case audience members die of fright; electric shocking devices built into seats; refunds for those who can't "take it"; ghosts flying over the heads of the audience. Waters's own use of a scratch-'n'-sniff card with his movie Polyester *was in the same cheerfully sleazy tradition. Castle (1914–1977), who late in his career astonished even himself by gaining respectability as the producer of* Rosemary's Baby, *was the king of the B movies, and these days, when horror and science fiction movies cost untold millions and are made and viewed with complete seriousness, his sideshow spirit would be a breath of sanity. Castle is the inspiration for John Goodman's sleaze merchant in* Matinee *(1993).*

from *Step Right Up*

"EMERGO"

"Bill, can't you come up with another gimmick as good as the insurance policy on *Macabre?*" We were seated in Steve Broidy's office at Allied Artists. Johnny Flynn, the publicity director, was sitting next to me. "How about some sort of sound effects? Like the wailing of ghosts that we can play in the lobby," Johnny suggested.

"It's a good idea," I said, "but we need something to really get the audiences excited."

"How about dressing the ushers as ghosts?" Steve asked.

"Fellas, what is the most exciting scene in the picture? When the skeleton comes out of the vat—right?" Johnny and Steve were in agreement. I continued. "Suppose—after coming out of the vat—we had the skeleton walk off the screen and go into the audience."

"That's impossible!" Broidy said.

Johnny Flynn smiled. "You're dreaming, Bill."

I paused. My mind was racing with an idea. "We build a separate black box and install it next to the screen. The audience won't be able to see it because it'll blend in with the black surrounding the screen. We build a plastic, twelve-foot skeleton and put it on a wire running over the audience's heads up to the projection booth. At the point where Vincent Price manipulates the skeleton on the screen, the projectionist pushes a button. The black box at the side opens, the skeleton lights up and moves on the wire, traveling electrically over the audience and up into the balcony. We time it exactly to the movement of the skeleton on the screen, and Price, with his contraption of wires, seems to pull the real skeleton from the balcony back into the screen."

"You're absolutely crazy!" screamed Broidy. Johnny Flynn laughed.

"It'll work," I said. "I'm sure."

"We'll have to manufacture hundreds of twelve-foot skeletons and to install them in the theatre will cost a fortune!" Broidy moaned.

"The theatres will pay for them. . . . I've even got a name for my gimmick," I said. "EMERGO!"

.   .   .   .

San Francisco was our first play date. The Golden Gate Theatre. Johnny Flynn and I had flown up. The theatre was packed, and Johnny and I stood in the back to watch the unveiling of "Emergo."

"Does the projectionist know when to push the button?" I asked Johnny nervously.

"I've told him three times."

"Maybe I'd better go up and tell him again."

"Relax . . . it'll work."

The image of Vincent Price flashed on the screen. He was manipulating his wire contraption and pulling his skeleton out of the vat. The skeleton onscreen was slowly walking toward the audience. Holding my breath, my gaze was riveted on the black box on the side of the screen. Now—*now*. Nothing happened.

"Oh, my God—it's not working!" My face was tense. Another few seconds passed—still nothing. "Johnny, for chrissake . . . what happened? I'll kill that projectionist! . . . Where's the goddamn skeleton?"

After what seemed like an eternity, the box opened slowly. Looking constipated, the skeleton staggered out, dangled for a few seconds, then bounced back into the box.

"Johnny, the sonofabitch skeleton is supposed to come *out*—not go back in—and the fucking thing doesn't light up."

The audience was howling. Suddenly the box opened again. The skeleton popped out and went halfway up the wire. Something snapped and it fell into the audience. The kids rose from their seats, grabbed the skeleton and, hollering, bounced it up into the air. The theatre was a madhouse!

We finally got "Emergo" working for the third show, and by evening, my skeleton was performing beautifully. The audience loved it.

Saturday I was home in Beverly Hills. Ellen was expecting our second baby any minute. The telephone rang. "It's for you, darling, San Francisco calling."

Picking up the phone, I waited for trouble. Larry Blanchard, the publicity director for the Golden Gate Theatre, informed me audiences were going wild and that I should get up there immediately.

I couldn't believe my eyes. The Golden Gate Theatre was sold out for the entire day. Thousands of kids had been waiting on line for hours for the evening performances. That night the line was six blocks long! Rushing to a telephone booth, I called Steve Broidy at his home. "Steve, we're completely sold out! We've done the biggest gross in the theatre's history!"

"THE TINGLER"

"What's a 'Tingler' look like?"

"Sort of like a lobster, but flat, and instead of claws it has long, slimy feelers. That's what I think a 'Tingler' looks like." I was in the art department at Columbia, talking to an artist. After the success of *The House on Haunted Hill,* I was back at Columbia. Only this time, I had my own independent production company and I was completely autonomous.

The artist finished sketching. "How's that?" he said.

"Perfect," I said. "People won't be eating lobster for the next five years."

.   .   .   .

"Vinnie, you've got to play the doctor in it. You'll be perfect!"

"Bill, I don't want to be typecast." Vincent Price puffed on his long, slender cigar.

"Vinnie, with the success of *Haunted Hill,* I think it'll open up a whole new career for you."

Price hesitated. "Well . . . maybe. Tell me a little more about it."

"The character you play has a theory that the 'Tingler' is in everyone's spine. Usually, people who are frightened scream, and screaming keeps their 'Tingler' from growing. Judith Evelyn will play the part of a deaf-mute who runs a silent movie theatre. Experimenting, you scare the hell out of her. Because she can't utter a sound—is unable to scream—her 'Tingler' grows, crushing her to death. You operate, remove the 'Tingler' from her spine, and keep it in a glass jar in your laboratory. Then it escapes and gets into the silent movie theatre. We'll then make believe that the theatre is where the picture is actually playing. The 'Tingler' will attack the projectionist and then get onto the screen. It'll be a movie within a movie. Audiences seeing it will think it's loose in the theatre they're in. We'll put your voice on the sound track and after the lights go out . . . you announce that the 'Tingler' is loose in the audience and ask them to scream for their lives. . . . All hell will break loose."

"Do you think it'll work?" Vinnie asked.

"I know it will."

But it wasn't enough. I was now becoming known as "The Master of Gimmicks." Exhibitors were inquiring what my gimmick for *The Tingler* would be. After the insurance policy and "Emergo," they wanted something bigger—more exciting.

One night the lamp beside my bed went out as I was reading. Getting a new bulb from the kitchen, I started to replace it. "Shit!" I yelled. "I got a helluva shock. Something's wrong with the wire." Suddenly I had my gimmick for *The Tingler*. I shook Ellen excitedly. "Wake up, wake up!"

"What's it now?" she mumbled.

"I'm going to buzz the asses of everyone in America by installing little motors under the seats of every theatre in the country. When the 'Tingler' appears on the screen, the projectionist will push a button. . . . The audiences will get a shock on their butts—and think the 'Tingler' is loose in the theatre!"

By now Ellen was fully awake. "You're stark raving mad!" she observed.

To get Columbia to go ahead with the idea was a herculean task. It meant the outlay of a fortune to design the equipment and to make the little boxes. Teams of special-effects men would have to be sent all over the country to install the complicated equipment in the theatres at night after closing. A manual was printed giving complete instructions with diagrams, etc.

My other gimmicks had proven so successful and paid off so handsomely at the box office that Columbia went along with me. Teams of experts were dispatched throughout the country to install the equipment. Dona Holloway, who had been Harry Cohn's executive secretary, was now my associate producer. She came up with the name of the gimmick—"PERCEPTO." Dona is a fantastic woman, and my production company couldn't have made it without her help and encouragement.

.   .   .   .

We were in Boston for the opening of *The Tingler* the following day. A snowstorm had delayed the special-effects crew, and when the theatre closed that night, they hadn't arrived. "Percepto" had to be installed.

Dona and I were under the theatre seats with our manuals. She was studying the manual. "Where does the 'B' wire go?"

"How the hell do I know?" I snapped. "Look in the manual."

"Oh, I see . . . it fits into the relay that goes to the projection booth."

"How many buzzers have you screwed underneath the seats?" I asked.

"About eight rows," Dona replied.

"I've done six. We've got eighteen more to go—oh, and fasten them to the seats tightly so the kids can't get at them."

All over the United States, when *The Tingler* got loose, people screamed for their lives. In one theatre in Philadelphia, one patron, a burly truckdriver, got so angry when the motor under his seat gave him a shock, that he ripped out the entire seat in a rage, and threw it at the screen. Five ushers had to control him.

A week before *The Tingler* opened in Boston, *The Nun's Story*, starring Audrey Hepburn, was playing. During a matinee filled with women, the bored projectionist decided to test the "Tingler" equipment. He pushed the switch during a scene where Hepburn and the nuns were praying. The proper Bostonian ladies got the shock of their lives.

In the final count, I think we must have buzzed 20,000,000 behinds.

LILLIAN ROSS

Lillian Ross's Picture *is a legendary work of reporting, a book-length 1952 study of one motion picture, John Huston's* The Red Badge of Courage, *from its first mention in a gossip column through its disastrous previews and eventual failure. It is ironic that Huston, who made so many successes (his next film was* The African Queen*), had his greatest flop so completely documented. Yet the book is all the more useful for showing how a major studio handled a film that its top executive, L. B. Mayer, resisted from the start—and how after the film performed poorly in previews, the studio desperately tried to change its very nature in the editing room. This excerpt begins with the first in-house screenings of the film. The major players here include Huston; Gottfried Reinhardt, the film's producer; and Dore Schary, the head of production at MGM.*

from *Picture*

"Well, boys," Dore Schary said when he received us, "I've got bad news for you. Hopper likes the picture."

"Christ, kid!" Huston said. He and Reinhardt both laughed.

"You're happy, huh?" Schary said.

"Christ!" said Huston.

"You're leaving for Africa," Schary said.

"Yeah," Huston said.

"I'll show you a couple of things when you get back," Schary said.

"Christ, kid," Huston said. "I've never had a reaction like this to a picture. Willie Wyler says it's the greatest picture he's ever seen."

"You had Willie there?" Schary said.

"Yeah, and——" Huston paused, as though his mind had gone blank. "Who else was there, Gottfried?"

"You look sort of gay in that cap," Schary said, not giving Reinhardt a chance to answer.

"Well, I'm kind of a sport," Huston said, taking off his cap and coat.

Schary ushered us into the living room. Huston said, "Dore, before you see any of this, I just want to tell you it's the best picture I ever made. I never, never had such a reaction before."

"Let's run it and we'll talk later," said Schary.

"You want to close the blind?" Reinhardt asked. The sun was streaming in.

"Pull it down, Gottfried," Schary said, and Reinhardt pulled down the blind.

The wide panel in the wall at one end of the room slid up, exposing the white screen, and the M-G-M lion appeared on the screen, and its roar dissolved in the sound of gunfire. The prologue of the picture started, showing the Youth on sentry duty near a river. Two of Schary's children bounded into the room and sat down facing the screen.

Schary got up and led them out of the room. "I told you to stay out. I want you to stay out," he said.

Nobody said anything during the showing, and except for some subdued laughter from Huston and Reinhardt at an early comic scene in the movie there was no sound in the room at all but what came from the sound track. At the end of the picture, the lights came on. Schary turned slowly to Reinhardt and Huston and said, "I think you ought to reprise these guys at the end."

"The faces," Huston said, nodding emphatically.

"Yeah," said Schary. "By the way, I'm glad to see you dubbed in 'gone goose' for 'gone coon.' " He was apparently taking his time about giving his opinion. After another long pause, he said, "Well, it's a wonderful picture."

Huston leaped to his feet and went over to Schary. Reinhardt shakily held a match to his cigar, which had gone out.

"I have two suggestions," Schary said as the heads of his children peered around the door. "I think some of the picture will be swallowed by the music. If it were *my* picture, I would yank the music out of the scene where the boy writes the letter. Close the door, kids!" The heads vanished. "Each time the music has the sense of warmth and nostalgia, it creates a mood that is helpful to the picture," Schary went on. "As soon as the music gets highly inventive, it hurts the picture. I think it'll hurt your picture, John. This picture is gonna stand up for years to come. It's a great, great picture."

Reinhardt and Huston did not interrupt. They were tense, and they were giving Schary their full attention.

"A great picture," Schary repeated. He glanced at some notes he had made. "The only scene I don't like—I still don't understand it, it destroys the mood— is the scene where the recruits are marchin' past the veterans and the veterans are laughin' at the guys." He had lapsed into an even more homespun and chatty manner than usual. "That irony at the end, when the guys think they're winnin' a battle and then it turns out they're not—that's accurate and real. I don't accept it in the other scene. It confuses me. I have to reorient myself. I think that scene should come out. I think it hurts you."

Huston started walking in small circles. "Uh-huh," he said. "Uh-huh. I'm just trying to orient the thought, Dore."

Reinhardt said nothing. He seemed to be making an effort to keep his face blank.

After a while, Huston said haltingly, "The only value the scene has, it's an interruption of that slam-bang of battle."

"That's not a valid argument," Schary said. "The mood of battle is sustained. You don't have to break it."

"You're right," Huston said. "It doesn't need to be there."

Schary looked pleased. "It just confuses you," he said. "The scene always bothered me."

Huston said, "You think it's an error, Dore, to take the view that the sole purpose of the scene is to give you a lift?"

"You don't need the scene," said Schary. "Boys, I think this picture is a great document. It's gonna be in the files. It's gonna be in the history books. It's a great picture."

"Then it comes off," Huston said.

"It must be sold as a great battle story," Schary said. "If we make it too special, you know—a great novel and all that—we'll drive away the kids who come to see a war story."

"The danger is it might be slapped into the big theatres for short runs," Reinhardt said.

"It won't be," said Schary.

"It ought to go to a big theatre that will give it time to build to a long run," said Reinhardt.

"You mean, Gottfried, like the Astor?" Huston asked.

"Yes. Show that the makers of the picture have faith in the picture," Reinhardt answered.

Huston said that reprising the faces at the end of the picture was a great idea.

"Just goes to prove the value of reading your mail," Schary said warmly. "A letter comes from a fella, he says, 'I run a theatre. Why don't you put the name of the picture at the *end*? All it ever says at the end is "The End." This is a great idea and it costs you nothing.' So I'm puttin' in this new thing at the studio." Schary seemed to be in especially high spirits. "I think this is the best picture you ever made, John."

"So do I," said Huston, laughing.

"So glad we made it," Schary said, and chuckled.

"Yeah, we finally made it," Huston said.

"It's a great picture, and it'll get great notices," said Schary. "I told you what your notices would be on "The Asphalt Jungle,' didn't I?"

"You did," said Huston. There was a moment of silence.

"You fellas call me right after the preview," said Schary.

"Jesus, I'd love to see this be a big success," Huston said. "You know why, Dore. After everything we've been through with L.B. on this picture."

"Don't worry about it, kiddy," Schary said, grinning.

"Dore, you like the picture?" Reinhardt asked.

"I told you—this picture is gonna be remembered," Schary said. "It's a great picture."

"It ought to run in a theatre like the Astor or the Music Hall," Reinhardt said.

"Not the Music Hall," Schary said. "It should go into a house where people will come to enjoy seeing it, not a place where it will be the object of concern about whether it will gross this much or that much."

"The thing is it's got to have time to grow," Huston said. "I'd go to towns where 'Asphalt' had just opened and the managers would tell me business was picking up, but they couldn't take the chance of keeping it on for five more days."

Schary said that this was the kind of picture that should have special showings, to special groups, who would promote it. Also, it should have a special, and dignified, kind of publicity campaign. "Too bad you're leaving," he said to Huston. "You could handle some special showings yourself."

Huston said it was imperative that he be in England in four days, on his way to Africa.

"I could send the picture to New York with you," Schary said.

"I'll be in New York only one day—Sunday," Huston said.

"Too bad," said Schary. "The press will go crazy about this picture. This is a magnificent picture. It has intelligence and it has art. It fulfills the purpose of the cinema as a medium of entertainment and education. Nothing is wrong except that one scene. And a few tiny places where you go out too quick or hold too long." His telephone rang. The call was from Benny Thau, one of the company's vice-presidents. "I feel pretty good, Benny," Schary said. "No, I can't be at the preview. I don't know whether you'll like it or not, but you're gonna see one of the greatest pictures ever made."

When Schary had hung up, Huston said, "Can he afford *not* to like it now?" Schary chuckled.

"I saw L.B. today," Reinhardt said slowly. "Mayer said to me, 'Maybe the picture is a good picture, but it can't possibly be a success at the box office.' I told him, 'I don't know if it is commercial, but it is a great picture.' "

Schary said dryly, "You played that scene wrong, Gottfried. If *I* had been playing that scene, *I* would have said, 'If I were starting all over again, I would now enter upon the making of this picture with greater confidence than ever before, with complete and unmitigated confidence.' "

"Too many people say that," Reinhardt said in a low voice.

"L.B. thinks a picture's no good if you don't say it," Huston said.

"I don't agree with you on the music," Reinhardt said suddenly to Schary.

Huston and Schary looked startled. Schary said, "I have no conviction. It's just my personal reaction."

"Audie is twice as good with the music under him, I tell you," said Reinhardt.

Schary replied coolly, "I think all music in pictures has to be cliché to be effective. Let's not debate it. I'll prove it to you. In Marine pictures, you play 'Halls of Montezuma.' In Navy pictures, you play 'Anchors Aweigh.' In this picture, the music that's effective is the sentimental-cliché music. It's a fact. Let's not debate it."

Schary quickly asked Huston whether he intended to sell his father's country house in the San Bernardino Mountains, and told him he'd be interested in it if Huston ever set a price on it.

"So you're going to have your Berchtesgaden," said Reinhardt.

Schary did not seem to hear him. "I'm getting to the point where I want a place of my own. A *place,*" he said. "With *things* on it." He stood up, and congratulated Huston and Reinhardt again. "Call me after the preview, kiddies," he said.

.   .   .   .

The preview was at the Picwood Theatre, a fifteen-minute drive from Schary's house. M-G-M often previewed pictures there. It was a modern, comfortable theatre, and on preview nights the lights on the marquee always read, "MAJOR

STUDIO PREVIEW TONIGHT." The purpose of a preview—usually called a sneak preview—is supposedly to spring a picture on an audience without warning, in order to get an uninfluenced reaction. Many previews are advertised on marquees, in newspapers, and by word of mouth, but even these are known in the trade as sneak previews, or sneaks.

The marquee of the Picwood said "HARVEY" as well as "MAJOR STUDIO PREVIEW TONIGHT."

"I hate previews," Reinhardt said to me as he and Huston and I got out of the car. "The smelly house. Popcorn. Babies crying. Ugh! I hate it."

Bronislau Kaper buttonholed Reinhardt in the lobby. "Tell me. What did he say? Tell me everything." Reinhardt led him aside to tell him what Schary had said.

Johnny Green, head of M-G-M's music department, and Margaret Booth came up to Huston and asked him what Schary had said.

"Who's got a nickel?" Huston said. "Albert! Get me some popcorn." Albert Band, who was now working as Reinhardt's assistant, made his way through the crowd to a gleaming popcorn machine, as streamlined as the Picwood Theatre itself.

A man asked Huston whether he had ever heard Tallulah Bankhead's radio show. "If I could find the right thing in the picture, I might get a spot for it on Tallulah's show," he said.

One of the company's vice-presidents, L. K. Sidney, came over to Huston, took a handful of his popcorn, and said, "Good luck, John."

A short man with a cherubic face came over to Huston and pumped his hand. "Remember me? Swifty," he said.

"How are you, Swifty?" said Huston.

"I know you're thinking of other important matters tonight, but this I gotta tell you," said Swifty.

"Of course, Swifty," Huston said, looking very interested.

"The latest about Jack Warner!" Swifty announced. "One of Jack's producers suggests he do a picture about Mexico. So Jack says, 'I don't like Mexican pictures. All the actors in them look too goddamn *Mexican.*'" Swifty let out a wild guffaw.

"A great story, Swifty," Huston said.

"I knew you'd appreciate it," said Swifty.

Huston tossed pieces of popcorn into his mouth. "Eddie Mannix!" he said, moving to greet a square-faced, hulking man who looked like a football coach—another of M-G-M's vice-presidents.

"Good luck, fella," said Mannix.

Mrs. Huston arrived breathlessly, having driven in from Malibu Beach with Pablo.

Mrs. Reinhardt turned up and said that she had reluctantly left her French poodle, Mocha, at home. "Gottfried!" she cried. "Mocha wanted to come to the preview."

"Silvia, please!" Reinhardt said.

"What's wrong with *Mocha's* opinion?" Mrs. Reinhardt asked.

"L. B. Mayer is here," someone said to Huston. "He just scooted inside."

"How are you? Glad to see you," Huston was saying, shaking hands with still another M-G-M vice-president, as Reinhardt took a stand at Huston's side.

I went in and sat down in the rear. When "The Red Badge of Courage" flashed on the screen, there was a gasp from the audience and a scattering of applause. As the showing went along, some of the preview-goers laughed at the right times, and some laughed at the wrong times, and some did not laugh at all. When John Dierkes, in the part of the Tall Soldier, and Royal Dano, in the part of the Tattered Man, played their death scenes, which had been much admired before, some people laughed and some murmured in horror. The audience at the private showing had been deeply and unanimously moved by the death scenes. There was no unanimity in the audience now. Several elderly ladies walked out. Now and then, there were irrelevant calls from the balcony; one masculine voice, obviously in the process of changing, called out, "Hooray for Red Skelton!" Two or three babies cried. Men posted at the exits counted all departures. I could not see where Huston and Reinhardt were sitting. Across the aisle from me I could see L. B. Mayer, white-haired and bespectacled, sitting with his arms folded, looking fiercely blank-faced. Several M-G-M people nearby were watching him instead of the movie. During a particularly violent battle scene, Mayer turned to a lady sitting on his right and said, "That's Huston for you." There was a slight stir in his vicinity, but Mayer said nothing more.

In the lobby, the Picwood manager, assisted by several M-G-M men, stood ready to hand out what are known as preview cards—questionnaires for the audience to fill out. The first question was: "How would you rate this picture?" Five alternatives were offered: "Outstanding," "Excellent," "Very Good," "Good," and "Fair." Other questions were: "Whom did you like best in the picture?" "Which scenes did you like most?" "Which scenes, if any, did you dislike?" "Would you recommend this picture to your friends?" Below the questions, there was this additional request:

> We don't need to know your name, but we would like to know the following facts about you:
> (A) Male
>   Female
> (B) Please check your age group:
>   Between 12 and 17
>   Between 18 and 30
>   Between 31 and 45
>   Over 45

When the showing ended, the preview-goers milled about in the lobby, filling out the cards under the resentful surveillance of the men who had made the movie. Mayer walked out of the theatre and stood at the curb out front, looking as though he would like to have somebody talk to him. Reinhardt and Huston went into the manager's office, off the lobby, and sat down to await the verdict. Johnny Green, Margaret Booth, Bronislau Kaper, and Albert Band alternately watched the people filling out cards and Mayer. Most of the other executives had already departed. Benny Thau joined Mayer at the curb. Mayer got into his town-and-country Chrysler, and his chauffeur drove him off. Benny Thau got into a black limousine, and *his* chauffeur drove *him* off. Band went into the manager's office. Huston and Reinhardt sat looking glumly at each other.

"Did Mayer talk to anybody?" Reinhardt asked.

Band reported that Mayer had talked to Benny Thau.

The manager came in and handed Reinhardt and Huston a batch of preview cards he had collected from the audience. Reinhardt read through them rapidly. Huston read some of the comments aloud. " 'This would be a wonderful picture on television,' " he read. " 'With all the money in Hollywood, why can't you make some good pictures?' "

" 'Fair.' 'Fair.' 'Good.' 'Fair,' " Band read. "Here's one with 'Fair' crossed out and 'Stinks' substituted."

"Here's an 'Excellent,' " Huston said.

"No 'Outstanding's yet," said Reinhardt. He was perspiring, and he looked grim. "Here's a 'Lousy,' " he said.

"The audience hated the picture," Band said.

Huston seemed dazed. "Call Dore, Gottfried," he said.

Reinhardt dialled the number. After getting Schary, he said, "Dore," in a low, shaking voice, and after listening for a moment he said, "You *know?* . . . Who told you? . . . Well, then you know. . . . Well, a lot of people walked out. . . . Well, a new batch of cards is coming in. . . . We've counted twenty-two 'Outstanding's so far, fourteen 'Excellent's, thirty 'Very Good's, fourteen 'Good's, and forty-three 'Fair's. . . . Well, Margaret Booth said the reaction was terrible. . . . No, I didn't talk to L.B. I didn't talk to Mannix. . . . Well, I think we should take it out again tomorrow, with a serious picture. Not with 'Harvey.' Maybe with 'The Steel Helmet.' . . . He is right here."

Reinhardt handed the telephone to Huston, who said, "Well. . . . Well, Jesus Christ. Dore, I had the feeling they'd rather be anywhere than in this theatre. Must have been a dozen people walked out on the scenes I think are the best—the two death scenes. Wait till you see the cards. They're extraordinary. They're either raves or they say it's the worst picture they've ever seen. They just hate it. It's extraordinary."

An M-G-M man put his head in at the door. "Thirty-two walkouts," he said.

The capacity of the Picwood was sixteen hundred, and it had been filled at the start of the showing.

The manager said sympathetically to Reinhardt, "How much did it cost? A million five?"

After Huston hung up, he said to Reinhardt, "Christ, Gottfried! I never saw one like this before, did you?"

"You can't force an audience to like a picture," Reinhardt said bleakly. "God! Tomorrow morning at the studio! How I hate to walk in there! They'll all be my enemies."

"Well, good night, Gottfried," Huston said. He was driving home with Mrs. Huston and Pablo.

Reinhardt walked to his car with his wife and me. "It's a cruel business," he said. "It isn't worth it. Almost a whole year." He looked at his half-smoked cigar with distaste. "M-G-M doesn't know what to do with a picture like this." He put the cigar in his mouth. "Did you see John? John was demolished tonight."

ELMORE LEONARD

The Shorty *in the title of Leonard's novel is Michael Weir, a short but popular movie star. Chili Palmer, the hero of the book, is a Miami loan shark who finds himself in an unlikely association with a third-rate Hollywood producer who needs Shorty for a movie. Leonard's dialogue here flows with such irresistible comic logic that it was employed with minimal changes in the 1995 movie, in which John Travolta is Chili, Danny DeVito is Shorty, and Gene Hackman is the producer.*

from *Get Shorty*

It took Chili a couple of minutes to figure Michael Weir out. He wanted people to think he was a regular guy, but was too used to being who he was to pull it off.

The two of them sitting at the table now, Chili asked him if he wanted a drink. Michael, watching Nicki and her band through the archway, said yeah, that sounded like a good idea. Chili asked him what he wanted. Michael said oh, anything. Did he want Scotch, bourbon, a beer? Michael said oh, and stopped and said no, he'd like a Perrier. Still watching Nicki and the band. They hadn't started to play. Chili looked over at the bar, not open yet, thinking he'd have to go all the way upstairs to get the movie star his soda water. Right then Michael said, "They're a tough audience."

Chili noticed the movie star's expression, eyebrows raised, like he'd just heard some bad news but was more surprised than hurt.

"My Michael Jackson went right by them."

Oh—meaning his moonwalk routine. Chili said, "It looked good to me." It did.

"To do it right you put on a touch of eye makeup, white socks, the glove . . . I was a little off on the voice too, the baby-doll whisper?"

Chili said, "I couldn't hear that part."

"But I can understand it, guys like that, their attitude. It has to do with territorial imperative."

Chili said, "That must be it," feeling more at ease with the movie star, knowing a bullshitter when he met one. It didn't mean the guy wasn't good.

"I'm not certain why," Michael said, "but it reminds me of the one, the third-rate actor doing Hamlet?" Michael smiling with his eyes now. "He's so bad that before long the audience becomes vocally abusive, yelling at him to get off the stage. They keep it up until the actor, finally, unable to take any more, stops the soliloquy and says to the audience, 'Hey, what're you blaming me for? I didn't write this shit.' "

Now they were both smiling, Michael still doing his with his eyes, saying, "I could tell those kids I didn't invent Michael Jackson . . . someone else did." Chili wondering, if it doesn't bother him, why didn't he just drop it? Chili looking for the right moment to bring up *Mr. Lovejoy*.

He was ready to get into it, said, "Oh, by the way . . ." and Nicki's band kicked off, filling the room with their sound, and Michael turned his chair to face the bandstand through the archway. They were loud at first, but then settled down and it wasn't too bad, more like rhythm and blues than rock and roll. The beat got the tips of Chili's fingers brushing the table. Michael sat with his hands folded in his lap, his legs in the baggy pants stretched out in front of him, ankles crossed, the laces of one of his Reeboks loose, coming untied. He looked more like in his thirties than forty-seven. Not a bad-looking guy, even with the nose, Chili studying his profile. There was no way to tell if Michael liked the beat or not. Chili thought of asking him, but had the feeling people waited for the movie star to speak first, give his opinion and then everybody would say yeah, that's right, always agreeing. Like with Momo, the few times Chili saw him in the social club years ago, noticing the way the guys hung on to whatever Momo said. It was like you had to put kneepads on to talk to this man who never worked in his life.

Chili leaned into the table saying, "You might not remember, but we met one time before."

He gave the movie star time to look over.

"In Brooklyn, when you were making *The Cyclone,* that movie."

Michael said, "You know, I had a feeling we'd met. I couldn't quite put my finger on it, the occasion. Chil, is it?"

"Chili Palmer. We met, it was at a club on 86th Street, Bensonhurst. You dropped by, you wanted to talk to some of the guys."

"Sure, I remember it very well," Michael said, turning his chair around to the table.

"You were, I guess you were seeing what it was like to be one of us," Chili said, locking his eyes on the movie star's the way he looked at a slow pay, a guy a week or two behind.

"Yeah, to listen more than anything else."

"Is that right?"

"Pick up your rhythms of speech."

"We talk different?"

"Well, different in that the way you speak is based on an attitude," the movie star said, leaning in with an elbow on the table and running his hand through his hair. Chili could see him doing it on the screen, acting natural. "It's like ya tone a voice," the movie star said, putting on an accent, "says weah ya comin' from." Then back to his normal voice, that had a touch of New York in it anyway, saying, "I don't mean where you're from geographically, I'm referring to attitude. Your tone, your speech patterns demonstrate a certain confidence in yourselves, in your opinions, your indifference to conventional views."

"Like we don't give a shit."

"More than that. It's a laid-back attitude, but with an intimidating edge. Cut-and-dried, no bullshit. Your way is the only way it's going to be."

"Well, you had it down cold," Chili said. "Watching you in the movie, if I didn't know better I'd have to believe you were a made guy and not acting. I mean you be*came* that fuckin guy. Even the fink part," Chili said, laying it on now. "I never met a fink and I hope to God I never do, but how you did it must be the way finks act."

The movie star liked that, starting to nod, saying, "It was a beautiful part. All I had to do was find the character's center, the stem I'd use to wind him up and he'd play, man, he'd play." The movie star nodding with Nicki's beat now, eyes half closed, like he was showing how to change into somebody else, saying,

"Once I have the authentic sounds of speech, the rhythms, man, the patois, I can actually begin to think the way those guys do, get inside their heads."

Like telling how he studied this tribe of natives in the jungles of Brooklyn. That's how it sounded to Chili.

He said, "Okay, I'm one of those guys you mention. What am I thinking?"

The movie star put on an innocent look first, surprised. What? Did I say something? The look gradually becoming a nice-guy smile. He ran both hands through his hair this time.

"Don't get me wrong, I'm not saying an actual metamorphosis takes place, I become one of you. That wouldn't be acting. I had the opportunity one time, years ago, to ask Dame Edith Evans how she approached her parts and she said, 'I pretend, dear boy, I pretend.' Well, I'll get involved in a certain life, observe all I can, because I want that feeling of realism, verisimilitude. But ultimately what I do is practice my craft, I act, I pretend to be someone else."

"So you don't know what I'm thinking," Chili said, staying with it.

It got another smile, a tired one. "No, I don't. Though I have to say, I'm curious."

"So, you want to know?"

"If you'd like to tell me, yeah."

"I'm thinking about a movie."

"One of mine?"

"One we're producing and we want you to be in," Chili said, seeing the movie star's eyebrows go up, and one of the arms in the worn-out leather jacket, raising his hand as Chili tried to tell him, "It's one you already know about, you read."

But Michael wasn't listening, he was saying, "Wait. Time out, okay?" before lowering his arm and settling back. "I don't want to come off sounding rude, because I appreciate your interest and I'm flattered, really, that you'd think of me for a part. But, and here's the problem. My agent won't let me go anywhere near an independently financed production, I'm sorry."

Chili got to say, "It isn't that kind—" and the hand shot up again.

"My manager along with my agent, the business heads, they've made it our policy. Otherwise, I'm sure you can understand, I'd have pitches coming at me from independents day and night." The movie star shrugged, helpless, his gaze moving off to the band.

"You think I'm talking about wiseguy money," Chili said. "No way. This one's gonna be made at a studio."

It brought the movie star partway back.

"I'm not connected to those people anymore. Not since I walked out of a loan-shark operation in Miami."

That brought the movie star all the way back with questions in his eyes, sitting up, interested in the real stuff.

"What happened? The pressure got to you?"

"Pressure? I'm the one applied the pressure."

"That's what I mean, the effect that must've had on you. What you had to do sometimes to collect."

"Like have some asshole's legs broken?"

"That, yeah, or some form of intimidation?"

"Whatever it takes," Chili said. "You're an actor, you like to pretend. Imagine you're the shylock. A guy owes you fifteen grand and he skips, leaves town."

"Yeah?"

"What do you do?"

Chili watched the movie star hunch over, narrowing his shoulders. For a few moments he held his hands together in front of him, getting a shifty look in his eyes. Then gave it up, shaking his head.

"I'm doing Shylock instead of *a* shylock. Okay, what's my motivation? The acquisition of money. To collect. Inflict pain if I have to." Michael half-closed his eyes. "My father used to beat me for no reason . . . Take the money I earned on my paper route, that I kept in a cigar box . . ."

"Hold it," Chili said. "I was a shylock—what do I look like?"

"That's right, yeah," Michael said, staring at Chili, his expression gradually becoming deadpan, sleepy.

"You the shylock now?"

"Guy owes me fifteen large and takes off, I go after him," the movie star said. "The fuck you think I do?"

"Try it again," Chili said. "Look at me."

"I'm looking at you."

"No, I want you to look at me the way I'm looking at you. Put it in your eyes, 'You're mine, asshole,' without saying it."

"Like this?"

"What're you telling me, you're tired? You wanta go to bed?"

"Wait. How about this?"

"You're squinting, like you're trying to look mean or you need glasses. Look at me. I'm thinking, You're mine, I fuckin own you. What I'm *not* doing is feeling anything about it one way or the other. You understand? You're not a person to me, you're a name in my collection book, a guy owes me money, that's all."

"The idea then," the movie star said, "I show complete indifference, until I'm crossed."

"Not even then. It's nothing personal, it's business. The guy misses, he knows what's gonna happen."

"How about this?" the movie star said, giving Chili a nice dead-eyed look.

"That's not bad."

"This's what I think of you, asshole. Nothing."

"I believe it," Chili said.

"I turn it on when I confront the guy."

"Yeah, but you haven't found him yet."

Chili watched the movie star wondering what he was supposed to do next, giving him a strange look, Chili wondering himself exactly what he was doing, except he could see it right there in his mind so he kept going.

"The guy took off for Las Vegas."

"How do I know that?" The movie star picking up on it.

"The guy's wife tells you."

Chili paused, the movie star waiting.

"Yeah?"

"The wife wants to go with you on account of her husband skipped with all her money . . . three hundred grand," Chili said, starting to roll and not seeing anywhere to stop, "they conned off an airline after this jet crashed the guy was supposed to be on but wasn't and everybody was killed."

The movie star was looking at him funny again.

"If the guy wasn't on the plane . . ."

"He was, but he got off just before it left and blew up. So his bag's on the plane, his name's on the passenger list . . ."

"The wife sues the airline," the movie star said, nodding. "This is a gutsy babe."

"Good-looking too."

"The husband takes off with the money, plus he still owes me the fifteen large," Michael the shylock said, "and the wife and I take off after him. Go on. When do I meet up with the guy and give him the look?"

Chili had to think about it. Tell Michael what actually happened or what he thought would sound better?

"It's not that simple," Chili said. "You have to be careful. Leo, the husband, isn't much to worry about, outside of he could try and nail you from behind if you get close. But there's another guy that comes along, a hard-on you happen to owe money to. A mob guy. He knows about the three hundred grand and would like to take you out anyway, on account of a past situation."

This time when Chili paused, wondering how to get back to where this thing had started, the movie star said, "This actually happened, didn't it? It's a true story."

"Basically," Chili said.

"You're the shylock."

"I was at one time."

"So, did you find the guy? What's his name, Leo?"

"I found him," Chili said, "yeah."

That was a fact. But now he didn't know what else to say, or how he actually got this far into it.

"You understand, you're pretending you're a shylock."

"Yeah? Go on."

"I mean that's all we're doing. You wanted to see if you can think like a shylock, get in his head. So I gave you a situation, that's all."

"You're not going to tell me the rest?"

"At this point, basically, that has to be it."

Michael was giving him a strange look again: not so confused this time, more like he was figuring something out. He said, "Well, if you won't, you won't," and started to grin. "I don't know how long you've been in the business, but that was the most ingenious pitch I've ever had thrown at me, and I mean in my entire career. You got me playing the guy, the shylock, before I even realized it was a pitch. So now I have to read the script to find out what happens. Beautiful. Really, that was artfully done."

Chili said, "Well, actually . . ." The movie star had his head turned and was watching Nicki and her group wailing away. "Actually, what I started to mention, the movie we want you to be in is *Mr. Lovejoy.* We understand you read the script and like it . . . a lot."

Now he had to wait for this to make sense, give the movie star time to think about it. Michael said, *"Lovejoy,"* looking over again. "That's the one, the florist sees his boy run over?"

"And goes after the guy, to catch him driving his car."

"What production company was that?"

"ZigZag, Harry Zimm."

"That's right, the slime-people guy. I read for Harry when I first started working in features. I didn't get the part."

Chili said, "He turned you down? Come on."

"I wasn't Michael Weir then," Michael said.

He wasn't kidding either. It sounded strange.

"Anyway, we're going to Tower Studios with it," Chili said, and that got a smile from Michael.

He said, "You know what they say about Elaine Levin. She fucked her Rolodex to get where she is. But I'll tell you something, she didn't have to if she did. Elaine knows what she's doing. She made an awful lot of money for Metro up to the time they forced that disaster on her. Did you see it, *San Juan Hill?"*

"I liked it," Chili said.

"It wasn't a bad picture," Michael said. "It had the facts right for once, the black troops saving Teddy Roosevelt's ass, but that didn't sell tickets and it was way overproduced. The picture cost more than the actual war, which hadn't been done to my knowledge since *A Message to Garcia* with John Boles. I remember a script called *Siboney,* the same war, I thought very seriously about doing. That was a fascinating period, the U.S. emerging as a world power, the enactment of the Monroe Doctrine, eminent domain . . . I might look at that script again, *Siboney.* That was where our troops landed in Cuba."

"Sounds good," Chili said, not having any idea what the guy was talking about. He tried to get back to *Lovejoy* with, "Listen, what we're thinking—"

But Michael was already saying, "The title does have a nice sound. Build the score around the song. Si-bo-ney, da da *da* da . . ."

Christ, now he was singing it, against the rock beat in the background.

"Da da *da* da, Si-bo-ney . . . It's an old piece but has all kinds of dramatic riffs in it. It can be stirring, romantic, militaristic. Someone like John Williams could score the ass off that picture."

Chili said, "What I wanted to mention . . ." and paused. The room was quiet again, the band finished with their number. "We're definitely gonna produce the movie at a studio."

Michael Weir nodded. But now he was getting up, looking over at Nicki raising her guitar strap over her head. He said, "I guess we're taking off. It was nice talking to you."

"You have to go, huh?"

"Nicki's waiting. We're going to duck out . . ."

"But you like *Lovejoy?*"

"I like the character, the guy, he has possibilities. But the way the plot develops it turns into a B movie by the time you're into the second act. Take a look at *The Cyclone* again, the way a visual fabric is maintained even while the metaphor plays on different levels, with the priest, with the mother . . . so that you never lose sight of the picture's thematic intent."

Chili said, "Yeah, well, we're already making changes. Getting a girl in it, fixing up the ending . . ."

"Sounds good."

"Can we talk about it, you get a chance?"

"Anytime," Michael Weir said, moving away. "Call Buddy and we'll set something up."

"Buddy?"

"My agent," the movie star said. "Harry knows him."

.   .   .   .

Chili opened the door to 325 to see the message light on the phone blinking on and off. He lit a cigarette before dialing the operator.

She said, "Just a minute." The one with maybe a Latin accent. She came back on saying, "A Mr. Zimm called. You have a meeting tomorrow, three P.M. at

Tower Studios. He'll call you in the morning. Let's see. And a Mr. Carlo called. He said he was going out for the evening and to tell you . . . Mr. Barboni will arrive tomorrow on Delta Flight Eighty-nine at twelve-oh-five. You like me to repeat that?"

Chili told her thanks anyway.

MICHAEL TOLKIN

Michael Tolkin's novel, made into one of the great Hollywood movies by Robert Altman, was an insider's book about an outsider. Its hero, a mid-level executive named Griffin, has committed murder shortly before this excerpt begins, killing a screenwriter outside a repertory theater in Pasadena, after becoming convinced that the man had sinister designs on him. Much of the dark humor of the book comes from the contrast between Griffin's guilt, as he feels a police net growing tighter, and the banality of his daily life at the studio. The amazing thing about Tolkin's dialogue here is that Hollywood producers and executives really do talk like this—not that it leads them to better ideas for movies.

from *The Player*

"Nobody leaves my office until we agree on fifteen reasons for why we go to the movies." Levison looked around the room. "Alison, when was the last time you bought a ticket to see a movie?"

Alison Kelly, his story editor, covered her face with her hands. "I am so embarrassed," she said. "But I just hate to stand in lines. I think it's been two months. What can I say, I go to screenings."

Levison stood up. "From now on, everyone in this room has to go to a movie theater and pay to see a movie, sneak previews don't count, at least once a month." He turned to Griffin. "Griffin, when was the last time you bought a ticket to see a movie?"

"*The Bicycle Thief,* last night." As soon as he said it, he realized what he had done. He had confessed.

"Okay," said Levison, "why did you go?"

"Because it's a classic and I've never seen it."

"And why didn't you have it screened?"

"I wanted to feel the audience reaction."

"What was the reaction?"

"They loved it."

"Who were they?"

"People who hate the movies we make." Better to go on the attack. Maybe not.

"Did you like it?"

"It's great. Of course."

"No remake potential?"

"We'd have to give it a happy ending."

"What if we set it in space, another planet. *The Rocket Thief*?" He was grinning. This was a joke.

"A poor planet?"

"There you go," said Levison. "Right away we're talking about something we've never seen in a science-fiction film, and that's a poor planet. How come space is always rich?"

"Luke Skywalker's farm in *Star Wars* was pretty run-down."

"Fine," said Levison. "And it worked, and what I'm saying is, that's why we have these meetings, to come up with images, to come up with characters and story ideas, so we're not at the mercy of whoever comes through the door. So we can contribute, so our own ideas can get made. Now. Let's start at the beginning. Why do we go to the movies? Give me some reasons."

Hands were raised. Levison ran to the always ready easel with its large tablet of clean poster paper and, with a marking pen, quickly scribbled one through fifteen.

"One," he said. "Griffin went to see a classic. This list should not be in any special order of priority. You'll notice I don't want to start with the clichés, like escape or entertainment. So we'll say—and this is a legitimate reason to go to the movies—we'll say, 'We go to see classics.' " He wrote CLASSICS on the paper. Then he wrote next to two, ENTERTAINMENT, and next to three, ESCAPE.

"Mysteries," someone said. MYSTERIES was added.

"Doesn't anyone go to the movies for sex?" asked Levison. "Don't guys choose movies that they hope will turn on their girlfriends?" Levison grinned and wrote SEXUAL PROVOCATION.

"New fashions?"

STYLE.

"I like driving fast after a James Bond film."

ENERGY.

"What about movie stars?"

STARS.

"I'm always happy looking at Paris."

TRAVEL.

"Comedy."

LAUGHS.

"Horror films."

SCREAMS.

"Songs."

SONGS.

"Love stories."

LOVE STORIES.

"Are we talking about types of movies or reasons that we go?" Drew asked.

"Whatever gets you to the theater," said Levison.

"I like the crowd," said Drew. "I like other people."

COMMUNITY.

Griffin pressed back into the green couch. He thought about excuses. First he would have to say something to the people in the room. Once the body was discovered, and it was already in a morgue, he knew that someone would say, "This writer was killed outside that theater you went to last night, Griffin, did you know that?" And he would answer, "That's the last time I go out in public." Some kind of light remark to get away from the specific murder into the territory of a world gone mad.

"Sometimes," said Drew Posner, "I have to admit I go to the movies not so much for escape—well, I guess it's a kind of escape, but it's more—it's for comfort. It's sort of everything, it doesn't matter what kind of film, just as long as it's a movie."

COMFORT.

"I know they're not popular now," said Mary, "but I've always liked big costume epics."

PERIOD.

"Fair enough," said Levison. "The point of this exercise is to think about what we like, not what we think we should like, or what we think the public will like or what we think the public already likes. And that's fifteen. Let's get sixteen. Who's going for it?"

Griffin raised his hand. "Usually I go to the movies to see what everyone else is seeing, so I can talk about it, so I don't feel left out. When I was in the fourth grade, all the cool kids in my class had seen *The Great Escape*. I hadn't. But I acted like I had."

Levison held the chalk to the board, trying to find the one word.

"Try lemmings," said Drew.

PEER PRESSURE.

"Now that we know why we go to the movies, the next step will be to look for projects that engage us on these basic levels. Class dismissed."

EVERETT WEINBERGER

It is possible in the film industry to make a great deal of money by doing nothing other than being the person to whom a great deal of money is paid. Michael Tolkin's novel and Robert Altman's film The Player *describe middle-level Hollywood executives with very high salaries but ill-defined skills and duties, who deftly network from one position to another without ever accomplishing anything except maintaining their position in the rat race. The challenge is to climb onto the spinning treadmill in the first place, and that is what Weinberger's* Wannabe *is about. He was a junior functionary trying to move up the ladder past others, who, because they were playing the same game, knew exactly who and what he was and understandably had no interest in helping him succeed.*

from *Wannabe*

Once on the Disney lot, I headed to the Animation Building, site of those disappointing rounds of interviews several months back. I climbed the stairs toward the rarefied air of the executive offices. If the rest of the building seemed squeaky clean, this floor was air-blasted. People there walked briskly with an air of hyper-importance. "I'm on a mission from God," they seemed to be saying.

I walked past Jeffrey Katzenberg, the diminutive head of Disney production, who administered and shaped every Disney release. He was famous in the industry for his workaholic schedule, his hundred phone calls a day, his pit-bull tenaciousness. Like Eisner, he had grown up as a rich kid in Manhattan, and by age fourteen he had begun working on what would become a seven-year stint for New York City Mayor John Lindsay, dropping out of New York University along the way. He eventually left politics for the movie industry, working as assistant to Barry Diller and moving his way up to head of production at Paramount.

Katzenberg was the counterbalance to Eisner, the nudger alongside the innovator. Eisner was known to call him the Golden Retriever for his consistent ability to sniff out new stars and profitable projects. Katzenberg moved with Eisner from Paramount to Disney in 1984. Referred to as "Sparky" in Celia Brady's acerbic column on the industry in *Spy* magazine, he was the embodiment of those Disney qualities many industry insiders hated: the pennypinching, the need for total control over creative elements, the formularization of the creative development process, and the nightmarish work schedules. Legend had it that when he showed up to work in the early morning hours and spotted other cars in the parking lot, he would feel their hoods to see if the other executives had just sneaked in ahead of him. Alec Baldwin was said to have called Katzenberg the eighth dwarf, Greedy.

Sparky Katzenberg was standing next to one of his secretaries' desks. I nodded at him and he nodded back, thinking I was someone important, given that I was headed purposefully toward the big cheeses' offices. Also, I looked pretty good in my business suit and Hollywood tie, like I belonged in the executive suite. He'd soon learn that I was just another peon, so I enjoyed it while I could.

I continued to the end of the hallway, and sucked my breath in as I saw a knockout blonde with a perfectly toned body. I assumed she was one of Frank Wells's two assistants.

"Hi, I'm from Right Connections. I'm Everett Weinberger." I smiled and extended my hand.

She shook it extremely hard and inspected me. "Tracy Taylor." Blunt, efficient, impassive. Hmmm, now where have I seen this type of person before? It hit me soon enough—she was the female version of Brad Dorman.

"Have a seat. I'll have some work for you in a minute."

I sat at the desk parallel to hers and waited, thinking what my opening line would be when I met Wells.

Tracy placed a huge bundle of mail on my desk. "Here, you can begin slitting the mail and stamping the date on it—always on the upper right-hand corner." So much for executive-level tasks. I was intrigued, however, by the prospect of reading Frank Wells's mail.

Several minutes later, Tracy flicked her eyes at me and noticed that I was doing slightly more reading than opening. "You'll have plenty of time to read later. For now, just stick to opening the letters."

There was a palpable sense of movement on the floor and I knew Wells was approaching. It wasn't that you could actually feel his power, but you could hear and see people's reactions as he passed by.

"Morning, Terry, Anne. That is the prettiest dress." I heard girlish laughter from down the hall. You don't become president of Disney without knowing how to flirt.

"Tracy, have you got the Euro-Disney file?" He called out even before he was in sight. This man knew how to maximize his time. Tracy, in turn, knew how to maximize her brownie points. She had the file stretched out in her hands before he even reached her desk.

"Morning, Frank. That is a great tie."

She pointed to me without taking her eyes off Wells. "Frank, this is Everett Weinberger replacing Sue for the week." I smiled and looked at him expectantly.

Wells grunted and barely turned his eyes in my direction. As he turned to go into his office, and with my heartbeat accelerating, I called out. "Mr. Wells?"

He and Tracy turned their heads toward me in surprise. Tracy immediately frowned and looked nervous. You don't speak until spoken to.

"I know your son Kevin from Stanford . . ."

He immediately smiled broadly, strode to my desk, and shook my hand.

"Hi! Welcome to Disney. So, you were in undergrad or business school with Kevin?"

"Business school. And I saw you speak on campus last spring." He had visited Stanford and given a speech in Bishop Auditorium on the Disney turnaround story.

He nodded and grinned. "Great, great. Good to have you here!" Touché, Tracy!

After he left, Tracy sullenly gave me some more mindless tasks to do. I realized that my encounter with Wells was strike one in her eyes.

My initial reaction would prove accurate. Tracy was like the hundreds of Brad Dormans who filled the junior ranks of Hollywood. But unlike him, she was a very pretty woman and a skilled flirt, at least with higher-ups she needed something from. The tone of her voice gave away whether she was addressing someone in a position of power or giving a minion an order.

Though Wells did not usher me in as a confidante and give me top-level strategic planning assignments, he did occasionally come directly to me and ask me to run some errands for him. This bugged Tracy, who, understandably, wanted me as far from her boss as possible.

Later that same day, when Tracy was away from her desk, Wells asked me to deliver a package across the lot. "No hurry on that, Everett—just make sure it gets there by two o'clock." I decided to wait and deliver it during my lunch break. Tracy returned, saw the package on my desk, and stood in front of me.

"Did Frank give you that to deliver?"

"Yes. He said to do it when I had a chance, so I'm going to deliver it at lunchtime in twenty minutes."

"I think you should go now and get it out of the way."

"Well, I think it makes sense to combine it with lunch at noon."

"You better go now. Believe me, I know when Frank says 'sometime during the day,' he means *now*."

"But Tracy, he would have said 'Now.' He said just to get it there by two. It's all the way across the lot and—"

"That's twice you snapped at me," she hissed, her face inches from mine. "Don't you *ever* contradict me again because you'll be out of here in ten seconds otherwise. I place one phone call to personnel and you're gone! So *don't* do that ever again! I won't stand for it! Do you understand?"

I stared at her. "I'm sorry, Tracy . . . I—I didn't mean anything by it." I caved in totally. I was shaking slightly, I was so angry. But if I displayed any of this rage, I'd be fired. Though she was wrong, I had to acquiesce. I managed a really pitiful look and hated myself for it.

"That's all right. Now after you deliver that, you can take lunch early." And with that, she actually smiled. Her transformation was frightening. One minute she was practically firing me; the next, she was my best friend.

Every day, Tracy would leave work with two canvas bags filled with piles of papers and breathlessly, but contentedly, complain to all who were within earshot. "Uhhh . . . I have so much work to do tonight . . . so much! Frank needs all of this by nine tomorrow morning." I never could figure out how mundane secretarial tasks could fill two bags with work every night. Wells, after all, had an executive assistant who worked on the more analytical projects. But Tracy was a dedicated Disney staffer, eager to follow company norms.

.   .   .   .

"Congratulations, Everett!" A female voice blared through the phone receiver, waking me up from an unfitful sleep on Friday, my last day at Frank Wells's office. Doesn't anyone sleep past seven in Hollywood? My mind went blank for a minute before I recognized Barbara Dreyfus's throaty voice. It had been six days since my first-round interview with her for the position of assistant to Alec Baldwin.

"You did very well. Let's just say that based on what I told him, Alec loved you—and *that's* an understatement . . . Heh-low! Are you there? Aaaa-lekk Baldwin wants to meet you!"

"Th-that's g-great," I stammered.

"You bet your (*crackle*) that's great. I'm having (*hiss*) see only three people (*crackle*) my number one choice (*crackle, hiss*) car phone (*crackle*) tunnel (*crackle*) today at five-thirty, okay?"

I thought of the horrors of having to ask Tracy if I could leave work early, and shuddered. "Actually, is Monday possible? I have to work for Frank Wells today at Disney until six." I thought name-dropping would aid my cause, but it had no effect on Barbara.

She seemed slightly miffed. "No, it most definitely isn't. Alec is in town just until tomorrow and is flying to Brazil with Kim for several weeks and then (*hiss, crackle, crackle, hiss*) when he'll be back. Now if you want this *amazing* position which is yours for the taking, I suggest you be there today. . . . All right?" Why doesn't she hype me just a little more about this job?

"Okay, okay. Today will be fine then."

"Terrific. Knock 'em dead, Ev!"

.   .   .   .

An hour later, I was on my way to Disney. I took the scenic route through Beverly Hills, as I needed extra time to think. I drove along Beverly Drive, one of my favorite streets in the city. It was L.A. as a picture postcard, a dizzying array of multi-million-dollar mansions built behind two perfectly spaced rows of fifty-foot palms that flanked the road. The street seemed to reach its apex at Sunset Boulevard with the otherworldly perfection of the lush, salmon-colored Beverly Hills Hotel, known as the Pink Palace. Built in 1912, the hotel was now owned by the Sultan of Brunei.

As I followed the stream of cars snaking north along Coldwater Canyon toward Burbank, I rehearsed the conversation I had to have with Tracy in my mind, not liking any of its variations. I needed to leave an hour early, and I knew that she was not going to like it.

"Tracy, I've got a very important interview." "Tracy, I'm feeling really sick." "Tracy, my brother is getting married tonight." "Tracy, I'm going to beat you to death with this stapler if you don't let me go."

I arrived at quarter to nine, a bit late due to the horrendous traffic. She hadn't come in yet. I frowned; clearly, something extraordinary had to have happened for Wonder Girl to show up late for work.

She rushed in at nine-thirty looking uncharacteristically disheveled and immediately got on the phone, sobbing to her friends: She had smacked her gorgeous red Jeep Wrangler into a school bus. She was fine, but the Jeep was a mess. I sympathized with her, but soon grew weary of the story, having heard it at least twenty times, as she told it to everyone who came in or called.

I waited until later in the morning when she had settled down to her work. "Uh, Tracy?"

"Uh-huh?" She didn't look up from her desk.

I opted for honesty. "Tracy, I need to leave an hour early today for a very important final-round interview." Her head jolted up and I spoke faster. "Believe me, I wouldn't ask if it weren't crucial or if I could get out of it. The interview's at five-thirty, so I need to leave here at five. I know today's a bad day for you, but is it okay with you?"

"Sure . . . sure, no problem. Don't worry about it—I'll be fine." Well, that seemed a tad too easy.

Ten minutes later, Tracy called me on the phone in the file room. "Harriet of Right Connections is on line two for you."

I picked up line two. "Everett, how can you do this to us?" Harriet wailed.

"It's just not professional," chimed in Pauline.

"Wh—what are you talking about?"

"You can't just leave a job in the middle." "It's just not professional." Two on one again.

"You have an obligation to Disney and to us." "It's your last day there, anyway. We know you'll do the right thing and stay."

"Wait a minute . . ." My hand involuntarily began massaging my suddenly throbbing temple. "First of all, it's just an hour early. Second of all, I asked Tracy for permission not ten minutes ago and she said okay—no problem."

"Please, Everett, Disney is our most important account and Frank Wells is the president, for God's sake." "Don't do it, Everett, you've gotta stay."

"But she just said it was totally okay! Wells is out of the office on business, anyway. There's not much to do here today. And why didn't she say anything to me?"

"She sure did say something. She immediately called the head of Human Resources at Disney and screamed about the temps at Right Connections." "She just had a very severe car accident, for God's sake. She may need to leave early for the hospital to get an X-ray."

"Hospital?" I sneered. "She looks fine to me. Listen, if it'll make you feel better I'll talk to her right now, and if she asks me to stay, I promise you I'll stay. No problem at all . . ."

"That's all we're asking." "Do the right thing."

I hung up the phone and walked slowly back into the office and stood in front of her desk.

"Tracy?"

She looked up at me with an angelic smile. A choir girl. "Yeah?"

"I didn't know you weren't feeling well. Do you need me to stay until six?"

"Well, I do have a little headache and I might also leave early, but don't worry about it. You go on to your interview."

"Tracy, that's not what I just heard. I got off the phone with Right Connections begging me to stay. Now, if you need me to stay, it's no problem at all— I swear. Just say the word and I'll stay."

"No, you can definitely go. Don't worry, I'll be all right."

"Are you sure, now? Because if there's any doubt at all . . ."

"Yes, I'm sure." She smiled broadly. "You can go . . . really."

"It's really okay? Because—"

"Listen," she said in a stern but friendly voice. "I'm telling you, it's all right. I wouldn't say it was all right if it wasn't. Now not another word on this."

She looked at me and smiled with total warmth, like a mother who has just reprimanded her son. I felt relieved. The head of personnel must have misunderstood. Tracy couldn't possibly have lied so convincingly. No one was *that* good—it would be too evil. Plus, I really needed to go on the interview.

Tracy left the office early, at four-thirty, with her usual two overstuffed canvas bags. A severe concussion could never stop Supergirl.

"Hey, feel better, Tracy!" I called out and grinned.

"Don't worry about me." She beamed at me with her Pepsodent smile. "And good luck on your interview!"

"Thanks." Maybe I had judged her unkindly after all.

. . . .

I was lying in bed at ten-thirty in the morning, several days after my interviews with Alec Baldwin and Kim Basinger, feeling restless and bored. It was my second day in a row without a temp assignment. I grabbed the remote control and began channel surfing. I could find nothing more amusing than the ending of a *Joy of Painting* episode with Bob Ross, a white guy with a seventies-style Afro and a soothing voice. I always found him hypnotic.

"Let's build us today a happy little cloud. I'm gonna take a little titanium white right on the ol' two-inch brush. And let's go up in here and just drop in an indication of some little clouds that live up here . . . Wherever . . . It doesn't matter where . . . Wherever you think they should live; that's *exactly* where they should be." That's why I liked him; in Bob Ross's microcosm, you could do no wrong.

I followed that with a repeat episode of *Lifestyles of the Rich and Famous.* I displaced all brain waves for the moment and listened while Robin Leach described today's fabulous story of excess.

"His name is Adnan Khashoggi," the Englishman began in stentorian tones. "This multi-billionaire is at home in any one of his twelve fabulous homes in the world's most glamorous cities. Whether driving around in one of his eighteen Rolls-Royces or jetting the globe in one of his five custom-made jets, Adnan Khashoggi is a true cosmopolitan!

"His hilltop retreat overlooking the beach at Saint Tropez," he continued, his voice rising to a crescendo, "is worth a fabulous thirty-five million dollars!"

I flicked the television off, comforting myself with the thought that if I had that kind of money, I would not flaunt it on national television.

The phone rang, and I lunged to answer it.

"I'm sorry, Everett." "We did what we could do." The Harriet and Pauline show.

"W-what are you talking about?"

"He doesn't know." "We better tell him."

"Tell me what?" I was starting to worry.

"Disney." "Tracy went ballistic."

I sat up in bed. "WHAT?"

"She called up the head of personnel yesterday and demanded that you be blacklisted from Disney." "We had no choice, Everett—it was either you or us."

"She did *what* now?"

"The head of personnel told us that either we blacklist you from future Disney temp assignments or we won't get any more Disney contracts." "They're our biggest client by far, you know."

I was sputtering with rage. "B-but you know that after we spoke she said it was okay to leave. I told her I'd stay, but she smiled at me and wished me luck. She practically ordered me to leave . . . Believe me, I wouldn't have left if she had told me to stay."

The Right Connections women were surprisingly supportive. "We know— it's not the first time she's given our temps trouble. She has a reputation." "We'll take care of you though. We'll have to keep you away from the creative side for now and see if we can work you into other areas at Disney."

"I can't believe this . . . it's—it's beyond evil."

"We know, honey." "Don't take it personally."

I hung up the phone, wanting to cry. I didn't even care that much about not being able to work at Disney. What enraged me was that Tracy, representative of many young people in Hollywood, was at least as mean as she was successful. Her beautiful facade hid her true disposition. I also couldn't stand the emasculating feeling of not being able to retaliate, utterly powerless in the face of such outrage. I wondered if Wells knew of Tracy's behavior outside of his presence and momentarily considered relating to him the whole episode.

.   .   .   .

I settled into a routine of single-day temp assignments, and the next few weeks passed in a blur. Then, several events shattered the calm.

At first I didn't recognize the pretty blonde sitting alone in the nearly empty Jack in the Box restaurant, but I knew I'd met her somewhere. I was bleary-eyed tired that Friday night from a week's worth of temping in the television commercial sales department at local station KTLA, and in no mood to think about what to eat, so I had allowed myself the cheap luxury of fast food. I was so hungry that I didn't even bother looking for a restaurant with a drive-thru window.

"Fries, filet of fish, Diet Coke and . . . that'll be it. To go, please." I glanced behind me again, my eyes focusing now on the blonde, her hair tied in a neat ponytail, an overstuffed tan canvas bag beside her. Tracy Sure-You-Can-Leave-Early Taylor! Good God! Alone, on a Friday night, hunched over a soggy burger in an antiseptic Jack in the Box on Santa Monica Boulevard. With a gentle look on her face, she barely resembled the Doberman who had barked at me so viciously.

Unconsciously, I pulled out bills and handed them to the cashier, my body turned sideways so I could continue watching her. Here was a portrait of the wannabe. No outsider who envisioned the career path of a movie executive would ever stop and consider the nights I, Tracy, and many other hopefuls spent in places like this.

I had built her up in my mind as a monster, and yet, seeing her in the vulnerable state, I forgave Tracy at that moment. Should I go over and talk to her? No, I decided. She'd be sure to resurrect her defenses and proffer some excuse for being there. She'd have said that she was doing top-secret research on fast-food chains for Frank. Then I'd hate her all over again. Instead, I grabbed my bag and headed home.

SEX AND SCANDAL

JOHN KOBAL

John Kobal was a writer, a critic and fan of the movies, and a gifted interviewer, whose People Will Talk *is an invaluable collection of interviews with Hollywood legends who opened up to a startling degree for him. Perhaps that was because he was also the founder and proprietor of the Kobal Collection, which began as his private collection of movie star photos and expanded until it became one of the largest archives of movie-related photographs in the world. He knew so much about his subjects that perhaps they thought he might as well know the rest. One of his most challenging subjects was Mae West, and here you can see how he wins her confidence and gets her talking and sits back, delighted.*

"Mae West"

Mae West was born into an era of America's history when signs of the new nation's success were forests of chimney stacks billowing pollution into the sky to herald the cities mushrooming up beneath. A man's worth then could be measured by his girth; a woman's charms by ample curves that made her look like a scenic railroad. When Mae (the woman who put the giggle into "gigolo") finally struck it big, it wasn't with the plays on contemporary themes that gave her early notoriety (*Sex, The Drag* and such), but by going back to her own roots on the Bowery and to the dreams that had fueled her rise from barroom boards to the heights of the legitimate stage, Broadway.

Mae's earliest theatrical experiences had been as Little Eva in *Uncle Tom's Cabin* and in other such celebrated child roles (Mae was always small for her years), but in between acts she entertained as a "coon-shouter"* from which she got that

---

*The term "coon-shouter" came from the Old South, where black slaves used to chase raccoons out of hiding to make them easier targets. The tag stuck, and when in vaudeville black music became acceptable entertainment for white audiences, performed by blacks, not in white- or black-face but as themselves, they became known as

sassy delivery, that sashaying walk—like a sailor back on dry land after months at sea—and her lifelong love for the black-soul sound that could have made her one of the great white blues-singers, a talent overshadowed by the immortality she gained, drawing on another of her earliest-learned skills as an impressionist of the famous vaudeville stars of her youth. She re-created the two most celebrated symbols of self-made wealth and beauty of her era, the legendary railroad tycoon "Diamond Jim" Brady and the beauty who set the standard for generations of young girls, Lillian Russell, the actress Brady showered with diamonds. Mae took the best parts of both and gave the world *Diamond Lil,* the first white woman with a black soul.

By the time she took the Silver Chief to Hollywood in 1932, Mae wasn't a little girl from a little town trying to make good in the big city, she was a big girl from a big town she'd already conquered. She'd come to save the ailing Paramount studio from going under with the box-office returns from her first starring film, a somewhat cleaned-up version of her nationally known *Diamond Lil.* To appease puritan outrage the film version was retitled *She Done Him Wrong,* and so that Mae's character wouldn't be confused with the notorious theatrical Lil, they renamed her Lou. The guardians of public morality were happy with their silly victory.

She Done Him Wrong rescued Paramount from an MGM takeover by grossing $2 million, a formidable sum considering that film tickets in 1933 cost 10 cents, and lent an additional meaning to the popular song "Brother, Can You Spare a Dime?" In the depths of the Depression, when people lived on nothing and sometimes less, for ten cents Mae gave them back confidence and the notion of a time in America when a man's, or a woman's, get-up-and-go was all that was needed to gain fame, fortune, a bed of roses and a safe full of diamonds. People by the millions, hungry and dispirited, shelled out their precious dimes (enough for a meal) to see her strut her stuff, lick the liars, outwit the politicians at their own game . . . and when she rolled her eyes over a good-looking guy, an audience could feel the goose on their own bottom. Mae's *Diamond Lil* was a raffish, healthy reaffirmation of what an American was capable of achieving in the home of the brave and the free.

Mae's arrival on screen is in a horse-drawn barouche pulling up in front of

---

"coon-shouters." Down, dirty, funky and blue, they chased white entertainment up the vaudeville tree. Mae even as a child knew a good thing when she heard it, and she took it for herself. By the time, years after, when she had hit her own stride, the term had dropped from the vocabulary, with Mae the sole and soul beneficiary. I'd always had a hunch—nothing sure, just an instinct from watching her perform, trading quips with the black help, not like mistress and servant but like two girls in the dressing room, and from the way she sang—that the oft-hinted-at secret in Mae's past was a touch of color in her blood. I could never get Mae to admit anything like that when I delicately broached the subject, because I felt that she shouldn't be making rock 'n' roll records, but rather the old blues the way they should be sung. The idea really appealed to Mae, but she just explained that her affinity for black music was because it's the best there is. She died with all her secrets intact.

her Bowery place of work. As she gets out, she greets a poor widow woman and her little girl with a tip and a friendly pat on the kid's head. As Mae née Lil now Lou saunters through the swinging doors into the bar, the widow woman says, "You're a good woman, Miss Lou," to which the nonchalant Mae replies, "Best woman ever walked the streets." In one swift establishing scene Mae had won over mothers (of which there were many) and the poor (of which there were more). Not everyone liked Mae, though. When somebody told her that the jam-packed premiere of *I'm No Angel* at Grauman's Chinese Theater was noticeably lacking Hollywood's elite, Mae put Tinsel Town in its place, saying she liked it that way because "I prefer to play to the best people." Hollywood's churlish attitude lasted no longer than it took to cash in on Mae's success. When MGM's sex star, Jean Harlow, started to sass her way to comedy success (black maids and all), Mae's victory was complete.

By the time I met Mae, in 1970, almost as many years had elapsed since she brought her most famous creation to the screen as had separated that film from the era of Brady and Russell, and by now she had become as much a legend on the American scene as the prototypes for her fame. Once Mae had found Lil, she never really deviated from it—it was the skin that suited her best, and subsequent roles, on stage or screen, whether in a contemporary setting or as a historical heroine like the Empress of Russia in *Catherine Was Great,* were really the further adventures and conquests of her Lil. Unlike other performers who made a name by impersonating famous faces and voices of the screen, especially herself (Mae always had a great fondness for male impressionists), neither Brady nor Lillian Russell was much more than a dim name to the people Mae appealed to on Broadway or in movies, and as a result she was never handicapped by comparisons. In the end, she believed in her creation and saw it as an extension of herself in much the same way the paying fans did. Talking to her about Lil was like talking to Mae about herself. It may have been the woman I met, but it was the legend I saw. She was Lil.

I did have an exceptional and unique illustration of Mae's gifts as an impressionist, in a location as bizarre and unexpected as the performer she momentarily re-created. I had no tape recorder to capture the moment for posterity, but I wasn't likely to forget Mae doing Sarah Bernhardt in a Chinese restaurant in downtown Los Angeles one night in 1974. There were four of us, Mae; Paul Novak, her friend, bodyguard, chauffeur, masseur, and, it was said, lover; Paul Morrissey, the Warhol director who'd been wanting to meet her; and I. Dinner was lively even though the subjects under discussion were the well-worn paths of her career and sayings. In the middle of our meal, a semi-drunk black man came over and stood by our table, not threatening, just waving on his feet. He addressed Mae without preamble, as if to continue a conversation they hadn't finished the day before.

"How's Ruby?" he asked. "Ruby," said Mae. "Yeah, she worked for you."

"Oh," said Mae, "yeah, she's gone." "When was that?" "Long ago now, deah." "Did she go back to New York?" "Yeah, I think so, deah." "You don't have her address, do you?" he wanted to know. "No, deah, no." "She was a nice girl." "Yeah, very nice. Sweet," Mae added. "Well, you're looking good." "Thanks, deah." "Well, it's been good seeing you." "Yeah, deah." "See you around." He tipped his hand in salutation and ambled off the way he came.

"Who's that?" we asked. "Don't know, deah." "Who's Ruby?" Mae had no idea. "But you sent her off to New York," we persisted. "He sounded as if he knew you." Mae chuckled, "Oh they all do, deah."

So, we were laughing and joking, and in that frame of mind I thought I'd see if Mae really did remember or if she was just parroting a lifetime's performance in the role of Mae West.

What was Lillian Russell like? I wanted to know. Mae wasn't totally sure any-more because in her mind she'd long ago confused Russell with her own mother, probably the single most influential force in her own life. So, then, had she ever seen Sarah Bernhardt, the legendary French tragedienne? I might just as well have said Eva Tanguay or Anna Held, but, well, Bernhardt was a name familiar to all. "Oh, sure," Mae drawled and told of the New York actors' benefit one Sunday afternoon before the war. World War I, that is. "1912," said Mae. We were riveted. "What was Sarah like?" I asked. "Well, you know," Mae said, maybe a bit put off by my persistence in wanting to know about anybody except Mae West, "it was so long ago, and she was talkin' in French, you know." But was she good? "Oh, yeah, deah, sure . . . she was a great actress." "What did she do?" Mae, instead of saying how or why she was good, went into an impression. Her little hands with their long, hard, clawlike nails took on the melodramatic ges-tures of the actors of Bernhardt's era that one can see in the pictures from those days, the hands held out front, one up over her face, the fingers slightly curled as if gripping some invisible force, and her voice became a low, rolling growl, full of long *rrrr*'s and words like "*royame . . . de royame . . . de royame. . . .*" When she had finished, one of the Paul's asked Mae whether this was before or after Bernhardt had lost her leg. "What's that, deah?" "Well," he explained, "Sarah had to have a leg amputated." "Oh, yeah, deah," she answered after a little re-flection. "Must have been aftah . . . 'cause she was draggin' things a bit."

So, after that evening I always believed Mae, whether it was a story she told for the first time or so often that everybody had lost count. Sort of her own "To be or not to be," like the story about the cop with the gun in his pocket, or her advice to skinny girls, when she told them, "What the good Lord has forgotten we'll put there with cotton." She never lost her timing for making things sound fresh; and nobody was ever quite as delighted with Mae's success story as Mae herself. Back in England, I told friends about her Bernhardt in the restaurant, and somebody asked me whether or not Mae had been any good. How the hell would I know? I've never heard Sarah Bernhardt, but it sure sounded amazing at the time.

Getting the interview on tape for posterity wasn't as easy as egg foo yung and a pair of chopsticks. Mae hesitated. She hadn't let anyone do a taped interview with her for more than a decade, and she didn't want to spoil the impact of her screen return by letting people hear her . . . "unless," as she said, "the interview is short and the questions are good. They have to be good, you know, whatever they are. You've got to ask the right questions. You know."

Mae had appeared at the Academy screening room, where they'd been having a seminar, showing a film followed by a question-and-answer session. After the screening of *I'm No Angel* they brought in a chaise-longue and placed it center stage beneath a large potted floral growth. George Cukor, who acted as moderator, escorted Mae on. Slowly. She was in her elevator heels, towering over him, her hair piled sky-high, looking like nobody else. She wowed the audience. It was just her and Cukor up there onstage, talking. The standing-room crowd screamed and hollered and made the whole thing into an event that was something of a first of its kind for that time: "camp" was in the air even though it hadn't yet pitched tent in every corner bar in the land. The questions were planted, the answers confident. The result was a triumph: the publicity for *Myra Breckinridge,* still in production, was enormous. Mae felt good. So good, in fact, that she lowered some of her reservations about letting me do the first "taped" interview she'd done in so many years. She promised to consider doing it. She had to approve the questions. I had to have the interview. She was still reluctant to be taped. We'd talk. She'd decide what questions she liked, which answers she liked. We'd tape later. It was a start.

MW: Ohhhhh. Did you see that picture *Dolly?* [*Hello, Dolly!* with Barbra Streisand.] Because I want to look at it. I understand that she's doing an imitation of me. That's a lot of nerve [pronounced "noive"]. Taking your mannerisms and everything, and puttin' it up there like it's hers.

JK: Don't you think it's really a big compliment?

MW: No, no. She's liable to continue doing everything that way, playing all her parts. First thing you know, people will think it's hers. Why should she dare do this? As an imitation, fine, but you can't imitate a person all through a picture. I understand she copies my style all through the picture. She didn't know how she wanted to play it and she thought of me, and it just stuck with her and she couldn't help it. I was never interested in seeing other performers for ideas for my act. I was an individual and I was developing my own personality, you see. I didn't want anything from anybody else that wasn't me. I saw all the shows when I wasn't working, but I never copied them. I mimicked Eddie Foy and George M. Cohan . . .

I did these great male impersonations . . . but that was mimicry, which is different from taking tricks from people.

JK: Your mannerisms are classics. It struck me again watching you the other night that, although you don't smoke, you always have these long cigarettes in your films.

MW: Ohhhh. I always have a cigarette for the characterizations. But I didn't like it. I used to have to hold it, but I never puffed. You never saw me inhalin' or anything. I couldn't wait till I got rid of it. But I had to do it, you know, it was for the characters. When I played these, you know, very few women smoked, they didn't smoke in public in the '20s. And they never had sex symbols in films till I came. Or they called it something else, 'cause nobody used the word "sex" till I used it in my play, except to differentiate between the male and female, like he's of the male sex. . . . So now, when the studio sees somebody who looks like a sex symbol, they build it up and stuff it down the public's throat and keep telling the public that this is a sex symbol till after a time people come to believe it. After I was called a sex symbol and the studios saw how much money my films made, they wanted others. But these were "synthetic." When MGM were building up Harlow, they came to me to ask me to write some stories for her, give her some funny dialogue. That was a joke. I was breakin' my neck writing, casting and starring in my own films. If I thought of something funny, I wasn't about to give it to them!

JK: Not only funny, but racy too. Not dirty, but you did make movies that helped bring the Hays Office down on Hollywood.

MW: Deah, when I knew that the censors were after my films and they had to come and okay everything, I wrote scenes for them to cut! These scenes were so rough that I'd never have used them. But they worked as a decoy. They cut them and left the stuff I wanted. I had these scenes in there about a man's fly and all that, and the censors would be sittin' in the projection room laughing themselves silly. Then they'd say "Cut it" and not notice the rest. Then when the film came out and people laughed at it and the bluenoses were outraged, they came and said, "Mae, you didn't show us that." But I'd show them the scripts they had okayed themselves!

JK: Where did you get this feeling for the underworld jargon? The way characters like Chick and Clogg and the others talked?

MW: Well . . . surely, you know . . . I met characters, I met people, you talk and listen to them, they talk that way, you know what I mean, slangy and all. And I knew all that slang. I come from Brooklyn, New York, and a lot of characters are there. I didn't base my characters, like Gus Jordan and those, on real people. They are all characters I made up. Yeah. No, the whole thing just came. Well, you gotta watch all the pictures I made, it's the same way . . . they came to me. I never stopped, you know, I just made one picture after another. You know, *Klondike Annie* and the circus picture you saw the other night, *I'm No Angel,* you know.

JK: There were so many young people there, did you like that?

MW: Oh, God, yeah. Well, I expect this picture *Myra Breckinridge* will get both; the older people will come out to see it, and I've got this young crowd. It can't miss.

At this point, nobody—including Mae—knew yet what the end of the film was going to be. She felt that it should end with a great last line . . . hers. But the film still had a week to shoot. At the moment she was still wondering what she'd do after the film. One of the plans was to do the play *Sextette* in England, but she said:

MW: I'd rather do another picture than do a spectacular for television. Because I think my value is when they've got to pay money to see me. When they start to see me on TV, they just turn you off and on, you know, they get satisfied and then they say, "Oh, she'll be on again," and they just wait. I want to make another picture before I do anything on TV. Somebody's talking to me about doin' *Sextette.* I want to get Christopher Plummer for that. Do you know him? I told Bob Wise after I saw that picture he did with him, you know, *Sound of Music,* I said, "There's your sex person. There's your box office. Him." He carried that picture. She was all right, you know, Julie Andrews, you know what I mean, to play a schoolmarm or a nun, but she hasn't got the sex personality. No, no, no. And unless you put somebody in there with him who has it, it's missin'. That's why I think that picture *Star* didn't do so well. She hasn't got *it.*

JK: I heard once that you rejected George Raft when you were making *Belle of the Nineties,* even though you had worked with him in *Night After Night,* your first film. Didn't he have it?

MW: Sure. Ah, no, I'd 'a had him. But, you see, I would have had to co-star with him again. This way I didn't have to co-star with anyone. I just featured them.

JK: Did you always cast your leading men yourself?

MW: Ohhh, yeah. Like I cast Cary Grant. And I cast Victor McLaglen for *Klondike Annie.* Why I cast Victor was I was up to 142 pounds in that picture, though you'd never know it. And I couldn't get the weight off in time, see, so I figured, well, I'd get McLaglen. He's not only tall but wide, a very thick look in his face, bulky, you know, big. And he'd make me look thin. That's how I put Victor McLaglen in. And then, of course, he was perfect for the part of Bull Brackett. I think he gave a great perfor-

mance. He got a sex personality. Ohhhhh, yes. He has it. That smile . . .
I always cast my leading men in my plays too. Of course, sometimes you
can't always get what you want, so you take second best.

JK: It's funny to hear you speak of "second best" . . . you've worked so hard
at maintaining your image, your "star."

MW: Deah, I've had an easy, successful and happy life. Show me anyone at my
age who can do what I'm doing now and look the way I do and play the
parts I play. You know, most women when they're forty [who is going to
argue with Mae West?] start having to play character parts. It should give
other people hope, deah. If I can do it, they can. It's the body and the mind.
Keep your mind youthful-thinking and your insides have to be healthy and
young. I have a cold once in ten years.

    I never wanted to be anyone else. I was satisfied to be myself. If I
wanted to be Florence Nightingale or Madame de Pompadour, I'd play
them for a short time till I got tired of the part. Well, I only ever wanted
to be a lion tamer. As a child I was always being told that the lion was the
king of animals and the most beautiful and ferocious beast, and my father
took me to see them and told me how they were the greatest. So years
later I wrote myself a part in *I'm No Angel* in which I played a lion tamer.
When I went into that cage, I felt at home because I had wanted to do this
so much since I was a child. There were about ten lions in the cage, if you
remember. That was no fake. They wouldn't let me put my head in the
lion's mouth, though. I wanted to, but they said they had to think of the
picture, and they got this woman who worked with the lions to do that.
I would've done it. Of course, when I think of it now, you couldn't get
me into a cage with a lion for anything. So you see, deah, if I want to be
something else, I write it as a part and play it, but I never wanted to be
anyone else but me for long.

JK: And you've played *that* part since . . . when?

MW: Ohhh, I was in shows and in vaudeville when I was a kid. While I was working, I had an aunt along to chaperone me, and there was a maid who
dressed me and all that stuff. I had a very proper family. We never used
any swearing or discussed sex at home. It's strange, that, but I never
talked about sex with my parents. Even today I don't like to discuss sex
with my sister . . . I'd feel dirty. The way I heard about sex first came from
a friend of mine when I was nine. Her mother was a doctor, and we were
playing in her house one day and there was this book lying there on the
table and after I read it I had a funny feeling about my parents. A peculiar
feeling—disgust, you might say. It took a long time for me to get over it.
They suddenly weren't gods anymore. Ohh, I wish they wouldn't teach
sex in the schools. They should teach *health*. Health is what is important.

But I never had much time to mix with other children, but I know I never missed them. You see, I was so carried away with myself, my dancing, my singing, that I didn't need other kids around. Besides, growing up in show business makes you a lot smarter, and it gave me a standing in the neighborhood.

JK: How did you break into show business?

MW: Well, I had a natural singing voice and my mother took me to singing and dancing schools. Nobody else in our family had ever been in show business, but she had wanted to go on the stage when she was a young girl. Her parents wouldn't let her, they were very strict like that. But she loved me being in the theater. I was crazy about my mother. But I never liked my father much when I was small. I don't know why, 'cause he never laid a hand on any of us, you know, and he always provided good for us. The only reason I can think of now why I wasn't crazy about him was that he smoked these big cigars. To this day I haven't been able to stand cigars. He was a prizefighter in the beginning, a very handsome man, and later he had a detective agency and then his own hansom-cab business.

JK: Is he the reason for your partiality to boxing and muscle men?

MW: No, I don't think it's because he was a fighter. I was never much around businessmen because I wasn't in that walk of life. I was in show biz and so I went for that kind of man. I attracted athletes because I don't smoke and I don't drink and I like to keep fit. That gets 'em. Yeah. . . .

Mae was always proud of her body. She maintained it and liked to have it appreciated and was not averse to having you feel her muscles. Back in the '30s Paramount photographer Bill Walling had done a couple of "at home" sessions with her, and he was present the day Mae came to the gallery for a portrait session soon after she'd signed with Paramount. "She was wearing a slinky low-cut dress that wasn't covering much as it was, and all that flesh was making Gene [the head of Paramount Portrait Gallery, who shot all the big stars like Dietrich, Lombard and, naturally, Mae West] a bit nervous. Gene was a staid sort of guy, not very lively. But he knew his job. Mae was leaning over a round, glass table cupping her head in her hands. The radio was on because she liked music. These sessions could take a long time, and the music helped her to relax. This was during the Depression, and there used to be a lot of these giveaway shows on the air. This guy was forever offering dumb things to his listeners. He was saying how he had these two cute little puppies to be given away. One had a cute little brown nose, and the other had a cute little pink nose. And you were to call in to say which one you wanted. Gene was behind the camera when Mae said, 'Hey, Gene.' She'd taken out one of her big beautiful bazooms and put it on the table. 'Which one do you want? The one with the cute little brown nose or the one with the cute little pink nose?' She was a real exhibitionist. Well, Gene was so shocked he nearly knocked the camera over. She thought that was real funny."

MW: But you asked me about me and show biz. Well, when I was twelve, I had gotten too mature for children's parts, so I went back to living at home in Brooklyn till I was sixteen, when I could get a work permit and go back on the stage. While I was living at home, I used to do Sunday concerts for various organizations like the Knights of Columbus. That sort of thing, you know. And the first boyfriend that I remember was Joe Schenk—he was about seventeen and I was fourteen. He was a pianist and had his own ragtime band, and Saturday nights they'd come up to our house to rehearse. But I had an awful lot of boyfriends in those years at home, Joe was just the first in long pants. I always had maybe one girlfriend at a time, but I wasn't much of a woman's woman. Even then. My sister, Beverly, was a lot younger than I was, so we never had much in common as children. But later we were very close.

JK: So you got your first man when you were fourteen. How old were you when you got married?

MW: I was seventeen. But I had lots of affairs before I married Frank Wallace. But they were just love affairs, not sex-love affairs. We'd neck and hug and kiss and play with each other, but no sex. Not till I got married. Probably one of the reasons I did get married then was because of sex. Frank and I were on the road at the time with our vaudeville act, so my parents didn't know, and before I agreed to marry him, I made him swear not to tell my mother. We never signed into a hotel as a married couple. And I'll say that for him, he never told her and she never knew I was married till the day she died. But Frank was a problem. Our marriage was a mistake anyhow, even if the judge had tied us with a sailor's knot, and Frank kept on pressing me, making demands, wanting me to live with him instead of at home, but I wanted to be free. So I made up this story that my mother wanted me to do a single act 'cause she thought it would be good for my career. As he'd promised to not tell her, he never went to ask her. I had really gotten this offer to work for the Shuberts in a show,* and I didn't want Frank around. While I was in their office one day, I heard that they were casting a show that was going on the road, and they hadn't a juvenile, so I suggested Frank. I told him to come right over and he got the

---

*Mae, still a brunette, played Maymie Dean, the "vamp," in the Rudolf Friml musical *Sometime,* in which she introduced the "Shimmy-Shake" and sang "What Do I Have to Do to Get It?" That was in 1918, and she found the answer.

part and went on the road for a year. We stayed apart after that. And I
never got married again because there were enough men to choose from.
Besides, I was already married. Even if nobody else knew that, I did.

I suppose I never loved one man enough to settle down to marriage. I
was fickle because I had too much temptation. Marriage and one man for
life is fine for some people, but for me it wasn't good. Every time I look
at myself, I become absorbed in myself, and I didn't want to get involved
with another person like that. I saw what it did to other people when they
loved another person the way I loved myself, and I didn't want that problem. Because of that, I never wanted children and I never had any. I like
other people's children, but I was my own baby. I had myself to do things
for. Get my act together, get my material, write my stuff, work. That's
what I wanted.*

JK: And you got it. You did write all of your own lines, didn't you, even in
your first movie?

MW: Yes, deah. You know, Louis B. Mayer never liked me because I wouldn't
go and work for MGM after I'd made this big success in *Night After Night*
over at Paramount. That film took sixteen weeks to shoot. When I first
came out to the Coast, I sat around for twelve weeks drawing money and
I never saw a script. This wasn't for me: either I worked or I wanted to
get back on the stage. But they kept begging me and telling me they had
a contract with me, so I told them to let me have a script and I would
rewrite it. "Hold it," they said, "just your own scenes." Well, it came to
shooting my first scene. Everybody was so slow with their delivery. The
film was going to sleep on me, I had to come in like a streak of lightning
or we'd all go to sleep. So I played my lines very smart, you know, never
giving the other actors time to think over their lines, and I'd be always
rolling on the axis and breaking into lines with an "Oh yeah" and an "Uh-
hummm." You know, to keep the action flowing. And I was mad at Paramount. I'd come from Broadway, where I'd been a top star, and here I
was playing this . . . you'd call it a guest part. And it wasn't even ready
till I started to rewrite it. The night they screened it, I didn't come along.
Then I got these phone calls telling me what a hit it was going to be and I
could have anything I wanted. They had no projects for me at Paramount,
so they came to me asking if I had anything I wanted to do. I had *Diamond
Lil* all ready and I gave it to them. The play department who got hold of a
copy wrote something on a foolscap-sized page to tell me why it wouldn't
work on film. Well, deah, we shot it in two weeks and they called it *She*

---

*In fact, though she didn't want it for her image, Mae was devoted to her sister, Beverly, and her brother, and
looked after them, supported them, till her death.

Done Him Wrong. It saved the studio. I found out afterwards that MGM were planning to buy Paramount if it went bust, and then my film made money and the studio was okay.

JK: In *Diamond Lil,* how much is the character of Lil—or Lou, as it ended up in the movie—based on you?

MW: Ohhh, well, if I were that character, if I were livin' in that time, I'd do exactly what I write about. That's the way my mind runs.

JK: But is she expressing your own philosophy when she says, "Diamonds have souls"?

MW: Oh, yeah, that's all mine. Well, when she meets up with this good man, he's with the Salvation Army, the one who tells her that "Diamonds have no souls." That's from his standpoint. Then she repeats it, you know what I mean? So she's learnin', you know. She says, "When you're dead, you're dead, that's the end of it." Then he gives her a little of the Bible. See, she's surrounded by all these rough guys. You know, she says, "I've always appreciated good men." I mean, good principle, good character, good in that sense. Because I've met a lot of the other type of man. I wasn't very religious as a child or anything. Every time I went to Sunday School, I used to come home with a headache. But, like I told you, we were brought up strict, and later, when I was on my own, I kept the Ten Commandments and that was enough. And I've always leaned towards . . . for myself, to really be satisfied with a man, I have to feel that he's right, and respect him, you see. And that's why I thought to put this character's line in. Then, as I was goin' through the story and everything, I said, "I need a good punch ending to follow all this great material, all this great stuff." And I didn't know what to do and I didn't want to introduce another character, so then that's when I figured that he was an undercover detective and I made a detective out of him. But I got all that goodness over, and her falling in love with him when she thought he was with the Salvation Army.

JK: Well, you re-created that whole period effectively.

MW: Yeah, and I'll tell you why. My mother was taken many times, when I was a child, for being Lillian Russell. She was the great American beauty for years. Nobody took her place. It wasn't like these, you know, movie stars, these Miss America things they run every year, somebody new. Here was a beauty that nobody could top. For years and years. And then she was in this period, the clothes that she wore and everything. And then I saw pictures of my mother when she was in her twenties or so, with all these kinds of clothes on her and everything, and I was always fascinated with it. That's when I started to write. And my main reason, like I told you, was I used to have 80 percent men in my audience, and I wanted more women. That's how I thought of that period. Then I got the grandmothers and grandfathers, I got three generations. That really made me break everybody's box-office records all over. So *Diamond Lil* did the trick.

JK: But earlier, in the story of the play more than the movie, you have her thinking only about her diamonds when Chick Clark almost kills her.

MW: Well, that character . . . she lived for her diamonds. I was that way when I was about fifteen years old. I saw a great big diamond on Fifth Avenue in one of those jewelry stores, hanging on one of those velvet busts, and it was on a fine chain. It was about twenty-five carats of diamond, and I fell in love with that diamond. And I've always thought of a diamond that size. I've got to have one that big. I've got to have that diamond. And I got lots of diamonds later, but every time I got one, I wasn't thrilled enough with it. I liked it, but I was still thinking thinking thinking of that one. Finally, I got them that size. Know what I mean? Diamonds, ohhh- hhh, they just did things for me. I wouldn't wear a rhinestone. I wouldn't wear anything else unless it was the real thing. See, it's only lately that you have duplicates on account of robbery, and on account of jewelry being so high to insure for. So for the stage I wear the imitation, you know. But Lil was a character just like that.

JK: Do you still value diamonds that much? Because one thinks of diamonds and one thinks of Mae West . . . and vice versa.

MW: Well, I've had so many, I've had so much diamonds, and now, because of all these rhinestones they wear, the imitations and all that stuff that almost look as good, I keep the real stuff in a vault. The last time I had my good big diamonds out was when I went over to the college.* Well, I have so many different sets that I wouldn't have room for all of them. I just keep them in a vault. When I took them out one day, it cost me $75 a week just to have one out. This was the $45,000 diamond. So I put it back. It made no sense. It was too expensive. It's sad, but then they've given me the imitations, which look almost as good.

JK: Mae, the public see your connection with diamonds as materialistic, yet you always had some spiritualistic connection with them.

MW: Yeah?

JK: Well, in *She Done Him Wrong* you sold diamonds to pay for the upkeep of an orphanage, and then sold more diamonds to pay for the lease on the Salvation Army shelter . . . and you did it all anonymously. You are very involved in the spiritual. . . .

MW: Ohhh, yeah. I see, yeah. Sure. And it was the strangest thing. I don't know

*I don't know what occasion she is referring to here, and, short of a fraternity panty-raid party, I can only think that she means one of the dinners in her honor that UCLA or USC gave as a result of the Mae West revival sweep- ing America at that time.

if I ever told you, but while I was writin' *Diamond Lil,* I had most of my characters but no lead. And I said, "Now I've got to get one man in here that she really falls in love with." I thought, Gee whiz, and I didn't know what I was going to put in, whether it was a young society boy or what, and I hesitated. And I was layin' my whole story out, and I went down to the Bowery just to look the place over because it was nothing like it was in the old days. And that day I just rode down there again, just drove around, you know, just, I don't know, to feel the place. And first thing I know, I saw this door that was open, and I saw an American flag in this dumpy place, this old building, you know. And then I looked, and I was drivin' slowly and, first thing you know, this handsome Salvation Army captain, without his cap on, came out. He walked out of this door, right to the gutter at the end of the sidewalk, and I passed him slowly. He looked into the car, and I said, "Uhmmmm, ahhhh, ohhhh," and I suddenly felt like drivin' around the block again to take another look, 'cause he was so handsome, and I thought, Gee, he should really be an actor. He was so handsome. Then it dawned on me. The forces, even though I didn't know so much about them in those days, I thought, he should be a leading man. Ohhhhh, yeah, a good man. A Salvation Army captain. He's the guy to come in and fall in love with her. He just walked out at the psychological moment, see? I went to see the buildings, and here he was. I had a mirror in my car, and as we were driving past, I looked in it, and I could see him looking after the car and then turning around and goin' back in. I don't know what he came out for, it was just the forces made him come out, now that I understand about the forces, they made him come out for me to see him.

You know, sometimes I just lie down in a semidark room and I see crowds, individuals coming in like a montage. Now, I'm a very normal, healthy person, I don't imagine things, so when I see things and hear voices, I know there is something that exists around us. Over the years I've developed my psychic powers. Everything was a thought before it was created . . . this table, this vase, they were a thought before we made them. But I really didn't get involved with ESP until I met Thomas Kelly in 1941. The forces for good and evil were coming in, I would hear psychic voices and see people all the time and they kept me awake at night. If you told this to people about hearing voices, they'd think you were mad or something. With Thomas Kelly, you know, he came to my house because I'd heard so much about him from friends who knew I was interested in ESP. He tied a bandage around his eyes while we all were told to ask questions by writing them on a piece of paper and put that paper in a blank envelope so he wouldn't know whose envelope he was feelin'. I wrote five questions: "When will we be in the war? For how long? Who'll win it?" and two other questions of a very personal nature. When we came to my envelope, he said, "In three months we'll be attacked by Mr. Jap when he blows up Pearl Harbor; we'll be in the war for five or six years and President Roosevelt will be up for a fourth term, but he won't outlive it." Then he told me the personal things that I knew nobody else knew. I figured to myself that if he could answer all those questions, there had to be forces guiding him. He passed on, but he introduced me to a wonderful friend, Dr. Richard Ireland.

Now, I know that I must have always had these voices telling me things: One time I got a whole picture, *Every Day's a Holiday,* it came to me in fifty-six seconds, the length of time it took to play a chorus on the piano. It took me fifteen minutes to tell it to my producer and director, who were there at the time, and another forty-five minutes to dictate it to a typist. It was one of my best pictures. When I began to understand more about ESP in 1941, I realized that my having had the idea so quickly, the complete story, had something to do with the forces around us. You see, they helped me several times when I was really in a problem and I didn't know how to get out of it. Like the court case I had. I was bein' sued for $100,000 and I knew I was innocent, but I didn't know how to handle the case. I was lyin' in my bed when suddenly this voice comes to me, a very beautiful, deep man's voice speakin' in that old English with "yea, thee and thous" and this was in 1948, and I knew I had heard that voice before . . . back in 1941 and I had always remembered it because it was very distinguished. And now it told me what to say when I went into court that day, and I won my case, so, you see, it works for you. It does good for you. Ohh, yeah, after it was over, I wanted to know for myself what kind of person the voice belonged to. I asked the dictionary about it and it opened where it said "clergy"—so I knew he was a man from the clergy, you know, back in the 18th or 19th century.

While we were driving back to her apartment after our Chinese meal, Mae was talking about projects she had in mind, plays she was thinking of reviving, other films she was going to do, and an offer from ABC for a television version of the celebrated *Diamond Lil.* She was toying with the idea of the TV production, musing about leading men she had in mind. She ran through a list of television stars who'd caught her eye. She thought Rock Hudson was too old (this was in 1974!). Unable to imagine who could fill her shoes, I blurted out: "But who could possibly play Diamond Lil?"

Mae, who had been lying back, drew herself up and broke the shocked silence: "Why, *Mae West* of course!" and looked at me as if I'd lost my senses.

KENNETH ANGER

Kenneth Anger has two reputations. The larger one involves his notorious books Hollywood Babylon *(1958) and* Hollywood Babylon II *(1984), lurid compilations of
Hollywood scandal and gossip, some of it learned from his grandmother, a studio costume
mistress, who, like so many crew members, remained invisible while hearing everything.
Anger's other reputation is as one of the most influential early figures in the American
underground film, with work such as* Fireworks *(1947) and* Scorpio Rising *(1964).
The first* Babylon *book, written with a breathless delight in the secrets behind Hollywood's
carefully defended images, helped create today's era of supermarket tabloids and gossip
television.*

from *Hollywood Babylon*

Just as an occasional sex-murder rendered some would-be starlet "front-page-
famous" for the space of one edition, sometimes a suicide would allow some obscure Hollywoodian those longed-for headlines for a brief flash of posthumous
fame.

In the grim, grinding years of the Depression, when even the once-famous
of the silents had their sleeping potion or gaspipe exits perfunctorily recorded
in the papers, it took some sob-sister angle or novel touch in technique of self-
destruction to make the blasé editors sit up and take notice.

The suicides in the ranks of the starlets were of two distinct categories. One
was the "bid" that had the cards stacked so there was little likelihood of a fatal
issue—these were the ill-famed "publicity stunt" suicide attempts which desperate climbers have resorted to in hope of achieving *some* form of public
notoriety—a last gamble. (Sleeping pills, preceded by a *"Goodbye cruel Hollywood"*
phone call were a favored method—but sometimes the "last-minute rescue" *did
not come off* and the starlet slept on—*into oblivion.*)

The other order of suicide was another manner entirely—the starlet was grimly earnest and determined to succeed, at least, in this one last melodramatic gesture. The measure of bitterness and heartbreak felt by these former beauty contest winners, screen-test winners, and would-be screen luminaries was revealed in the pains they took that the bizarre trappings or circumstances of their murder scene played with themselves should not escape the eye of the film colony that had found no use for them, and that their name—*just once*—should blaze forth from the fourth estate.

Thus it was that a lovely young brunette named Arletta Duncan planned to quit the scene in the grand manner, in the middle Thirties. Arletta's tale was typical of many others. In a "Girl from Every State Talent Contest" trumped up by Universal Studios, Arletta, who had achieved local renown as Harvest Queen in her home town of Belle Plaine, was brought to Hollywood as Miss Iowa.

Winning by the same roulette that had brought Clara Bow to Hollywood, Arletta arrived in 1930 to a welcoming committee of Universal stars. Her screen and voice tests were deemed promising enough—she had a good body and a pretty face that Hollywood could gimmick up any way it chose. She was signed to a starlet contract, and enmeshed in the Universal machine known as "The Treatment." This meant studio flacks got her picture and mention in the fan magazines; a series of walk-on bits with a line or two in Universal films; gossip-column mention through plants about a studio-manufactured romance with featured-player Tom Brown, with whom she was seen wining, dining, and dancing.

Arletta began to receive fan mail; she did well enough in another small part to be considered for a featured role in James Whale's *The Bride of Frankenstein*. She was tested; publicity shots were taken picnicking with Boris Karloff—*somebody else got the part*. Arletta had been in Hollywood five years and—from her viewpoint—had gotten exactly nowhere. She couldn't go back to Belle Plaine. Her Hollywood caper had met with strong disapproval from her family. She'd never live it down.

When Arletta Duncan decided to bow out, she loaded every vestige of her Hollywood career in her roadster, and drove out Sunset Boulevard to Santa Monica canyon, where she parked near a deserted field. She unloaded the messy accumulation of five years' memorabilia in the Film Mecca and carried it armload by armload to the center of the field. There she made a pyre—feeding to the flames her original Universal contract, clippings of herself as Harvest Queen and Miss Iowa, a souvenir program from the *Cocoanut Grove* signed, "To Arletta— In Memory of a Swell Evening—Tom Brown." Also into the fire went bundles of fan mail which included offers of marriage from Alaska and Singapore; shooting-scripts with her few scenes underscored in red; stacks of standardized, posed, publicity photographs. (Enough ill-consumed remnants were discovered later to identify the violator of the Santa Monica public trash-burning ordinance—but Arletta was beyond reprimand at that time.)

As the afternoon declined, Arletta drove back into Hollywood for the last time, this time parking her car in the Hollywood hills, at the base of that steep hillside which bore thirteen gigantic, lethal letters: each the size of a house, they spelled out

HOLLYWOODLAND

constructed of metal scaffolding faced with sheet-iron. (The fancy nomenclature and its cumbersome erection on the hillside was the doing of Mack Sennett, who sunk much capital in a real-estate scheme in the late Twenties to promote the hillside area for fashionable Spanish villa homesites. The Crash made quick work of the grandiose project and left Sennett without either property or bank account.)

Arriving beneath the spelled-out taunt of the realm she could not conquer, Arletta stripped off her skirt and blouse to uncover a brief little two-piece outfit that had shown her advantages fetchingly in publicity photos.

It was as if all the publicity photographers in Hollywood were amassed below as Arletta deftly climbed up the scaffolding supporting the towering **"H."** On the summit—in the orange rays of the setting sun, Arletta then performed an act never witnessed by the Universal publicity department: she peeled off her skimpy bra, flung it to imaginary fans below, and the scanty panties followed.

Nude, facing the city which refused her a crown, Arletta flung herself into thin air.

That should have been a merciful conclusion to her gesture. But no: Arletta's leap into space landed her square in a clump of prickly-pear cactus. When the reporters turned up the next day to check out her letters—opened that morning—telling them where to go to find "a broken body hiding a broken heart," they found instead a still-living though battered Arletta, whose delirious thrashings, all night long in the cactus clump, had turned her into a livid human pin-cushion.

Arletta's agony lasted four days, during which a team of interns extracted thousands of spines from her graceful, dying body. *Qualis artifex pereo!*

Around 1930 there appeared in the United States a pharmaceutical product which immediately became immensely popular, a sleeping pill called *Seconal*. About ten pills were enough for a painless slumber that would last forever. There were hundreds of *Seconal suicides* in Hollywood, where it was assured—for special reasons!—that the product would be well received. Starving extras, victims of blackmailers, fucked and forgotten little *hopefuls*—but also many, many celebrities!

Among these candidates for death were, first of all, the drug-ridden star Jeanne Eagels, 1929; Milton Sills, 1930; the young leading man Robert Ames, 1931; dope-addicted Alma Rubens, 1931; the comic, Karl Dane, 1932; silent star Marie Prevost, 1934; director George Hill, 1934; fallen star John Gilbert, 1935; the star of *The Crowd,* James Murray, 1937; the young Warner Brothers leading man, Ross Alexander, 1937; the director Tom Forman, 1938. A *second* wave carried off female impersonator Julian Eltinge, 1941; comedian Joe Jackson, 1942; the comedienne Lupe Velez, 1944; the character actor Laird Cregar, 1945; Hal Roach star Carole Landis, 1948; Hitchcock's actor Robert Walker, 1951; and the Madame Gin Sling of Sternberg, Ona Munson, 1956.

The most recent spectacular attempts have been those of Susan Hayward, saved by having her stomach pumped out, as well as Diana Barrymore in 1955; Martha Raye and Judy Garland in the following year, and in 1957 Montgomery Clift and Marie MacDonald,—known as *The Body*—a starlet suffering from constant bad publicity following her famous bungled "kidnaping attempt."

The palm for *perseverance* in this department should go to Judy Garland, who was dropped by M-G-M and who has tried on *several* occasions to end it all by *Seconal,* by gas, or with a razor, in between stays at various withdrawal sanitariums.

The friend and assistant of Murnau, Herman Bing, put an end to his life by means of a pistol shot in 1947, as had Paul Bern in 1932 and Robert Harron, Griffith's ex-protege, in 1920.

Also in 1935, the ex-star of silent pictures, Lou Tellegen, staged the most *revolting* of all Hollywood suicides; surrounded by posters of his successes and his most beautiful stills, he ripped open his chest with scissors, just like Max Linder, ten years before.

"There's no come-back for a *HAS BEEN.*"

The suicide of Lupe Velez is possibly the most revealing and the one giving the deepest insight. Her hot temperament at all times has earned this comedienne, introduced by Douglas Fairbanks in *The Gaucho,* Leon Errol's leading lady in Hal Roach Comedies, the surname of "The Mexican Bombshell." Famous for her stormy love affairs, Lupe, upon being deserted by Gary Cooper, got hold of young Johnny Weissmuller—hero of the Olympic Games and the fastest swimmer in the world—who had been called to Hollywood to play *Tarzan.* The marks of their violent physical encounters left marks on Tarzan's Olympian torso which created a problem for the makeup man, who had to camouflage scratches, bruises and bites—not *all* of them, of course, only the ones which would show on film! It should be added that Johnny took spectacular revenge one night at Ciro's, the most exclusive nightclub on Sunset Boulevard, by throwing a table—and everything on it!—at the head of this ravening *she-wolf.*

When Lupe no longer saw a way out of her troubles—after so many quarrels and stories—she decided to kill herself, and determined to turn it into one of the most beautiful moments of her life; to turn tragedy into *apotheosis.*

She ordered hundreds of flower arrangements, and when her house had been turned into a greenhouse of the very loveliest ones, she called in her make-up man and her hairdresser to turn her out more magnificently than ever before for this last time. Then, in the huge Spanish-style house, she put on a lamé dress and lots of jewelry. After a solitary banquet, during which she had herself served with the spiced dishes of her native country, she dismissed the servants and went upstairs to her room. Alone among the flowers, she swallowed a *tubeful* of *Seconal* and lay down on her bed.

Half an hour later, the meticulous staging suddenly took an unforseen turn which would have been worthy of Buñuel. All the effects planned by the fiery Mexican had been ordered; the flowers paid her a final homage, the glistening chandeliers shone on the lamé of her dress. Lupe died in *beauty.*

The harmony was complete, with the sole exception of the *Seconal* and the spicy food, when the solemn lights around her body were abruptly bespattered. Lupe obeyed an instinct even stronger than death and ran, teetering on her high heels, toward the bathroom. But she slipped on the marble tiles as she ran up to the toilet bowl—which turned out to be her last mirror!—and head first, she fell in and broke her neck. Thus she was found, stuck and half-submerged in this *bowl,* strange and macabre. And thus was extinguished one of Hollywood's glories!

PARKER TYLER

Parker Tyler was one of the most eclectic and eccentric of film critics, and one of the most valuable, because although his essays often read like free association involving all the movies he had seen, there was always an underlying logic, detonated at the end of the journey. By the time we get to the end of this essay about sex goddesses in the movies, we understand why they are not to be slept with, or on, but about.

"The Awful Fate of the Sex Goddess"

What, by virtue of the movies, is a sex goddess? It is easy to point, say, to Sophia Loren, imagine her quite naked (as may be done without the camera's assistance) and have the right answer. But Miss Loren's case is relatively simple and unaffected. The matter, with regard to the movies' history of sex, is too complex for mere pointing. The sex goddess's mutation, starting with the celebrated Vampire, is something to arrest and fascinate movie buffs and other susceptible scholars. Its ups and downs, turnabouts and triumphs, take on cosmic dimensions. Going in as straight a line as possible from Theda Bara to Greta Garbo, one's wits are staggered by so vast a change visible in one stroke of the imagination—and that stroke takes us only to 1941. . . . Technically, Garbo is a direct descendant of her distant Hollywood predecessor: the fatal Queen of Love and Ruler of Man which a sex goddess is—or was—supposed to be.

I change the tense and *there's* the rub. For whatever reasons, a sharp decline of divine dimensions in nominal sex goddesses has come about; it is as if "sex" and "goddess" were terms that, idiomatically, no longer agreed. Take the case of one who bore a notable physical resemblance to Sophia Loren, Jane Russell, a goddess ephemeral and now long extinct. Miss Russell was two great breasts mounted upon a human pedestal with a doll's head to top it off. Besides being no actress at all (which Loren, after all, *is*), Russell was hardly a sound recipe for a sex goddess. Her peculiar weakness may have lain in the very fact that a California judge, passing on the claim that her film, *The Outlaw,* was obscene owing largely to her salient and partly exposed mammary equipment, decided that anything God-given, such as breasts, could not be "obscene." Goddesses, by definition, *are* beyond the law. But voluptuous breasts are but the window-dressing of sex divinity. Jane represented one of the last historic efforts to invent a great personality on the basis of sex-appeal alone.

Plausibly, the physical dimensions of sex goddesses first tended to be ample. Theda Bara had a maternal figure. She was, in fact, remarkably like a suburban housewife circa World War I, bitten by the glamor bug into imagining herself supreme seductress of men, and by some weird turn of fate succeeding at it. Today, an Elizabeth Taylor also succeeds though *her* proportions and personality start by being those of the reigning office minx, from whom neither president of the company nor errand boy is safe. By another weird turn of fate we get instead, in this actress, a universal Miss Sexpot—for a sex goddess, one is obliged to call that a comedown. Nowadays sex-goddessing is more a trade than something, as it were, acquired by divine privilege. Another Italian star, Gina Lollobrigida, oddly resembles Miss Taylor although she is better-looking. Lollobrigida is simply Sophia Loren seen a few paces further off: a sort of reproduction in minor scale. But big and beautiful as La Loren is, we must face the fact that sheer majesty in the female body has become, historically, badly compromised as a glamor asset. Being a sex goddess has nothing whatever to do with the sexual act as such. Getting laid is a strictly human, quite unglamorous occupation.

Mediating between Bara and Garbo, Mae West turned up as an eccentric, utterly unexpected manifestation of sex divinity. Like the old gods of the Greek plays, she appeared with the primal authority of "Here I am!" Part of the majesty of Mae's corseted figure, hefty of hip and bosom, was its anachronism: she duplicated the physical image of the late 19th century stage, where even chorus girls were girthy. The very pathos of distance helped make West a goddess, and historic. I confess to having been, in 1944, the first to describe what her style owed to the female impersonator: just about everything basic. A true parody of sex divinity, Mae was the opposite of the classic Vampire because she aimed at being both funny and good-natured: qualities more plebeian than royal or divine.

The movie canon of the teens and twenties had it that personified sex-appeal was a destroyer of men. Hence the Vampire embodied irresistible sexual evil. She was no laughing matter till time gave us the modern perspective, in which she's little *but* that. Vintage eroticism, regally portrayed by beautiful ladies throughout the twenties, automatically evokes titters when seen today. Mae West's sudden greatness was to have introduced a *deliberately* comic parody of the sex goddess. Her unique blend of sexiness and vulgar comedy, in other words, was the screen's first sterling brand of conscious sex camp. Other brands developed but these were the cynical farcing of tired-out actresses who had never quite believed in their own eroticism. Mae *did* believe in hers. That was the wonder of the spectacle she made. Few others actually did—probably not even her leading men! What her public believed in was the raw, happy camp of it. That incredible nasality, that incredible accent!

Garbo is virtually unique among the remoter goddesses because, even in some of her earlier roles (such as that in *Romance*), she can still be taken seriously. And yet even Garbo is not foolproof against the sensibility of what once a very few called, and now the world calls, camp. (Camp, one must note, is a proved culture virus affecting non-deviates as well as deviates.) Seeing Greta gotten up as an innocent country girl in *The Torrent,* one understands better that creeping parody of passion that meant her downfall in *Two-Faced Woman,* her last picture. The "two-faced" was painfully exact. A split personality may have suited the being termed by Robert Graves the Triple Goddess of archaic times on earth. But for our times, even one extra personality makes *The Divine Woman* (the title of a Garbo film) into a schizophrenic with professional delusion-of-grandeur. Film myths of the making and unmaking of a star began to appear as early as the thirties and their climax, in the sixties, was explicitly labelled *The Goddess*—no accident that an actress with superficial sex-appeal and no real ability, Kim Novak, was featured in it.

The sex goddess, supposedly, satisfies a basic human need: she would and should be the sanctified, superhuman symbol of bedroom pleasure, and bedroom pleasure as such seems here to stay. Europe, however, held a more tangible appreciation of sex as sex. Thus, a Brigitte Bardot came as no surprise at all. This legitimate goddess, after fifteen years' hard labor, has faded. Yet while she was at her international peak (somewhat pre-Loren), she had the simplicity and stark presence natural to erotic greatness. B.B., with canonic plenitude up front, facile nudity and long, tumbling blonde hair, was an impressive paradox: a cheerful Magdalene. Repentance and guilt were alien to her if only because her assets (like Jane Russell's before her) were so unmistakably God-given. Unworldly innocence imparted to B. B.'s sexiness a gay pathos; worldly sophistication imparted to Mae West's a more complex gaiety, a more complex pathos. B. B. was a symbol that implied nothing but reality, Mae a reality that implied nothing but a symbol. . . .

When the self-farcing tendency began overtaking stars and films in the late fifties and sixties, even bouncy B. B. began parodying her rather down-to-earth divinity. As of now, screen nudity (to take sex at its simplest) has begun to be so proliferant as to look common. Arty, self-conscious, coyly denuding camera shots of the sexual clutch (one has had to creep up on body-candor in the movies) has become, by 1969, a cliché. Sex goddesses inevitably were victimized by the big breakthrough toward sexual realism. Currently, we are down to the nitty-gritty of the postures, the paintings, the in-plain-view of sex—down, in other words, to its profanity, including the garniture of those four-letter words. The sex goddesses have become sitting ducks for the exploding peephole of a film frame. In *La Dolce Vita* (1960), Fellini's genius for casting cannily registered the fatal downwardness then true of sex-goddessing. We found a perfect big-blonde-goddess type, Anita Ekberg, playing a parody movie star with a bust like a titaness, a baby voice and the courage of Minnie Mouse.

Sexy even so? Well, yes. Fellini pressed some delicate poetry no less than some satire from the combination of Miss Ekberg's shape, poundage and sweet, naïve femininity. Yet when, in the film, her husband whacks her for moonlighting with Mastroianni and she slinks off to bed, La Ekberg is just another silly woman—and "divine" only as a young man's midnight fancy. Even when she had answered in kind to the baying of neighborhood dogs, it was more a chorus than a command: the gorgeous bitch fled in an auto when the baying became serious. Fellini thereby branded the explicit profession of sex goddess a benignly comic fraud. Whyever should sex goddesses have fallen so low as to be "caught out" like that? The way they were caught out is clear enough: their regal posture was shown as an imposture: a fabricated illusion based on physical pretensions and almost nothing else. The method was to expose the base fleshly mechanism behind a grand illusion. In Hollywood, both sex goddesses and other stars were, it seemed, manufactured. Essentially, the goddesses had been lovely hoaxes foisted upon a naïve, gullible and dated public of both sexes: the gaga identifiers (female) and the gasping adorers (male).

It is a pause-giving irony that the truly great among sex goddesses were the first to show glaring symptoms of the decline and fall of the movie line. Was there something too *façadelike* about the Very Greats? Gazing back, one can detect one of the handsomest, Nita Naldi (who played opposite Valentino in *Blood and Sand*), unable to be anything from head to foot but a striking mask. In the teens and early twenties, statuesque feminine fulsomeness was still bona fide; it was the sweet and pure star actresses who were petite. Today, like Bara, Naldi must seem a rather puffy anachronism; if not downright absurd, at least strangely pathetic—a period clotheshorse, stunning but quite without humor. And take Mae West as a "mask" rather than a comedienne: physically she seems made from a mold, as if her whole body were a layer of simulated flesh about an inch thick, with nothing whatever inside. It took wit, humor and an interesting face to make La West a real "divine woman."

Historically, humor came into Hollywood supersex with the later twenties in the personnel of Flaming Youth: chiefly the "It Girl," Clara Bow. And then, of course, came Jean Harlow, who created a totally new standard for sex goddesses. Jean was a sacred-whore type whose unabashed vulgarity (even as West's) was integral with the spell she cast. Yet a few veils of illusion had been brutally torn off: evidently the sex goddess was no lady if, as Harlow, she could be a downright slut. Nobody sensed it then, I think, but a great symbol was being debunked. There could be no question about *Harlow's* real fleshliness, all over and through and through, if only because nothing seemed to exist between her and her filmy dresses but a little perspiration.

Like Mae, Jean was funny—more professionally and seriously so than Clara Bow, who was only a rampaging teenager with sex-appeal; essentially, that is, Clara was *decent*. Both West and Harlow let a certain middle-class decency (allied with basic chastity) simply go by the board. Both gloried in being, at least potentially, unchaste. They weren't exactly prostitutes (or but rarely) yet that they exploited sex professionally hit one between the eyes. They were Gimme Girls as much as Glamor Girls and quite beyond morality in those vocations. It would be humanly unnatural should beautiful ladies, every bare inch of them, cease to be darlings of the camera's eye. But capitalized Lust is either a mad holiday or a deadly sin. Once, being a sex goddess was to skip all mundane considerations and assume that Lust meant Glorious Aphrodite. In the movies' advanced age (they are well over seventy), sex and other sorts of violence keep the film cameras grinding. But make no mistake: the goddessing of movie sex, subtly and brutally too, has met an awful fate.

In West, parody was a divine she-clown act; in Harlow, sex bloomed miraculously, nakedly, gaudily from the gutter. *The Queen,* a documentary about classy transvestites competing for the title of Miss All-American, offers (at the moment I write) the most eloquent evidence anywhere that sex-goddessing can still be taken seriously. Yet among those to whom queendom is synonymous with homosexuality, the divinity of sex as a public symbol carries a necessary irony and a necessary narrowness. "Harlow" has become a sort of trade name among professional transvestites. The winner of the contest in *The Queen* calls himself just Harlow, and one of Andy Warhol's home-made films is titled *Harlot* because it features an Underground transvestite's camp act in a blonde wig.

This "superstar," Mario Montez, has attached the name of a minor sex goddess (extinct) who was lately honored with an Underground cult: Maria Montez. The camp symbolism of the Warhol film, whose action takes place entirely on and about a couch where four people are grouped—two young men, a "lesbian" and "Harlow"—is to have Montez extract first one banana then another from various caches and munch them deliberately, in voluptuous leisure, for about an hour. This is the principal "action." Get the picture? If you do, you qualify for the Underground sex scene. It's this way: one is to imagine a camp queen of sex, even when genuinely female, not with an adoring male crawling up her knees, but an adored male with *her* crawling up *his* knees. In her early days, Garbo herself used to slither over her men like a starved python. But she was only combatting Old Man Morality: her erotic power, and its authenticity, were never in question.

Today everything is in question about the sex goddess but the blunt mechanism any woman offers a man. Personally, I find the progressive demoralization of the s. g. in females rather desperately saddening. Two acting celebrities, Bette Davis and Tallulah Bankhead (while neither was ever a sex goddess), have parodied neurotic and unconsciously funny females so often and so emphatically that they represent an historic attack on high feminine seductiveness. Sex-parody became, rather early, an integral part of Miss Davis' style till it exploded in her 100 per cent camp films, *Whatever Happened to Baby Jane?* and *Hush, Hush, Sweet Charlotte.* The aging Miss Bankhead's failure as a serious actress was suavely turned into success on the radio as a bass-voiced caricature. In the movies, finally, Bankhead followed suit to *Hush, Hush, Sweet Charlotte* with *Die, Die, My Darling* (Ugh!). Yet she (a handsome woman in her own right) had once in her career, if transiently, vied with Garbo.

We find a rich clue to the fate of the sex goddesses if we look at the way classic beauty currently serves movie sex. If the physical proportions and personalities of Sophia Loren and Anita Ekberg lend themselves easily to light sex-comedy with a wedge of farce and satire, the face and figure of Ursula Andress (taken in themselves) have a pure, invulnerable classic beauty. In the 19th century and the first quarter of the 20th, Ursula would have been destined as a sex goddess of real if removed divinity, surrounded with protocol and awe, a queen of fashion as of sex. On looks and style alone, Andress would do as well in society as in the acting profession. But what, alas! was her fate? To be an ultra-classy foil for a James Bond—a lesbianlike Pussy Galore! A "destroyer of men," by all means, but stamped with the comicstrip sensibility (see *Modesty Blaise,* et al.) that informs all Pop versions of camp sex.

The newest archetype of the sex goddess, robbing her of her former dignity and classic authority, inhabits the comic strip itself, where Barbarella (played by Jane Fonda) has been enshrined as the supreme Vinyl Girl of sex-appeal. Fundamentally, she is the oldtime serial queen, *rediviva.* Remember that serials (take *The Perils of Pauline*) were always animated comic strips with real performers. Even more significantly, there has been the completely nude Phoebe Zeit-Geist, the comicstrip heroine introduced by the Evergreen Review. Like a metaphysical idea, Phoebe seemed not to know what clothes are. Her sole function, naked and attractive as she was, was to be camp sacrificial victim *in perpetuo* for the historic villains and most grandiose, come-lately freaks of comicstripdom (for more clarification on this theme, consult the well-thumbed dictionary of sado-masochism at your local library).

Maybe no fate is really awful so long as, like Phoebe's, it's also fun. Yet the point is erotically disputable. To those tending to think the female sex represents a supreme power, like antiquity's Ruler of Men, the latterday Pop versions of sex goddesses partake more of existential gloom than existential fun. The "fun" is slightly sick. Shouldn't the put-it-on-the-line psychology of sex-presentation be left for the hardcore geeks in the audience? Actually the transvestites, with their delusions of reincarnating extinct sex goddesses, are truer queens of beauty and sex than Ursula Andress—who looks more and more as if she had been cut out of cardboard and achieved her classic volumes by courtesy of 3-D (flesh-tones by Technicolor). I, for one, think it an awful fate that the grand profession of sex-goddessing should have sunk to the petty profession of sex-shoddessing. The robotizing trend of female charms (against which only that cartoon pair of *Playboy* tits seems holding out) must not be underrated. Think, ladies and gentlemen! The supreme goal of male propulsion, as foreseen in *2001: a Space Odyssey,* is a geometric black slab with unproved sexual capacities. Theda Bara would, tacitly, be more negotiable than that; and shapelier.

Come to think of it, Marilyn Monroe came along in those fidgety 'fifties and altered the whole set-up. There was something genuine about her, and really pathetic, as if she were all too human to exercise the great craft of queening it for the tradition. We know what finally happened to her. Maybe she was the last "goddess" actually seeming to be made out of flesh rather than foamrubber: something to sleep *with*, not *on*. And that was probably her fatal mistake. Goddesses are to be slept *about*.

BRENDAN GILL

Although the history of filmed pornography is almost as long as the history of film, it was not until the late 1960s, with the advent of films like I am Curious (Yellow) *and* Deep Throat, *that porn began to be openly advertised and exhibited in movie theaters. Brendan Gill, for many years a film critic at* The New Yorker *and then its theater critic, described his porn-going experiences in 1973 for* Film Comment. *"I was known there as the grey eminence of porn," he wrote me recently. "As I predicted (I wouldn't mention this, of course, except that it reflects credit on me!), what was then thought to be pornographic moved into the mainstream—when boy and girl meet 'cute' nowadays it is often the case that she is going down on him. And nobody says a word about it. The world is full of wonders, is it not?"*

"Blue Notes"

I

For a good many years, I was a movie reviewer for the *New Yorker,* and I continue to go to movies with an undiminished and evidently incorrigible zeal, which is to say that I am upset if I fail to see most of the important movies of a given season and that I feel from time to time a nagging desire not merely to have seen certain movies but also to be known to have seen them—to put in my two cents' worth of criticism along with that of my former colleagues. I try to resist this temptation, but there are areas of moviemaking that my old friends curiously neglect, and with pleasure I now volunteer to walk the bounds of one such area, calling attention to a few of the more notable features of a landscape apparently as foreign to most newspaper and magazine reviewers as Cockaigne. What I have in mind are those commercial blue movies that have become a commonplace of our contemporary culture and about which, up to now, there has been an almost total lack of critical discussion. Whenever I raise the question of the radical changes that have taken place in their manufacture and distribution in recent years, it will usually turn out that my friends among the reviewers have no first-hand knowledge of these changes and that what little they possess in the way of opinions is based on hearsay. All this for the reason that they simply do not go to blue movies, indeed, they are, or affect to be, aggressively indifferent to them. Sometimes they protest that the reason for their indifference is that blue movies are so boring. How can they be sure of this, I ask them, if they refuse to see any? Unhappy at being caught out in a child's dodge, they offer a child's riposte: *everyone* knows that blue movies are boring, and the only mystery is what a person of my supposedly refined perceptions finds of interest in them. With a patience that they no doubt consider irritating, I point out that they have misconstrued the argument, a sure sign of unease: up to that moment, I had not claimed that blue movies were interesting in themselves but only that they could not be ignored as a phenomenon. Lest I be thought to be masking a Puritan prurience behind sociological cant (one thinks of Bishop Potter leapfrogging among the whores in order to improve his education), I then quickly add that a large portion of the blue movies I go to strike me as being at once boring *and* fascinating, and that what proves fascinating in them nearly always encourages me to sit through what proves boring. In that respect, if perhaps in no other, blue movies are not unlike the works of George Eliot.

II

I go to as many blue movies as I can find time for, and it amounts to a blessing that two of the most important theatres housing hard-core porn in New York City—the Hudson/Avon, for heterosexual blue movies, and the Park/Miller, for homosexual ones—are within a couple of hundred yards of my office. At the moment of writing, another fifteen or twenty porn houses are but five minutes away. How lucky I am that this unexpected period of permissiveness in pornography should have coincided with my life, and how unready I am to have the period brought to a close by some new ruling of the courts! The President's Commission on Obscenity and Pornography, appointed by Johnson, submitted a report to Nixon so little disapproving of pornography and therefore so little to his liking that Nixon immediately rejected it. Open pornography openly arrived at has been in increasing jeopardy during the Nixon administration. A permissive society makes people like Nixon nervous, because they feel sure of themselves only under conditions of repression. These conditions need not be the ones they favor; if they exist, they can be manipulated and made to serve. The threat to freedom of the press and the threat to a continued easy access to pornography are scarcely to be spoken of in the same breath, but they occupy the same ground and will often be found to have the same defenders.

III

History may see the early nineteen-seventies as the high-water mark of permissiveness in the arts in this country. At present, there is nothing I can think of that a novel or poem is not free to describe, that a play or dance cannot embody, that a movie cannot depict. We are no longer at the mercy of the Irish Catholic policeman who stops a movie, arrests the projectionist, and testifies in court that the movie must have been obscene because it gave him an erection. (What does that make his wife, who presumably is capable of securing the same response? Or his sacred old mother, who, if she had lacked this ability, would have failed to conceive him?) Still, we remain a Jansenist country, in which, as Henry Adams noted long ago, sex remains a species of crime. The police and the courts are eager to resume control over our appetites; prosecutors who should know better continue to equate morality with law. The grating insistence on the part of clergymen and big real-estate operators that the city clean up Times Square may be a hint of hard times to come. The Times Square that these groaners pretend to look back upon with affection never existed; it was a squalid and ramshackle honky-tonk fifty years ago, as it is today, and the groaners were already in full—and, thank goodness, ineffectual—voice. The metaphor for the Square is the statue of Father Duffy there: pigeons shitting on the bronze head of a priest. The question is not "What are they doing there?" but "What is he doing there?" I grant that the Square is more dangerous now than it was in the twenties, but then so is Fifth Avenue, so is Main Street everywhere. The groaners do not really want the Square to be cleaned up; they want it to be wiped out. Their cure for what they consider all the uglier manifestations of the life-force is extermination.

IV

Yeats says that love pitches its mansion in the place of excrement, and this is precisely what all blue movies, even the worst of them, say again and again; ideally, it is all they have to say. And *I* say that we are a timid and fastidious people and are far from having heard the message as often as we need to. But in saying even that much I risk striking the note of the Puritan bully: the mutilating didact, sure that he knows what is good for everyone else, and who, if he likes eating dung, would turn us into a nation of dung-eaters.

V

Many otherwise sophisticated men are embarrassed to be seen entering or leaving a blue movie house. Hard as it is to believe, this sense of shame is surely one of the reasons that so few of my former colleagues have kept up with the revolution in the genre. By and large, movie reviewers are a bourgeois lot, and while they would not be averse to catching a blue movie or two at the home of that quintessence of bourgeois chic, George Plimpton, they are unwilling to stand at the turnstiles of the not very fashionable little boutique pornie houses—former hardware stores, shoe shops, and delicatessens—that bespeckle the West Forties. They would feel that the eyes of the world were upon them, glittering with disapprobation. ("Nanny spank!") Myself, what I usually feel at the turnstiles is a rueful sense of outrage at the price of admission: three or four dollars at most midtown heterosexual blue movie houses and five dollars at most midtown homosexual houses. In the light of how little the movies have cost to make compared with, say, RYAN'S DAUGHTER, I cannot fail to feel that I am being flimflammed. Nevertheless, I pay, for nevertheless it is worth it. On leaving the theatre, many people dart sidelong into the crowd, seeking to efface themselves and their immediate past as quickly as possible. My own tendency is to saunter. Since I have the reputation of being an exceptionally fast walker, my slow pace under the marquee must be a way of affirming that attendance at blue movies is not to my mind a clandestine activity. Grubby, yes, it may be that, but I have long since made my peace with grubbiness. There are a number of things in my life that I cherish and that lack elegance.

VI

Some titles: *The Odd Mother, Little Women, The Coming Thing, Gland Hotel, Cheek to Cheek, All Balled Up.* And in just tribute to that early capital of movie porn, on every blazing marquee: *San Francisco Femmes.*

VII

Nowhere in these notes have I tried to define the word "pornography." And this is wise and not merely craven, for if two people were to discuss the matter face to face it is possible that they could arrive at last at a rough meaning, hedged round with all manner of provisos concerning its applicability to such and such a state of affairs in such and such a time and place. Three people, though they met face to face, would be unlikely to agree on a definition. Pornography is whatever one thinks it is, and what *I* think it is will have to be guessed from the way I write about it. In his biography of Mark Twain, Justin Kaplan speaks of the pornography of the dollar. I think I know what the phrase means, but I doubt if J. Paul Getty would know what it means. Or, rather, to be fair to Mr. Getty (for the evidence is clear that he is far more acute about money than I am), if he were to be right about what the phrase means, then I would be sure to be wrong. In the same fashion, Pope Paul and I do not mean the same thing when we speak of the sacredness of the body. To me that means its continuous, joyous use, in all its passionate carnality; to the Pope it means chastity, the highest expression of which is virginity, both in men and in women. In short, non-use: a gathering of cob-webs, to be broken only by the furtive, unruly finger.

VIII

If I am being fair to J. Paul Getty, I may as well try to be fair to the Papacy as well. Paul's predecessor, the jolly and sensual John, would have granted me my definition of the sacredness of the body, only adding that eating and drinking and working and playing and making love must be to the greater glory of God. "No harm in that?" he would have asked me, and "No harm in that," I would have been obliged to reply. John once granted an audience to a large body of journalists meeting in Rome. His message to them: "Now, you gentlemen are journalists, and there is one commandment—'Thou shalt not bear false witness'—that is to be followed with a particular fidelity by you. As for the other nine, pay as little attention as possible to them."

IX

A good deal of nonsense has been written about the audiences at blue movies. As a veteran champion of Women's Lib, I am sorry to say that the most inaccurate articles I have read on the subject have been by women reporters, who in most cases describe what they expected to find and not what, according to my greater experience in this field, actually exists. What Dwight Macdonald has called the parajournalism of Tom Wolfe has infected a younger generation of writers: in Wolfe's terms, serendipity is not the happy faculty of stumbling by chance upon something one wants but the inventing of something one wants

that is then stumbled upon by calculation. Writers in the *Village Voice* and elsewhere would have you believe that audiences at blue movies consist largely of
lonely, middle-aged men bringing themselves off under rustling raincoats. Let
me testify that the pleasure of masturbation appears to be no more commonly
indulged in at blue movies than at straight ones. It could be argued, indeed, that
the rate of indulgence would be likely to be higher at straight movies, on the
grounds that one's fantasy in respect to a desirable but wholly unattainable sex
object would be far more intense than one's fantasy in respect to women who
combine an appearance of immediate availability with comparatively little allure. (In a similar way, the underwear advertisements in the Sunday *Times*
magazine section may be more stimulating to many men and women than the
photographs of genitalia in the magazines sold in the shabby storefronts on
Forty-second Street.) Nor does the average audience consist of middle-aged
men—the range in age will extend from, say, very young, non-English-speaking
Argentinian sailors, who are spending a few days in port and can think of
nothing better to do at the moment, to very old men, who also have nothing
better to do and who tend to fall asleep almost as soon as they sit down, hypnotized not by what they see on the screen but by its harsh light. As for the loneliness of the men in the audience, that is surely in the mind of the beholder; if
it is not, then I am at a loss to understand the method by which, in a darkened
auditorium, a reporter succeeds in detecting such a characteristic. Loneliness
is something I am unable to make out with any degree of confidence in the faces
of strangers passing me on a sunlit Madison Avenue, to say nothing of the faces
of old friends passing me in the corridor outside my office. My guess is that the
audiences at blue movies would be scarcely different in appearance, aptitudes,
and appetites from the male portion of any crowd in a subway car or a political rally or a meeting of the P.T.A. I suspect, but cannot be sure, that many of
the audience are salesmen idling between appointments; others—those who,
glancing at their watches around five in the afternoon, hastily jump to their feet
and race up the aisle—may be commuters, on their way home to voluptuous
wives in Scarsdale.

X

What all reporters can agree on is that the great majority of the audiences at blue
movies is male. White middle-class women of any age are conspicuously absent.
Only one white woman of my acquaintance—a brilliant Englishwoman of
twenty-seven—has seen as many as three or four blue movies. "They make me
feel sexy," she says. "I was very strictly brought up, so the feeling may come as
much from my sense of doing a forbidden thing as from watching sex. I go to
skinflicks with a man from the office—married; no big deal—to kill a couple

of hours at lunchtime. We bring hot dogs and cokes and relax. I like everything about skinflicks except the way the man always has to ejaculate outside the woman. I suppose that's to prove he isn't cheating the audience. Naturally, I think of him as cheating the woman."

XI

A good many Puerto Ricans and blacks come in couples to blue movies, nearly always seating themselves at the rear of the theatre and appearing more interested in nuzzling each other than in watching the screen. At homosexual blue movies one sees, understandably, no women at all. As far as I know, there is not a single blue movie theatre in New York that caters to Lesbians; they must make do with the occasional movie of women having intercourse that one encounters in programs combining six or eight so-called "featurettes" or "stagette loops." Even in these movies, the two or more women making love will sooner or later be joined by two or more men, and a heterosexual frolic will then ensue. (In such cases, the men never make love to other men; it is a tradition in blue movies that women are permitted to be indiscriminate in regard to the sex of their partners but that men are not.) Women play no part in homosexual blue movies; one might expect them to be introduced into a plot as possible rivals or as sexual objects to be repudiated, but no—the only authentic feminine note struck is by drag-queens. A large portion of the audience at both heterosexual and homosexual blue movies is Oriental. Unlike white males, Oriental males come into the theatre by two's and three's and talk and laugh freely throughout the course of the program. At heterosexual blue movies, white males ordinarily enter and leave alone, speak to no one, and manifest as little emotion as possible. If some especially gauche sexual gesture is enacted on screen, there may be scattered laughter, almost instantly suppressed; and sometimes, as when an ardent act of fellatio fails to have the desired result and the fellator increases her efforts with evident impatience and a speed of thrusting that seems to threaten actual injury, a universal groan will go up. Otherwise, the conventional posture of the audience is that of the herd: calculatedly impassive, taking everything in with fixed eyes and giving nothing back.

XII

The behavior of audiences at homosexual blue movies is radically unlike that of audiences at heterosexual ones. Each kind of audience has its favorite rituals and taboos, and although it is a topic risky to speculate on, it would seem to be the case that the homosexual audience, enjoying a much greater freedom of action than the heterosexual audience, is likely to be having a much better time. For the homosexual, it is the accepted thing that the theatre is there to be cruised in; this is one of the advantages he has purchased with his expensive ticket of admission. The atmosphere is perhaps not quite that of a tea-dance on a terrace in the Hamptons, but neither is it that of the Meditation Room at Frank Campbell's. Far from sitting slumped motionless in one's chair, one moves about at will, sizing up possibilities. Often there will be found standing at the back of the theatre two or three young men, any of whom, for a fee, will accompany one to seats well down front and there practice upon one the same arts that are being practiced upon others on screen. One is thus enabled to enjoy two very different sorts of sexual pleasure simultaneously—a boon that Edison, though himself of strongly homosexual tendencies (one remembers those camping trips with Henry Ford), was too inhibited to have made his goal when he set about inventing a practicable motion-picture camera.

XIII

It is a sign of the increasing acceptance of blue movies in our culture that *Variety* now lists the most successful of them in its weekly chart of big movie grossers. Throughout the autumn, *Deep Throat* was averaging something like $35,000 a week at the box-office, giving it a place of importance not far below *Whats Up Doc* and *The Straw Dogs*. Legman's now widely accepted theory that Americans, in their arts as in their lives, prefer violence to sex, is borne out by the fact that there has yet to be a really substantial box-office hit among blue movies. The figures speak for themselves; in the time that it took *Deep Throat* to gross $500,000, *The Godfather* grossed $42,000,000. *Deep Throat* is a silly little fable celebrating life; *The Godfather* is a celebration of blood and death.

XIV

Another sign of a general acceptance of blue movies is the number of Upper East Side people who are venturing into Times Square to catch blue movies often at what they believe to be the risk of their lives. A ticket-seller in the box-office at the Cameo was quoted recently as saying, "We're getting an altogether different class of people in here these days—the kind of people who call up and ask what time the feature starts."

XV

As blue movies gain in popularity, they become more and more profitable to manufacture and distribute. Already they are claiming attention as a growth industry, like mobile homes and male cosmetics. In a fashion often praised by big business but rarely practiced by it, the money to be made in blue movies has led to increased competition in the marketplace, which has led in turn to a notable improvement in the quality of the product. Of course I do not mean an improvement in its artistic quality. On the contrary, I would be tempted to argue that, following the principle that it is the difficulty of the sonnet that makes for excellence in that form, the present license to depict anything one pleases on the screen has led to a falling off in the ingenuity of the plots of blue movies—never a strong point in the best of circumstances—therefore to a lessening of sympathetic interest on the part of the spectator. In the old Mrs. Grundy days, one had to find some means, however clumsy, to get the performers down to their skins, in order that they could set about making love or at least—and how sad this always seemed!—to simulate making love, with the man's shadowy genitalia just out of camera range and the girl's tongue licking her lips in transports of passion that she was all too evidently far from feeling. We had time to become familiar with the amateur actors, squeaking away uneasily in their poor little paper-thin roles, and even to identify with their often grotesque problems. We wanted them to be happy, which is to say that we wanted them to score, and we knew that sooner or later they would be able to do so. Nowadays, the protagonists are often to be seen scoring as the movie opens, and scoring in gigantic close-ups of great technical resourcefulness, well-lighted and (to the extent that scoring is subject to instruction) well-directed, and at the same time hard to recognize as human. For the camerawork may well be so superb that at first we will simply not know where we are—can we be approaching the nave of some great Gothic cathedral, hung with pink moss, or is this only a vagina? That immense veined wet redwood, straining to resist the force of some incalculable gale—is it only, at second glance, a penis? A few years ago, we would not have thought "only" a vagina, "only" a penis. The bolder the movie and the better made it is, the more it risks, in 1972, boring us. The threat of anti-climax hovers over the latest and most skilled handiwork of young blue movie makers, prompting us to observe that in the field of pornography, as in so many other fields, prosperity is often the enemy of promise.

XVI

Simply as theatre, cunnilingus isn't a patch on fellatio, and it is difficult to see what even the most ardent Women's Lib maker of blue movies can do about it.

XVII

People like me, who champion pornography on the grounds that it is life-enhancing are constantly being told that it isn't *truly* life-enhancing, because it is only a travesty of the real thing. The difficulty with that argument is knowing what the real thing is. Wherever I ask for a definition, my interlocutor begins to sputter; precisely as "everyone" knows that blue movies are boring, "everyone" knows what the real thing is. But I don't. Or I do and I don't. I live bathed in a continuous erotic glow, and I recognize pornography as among the thousand blessed things that heighten this glow. Like sunlight, like water, like the smell and taste of skin, it helps make me happy. I foresee that with every passing year it will become increasingly precious to me: a vade mecum when the adventure of old age begins.

PAULINE KAEL

Pauline Kael was the film critic of The New Yorker *from 1968 to 1991, and during those years hers were the most read, most quoted, most influential film reviews in the world. Although her outspoken opinions were known much earlier to the readers of the film magazines and literary quarterlies, she first found a larger audience in 1965, with the publication of her first book,* I Lost It at the Movies. *Even her titles announced her irreverence. "Is There a Cure for Film Criticism?" she asked, and went on to answer in an outpouring of words, collected in fourteen books that represent the most important sustained contribution in the history of film criticism. It was that word "movies" in the title of her first book that announced her basic orientation: She went to movies, not films, and she scorned abstract theory as a barrier between the moviegoer and the actual experience of losing it at the movies. Kael's support of the films and directors she loved led to direct involvement: She campaigned; she plotted; she enlisted support from other critics. Less public is her generosity toward younger critics. As one of many novices who learned from Kael and benefited from her friendship, I was moved to learn that she was still offering encouragement to young writers in 1995, four years after Parkinson's disease had forced her to retire from* The New Yorker. *A teenage film critic in Florida wrote me that he'd sent Kael a sampling of his work. Her health made it difficult for her to write back—so, he said, she phoned him. Kael's writings include many pieces that have become famous, including her review of* Nashville, *her piece on Cary Grant, and her essay "Trash, Art and the Movies." None caused a greater stir than her rave review for Bernardo Bertolucci's* Last Tango in Paris *(1972), which I'm pairing with Norman Mailer's equally personal assessment of the same movie.*

"Last Tango in Paris"

Bernardo Bertolucci's *Last Tango in Paris* was presented for the first time on the closing night of the New York Film Festival, October 14, 1972; that date should become a landmark in movie history comparable to May 29, 1913—the night *Le Sacre du Printemps* was first performed—in music history. There was no riot, and no one threw anything at the screen, but I think it's fair to say that the audience was in a state of shock, because *Last Tango in Paris* has the same kind of hypnotic excitement as the *Sacre,* the same primitive force, and the same thrusting, jabbing eroticism. The movie breakthrough has finally come. Exploitation films have been supplying mechanized sex—sex as physical stimulant but without any passion or emotional violence. The sex in *Last Tango in Paris* expresses the characters' drives. Marlon Brando, as Paul, is working out his aggression on Jeanne (Maria Schneider), and the physical menace of sexuality that is emotionally charged is such a departure from everything we've come to expect at the movies that there was something almost like fear in the atmosphere of the party in the lobby that followed the screening. Carried along by the sustained excitement of the movie, the audience had given Bertolucci an ovation, but afterward, as individuals, they were quiet. This must be the most powerfully erotic movie ever made, and it may turn out to be the most liberating movie ever made, and so it's probably only natural that an audience, anticipating a voluptuous feast from the man who made *The Conformist,* and confronted with this unexpected sexuality and the new realism it requires of the actors, should go into shock. Bertolucci and Brando have altered the face of an art form. Who was prepared for that?

Many of us had expected eroticism to come to the movies, and some of us had even guessed that it might come from Bertolucci, because he seemed to have the elegance and the richness and the sensuality to make lushly erotic movies. But I think those of us who had speculated about erotic movies had tended to think of them in terms of Terry Southern's deliriously comic novel on the subject, *Blue Movie;* we had expected *artistic* blue movies, talented directors taking over from the *Shlockmeisters* and making sophisticated voyeuristic fantasies that would be gorgeous fun—a real turn-on. What nobody had talked about was a sex film that would churn up everybody's emotions. Bertolucci shows his masterly elegance in *Last Tango in Paris,* but he also reveals a master's substance.

The script (which Bertolucci wrote with Franco Arcalli) is in French and English; it centers on a man's attempt to separate sex from everything else. When his wife commits suicide, Paul, an American living in Paris, tries to get away from his life. He goes to look at an empty flat and meets Jeanne, who is also looking at it. They have sex in an empty room, without knowing anything about each other—not even first names. He rents the flat, and for three days they meet there. She wants to know who he is, but he insists that sex is all that matters. We see both of them (as they don't see each other) in their normal lives—Paul back at the flophouse-hotel his wife owned, Jeanne with her mother, the widow of a colonel, and with her adoring fiancé (Jean-Pierre Léaud), a TV director, who is relentlessly shooting a sixteen-millimeter film about her, a film that is to end in a week with their wedding. Mostly, we see Paul and Jeanne together in the flat as they act out his fantasy of ignorant armies clashing by night, and it *is* warfare—sexual aggression and retreat and battles joined.

The necessity for isolation from the world is, of course, his, not hers. But his life floods in. He brings into this isolation chamber his sexual anger, his glorying in his prowess, and his need to debase her and himself. He demands total subservience to his sexual wishes; this enslavement is for him the sexual truth, the real thing, sex without phoniness. And she is so erotically sensitized by the rounds of lovemaking that she believes him. He goads her and tests her until when he asks if she's ready to eat vomit as a proof of love, she is, and gratefully. He plays out the American male tough-guy sex role—insisting on his power in bed, because that is all the "truth" he knows.

What they go through together in their pressure cooker is an intensified, speeded-up history of the sex relationships of the dominating men and the adoring women who have provided the key sex model of the past few decades—the model that is collapsing. They don't know each other, but their sex isn't "primitive" or "pure"; Paul is the same old Paul, and Jeanne, we gradually see, is also Jeanne, the colonel's daughter. They bring their cultural hangups into sex, so it's the same poisoned sex Strindberg wrote about: a battle of unequally matched partners, asserting whatever dominance they can, seizing any advantage. Inside the flat, his male physical strength and the mythology he has built on it are the primary facts. He pushes his morose, romantic insanity to its limits; he burns through the sickness that his wife's suicide has brought on—the self-doubts, the need to prove himself and torment himself. After three days, his wife is laid out for burial, and he is ready to resume his identity. He gives up the flat: he wants to live normally again, and he wants to love Jeanne as a *person*. But Paul is forty-five, Jeanne is twenty. She lends herself to an orgiastic madness, shares it, and then tries to shake it off—as many another woman has, after a night or a twenty years' night. When they meet in the outside world, Jeanne sees Paul as a washed-up middle-aged man—a man who runs a flophouse.

Much of the movie is American in spirit. Brando's Paul (a former actor and journalist who has been living off his French wife) is like a drunk with a literary turn of mind. He bellows his contempt for hypocrisies and orthodoxies; he keeps trying to shove them all back down other people's throats. His profane humor and self-loathing self-centeredness and street "wisdom" are in the style of the American hardboiled fiction aimed at the masculine-fantasy market, sometimes by writers (often good ones, too) who believe in more than a little of it. Bertolucci has a remarkably unbiased intelligence. Part of the convulsive effect of *Last Tango in Paris* is that we are drawn to Paul's view of society and yet we can't help seeing him as a self-dramatizing, self-pitying clown. Paul believes that his animal noises are more honest than words, and that his obscene vision of things is the way things really are; he's often convincing. After Paul and Jeanne have left the flat, he chases her and persuades her to have a drink at a ballroom holding a tango contest. When we see him drunkenly sprawling on the floor among the bitch-chic mannequin-dancers and then baring his bottom to the woman official who asks him to leave, our mixed emotions may be like those some of us experienced when we watched Norman Mailer put himself in an in-defensible position against Gore Vidal on the Dick Cavett show, justifying all the people who were fed up with him. Brando's Paul carries a yoke of mascu-line pride and aggression across his broad back; he's weighed down by it and hung on it. When Paul is on all fours barking like a crazy man-dog to scare off a Bible salesman who has come to the flat,* he may—to the few who saw Mailer's *Wild 90*—be highly reminiscent of Mailer on his hands and knees bark-ing at a German shepherd to provoke it. But Brando's barking extends the terms of his character and the movie, while we are disgusted with Mailer for needing to prove himself by teasing an unwilling accomplice, and his barking throws us outside the terms of his movie.

Realism with the terror of actual experience still alive on the screen—that's what Bertolucci and Brando achieve. It's what Mailer has been trying to get at in his disastrous, ruinously expensive films. He was right about what was needed

*This scene was deleted by the director after the New York Film Festival showing.

but hopelessly wrong in how he went about getting it. He tried to pull a new realism out of himself onto film, without a script, depending wholly on improvisation, and he sought to bypass the self-consciousness and fakery of a man acting himself by improvising within a fictional construct—as a gangster in *Wild 90,* as an Irish cop in *Beyond the Law* (the best of them), and as a famous director who is also a possible Presidential candidate in *Maidstone.* In movies, Mailer tried to will a work of art into existence without going through the steps of making it, and his theory of film, a rationale for this willing, sounds plausible until you see the movies, which are like Mailer's shambling bouts of public misbehavior, such as that Cavett show. His movies trusted to inspiration and were stranded when it didn't come. Bertolucci builds a structure that supports improvisation. Everything is prepared, but everything is subject to change, and the whole film is alive with a sense of discovery. Bertolucci builds the characters "on what the actors are in themselves. I never ask them to interpret something preëxistent, except for dialogue—and even that changes a lot." For Bertolucci, the actors "make the characters." And Brando knows how to improvise: it isn't just Brando improvising, it's Brando improvising as Paul. This is certainly similar to what Mailer was trying to do as the gangster and the cop and the movie director, but when Mailer improvises, he expresses only a bit of himself. When Brando improvises within Bertolucci's structure, his full art is realized. His performance is not like Mailer's acting but like Mailer's best writing: intuitive, rapt, princely. On the screen, Brando is our genius as Mailer is our genius in literature. Paul is Rojack's expatriate-failure brother, and Brando goes all the way with him.

We all know that movie actors often merge with their roles in a way that stage actors don't, quite, but Brando did it even on the stage. I was in New York when he played his famous small role in *Truckline Café* in 1946; arriving late at a performance, and seated in the center of the second row, I looked up and saw what I thought was an actor having a seizure onstage. Embarrassed for him, I lowered my eyes, and it wasn't until the young man who'd brought me grabbed my arm and said "Watch this guy!" that I realized he was *acting.* I think a lot of people will make my old mistake when they see Brando's performance as Paul; I think some may prefer to make this mistake, so they won't have to recognize how deep down he goes and what he dredges up. Expressing a character's sexuality makes new demands on an actor, and Brando has no trick accent to play with this time, and no putty on his face. It's perfectly apparent that the role was conceived for Brando, using elements of his past as integral parts of the character. Bertolucci wasn't surprised by what Brando did; he was ready to use what Brando brought to the role. And when Brando is a full creative presence on the screen, the realism transcends the simulated actuality of any known style of *cinéma vérité,* because his surface accuracy expresses what's going on underneath. He's an actor:

when he shows you something, he lets you know what it means. The torture of seeing Brando—at his worst—in *A Countess from Hong Kong* was that it was a *reductio ad absurdum* of the wastefulness and emasculation (for both sexes) of Hollywood acting; Chaplin, the director, obviously allowed no participation, and Brando was like a miserably obedient soldier going through drill. When you're nothing but an inductee, you have no choice. The excitement of Brando's performance here is in the revelation of how creative screen acting can be. At the simplest level, Brando, by his inflections and rhythms, the right American obscenities, and perhaps an improvised monologue, makes the dialogue his own and makes Paul an authentic American abroad, in a way that an Italian writer-director simply couldn't do without the actor's help. At a more complex level, he helps Bertolucci discover the movie in the process of shooting it, and that's what makes moviemaking an art. What Mailer never understood was that his *macho* thing prevented flexibility and that in terms of his own personality he *couldn't* improvise—he was consciously acting. And he couldn't allow others to improvise, because he was always challenging them to come up with something. Using the tactics he himself compared to "a commando raid on the nature of reality," he was putting a gun to their heads. Lacking the background of a director, he reduced the art of film to the one element of acting, and in his confusion of "existential" acting with improvisation he expected "danger" to be a spur. But acting involves the joy of self-discovery, and to improvise, as actors mean it, is the most instinctive, creative part of acting—to bring out and give form to what you didn't know you had in you; it's the surprise, the "magic" in acting. A director has to be supportive for an actor to feel both secure enough and free enough to reach into himself. Brando here, always listening to an inner voice, must have a direct pipeline to the mystery of character.

Bertolucci has an extravagant gift for sequences that are like arias, and he has given Brando some scenes that really sing. In one, Paul visits his dead wife's lover (Massimo Girotti), who also lives in the run-down hotel, and the two men, in identical bathrobes (gifts from the dead woman), sit side by side and talk. The scene is miraculously basic—a primal scene that has just been discovered. In another, Brando rages at his dead wife, laid out in a bed of flowers, and then, in an excess of tenderness, tries to wipe away the cosmetic mask that defaces her. He has become the least fussy actor. There is nothing extra, no flourishes in these scenes. He purifies the characterization beyond all that: he brings the character a unity of soul. Paul feels so "real" and the character is brought so close that a new dimension in screen acting has been reached. I think that if the actor were anyone but Brando many of us would lower our eyes in confusion.

His first sex act has a boldness that had the audience gasping, and the gasp was caused—in part—by our awareness that this was Marlon Brando doing it, not an unknown actor. In the flat, he wears the white T-shirt of Stanley Kowal-

ski, and he still has the big shoulders and thick-muscled arms. Photographed looking down, he is still tender and poetic; photographed looking up, he is ravaged,
like the man in the Francis Bacon painting under the film's opening titles. We
are watching *Brando* throughout this movie, with all the feedback that that implies, and his willingness to run the full course with a study of the aggression in
masculine sexuality and how the physical strength of men lends credence to the
insanity that grows out of it gives the film a larger, tragic dignity. If Brando knows
this hell, why should we pretend we don't?

The colors in this movie are late-afternoon orange-beige-browns and pink—
the pink of flesh drained of blood, corpse pink. They are so delicately modulated (Vittorio Storaro was the cinematographer, as he was on *The Conformist*)
that romance and rot are one; the lyric extravagance of the music (by Gato Bar-
bieri) heightens this effect. Outside the flat, the gray buildings and the noise are
certainly modern Paris, and yet the city seems muted. Bertolucci uses a feedback of his own—the feedback of old movies to enrich the imagery and associations. In substance, this is his most American film, yet the shadow of Michel
Simon seems to hover over Brando, and the ambience is a tribute to the early
crime-of-passion films of Jean Renoir, especially *La Chienne* and *La Bête Humaine*.
Léaud, as Tom, the young director, is used as an affectionate takeoff on Godard,
and the movie that Tom is shooting about Jeanne, his runaway bride, echoes Jean
Vigo's *L'Atalante*. Bertolucci's soft focus recalls the thirties films, with their lyri-
cally kind eye for every variety of passion; Marcel Carné comes to mind, as well
as the masters who influenced Bertolucci's technique—von Sternberg (the controlled lighting) and Max Ophuls (the tracking camera). The film is utterly
beautiful to look at. The virtuosity of Bertolucci's gliding camera style is such
that he can show you the hype of the tango-contest scene (with its own echo
of *The Conformist*) by stylizing it (the automaton-dancers do wildly fake head
turns) and still make it work. He uses the other actors for their associations,
too—Girotti, of course, the star of so many Italian films, including *Senso* and
Ossessione, Visconti's version of *The Postman Always Rings Twice,* and, as Paul's
mother-in-law, Maria Michi, the young girl who betrays her lover in *Open City*.
As a maid in the hotel (part of a weak, diversionary subplot that is soon dispensed
with), Catherine Allegret, with her heart-shaped mouth in a full, childishly
beautiful face, is an aching, sweet reminder of her mother, Simone Signoret, in
her *Casque d'Or* days. Bertolucci draws upon the movie background of this movie
because movies are as active in him as direct experience—perhaps more active,
since they may color everything else. Movies are a past we share, and, whether
we recognize them or not, the copious associations are at work in the film and
we feel them. As Jeanne, Maria Schneider, who has never had a major role before, is like a bouquet of Renoir's screen heroines and his father's models. She
carries the whole history of movie passion in her long legs and baby face.

Maria Schneider's freshness—Jeanne's ingenuous corrupt innocence—gives the film a special radiance. When she lifts her wedding dress to her waist, smiling coquettishly as she exposes her pubic hair, she's in a great film tradition of irresistibly naughty girls. She has a movie face—open to the camera, and yet no more concerned about it than a plant or a kitten. When she speaks in English, she sounds like Leslie Caron in *An American in Paris,* and she often looks like a plump-cheeked Jane Fonda in her *Barbarella* days. The role is said to have been conceived for Dominique Sanda, who couldn't play it, because she was pregnant, but surely it has been reconceived. With Sanda, a tigress, this sexual battle might have ended in a draw. But the pliable, softly unprincipled Jeanne of Maria Schneider must be the winner: it is the soft ones who defeat men and walk away, consciencelessly. A Strindberg heroine would still be in that flat, battling, or in another flat, battling. But Jeanne is like the adorably sensual bitch-heroines of French films of the twenties and thirties—both shallow and wise. These girls know how to take care of themselves; they know who No. 1 is. Brando's Paul, the essentially naïve outsider, the romantic, is no match for a French bourgeois girl.

Because of legal technicalities, the film must open in Italy before it opens in this country, and so *Last Tango in Paris* is not scheduled to play here until January. There are certain to be detractors, for this movie represents too much of a change for people to accept it easily or gracefully. They'll grab at aesthetic flaws—a florid speech or an oddball scene—in order to dismiss it. Though Americans seem to have lost the capacity for being scandalized, and the Festival audience has probably lost the cultural confidence to admit to being scandalized, it might have been easier on some if they could have thrown things. I've tried to describe the impact of a film that has made the strongest impression on me in almost twenty years of reviewing. This is a movie people will be arguing about, I think, for as long as there are movies. They'll argue about how it is intended, as they argue again now about *The Dance of Death.* It is a movie you can't get out of your system, and I think it will make some people very angry and disgust others. I don't believe that there's *anyone* whose feelings can be totally resolved about the sex scenes and the social attitudes in this film. For the very young, it could be as antipathetic as *L'Avventura* was at first—more so, because it's closer, more realistic, and more emotionally violent. It could embarrass them, and even frighten them. For adults, it's like seeing pieces of your life, and so, of course, you can't resolve your feelings about it—our feelings about life are never resolved. Besides, the biology that is the basis of the "tango" remains.

NORMAN MAILER

"One might as well be in the crowd just before an important fight commences"—Mailer's high praise before the lights go down for Last Tango in Paris. *And then comes his disappointment at the lack of gynecological detail; Mailer, like so many before and since, awaits the cinematic marriage of Sex and Art. I am not convinced such a thing is possible. In traditional fiction films, art involves the filmmakers in creating a fiction about characters whose lives we care about. Sex, to the degree that it involves nudity and explicit detail, brings the whole story crashing down to the level of documentary. The actors lose not only their clothes but their characters, and stand (or recline) revealed as only themselves.*

"Tango, Last Tango"

To pay one's $5.00 and join the full house at the Translux for the evening show of *Last Tango in Paris* is to be reminded once again that the planet is in a state of pullulation. The seasons accelerate. The snow which was falling in November had left by the first of March. Would our summer arrive at Easter and end with July? It is all that nuclear radiation, says every aficionado of the occult. And we pullulate. Like an ant-hive beginning to feel the heat.

We know that Spengler's thousand-year metamorphosis from Culture to Civilization is gone, way gone, and the century required for a minor art to move from commencement to decadence is off the board. Whole fashions in film are born, thrive, and die in twenty-four months. Still! It is only a half year since Pauline Kael declared to the readers of *The New Yorker* that the presentation of *Last Tango in Paris* at the New York Film Festival on October 14, 1972, was a date that "should become a landmark in movie history—comparable to May 29, 1913—the night *Le Sacre du Printemps* was first performed—in music history," and then went on to explain that the newer work had "the same kind of hypnotic excitement as the *Sacre,* the same primitive force, and the same jabbing, thrusting eroticism. . . . Bertolucci and Brando have altered the face of an art form." Whatever could have been shown on screen to make Kael pop open for a film? "This must be the most powerfully erotic movie ever made, and it may turn out to be the most liberating movie ever made. . . ." Could this be our own Lady Vinegar, our quintessential cruet? The first frigid of the film critics was treating us to her first public reception. Prophets of Baal, praise Kael! We had obviously no ordinary hour of cinema to contemplate.

. . . .

Now, a half year later, the movie is history, has all the palpability of the historic. Something just discernible has already happened to humankind as a result of it, or at least to that audience who are coming in to the Translux to see it. They are a crew. They have unexpected homogeneity for a movie audience, compose, indeed, so thin a sociological slice of the New York and suburban sausage that you cannot be sure your own ticket isn't what was left for the toothpick, while the rest of the house has been bought at a bite. At the least, there is the same sense of aesthetic oppression one feels at a play when the house is filled with a theater party. So, too, is the audience at *Tango* an infarct of middle-class anal majesties—if Freud hadn't given us the clue, a reader of faces could decide all on his own that there had to be some social connection between sex, shit, power, violence, and money. But these middle-class faces have advanced their historical inch from the last time one has seen them. They are this much closer now to late Romans.

Whether matrons or young matrons, men or boys, they are *swingers.* The males have wife-swapper mustaches, the women are department-store boutique. It is as if everything recently and incongruously idealistic in the middle class has been used up in the years of resistance to the Vietnamese War—now, bring on the Caribbean. Amazing! In America, even the Jews have come to look like the French middle class, which is to say that the egocentricity of the Fascist mouth is on the national face. Perhaps it is the five-dollar admission, but this audience has an obvious obsession with sex as the confirmed core of a wealthy life. It is enough to make one ashamed of one's own obsession (although where would one delineate the difference?). Maybe it is that this audience, still in March, is suntanned, or at the least made up to look suntanned. The red and orange of their skins will match the famous "all uterine" colors—so termed by the set designer—of the interiors in *Last Tango.*

. . . .

In the minute before the theater lights are down, what a tension is in the house. One might as well be in the crowd just before an important fight commences.

It is years since one has watched a movie begin with such anticipation. And the tension holds as the projection starts. We see Brando and Schneider pass each other in the street. Since we have all been informed—by *Time* no less—we know they are going to take carnal occupation of each other, and very soon. The audience watches with anxiety as if it is also going to be in the act with someone new, and the heart (and for some, the bowels) shows a tremor between earthquake and expectation. Maria Schneider is so sexual a presence. None of the photographs has prepared anybody for this. Rare actresses, just a few, have flesh appeal. You feel as if you can touch them on the screen. Schneider has nose appeal—you can smell her. She is every eighteen-year-old in a mini-skirt and a maxi-coat who ever promenaded down Fifth Avenue in the inner arrogance that proclaims, "My cunt is my chariot."

We have no more than a few minutes to wait. She goes to look at an apartment for rent, Brando is already there. They have passed in the street, and by a telephone booth; now they are in an empty room. Abruptly Brando cashes the check Stanley Kowalski wrote for us twenty-five years ago—he fucks the heroine standing up. It solves the old snicker of how do you do it in a telephone booth?—he rips her panties open. In our new line of *New Yorker*–approved superlatives, it can be said that the cry of the fabric is the most thrilling sound to be heard in World Culture since the four opening notes of Beethoven's Fifth.* It is, in fact, a hell of a sound, small, but as precise as the flash of a match above a pile of combustibles, a way for the director to say, "As you may already have guessed from the way I established my opening, I am very good at movie making, and I have a superb pair, Brando and Schneider—they are sexual heavyweights. Now I place my director's promise upon the material: you are going to be in for a grave and wondrous experience. We are going to get to the bottom of a man and a woman."

So intimates Bertolucci across the silence of that room, as Brando and Schneider, fully dressed, lurch, grab, connect, hump, scream, and are done in less than a minute, their orgasms coming on top of one another like trash cans tumbling down a hill. They fall to the floor, and fall apart. It is as if a hand grenade has gone off in their entrails. A marvelous scene, good as a passionate kiss in real life, then not so good because there has been no shot of Brando going up Schneider, and since the audience has been watching in all the somber awe one would bring to the first row of a medical theater, it is like seeing an operation without the entrance of the surgeon's knife.

One can go to any hard-core film and see fifty phalluses going in and out of

---

*John Simon, as predictable in his critical reactions as a headwaiter, naturally thought *Last Tango* was part of the riff-raff. Since it is Simon's temper to ignore details, he not only does not hear the panties tearing (some ears reside in the music of the spheres) but announces that Schneider, beasty abomination, is wearing none.

as many vaginas in four hours (if anyone can be found who stayed four hours). There is a monumental abstractedness about hard core. It is as if the more a player can function sexually before a camera, the less he is capable of offering any other expression. Finally, the sexual organs show more character than the actors' faces. One can read something of the working conditions of a life in some young girl's old and irritated cunt, one can even see triumphs of the human spirit—old and badly burned labia which still come to glisten with new life, capital! There are phalluses in porno whose distended veins speak of the integrity of the hard-working heart, but there is so little specific content in the faces! Hard core lulls after it excites, and finally it puts the brain to sleep.

But Brando's real cock up Schneider's real vagina would have brought the history of film one huge march closer to the ultimate experience it has promised since its inception (which is to re-embody life). One can even see how on opening night at the Film Festival, it did not matter so much. Not fully prepared for what was to come, the simulated sex must have quivered like real sex the first time out. Since then we have been told the movie is great, so we are prepared to resist greatness, and have read in *Time* that Schneider said, " 'We were never screwing on stage. I never felt any sexual attraction for him . . . he's almost fifty you know, and'—she runs her hand from her torso to her midriff, 'he's only beautiful to here!' "

So one watches differently. Yes, they *are* simulating. Yes, there is something slightly unnatural in the way they come and fall apart. It is too stylized, as if paying a few subtle respects to Kabuki. The real need for the real cock of Brando into the depths of the real actress might have been for those less exceptional times which would follow the film long after it opened and the reaction had set in.

Since *Tango* is, however, the first major film with a respectable budget, a superbly skilled young director, an altogether accomplished cameraman, and a great actor who is ready to do more than dabble in improvisation, indeed will enter heavily into such near to untried movie science, so the laws of improvisation are before us, and the first law to recognize is that it is next to impossible to build on too false a base. The real problem in movie improvisation is to find some ending that is true to what has gone before and yet is sufficiently untrue to enable the actors to get out alive.

.   .   .   .

We will come back to that. It is, however, hardly time to let go of our synopsis. Real or simulated, opening night or months later, we know after five minutes that, at the least, we are in for a thoroughgoing study of a man and a woman, and the examination will be close. Brando rents the empty apartment; they will visit each other there every day. His name is Paul, hers is Jeanne, but they are not to learn each other's names yet. They are not to tell one another such things, he informs her. "We don't need names here . . . we're going to forget everything we knew. . . . Everything outside this place is bullshit."

They are going to search for pleasure. We are back in the existential confrontation of the century. Two people are going to fuck in a room until they arrive at a transcendent recognition or some death of themselves. We are dealing not with a plot but with a theme that is open range for a hundred films. Indeed we are face to face with the fundamental structure of porno—the difference is that we have a director who by the measure of porno is Eisenstein, and actors who are as gods. So the film takes up the simplest and richest of structures. To make love in an empty apartment, then return to a separate life. It is like every clandestine affair the audience has ever had, only more so—no names! Every personal demon will be scourged in the sex—one will obliterate the past! That is the huge sanction of anonymity. It is equal to a new life.

What powerful biographical details we learn, however, on the instant they part. Paul's wife is a suicide. Just the night before, she has killed herself with a razor in a bathtub; the bathroom is before us, red as an abattoir. A sobbing chambermaid cleans it while she speaks in fear to Paul. It is not even certain whether the wife is a suicide or he has killed her—that is almost not the point. It is the bloody death suspended above his life like a bleeding amputated existence—it is with that crimson torso before his eyes that he will make love on the following days.

Jeanne, in her turn, is about to be married to a young TV director. She is the star in a videofilm he is making about French youth. She pouts, torments her fiancé, delights in herself, delights in the special idiocy of men. She can cuckold her young director to the roots of his eyes. She also delights in the violation she will make of her own bourgeois roots. In this TV film she makes within the movie she presents her biography to her fiancé's camera: she is the daughter of a dead Army officer who was sufficiently racist to teach his dog to detect Arabs by smell. So she is well brought up—there are glimpses of a suburban villa on a small walled estate—it is nothing less than the concentrated family honor of the French Army she will surrender when Brando proceeds a little later to bugger her.

These separate backgrounds divide the film as neatly between biography and fornication as those trick highball glasses which present a drawing of a man or a woman wearing clothes on the outside of the tumbler and nude on the inside. Each time Brando and Schneider leave the room we learn more of their lives beyond the room; each time they come together, we are ready to go further. In addition, as if to enrich his theme for students of film, Bertolucci offers touches from the history of French cinema. The life preserver in *Atalante* appears by way of homage to Vigo, and Jean-Pierre Léaud of *The 400 Blows* is the TV director, the boy now fully grown. Something of the brooding echo of *Le Jour Se Lève* and

Arletty is also with us, that somber memory of Jean Gabin wandering along the wet docks in the dawn, waiting for the police to pick him up after he has murdered his beloved. It is as if we are to think not only of this film but of other sexual tragedies French cinema has brought us, until the sight of each gray and silent Paris street is ready to evoke the lost sound of the *Bal musette* and the sad near-silent wash of the Seine. Nowhere as in Paris can doomed lovers succeed in passing sorrow, drop by drop, through the blood of the audience's heart.

. . . .

Yet as the film progresses with every skill in evidence, while Brando gives a performance that is unforgettable (and Schneider shows every promise of becoming a major star), as the historic buggeries and reamings are delivered, and the language breaks through barriers not even yet erected—no general of censorship could know the armies of obscenity were so near!—as these shocks multiply, and lust goes up the steps to love, something bizarre happens to the film. It fails to explode. It is a warehouse of dynamite and yet something goes wrong with the blow-up.

One leaves the theater bewildered. A fuse was never ignited. But where was it set? One looks to retrace the line of the story.

So we return to Paul trying to rise out of the bloody horizon of his wife's death. We even have some instinctive comprehension of how he must degrade his beautiful closet-fuck, indeed we are even given the precise detail that he will grease her ass with butter before he buggers her family pride. A scene or two later, he tricks forth her fear of him by dangling a dead rat which he offers to eat. "I'll save the asshole for you," he tells her. "Rat's asshole with mayonnaise."* (The audience roars—Brando knows audiences.) She is standing before him in a white wedding gown—she has run away from a TV camera crew that was getting ready to film her pop wedding. She has rushed to the apartment in the rain. Now shivering, but recovered from her fear, she tells him she has fallen in love with somebody. He tells her to take a hot bath, or she'll catch pneumonia, die, and all he'll get is "to fuck the dead rat."

No, she protests, she's in love.

"In ten years," says Brando looking at her big breasts, "you're going to be playing soccer with your tits." But the thought of the other lover is grinding away at him. "Is he a good fucker?"

"Magnificent."

"You know, you're a jerk. 'Cause the best fucking you're going to get is right here in this apartment."

---

*Dialogue from *Last Tango in Paris* was not entirely written in advance, but was in part an improvisation. In other words, a small but important part of the screenplay has in effect been written by Brando.

No, no, she tells him, the lover is wonderful, a mystery . . . different.

"A local pimp?"

"He could be. He looks it."

She will never, he tells her, be able to find love until she goes "right up into the ass of death." He is one lover who is not afraid of metaphor. "Right up his ass—till you find a womb of fear. And then maybe you'll be able to find him."

"But I've found this man," says Jeanne. Metaphor has continued long enough for her. "He's you. You're that man."

In the old scripted films, such a phrase was plucked with a movie composer's chord. But this is improvisation. Brando's instant response is to tell her to get a scissors and cut the fingernails on her right hand. Two fingers will do. Put those fingers up his ass.

"*Quoi?*"

"Put your fingers up my ass, are you deaf? Go on."

No, he is not too sentimental. Love is never flowers, but farts and flowers. Plus every superlative test. So we see Brando's face before us—it is that tragic angelic mask of incommunicable anguish which has spoken to us across the years of his uncharted heroic depths. Now he is entering that gladiator's fundament again, and before us and before millions of faces yet to come she will be his surrogate bugger, real or simulated. What an entrance into the final images of history! He speaks to us with her body behind him, and her fingers just conceivably up him. "I'm going to get a pig," are the words which come out of his tragic face, "and I'm going to have a pig fuck you,"—yes, the touch on his hole has broken open one gorgon of a fantasy—"and I want the pig to vomit in your face. And I want you to swallow the vomit. You going to do that for me?"

"Yeah."

"Huh?"

"Yeah!"

"And I want the pig to die while,"—a profound pause—"while you're fucking him. And then you have to go behind, and I want you to smell the dying farts of the pig. Are you going to do that for me?"

"Yes, and more than that. And worse than before."

.   .   .   .

He has plighted a troth. In our year of the twentieth century how could we ever contract for love with less than five hundred pounds of pig shit? With his courage to give himself away, we finally can recognize the tragedy of his expression across these twenty-five years. That expression has been locked into the impossibility of ever communicating such a set of private thoughts through his beggar's art as an actor. Yet he has just done it. He is probably the only actor in the world who could have done it. He is taking the shit that is in him and leaving it on us. How the audience loves it. They have come to be covered. The world is not polluted for nothing. There is some profound twentieth-century malfunction in the elimination of waste. And Brando is on to it. A stroke of genius to have made a speech like that. Over and over, he is saying in this film that one only arrives at love by springing out of the shit in oneself.

So he seeks to void his eternal waste over the wife's suicide. He sits by her laid-out corpse in a grim hotel room, curses her, weeps, proceeds to wipe off the undertaker's lipstick, broods on her lover (who lives upstairs in the hotel), and goes through some bend of the obscure, for now, off-stage, he proceeds to remove his furniture from the new apartment. We realize this as we see Jeanne in the empty rooms. Paul has disappeared. He has ordered her to march into the farts of the pig for nothing. So she calls her TV director to look at the empty apartment—should they rent it? The profound practicality of the French bourgeoisie is squatting upon us. She appreciates the value of a few memories to offer sauce for her lean marriage. But the TV director must smell this old cooking for he takes off abruptly after telling her he will look for a better apartment.

Suddenly Brando is before her again on the street. Has he been waiting for her to appear? He looks rejuvenated. "It's over," she tells him. "It's over," he replies. "Then it begins again." He is in love with her. He reveals his biography, his dead wife, his unromantic details. "I've got a prostate like an Idaho potato but I'm still a good stick man. . . . I suppose if I hadn't met you I'd probably settle for a hard chair and a hemorrhoid." They move on to a hall, some near mythical species of tango palace where a dance contest is taking place. They get drunk and go on the floor. Brando goes in for a squalid parody of the tango. When they're removed by the judges, he flashes his bare ass.

Now they sit down again and abruptly the love affair is terminated. Like that! She is bored with him. Something has happened. We do not know what. Is she a bourgeoise repelled by his flophouse? Or did his defacement of the tango injure some final nerve of upper French deportment? Too small a motive. Must we decide that sex without a mask is no longer love, or conclude upon reflection that no mask is more congenial to passion than to be without a name in the bed of a strange lover?

There are ten reasons why her love could end, but we know none of them. She merely wants to be rid of him. Deliver me from a fifty-year-old, may even be her only cry.

She tries to flee. He follows. He follows her on the Métro and all the way to her home. He climbs the spiraling stairs as she mounts in the slow elevator, he rams into her mother's apartment with her, breathless, chewing gum, leering. Now he is all cock. He is the memory of every good fuck he has given her. "This is the title shot, baby. We're going all the way."

She takes out her father's army pistol and shoots him. He murmurs, "Our children, our children, our children will remember . . ." and staggers out to the balcony, looks at the Paris morning, takes out his chewing gum, fixes it carefully to the underside of the iron railing in a move that is pure broth of Brando—culture is a goat turd on the bust of Goethe—and dies. The angel with the tragic face slips off the screen. And proud Maria Schneider is suddenly and most unbelievably reduced to a twat copping a plea. "I don't know who he is," she mutters in her mind to the oncoming *flics,* "he followed me in the street, he tried to rape me, he is insane. I do not know his name. I do not know who he is. He wanted to rape me."

. . . .

The film ends. The questions begin. We have been treated to more cinematic breakthrough than any film—at the least—since *I Am Curious, Yellow.* In fact we have gone much further. It is hard to think of any film that has taken a larger step. Yet if this is "the most powerful erotic film ever made" then sex is as Ex-Lax to the lady. For we have been given a bath in shit with no reward. The film, for all its power, has turned inside out by the end. We have been asked to follow two serious and more or less desperate lovers as they go through the locks of lust and defecation, through some modern species of homegrown cancer cure, if you will, and have put up with their modern depths—shit on the face of the beloved and find love!—only to discover a peculiar extortion in the aesthetic. We have been taken on this tour down to the prostate big as an Idaho potato only to recognize that we never did get into an exploration of the catacombs of love, passion, infancy, sodomy, tenderness, and the breaking of emotional ice, instead only wandered from one onanist's oasis to another.

It is, however, a movie that has declared itself, by the power of its opening, as equal in experience to a great fuck, and so the measure of its success or failure is by the same sexual aesthetic. Rarely has a film's value depended so much on the power or lack of power of its ending, even as a fuck that is full of promise is ready to be pinched by a poor end. So, in *Tango,* there is no gathering of forces for the conclusion, no whirling of sexual destinies (in this case, the audience and the actors) into the same funnel of becoming, no flying out of the senses in pursuit of a new vision, no, just the full charge into a blank wall, a masturbator's spasm—came for the wrong reason and on the wrong thought—and one is thrown back, shattered, too ubiquitously electrified, and full of criticism for the immediate past. Now the recollected flaws of the film eat at the pleasure, even as the failed orgasm of a passionate act will call the character of the passion into question.

So the walk out of the theater is with anger. The film has been in reach of the greatness Kael has been talking about, but the achievement has only been partial. Like all executions less divine than their conception *Tango* will give rise to mutations that are obliged to explore into dead ends. More aesthetic pollution to come! The performance by Brando has been unique, historic, without compare—it is just possible, however, that it has gone entirely in the wrong direction. He has been like a lover who keeps telling consummate dirty jokes until the ravaged dawn when the girl will say, "Did you come to sing or to screw?" He has come with great honor and dignity and exceptional courage to bare his soul. But in a solo. We are being given a fuck film without the fuck. It is like a Western without the horses.

MARIO PUZO

Did Mario Puzo really model Johnny Fontane on the life of Frank Sinatra? What was important was that everyone thought so, just as The Godfather's *millions of readers believed that Puzo was revealing the inside workings of the mob in America. Here are two excerpts, one about Fontane, the other leading up to what became the movie's most shocking image.*

from *The Godfather*

They were all proud of him. He was of them and he had become a famous singer, a movie star who slept with the most desired women in the world. And yet he had shown proper respect for his Godfather by traveling three thousand miles to attend this wedding. He still loved old friends like Nino Valenti. Many of the people there had seen Johnny and Nino singing together when they were just boys, when no one dreamed that Johnny Fontane would grow up to hold the hearts of fifty million women in his hands.

Johnny Fontane reached down and lifted the bride up on to the bandstand so that Connie stood between him and Nino. Both men crouched down, facing each other, Nino plucking the mandolin for a few harsh chords. It was an old routine of theirs, a mock battle and wooing, using their voices like swords, each shouting a chorus in turn. With the most delicate courtesy, Johnny let Nino's voice overwhelm his own, let Nino take the bride from his arm, let Nino swing into the last victorious stanza while his own voice died away. The whole wedding party broke into shouts of applause, the three of them embraced each other at the end. The guests begged for another song.

Only Don Corleone, standing in the corner entrance of the house, sensed something amiss. Cheerily, with bluff good humor, careful not to give offense to his guests, he called out, "My godson has come three thousand miles to do us honor and no one thinks to wet his throat?" At once a dozen full wine glasses were thrust at Johnny Fontane. He took a sip from all and rushed to embrace his Godfather. As he did so he whispered something into the older man's ear. Don Corleone led him into the house.

Tom Hagen held out his hand when Johnny came into the room. Johnny shook it and said, "How are you, Tom?" But without his usual charm that consisted of a genuine warmth for people. Hagen was a little hurt by this coolness but shrugged it off. It was one of the penalties for being the Don's hatchet man.

Johnny Fontane said to the Don, "When I got the wedding invitation I said to myself, 'My Godfather isn't mad at me anymore.' I called you five times after my divorce and Tom always told me you were out or busy so I knew you were sore."

Don Corleone was filling glasses from the yellow bottle of Strega. "That's all forgotten. Now. Can I do something for you still? You're not too famous, too rich, that I can't help you?"

Johnny gulped down the yellow fiery liquid and held out his glass to be refilled. He tried to sound jaunty. "I'm not rich, Godfather. I'm going down. You were right. I should never have left my wife and kids for that tramp I married. I don't blame you for getting sore at me."

The Don shrugged. "I worried about you, you're my godson, that's all."

Johnny paced up and down the room. "I was crazy about that bitch. The biggest star in Hollywood. She looks like an angel. And you know what she does after a picture? If the makeup man does a good job on her face, she lets him bang her. If the cameraman made her look extra good, she brings him into her dressing room and gives him a screw. Anybody. She uses her body like I use the loose change in my pocket for a tip. A whore made for the devil."

Don Corleone curtly broke in. "How is your family?"

Johnny sighed. "I took care of them. After the divorce I gave Ginny and the kids more than the courts said I should. I go see them once a week. I miss them. Sometimes I think I'm going crazy." He took another drink. "Now my second wife laughs at me. She can't understand my being jealous. She calls me an old-fashioned guinea, she makes fun of my singing. Before I left I gave her a nice beating but not in the face because she was making a picture. I gave her cramps,

I punched her on the arms and legs like a kid and she kept laughing at me." He lit a cigarette. "So, Godfather, right now, life doesn't seem worth living."

Don Corleone said simply. "These are troubles I can't help you with." He paused, then asked, "What's the matter with your voice?"

All the assured charm, the self-mockery, disappeared from Johnny Fontane's face. He said almost brokenly, "Godfather, I can't sing anymore, something happened to my throat, the doctors don't know what." Hagen and the Don looked at him with surprise, Johnny had always been so tough. Fontane went on. "My two pictures made a lot of money. I was a big star. Now they throw me out. The head of the studio always hated my guts and now he's paying me off."

Don Corleone stood before his godson and asked grimly, "Why doesn't this man like you?"

"I used to sing those songs for the liberal organizations, you know, all that stuff you never liked me to do. Well, Jack Woltz didn't like it either. He called me a Communist, but he couldn't make it stick. Then I snatched a girl he had saved for himself. It was strictly a one-night stand and she came after me. What the hell could I do? Then my whore second wife throws me out. And Ginny and the kids won't take me back unless I come crawling on my hands and knees, and I can't sing anymore. Godfather, what the hell can I do?"

Don Corleone's face had become cold without a hint of sympathy. He said contemptuously, "You can start by acting like a man." Suddenly anger contorted his face. He shouted. "LIKE A MAN!" He reached over the desk and grabbed Johnny Fontane by the hair of his head in a gesture that was savagely affectionate. "By Christ in heaven, is it possible that you spent so much time in *my* presence and turned out no better than this? A Hollywood *finocchio* who weeps and begs for pity? Who cries out like a woman—'What shall I do? Oh, what shall I do?' "

The mimicry of the Don was so extraordinary, so unexpected, that Hagen and Johnny were startled into laughter. Don Corleone was pleased. For a moment he reflected on how much he loved this godson. How would his own three sons have reacted to such a tongue-lashing? Santino would have sulked and behaved badly for weeks afterward. Fredo would have been cowed. Michael would have given him a cold smile and gone out of the house, not to be seen for months. But Johnny, ah, what a fine chap he was, smiling now, gathering strength, knowing already the true purpose of his Godfather.

Don Corleone went on. "You took the woman of your boss, a man more powerful than yourself, then you complain he won't help you. What nonsense. You left your family, your children without a father, to marry a whore and you weep because they don't welcome you back with open arms. The whore, you don't hit her in the face because she is making a picture, then you are amazed because she laughs at you. You lived like a fool and you have come to a fool's end."

Don Corleone paused to ask in a patient voice, "Are you willing to take my advice this time?"

Johnny Fontane shrugged. "I can't marry Ginny again, not the way she wants. I have to gamble, I have to drink, I have to go out with the boys. Beautiful broads run after me and I never could resist them. Then I used to feel like a heel when I went back to Ginny. Christ, I can't go through all that crap again."

It was rare that Don Corleone showed exasperation. "I didn't tell you to get married again. Do what you want. It's good you wish to be a father to your children. A man who is not a father to his children can never be a real man. But then, you must make their mother accept you. Who says you can't see them every day? Who says you can't live in the same house? Who says you can't live your life exactly as you want to live it?"

Johnny Fontane laughed. "Godfather, not all women are like the old Italian wives. Ginny won't stand for it."

Now the Don was mocking. "Because you acted like a *finocchio*. You gave her *more* than the court said. You didn't hit the other in the face because she was making a picture. You let women dictate your actions and they are not competent in this world, though certainly they will be saints in heaven while we men burn in hell. And then I've watched you all these years.'" The Don's voice became earnest. "You've been a fine godson, you've given me all the respect. But what of your other old friends? One year you run around with this person, the next year with another person. That Italian boy who was so funny in the movies, he had some bad luck and you never saw him again because you were more famous. And how about your old, old comrade that you went to school with, who was your partner singing? Nino. He drinks too much out of disappointment but he never complains. He works hard driving the gravel truck and sings weekends for a few dollars. He never says anything against you. You couldn't help him a bit? Why not? He sings well."

Johnny Fontane said with patient weariness, "Godfather, he just hasn't got enough talent. He's OK, but he's not big time."

Don Corleone lidded his eyes almost closed and then said, "And you, godson, you now, you just don't have talent enough. Shall I get you a job on the gravel truck with Nino?" When Johnny didn't answer, the Don went on. "Friendship is everything. Friendship is more than talent. It is more than government. It is almost the equal of family. Never forget that. If you had built up a wall of friendships you wouldn't have to ask me to help. Now tell me, why can't you sing? You sang well in the garden. As well as Nino."

Hagen and Johnny smiled at this delicate thrust. It was Johnny's turn to be patronizingly patient. "My voice is weak. I sing one or two songs and then I can't sing again for hours or days. I can't make it through the rehearsals or the retakes. My voice is weak, it's got some sort of sickness."

"So you have woman trouble. Your voice is sick. Now tell me the trouble you're having with this Hollywood *pezzonovante* who won't let you work." The Don was getting down to business.

"He's bigger than one of your *pezzonovantes,*" Johnny said. "He owns the studio. He advises the President on movie propaganda for the war. Just a month ago he bought the movie rights to the biggest novel of the year. A best seller. And the main character is a guy just like me. I wouldn't even have to act, just be myself. I wouldn't even have to sing. I might even win the Academy Award. Everybody knows it's perfect for me and I'd be big again. As an actor. But that bastard Jack Woltz is paying me off, he won't give it to me. I offered to do it for nothing, for a minimum price and he still says no. He sent the word that if I come and kiss his ass in the studio commissary, maybe he'll think about it."

Don Corleone dismissed this emotional nonsense with a wave of his hand. Among reasonable men problems of business could always be solved. He patted his godson on the shoulder. "You're discouraged. Nobody cares about you, so you think. And you've lost a lot of weight. You drink a lot, eh? You don't sleep and you take pills?" He shook his head disapprovingly.

"Now I want you to follow my orders," the Don said. "I want you to stay in my house for one month. I want you to eat well, to rest and sleep. I want you to be my companion, I enjoy your company, and maybe you can learn something about the world from your Godfather that might even help you in the great Hollywood. But no singing, no drinking and no women. At the end of the month you can go back to Hollywood and this *pezzonovante,* this .90 caliber will give you that job you want. Done?"

Johnny Fontane could not altogether believe that the Don had such power. But his Godfather had never said such and such a thing could be done without having it done. "This guy is a personal friend of J. Edgar Hoover," Johnny said. "You can't even raise your voice to him."

"He's a businessman," the Don said blandly. "I'll make him an offer he can't refuse."

"It's too late," Johnny said. "All the contracts have been signed and they start shooting in a week. It's absolutely impossible."

Don Corleone said, "Go, go back to the party. Your friends are waiting for you. Leave everything to me." He pushed Johnny Fontane out of the room.

Hagen sat behind the desk and made notes. The Don heaved a sigh and asked, "Is there anything else?"

"Sollozzo can't be put off any more. You'll have to see him this week." Hagen held his pen over the calendar.

The Don shrugged. "Now that the wedding is over, whenever you like."

This answer told Hagen two things. Most important, that the answer to Virgil Sollozzo would be no. The second, that Don Corleone, since he would not give the answer before his daughter's wedding, expected his no to cause trouble.

Hagen said cautiously, "Shall I tell Clemenza to have some men come live in the house?"

The Don said impatiently, "For what? I didn't answer before the wedding because on an important day like that there should be no cloud, not even in the distance. Also I wanted to know beforehand what he wanted to talk about. We know now. What he will propose is an *infamita*."

Hagen asked, "Then you will refuse?" When the Don nodded, Hagen said, "I think we should all discuss it—the whole Family—before you give your answer."

The Don smiled. "You think so? Good, we will discuss it. When you come back from California. I want you to fly there tomorrow and settle this business for Johnny. See that movie *pezzonovante*. . . ."

.   .   .   .

It was still dark when the plane landed in Los Angeles. Hagen checked into his hotel, showered and shaved, and watched dawn come over the city. He ordered breakfast and newspapers to be sent up to his room and relaxed until it was time for his ten A.M. appointment with Jack Woltz. The appointment had been surprisingly easy to make.

The day before, Hagen had called the most powerful man in the movie labor unions, a man named Billy Goff. Acting on instructions from Don Corleone, Hagen had told Goff to arrange an appointment on the next day for Hagen to call on Jack Woltz, that he should hint to Woltz that if Hagen was not made happy by the results of the interview, there could be a labor strike at the movie studio. An hour later Hagen received a call from Goff. The appointment would be at ten A.M. Woltz had gotten the message about the possible labor strike but hadn't seemed too impressed, Goff said. He added, "If it really comes down to that, I gotta talk to the Don myself."

"If it comes to that he'll talk to you," Hagen said. By saying this he avoided making any promises. He was not surprised that Goff was so agreeable to the Don's wishes. The family empire, technically, did not extend beyond the New York area but Don Corleone had first become strong by helping labor leaders. Many of them still owed him debts of friendship.

But the ten A.M. appointment was a bad sign. It meant that he would be first on the appointment list, that he would not be invited to lunch. It meant that Woltz held him in small worth. Goff had not been threatening enough, probably because Woltz had him on his graft payroll. And sometimes the Don's success in keeping himself out of the limelight worked to the disadvantage of the family business, in that his name did not mean anything to outside circles.

His analysis proved correct. Woltz kept him waiting for a half hour past the appointed time. Hagen didn't mind. The reception room was very plush, very comfortable, and on a plum-colored couch opposite him sat the most beautiful child Hagen had ever seen. She was no more than eleven or twelve, dressed in a very expensive but simple way as a grown woman. She had incredibly golden hair, huge deep sea-blue eyes and a fresh raspberry-red mouth. She was guarded by a woman obviously her mother, who tried to stare Hagen down with a cold arrogance that made him want to punch her in the face. The angel child and the dragon mother, Hagen thought, returning the mother's cold stare.

Finally an exquisitely dressed but stout middle-aged woman came to lead him through a string of offices to the office-apartment of the movie producer. Hagen was impressed by the beauty of the offices and the people working in them. He smiled. They were all shrewdies, trying to get their foot in the movie door by taking office jobs, and most of them would work in these offices for the rest of their lives or until they accepted defeat and returned to their home towns.

Jack Woltz was a tall, powerfully built man with a heavy paunch almost concealed by his perfectly tailored suit. Hagen knew his history. At ten years of age Woltz had hustled empty beer kegs and pushcarts on the East Side. At twenty he helped his father sweat garment workers. At thirty he had left New York and moved West, invested in the nickelodeon and pioneered motion pictures. At forty-eight he had been the most powerful movie magnate in Hollywood, still rough-spoken, rapaciously amorous, a raging wolf ravaging helpless flocks of young starlets. At fifty he transformed himself. He took speech lessons, learned how to dress from an English valet and how to behave socially from an English butler. When his first wife died he married a world-famous and beautiful actress who didn't like acting. Now at the age of sixty he collected old master paintings, was a member of the President's Advisory Committee, and had set up a multimillion-dollar foundation in his name to promote art in motion pictures. His daughter had married an English lord, his son an Italian princess.

His latest passion, as reported dutifully by every movie columnist in America, was his own racing stables on which he had spent ten million dollars in the past year. He had made headlines by purchasing the famed English racing horse Khartoum for the incredible price of six hundred thousand dollars and then announcing that the undefeated racer would be retired and put to stud exclusively for the Woltz stables.

He received Hagen courteously, his beautifully, evenly tanned, meticulously barbered face contorted with a grimace meant to be a smile. Despite all the money spent, despite the ministrations of the most knowledgeable technicians, his age showed; the flesh of his face looked as if it had been seamed together. But there was an enormous vitality in his movements and he had what Don Corleone had, the air of a man who commanded absolutely the world in which he lived.

Hagen came directly to the point. That he was an emissary from a friend of Johnny Fontane. That this friend was a very powerful man who would pledge his gratitude and undying friendship to Mr. Woltz if Mr. Woltz would grant a small favor. The small favor would be the casting of Johnny Fontane in the new war movie the studio planned to start next week.

The seamed face was impassive, polite. "What favors can your friend do me?" Woltz asked. There was just a trace of condescension in his voice.

Hagen ignored the condescension. He explained. "You've got some labor trouble coming up. My friend can absolutely guarantee to make that trouble disappear. You have a top male star who makes a lot of money for your studio but he just graduated from marijuana to heroin. My friend will guarantee that your male star won't be able to get any more heroin. And if some other little things come up over the years a phone call to me can solve your problems."

Jack Woltz listened to this as if he were hearing the boasting of a child. Then he said harshly, his voice deliberately all East Side, "You trying to put muscle on me?"

Hagen said coolly, "Absolutely not. I've come to ask a service for a friend. I've tried to explain that you won't lose anything by it."

Almost as if he willed it, Woltz made his face a mask of anger. The mouth curled, his heavy brows, dyed black, contracted to form a thick line over his glinting eyes. He leaned over the desk toward Hagen. "All right, you smooth son of a bitch, let me lay it on the line for you and your boss, whoever he is. Johnny Fontane never gets that movie. I don't care how many guinea Mafia goombahs come out of the woodwork." He leaned back. "A word of advice to you, my friend. J. Edgar Hoover, I assume you've heard of him"—Woltz smiled sardonically—"is a personal friend of mine. If I let him know I'm being pressured, you guys will never know what hit you."

Hagen listened patiently. He had expected better from a man of Woltz's stature. Was it possible that a man who acted this stupidly could rise to the head of a company worth hundreds of millions? That was something to think about since the Don was looking for new things to put money into, and if the top brains of this industry were so dumb, movies might be the thing. The abuse itself bothered him not at all. Hagen had learned the art of negotiation from the Don himself. "Never get angry," the Don had instructed. "Never make a threat. Reason with people." The word "reason" sounded so much better in Italian, *rajunah,* to rejoin. The art of this was to ignore all insults, all threats; to turn the other cheek. Hagen had seen the Don sit at a negotiating table for eight hours, swallowing insults, trying to persuade a notorious and megalomaniac strong-arm man to mend his ways. At the end of the eight hours Don Corleone had thrown up his hands in a helpless gesture and said to the other men at the table, "But no one can reason with this fellow," and had stalked out of the meeting room. The strong-arm man had turned white with fear. Emissaries were sent to bring the Don back into the room. An agreement was reached but two months later the strong-arm was shot to death in his favorite barbershop.

So Hagen started again, speaking in the most ordinary voice. "Look at my card," he said. "I'm a lawyer. Would I stick my neck out? Have I uttered one threatening word? Let me just say that I am prepared to meet any condition you name to get Johnny Fontane that movie. I think I've already offered a great deal for such a small favor. A favor that I understand it would be in your interest to grant. Johnny tells me that you admit he would be perfect for that part. And let me say that this favor would never be asked if that were not so. In fact, if you're worried about your investment, my client would finance the picture. But please let me make myself absolutely clear. We understand your no is no. Nobody can force you or is trying to. We know about your friendship with Mr. Hoover, I may add, and my boss respects you for it. He respects that relationship very much."

Woltz had been doodling with a huge, red-feathered pen. At the mention of money his interest was aroused and he stopped doodling. He said patronizingly, "This picture is budgeted at five million."

Hagen whistled softly to show that he was impressed. Then he said very casually, "My boss has a lot of friends who back his judgment."

For the first time Woltz seemed to take the whole thing seriously. He studied Hagen's card. "I never heard of you," he said. "I know most of the big lawyers in New York, but just who the hell are you?"

"I have one of those dignified corporate practices," Hagen said dryly. "I just handle this one account." He rose. "I won't take up any more of your time." He held out his hand, Woltz shook it. Hagen took a few steps toward the door and turned to face Woltz again. "I understand you have to deal with a lot of people who try to seem more important than they are. In my case the reverse is true. Why don't you check me out with our mutual friend? If you reconsider, call me at my hotel." He paused. "This may be sacrilege to you, but my client can do things for you that even Mr. Hoover might find out of his range." He saw the movie producer's eyes narrowing. Woltz was finally getting the message. "By the way, I admire your pictures very much," Hagen said in the most fawning voice he could manage. "I hope you can keep up the good work. Our country needs it."

Late that afternoon Hagen received a call from the producer's secretary that a car would pick him up within the hour to take him out to Mr. Woltz's country home for dinner. She told him it would be about a three-hour drive but that the car was equipped with a bar and some hors d'oeuvres. Hagen knew that Woltz made the trip in his private plane and wondered why he hadn't been invited to make the trip by air. The secretary's voice was adding politely, "Mr.

Woltz suggested you bring an overnight bag and he'll get you to the airport in the morning."

"I'll do that," Hagen said. That was another thing to wonder about. How did Woltz know he was taking the morning plane back to New York? He thought about it for a moment. The most likely explanation was that Woltz had set private detectives on his trail to get all possible information. Then Woltz certainly knew he represented the Don, which meant that he knew something about the Don, which in turn meant that he was now ready to take the whole matter seriously. Something might be done after all, Hagen thought. And maybe Woltz was smarter than he had appeared this morning.

.   .   .   .

The home of Jack Woltz looked like an implausible movie set. There was a plantation-type mansion, huge grounds girdled by a rich black-dirt bridle path, stables and pasture for a herd of horses. The hedges, flower beds and grasses were as carefully manicured as a movie star's nails.

Woltz greeted Hagen on a glass-panel air-conditioned porch. The producer was informally dressed in blue silk shirt open at the neck, mustard-colored slacks, soft leather sandals. Framed in all this color and rich fabric his seamed, tough face was startling. He handed Hagen an outsized martini glass and took one for himself from the prepared tray. He seemed more friendly than he had been earlier in the day. He put his arm over Hagen's shoulder and said, "We have a little time before dinner, let's go look at my horses." As they walked toward the stables he said, "I checked you out, Tom; you should have told me your boss is Corleone. I thought you were just some third-rate hustler Johnny was running in to bluff me. And I don't bluff. Not that I want to make enemies, I never believed in that. But let's just enjoy ourselves now. We can talk business after dinner."

Surprisingly Woltz proved to be a truly considerate host. He explained his new methods, innovations that he hoped would make his stable the most successful in America. The stables were all fire-proofed, sanitized to the highest degree, and guarded by a special security detail of private detectives. Finally Woltz led him to a stall which had a huge bronze plaque attached to its outside wall. On the plaque was the name "Khartoum."

The horse inside the stall was, even to Hagen's inexperienced eyes, a beautiful animal. Khartoum's skin was jet black except for a diamond-shaped white patch on his huge forehead. The great brown eyes glinted like golden apples, the black skin over the taut body was silk. Woltz said with childish pride, "The greatest racehorse in the world. I bought him in England last year for six hundred grand. I bet even the Russian Czars never paid that much for a single horse. But I'm not going to race him, I'm going to put him to stud. I'm going to build the greatest racing stable this country has ever known." He stroked the horse's mane and called out softly, "Khartoum, Khartoum." There was real love in his voice and the animal responded. Woltz said to Hagen, "I'm a good horseman, you know, and the first time I ever rode I was fifty years old." He laughed. "Maybe one of my grandmothers in Russia got raped by a Cossack and I got his blood." He tickled Khartoum's belly and said with sincere admiration, "Look at that cock on him. I should have such a cock."

They went back to the mansion to have dinner. It was served by three waiters under the command of a butler, the table linen and ware were all gold thread and silver, but Hagen found the food mediocre. Woltz obviously lived alone, and just as obviously was not a man who cared about food. Hagen waited until they had both lit up huge Havana cigars before he asked Woltz, "Does Johnny get it or not?"

"I can't," Woltz said. "I can't put Johnny into that picture even if I wanted to. The contracts are all signed for all the performers and the cameras roll next week. There's no way I can swing it."

Hagen said impatiently, "Mr. Woltz, the big advantage of dealing with a man at the top is that such an excuse is not valid. You can do anything you want to do." He puffed on his cigar. "Don't you believe my client can keep his promises?"

Woltz said dryly, "I believe that I'm going to have labor trouble. Goff called me up on that, the son of a bitch, and the way he talked to me you'd never guess I pay him a hundred grand a year under the table. And I believe you can get that fag he-man star of mine off heroin. But I don't care about that and I can finance my own pictures. Because I hate that bastard Fontane. Tell your boss this is one favor I can't give but that he should try me again on anything else. Anything at all."

Hagen thought, you sneaky bastard, then why the hell did you bring me all the way out here? The producer had something on his mind. Hagen said coldly, "I don't think you understand the situation. Mr. Corleone is Johnny Fontane's godfather. That is a very close, a very sacred religious relationship." Woltz bowed his head in respect at this reference to religion. Hagen went on. "Italians have a little joke, that the world is so hard a man must have two fathers to look after him, and that's why they have godfathers. Since Johnny's father died, Mr. Corleone feels his responsibility even more deeply. As for trying you again, Mr. Corleone is much too sensitive. He never asks a second favor where he has been refused the first."

Woltz shrugged. "I'm sorry. The answer is still no. But since you're here, what will it cost me to have that labor trouble cleared up? In cash. Right now."

That solved one puzzle for Hagen. Why Woltz was putting in so much time on him when he had already decided not to give Johnny the part. And that could not be changed at this meeting. Woltz felt secure; he was not afraid of the power of Don Corleone. And certainly Woltz with his national political connections, his acquaintanceship with the FBI chief, his huge personal fortune and his absolute power in the film industry, could not feel threatened by Don Corleone. To any intelligent man, even to Hagen, it seemed that Woltz had correctly assessed his position. He was impregnable to the Don if he was willing to take the losses the labor struggle would cost. There was only one thing wrong with the whole equation. Don Corleone had promised his godson he would get the part and Don Corleone had never, to Hagen's knowledge, broken his word in such matters.

Hagen said quietly, "You are deliberately misunderstanding me. You are trying to make me an accomplice to extortion. Mr. Corleone promises only to speak in your favor on this labor trouble as a matter of friendship in return for your speaking in behalf of his client. A friendly exchange of influence, nothing more. But I can see you don't take me seriously. Personally, I think that is a mistake."

Woltz, as if he had been waiting for such a moment, let himself get angry. "I understood perfectly," he said. "That's the Mafia style, isn't is? All olive oil and sweet talk when what you're really doing is making threats. So let me lay it on the line. Johnny Fontane will never get that part and he's perfect for it. It would make him a great star. But he never will be because I hate that pinko punk and I'm going to run him out of the movies. And I'll tell you why. He ruined one of my most valuable protégés. For five years I had this girl under training, singing, dancing, acting lessons, I spent hundreds of thousands of dollars. I was going to make her a star. I'll be even more frank, just to show you that I'm not a hard-hearted man, that it wasn't all dollars and cents. That girl was beautiful and she was the greatest piece of ass I've ever had and I've had them all over the world. She could suck you out like a water pump. Then Johnny comes along with that olive-oil voice and guinea charm and she runs off. She threw it all away just to make me ridiculous. A man in my position, Mr. Hagen, can't afford to look ridiculous. I have to pay Johnny off."

For the first time, Woltz succeeded in astounding Hagen. He found it inconceivable that a grown man of substance would let such trivialities affect his judgment in an affair of business, and one of such importance. In Hagen's world, the Corleones' world, the physical beauty, the sexual power of women, carried not the slightest weight in worldly matters. It was a private affair, except, of course, in matters of marriage and family disgrace. Hagen decided to make one last try.

"You are absolutely right, Mr. Woltz," Hagen said. "But are your grievances that major? I don't think you've understood how important this very small favor is to my client. Mr. Corleone held the infant Johnny in his arms when he was baptized. When Johnny's father died, Mr. Corleone assumed the duties of parenthood, indeed he is called 'Godfather' by many, many people who wish to show their respect and gratitude for the help he has given them. Mr. Corleone never lets his friends down."

Woltz stood up abruptly. "I've listened to about enough. Thugs don't give me orders, I give them orders. If I pick up this phone, you'll spend the night in jail. And if that Mafia goombah tries any rough stuff, he'll find out I'm not a band leader. Yeah, I heard that story too. Listen, your Mr. Corleone will never know what hit him. Even if I have to use my influence at the White House."

The stupid, stupid son of a bitch. How the hell did he get to be a *pezzonovante*, Hagen wondered. Advisor to the President, head of the biggest movie studio in the world. Definitely the Don should get into the movie business. And the guy was taking his words at their sentimental face value. He was not getting the message.

"Thank you for the dinner and a pleasant evening," Hagen said. "Could you give me transportation to the airport? I don't think I'll spend the night." He smiled coldly at Woltz. "Mr. Corleone is a man who insists on hearing bad news at once."

While waiting in the floodlit colonnade of the mansion for his car, Hagen saw two women about to enter a long limousine already parked in the driveway. They were the beautiful twelve-year-old blond girl and her mother he had seen in Woltz's office that morning. But now the girl's exquisitely cut mouth seemed to have smeared into a thick, pink mass. Her sea-blue eyes were filmed over and when she walked down the steps toward the open car her long legs tottered like a crippled foal's. Her mother supported the child, helping her into the car, hissing commands into her ear. The mother's head turned for a quick furtive look at Hagen and he saw in her eyes a burning, hawklike triumph. Then she too disappeared into the limousine.

So that was why he hadn't got the plane ride from Los Angeles, Hagen thought. The girl and her mother had made the trip with the movie producer. That had given Woltz enough time to relax before dinner and do the job on the little kid. And Johnny wanted to live in this world? Good luck to him, and good luck to Woltz.

.   .   .   .

Jack Woltz always slept alone. He had a bed big enough for ten people and a bedroom large enough for a movie ballroom scene, but he had slept alone since the death of his first wife ten years before. This did not mean he no longer used women. He was physically a vigorous man despite his age, but he could be aroused now only by very young girls and had learned that a few hours in the evening were all the youth of his body and his patience could tolerate.

On this Thursday morning, for some reason, he awoke early. The light of dawn made his huge bedroom as misty as a foggy meadowland. Far down at the foot of his bed was a familiar shape and Woltz struggled up on his elbows to get a clearer look. It had the shape of a horse's head. Still groggy, Woltz reached and flicked on the night table lamp.

The shock of what he saw made him physically ill. It seemed as if a great sledgehammer had struck him on the chest, his heartbeat jumped erratically and he became nauseous. His vomit spluttered on the thick flair rug.

Severed from its body, the black silky head of the great horse Khartoum was stuck fast in a thick cake of blood. White, reedy tendons showed. Froth covered the muzzle and those apple-sized eyes that had glinted like gold, were mottled the color of rotting fruit with dead, hemorrhaged blood. Woltz was struck by a purely animal terror and out of that terror he screamed for his servants and out of that terror he called Hagen to make his uncontrolled threats. His maniacal raving alarmed the butler, who called Woltz's personal physician and his second in command at the studio. But Woltz regained his senses before they arrived.

He had been profoundly shocked. What kind of man could destroy an animal worth six hundred thousand dollars? Without a word of warning. Without any negotiation to have the act, its order, countermanded. The ruthlessness, the sheer disregard for any values, implied a man who considered himself completely his own law, even his own God. And a man who backed up this kind of will with the power and cunning that held his own stable security force of no account. For by this time Woltz had learned that the horse's body had obviously been heavily drugged before someone leisurely hacked the huge triangular head off with an ax. The men on night duty claimed that they had heard nothing. To Woltz this seemed impossible. They could be made to talk. They had been bought off and they could be made to tell who had done the buying.

Woltz was not a stupid man, he was merely a supremely egotistical one. He had mistaken the power he wielded in his world to be more potent than the power of Don Corleone. He had merely needed some proof that this was not true. He understood this message.

EARLY DAYS

New York Times

"Edison's Vitascope Cheered"

Philadelphia Inquirer

"The Great Train Robbery"

The notion of film criticism as a discrete line of work is fairly modern, establishing itself with the work of James Agee, Stark Young, Graham Greene, and others in the late 1930s. But films have always attracted journalism, and some of the early fan magazines, like Photoplay, *were surprisingly sophisticated in their discussions of new movies. Stanley Kauffmann and Bruce Henstell went on an archaeological dig through old newspaper and magazine files to find early examples of film criticism, all the way back to these reports, from the* New York Times *of April 24, 1896, and the* Philadelphia Inquirer *of June 26, 1904, written at the dawning of the medium.*

Edison's Vitascope Cheered

The new thing at Koster and Bial's last night was Edison's vitascope, exhibited for the first time. The ingenious inventor's latest toy is a projection of his kinetescope figures, in stereopticon fashion, upon a white screen in a darkened hall. In the center of the balcony of the big music hall is a curious object, which looks from below like the double turret of a big monitor. In the front of each half of it are two oblong holes. The turret is neatly covered with the blue velvet brocade which is the favorite decorative material in this house. The white screen used on the stage is framed like a picture. The moving figures are about half life-size.

When the hall was darkened last night a buzzing and roaring were heard in the turret, and an unusually bright light fell upon the screen. Then came into view two precious blonde young persons of the variety stage, in pink and blue dresses, doing the umbrella dance with commendable celerity. Their motions were clearly defined. When they vanished, a view of an angry surf breaking on a sandy beach near a stone pier amazed the spectators. The waves tumbled in furiously, and the foam of the breakers flew high in the air. A burlesque boxing match between a tall, thin comedian and a short, fat one, a comic allegory called *The Monroe Doctrine,* an instant of motion in Hoyt's farce, *A Milk White Flag,* repeated over and over again, and a skirt dance by a tall blonde completed the views, which were all wonderfully real and singularly exhilarating. For the spectator's imagination filled the atmosphere with electricity, as sparks crackled around the swiftly moving, lifelike figures.

So enthusiastic was the appreciation of the crowd long before this extraordinary exhibition was finished that vociferous cheering was heard. There were loud calls for Mr. Edison, but he made no response.

The vitascope is only one feature of an excellent bill at Koster and Bial's, in which, of course, the admirable art of the London monologue man, [Albert] Chevalier, is a notable item. There are persons who admire and understand stage art who do not go to the music halls. For their sake it is well to say that to hear and see Chevalier in such selections as "The Nipper's Lullaby," "My Old Dutch," and "The Old Kent Road" amply atones for any irritation an over-sensitive mind may receive from, say, Miss Florrie West's expression of her opinion of Eliza, and her juvenile confidences as to the information on delicate subjects imparted to her by Johnny Jones. People whose minds are not oversensitive find Miss West intensely amusing. But everybody likes Chevalier, though it is doubtful if the perfect naturalness and delicate finish of his impersonations are generally appreciated. He is not "sensational."

The Great Train Robbery

What *The Philadelphia Inquirer* of June 26th, 1904 has to say about Lubin's Great Picture

The Great Train Robbery has proved a "thriller" in nearly all the larger cities of the United States. They have been a source of wonder as to how photographs of such a drama could have been taken in the Rocky Mountains.

The picture play begins with a view in the lonesome telegraph station, in which an operator, receiving train orders, is overcome, bound hand and foot, gagged, and left unconscious on the floor by the desperadoes; proceeds with the capture of the train, murder of the fireman, killing of the express messenger, blowing open of the safe, holdup of passengers, and shooting of one who attempts to escape; and winds up with a horseback ride through the mountains with bags of booty, a wild, weird dance in a log cabin, pursuit by the sheriff's posse, and death of all the robbers.

There is a great amount of shooting. The smoke of the pistols is plainly seen, and men drop dead right and left, but no sound is heard. Nevertheless, while witnessing the exhibition women put their fingers in their ears to shut out the noise of the firing.

The fireman attacks his assailants, with six shooters in his face, while his only weapon is the shovel, and he fails to brain his man by a narrow margin.

After one of the robbers gets him down and beats his brains out with a lump of coal, his body is picked up and thrown off the tender.

The desperadoes are a tough-looking lot. The horses look like some of Colonel Cody's bronchos. They dash through the Orange Mountains with the surefootedness of burros. The men are good riders. In the pursuit by the sheriff one is shot in the back as he dashes madly downhill, and the way in which he tumbles from his horse and strikes the ground leaves the spectators wondering if he is not a dummy, for it does not seem possible that a man could take such a fall and live.

MAXIM GORKY

This is the astonishing outpouring of a great writer's first impressions on encountering the new medium. Maxim Gorky (1868–1936) saw a program of Lumière films at a Russian fair and published this article on July 4, 1896. It is written on a completely clear slate, by someone who had not already been taught how to regard the cinema by a thousand other writers, and the newness of it all leaps from the page. What is remarkable is Gorky's prescience in the last two paragraphs, as he leaps ahead from his description of the first films to speculation on what directions the cinema might eventually take, toward sex and violence. How did he know?

Lumière

Last night I was in the Kingdom of Shadows.

If you only knew how strange it is to be there. It is a world without sound, without colour. Everything there—the earth, the trees, the people, the water and the air—is dipped in monotonous grey. Grey rays of the sun across the grey sky, grey eyes in grey faces, and the leaves of the trees are ashen grey. It is not life but its shadow, it is not motion but its soundless spectre.

Here I shall try to explain myself, lest I be suspected of madness or indulgence in symbolism. I was at Aumont's and saw Lumière's cinematograph—moving photography. The extraordinary impression it creates is so unique and complex that I doubt my ability to describe it with all its nuances. However, I shall try to convey its fundamentals.

When the lights go out in the room in which Lumière's invention is shown, there suddenly appears on the screen a large grey picture, "A Street in Paris"—shadows of a bad engraving. As you gaze at it, you see carriages, buildings and people in various poses, all frozen into immobility. All this is in grey, and the sky above is also grey—you anticipate nothing new in this all too familiar scene, for you have seen pictures of Paris streets more than once. But suddenly a strange flicker passes through the screen and the picture stirs to life. Carriages coming from somewhere in the perspective of the picture are moving straight at you, into the darkness in which you sit; somewhere from afar people appear and loom larger as they come closer to you; in the foreground children are playing with a dog, bicyclists tear along, and pedestrians cross the street picking their way among the carriages. All this moves, teems with life and, upon approaching the edge of the screen, vanishes somewhere beyond it.

And all this in strange silence where no rumble of the wheels is heard, no sound of footsteps or of speech. Nothing. Not a single note of the intricate symphony that always accompanies the movements of people. Noiselessly, the ashen-grey foliage of the trees sways in the wind, and the grey silhouettes of the people, as though condemned to eternal silence and cruelly punished by being deprived of all the colours of life, glide noiselessly along the grey ground.

Their smiles are lifeless, even though their movements are full of living energy and are so swift as to be almost imperceptible. Their laughter is soundless, although you see the muscles contracting in their grey faces. Before you a life is surging, a life deprived of words and shorn of the living spectrum of colours— the grey, the soundless, the bleak and dismal life.

It is terrifying to see, but it is the movement of shadows, only of shadows. Curses and ghosts, the evil spirits that have cast entire cities into eternal sleep, come to mind and you feel as though Merlin's vicious trick is being enacted before you. As though he had bewitched the entire street, he compressed its many-storied buildings from roof-tops to foundations to yard-like size. He dwarfed the people in corresponding proportion, robbing them of the power of speech and scraping together all the pigment of earth and sky into a monotonous grey colour.

Under this guise he shoved his grotesque creation into a niche in the dark room of a restaurant. Suddenly something clicks, everything vanishes and a train appears on the screen. It speeds straight at you—watch out! It seems as though it will plunge into the darkness in which you sit, turning you into a ripped sack full of lacerated flesh and splintered bones, and crushing into dust and into broken fragments this hall and this building, so full of women, wine, music and vice.

But this, too, is but a train of shadows.

Noiselessly, the locomotive disappears beyond the edge of the screen. The train comes to a stop, and grey figures silently emerge from the cars, soundlessly greet their friends, laugh, walk, run, bustle, and . . . are gone. And here is another picture. Three men seated at the table, playing cards. Their faces are tense, their hands move swiftly. The cupidity of the players is betrayed by the trembling fingers and by the twitching of their facial muscles. They play. . . . Suddenly, they break into laughter, and the waiter who has stopped at their table with beer, laughs too. They laugh until their sides split but not a sound is heard. It seems as if these people have died and their shadows have been condemned to play cards in silence unto eternity. Another picture. A gardener watering flowers. The light grey stream of water, issuing from a hose, breaks into a fine spray. It falls upon the flowerbeds and upon the grass blades weighted down by the water. A boy enters, steps on the hose, and stops the stream. The gardener stares into the nozzle of the hose, whereupon the boy steps back and a stream of water hits the gardener in the face. You imagine the spray will reach you, and you want to shield yourself. But on the screen the gardener has already begun to chase the rascal all over the garden and having caught him, gives him a beating. But the beating is soundless, nor can you hear the gurgle of the water as it gushes from the hose left lying on the ground.

This mute, grey life finally begins to disturb and depress you. It seems as though it carries a warning, fraught with a vague but sinister meaning that makes your heart grow faint. You are forgetting where you are. Strange imaginings invade your mind and your consciousness begins to wane and grow dim. . . .

But suddenly, alongside of you, a gay chatter and a provoking laughter of a woman is heard . . . and you remember that you are at Aumont's, Charles Aumont's. . . . But why of all places should this remarkable invention of Lumière find its way and be demonstrated here, this invention which affirms once again the energy and the curiosity of the human mind, forever striving to solve and grasp all, and . . . while on the way to the solution of the mystery of life, incidentally builds Aumont's fortune? I do not yet see the scientific importance of Lumière's invention but, no doubt, it is there, and it could probably be applied to the general ends of science, that is, of bettering man's life and the developing of his mind. This is not to be found at Aumont's where vice alone is being encouraged and popularized. Why then at Aumont's, among the "victims of social needs" and among the loafers who here buy their kisses? Why here, of all places, are they showing this latest achievement of science? And soon probably Lumière's invention will be perfected, but in the spirit of Aumont-Toulon and Company.

Besides those pictures I have already mentioned, is featured "The Family Breakfast," an idyll of three. A young couple with its chubby first-born is seated at the breakfast table. The two are so much in love, and are so charming, gay and happy, and the baby is so amusing. The picture creates a fine, felicitous impression. Has this family scene a place at Aumont's?

And here is still another. Women workers, in a thick, gay and laughing crowd, rush out of the factory gates into the street. This too is out of place at Aumont's. Why remind here of the possibility of a clean, toiling life? This reminder is useless. Under the best of circumstances this picture will only painfully sting the woman who sells her kisses.

I am convinced that these pictures will soon be replaced by others of a genre more suited to the general tone of the "Concert Parisien." For example, they will show a picture titled: "As She Undresses," or "Madam at Her Bath," or "A Woman in Stockings." They could also depict a sordid squabble between a husband and wife and serve it to the public under the heading of "The Blessings of Family Life."

Yes, no doubt, this is how it will be done. The bucolic and the idyll could not possibly find their place in Russia's markets thirsting for the piquant and the extravagant. I also could suggest a few themes for development by means of a cinematograph and for the amusement of the market place. For instance: to impale a fashionable parasite upon a picket fence, as is the way of the Turks, photograph him, then show it.

It is not exactly piquant but quite edifying.

A Conversation on Film with Leo Tolstoy

It is difficult to think of Leo Tolstoy (1828–1910) and the cinema as having overlapped; the movies based on his books, including at least two versions of War and Peace, *belong to the twentieth century of movie stars and elaborate sets; his novels belong to the nineteenth century of long, ruminative stories. Yet Tolstoy not only loved to see movies but was prescient about the way they would develop as an industry. His image of the businessman-toad devouring the artist-insect is remarkable for the way he finds an optimistic way to conclude it. This conversation was found in an appendix to* Kino, *Jay Leyda's history of Soviet films.*

"You will see that this little clicking contraption with the revolving handle will make a revolution in our life–in the life of writers. It is a direct attack on the old methods of literary art. We shall have to adapt ourselves to the shadowy screen and to the cold machine. A new form of writing will be necessary. I have thought of that and I can feel what is coming.

"But I rather like it. This swift change of scene, this blending of emotion and experience—it is much better than the heavy, long-drawn-out kind of writing to which we are accustomed. It is closer to life. In life, too, changes and transitions flash by before our eyes, and emotions of the soul are like a hurricane. The cinema has divined the mystery of motion. And that is greatness.

"When I was writing 'The Living Corpse,' I tore my hair and chewed my fingers because I could not give enough scenes, enough pictures, because I could not pass rapidly enough from one event to another. The accursed stage was like a halter choking the throat of the dramatist; and I had to cut the life and swing of the work according to the dimensions and requirements of the stage. I remember when I was told that some clever person had devised a scheme for a revolving stage, on which a number of scenes could be prepared in advance. I rejoiced like a child, and allowed myself to write ten scenes into my play. Even then I was afraid the play would be killed.

"But the films! They are wonderful! Drr! and a scene is ready! Drr! and we have another! We have the sea, the coast, the city, the palace—and in the palace there is tragedy (there is always tragedy in palaces, as we see in Shakespeare).

"I am seriously thinking of writing a play for the screen. I have a subject for it. It is a terrible and bloody theme. I am not afraid of bloody themes. Take

Homer or the Bible, for instance. How many bloodthirsty passages there are in them—murders, wars. And yet these are the sacred books, and they ennoble and uplift the people. It is not the subject itself that is so terrible. It is the propagation of bloodshed, and the justification for it, that is really terrible! Some friends of mine returned from Kursk recently and told me a shocking incident. It is a story for the films. You couldn't write it in fiction or for the stage. But on the screen it would be good. Listen—it may turn out to be a powerful thing!"

And Leo Tolstoy related the story in detail. He was deeply agitated as he spoke. But he never developed the theme in writing. Tolstoy was always like that. When he was inspired by a story he had been thinking of, he would become excited by its possibilities. If some one happened to be near by, he would unfold the plot in all its details. Then he would forget all about it. Once the gestation was over and his brain-child born, Tolstoy would seldom bother to write about it.

Some one spoke of the domination of the films by business men interested only in profits. "Yes, I know, I've been told about that before," Tolstoy replied. "The films have fallen into the clutches of business men and art is weeping! But where aren't there business men?" And he proceeded to relate one of those delightful little parables for which he is famous.

"A little while ago I was standing on the banks of our pond. It was noon of a hot day, and butterflies of all colours and sizes were circling around, bathing and darting in the sunlight, fluttering among the flowers through their short—their very short—lives, for with the setting of the sun they would die.

"But there on the shore near the reeds I saw an insect with little lavender spots on its wings. It, too, was circling around. It would flutter about, obstinately, and its circles became smaller and smaller. I glanced over there. In among the reeds sat a great green toad with staring eyes on each side of his flat head, breathing quickly with his greenish-white, glistening throat. The toad did not look at the butterfly, but the butterfly kept flying over him as though she wished to be seen. What happened? The toad looked up, opened his mouth wide and—remarkable!—the butterfly flew in of her own accord! The toad snapped his jaws shut quickly, and the butterfly disappeared.

"Then I remembered that thus the insect reaches the stomach of the toad, leaves its seed there to develop and again appear on God's earth, become a larva, a chrysalis. The chrysalis becomes a caterpillar, and out of the caterpillar springs a new butterfly. And then the playing in the sun, the bathing in the light, and the creating of new life, begin all over again.

"Thus it is with the cinema. In the reeds of film art sits the toad—the business man. Above him hovers the insect—the artist. A glance, and the jaws of the business man devour the artist. But that doesn't mean destruction. It is only one of the methods of procreation, or propagating the race; in the belly of the business man is carried on the process of impregnation and the development of the seeds of the future. These seeds will come out on God's earth and will begin their beautiful, brilliant lives all over again."

JOSEPH MEDILL PATTERSON

When the movies were first invented, mere spectacle was enough; audiences were astonished to see movement on the screen. Was there something about film itself that forced it to extend itself and tell stories? In 1907, when the Saturday Evening Post *was itself the greatest mass medium in American history, the magazine looked curiously at the new medium. Charting the rise of film from a novelty to a new entertainment medium, the* Post *took a pragmatic approach, reporting on the logistics, costs, and audiences.*

"The Nickelodeons"

Three years ago there was not a nickelodeon, or five-cent theatre devoted to moving-picture shows, in America. To-day there are between four and five thousand running and solvent, and the number is still increasing rapidly. This is the boom time in the moving-picture business. Everybody is making money—manufacturers, renters, jobbers, exhibitors. Overproduction looms up as a certainty of the near future; but now, as one press-agent said enthusiastically, "this line is a Klondike."

The nickelodeon is tapping an entirely new stratum of people, is developing into theatregoers a section of population that formerly knew and cared little about the drama as a fact in life. That is why "this line is a Klondike" just at present.

Incredible as it may seem, over two million people on the average attend the nickelodeons *every day of the year,* and a third of these are children.

Let us prove up this estimate. The agent for the biggest firm of film renters in the country told me that the average expense of running a nickelodeon was from $175 to $200 a week, divided as follows:

Wage of manager	$25
Wage of operator	20
Wage of doorman	15
Wage of porter or musician	12
Rent of films (two reels changed twice a week)	50
Rent of projecting machine	10
Rent of building	40
Music, printing, "campaign contributions," etc.	18
Total	$190

Merely to meet expenses, then, the average nickelodeon must have a weekly attendance of 4000. This gives all the nickelodeons 16,000,000 a week, or over 2,000,000 a day. Two million people a day are needed before profits can begin, and the two million are forthcoming. It is a big thing, this new enterprise.

The nickelodeon is usually a tiny theatre, containing 199 seats, giving from twelve to eighteen performances a day, seven days a week. Its walls are painted red. The seats are ordinary kitchen chairs, not fastened. The only break in the red color scheme is made by half a dozen signs, in black and white,

> NO SMOKING   HATS OFF

and sometimes, but not always,

> STAY AS LONG
> AS YOU LIKE

The spectatorium is one story high, twenty-five feet wide and about seventy feet deep. Last year or the year before it was probably a second-hand clothier's, a pawnshop or cigar store. Now, the counter has been ripped out, there is a ticket-seller's booth where the show-window was, an automatic musical barker somewhere up in the air thunders its noise down on the passersby, and the little store has been converted into a theatrelet. Not a theatre, mind you, for theatres must take out theatrical licenses at $500 a year. Theatres seat two hundred or more people. Nickelodeons seat 199, and take out amusement licenses. This is the general rule.

But sometimes nickelodeon proprietors in favorable locations take out theatrical licenses and put in 800 or 1000 seats. In Philadelphia there is, perhaps, the largest nickelodeon in America. It is said to pay not only the theatrical license, but also $30,000 a year ground rent and a handsome profit.

To-day there is cutthroat competition between the little nickelodeon owners, and they are beginning to compete each other out of existence. Already consolidation has set in. Film-renting firms are quietly beginning to pick up, here and there, a few nickelodeons of their own; presumably they will make better rates and give prompter service to their own theatrelets than to those belonging to outsiders. The tendency is clearly toward fewer, bigger, cleaner five-cent theatres and more expensive shows. Hard as this may be on the little showman who is forced out, it is good for the public, who will, in consequence, get more for their money.

. . . .

The character of the attendance varies with the locality, but, whatever the locality, children make up about thirty-three per cent of the crowds. For some reason, young women from sixteen to thirty years old are rarely in evidence, but many middle-aged and old women are steady patrons, who never, when a new film is to be shown, miss the opening.

In cosmopolitan city districts the foreigners attend in larger proportion than the English-speakers. This is doubtless because the foreigners, shut out as they are by their alien tongues from much of the life about them, can yet perfectly understand the pantomime of the moving pictures.

As might be expected, the Latin races patronize the shows more consistently than Jews, Irish or Americans. Sailors of all races are devotees.

Most of the shows have musical accompaniments. The enterprising manager usually engages a human pianist with instructions to play Eliza-crossing-the-ice when the scene is shuddery, and fast ragtime in a comic kid chase. Where there is little competition, however, the manager merely presses the button and starts the automatic going, which is as apt as not to bellow out, I'd Rather Two-Step Than Waltz, Bill, just as the angel rises from the brave little hero-cripple's corpse.

The moving pictures were used as chasers in vaudeville houses for several years before the advent of the nickelodeon. The cinematograph or vitagraph or biograph or kinetoscope (there are seventy-odd names for the same machine) was invented in 1888–1889. Mr. Edison is said to have contributed most toward it, though several other inventors claim part of the credit.

The first very successful pictures were those of the Corbett-Fitzsimmons fight at Carson City, Nevada, in 1897. These films were shown all over the country to immense crowds and an enormous sum of money was made by the exhibitors.

The Jeffries-Sharkey fight of twenty-five rounds at Coney Island, in November, 1899, was another popular success. The contest being at night, artificial light was necessary, and 500 arc lamps were placed above the ring. Four cameras were used. While one was snapping the fighters, a second was being focused at them, a third was being reloaded, and a fourth was held in reserve in case of breakdown. Over seven miles of film were exposed and 198,000 pictures, each 2 by 3 inches, were taken. This fight was taken at the rate of thirty pictures to the second.

The 500 arc lamps above the ring generated a temperature of about 115 degrees for the gladiators to fight in. When the event was concluded, Mr. Jeffries was overheard to remark that for no amount of money would he ever again in his life fight in such heat, pictures or no pictures. And he never has.

Since that mighty fight, manufacturers have learned a good deal about cheapening their process. Pictures instead of being 2 by 3 inches are now 5/8 by 1 1/8 inches, and are taken sixteen instead of thirty to the second, for the illusion to the eye of continuous motion is as perfect at one rate as the other.

By means of a ratchet each separate picture is made to pause a twentieth of a second before the magic-lantern lens, throwing an enlargement to life size upon the screen. Then, while the revolving shutter obscures the lens, one picture is dropped and another substituted, to make in turn its twentieth of a second display.

The films are, as a rule, exhibited at the rate at which they are taken, though chase scenes are usually thrown faster, and horse races, fire-engines and fast-moving automobiles slower, than the life-speed.

.   .   .   .

Within the past year an automatic process to color films has been discovered by a French firm. The pigments are applied by means of a four-color machine stencil. Beyond this bare fact, the process remains a secret of the inventors. The stencil must do its work with extraordinary accuracy, for any minute error in the application of color to outline made upon the 5/8 by 1 1/8 inches print is magnified 200 times when thrown upon the screen by the magnifying lens. The remarkable thing about this automatic colorer is that it applies the pigment in slightly different outline to each successive print of a film 700 feet long. Colored films sell for about fifty per cent more than black and whites. Tinted films—browns, blues, oranges, violets, greens and so forth—are made by washing, and sell at but one per cent over the straight price.

The films are obtained in various ways. "Straight" shows, where the interest depends on the dramatist's imagination and the setting, are merely playlets acted out before the rapid-fire camera. Each manufacturing firm owns a studio with property-room, dressing-rooms and a completely-equipped stage. The actors are experienced professionals of just below the first rank, who are content to make from $18 to $25 a week. In France a class of moving-picture specialists has grown up who work only for the cameras, but in this country most of the artists who play in the film studios in the daytime play also behind the foot-lights at night.

The studio manager orders rehearsals continued until his people have their parts "face-perfect," then he gives the word, the lens is focused, the cast works rapidly for twenty minutes while the long strip of celluloid whirs through the camera, and the performance is preserved in living, dynamic embalmment (if the phrase may be permitted) for decades to come.

Eccentric scenes, such as a chalk marking the outlines of a coat upon a piece of cloth, the scissors cutting to the lines, the needle sewing, all automatically without human help, often require a week to take. The process is ingenious. First the scissors and chalk are laid upon the edge of the cloth. The picture is taken. The camera is stopped, the scissors are moved a quarter of an inch into the cloth, the chalk is drawn a quarter of an inch over the cloth. The camera is opened again and another picture is taken showing the quarter-inch cut and quarter-inch mark. The camera is closed, another quarter inch is cut and chalked; another exposure is made. When these pictures so slowly obtained are run off rapidly, the illusion of fast self-action on the part of the scissors, chalk and needle is pro-duced.

Sometimes in a nickelodeon you can see on the screen a building completely wrecked in five minutes. Such a film was obtained by focusing a camera at the building, and taking every salient move of the wreckers for the space, perhaps, of a fortnight. When these separate prints, obtained at varying intervals, some of them perhaps a whole day apart, are run together continuously, the appear-ance is of a mighty stone building being pulled to pieces like a house of blocks.

Such eccentric pictures were in high demand a couple of years ago, but now the straight-story show is running them out. The plots are improving every year in dramatic technique. Manufacturing firms pay from $5 to $25 for good sto-ries suitable for film presentation, and it is astonishing how many sound dramatic ideas are submitted by people of insufficient education to render their thoughts into English suitable for the legitimate stage.

The moving-picture actors are becoming excellent pantomimists, which is natural, for they cannot rely on the playwright's lines to make their meanings. I remember particularly a performance I saw near Spring Street on the Bowery, where the pantomime seemed to me in nowise inferior to that of Mademoiselle Pilar-Morin, the French pantomimist.

The nickelodeon spectators readily distinguish between good and bad acting, though they do not mark their pleasure or displeasure audibly, except very rarely, in a comedy scene, by a suppressed giggle. During the excellent show of which I have spoken, the men, women and children maintained a steady stare of fascination at the changing figures on the scene, and toward the climax, when forgiveness was cruelly denied, lips were parted and eyes filled with tears. It was as much a tribute to the actors as the loudest bravos ever shouted in the Metropolitan Opera House.

To-day a consistent plot is demanded. There must be, as in the drama, exposition, development, climax and dénouement. The most popular films run from fifteen to twenty minutes and are from five hundred to eight hundred feet long. One studio manager said: "The people want a story. We run to comics generally; they seem to take best. So-and-so, however, lean more to melodrama. When we started we used to give just flashes—an engine chasing to a fire, a base-runner sliding home, a charge of cavalry. Now, for instance, if we want to work in a horse race it has to be as a scene in the life of the jockey, who is the hero of the piece—we've got to give them a story; they won't take anything else—a story with plenty of action. You can't show large conversation, you know, on the screen. More story, larger story, better story with plenty of action—that is our tendency."

.   .   .   .

Civilization, all through the history of mankind, has been chiefly the property of the upper classes, but during the past century civilization has been permeating steadily downward. The leaders of this democratic movement have been general education, universal suffrage, cheap periodicals and cheap travel. To-day the moving-picture machine cannot be overlooked as an effective protagonist of democracy. For through it the drama, always a big fact in the lives of the people at the top, is now becoming a big fact in the lives of the people at the bottom. Two million of them a day have so found a new interest in life.

The prosperous Westerners, who take their week or fortnight, fall and spring, in New York, pay two dollars and a half for a seat at a problem play, a melodrama, a comedy or a show-girl show in a Broadway theatre. The stokers who have driven the Deutschland or the Lusitania from Europe pay five cents for a seat at a problem play, a melodrama, a comedy or a show-girl show in a Bowery nickelodeon. What is the difference?

The stokers, sitting on the hard, wooden chairs of the nickelodeon, experience the same emotional flux and counter-flux (more intense is their experience, for they are not as blasé) as the prosperous Westerners in their red plush orchestra chairs, uptown.

The sentient life of the half-civilized beings at the bottom has been enlarged and altered, by the introduction of the dramatic motif, to resemble more closely the sentient life of the civilized beings at the top.

Take an analogous case. Is aimless travel "beneficial" or not? It is amusing, certainly; and, therefore, the aristocrats who could afford it have always traveled aimlessly. But now, says the Democratic Movement, the grand tour shall no longer be restricted to the aristocracy. Jump on the rural trolley-car, Mr. Workingman, and make a grand tour yourself. Don't care, Mr. Workingman, whether it is "beneficial" or not. Do it because it is amusing; just as the aristocrats do.

The film makers cover the whole gamut of dramatic attractions. The extremes in the film world are as far apart as the extremes in the theatrical world—as far apart, let us say, as The Master Builder and The Gay White Way.

If you look up the moving-picture advertisements in any vaudeville trade paper you cannot help being struck with this fact. For instance, in a current number, one firm offers the following variety of attractions:

Romany's Revenge (very dramatic)	300 feet
Johnny's Run (comic kid chase)	300 "
Roof to Cellar (absorbing comedy)	782 "
Wizard's World (fantastic comedy)	350 "
Sailor's Return (highly dramatic)	535 "
A Mother's Sin (beautiful, dramatic and moral)	392 "
Knight Errant (old historical drama)	421 "
Village Fire Brigade (big laugh)	325 "
Catch the Kid (a scream)	270 "
The Coroner's Mistake (comic ghost story)	430 "
Fatal Hand (dramatic)	432 "

Another firm advertises in huge type, in the trade papers:

LIFE AND PASSION OF CHRIST

Five Parts, Thirty-nine Pictures,	
3114feet	Price, $373.68
Extra for coloring	125.10

The presentation by the picture machines of the Passion Play in this country was undertaken with considerable hesitation. The films had been shown in France to huge crowds, but here, so little were even professional students of American lower-class taste able to gauge it in advance, that the presenters feared the Passion Play might be boycotted, if not, indeed, in some places, mobbed. On the contrary, it has been the biggest success ever known to the business.

Last year incidents leading up to the murder of Stanford White were shown, succeeded enormously for a very few weeks, then flattened out completely and were withdrawn. Film people are as much at sea about what their crowds will like as the managers in the "legitimate."

Although the gourdlike growth of the nickelodeon business as a factor in the conscious life of Americans is not yet appreciated, already a good many people are disturbed by what they do know of the thing.

Those who are "interested in the poor" are wondering whether the five-cent theatre is a good influence, and asking themselves gravely whether it should be encouraged or checked (with the help of the police).

Is the theatre a "good" or a "bad" influence? The adjectives don't fit the case. Neither do they fit the case of the nickelodeon, which is merely the theatre democratized.

Take the case of the Passion Play, for instance. Is it irreverent to portray the Passion, Crucifixion, Resurrection and Ascension in a vaudeville theatre over a darkened stage where half an hour before a couple of painted, short-skirted girls were doing a "sister-act"? What is the motive which draws crowds of poor people to nickelodeons to see the Birth in the Manger flashed magic-lanternwise upon a white cloth? Curiosity? Mere mocking curiosity, perhaps? I cannot answer.

Neither could I say what it is that, every fifth year, draws our plutocrats to Oberammergau, where at the cost, from first to last, of thousands of dollars and days of time, they view a similar spectacle presented in a sunny Bavarian setting.

It is reasonable, however, to believe that the same feelings, whatever they are, which drew our rich to Oberammergau draw our poor to the nickelodeons. Whether the powerful emotional reactions produced in the spectator by the Passion Play are "beneficial" or not is as far beyond decision as the question whether a man or an oyster is happier. The man is more, feels more, than the oyster. The beholder of the Passion Play is more, feels more, than the non-beholder.

Whether for weal or woe, humanity has ceaselessly striven to complicate life, to diversify and make subtle the emotions, to create and gratify the new and artificial spiritual wants, to know more and feel more both of good and evil, to attain a greater degree of self-consciousness; just as the one fundamental instinct of the youth, which most systems of education have been vainly organized to eradicate, is to find out what the man knows.

In this eternal struggle for more self-consciousness, the moving-picture machine, uncouth instrument though it be, has enlisted itself on especial behalf of the least enlightened, those who are below the reach even of the yellow journals. For although in the prosperous vaudeville houses the machine is but a toy, a "chaser," in the nickelodeons it is the central, absorbing fact, which strengthens, widens, vivifies subjective life; which teaches living other than living through the senses alone. Already, perhaps, touching him at the psychological moment, it has awakened to his first, groping, necessary discontent the spirit of an artist of the future, who otherwise would have remained mute and motionless.

The nickelodeons are merely an extension course in civilization, teaching both its "badness" and its "goodness." They have come in obedience to the law of supply and demand; and they will stay as long as the slums stay, for in the slums they are the fittest and must survive.

VACHEL LINDSAY

Writing at the dawn of the cinema, in 1915, the poet Vachel Lindsay (1870–1931) supplies a description of the action genre, in which the fundamental outlines were already so firmly established that he could be describing an action film of the 1990s.

"The Photoplay of Action"

Let us assume, friendly reader, that it is eight o'clock in the evening when you make yourself comfortable in your den, to peruse this chapter. I want to tell you about the Action Film, the simplest, the type most often seen. In the mind of the habitué of the cheaper theatre it is the only sort in existence. It dominates the slums, is announced there by red and green posters of the melodrama sort, and retains its original elements, more deftly handled, in places more expensive. The story goes at the highest possible speed to be still credible. When it is a poor thing, which is the case too often, the St. Vitus dance destroys the pleasure-value. The rhythmic quality of the picture-motions is twitched to death. In the bad photoplay even the picture of an express train more than exaggerates itself. Yet when the photoplay chooses to behave it can reproduce a race far more joyously than the stage. On that fact is based the opportunity of this form. Many Action Pictures are indoors, but the abstract theory of the Action Film is based on the out-of-door chase. You remember the first one you saw where the policeman pursues the comical tramp over hill and dale and across the town lots. You remember that other where the cowboy follows the horse thief across the desert, spies him at last and chases him faster, faster, faster, and faster, and finally catches him. If the film was made in the days before the National Board of Censorship, it ends with the cowboy cheerfully hanging the villain; all details given to the last kick of the deceased.

One of the best Action Pictures is an old Griffith Biograph, recently reissued, the story entitled "Man's Genesis." In the time when cave-men-gorillas had no weapons, Weak-Hands (impersonated by Robert Harron) invents the stone club. He vanquishes his gorilla-like rival, Brute-Force (impersonated by Wilfred Lucas). Strange but credible manners and customs of the cave-men are detailed. They live in picturesque caves. Their half-monkey gestures are wonderful to see. But these things are beheld on the fly. It is the chronicle of a race between the brain of Weak-Hands and the body of the other, symbolized by the chasing of poor Weak-Hands in and out among the rocks until the climax. Brain desperately triumphs. Weak-Hands slays Brute-Force with the startling invention. He wins back his stolen bride, Lily-White (impersonated by Mae Marsh). It is a Griffith masterpiece, and every actor does sound work. The audience, mechanical Americans, fond of crawling on their stomachs to tinker their automobiles, are eager over the evolution of the first weapon from a stick to a hammer. They are as full of curiosity as they could well be over the history of Langley or the Wright brothers.

The dire perils of the motion pictures provoke the ingenuity of the audience, not their passionate sympathy. When, in the minds of the deluded producers, the beholders should be weeping or sighing with desire, they are prophesying the next step to one another in worldly George Ade slang. This is illustrated in another good Action Photoplay: the dramatization of The Spoilers. The original novel was written by Rex Beach. The gallant William Farnum as Glenister dominates the play. He has excellent support. Their team-work makes them worthy of chronicle: Thomas Santschi as McNamara, Kathlyn Williams as Cherry Malotte, Bessie Eyton as Helen Chester, Frank Clark as Dextry, Wheeler Oakman as Bronco Kid, and Jack McDonald as Slapjack.

There are, in The Spoilers, inspiriting ocean scenes and mountain views. There are interesting sketches of mining-camp manners and customs. There is a well-acted love-interest in it, and the element of the comradeship of loyal pals. But the chase rushes past these things to the climax, as in a policeman picture it whirls past blossoming gardens and front lawns till the tramp is arrested. The difficulties are commented on by the people in the audience as rah-rah boys on the side lines comment on hurdles cleared or knocked over by the men running in college field-day. The sudden cut-backs into side branches of the story are but hurdles also, not plot complications in the stage sense. This is as it should be. The pursuit progresses without St. Vitus dance or hysteria to the end of the film. There the spoilers are discomfited, the gold mine is recaptured, the incidental girls are won, in a flash, by the rightful owners.

These shows work like the express elevators in the Metropolitan Tower. The ideal is the maximum of speed in descending or ascending, not to be jolted into insensibility. There are two girl parts as beautifully thought out as the parts of ladies in love can be expected to be in Action Films. But in the end the love is not much more romantic in the eye of the spectator than it would be to behold a man on a motorcycle with the girl of his choice riding on the same machine behind him. And the highest type of Action Picture romance is not attained by having Juliet triumph over the motorcycle handicap. It is not achieved by weaving in a Sherlock Holmes plot. Action Picture romance comes when each hurdle is a tableau, when there is indeed an art-gallery-beauty in each one of these swift glimpses: when it is a race, but with a proper and golden-linked grace from action to action, and the goal is the most beautiful glimpse in the whole reel.

In the Action Picture there is no adequate means for the development of any full grown personal passion. The distinguished character-study that makes genuine the personal emotions in the legitimate drama, has no chance. People are but types, swiftly moved chessmen. . . . But here, briefly: the Action Pictures are falsely advertised as having heart-interest, or abounding in tragedy. But though the actors glower and wrestle and even if they are the most skilful lambasters in the profession, the audience gossips and chews gum.

Why does the audience keep coming to this type of photoplay if neither lust, love, hate, nor hunger is adequately conveyed? Simply because such spectacles gratify the incipient or rampant speed-mania in every American.

To make the elevator go faster than the one in the Metropolitan Tower is to destroy even this emotion. To elaborate unduly any of the agonies or seductions in the hope of arousing lust, love, hate, or hunger, is to produce on the screen a series of misplaced figures of the order Frankenstein.

How often we have been horrified by these galvanized and ogling corpses. These are the things that cause the outcry for more censors. It is not that our moral codes are insulted, but what is far worse, our nervous systems are temporarily racked to pieces. These wriggling half-dead men, these over-bloody burglars, are public nuisances, no worse and no better than dead cats being hurled about by street urchins.

The cry for more censors is but the cry for the man with the broom. Sometimes it is a matter as simple as when a child is scratching with a pin on a slate. While one would not have the child locked up by the chief of police, after five minutes of it almost every one wants to smack him till his little jaws ache. It is the very cold-bloodedness of the proceeding that ruins our kindness of heart. And the best Action Film is impersonal and unsympathetic even if it has no scratching pins. Because it is cold-blooded it must take extra pains to be tactful. Cold-blooded means that the hero as we see him on the screen is a variety of amiable or violent ghost. Nothing makes his lack of human charm plainer than when we as audience enter the theatre at the middle of what purports to be the most passionate of scenes when the goal of the chase is unknown to us and the alleged "situation" appeals on its magnetic merits. Here is neither the psychic telepathy of Forbes Robertson's Cæsar, nor the fire-breath of E. H. Sothern's Don Quixote. The audience is not worked up into the deadly still mob-unity of the speaking theatre. We late comers wait for the whole reel to start over and the goal to be indicated in the preliminary, before we can get the least bit wrought up. The prize may be a lady's heart, the restoration of a lost reputation, or the ownership of the patent for a churn. In the more effective Action Plays it is often what would be secondary on the stage, the recovery of a certain glove, spade, bull-calf, or rock-quarry. And to begin, we are shown a clean-cut picture of said glove, spade, bull-calf, or rock-quarry. Then when these disappear from ownership or sight, the suspense continues till they are again visible on the screen in the hands of the rightful owner.

In brief, the actors hurry through what would be tremendous passions on the stage to recover something that can be really photographed. For instance, there came to our town long ago a film of a fight between Federals and Confederates, with the loss of many lives, all for the recapture of a steam-engine that took on more personality in the end than private or general on either side, alive or dead. It was based on the history of the very engine photographed, or else that engine was given in replica. The old locomotive was full of character and humor amidst the tragedy, leaking steam at every orifice. The original is in one of the Southern Civil War museums. This engine in its capacity as a principal actor is going to be referred to more than several times in this work.

The highest type of Action Picture gives us neither the quality of Macbeth or Henry Fifth, the Comedy of Errors, or the Taming of the Shrew. It gives us rather that fine and special quality that was in the ink-bottle of Robert Louis Stevenson, that brought about the limitations and the nobility of the stories of Kidnapped, Treasure Island, and the New Arabian Nights. . . .

Having read thus far, why not close the book and go round the corner to a photoplay theatre? Give the preference to the cheapest one. *The Action Picture will be inevitable. Since this chapter was written, Charlie Chaplin and Douglas Fairbanks have given complete department store examples of the method, especially Chaplin in the brilliantly constructed Shoulder Arms, and Fairbanks in his one great piece of acting, in The Three Musketeers.*

CHARLIE CHAPLIN

Charlie Chaplin arrives in Los Angeles, finds a job, and creates history. It was all so simple, the way Chaplin describes it. He was hanging around Mack Sennett's set, hoping to catch his eye, and when Sennett told him, "We need some gags here," Chaplin went to wardrobe and emerged as . . . the Little Tramp, the most famous character in the first fifty years of film. It was a matter of the right clothes and makeup, Chaplin seems to believe: "By the time I walked on to the stage he was fully born." Of course inspiration could strike like that when the movies were young and you needed a gag, fast. Today six studio executives would feel it necessary to improve the Little Tramp with their input.

from *My Autobiography*

Eager and anxious, I arrived in Los Angeles and took a room at a small hotel, the Great Northern. The first evening I took a busman's holiday and saw the second show at the Empress, where the Karno Company had worked. The attendant recognized me and came a few moments later to tell me that Mr. Sennett and Miss Mabel Normand were sitting two rows back and had asked if I would join them. I was thrilled, and after a hurried, whispered introduction we all watched the show together. When it was over, we walked a few paces down Main Street, and went to a rathskeller for a light supper and a drink. Mr. Sennett was shocked to see how young I looked. "I thought you were a much older man," he said. I could detect a tinge of concern, which made me anxious, remembering that all Sennett's comedians were oldish-looking men. Fred Mace was over fifty and Ford Sterling in his forties. "I can make up as old as you like," I answered. Mabel Normand, however, was more reassuring. Whatever her reservations were about me, she did not reveal them. Mr. Sennett said that I would not start immediately, but should come to the studio in Edendale and get acquainted with the people. When we left the café, we bundled into Mr. Sennett's glamorous racing car and I was driven to my hotel.

The following morning I boarded a street-car for Edendale, a suburb of Los Angeles. It was an anomalous-looking place that could not make up its mind whether to be a humble residential district or a semi-industrial one. It had small lumber-yards and junk-yards, and abandoned-looking small farms on which were built one or two shacky wooden stores that fronted the road. After many enquiries I found myself opposite the Keystone Studio. It was a dilapidated affair with a green fence round it, one hundred and fifty feet square. The entrance to it was up a garden path through an old bungalow—the whole place looked just as anomalous as Edendale itself. I stood gazing at it from the opposite side of the road, debating whether to go in or not.

It was lunch-time and I watched the men and women in their make-up come pouring out of the bungalow, including the Keystone Cops. They crossed the road to a small general store and came out eating sandwiches and hot dogs. Some called after each other in loud, raucous voices: "Hey, Hank, come on!" "Tell Slim to hurry!"

Suddenly I was seized with shyness and walked quickly to the corner at a safe distance, looking to see if Mr. Sennett or Miss Normand would come out of the bungalow, but they did not appear. For half an hour I stood there, then decided to go back to the hotel. The problem of entering the studio and facing all those people became an insuperable one. For two days I arrived outside the studio, but I had not the courage to go in. The third day Mr. Sennett telephoned and wanted to know why I had not shown up. I made some sort of excuse. "Come down right away, we'll be waiting for you," he said. So I went down and boldly marched into the bungalow and asked for Mr. Sennett.

He was pleased to see me and took me immediately into the studio. I was enthralled. A soft even light pervaded the whole stage. It came from broad streams of white linen that diffused the sun and gave an ethereal quality to everything. This diffusion was for photographing in daylight.

After being introduced to one or two actors I became interested in what was going on. There were three sets side by side, and three comedy companies were at work in them. It was like viewing something at the World's Fair. In one set Mabel Normand was banging on a door shouting: "Let me in!" Then the camera stopped and that was it—I had no idea films were made piecemeal in this fashion.

On another set was the great Ford Sterling whom I was to replace. Mr. Sennett introduced me to him. Ford was leaving Keystone to form his own company with Universal. He was immensely popular with the public and with everyone in the studio. They surrounded his set and were laughing eagerly at him.

Sennett took me aside and explained their method of working. "We have no scenario—we get an idea then follow the natural sequence of events until it leads up to a chase, which is the essence of our comedy."

This method was edifying, but personally I hated a chase. It dissipates one's personality; little as I knew about movies, I knew that nothing transcended personality.

That day I went from set to set watching the companies at work. They all seemed to be imitating Ford Sterling. This worried me, because his style did not suit me. He played a harassed Dutchman, ad-libbing through the scene with a Dutch accent, which was funny but was lost in silent pictures. I wondered what Sennett expected of me. He had seen my work and must have known that I was not suitable to play Ford's type of comedy; my style was just the opposite. Yet every story and situation conceived in the studio was consciously or unconsciously made for Sterling; even Roscoe Arbuckle was imitating Sterling.

The studio had evidently been a farm. Mabel Normand's dressing-room was situated in an old bungalow and adjoining it was another room where the ladies of the stock company dressed. Across from the bungalow was what had evidently been a barn, the main dressing-room for minor members of the stock company and the Keystone Cops, the majority of whom were ex-circus clowns and prize-fighters. I was allotted the star dressing-room used by Mack Sennett, Ford Sterling and Roscoe Arbuckle. It was another barn-like structure which might have been the harness-room. Besides Mabel Normand, there were several other beautiful girls. It was a strange and unique atmosphere of beauty and beast.

For days I wandered around the studio, wondering when I would start work. Occasionally I would meet Sennett crossing the stage, but he would look through me, preoccupied. I had an uncomfortable feeling that he thought he had made a mistake in engaging me which did little to ameliorate my nervous tension.

Each day my peace of mind depended on Sennett. If perchance he saw me and smiled, my hopes would rise. The rest of the company had a wait-and-see attitude but some, I felt, considered me a doubtful substitute for Ford Sterling.

When Saturday came Sennett was most amiable. Said he: "Go to the front office and get your cheque." I told him I was more anxious to get to work. I wanted to talk about imitating Ford Sterling, but he dismissed me with the remark: "Don't worry, we'll get round to that."

Nine days of inactivity had passed and the tension was excruciating. Ford, however, would console me and after work he would occasionally give me a lift down-town, where we would stop in at the Alexandria Bar for a drink and meet several of his friends. One of them, a Mr. Elmer Ellsworth; whom I disliked at first and thought rather crass, would jokingly taunt me: "I understand you're taking Ford's place. Well, are you funny?"

"Modesty forbids," I said squirmishly. This sort of ribbing was most embarrassing, especially in the presence of Ford. But he graciously took me off the hook with a remark. "Didn't you catch him at the Empress playing the drunk? Very funny."

"Well, he hasn't made me laugh yet," said Ellsworth.

He was a big, cumbersome man, and looked glandular, with a melancholy, hangdog expression, hairless face, sad eyes, a loose mouth and a smile that showed two missing front teeth. Ford whispered impressively that he was a great authority on literature, finance and politics, one of the best-informed men in the country, and that he had a great sense of humour. However I did not appreciate it and would try to avoid him. But one night at the Alexandria bar, he said: "Hasn't this limey got started yet?"

"Not yet," I laughed uncomfortably.

"Well, you'd better be funny."

Having taken a great deal from the gentleman, I gave him back some of his own medicine: "Well, if I'm half as funny as you look, I'll do all right."

"Blimey! A sarcastic wit, eh? I'll buy him a drink after that."

DJUNA BARNES

John Bunny (1863–1915) died of Bright's disease one month after conducting this haunting interview with the writer and bohemian legend Djuna Barnes (1892–1982). Did he already know he was ill? He seems preoccupied with how he will be remembered after he is dead and reassures himself that film will grant him immortality. And so it has, but only among the handful of silent comedy lovers who know who he was. I first read this piece at about the same time John Candy died, and was filled with reflection.

John Bunny

Having pieced together necessities of the soul and the humor that gets past with the solemnity that holds the two down to earth as ballast, and having attained with the piecing a weight nearing the 300 mark, John Bunny, moving picture actor and little friend to the thin, looks at you out of prolonged almond eyes wherein is the shadow of the veil drawn aside, and a great sadness that seldom reaches his public.

Ask him what his nationality is and he will answer half-and-half, as though he were ordering a drink; ask him half of what and half of what again, and he will smile, "Half English, half Irish," and then ask him what he thinks of the Irish and he will answer, "Now, start something."

For half-an-hour I walked in John Bunny's footsteps, for he always walks ahead, and you must of necessity amble slowly behind, like a dog at the heels of a star.

Over his short, sandy hair he wears a cap of a check diminutive; over his sternum bone a shirt of a stripe majestic, and over the insteps of his jaunty, slow-moving feet the best of canvas not used in the making of the tents of Anthony.

This was the joy of the screen with the screen folded and laid aside, so I gripped him by the hand and looked into the face called funny, and wondered to see the mouth drawn down into the lines of slack net, sadly unfulfilling the purposes of its mesh.

"Humor," I said, "where art thou—as you live for us in the moving picture house?"

"No," he said, "I am not a humorous man. Many think I must be to get away with my laughs, but it is not because of my size nor because of my face that I have made my life a success; it is because I have intelligence. You can't make everyone understand that; nevertheless, it is the case. If I were merely funny and pounds I would have gone down at five-per day ages ago. It is the intelligence, the brain behind the mass, that makes the populace proclaim and desire. Twenty-six years I've been acting, everything from Shakespeare to a clown; Nick Bottom with Annie Russell to a darn fool with Hitchcock, and I found that it didn't pay.

"Have you ever realized," Bunny continued, in that slow drawl that sometimes broke into a lisp and sometimes into a deep, throaty chuckle, "that actors are merely public toys, playthings for the people to handle and grow tired of, toys that amuse for a time, toys that lure with the brightness of their paint, to be patronized just so long as the paint is new and bright and attractive, dropped and forgotten when it is worn off and the toy is broken and old? Dead, never to be resurrected; discarded and thrown aside for a toy more amply shaded with varnish and crimson, forgotten for a new face, a newer, larger smile, a greater capacity for tears. Who of us ever thinks of Booth? Who of us ever mentions Irving?

"Did you ever stop to think that if some ill-disposed person were to throw vitriol into this funny face that the thousands who had rocked with laughter would turn away and forget all the laughs and hours of merriment, would turn me loose into the realm of the great forgotten; that is, if I had remained an actor of the legitimate stage.

"But I have chosen a better thing. I shall live longer than Irving and Booth, not because I deserve to, but because there is a record of me that they did not leave; the public can have me always the same, so long as the pictures are preserved. To be remembered. To be remembered the feet must move. It is the single photograph that gets put away, but throw me on the screen when I'm only ashes and the people will respond the way they have always responded. Indeed, I would wager that they would rise up and become enthusiastic toward a dead comedy actor who, in pictures, went right on amusing them with overcountry rides in pursuit of a runaway daughter. It has a tang of the game in it. Most dead people are dead for a long while, but the moving picture actor goes right on living and loving and laughing and walking, even if he is languidly strumming upon a stringed instrument in another world.

"Oh, don't tell me," Bunny added, wiping his brow, "that the moving picture actor hasn't got it over the regular actor fifty ways. Why, in the mere matter of rehearsing and touring, every well-known actor has had to go on the road, has had to foot traveling bills, has had to listen to the temper which is called temperament of his leading lady, and has to listen to the railing of the stage manager, who is nothing but a clerk out front. He is denied his home, his church, his club. He subjects himself to all sorts of things that the moving picture actor never knows about, and wouldn't want to know, and in the end the play may be a failure. And he doesn't get the big pay that a moving picture actor gets. I get $50,000 a year. How many other legitimate actors get that?"

"But," I interrupted, "moving picture actors are looked down upon by the legitimate actors, are they not?"

"Once," he said, "the regular actor shunned us, until one day, looking to the cause of their slackness of trade, they saw us. Since then they have not crossed to the other side of the street.

"Yet the moving pictures will never take the place of the stage. They are simply a new kind of amusement. Moving pictures give you only two sides of a room, and out of your own imagination you supply the roof and the other sides. You make the actors talk. You are proud of the moving picture, yet it is not the moving pictures that you are proud of at all. It is the amount of yourself that you have put into them.

"And returning to the attitude of actors and public in general toward a moving picture star, I may say that I can pick my friends. Those that I do not like do not know me, because I won't be known. Those that I do not like may speak to me and receive a civil 'How do you do?' but they do not know my house, they do not read my books, they do not look at my pictures, they don't know my dog, they may not take me by the hand and call me comrade. If I dislike a person I don't see him, that's all. There are many that want to know me that I don't want to know. I get hundreds of letters; some of them are very pleasant, all of them are complimentary, and most of them make a touch for an autographed picture—which they get only when the letter sounds sincere. People walk up to me in the street and tell me how I have made their lives a little brighter; people come to me in the cafes and speak of my funny face; others turn about and look when they do not approach."

"What is your greatest ambition?" I asked.

"I hope to improve the moving pictures. Just how I don't want to say, but they are not nearly as perfect as they should be. I am going to experiment and try to make them better. Also, I am going to set out some rules for the improvement of the scenarios; they are often very inadequate. If I light a few more matches," he said irrelevantly, "you will think I buy them by the tree."

"What do you love more than anything else in the world, Mr. Bunny?"

"Baseball and the sea, and my wife and two boys—and my friends. But, best of all, set me adrift on a log." He laughed then and tipped his cap over his only-pair-of-eyes-in-the-world-like-them.

So let us leave him.

LOUISE BROOKS

Had Louise Brooks stopped making films after she walked out of Paramount Pictures, she would be forgotten today, except by silent movie buffs. But fate matched her with the German director G. W. Pabst, and with him she did two films—Pandora's Box and Diary of a Lost Girl, both in 1929—and they made her a screen immortal. The films retain their shocking erotic charge, both because of Brooks's incredibly expressive performances and because Pabst insisted that every action have a motivation (see Brooks's discussion of the difference between Griffith's "giggling virgins" and Pabst's). Brooks drifted back to Hollywood, acted in B pictures, quit Hollywood forever in 1940, and by 1943, she wrote, "found that the only well-paying career open to me, as an unsuccessful actress of thirty-six, was that of a call girl." (It is typical of Brooks that she deliberately left it unclear whether she worked at that career.) In 1956 she was persuaded to move to Rochester by James Card, the curator of the Eastman House film center, and there she began to write the essays that make up Lulu in Hollywood, one of the wittiest and most truthful books ever written about the movies.

"Pabst and Lulu"

Frank Wedekind's play *Pandora's Box* opens with a prologue. Out of a circus tent steps the Animal Tamer, carrying in his left hand a whip and in his right hand a loaded revolver. "Walk in," he says to the audience. "Walk into my menagerie!" The finest job of casting that G. W. Pabst ever did was casting himself as the director, the Animal Tamer, of his film adaptation of Wedekind's "tragedy of monsters." Never a sentimental trick did this whip hand permit the actors assembled to play his beasts. The revolver he shot straight into the heart of the audience. At the time Wedekind produced *Pandora's Box,* in Berlin around the turn of the century, it was detested, condemned, and banned. It was declared to be "immoral and inartistic." If in that period when the sacred pleasures of the ruling class were comparatively private, a play exposing them had called out the dogs of law, how much more savage would be the attack upon a film faithful to Wedekind's text which was made in 1928 in Berlin, where the ruling class publicly flaunted its pleasures as a symbol of wealth and power. And since nobody truly knows what a director is doing till he is done, nobody who was connected with the film dreamed that Pabst was risking commercial failure with the story of an "immoral" prostitute who wasn't crazy about her work and was surrounded by the "inartistic" ugliness of raw bestiality. Only five years earlier, the famous Danish actress Asta Nielsen had condensed Wedekind's play into the film *Loulou.* There was no lesbianism in it, no incest. Loulou the man-eater devoured her sex victims—Dr. Goll, Schwarz, and Schön—and then dropped dead in an acute attack of indigestion. This kind of film, with Pabst improvements, was what audiences were prepared for. Set upon making their disillusionment inescapable, hoping to avoid even any duplication of the straight bob and bangs that Nielsen had worn as Loulou, Mr. Pabst tested me with my hair curled. But after seeing the test he gave up this point and left me with my shiny black helmet, except for one curled sequence on the gambling ship.

Besides daring to film Wedekind's problem of abnormal psychology—in Wedekind's own words, "this fatal destiny which is the subject of the tragedy"—besides daring to show the prostitute as the victim, Mr. Pabst went on to the final, damning immorality of making his Lulu as "sweetly innocent" as the flowers that adorned her costumes and filled the scenes of the play. "Lulu is not a real character," Wedekind said in a commentary, "but the personification of primitive sexuality who inspires evil unaware. She plays a purely passive role." In the middle of the prologue, dressed in her boy's costume of Pierrot, she is carried by a stage hand before the Animal Tamer, who tells her, "Be unaffected, and not pieced out with distorted, artificial folly/even if the critics praise you

for it less wholly./And mind—all foolery and making faces/the childish sim-
pleness of vice disgraces." This was the Lulu, when the film was released, whom
the critics praised not less wholly, but not at all. "Louise Brooks cannot act,"
one critic wrote. "She does not suffer. She does nothing." As far as they were
concerned, Pabst had fired a blank. It was I who was struck down by my failure, although he had done everything possible to protect and strengthen me
against this deadly blow. He never allowed me to be publicly identified with the
film after the night, during production, when we appeared as guests at the opening of an UFA film, at the Gloria Palast. As we left the theatre, and he hurried
me through a crowd of hostile moviegoers, I heard a girl saying something loud
and nasty. In the cab, I began pounding his knee, insisting, "What did she say?
What did she say?" Finally, he translated: "That is the American girl who is playing our German Lulu!"

In the studio, Pabst, who had a special, pervasive sense that penetrated minds
and walls alike, put down all overt acts of contempt. Although I never complained, he substituted another assistant for an assistant who woke me out of my
dressing-room naps by beating the door and bellowing, "Fräulein Brooks!
Come!" Sitting on the set day after day, my darling maid, Josifine Müller, who
had worked for Asta Nielsen and thought she was the greatest actress in the
world, came to love me tenderly because I was the world's worst actress. For
the same reason, the great actor Fritz Kortner, who played Schön, never spoke
to me at all. Using Pabst's strength, I learned to block off painful impressions.
Kortner, like everybody else on the production, thought I had cast some blinding spell over Pabst which allowed me to walk through my part. To them, it
was a sorry outcome of Pabst's difficult search for Lulu, about which one of his
assistants, Paul Falkenberg, said in 1955, "Preparation for *Pandora's Box* was quite
a saga, because Pabst couldn't find a Lulu. He wasn't satisfied with any actress
at hand, and for months everybody connected with the production went around
looking for a Lulu. I talked to girls on the street, on the subway, in railway stations—'Would you mind coming up to our office? I would like to present you
to Mr. Pabst.' He looked all of them over dutifully and turned them all down.
And eventually he picked Louise Brooks."

How Pabst determined that I was his unaffected Lulu, with the childish sim-
pleness of vice, was part of a mysterious alliance that seemed to exist between
us even before we met. He knew nothing more of me than an unimportant part
he saw me play in the Howard Hawks film *A Girl in Every Port* (1928). I had never
heard of him, and had no idea he had made unsuccessful negotiations to borrow
me from Paramount until I was called to the front office on the option day of
my contract. My salary wasn't going to be increased. B. P. Schulberg told me
that I could stay on at my old salary or quit. It was the time of the switchover
to talkies, and studios were taking ugly advantage of this fact to cut contract play-

ers' salaries. Refusing to take what amounted to a cut, I quit Paramount. Almost as an afterthought, Schulberg told me about the Pabst offer, which I was now free to accept. I said I would accept it, and he sent off a cable to Pabst. All this took about ten minutes, and I left Schulberg somewhat dazed by my composure and my quick decisions.

If I had not acted at once, I would have lost the part of Lulu. At that very hour in Berlin Marlene Dietrich was waiting with Pabst in his office. Pabst later said, "Dietrich was too old and too obvious—one sexy look and the picture would become a burlesque. But I gave her a deadline, and the contract was about to be signed when Paramount cabled saying I could have Louise Brooks." It must be remembered that Pabst was speaking about the pre–Josef-von-Sternberg Dietrich. She was the Dietrich of *I Kiss Your Hand, Madame,* a film in which, caparisoned variously in beads, brocade, ostrich feathers, chiffon ruffles, and white rabbit fur, she galloped from one lascivious stare to another. Years after another trick of fate had made her a top star—for Sternberg's biographer, Herman Weinberg, told me that it was only because Brigitte Helm was not available that Sternberg looked further and found Dietrich for *The Blue Angel*—she said to Travis Banton, the Paramount dress designer who transformed her spangles and feathers into glittering, shadowed beauty, "Imagine Pabst choosing Louise Brooks for Lulu when he could have had me!"

So it is that my playing of the tragic Lulu with no sense of sin remained generally unacceptable for a quarter of a century.

Not long ago, after seeing *Pandora's Box* at Eastman House, a priest said to me, "How did you feel, playing—*that girl?*"

"Feel? I felt fine! It all seemed perfectly normal to me."

Seeing him start with distaste and disbelief, and unwilling to be mistaken for one of those women who like to shock priests with sensational confessions, I went on to prove the truth of Lulu's world by telling him of my own experience in the 1925 *Ziegfeld Follies,* when my best friend was a lesbian and I knew two millionaire publishers who, much like Schön in the film, backed shows to keep themselves well supplied with Lulus. But the priest rejected my reality exactly as Berlin had rejected its reality when we made *Pandora's Box* and sex was the business of the town. At the Eden Hotel, where I lived in Berlin, the café bar was lined with the higher-priced trollops. The economy girls walked the street outside. On the corner stood the girls in boots, advertising flagellation. Actors' agents pimped for the ladies in luxury apartments in the Bavarian Quarter. Race-track touts at the Hoppegarten arranged orgies for groups of sportsmen. The nightclub Eldorado displayed an enticing line of homosexuals dressed as women. At the Maly, there was a choice of feminine or collar-and-tie lesbians. Collective lust roared unashamed at the theatre. In the revue *Chocolate Kiddies,* when Josephine Baker appeared naked except for a girdle of bananas, it was precisely as Lulu's stage entrance was described by Wedekind: "They rage there as in a menagerie when the meat appears at the cage."

Every actor has a natural animosity toward every other actor, present or absent, living or dead. Most Hollywood directors did not understand that, any more than they understood why an actor might be tempted to withhold the rapt devotion to the master which they considered essential to their position of command. When I went to Berlin to film *Pandora's Box*, what an exquisite release, what a revelation of the art of direction, was the Pabst spirit on the set! He actually encouraged actors' disposition to hate and back away from each other, and thus preserved their energy for the camera; and when actors were not in use, his ego did not command them to sit up and bark at the sight of him. The behavior of Fritz Kortner was a perfect example of how Pabst used an actor's true feelings to add depth and breadth and power to his performance. Kortner hated me. After each scene with me, he would pound off the set and go to his dressing room. Pabst himself, wearing his most private smile, would go there to coax him back for the next scene. In the role of Dr. Schön, Kortner had feelings for me (or for the character Lulu) that combined sexual passion with an equally passionate desire to destroy me. One sequence gave him an opportunity to shake me with such violence that he left ten black-and-blue fingerprints on my arms. Both he and Pabst were well pleased with that scene, because Pabst's feelings for me, like Kortner's, were not unlike those of Schön for Lulu. I think that in the two films Pabst made with me—*Pandora's Box* and *Diary of a Lost Girl*—he was conducting an investigation into his relations with women, with the object of conquering any passion that interfered with his passion for his work. He was not aroused by sexual love, which he dismissed as an enervating myth. It was sexual hate that engrossed his whole being with its flaming reality.

With adroit perversity, Pabst selected Gustav Diessl to play Jack the Ripper in *Pandora's Box*, and Fritz Rasp to play the lascivious chemist's assistant in *Diary of a Lost Girl*. They were the only actors in those films whom I found beautiful and sexually alluring. There was no complexity in Pabst's direction of the Jack the Ripper scenes. He made them a tender love passage until that terrible moment when Diessl saw the knife on the edge of the table, gleaming in the candlelight. But, conceiving the seduction scenes in *Diary of a Lost Girl* as a ballet, with me (Thymiane) as the seductress, he directed them as a series of subtle, almost wordless maneuvers between an "innocent" young girl and a wary lecher. He chose Fritz Rasp not only for the restraint with which he would play a part verging on burlesque but also for his physical grace and strength. When I collapsed in his embrace, he swept me up into his arms and carried me off to bed as lightly as if I weighed no more than my silken nightgown and robe.

Unlike most directors, Pabst had no catalogue of characters, with stock emotional responses. D. W. Griffith required giggling fits from all sexually excited virgins. If Pabst had ever shot a scene showing a virgin giggling, it would have been because someone was tickling her. It was the stimulus that concerned him. If he got that right, the actor's emotional reaction would be like life itself—often strange and unsatisfactory to an audience that was used to settled acting conventions. When *Pandora's Box* was released, in 1929, film critics objected because Lulu did not suffer after the manner of Sarah Bernhardt in *Camille*. Publicity photographs taken before the filming of *Pandora's Box* show Pabst watching me with scientific intensity. Anticipating all my scenes in his films, he contrived to put me in similar situations in real life. A well-timed second visit to the set by the actress and future filmmaker Leni Riefenstahl—gabbing and laughing off in a corner with Pabst—guaranteed my look of gloomy rejection in a closeup in *Diary of a Lost Girl*. His tested knowledge of cause and effect is part of the answer to how Pabst could shoot very fast, with little rehearsal and few takes.

I revered Pabst for his truthful picture of this world of pleasure which let me play Lulu naturally. The other members of the cast were tempted to rebellion. And perhaps that was his most brilliant directorial achievement—getting a group of actors to play unsympathetic characters, whose only motivation was sexual gratification. Fritz Kortner, as Schön, wanted to be the victim. Franz Lederer, as the incestuous son Alva Schön, wanted to be adorable. Carl Goetz wanted to get laughs playing the old pimp Schigolch. Alice Roberts, the Belgian actress who played the screen's first lesbian, the Countess Geschwitz, was prepared to go no further than repression in mannish suits. Her first day's work was in the wedding sequence. She came on the set looking chic in her Paris evening dress and aristocratically self-possessed. Then Mr. Pabst began explaining the action of the scene in which she was to dance the tango with me. Suddenly, she understood that she was to touch, to embrace, to make love to another woman. Her blue eyes bulged and her hands trembled. Anticipating the moment of explosion, Mr. Pabst, who proscribed unscripted emotional outbursts, caught her arm and sped her away out of sight behind the set. A half hour later, when they returned, he was hissing soothingly to her in French and she was smiling like the star of the picture—which she was in all her scenes with me. I was just there obstructing the view. Both in two-shots and in her close-ups photographed over my shoulder, she cheated her look past me to Mr. Pabst, who was making love to her off camera. Out of the funny complexity of this design Mr. Pabst extracted his tense portrait of sterile lesbian passion, and Mme. Roberts satisfactorily preserved her reputation. At the time, her conduct struck me as silly. The fact that the public could believe an actress's private life to be like one role in one film did not come home to me till 1964, when I was visited by a French boy. Explaining why the young people in Paris loved *Pandora's Box,* he put an uneasy thought in my mind.

"You talk as if I were a lesbian in real life," I said.

"But of course!" he answered, in a way that made me laugh to realize I had been living in cinematic perversion for thirty-five years.

It had pleased me on the day I finished the silent version of *The Canary Murder Case* for Paramount to leave Hollywood for Berlin to work for Pabst. When I got back to New York after finishing *Pandora's Box,* Paramount's New York office called to order me to get on the train at once for Hollywood. They were making *The Canary Murder Case* into a talkie and needed me for retakes. When I said I wouldn't go, they sent a man round with a contract. When I still said I wouldn't go, they offered me any amount of money I might ask, to save the great expense of reshooting and dubbing in another voice. In the end, after they were finally convinced that nothing would induce me to do the retakes, I signed a release (gratis) for all my pictures, and they dubbed in Margaret Livingston's voice in *The Canary Murder Case.* But the whole thing—the money that Paramount was forced to spend, the affront to the studio—made them so angry that they sent out a story, widely publicized and believed, that they had let me go because I was no good in talkies.

In Hollywood, I was a pretty flibbertigibbet whose charm for the executive department decreased with every increase in her fan mail. In Berlin, I stepped onto the station platform to meet Pabst and became an actress. I would be treated by him with a kind of decency and respect unknown to me in Hollywood. It was just as if Pabst had sat in on my whole life and career and knew exactly where I needed assurance and protection. And, just as his understanding of me reached back to his knowledge of a past we did not have to speak about, so it was with the present. For although we were together constantly—on the set, at lunch, often for dinner and the theatre—he seldom spoke to me. Yet he would appear at the dressmaker's at the moment I was about to go into the classic act of ripping off an offensive wedding dress; he would banish a call boy who roared at me through the dressing-room door; he would refuse, after the first day's rushes, which secretly upset me, to let me see the rushes ever again. All that I thought and all his reactions seemed to pass between us in a kind of wordless communication. To other people surrounding him, he would talk endlessly in that watchful way of his, smiling, intense; speaking quietly, with his wonderful, hissing precision. But to me he might speak never a word all morning, and then at lunch turn suddenly and say, "Loueess, tomorrow morning you must be ready to do a big fight scene with Kortner," or "This afternoon, in the first scene, you are going to cry." That was how he directed me. With an intelligent actor, he would sit in exhaustive explanation; with an old ham, he would speak the language of the theatre. But in my case, by some magic, he would saturate me with one clear emotion and turn me loose. And it was the same with the plot. Pabst never strained my mind with anything not pertinent to the immediate action. But if I made that picture with only the dimmest notion of what it was about, on my second picture with Pabst, *Diary of a Lost Girl,* I had no idea at all of its plot or meaning till I saw it twenty-seven years later, at Eastman House.

And it was during the making of *Diary of a Lost Girl*—on the last day of shooting, to be exact—that Pabst moved into my future. We were sitting gloomily at a table in the garden of a little café, watching the workmen while they dug the grave for a burial scene, when he decided to let me have it. Several weeks before, in Paris, he had met some friends of mine—rich Americans with whom I spent every hour away from work. And he was angry: first, because he thought they prevented me from staying in Germany, learning the language, and becoming a serious actress, as he wanted; and, second, because he looked upon them as spoiled children who would amuse themselves with me for a time and then discard me like an old toy. "Your life is exactly like Lulu's," he said, "and you will end the same way."

At that time, knowing so little of what he meant by "Lulu," I just sat sullenly glaring at him, trying not to listen. Fifteen years later, in Hollywood, with all his predictions closing in on me, I heard his words again—hissing back to me. And, listening this time, I packed my trunks and went home to Kansas. But the strangest thing of all in my relationship with Mr. Pabst was the revelation tucked away in a footnote written by Richard Griffith in his book *The Film since Then.* He identified me as "Louise Brooks, whom Pabst brought to Germany from Hollywood to play in *Pandora's Box,* whose whole life and career were altered thereby." When I read that, thirty years after I refused to go back to Hollywood to do those retakes on *The Canary Murder Case,* I finally understood why.

KEVIN BROWNLOW

At a time when many of the great silent stars and a few of the directors were still alive but might not be for much longer Kevin Brownlow embarked on his irreplaceable book The Parade's Gone By. *His feeling was that the motion picture reached its greatest heights in the silent era and had been in decline since; it was a theory many of his subjects agreed with, and so they opened up to him and told stories they had in some cases been keeping private for decades. Here are two excerpts: Mary Pickford (1893–1979), who was one of silent Hollywood's most powerful producers as well as its greatest female star, brings Ernst*

Lubitsch over from Germany, differs with him, and many years later has reduced the experience to hilarious anecdotes. And Gloria Swanson (1897–1983), who adores Cecil B. De Mille, finds herself sitting on his knee and being called his brave boy.

Mary Pickford and Gloria Swanson

Mary Pickford

I will not allow one picture to be shown: *Rosita*. Oh, I detested that picture! I disliked the director, Ernst Lubitsch, as much as he disliked me. We didn't show it, of course, but it was a very unhappy and very costly experience.

Lubitsch was on his way over from Germany when the American Legion held a big meeting. I was on the platform. The supreme officer of the Legion got up and said, "I hear the son of the Kaiser is coming here. I would to God that the American Legion would go down to meet him—and throw him in the water. He doesn't belong here. He's still our enemy. And why are they bringing German singers over here? Do we not have enough good singers here, in the United States, without going to Germany?"

"Oh," I thought, "here it comes. I'll be next. 'What is she doing bringing Lubitsch over here? Do we not have good American directors?' " I wasn't going to take it sitting down. I decided that I would get up and speak. Perspiration began to break out on my forehead. This is what I planned to say:

"General, ladies and gentlemen. Since when has art borderlines? Art is universal, and for my pictures I will get the finest, no matter which country they come from. The war is over. And it is very ill-bred and stupid for the General to stand up and talk like that. A German voice is God-given if it's beautiful.

"Yes, I am bringing Mr. Lubitsch over here. Yes! I'm proud that I can. And General, you be grown up, you be a good boy and don't you say that to me, because I'm white, twenty-one, and an American citizen, and I contributed to the war as you did. But you're not contributing to anything with opinions like that."

I remember that speech to this day. I had it all set—and he never called on me. I was very disappointed.

Lubitsch was on the water, coming over, so I said, "We're in trouble. The American Legion may meet him." We arranged for a little pilot boat to take him off the ship. He was instructed not to mention Mary Pickford, where he was going, or what he was doing, and above all he was told not to mention Germany.

When he arrived in Hollywood I naturally sent Mrs. Lubitsch a large bunch of flowers. The newspaper people immediately wanted to know about it.

"What are you doing here, Mr. Lubitsch?"

Putting the card in his pocket, Lubitsch replied, "I'm not talking."

"Are you going to work?"

"*Nein.*"

I first met him on the studio lot, with Edward Knoblock and Douglas Fairbanks. Knoblock spoke perfect German, and he introduced us. Lubitsch took my hand, and suddenly threw it away from him.

"*Ach, mein Gott!*" he exclaimed. "She is cold!"

"Oh, he's just nervous," I thought.

"*Ja,* cold!" he repeated. "She cannot be an actress!"

"Our actresses are paid to act," said Knoblock. "They don't act when offstage, or away from the camera. You're judging her by German actresses."

Lubitsch was watching me all the time, to see if I would blow up. I kept my temper.

Our first production together was to be *Dorothy Vernon of Haddon Hall,* and he had read the script. I had spent a quarter of a million dollars in preparation. I remember seeing Knoblock and Lubitsch moving through the wheatfield at the back of the studio—the wheat was chest high, and they were swimming through it. "There goes trouble," I said to my mother.

Knoblock approached us and said, "I'm sorry. Lubitsch won't do *Dorothy Vernon.*"

"Edward!" I said. "Why not? He read the script in Germany, he came over here, he's been receiving salary, I paid his fare, and that of his wife . . ."

"Will you see him?" asked Knoblock.

"Of course," I said. "I'll have to."

I went over to my bungalow, which I had just had painted a dove gray. Lubitsch used to eat German-fried potatoes three times a day, and I was dismayed when the grease on his hands left little frescoes all around the room.

"All right, Mr. Lubitsch," I said. "What's wrong?"

He pounded my beautiful table with his fist and he shouted "I'm not making *Dorothy Vernon!*"

"Well," I said, "you read the script . . ."

"*Ja.* I don't like it."

"Why didn't you say that in Germany?"

"Vell, now I'm telling you."

"What's wrong with *Dorothy Vernon?*"

"Der iss too many qveens and not enough qveens."

Elizabeth and Mary; he objected to their story being more interesting than that of Dorothy Vernon. Queen Elizabeth and Mary Queen of Scots could have been a story on their own, but there wasn't enough in the script to make that possible.

"All right," I said. "I can't force you to do something you don't want to do."
"I go back to Germany."

I told him he could if he wished to. When he'd cooled down I said to Edward, "Let's find another story." We settled on *Rosita*. What an ordeal! I had to fight to get the story right. Lubitsch was a man's director, he had no sensitivity about women. He figured himself in every scene—as the man.

We had some amusing things, though. Lubitsch spoke very bad English; he would say the most censorable things on the set, and everybody would roar with laughter.

One morning I got onto the set early.

"Now look, boys and girls, if you went to Germany and tried to direct, you might say things that weren't proper yourselves. But you wouldn't like everybody to laugh at you. Now the first person that laughs on this stage will have to leave."

Lubitsch came in, and promptly said something and everybody disappeared. Charlie Rosher, my cameraman, hid his face under the black cloth of the stills camera, other people climbed up the walls of the set, and the only person who laughed was me. I can't remember this particular remark, but another occasion was equally amusing.

It was the big cathedral scene. I guess there were two or three hundred extras there. I was in my little dressing room, with my Alsatian maid, who spoke perfect German.

Lubitsch was outside. He was very pompous and very important, like all little men. "Komm, pliss," he called, clapping his hands. "Dis is de scenes vere Miss Pickford goes mit der beckside to ze altar!"

There was an explosion of laughter. "Bordermayer," I said, "please go out and tell Mr. Lubitsch that he's not to say that." He came in and apologized.

"That's all right, Mr. Lubitsch. I understand. You're trying to learn the language."

"So," he said. "Correct, pliss, Miss Pickford, is it right to say 'Go mit der beck to ze altar?' "

"Perfectly good."

"So!" he said. He went outside, clapped his hands again, and announced: "Dis is de scenes vere Miss Pickford goes mit der . . . beck . . . to ze altar."

Lubitsch was a nice enough man, but he was stubborn. He walked off the set when Edward Knoblock questioned the accuracy of a scene. He let out a torrent of German, and then looked around at everyone. He evidently wanted to say "Oh, good *night*!" Instead of which, all he could remember was "Oh, how do you do!" And he stalked off the set. We waited till the door had shut, and then you never heard such a roar of laughter.

In the story, Don Diego [George Walsh] is shot by a firing squad with blank cartridges. He's lying on the ground, and I'm supposed to think he's dead. Lubitsch was a frustrated actor, and he had to act out everything: "You say, 'Don Diego, Don Diego, anschver me! Anschver me!' "

I tried not to imitate him. "Don Diego!" I cried. "Answer me!" But Lubitsch corrected me. He called from behind the camera, "Miss Pickford! Again, pliss— 'anschver me!' "

To keep him happy I imitated him, and George Walsh's stomach started going up and down in convulsions of suppressed laughter.

"George," I said, "I'll kill you!"

"I'm not making a sound," he giggled.

"Your stomach's moving all over the place! I can't act!"

Mr. Lubitsch cried, "Stop! Stop! Miss Pickford—vat iss to laugh?"

"Nothing, Mr. Lubitsch. I'm sorry."

"Don't make mit der laugh!"

I tried once more: "Don Diego! Anschver me!"

It was no good. George's stomach went up and down again, and I fell across him and we both laughed till we cried.

Poor Mr. Lubitsch.

The climax came toward the end of production.

"Look, Mr. Lubitsch," I said. "This is a love story. You've got to put in a sequence that makes the ending important."

"*Nein,*" he said. "I'm not making it!"

I thought it over, and I went to his office.

"Mr. Lubitsch. This is the first time you've met me as the financial backer and producer."

"Vatt iss dis?"

"I'm telling you that I am the Court of Last Appeal. I'm putting up the money, I am the star, and I am the one that's known. I won't embarrass you; I will never say anything before the company. If I have anything to say, I'll say it as I'm saying it now. I didn't ask you to come to me, I came to your office. But you are not going to have the last word."

"Not for a million dollars!"

"I don't care if it's for ten million. You are not going to have that privilege."

With that he started tearing all the buttons off his clothes. Well, I wasn't losing *my* temper.

"That's final, Mr. Lubitsch."

He went to Edward Knoblock's desk and began tearing up valuable papers— papers that had been written in longhand. What a man. He shook his fist at me, and he really lost control.

We were going to do *Faust* with Lubitsch supervising. But Mother didn't know the story of *Faust,* so Lubitsch told her. "*Ja,*" he said. "She has a bebby, and she's not married, so she stringles the bebby."

Mother said, "What! What was that?"

"Well, Marguerite is not married, she has a bebby, so she stringles it."

"Not my daughter!" said my mother, outraged. "No sir!" So I didn't make *Faust*. . . .

I parted company with him as soon as I could. I thought he was a very uninspired director. He was a director of doors. Everybody came in and out of doors . . . He was a good man's director—good for Jannings and people like that. But for me he was terrible. To tell you the truth, I never saw his later pictures, because of my miserable experience on *Rosita*. He was very self-assertive, but then all little men are. . . .

GLORIA SWANSON

"He was a man I respected tremendously," said Gloria Swanson. "He demanded discipline, and got it. He never said a cruel thing to me in the three years I worked for him. He had great gentleness and appreciated anybody who tried to do a good job.

"In the Babylonian sequence on *Male and Female* one of the lions got loose and came within ten feet of me. The next day, when I came on the set, I was rather shaken from this experience. I'm a Swede, you see, so there's a delayed reaction. Mr. De Mille decided to cut out the shot where the lion is on my back.

" 'Mr. De Mille,' I said, 'you can't do that. I want to do it. Please—you promised me I could.'

" 'Young fellow,' he said, 'why do you want to do this?'

" 'Well,' I said, 'when I was a little girl, I used to sit at my grandmother's piano. On the left-hand side there was a copy of a famous painting called *A Lion's Bride*. You told me you wanted to reproduce this painting, and I'd like to take part.'

" 'All right,' he said, 'I thought maybe it was a little too much for you.'

"In the arena, there was Mr. De Mille, the cameraman and his assistant—and my father, in army officer's uniform, standing on top of this arena, looking at his one and only with his eyes bulging out of his head. There were also two trainers, armed with whips. They folded up canvas and put this on my back, which was bare to the waist. They put the animal so that his front legs were resting on me, and little by little they eased the canvas out from under his paws. Then they cracked their whips till he roared. It felt like thousands of vibrators. Every hair on my body was standing straight up. I had to close my eyes. The last thing I saw was Mr. De Mille with a gun.

"There is a postscript to that incident. We had been on Catalina Island, doing a lot of sea scenes, which were dangerous for me because I don't swim. Then came the incident with the lion—and they wanted me to change into another gown for another sequence. I just couldn't do it. I went to see Mr. De Mille in his office and I started to cry.

"He put me on his knee and treated me like a young child. Well, what was I? Eighteen, nineteen years old.

" 'At last,' he said, 'you're a woman. Now I know it.' He'd always thought of me as a young boy, which was why, I suppose, he called me 'young fellow.'

" 'I was going to give you this after the picture,' he said, 'because of all the things that have happened to you—and because you never complained even when your blood was running to your knees.'

"And he brought out a tray of jewels from a jewelry store. 'I want you to choose one as a memento of this picture.'

"My eyes were popping out of my head. I saw a tiny gold-mesh change purse, not more than four inches square. In the center was a beautiful sapphire. He said, 'Is this what you really want? Be sure. Look again.' I did.

" 'Yes, Mr. De Mille, I would like this.'

" 'That,' he said, 'is your gift for being a brave boy.' "

JOHN GILLETT AND JAMES BLUE

Buster Keaton (1895–1966) is one of the small number of great creators in the cinema, and of course there is a wealth of material that could be included here about him or by him. I had looked at a lot of it before I found this interview, the record of some time that John Gillett and James Blue spent with him at the Venice Film Festival, when his active career was long over but his reputation was just coming back into bloom. It must have been clear to Keaton then that his silent films would never be forgotten, although it was equally clear that his current services were no longer in demand. His interview is very much in the spirit of the silent clowns, who were as proud, maybe prouder, of how they had created great scenes than in why.

"Keaton at Venice"

Saturday, 4 September 1965 was Buster Keaton day at the Venice Festival. At the Press Conference after the preview of *Film* (in which Keaton interprets a Beckett script), the appearance of the familiar stocky figure determinedly stumping on to the platform was the signal for a standing ovation of wild affection from the press. "Caro Buster . . ." said somebody happily, after a long pause while Keaton blandly seated himself among a line of fussing officials, and went on to ask what he thought of the Beckett film. "I don't know what it was all about," the hoarsely grating voice promptly replied, "perhaps you can tell me." A hand waved expressively in the air: "The camera was *behind* me all the time. I ain't used to that."

What was he doing in Italy? He was making a comedy called *Two Marines and a General*—"I'm the General." Loud cheers made it clear that the audience agreed, and an attempt by the young lady valiantly struggling with three languages to translate this as "Ill Maresciallo" was drowned by roars of protest.

Keaton was obviously warming to his task. He stood up and started talking without waiting for questions, and spoke of the new Dick Lester film he was shortly joining in Spain. "I've had several other offers, but couldn't take 'em. No time to spare"—and there was a certain satisfaction in the way he said these last words, as if his present activity made up a little for the waste and neglect of the last twenty years. One notes that, unlike certain comedians, Keaton does not need to keep up a stream of wisecracks. Buster himself had taken over the Palazzo, in full command of his audience once again.

At the evening gala show, more unexpectedly, the smart Venetian audience also rose to their feet with delighted applause as the celebrities took their places. Somebody in the next seat poked Keaton. He looked surprised. "For me?" one could almost hear that dead-pan eyebrow exclaim; and he got up and bowed, beautifully.

Next day, we were able to interview Keaton at the Excelsior Hotel. Several other papers and television networks also had the same idea, and we had to wait a little while. Eventually we saw him peering through a door off the main foyer, apparently wiping down the glass panel with his handkerchief for the benefit of a lady admirer. It was only when he put his head through the space and started cleaning the "glass" from the other side that we realised that it was a beautiful Buster gag.

Keaton started talking almost before we got our equipment ready, and insisted on giving us the most comfortable chairs. He sat bolt upright on the other side of the table, large eyes staring straight ahead, with the Great Stone Face set throughout in expressive immobility except for one charming moment duly noted in the interview. Our questions triggered off an immediate response, precise down to the last little detail, almost as if his films were parading before him as he talked. And in his mind, Keaton the director seemed quite inseparable from Buster the actor.

BUSTER KEATON: I ought to do something about the new release print of *The General* that was shown in London. When the film was to be revived in Europe we brought over as many old prints as we could find, in order to pick out the best reels—to find the ones that hadn't faded, or been chewed up by the machine. We gave them to the outfit in Munich who were handling the film, and they made a duped negative. They did a beautiful job of it. The first thing they wanted to do, as an experiment, was to translate all the English titles into German so that they could release the film in Germany. It did a beautiful business there, so immediately they made some more prints with French titles for release in France. Now they must have lost the original list of English titles, so they put them back again into English from their own German translation.

I happened to see a print of this new English version in Rome last week—the same version you had in London—and the titles are misleading. For instance, when I'm trying to enlist and I'm asked "What is your occupation?" I say "bartender." Well, that type of man gets drafted into the army immediately. In the new version the title reads "barkeep"—that means you own the place. And it doesn't sound as funny anyway in English: it might in German, I don't know. Then they put "sir" on to the ends of sentences because I'm talking to an officer, but there's no "sirring' at all in our titles. Some of the explanatory titles were changed or dropped as well. Do you remember, for instance, the scene where we all got off the train and while we were away the engine was stolen? We actually stopped off there for lunch: the conductor comes into the car and says "This is Marietta: one hour for lunch." But they left that title off, and without it you'd think the train had emptied out because it was the end of the run. In which case there's no reason to steal the engine then: they could have waited until everyone had gone and the place was deserted.

J.G.:   *Apart from the comedy values, the most impressive thing about all the features you made during the Twenties is their distinctive visual style. They all have a kind of look which one associates with a Keaton film. How did you work with your various co-directors to achieve this? Who actually did what?*

Number one, I was practically my own producer on all those silent pictures. I used a co-director on some of them, but the majority I did alone. And I cut them all myself: I cut all my own pictures.

J.G.: *What exactly would the co-director do?*

Co-direct with me, that's all. He would be out there looking through the camera, and I'd ask him what he thought. He would maybe say "That scene looks a little slow"; and then I'd do it again and speed it up. As a rule, when I'm working alone, the cameraman, the prop man, the electrician, these are my eyes out there. I'd ask, "Did that work the way I wanted it to?" and they'd say yes or no. They knew what they were talking about.

J.G.: *You would choose the actual camera set-ups yourself?*

Always, when it was important for the scene I was going to do. If I had an incidental scene—someone runs in, say, and says "here, you've got to go and do this"—the background wasn't important. Then I generally just told the cameraman that I had these two characters in the scene, two full-length figures, and asked him to pick a good-looking background. He would go by the sun. He'd say, "I like that back crosslight coming in through the trees. There are clouds over there right now, so if we hurry up we can still get them before they disappear." So I would say "Swell," and go and direct the scene in front of the cameraman's set-up. We took pains to get good-looking scenery whenever we possibly could, no matter what we were shooting.

J.G.: *What about the visual idea of the films? Take, for instance, a picture like* Our Hospitality, *which has a beautiful period feeling.*

We were very conscious of our stories. We learned in a hurry that we couldn't make a feature-length picture the way we had done the two-reelers; we couldn't use impossible gags, like the kind of things that happen to cartoon characters. We had to eliminate all these things because we had to tell a logical story that an audience would accept. So story construction became a very strong point with us.

On *Our Hospitality* we had this one idea of an old-fashioned Southern feud. But it looks as though this must have died down in the years it took me to grow up from being a baby, so our best period for that was to go back something like eighty years. "All right," we say. "We go back that far. And now when I go South, am I travelling in a covered wagon, or what? Let's look up the records and see when the first railroad train was invented." Well, we find out: we've got the Stephenson Rocket for England and the De Witt Clinton for the United States. And we chose the Rocket engine because it's funnier looking. The passenger coaches were stage coaches with flanged wheels put on them. So we built that entire train and that set our period for us: 1825 was the actual year of the invention of the railroad. Now we dress our people to that period. And that was fine because we liked the costumes: you've got away there from the George

Washington short pants and into the more picturesque Johnny Walker type
of costume.

J.G.: *One of the best gags in the film is the moment when you swing out by a rope from
the river-bank and catch the girl almost in mid-air as she goes over the big waterfall. How did you stage this very tricky shot?*

We had to build that dam: we built it in order to fit that trick. The set
was built over a swimming pool, and we actually put up four eight-inch
water pipes, with big pumps and motors to run them, to carry the water
up from the pool to create our waterfall. That fall was about six inches
deep. A couple of times I swung out underneath there and dropped upside down when I caught her. I had to go down to the doctor right there
and then. They pumped out my ears and nostrils and drained me, because
when a full volume of water like that comes down and hits you and you're
upside down—then you really get it.

J.G.: *How long did it take to shoot the scene? How many takes were there?*

I think I got it on the third take. I missed the first two, but the third
one I got it . . . And it's hard to realise that it was shot in 1923. It sounds
like going back into ancient history.

J.B.: *But it still works. Two weeks ago in Paris I saw* The Three Ages, *which is also
forty-two years old, and the audience were rolling in the aisles. Presumably you did
this as a take-off on films like* Intolerance?

I was thinking of *Intolerance* when I made it. I told the three separate
stories the same as Griffith did; and of course in that film I did take liber-
ties, because it was more of a travesty than a burlesque. That's why I used
a wristwatch that was a sun-dial, and why I used my helmet the way I did.
Fords at that time had a safety device to stop people from stealing the cars:
a thing with a big spike which you locked on the back wheel and which
looked just like my Roman helmet. So I unlocked my Roman helmet off
me and locked it on to the wheel of my chariot. At that time the audience
all compared it with the safety gadget for a Ford.

J.B.: *This seems to lead to the question of how you find your gags. Do you get them from
the set, things in the decor . . . ?*

Yes, props, and characters, and everything, and then look for the simplest things to go wrong. And that leads to bigger things. But there is nothing worse with us than a misplaced gag. Someone may suggest a good gag,
or even an excellent one, but if it doesn't fit the story I'm doing and I try
to drag it in, then it looks dragged in on the screen. So it's much better
to save it, until some time when it does fit what I'm doing.

J.B.: *Quite often you start off a film rather slowly, and the camera movement increases
as the action builds up.*

Deliberately. I always do that. I use the simplest little things in the world, and I never look for big gags to start a picture. I don't want them in the first reel, because if I ever get a big laughing sequence in the first reel, then I'm going to have trouble following it later. The idea that I had to have a gag or get a laugh in every scene . . . I lost that a long time ago. It makes you strive to be funny and you go out of your way trying. It's not a natural thing.

J.G.: *In the short films it was different, of course, because you had to make it funny all the way.* Playhouse—*the one about the theatre in which you play almost every part—is absolutely packed with jokes. Was it in some ways easier to think up these separate gags for the short films, or did you prefer to have time to work out a story?*

We didn't rush. When we thought we had what we wanted, we went ahead and ordered the sets built. But I made one very bad mistake with that picture *The Playhouse*. I could have made the whole two-reeler just by myself, without any trouble. But we were a little scared to do it, because it might have looked as though we were trying to show how versatile I was—that I could make a whole half-hour picture all alone, without another soul in the cast. That's the reason why we brought other people into the second reel, and that was a mistake.

J.B.: *By the time you came to the features, the action was no longer just the basis for the gags but thoroughly integrated with them. Do you consistently look for a gag that will help to advance the action?*

Take one from a picture that I am about to re-release, *The Seven Chances*. I am running away from a batch of women who are chasing me. A friend has put it in the paper that I'll marry anybody so long as I can be married by five o'clock—it has to do with inheriting an estate or whatever. So all the women in the world show up to get married. They chase me out of the church, and so on. I went down to the dunes just off the Pacific Ocean out at Los Angeles, and I accidentally dislodged a boulder in coming down. All I had set up for the scene was a camera panning with me as I came over the skyline and was chased down into the valley. But I dislodged this rock, and it in turn dislodged two others, and they chased me down the hill.

That's all there was: just three rocks. But the audience at the preview sat up in their seats and expected more. So we went right back and ordered 1,500 rocks built, from bowling alley size up to boulders eight feet in diameter. Then we went out to the Ridge Route, which is in the High Sierras, to a burnt mountain steeper than a forty-five degree angle. A couple of truckloads of men took those rocks up and planted them; and then I went up to the top, and came down with the rocks. That gag gave me the whole final chase, and it was an accident in the first place.

J.G.: *The great thing about that chase is that a lot of it is shot from a long way away, so that you get the effect of the tiny figure with the rocks all round. You often seem to prefer to work within a rather large shot, rather than using a lot of close-ups.*

When I've got a gag that spreads out, I hate to jump a camera into close-ups. So I do everything in the world I can to hold it in that long-shot and keep the action rolling. When I do use cuts I still won't go right into a close-up: I'll just go in maybe to a full figure, but that's about as close as I'll come. Close-ups are too jarring on the screen, and this type of cut can stop an audience from laughing.

If I were going to show you this hotel lobby where we are now, for instance, I'd go back and show you the whole lobby on that first shot, and then move in closer. But the main thing is that I want you to be familiar with the atmosphere, so that you know what my location is and where I am. From then on I never have to go back to the long shot again unless I get into action where I am going to cover space in a hurry.

J.G.: *Could you tell us something about* Steamboat Bill Jr., *with the big cyclone at the end when you get the impression that the whole set is being systematically destroyed? It must have been one of the most elaborate of all your films to stage.*

The original story I had was about the Mississippi, but we actually used the Sacramento River in California, some six hundred miles north of Los Angeles. We went up there and built that street front, three blocks of it, and built the piers and so on. We found the river boats right there in Sacramento: one was brand new, and we were able to age the other one up to make it look as though it was ready to fall apart. My original situation in that film was a flood. But my so-called producer on that film was Joe Schenck, who at that time was producing Norma Talmadge, Constance Talmadge and myself, and who later became president of United Artists. Then later on 20th Century-Fox was Joe Schenck, and his brother Nicholas Schenck was head man of Metro-Goldwyn-Mayer. Schenck was supposed to be my producer but he never knew when or what I was shooting. He just turned me loose.

Well, the publicity man on *Steamboat Bill* goes to Schenck and he says: "He can't do a flood sequence because we have floods every year and too many people are lost. It's too painful to get laughs with." So Schenck told me, "You can't do a flood." I said, "That's funny, since it seems to me that Chaplin during World War One made a picture called *Shoulder Arms,* which was the biggest money-maker he'd made at that time. You can't get a bigger disaster than that, and yet he made his biggest laughing picture out of it." He said, "Oh, that's different." I don't know why it was different. I asked if it was all right to make it a cyclone, and he agreed that was better. Now he didn't know it, but there are four times more people killed in the United States by hurricanes and cyclones than by floods. But it was all right as long as he didn't find that out, and so I went ahead with my technical man and did the cyclone.

J.G.: *How about the technical side? The marvellous shot, for instance, of the front of the building falling on you, so that you are standing in the windows as it hits the ground. What were the problems in staging that scene?*

First I had them build the framework of this building and make sure that the things were all firm and solid. It was a building with a tall V-shaped roof, so that we could make this window up in the roof exceptionally high. An average second storey window would be about 12 feet, but we're up about 18 feet. Then you lay this framework down on the ground, and build the window round me. We built the window so that I had a clearance of two inches on each shoulder, and the top missed my head by two inches and the bottom my heels by two inches. We mark that ground out and drive big nails where my two heels are going to be. Then you put that house back up in position while they finish building it. They put the front on, painted it, and made the jagged edge where it tore away from the main building; and then we went in and fixed the interiors so that you're looking at a house that the front has blown off. Then we put up our wind machines with the big Liberty motors. We had six of them and they are pretty powerful: they could lift a truck right off the road. Now we had to make sure that we were getting our foreground and background wind effect, but that no current ever hit the front of that building when it started to fall, because if the wind warps her she's not going to fall where we want her, and I'm standing right out in front. But it's a one-take scene and we got it that way. You don't do those things twice.

J.B.: *Your usual method was to start with a story and then look for the gags. Where did you begin with a film like* The General?

I took that first page out of the history book. Disney did it about nine years ago and called it by its original name—*The Great Locomotive Chase*, with Fess Parker. But he made a mistake and told it from a Northerner's standpoint. And you can always make villains out of the Northerners, but you cannot make a villain out of the South. That was the first mistake he made.

In *The General* I took that page of history and I stuck to it in all detail. I staged it exactly the way it happened. The Union agents intended to enter from the State of Kentucky, which was neutral territory, pretending that they were coming down to fight for the Southern cause. That was an excuse to get on that train which takes them up to an army camp. Their leader took seven men with him, including two locomotive engineers and a telegraph operator; and he told them that if anything went wrong they were to scatter individually, stick to their stories that they were Kentuckians down to enlist in the Southern army, and then watch for the first opportunity to desert and get back over the line to the North. As soon as they stole that engine, they wanted to pull out of there, to disconnect the telegraph and burn bridges and destroy enough track to cripple the Southern army supply route. That was what they intended to do. And I staged the chase exactly the way it happened. Then I rounded out the story of stealing my engine back. When my picture ended the South was winning, which was all right with me.

J.B.: *How did the plot develop apart from the historical story line—the involvement with the girl and so on?*

Well, the moment you give me a locomotive and things like that to play with, as a rule I find some way of getting laughs with it. But the original locomotive chase ended when I found myself in Northern territory and had to desert. From then on it was my invention, in order to get a complete plot. It had nothing to do with the Civil War.

J.G.: *What many of us like about your films is the treatment of the women. These poor ladies, like Marian Mack in* The General, *are subjected to all kinds of humiliations and yet they battle on. They get pulled and pushed around, but they always stand by you. Did they mind at all?*

No, no. They didn't mind at all. Oh God, that girl in *The General* had more fun with that picture than any film she'd made in her life. (*At this point Keaton's face, hitherto frozen as usual, eased into a wide, knowing smile.*) I guess it's because so many leading ladies in those days looked as though they had just walked out of a beauty parlour. They always kept them looking that way—even in covered wagons, they kept their leading ladies looking beautiful at all times. We said to thunder with that, we'll dirty ours up a bit and let them have some rough treatment.

J.B.: *There is a moment of almost pathetic beauty, which is a gag at the same time, when you are both sitting on the steering rod of the wheel and the train starts to move. Not at the very end, but towards the middle of the film.*

I was alone on it when it moved. We were afraid to put her on it, or I would have moved it at the finish.

J.B.: *Can you remember how that gag came to you, out of the film's situation?*

Well, the situation of the picture at that point is that she says "never speak to me again until you're in uniform." So the bottom has dropped out of everything, and I've got nothing to do but sit down on my engine and think. I don't know why they rejected me: they didn't tell me it was because they didn't want to take a locomotive engineer off his duty. My fireman wants to put the engine away in the round-house and doesn't know that I'm sitting on the cross bar, and starts to take it in.

I was running that engine myself all through the picture: I could handle that thing so well I was stopping it on a dime. But when it came to this shot I asked the engineer whether we could do it. He said: "There's only one danger. A fraction too much steam with these old-fashioned engines and the wheel spins. And if it spins it will kill you right then and there."

We tried it out four or five times, and in the end the engineer was satisfied that he could handle it. So we went ahead and did it. I wanted a fade-out laugh for that sequence: although it's not a big gag it's cute and funny enough to get me a nice laugh.

J.G.: *It's also beautiful: it has another quality than just a laugh. On this question of emotion, there is the difference between your films and those of Chaplin, who sometimes seems to go into a sequence with the intention of milking it for all the emotion it can stand. You are rarely deliberately pathetic. In* Go West, *however, there is a slight element of conscious pathos. Did you feel you needed something more emotional there than in the other films?*

I was going to do everything I possibly could to keep that cow from being sent to the slaughter-house: I only had that one thing in mind. And I ran into one disappointment on that film. One of the most famous Western shows ever seen in the United States was called "The Heart of Maryland," in which these two guys are playing cards, and one guy calls the other a name, and he takes out his six-shooter and lays it down on the table, pointing right at this fellow's middle, and says, "When you call me that, smile . . . " Well, because I'm known as frozen face, blank pan, we thought that if you did that to me an audience would say, "Oh my God, he can't smile: he's gone; he's dead." But it didn't strike an audience as funny at all: they just felt sorry for me. We didn't find that out until the preview, and it put a hole in my scene right there and then. Of course I got out of it the best way I could, but we run into these lulls every now and then.

J.B.: *And you look for a gag to get yourself out of a situation: the pole-vault gag with the spear for instance in* The Three Ages. *There you were in a situation where you had to get the girl out of the hands of Wallace Beery. How did you work your way to the spear vault from that?*

I couldn't just run over a batch of rocks or something to get to her: I had to invent something, find something unexpected, and pole-vaulting with a spear seemed to be it.

J.G.: *You very often use gags which couldn't be managed except in films. For instance the scene in* Sherlock Jr. *where you are dreaming yourself into the picture, and the scenery keeps changing. How did you get the idea of this scene?*

That was the reason for making the whole picture. Just that one situation: that a motion picture projectionist in a theatre goes to sleep and visualises himself getting mixed up with the characters on the screen. All right, then my job was to transform those characters on the screen into my (the projectionist's) characters at home, and then I've got my plot. Now to make it work was another thing; and after that picture was made every cameraman in Hollywood spent more than one night watching it and trying to figure out just how we got some of those scenes.

J.G.:   *How did you actually do the sequence where you are near a tree, and then you are on a rock in the middle of the ocean. Was it some kind of back projection?*

No, that hadn't been invented then. We call it processing, but back projection is correct. But it hadn't been invented. We used measuring instruments for that sequence. When I stood on that rock I was going to jump into the ocean, but as I jumped the sea changed to something else. As I looked down I held still for a moment, and we ended that scene. Then we brought out tape-measures, put a cross-bar in front of the camera to square it off, and measured me from two angles. That made sure that I was in exactly the same spot as far as the camera was concerned. We also used surveyor's instruments to get me the same height, so that when we changed the scene and I went back on the set I was in exactly the same place as in the first shot. Then the cameraman just starts to crank and I jump; and when I jump I hit something else. I don't remember what I hit, but I hit something. This was all done just by changing the sets. But I on the screen never changed.

S. J. PERELMAN

Having been devastated by Griffith's Way Down East *as a youth, S. J. Perelman (1904–1979) revisited it in the 1950s, finding he had become more jaded in the meantime and now appreciated the innocence of Lillian Gish less than the malevolence of Lowell Sherman. There may never have been a better one-sentence description of a movie villain than "They had to spray him with fungicide between takes to keep the mushrooms from forming on him."*

"I'm Sorry I Made Me Cry"

The consulting room I sat in that dun December afternoon in 1920 was a perfect setting for a senior Rhode Island eye specialist, and Dr. Adrian Budlong was perfectly cast in the role of the specialist. A septuagenarian with a sunken, emaciated face, and as angular as a praying mantis, Dr. Budlong bore a chilling re-semblance to the mummified Rameses II, and it would not have surprised me to learn that he kept his entrails in an alabaster canopic jar under his desk. The room itself was rather like a crypt, dark and redolent of musty bindings and io-doform; behind the Doctor's head, in the shadows, a bust of Galen just large enough for a raven to perch on scowled down at me balefully. For forty-five min-utes, Dr. Budlong, in an effort to discover why my eyelids were swollen like Smyrna figs, had submitted me to every test known to ophthalmology. He had checked my vision with all manner of graduated charts and images, made me swivel my eyeballs until they bellied from their sockets, peered endlessly into my irises with sinister flashlights. The examination, clearly, had been fruitless, for he was now bombarding me with questions that struck me as irrelevant, if not fatuous. Had I eaten any toadstools recently, been stung by any wasps or hornets? Had I wittingly stepped on a rattlesnake or serpent of any description?

"I—I swim under water a lot at the Y.M.C.A.," I faltered. "Maybe the dis-infectant—"

"Chlorine never hurt anybody," he snapped. "Clears the brain." With a palsied clawlike hand, he plucked the optical mirror from his death's-head and dropped it on the blotter. "Humph—no reason a boy of your age should suddenly start looking like a bullfrog. Have you been under any mental strain lately? What kind of stuff d'ye read?"

"Er—mostly history," I said evasively. "Balzac's *Droll Stories,* the *Decameron,* Brantôme's *Lives of Fair and Gallant Ladies*—"

"Nothing there that would affect the lids especially," he said, with what I con-sidered unnecessary coarseness. "Now let's stop paltering around, young man. What have you been crying about?" Somewhere deep in my consciousness, a lou-ver flew open and I saw the façade of the Providence Opera House, the temple where every moviegoer in town had been snuffling uncontrollably over D. W. Griffith's great tear-jerker *Way Down East.* Choking back a sob, I confessed shamefacedly that I had seen the picture three times. Dr. Budlong regarded me for a full twenty minutes in silence, patently undecided whether to have me cer-tified or bastinadoed. Then, making no effort to conceal his spleen, he prescribed cold poultices and a moratorium on cinematic pathos, and flung me out. By an evil circumstance, the trolley car that bore me homeward passed the Opera House. Hours later, streaked with tears, and blubbering from my fourth expo-sure to the masterpiece, I informed my folks that Budlong had pronounced me a victim of winter hay fever. The diagnosis aroused no visible furor. By then the family was impervious to shock.

. . . .

Not long ago, examining the network of laughter lines around my eyes in the mirror, it occurred to me that I was in peril of becoming a slippered popinjay.

Life since forty had been so rollicking and mirthful that I had allowed my sentimental, nobler instincts to retrogress; what I needed, and pronto, was a profound emotional *nettoyage*. Accordingly, I downed twenty pages of Thomas Merton, the spiritual equivalent of sulphur and molasses, listened to Jan Peerce's superbly emetic recording of "What Is a Boy?" and topped it off with a matinée of *Way Down East* at the Museum of Modern Art. I can get around the house passably by holding on to the furniture, but I still feel a mite queasy.

The leitmotiv of *Way Down East,* like that of so many early film melodramas, was innocence betrayed, virtue—doggedly sullied through ten reels—rising triumphant and kneeing its traducer in the groin. The sweet resignation with which Lillian Gish, the heroine, underwent every vicissitude of fortune from bastardy to frostbite, and the lacquered, mandarin composure of Richard Barthelmess in the face of ostracism and blizzard, have rarely been surpassed on celluloid. It was, however, Lowell Sherman, that peerless actor, who, in his delineation of the villain, copped the honors. Exquisitely groomed, a trifle flaccid, the epitome of the jaded roué, he moved catlike through the action, stalking his prey, his face a mask of smiling insincerity that occasionally let slip a barbered sneer. When he tapped a cigarette deliberately on his silver case and cast a cool, speculative glance into a woman's bodice, you knew she would never survive the rabbit test. Sidney Blackmer, Henry Daniell, Robert Morley—there have been many able varmints since, but none quite as silky or loathsome as Lowell Sherman. They had to spray him with fungicide between takes to keep the mushrooms from forming on him.

Way Down East, billed in its opening title as "a simple story for plain people" (the adjectives would seem to be interchangeable), starts off with a windy hundred-and-twenty-two-word essay containing far less juice than pulp and seeds. Its general content is that while polygamy is on the wane, monogamy is not yet worldwide—an assertion calculated to lacerate nobody's feelings, whether Bedouin or Baptist. The locale of the drama, continues the preamble, is "in the story world of make-believe; characters nowhere, yet everywhere." Having slaked the passion for universality that constantly assailed him, Griffith yielded the stage to his puppets. Anna Moore (Miss Gish) and her widowed mother, destitute in a New England village, decide to put the sleeve on the Tremonts, their rich Boston relatives. Clad in gingham and a black wide-awake straw, Anna sets off for their mansion, bumbling into a stylish musicale they are giving and discomfiting her snobbish female cousins. In order to make character with a rich, eccentric aunt, however, the Tremonts swallow their resentment and take Anna in. Simultaneously, the girl has a fleeting encounter with her seducer-to-be, dashing Lennox Sanderson (Lowell Sherman), who smirks into her cleavage and earmarks her for future spoliation. We now whisk to the countervailing influence in Anna's life, David Bartlett (Richard Barthelmess), as he scratches a pigeon's neck on his father's farm, adjacent to Sanderson's country estate. "Though of plain stock," the subtitle explains, "he has been tutored by poets and vision wide as the world." He has also had access, it might be noted, to a remarkable pomade, which keeps his hair snugly plastered to his scalp no matter how turbulent the action becomes. The secret of Barthelmess's hair has never ceased to fascinate me. In every picture I recall him in, from *Broken Blossoms* and *Tol'able David* to *The Idol Dancer* and *The Love Flower,* nothing ever disturbed that sleek coiffure. Cockney bruisers beat the daylights out of Barthelmess, bullying mates kicked him down hatchways and flailed him with marlinspikes, and Papuans boiled him in kettles, but he always looked as though he had just emerged from the Dawn Patrol Barbershop. Of course, there is no external evidence that his hair was real; it may merely have been Duco, sprayed on him between takes, like Sherman's fungicide, but how they ever prevented it from cracking is beyond me.

Anna's downfall, the next item on the agenda, is one of the most precipitous and brutal since the sack of Constantinople by the Turks. Sanderson spies her at a society rout, almost unbearably ethereal in soft focus and a cloud of tulle, and, closing in, murmurs thickly, "In your beauty lives again Elaine, the Lily Maid, love-dreaming at Astolat." Enchanted by this verbal zircon, Anna dimples from head to toe and implores, "Tell me more." He obliges, with such notable effect that she ultimately agrees to a secret marriage ceremony, unaware that the parson is bogus and the witnesses fixed. From then on, the poor creature is fed through the dramatic wringer with relentless ferocity. After her return home, she finds she is gravid, appeals to Sanderson—who, meanwhile, has gone on to other amorous diversions—and discovers that she has been euchred. Sanderson callously deserts her, on the pretext that he will be disinherited if their liaison comes to light, and Anna's mother, with typical maternal spitefulness, dies off just when she is most needed. The baby languishes from birth; when it succumbs, giving Anna endless golden opportunities for histrionics, she is expelled from her lodgings by a righteous landlady, and the first portion of her Gethsemane concludes. The least sophisticated movie fan senses, though, that his tear ducts are being permitted only the briefest respite. Better than any director before or since, Griffith understood the use of the bean ball, and he now prepares to pitch it square at his leading lady and reduce everyone to jelly.

Drawn by the peculiar magnetism that polarizes movie characters, Anna wanders to the Bartlett farm, meets David, and so generally excites pity that Squire Bartlett, his gruff, bigoted father, gives her a minor post agitating a churn. The farm hums with all sorts of romantic activity. There is, for instance, a visiting niece named Kate who is alternately being courted by Hi Holler, the hired man, and the Professor, an absent-minded pedagogue with a butterfly net. Gusty bucolic comedy ensues when the former, daubing his shoes and hair with axle grease to enhance his charm, is struck on the head by a new-laid egg and backs into a pitchfork. Also on hand to provoke chuckles is a rustic twosome made up of Martha Perkins, the village gossip, and her perennial admirer, a hayseed in a linen duster who quaffs Long Life Bitters. The story meanders sluggishly along for a spell, washing up tender symbols like cooing buds and bursting doves to blueprint David's bias for Anna, and then Lennox Sanderson pops in again, this time mousing around after Kate. He berates Anna for remaining in his bailiwick and, in truly heartless fashion, orders her to clear off. As she is about to, though, David shyly confesses his *béguin* for her (and nobody could confess a *béguin* more shyly than Barthelmess, without moving so much as a muscle in his face). At length, sorely troubled, she decides to stay—a difficult decision and similar to one that I myself, by a coincidence, was having to make. Confidentially, it was touch and go.

Except for love's gradual ripening, the next thousand feet of the film are as devoid of incident as a Fitzpatrick travel talk on Costa Rica, Land of the Coffee Bean. There is a plethora of fields choked with daisies, misty-eyed colloquies, and orotund subtitles like "One heart for one heart, one soul for one soul, one love, even through eternity. At last the great overwhelming love, only to be halted by the stark ghost of her past." With the onset of winter, the plot registers a sudden galvanic twitch. Just as Anna is stalemated between David's proposal, which she cannot bring herself to accept, and Sanderson's renewed persecutions, her onetime landlady happens into the village, recognizes her, and recounts her shame to the sewing circle. Martha Perkins, of course, instantly hurries to the Squire to apprise him that he is harboring a Jezebel, and the fat is in the fire. Anna is excoriated in front of the entire household and driven forth despite David's protestations, but not before she castigates Sanderson as her betrayer. A blizzard, which has been picking its teeth in the wings, now comes in on cue, and enfolding the outcast, whirls her toward the icebound river. David, who meanwhile has been locked in mortal combat with Sanderson (without having his hair mussed, naturally), flattens his adversary and runs to intercept Anna; the ice goes out, she is swept to the brink of the falls, and her lover, exhibiting the nimblest footwork since Packy McFarland, saves her from annihilation. The rest of the spool portrays Sanderson, surprisingly natty after his drubbing, offering his dupe legitimate wedlock and sighing with relief when she disdains him, and a multiple marriage in which Anna and David, Kate and the Professor, and Martha and her apple-knocker are united. So ends the morality, with no hard feelings except in the gluteus, and with that unique sense of degradation that attends a trip to the movies during daylight.

.   .   .   .

As it happens, the only known antidote for the foregoing is a double banana split with oodles of fudge sauce, and immediately on quitting *Way Down East* I sought one out at a neighboring drugstore. As I was burrowing into it like a snowplow,

I became conscious of the soda jerker's intent scrutiny. "Say, din I use to see you around the old Opera House in Providence?" he inquired narrowly. "I took tickets there when I was a kid." Judging from the man's decrepitude, I would have had to dandle Bronson Alcott on my knee to be his contemporary, but I waived the point and held still for a spate of theatrical reminiscence. At last, as a sort of tourniquet, I mentioned *Way Down East* and suggested he might enjoy seeing it again. He drew himself up, offended. "Listen, wise guy," he retorted. "I may handle slop for a living, but I don't have to look at it." I slunk out with flaming cheeks, made even pinker by the cashier's recalling me to settle the check. Altogether, it was a shattering afternoon. The next time my nobler nature gets the upper hand, I aim for the nearest Turkish bath.

GENRES

E. M. FORSTER

"But is Mickey a mouse?" the novelist E. M. Forster (1879–1970) asked. "Certainly one would not recognize him in a trap." In the early days of animation, cartoons by Disney and others were prized not as family entertainment but as a wholly new art form; the Soviet director Eisenstein called Snow White and the Seven Dwarfs *the greatest film ever made. I remember asking Marcello Mastroianni once what his favorite movie love scene was. He could think of no candidates. Then suddenly he smiled. "I like it," he said, "when Minnie kisses Mickey, and little red hearts go pop-pop-pop, over their heads, in the air."*

"Minnie and Mickey"

I am a film-fanned rather than a film-fan, and oh the things I have had to see and hear because other people wanted to! About once a fortnight a puff of wind raises me from the seat where I am meditating upon life or art, and wafts me in amiability's name towards a very different receptacle. Call it a fauteuil. Here art is not, life not. Not happy, not unhappy, I sit in an up-to-date stupor, while the international effort unrolls. American women shoot the hippopotamus with eyebrows made of platinum. British ladies and gentlemen turn the movies into the stickies for old Elstree's sake. Overrated children salute me from Germany and France, steam-tractors drone across the lengths and breadths of unholy Russia, with the monotony of wedding chimes. All around me, I have reason to believe, sit many fellow film-fanneds, chaff from the winnowing like myself, but we do not communicate with one another, and are indistinguishable from ecstasy in the gloom. Stunned by the howls of the Wurlitzer organ, choked by the fumes of the cigars—and here I break off again, in a style not unsuited to the subject. Why do cigars and cigarettes in a cinema function like syringes? Why do they squirt smoke with unerring aim down my distant throat and into my averted eyes? Where are they coming from? Where are we going to? Before I can decide, the greatest super-novelty of all time has commenced, Ping Pong, and the toy counter at Gamage's is exhibited as a prehistoric island. Or mayn't I have a good laugh? Why certainly, why sure, that's what we take your money for, a good laugh, so here's a guy who can't swim and finds he can racing a guy who can swim and pretends he can't, and the guy who can't get a laugh out of that had better—

But now the attendant beckons, a wraith in beach pyjamas, waving her electric wand. She wants someone, and can it be me? No—she wants no one, it is just a habit she has got into, poor girlie, she cannot stop herself, wave she must, it is a cinema. And when she is off duty she still cannot stop herself, but fanned by she knows not what sits skirted and bloused in the audience she lately patrolled. I do think though—for it is time for optimism to enter—I do think that she will choose a performance which bills a Mickey Mouse. And I do hope that Mickey, on his side, will observe her fidelity and will introduce her into his next Silly Symphony, half-glow-worm and half-newt, waving, waving. . . .

What fun it would be, a performance in which Mickey produced the audience as well as the film! Perhaps Mr. Walt Disney will suggest it to him, and I will provide the title gratis: "Plastic Pools." We should see some gay sights in his semidarkness, and more would get squirted about than smoke. Siphons that pour zig-zag, chocolates exploding into fleas—there are rich possibilities in the refreshments alone, and when it comes to Miss Cow's hatpins and fauteuils for the dachshund sisters, why should there be any limits? Yet I don't know. Perhaps not. "Plastic Pools" is withdrawn. For much as I admire Mickey as a producer, I like him as a lover most, and rather regret these later and more elaborate efforts, for the reason that they keep him too much from Minnie. Minnie is his all, his meinie, his moon. Perhaps even the introduction of Pluto was a mistake. Have you forgotten that day when he and she strolled with their Kodaks through an oriental bazaar, snapping this and that, while their camel drank beer and galloped off on both its humps across the desert? Have you forgotten *Wild Waves?* Mickey's great moments are moments of heroism, and when he carries Minnie out of the harem as a pot-plant or rescues her as she falls in foam, herself its fairest flower, he reaches heights impossible for the *entrepreneur*. I would not even have the couple sing. The duets in which they increasingly indulge are distracting. Let them confine themselves to raptures for mice, and let them play their piano less.

But is Mickey a mouse? Well, I am hard put to it at moments certainly, and have had to do some thinking back. Certainly one would not recognize him in a trap. It is his character rather than his species that signifies, which one could surely recognize anywhere. He is energetic without being elevating, and although he is assuredly one of the world's great lovers he must be placed at some distance from Charlie Chaplin or Sir Philip Sidney. No one has ever been softened after seeing Mickey or has wanted to give away an extra glass of water to the poor. He is never sentimental, indeed there is a scandalous element in him which I find most restful. Why does he not pick up one of the coins thrown to him in that Texas bar? Why does one of the pillows in *Mickey's Nightmare* knock him down? Why does Pluto—Or there is that moment in *Wild Waves* when Minnie through some miscalculation on her part is drowning, and he rushes for a boat. As he heaves it out of the sand two little blobs are revealed beneath it, creatures too tiny to be anything but love-items, and they scuttle away into a world which will scarcely be as severe on them as ours. There are said to be "privately shown" Mickeys, and though I do not want to see one, imagination being its own kingdom, I can well believe that anyone who goes so far goes further.

About Minnie too little has been said, and her name at the top of this article is an act of homage which ought to have been paid long ago. Nor do we know anything about her family. When discovered alone, she appears to be of independent means, and to own a small house in the midst of unattractive scenery, where, with no servant and little furniture, she busies herself about trifles until Mickey comes. For he is her Rajah, her Sun. Without him, her character shines not. As he enters she expands, she becomes simple, tender, brave, and strong, and her coquetterie is of the delightful type which never conceals its object. Ah, that squeak of greeting! As you will have guessed from it, her only fault is hysteria. Minnie does not always judge justly, and she was ill advised, in *Puppy Love,* to make all that fuss over a bone. She ought to have known it belonged to the dogs. It is possible that, like most of us, she is deteriorating. To be approached so often by Mickey, and always for the first time, must make any mouse mechanical. Perhaps sometimes she worries whether she has ever been married or not, and her doubts are not easy to allay, and the wedding chimes in *Mickey's Nightmare* are no guide or a sinister one. Still, it seems likely that they have married one another, since it is unlikely that they have married anyone else, since there is nobody else for them to marry.

What of their future? At present Mickey is everybody's god, so that even members of the Film Society cease despising their fellow members when he appears. But gods are not immortal. There was an Egyptian called Bes, who was once quite as gay, and Brer Rabbit and Felix the Cat have been forgotten too, and Ganesh is being forgotten. Perhaps he and Minnie will follow them into oblivion. I do not care two hoots. I am all for the human race. But how fortunate that it should have been accompanied, down the ages, by so many cheerful animals, and how lucky that the cinema has managed to catch the last of them in its questionable reels!

ANDRÉ BAZIN

André Bazin (1918–1958) was the father of the auteur theory of film criticism and the patron saint of the French New Wave. He was also a kind man who befriended the confused and rebellious young François Truffaut and set him on the path toward film criticism and directing. Bazin's great gift was the ability to look at discredited genres, especially from Hollywood, and see beneath the clichés and convention an artistic hand that touched the films of some directors and not those of others.

"The Western: or the American Film *par Excellence*"

The western is the only genre whose origins are almost identical with those of the cinema itself and which is as alive as ever after almost half a century of uninterrupted success. Even if one disputes the quality of its inspiration and of its style since the thirties, one is amazed at the steady commercial success which is the measure of its health. Doubtless the western has not entirely escaped the evolution of cinema taste—or indeed taste, period. It has been and will again be subjected to influences from the outside—for instance the crime novel, the detective story, or the social problems of the day—and its simplicity and strict form have suffered as a result. We may be entitled to regret this, but not to see in it a state of decay. These influences are only felt in a few productions of relatively high standing and do not affect the low-budget films aimed principally at the home market. Furthermore, it is as important for us to marvel at the western's capacity to resist them as to deplore these passing moments of contamination. Every influence acts on them like a vaccine. The microbe, on contact, loses its deadly virulence. In the course of fifteen years, the American comedy has exhausted its resources. If it survives in an occasional success, it is only to the extent that, in some way, it abandons the rules that before the war made for successful comedy. From *Underworld* (1927) to *Scarface* (1932) the gangster film had already completed the cycle of its growth. The scenarios of detective stories have developed rapidly, and if it is still possible to rediscover an aesthetic of violence within the framework of the criminal adventure which they share with *Scarface*, we would be hard put to see in the private eye, the journalist, or the G-man the reflection of the original hero. Furthermore, if there is such a genre as the American detective film one cannot attribute to it the independent identity of the western; the literature which preceded it has continued to influence it, and the latest interesting variants of the crime film derive directly from it.

On the contrary, the durability of the western heroes and plots has been demonstrated recently by the fabulous success on television of the old Hopalong Cassidy films. The western does not age.

Its world-wide appeal is even more astonishing than its historical survival. What can there possibly be to interest Arabs, Hindus, Latins, Germans, or Anglo-Saxons, among whom the western has had an uninterrupted success, about evocations of the birth of the United States of America, the struggle between Buffalo Bill and the Indians, the laying down of the railroad, or the Civil War!

The western must possess some greater secret than simply the secret of youthfulness. It must be a secret that somehow identifies it with the essence of cinema.

. . . .

It is easy to say that because the cinema is movement the western is cinema *par excellence*. It is true that galloping horses and fights are its usual ingredients. But in that case the western would simply be one variety of adventure story. Again, the continuous movement of the characters, carried almost to a pitch of frenzy, is inseparable from its geographical setting and one might just as well define the western by its set—the frontier town and its landscapes; but other genres and schools of filmmaking have made use of the dramatic poetry of the landscape, for example the silent Swedish film, but although it contributed to their greatness it did not insure their survival. Better still, sometimes, as in *The Overlanders*, a western theme is borrowed—in this case the traditional cattle drive—and set in a landscape, central Australia, reasonably like the American West. The result, as we know, was excellent. But fortunately no attempt was made to follow up this paradoxical achievement, whose success was due to an unusual combination of circumstances. If in fact westerns have been shot in France against the landscapes of the Camargue, one can only see in this an additional proof of the popularity and healthiness of a genre that can survive counterfeiting, pastiche, or even parody.

It would be hopeless to try to reduce the essence of the western to one or other of these manifest components. The same ingredients are to be found elsewhere but not the same benefits that appear to go with them. Therefore, the western must be something else again than its form. Galloping horses, fights, strong and brave men in a wildly austere landscape could not add up to a definition of the genre nor encompass its charms.

Those formal attributes by which one normally recognizes the western are simply signs or symbols of its profound reality, namely the myth. The western was born of an encounter between a mythology and a means of expression: the saga of the West existed before the cinema in literary or folklore form, and the multiplication of western films has not killed off western literature which still retains its public, and continues to provide screenwriters with their best material. But there is no common measure between the limited and national audience for western stories and the worldwide audience for the films which they inspire. Just as the miniatures of the *Books of Hours* served as models for the statuary and the stained-glass windows of the cathedrals, this western literature, freed from the bonds of language, finds a distribution on the screen in keeping with its size—almost as if the dimensions of the image had become one with those of the imagination.

This book [J.–L. Rieupeyrout's *La Grande Adventure du western 1894–1964,* for which Bazin was here writing the Preface] will emphasize a little-known aspect of the western: its faithfulness to history. This is not generally recognized—primarily, doubtless, because of our ignorance, but still more because of the deeply rooted prejudice according to which the western can only tell extremely puerile stories, fruits of a naïve power of invention that does not concern itself with psychological, historical, or even material verisimilitude. True, few westerns are explicitly concerned with historical accuracy. True, too, these are not the only ones of any value. It would be absurd to judge the characters of Tom Mix—still more of his magic white horse—or even of William Hart or Douglas Fairbanks, all of whom made lovely films in the great primitive period of the western, by the yardstick of archeology.

After all, many current westerns of honorable standing—I am thinking of *Beyond the Great Divide, Yellow Sky*, or *High Noon*—have only a tenuous relation to historical fact. They are primarily works of imagination. But one would be as much in error not to recognize the historical references in the western as to deny the unabashed freedom of its screenplays. J.–L. Rieupeyrout gives a complete account of the birth of its epiclike idealization, based on comparatively recent history, yet it could be that his study, concerned to recall to us what is ordinarily forgotten, or even not known, and confining itself to films that justify his thesis, discards by implication the other side of the aesthetic reality. Still, this would show him to be doubly right. For the relations between the facts of history and the western are not immediate and direct, but dialectic. Tom Mix is the opposite of Abraham Lincoln, but after his own fashion he perpetuates Lincoln's cult and his memory. In its most romantic or most naïve form, the western is the opposite of a historical reconstruction. There is no difference between Hopalong Cassidy and Tarzan except for their costume and the arena in which they demonstrate their prowess. However, if one wanted to take the trouble to compare these delightful but unlikely stories and to superimpose on them, as is done in modern physiognomy, a number of negatives of faces, an ideal western would come through, composed of all the constants common to one and to the other: a western made up solely of unalloyed myth. Let us take one example, that of the woman.

In the first third of the film, the good cowboy meets the pure young woman—the good and strong virgin, let us call her—with whom he falls in love. Despite its chasteness we are able to guess this love is shared. However, virtually insurmountable obstacles stand in its way. One of the most significant and most frequent comes from the family of the beloved—for example, her brother is a sinister scoundrel and the good cowboy is forced to rid society of him, man to man. A modern Chimène, our heroine refuses to see in her brother's assassin any sort of a fine fellow. In order to redeem himself in his charmer's eyes and merit forgiveness, our knight must now pass through a series of fabulous trials. He ends by saving his elected bride from a danger that could be fatal to her person, her virtue, her fortune, or all three at once. Following which, since we are now near the end of the film, the damsel would indeed be ungrateful if she did not feel that her suitor had repaid his debt, and allow him to start dreaming of lots of children.

Up to this point, this outline into which one can weave a thousand variants—for example, by substituting the Civil War for the Indian threat, cattle rustlers—comes close to reminding us of the medieval courtly romances by virtue of the preeminence given to the woman and the trials that the finest of heroes must undergo in order to qualify for her love.

But the story is often complicated by a paradoxical character—the saloon B-girl—who as a rule, is also in love with the cowboy. So there would be one woman too many if the god of the screenwriter was not keeping watch. A few minutes before the end, the prostitute with the heart of gold rescues the man she loves from some danger or another, sacrificing her life and her hopeless love for the happiness of her cowboy. This also serves to redeem her in the eyes of the spectators.

There is food for thought here. Note, first of all, that the distinction between good and bad applies only to the men. Women, all up and down the social scale, are in every case worthy of love or at least of esteem or pity. The least little prostitute is redeemed by love and death—although she is spared the latter in *Stage-*

coach with its resemblance to de Maupassant's *Boule de Suif.* It is true that the good cowboy is more or less a reformed offender so that henceforth the most moral of marriages with his heroine becomes possible.

Furthermore, in the world of the western, it is the women who are good and the men who are bad, so bad that the best of them must redeem themselves from the original sin of their sex by undergoing various trials. In the Garden of Eden, Eve led Adam into temptation. Paradoxically Anglo-Saxon puritanism, under the pressure of historical circumstances, reverses the Biblical situation. The downfall of the woman only comes about as a result of the concupiscence of men.

Clearly, this theory derives from the actual sociological conditions obtaining in primitive western society which, because of the scarcity of women and the perils of a too harsh existence in this burgeoning world, make it imperative to safeguard its female members and its horses. Hanging was considered enough punishment for stealing a horse. To engender respect for women more was needed than the fear of a risk as trifling as the loss of one's life, namely the positive power of a myth. The myth of the western illustrates, and both initiates and confirms woman in her role as vestal of the social virtues, of which this chaotic world is so greatly in need. Within her is concealed the physical future, and, by way of the institution of the family to which she aspires as the root is drawn to the earth, its moral foundation.

These myths, of which we have just examined what is perhaps the most significant example (the next is the myth of the horse) may themselves doubtless be reduced to an even more essential principle. Basically each of these particularize, by way of an already specific dramatic plot, the great epic Manicheism which sets the forces of evil over against the knights of the true cause. These immense stretches of prairie, of deserts, of rocks to which the little wooden town clings precariously (a primitive amoeba of a civilization), are exposed to all manner of possible things. The Indian, who lived in this world, was incapable of imposing on it man's order. He mastered it only by identifying himself with its pagan savagery. The white Christian on the contrary is truly the conqueror of a new world. The grass sprouts where his horse has passed. He imposes simultaneously his moral and his technical order, the one linked to the other and the former guaranteeing the latter. The physical safety of the stagecoaches, the protection given by the federal troops, the building of the great railroads are less important perhaps than the establishment of justice and respect for the law. The relations between morality and law, which in our ancient civilization are just a subject for an undergraduate paper, were half a century ago the most vital thing confronting the youthful United States. Only strong, rough, and courageous men could tame these virgin lands. Everyone knows that familiarity with death does not keep alive the fear of hell, nor do scruples or moral debate. Policemen and judges are of most help to the weak. It was the force of this conquering humanity that constituted its weakness. Where individual morality is precarious it is only law that can impose the order of the good and the good of order.

But the law is unjust to the extent that it pretends to guarantee a moral society but ignores the individual merits of those who constitute that society. If it is to be effective, this justice must be dispensed by men who are just as strong and just as daring as the criminals. These virtues, as we have said, are in no way compatible with virtue in the absolute sense. The sheriff is not always a better person than the man he hangs. This begets and establishes an inevitable and necessary contradiction. There is often little moral difference between the outlaw and the man who operates within the law. Still, the sheriff's star must be seen as constituting a sacrament of justice, whose worth does not depend on the worthiness of the man who administers it. To this first contradiction a second must be added, the administration of justice which, if it is to be effective, must be drastic and speedy—short of lynching, however—and thus must ignore extenuating circumstances, such as alibis that would take too long to verify. In protecting society, such a form of justice runs the risk of unkindness to the most turbulent though not perhaps the least useful nor even the least deserving of its children.

Although the need for law was never more clearly allied to the need for morality, at the same time never was their antagonism more concrete and more evident. It is this which provides a basis, within a slapstick framework, for Charlie's *Pilgrim,* at the conclusion of which we see our hero riding his horse along the borderline between good and evil, which also happens to be the Mexican border.

John Ford's *Stagecoach,* which is a fine dramatic illustration of the parable of the pharisee and the publican, demonstrates that a prostitute can be more respectable than the narrow-minded people who drove her out of town and just as respectable as an officer's wife; that a dissolute gambler knows how to die with all the dignity of an aristocrat; that an alcoholic doctor can practice his profession with competence and devotion; that an outlaw who is being sought for the payment of past and possibly future debts can show loyalty, generosity, courage, and refinement, whereas a banker of considerable standing and reputation runs off with the cashbox.

So we find at the source of the western the ethics of the epic and even of tragedy. The western is in the epic category because of the superhuman level of its heroes and the legendary magnitude of their feats of valor. Billy the Kid is as invulnerable as Achilles and his revolver is infallible. The cowboy is a knight-at-arms. The style of the *mise en scène* is in keeping with the character of the hero. A transformation into an epic is evident in the set-ups of the shots, with their predilection for vast horizons, all-encompassing shots that constantly bring to mind the conflict between man and nature. The western has virtually no use for the closeup, even for the medium shot, preferring by contrast the traveling shot and the pan which refuse to be limited by the frameline and which restore to space its fullness.

True enough. But this epic style derives its real meaning only from the morality which underlies and justifies it. It is the morality of a world in which social good and evil, in their simplicity and necessity, exist like two primary and basic elements. But good in its natal state engenders law in all its primitive rigor; epic becomes tragedy, on the appearance of the first conflict between the transcendence of social justice and the individual character of moral justice, between the categorical imperative of the law which guarantees the order of the future city, and the no less unshakeable order of the individual conscience.

The Corneille-like simplicity of western scripts has often been a subject for parody. It is easy to see the analogy between them and the text of *Le Cid:* there is the same conflict between love and duty, the same knightly ordeals on the completion of which the wise virgin will consent to forget the insult to her family; the same chaste sentiments which are based on a concept of love subordinated to respect for the laws of society and morality. But this comparison is double-edged: to make fun of the western by comparing it to Corneille is also to draw attention to its greatness, a greatness near perhaps to the child-like, just as childhood is near to poetry.

Let there be no doubt about it. This naïve greatness is recognized in westerns by simple men in every clime—together with the children—despite differences of language, landscape, customs, and dress. The epic and tragic hero is a universal character. The Civil War is part of nineteenth century history, the western has turned it into the Trojan War of the most modern of epics. The migration to the West is our Odyssey.

Not only is the historicity of the western not at odds with the no less evident penchant of the genre for outlandish situations, exaggerations of fact and the use of the *deus ex machina* (in short, everything that makes for improbability); it is, on the contrary, the foundation of its aesthetic and its psychology. The history of film has only known one other epic cinema and that too is a historical cinema. Our purpose here is not to compare epic form in the Russian and in the American film, and yet an analysis of their styles would shed an unexpected light on the historical meaning of the events reconstructed in the two of them. Our only purpose is to point out that it is not their closeness to the facts that has given them their styles. There are legends that come into being almost instantaneously, that half a generation suffices to ripen into an epic. Like the conquest of the West, the Soviet revolution is a collection of historical events which signal the birth of a new order and a new civilization. Both have begotten the myths necessary for the confirmation of history, both had to reinvent a morality to rediscover at their living source and before mixture or pollution took place, the foundation of the law which would make order out of chaos, separate heaven from earth. But perhaps the cinema was the only language capable of expressing this, above all of giving it its true aesthetic dimension. Without the cinema the conquest of the West would have left behind, in the shape of the western story, only a minor literature, and it is neither by its painting nor its novels that Soviet art has given the world a picture of its grandeur. The fact is that henceforth the cinema is the specifically epic art.

ROBERT WARSHOW

I read Warshow's book The Immediate Experience *soon after starting to work as a film critic and have always remembered two sentences in particular: "A man goes to the movies. The critic must be honest enough to admit that he is that man." In other words, a review must reflect one's actual experience at the movies, not that experience filtered through ideology, fashion, or political correctness. In this view of the gangster movie, that is what Warshow does, seeing clearly the meaning of what was, when he wrote, a problematic genre.*

"The Gangster as Tragic Hero"

America, as a social and political organization, is committed to a cheerful view of life. It could not be otherwise. The sense of tragedy is a luxury of aristocratic societies, where the fate of the individual is not conceived of as having a direct and legitimate political importance, being determined by a fixed and supra-political—that is, non-controversial—moral order or fate. Modern equalitarian societies, however, whether democratic or authoritarian in their political forms, always base themselves on the claim that they are making life happier; the avowed function of the modern state, at least in its ultimate terms, is not only to regulate social relations, but also to determine the quality and the possibilities of human life in general. Happiness thus becomes the chief political issue—in a sense, the only political issue—and for that reason it can never be treated as an issue at all. If an American or a Russian is unhappy, it implies a certain reprobation of his society, and therefore, by a logic of which we can all recognize the necessity, it becomes an obligation of citizenship to be cheerful; if the authorities find it necessary, the citizen may even be compelled to make a public display of his cheerfulness on important occasions, just as he may be conscripted into the army in time of war.

Naturally, this civic responsibility rests most strongly upon the organs of mass culture. The individual citizen may still be permitted his private unhappiness so long as it does not take on political significance, the extent of this tolerance being determined by how large an area of private life the society can accommodate. But every production of mass culture is a public act and must conform with accepted notions of the public good. Nobody seriously questions the principle that it is the function of mass culture to maintain public morale, and certainly nobody in the mass audience objects to having his morale maintained.* At a time when the normal condition of the citizen is a state of anxiety, euphoria spreads over our culture like the broad smile of an idiot. In terms of attitudes towards life, there is very little difference between a "happy" movie like *Good News,* which ignores death and suffering, and a "sad" movie like *A Tree Grows in Brooklyn,* which uses death and suffering as incidents in the service of a higher optimism.

But, whatever its effectiveness as a source of consolation and a means of pressure for maintaining "positive" social attitudes, this optimism is fundamentally satisfying to no one, not even to those who would be most disoriented without its support. Even within the area of mass culture, there always exists a current of opposition, seeking to express by whatever means are available to it that sense of desperation and inevitable failure which optimism itself helps to create. Most often, this opposition is confined to rudimentary or semiliterate forms: in mob politics and journalism, for example, or in certain kinds of religious enthusiasm. When it does enter the field of art, it is likely to be disguised or attenuated: in an unspecific form of expression like jazz, in the basically harmless nihilism of the Marx Brothers, in the continually reasserted strain of hopelessness that often seems to be the real meaning of the soap opera. The gangster film is remarkable in that it fills the need for disguise (though not sufficiently to avoid arousing uneasiness) without requiring any serious distortion. From its beginnings, it has

---

*In her testimony before the House Committee on Un-American Activities, Mrs. Leila Rogers said that the movie *None but the Lonely Heart* was un-American because it was gloomy. Like so much else that was said during the unhappy investigation of Hollywood, this statement was at once stupid and illuminating. One knew immediately what Mrs. Rogers was talking about; she had simply been insensitive enough to carry her philistinism to its conclusion.

been a consistent and astonishingly complete presentation of the modern sense of tragedy.*

In its initial character, the gangster film is simply one example of the movies' constant tendency to create fixed dramatic patterns that can be repeated indefinitely with a reasonable expectation of profit. One gangster film follows another as one musical or one Western follows another. But this rigidity is not necessarily opposed to the requirements of art. There have been very successful types of art in the past which developed such specific and detailed conventions as almost to make individual examples of the type interchangeable. This is true, for example, of Elizabethan revenge tragedy and Restoration comedy.

For such a type to be successful means that its conventions have imposed themselves upon the general consciousness and become the accepted vehicles of a particular set of attitudes and a particular aesthetic effect. One goes to any individual example of the type with very definite expectations, and originality is to be welcomed only in the degree that it intensifies the expected experience without fundamentally altering it. Moreover, the relationship between the conventions which go to make up such a type and the real experience of its audience or the real facts of whatever situation it pretends to describe is of only secondary importance and does not determine its aesthetic force. It is only in an ultimate sense that the type appeals to its audience's experience of reality; much more immediately, it appeals to previous experience of the type itself: it creates its own field of reference.

Thus the importance of the gangster film, and the nature and intensity of its emotional and aesthetic impact, cannot be measured in terms of the place of the gangster himself or the importance of the problem of crime in American life. Those European movie-goers who think there is a gangster on every corner in New York are certainly deceived, but defenders of the "positive" side of American culture are equally deceived if they think it relevant to point out that most Americans have never seen a gangster. What matters is that the experience of the gangster *as an experience of art* is universal to Americans. There is almost nothing we understand better or react to more readily or with quicker intelligence. The Western film, though it seems never to diminish in popularity, is for most of us no more than the folklore of the past, familiar and understandable only because it has been repeated so often. The gangster film comes much closer. In ways that we do not easily or willingly define, the gangster speaks for us, expressing that part of the American psyche which rejects the qualities and the demands of modern life, which rejects "Americanism" itself.

---

*Efforts have been made from time to time to bring the gangster film into line with the prevailing optimism and social constructiveness of our culture; *Kiss of Death* is a recent example. These efforts are usually unsuccessful; the reasons for their lack of success are interesting in themselves, but I shall not be able to discuss them here.

The gangster is the man of the city, with the city's language and knowledge, with its queer and dishonest skills and its terrible daring, carrying his life in his hands like a placard, like a club. For everyone else, there is at least the theoretical possibility of another world—in that happier American culture which the gangster denies, the city does not really exist; it is only a more crowded and more brightly lit country—but for the gangster there is only the city; he must inhabit it in order to personify it: not the real city, but that dangerous and sad city of the imagination which is so much more important, which is the modern world. And the gangster—though there are real gangsters—is also, and primarily, a creature of the imagination. The real city, one might say, produces only criminals; the imaginary city produces the gangster: he is what we want to be and what we are afraid we may become.

Thrown into the crowd without background or advantages, with only those ambiguous skills which the rest of us—the real people of the real city—can only pretend to have, the gangster is required to make his way, to make his life and impose it on others. Usually, when we come upon him, he has already made his choice or the choice has already been made for him, it doesn't matter which: we are not permitted to ask whether at some point he could have chosen to be something else than what he is.

The gangster's activity is actually a form of rational enterprise, involving fairly definite goals and various techniques for achieving them. But this rationality is usually no more than a vague background; we know, perhaps, that the gangster sells liquor or that he operates a numbers racket; often we are not given even that much information. So his activity becomes a kind of pure criminality: he hurts people. Certainly our response to the gangster film is most consistently and most universally a response to sadism; we gain the double satisfaction of participating vicariously in the gangster's sadism and then seeing it turned against the gangster himself.

But on another level the quality of irrational brutality and the quality of rational enterprise become one. Since we do not see the rational and routine aspects of the gangster's behavior, the practice of brutality—the quality of unmixed criminality—becomes the totality of his career. At the same time, we are always conscious that the whole meaning of this career is a drive for success: the typical gangster film presents a steady upward progress followed by a very precipitate fall. Thus brutality itself becomes at once the means to success and the content of success—a success that is defined in its most general terms, not as accomplishment or specific gain, but simply as the unlimited possibility of aggression. (In the same way, film presentations of businessmen tend to make it appear that they achieve their success by talking on the telephone and holding conferences and that success *is* talking on the telephone and holding conferences.)

From this point of view, the initial contact between the film and its audience is an agreed conception of human life: that man is a being with the possibilities of success or failure. This principle, too, belongs to the city; one must emerge from the crowd or else one is nothing. On that basis the necessity of the action is established, and it progresses by inalterable paths to the point where the gangster lies dead and the principle has been modified: there is really only one possibility—failure. The final meaning of the city is anonymity and death.

In the opening scene of *Scarface,* we are shown a successful man; we know he is successful because he has just given a party of opulent proportions and because he is called Big Louie. Through some monstrous lack of caution, he permits himself to be alone for a few moments. We understand from this immediately that he is about to be killed. No convention of the gangster film is more strongly established than this: it is dangerous to be alone. And yet the very conditions of success make it impossible not to be alone, for success is always the establishment of an *individual* pre-eminence that must be imposed on others, in whom it automatically arouses hatred; the successful man is an outlaw. The gangster's whole life is an effort to assert himself as an individual, to draw himself out of the crowd, and he always dies *because* he is an individual; the final bullet thrusts him back, makes him, after all, a failure. "Mother of God," says the dying Little Caesar, "is this the end of Rico?"—speaking of himself thus in the third person because what has been brought low is not the undifferentiated *man,* but the individual with a name, the gangster, the success; even to himself he is a creature of the imagination. (T. S. Eliot has pointed out that a number of Shakespeare's tragic heroes have this trick of looking at themselves dramatically; their true identity, the thing that is destroyed when they die, is something outside themselves—not a man, but a style of life, a kind of meaning.)

At bottom, the gangster is doomed because he is under the obligation to succeed, not because the means he employs are unlawful. In the deeper layers of the modern consciousness, *all* means are unlawful, every attempt to succeed is an act of aggression, leaving one alone and guilty and defenseless among enemies: one is *punished* for success. This is our intolerable dilemma: that failure is a kind of death and success is evil and dangerous, is—ultimately—impossible. The effect of the gangster film is to embody this dilemma in the person of the gangster and resolve it by his death. The dilemma is resolved because it is *his* death, not ours. We are safe; for the moment, we can acquiesce in our failure, we can choose to fail.

MANNY FARBER

*Manny Farber is a San Diego–based painter who has worked in many other fields and has
written a lot of film criticism for art magazines. His collected essays (*Negative Space*)
are provocative and quirky and cause you suddenly to see movies from unexpected angles.
This piece, titled "Underground Films," was published in 1957, before the term took on
its 1960s connotation of low-budget 8 and 16 mm experimental films. What he is actually describing here is the kind of Hollywood film that came to be valued by the auteur
critics, although he has arrived at his own auteur theory by other roads and entirely on
his own terms. He is writing an elegy for spare, muscular, non-self-conscious male-oriented
action movies, the "itch houses" where they played, and the audiences that sought them
there for all sorts of reasons, none of them having to do with Art. His championing of the
values of Hawks, Wellman, Sturges, and Aldrich—which were taken up by countless other
writers after Andrew Sarris brought the auteur theory to America—was original and new
when he wrote it, as was his gritty style, which seems to have been scratched out by the
kind of person who already knew what those movies were telling him.*

"Underground Films"

The saddest thing in current films is watching the long-neglected action directors fade away as the less talented De Sicas and Zinnemanns continue to fascinate the critics. Because they played an anti-art role in Hollywood, the true
masters of the male action film—such soldier-cowboy-gangster directors as
Raoul Walsh, Howard Hawks, William Wellman, William Keighley, the early,
pre-*Stagecoach* John Ford, Anthony Mann—have turned out a huge amount of
unprized, second-gear celluloid. Their neglect becomes more painful to behold
now that the action directors are in decline, many of them having abandoned
the dry, economic, life-worn movie style that made their observations of the
American he-man so rewarding. Americans seem to have a special aptitude for

allowing History to bury the toughest, most authentic native talents. The same
tide that has swept away Otis Ferguson, Walker Evans, Val Lewton, Clarence
Williams, and J. R. Williams into near oblivion is now in the process of bury-
ing a group that kept an endless flow of interesting roughneck film passing
through the theaters from the depression onward. The tragedy of these filmmakers lies in their having been consigned to a Sargasso Sea of unmentioned talent by film reviewers whose sole concern is not continuous flow of quality but
the momentary novelties of the particular film they are reviewing.

Howard Hawks is the key figure in the male action film because he shows a
maximum speed, inner life, and view, with the least amount of flat foot. His
best films, which have the swallowed-up intricacy of a good soft-shoe dance, are
Scarface, Only Angels Have Wings, His Girl Friday, and *The Big Sleep.* Raoul Walsh's
films are melancholy masterpieces of flexibility and detailing inside a lower-
middle-class locale. Walsh's victories, which make use of tense, broken-field
journeys and nostalgic background detail, include *They Drive by Night, White Heat,*
and *Roaring Twenties.* In any Bill Wellman operation, there are at least four directors—a sentimentalist, deep thinker, hooey vaudevillian, and an expedient
short-cut artist, whose special love is for mulish toughs expressing themselves
in drop-kicking heads and somber standing around. Wellman is at his best in stiff,
vulgar, low-pulp material. In that setup, he has a low-budget ingenuity, which
creates flashes of ferocious brassiness, an authentic practical-joke violence (as in
the frenzied inadequacy of Ben Blue in *Roxie Hart*), and a brainless hell-raising.
Anthony Mann's inhumanity to man, in which cold mortal intentness is the trademark effect, can be studied best in *The Tall Target, Winchester 73, Border Incident,*
and *Railroaded.* The films of this tin-can de Sade have a Germanic rigor, caterpillar intimacy, and an original dictionary of ways in which to punish the human
body. Mann has done interesting work with scissors, a cigarette lighter, and
steam, but his most bizarre effect takes place in a taxidermist's shop. By intricate manipulation of athletes' bodies, Mann tries to ram the eyes of his com-
batants on the horns of a stuffed deer stuck on the wall.

The film directors mentioned above did their best work in the late 1940's,
when it was possible to be a factory of unpretentious picture-making without
frightening the front office. During the same period and later, less prolific directors also appear in the uncompromising action film. Of these, the most important is John Farrow, an urbane vaudevillian whose forte, in films like *The Big
Clock* and *His Kind of Woman,* is putting a fine motoring system beneath the veer-
ing slapstick of his eccentric characterizations. Though he has tangled with such
heavyweights as Book-of-the-Month and Hemingway, Zoltan Korda is an authentic hard-grain cheapster telling his stories through unscrubbed action, masculine characterization, and violent explorations inside a fascinating locale.
Korda's best films—*Sahara, Counterattack, Cry the Beloved Country*—are strangely

active films in which terrain, jobs, and people get curiously interwoven in a ravening tactility. William Keighley, in *G-Men* and *Each Dawn I Die,* is the least sentimental director of gangster careers. After the bloated philosophical safe-crackers in Huston's *Asphalt Jungle,* the smallish cops and robbers in Keighley's work seem life-size. Keighley's handling is so right in emphasis, timing, and shrewdness that there is no feeling of the director breathing, gasping, snoring over the film.

The tight-lipped creators whose films are mentioned above comprise the most interesting group to appear in American culture since the various groupings that made the 1920's an explosive era in jazz, literature, silent films. Hawks and his group are perfect examples of the anonymous artist, who is seemingly afraid of the polishing, hypocrisy, bragging, fake educating that goes on in serious art. To go at his most expedient gait, the Hawks type must take a withdrawn, al-most hidden stance in the industry. Thus, his films seem to come from the most neutral, humdrum, monotonous corner of the movie lot. The fascinating thing about these veiled operators is that they are able to spring the leanest, shrewdest, sprightliest notes from material that looks like junk, and from a creative posi-tion that, on the surface, seems totally uncommitted and disinterested. With striking photography, a good car for natural dialogue, an eye for realistic detail, a skilled inside-action approach to composition, and the most politic hand in the movie field, the action directors have done a forbidding stenography on the hard-boiled American handyman as he progresses through the years.

It is not too remarkable that the underground films, with their twelve-year-old's adventure-story plot and endless palpitating movement, have lost out in the film system. Their dismissal has been caused by the construction of solid con-fidence built by daily and weekly reviewers. Operating with this wall, the critic can pick and discard without the slightest worry about looking silly. His choice of best salami is a picture backed by studio build-up, agreement amongst his colleagues, a layout in *Life* mag (which makes it officially reasonable for an American award), and a list of ingredients that anyone's unsophisticated aunt in Oakland can spot as comprising a distinguished film. This prize picture, which has philosophical undertones, pan-fried domestic sights, risqué crevices, sporty actors and actresses, circuslike gymnastics, a bit of tragedy like the main fall at Niagara, has every reason to be successful. It has been made for that purpose. Thus, the year's winner is a perfect film made up solely of holes and evasions, covered up by all types of padding and plush. The cavity-filling varies from one prize work to another, from *High Noon* (cross-eyed artistic views of a clock, sil-houettes against a vaulting sky, legend-toned walking, a big song), through *From Here to Eternity* (Sinatra's private scene-chewing, pretty trumpeting, tense shots in the dark and at twilight, necking near the water, a threatening hand with a broken bottle) to next year's winner, which will probably be a huge ball of cotton candy containing either Audrey Hepburn's cavernous grin and stiff behind or more of Zinnemann's glacéed picture-making. In terms of imaginative photography, honest acting, and insight into American life, there is no comparison between an average underground triumph (*Phenix City Story*) and the trivia that causes a critical salaam across the land. The trouble is that no one asks the critics' alliance to look straight backward at its "choices," for example, a horse-drawn truckload of liberal schmaltz called *The Best Years of Our Lives*. These ridiculously maltreated films sustain their place in the halls of fame simply because they bear the label of ART in every inch of their reelage. Praising these solemn goiters has produced a climate in which the underground picture-maker, with his modest entry and soft-shoe approach, can barely survive.

However, any day now, Americans may realize that scrambling after the obvious in art is a losing game. The sharpest work of the last thirty years is to be found by studying the most unlikely, self-destroying, uncompromising, roundabout artists. When the day comes for praising infamous men of art, some great talent will be shown in true light: people like Weldon Kees, the rangy Margie Israel, James Agee, Isaac Rosenfeld, Otis Ferguson, Val Lewton, a dozen comic-strip geniuses like the creator of "Harold Teen," and finally a half-dozen directors such as the master of the ambulance, speedboat, flying-saucer movie: Howard Hawks.

The films of the Hawks-Wellman group are *underground* for more reasons than the fact that the director hides out in subsurface reaches of his work. The hard-bitten action film finds its natural home in caves: the murky, congested theaters, looking like glorified tattoo parlors on the outside and located near bus terminals in big cities. These theaters roll action films in what, at first, seems like a nightmarish atmosphere of shabby transience, prints that seem overgrown with jungle moss, sound tracks infected with hiccups. The spectator watches two or three action films go by and leaves feeling as though he were a pirate discharged from a giant sponge.

The cutthroat atmosphere in the itch house is reproduced in the movies shown there. Hawks's *The Big Sleep* not only has a slightly gaseous, subsurface, Baghdadish background, but its gangster action is engineered with a suave, cutting efficacy. Walsh's *Roaring Twenties* is a jangling barrelhouse film, which starts with a top gun bouncing downhill, and, at the end, he is seen slowly pushing his way through a lot of Campbell's scotch broth. Wellman's favorite scene is a group of hard-visaged ball bearings standing around—for no damned reason and with no indication of how long or for what reason they have been standing. His worst pictures are made up simply of this moody, wooden standing around. All that saves the films are the little flurries of bulletlike acting that give the men an inner look of credible orneriness and somewhat stupid mulishness. Mann likes to stretch his victims in crucifix poses against the wall or ground and then to peer intently at their demise with an icy surgeon's eye. Just as the harrowing machine is about to run over the wetback on a moonlit night, the camera catches him sprawled out in a harrowing image. At heart, the best action films are slicing journeys into the lower depths of American life: dregs, outcasts, lonely hard wanderers caught in a buzzsaw of niggardly, intricate, devious movement.

The projects of the underground directors are neither experimental, liberal, slick, spectacular, low-budget, epical, improving, or flagrantly commercial like Sam Katzman two-bitters. They are faceless movies, taken from a type of half-polished trash writing, that seem like a mixture of Burt L. Standish, Max Brand, and Raymond Chandler. Tight, cliché-ridden melodramas about stock muscle-men. A stool pigeon gurgling with scissors in his back; a fat, nasal-voiced gang leader; escaped convicts; power-mad ranch owners with vengeful siblings; a mean gun with an Oedipus complex and migraine headaches; a crooked gambler trading guns to the redskins; exhausted GI's; an incompetent kid hoodlum hiding out in an East Side building; a sickly-elegant Italian barber in a plot to kill Lincoln; an underpaid shamus signing up to stop the blackmailing of a tough millionaire's depraved thumb-sucking daughter.

The action directors accept the role of hack so that they can involve themselves with expedience and tough-guy insight in all types of action: barnstorming, driving, bulldogging. The important thing is not so much the banal-seeming journeys to nowhere that make up the stories, but the tunneling that goes on inside the classic Western-gangster incidents and stock hoodlum-dogface-cowboy types. For instance, Wellman's lean, elliptical talents for creating brassy cheapsters and making gloved references to death, patriotism, masturbation, suggest that he uses private runways to the truth, while more famous directors take a slow, embalming surface route.

The virtues of action films expand as the pictures take on the outer appearance of junk jewelry. The underground's greatest mishaps have occurred in art-infected projects where there is unlimited cash, studio freedom, an expansive story, message, heart, and a lot of prestige to be gained. Their flattest, most sentimental works are incidentally the only ones that have attained the almond-paste-flavored eminence of the Museum of Modern Art's film library, i.e., *GI Joe, Public Enemy*. Both Hawks and Wellman, who made these overweighted mistakes, are like basketball's corner man: their best shooting is done from the deepest, worst angle. With material that is hopelessly worn out and childish (*Only Angels Have Wings*), the underground director becomes beautifully graphic and modestly human in his flexible detailing. When the material is like drab concrete, these directors become great on-the-spot inventors, using their curiously niggling, reaming style for adding background detail (Walsh); suave grace (Hawks); crawling, mechanized tension (Mann); veiled gravity (Wellman); svelte semicaricature (John Farrow); modern Gothic vehemence (Phil Karlson); and dark, modish vaudeville (Robert Aldrich).

In the films of these hard-edged directors can be found the unheralded ripple of physical experience, the tiny morbidly life-worn detail which the visitor to a strange city finds springing out at every step. The Hawks film is as good on the mellifluous grace of the impudent American hard rock as can be found in any art work; the Mann films use American objects and terrain—guns, cliffs, boulders, an 1865 locomotive, telephone wires—with more cruel intimacy than any other film-maker; the Wellman film is the only clear shot at the mean, brassy, clawlike soul of the lone American wolf that has been taken in films. In other words, these actioneers—Mann and Hawks and Keighley and, in recent times, Aldrich and Karlson—go completely underground before proving themselves more honest and subtle than the water buffaloes of film art: George Stevens, Billy Wilder, Vittorio De Sica, Georges Clouzot. (Clouzot's most successful work, *Wages of Fear,* is a wholesale steal of the mean physicality and acrid highway inventions in such Walsh-Wellman films as *They Drive by Night.* Also, the latter film is a more flexible, adroitly ad-libbed, worked-in creation than Clouzot's eclectic money-maker.)

Unfortunately, the action directors suffer from presentation problems. Their work is now seen repeatedly on the blurred, chopped, worn, darkened, commercial-ridden movie programs on TV. Even in the impossible conditions of the "Late Show," where the lighting is four shades too dark and the porthole-shaped screen defeats the movie's action, the deep skill of Hawks and his tribe shows itself. Time has dated and thinned out the story excitement, but the ability to capture the exact homely-manly character of forgotten locales and misanthropic figures is still in the pictures along with pictorial compositions (Ford's *Last of the Mohicans*) that occasionally seem as lovely as anything that came out of the camera box of Billy Bitzer and Matthew Brady. The conditions in the outcast theaters—the Lyric on Times Square, the Liberty on Market Street, the Victory on Chestnut—are not as bad as TV, but bad enough. The screen image is often out of plumb, the house lights are half left on during the picture, the broken seats are only a minor annoyance in the unpredictable terrain. Yet, these action-film homes are the places to study Hawks, Wellman, Mann, as well as their near and distant cousins.

The underground directors have been saving the American male on the screen for three decades without receiving the slightest credit from critics and prize committees. The hard, exact defining of male action, completely lacking in acting fat, is a common item *only* in underground films. The cream on the top of a *Framed* or *Appointment with Danger* (directed by two first cousins of the Hawks-Walsh strain) is the eye-flicking action that shows the American body—arms, elbows, legs, mouths, the tension profile line—being used expediently, with grace and the suggestion of jolting hardness. Otherwise, the Hollywood talkie seems to have been invented to give an embarrassingly phony impression of the virile action man. The performance is always fattened either by coyness (early

Robert Taylor), unction (Anthony Quinn), histrionic conceit (Gene Kelly), liberal knowingness (Brando), angelic stylishness (Mel Ferrer), oily hamming (José Ferrer), Mother's Boy passivity (Rock Hudson), or languor (Montgomery Clift). Unless the actor lands in the hands of an underground director, he causes a candy-coated effect that is misery for any spectator who likes a bit of male truth in films.

After a steady diet of undergrounders, the spectator realizes that these are the only films that show the tension of an individual intelligence posing itself against the possibilities of monotony, bathos, or sheer cliché. Though the action film is filled with heroism or its absence, the real hero is the small detail which has arisen from a stormy competition between lively color and credibility. The hardness of these films arises from the esthetic give-and-go with banality. Thus, the philosophical idea in underground films seems to be that nothing is easy in life or the making of films. Jobs are difficult, even the act of watching a humdrum bookstore scene from across the street has to be done with care and modesty to evade the type of butter-slicing glibness that rots the Zinnemann films. In the Walsh film, a gangster walks through a saloon with so much tight-roped ad-libbing and muscularity that he seems to be walking backward through the situation. Hawks's achievement of moderate toughness in *Red River,* using Clift's delicate languor and Wayne's claylike acting, is remarkable. As usual, he steers Clift through a series of cornball fetishes (like the Barney Google Ozark hat and the trick handling of same) and graceful, semicollegiate business: stances and kneelings and snake-quick gunmanship. The beauty of the job is the way the cliché business is kneaded, strained against without breaking the naturalistic surface. One feels that this is the first and last hard, clamped-down, imaginative job Clift does in Hollywood—his one nonmush performance. Afterward, he goes to work for Zinnemann, Stevens, Hitchcock.

The small buried attempt to pierce the banal pulp of underground stories with fanciful grace notes is one of the important feats of the underground director. Usually, the piercing consists in renovating a cheap rusty trick that has been slumbering in the "thriller" director's handbook—pushing a "color" effect against the most resistant type of unshowy, hard-bitten direction. A mean butterball flicks a gunman's ear with a cigarette lighter. A night-frozen cowboy shudders over a swig of whisky. A gorilla gang leader makes a cannonaded exit from a barber chair. All these bits of congestion are like the lines of a hand to a good gun movie; they are the tracings of difficulty that make the films seem uniquely hard and formful. In each case, the director is taking a great chance with clichés and forcing them into a hard natural shape.

People don't notice the absence of this hard combat with low, commonplace ideas in the Zinnemann and Huston epics, wherein the action is a game in which the stars take part with confidence and glee as though nothing can stop them. They roll in parts of drug addicts, tortured sheriffs; success depending on how much sentimental bloop and artistic japery can be packed in without encountering the demands of a natural act or character. Looking back on a Sinatra film, one has the feeling of a private whirligig performance in the center of a frame rather than a picture. On the other hand, a Cagney performance under the hands of a Keighley is ingrained in a tight, malignant story. One remembers it as a sinewy, life-marred exactness that is as quietly laid down as the smaller jobs played by the Barton MacLanes and Frankie Darros.

A constant attendance at the Lyric-Pix-Victory theaters soon impresses the spectator with the coverage of locales in action films. The average gun film travels like a shamus who knows his city and likes his private knowledges. Instead of the picture-postcard sights, the underground film finds the most idiosyncratic spot of a city and then locates the niceties within the large nicety. The California Street hill in San Francisco (*Woman in Hiding*) with its old-style mansions played in perfect night photography against a deadened domestic bitching. A YMCA scene that emphasizes the wonderful fat-waisted, middle-aged physicality of people putting on tennis shoes and playing handball (*Appointment with Danger*). The terrorizing of a dowdy middle-aged, frog-faced woman (*Born to Kill*) that starts in a decrepit hotel and ends in a bumbling, screeching, crawling murder at midnight on the shore. For his big shock effect, director Robert Wise (a sometime member of the underground) uses the angle going down to the water to create a middle-class mediocrity that out-horrors anything Graham Greene attempted in his early books on small-time gunsels.

Another fine thing about the coverage is its topographic grimness, the fact that the terrain looks worked over. From Walsh's *What Price Glory?* to Mann's *Men in War,* the terrain is special in that it is used, kicked, grappled, worried, sweated up, burrowed into, stomped on. The land is marched across in dark, threading lines at twilight, or the effect is reversed with foot soldiers in white parkas (*Fixed Bayonets*) curving along a snowed-in battleground as they watch troops moving back—in either case, the cliché effect is worked credibly inward until it creates a haunting note like the army diagonals in *Birth of a Nation*. Rooms are boxed, crossed, opened up as they are in few other films. The spectator gets to know these rooms as well as his own hand. Years after seeing the film, he remembers the way a dulled waitress sat on the edge of a hotel bed, the weird elongated adobe in which ranch hands congregate before a Chisholm Trail drive. The rooms in big-shot directors' films look curiously bulbous, as though inflated with hot air and turned toward the audience, like the high school operetta of the 1920's.

Of all these poet-builders, Wellman is the most interesting, particularly with Hopper-type scenery. It is a matter of drawing store fronts, heavy bedroom boudoirs, the heisting of a lonely service station, with light, furious strokes. Also, in mixing jolting vulgarity (Mae Clarke's face being smashed with a grapefruit) with a space composition dance in which the scene seems to be constructed before your eyes. It may be a minor achievement, but, when Wellman finishes with a service station or the wooden stairs in front of an ancient saloon, there is no reason for any movie realist to handle the subject again. The scene is kept light, textural, and as though it is being built from the outside in. There is no sentiment of the type that spreads lugubrious shadows (Kazan), builds tensions of perspective (Huston), or inflates with golden sunlight and finicky hot air (Stevens).

Easily the best part of underground films are the excavations of exciting-familiar scenery. The opening up of a scene is more concerted in these films than in other Hollywood efforts, but the most important thing is that the opening is done by road-mapped strategies that play movement against space in a cunning way, building the environment and event before your eyes. In every underground film, these vigorous ramifications within a sharply seen terrain are the big attraction, the main tent. No one does this anatomization of action and scene better than Hawks, who probably invented it—at least, the smooth version—in such 1930's gunblasts as *The Crowd Roars.* The control of Hawks's strategies is so ingenious that, when a person kneels or walks down the hallway, the movement seems to click into a predetermined slot. It is an uncanny accomplishment that carries the spectator across the very ground of a giant ranch, into rooms and out again, over to the wall to look at some faded fight pictures on a hotel wall—as though he were in the grip of a spectacular, mobile "eye." When Hawks landscapes action—the cutting between light tower and storm-caught plane in *Ceiling Zero,* the vegetalizing in *The Thing,* the shamus sweating in a greenhouse in *The Big Sleep*—the feeling is of a clever human tunneling just under the surface of terrain. It is as though the film has a life of its own that goes on beneath the story action.

However, there have been many great examples of such veining by human interactions over a wide plane. One of the special shockers, in *Each Dawn I Die,* has to do with the scissoring of a stooly during the movie shown at the penitentiary. This Keighley-Cagney effort is a wonder of excitement as it moves in great leaps from screen to the rear of a crowded auditorium: crossing contrasts of movement in three points of the hall, all of it done in a sinking gloom. One of the more ironic crisscrossings has to do with the coughings of the stuck victim played against the screen image of zooming airplanes over the Pacific.

In the great virtuoso films, there is something vaguely resembling this underground maneuvering, only it goes on above the story. Egocentric padding that builds a great bonfire of pyrotechnics over a gapingly empty film. The perfect example is a pumped-up fist fight that almost closes the three-hour *Giant* film. This ballroom shuffle between a reforming rancher and a Mexican-hating luncheonette owner is an entertaining creation in spectacular tumbling, swinging, back arching, bending. However, the endless masturbatory "building" of excitement—beautiful haymakers, room-covering falls, thunderous sounds—is more than slightly silly. Even if the room were valid, which it isn't (a studio-built chromium horror plopped too close to the edge of a lonely highway), the room goes unexplored because of the jumbled timing. The excess that is so noticeable in Stevens's brawl is absent in the least serious undergrounder, which attains most of its crisp, angular character from the modesty of a director working skillfully far within the earthworks of the story.

Underground films have almost ceased to be a part of the movie scene. The founders of the action film have gone into awkward, big-scaled productions involving pyramid-building, a passenger plane in trouble over the Pacific, and postcard Westerns with Jimmy Stewart and his harassed Adam's apple approach to gutty acting. The last drainings of the underground film show a tendency toward moving from the plain guttural approach of *Steel Helmet* to a Germanically splashed type of film. Of these newcomers, Robert Aldrich is certainly the most exciting—a lurid, psychiatric stormer who gets an overflow of vitality and sheer love for movie-making into the film. This enthusiasm is the rarest item in a dried, decayed-lemon type of movie period. Aldrich makes viciously anti-Something movies—*Attack* stomps on Southern rascalism and the officer sect in war, *The Big Knife* impales the Zanuck-Goldwyn big shot in Hollywood. The Aldrich films are filled with exciting characterizations—by Lee Marvin, Rod Steiger, Jack Palance—of highly psyched-up, marred, and bothered men. Phil Karlson has done some surprising modern Gothic treatments of the Brinks hold-up (*Kansas City Confidential*) and the vice-ridden Southern town (*The Phenix City Story*). His movies are remarkable for their endless outlay of scary cheapness in detailing the modern underworld. Also, Karlson's work has a chilling documentary exactness and an exciting shot-scattering belligerence.

There is no longer a literate audience for the masculine picture-making that Hawks and Wellman exploited, as there was in the 1930's. In those exciting movie years, a smart audience waited around each week for the next Hawks, Preston Sturges, or Ford film—shoe-stringers that were far to the side of the expensive Hollywood film. That underground audience, with its expert voice in Otis Ferguson and its ability to choose between perceptive trash and the Thalberg pepsin-flavored sloshing with Tracy and Gable, has now oozed away. It seems ridiculous, but the Fergusonite went into fast decline during the mid-1940's when the movie market was flooded with fake underground films—plushy thrillers with neo-Chandler scripts and a romantic style that seemed to pour the gore, histrionics, decor out of a giant catsup bottle. The nadir of these films: an item called *Singapore* with Fred MacMurray and Ava Gardner.

The straw that finally breaks the back of the underground film tradition is the dilettante behavior of intellectuals on the subject of oaters. Esthetes and upper bohemians now favor horse operas almost as wildly as they like the cute, little-guy worshipings of De Sica and the pedantic, interpretive reading of Alec Guinness. This fad for Western films shows itself in the inevitable little-magazine review, which finds an affinity between the subject matter of cowboy films and the inner esthetics of Cinemah. The Hawks-Wellman tradition, which is basically a subterranean delight that looks like a cheap penny candy on the outside, hasn't a chance of reviving when intellectuals enthuse in equal amounts over Westerns by Ford, Nunnally Johnson, J. Sturges, Stevens, Delmer Daves. In Ferguson's day, the intellectual could differentiate between a stolid genre painter (Ford), a long-winded cuteness expert with a rotogravure movie scene (Johnson), a scene-painter with a notions-counter eye and a primly naïve manner with sun-hardened bruisers (John Sturges), and a *Boys' Life* nature lover who intelligently half-prettifies adolescents and backwoods primitives (Daves). Today, the audience for Westerns and gangster careers is a sickeningly frivolous one that does little more than play the garbage collector or make a night court of films. With this high-brow audience that loves banality and pomp more than the tourists at Radio City Music Hall, there is little reason to expect any stray director to try for a hidden meager-looking work that is directly against the serious art grain.

Susan Sontag

This essay is doubly fascinating, first for what Sontag has to say about the science fiction film and second for how she phrases it, as if she too were somehow a visitor from another world, encountering an alien phenomenon. It is impossible, when one reads these words, to imagine her ever huddled in the dark of a movie theater, eating popcorn, and jumping with fright when the bug-eyed monster appears. There is not a single sentence that suggests she has ever enjoyed one of the films she is discussing, yet one suspects she would not have attended so many of them, and paid such close attention, if all she had hoped to get out of them was an essay.

"The Imagination of Disaster"

The typical science fiction film has a form as predictable as a Western, and is made up of elements which, to a practiced eye, are as classic as the saloon brawl, the blonde schoolteacher from the East, and the gun duel on the deserted main street.

One model scenario proceeds through five phases.

(1) The arrival of the thing. (Emergence of the monsters, landing of the alien spaceship, etc.) This is usually witnessed or suspected by just one person, a young scientist on a field trip. Nobody, neither his neighbors nor his colleagues, will believe him for some time. The hero is not married, but has a sympathetic though also incredulous girl friend.

(2) Confirmation of the hero's report by a host of witnesses to a great act of destruction. (If the invaders are beings from another planet, a fruitless attempt to parley with them and get them to leave peacefully.) The local police are summoned to deal with the situation and massacred.

(3) In the capital of the country, conferences between scientists and the military take place, with the hero lecturing before a chart, map, or blackboard. A national emergency is declared. Reports of further destruction. Authorities from other countries arrive in black limousines. All international tensions are suspended in view of the planetary emergency. This stage often includes a rapid montage of news broadcasts in various languages, a meeting at the UN, and more conferences between the military and the scientists. Plans are made for destroying the enemy.

(4) Further atrocities. At some point the hero's girl friend is in grave danger. Massive counter-attacks by international forces, with brilliant displays of rocketry, rays, and other advanced weapons, are all unsuccessful. Enormous military casualties, usually by incineration. Cities are destroyed and/or evacuated. There is an obligatory scene here of panicked crowds stampeding along a highway or a big bridge, being waved on by numerous policemen who, if the film is Japanese, are immaculately white-gloved, preternaturally calm, and call out in dubbed English, "Keep moving. There is no need to be alarmed."

(5) More conferences, whose motif is: "They must be vulnerable to something." Throughout the hero has been working in his lab to this end. The final strategy, upon which all hopes depend, is drawn up; the ultimate weapon—often a super-powerful, as yet untested, nuclear device—is mounted. Countdown. Final repulse of the monster or invaders. Mutual congratulations, while the hero and girl friend embrace cheek to cheek and scan the skies sturdily. "But have we seen the last of them?"

. . . .

The film I have just described should be in color and on a wide screen. Another typical scenario, which follows, is simpler and suited to black-and-white films with a lower budget. It has four phases.

(1) The hero (usually, but not always, a scientist) and his girl friend, or his wife and two children, are disporting themselves in some innocent ultra-normal middle-class surroundings—their house in a small town, or on vacation (camping, boating). Suddenly, someone starts behaving strangely; or some innocent form of vegetation becomes monstrously enlarged and ambulatory. If a character is pictured driving an automobile, something gruesome looms up in the middle of the road. If it is night, strange lights hurtle across the sky.

(2) After following the thing's tracks, or determining that It is radioactive, or poking around a huge crater—in short, conducting some sort of crude investigation—the hero tries to warn the local authorities, without effect; nobody believes anything is amiss. The hero knows better. If the thing is tangible, the house is elaborately barricaded. If the invading alien is an invisible parasite, a doctor or friend is called in, who is himself rather quickly killed or "taken possession of" by the thing.

(3) The advice of whoever further is consulted proves useless. Meanwhile, It continues to claim other victims in the town, which remains implausibly isolated from the rest of the world. General helplessness.

(4) One of two possibilities. Either the hero prepares to do battle alone, accidentally discovers the thing's one vulnerable point, and destroys it. Or, he somehow manages to get out of town and succeeds in laying his case before competent authorities. They, along the lines of the first script but abridged, deploy a complex technology which (after initial setbacks) finally prevails against the invaders.

. . . .

Another version of the second script opens with the scientist-hero in his laboratory, which is located in the basement or on the grounds of his tasteful, prosperous house. Through his experiments, he unwittingly causes a frightful metamorphosis in some class of plants or animals which turn carnivorous and go on a rampage. Or else, his experiments have caused him to be injured (sometimes irrevocably) or "invaded" himself. Perhaps he has been experimenting with radiation, or has built a machine to communicate with beings from other planets or transport him to other places or times.

Another version of the first script involves the discovery of some fundamental alteration in the conditions of existence of our planet, brought about by nuclear testing, which will lead to the extinction in a few months of all human life. For example: the temperature of the earth is becoming too high or too low to support life, or the earth is cracking in two, or it is gradually being blanketed by lethal fallout.

A third script, somewhat but not altogether different from the first two, concerns a journey through space—to the moon, or some other planet. What the space-voyagers discover commonly is that the alien terrain is in a state of dire emergency, itself threatened by extra-planetary invaders or nearing extinction through the practice of nuclear warfare. The terminal dramas of the first and second scripts are played out there, to which is added the problem of getting away from the doomed and/or hostile planet and back to Earth.

. . . .

I am aware, of course, that there are thousands of science fiction novels (their heyday was the late 1940s), not to mention the transcriptions of science fiction themes which, more and more, provide the principal subject-matter of comic books. But I propose to discuss science fiction films (the present period began in 1950 and continues, considerably abated, to this day) as an independent sub-genre, without reference to other media—and, most particularly, without reference to the novels from which, in many cases, they were adapted. For, while novel and film may share the same plot, the fundamental difference between the resources of the novel and the film makes them quite dissimilar.

Certainly, compared with the science fiction novels, their film counterparts have unique strengths, one of which is the immediate representation of the extraordinary: physical deformity and mutation, missile and rocket combat, toppling skyscrapers. The movies are, naturally, weak just where the science fiction novels (some of them) are strong—on science. But in place of an intellectual workout, they can supply something the novels can never provide—sensuous elaboration. In the films it is by means of images and sounds, not words that have to be translated by the imagination, that one can participate in the fantasy of living through one's own death and more, the death of cities, the destruction of humanity itself.

Science fiction films are not about science. They are about disaster, which is one of the oldest subjects of art. In science fiction films disaster is rarely viewed intensively; it is always extensive. It is a matter of quantity and ingenuity. If you will, it is a question of scale. But the scale, particularly in the wide-screen color films (of which the ones by the Japanese director Inoshiro Honda and the American director George Pal are technically the most convincing and visually the most exciting), does raise the matter to another level.

Thus, the science fiction film (like that of a very different contemporary genre, the Happening) is concerned with the aesthetics of destruction, with the peculiar beauties to be found in wreaking havoc, making a mess. And it is in the imagery of destruction that the core of a good science fiction film lies. Hence, the disadvantage of the cheap film—in which the monster appears or the rocket lands in a small dull-looking town. (Hollywood budget needs usually dictate that the town be in the Arizona or California desert. In *The Thing from Another World* [1951] the rather sleazy and confined set is supposed to be an encampment near the North Pole.) Still, good black-and-white science fiction films have been made. But a bigger budget, which usually means color, allows a much greater play back and forth among several model environments. There is the populous city. There is the lavish but ascetic interior of the spaceship—either the invaders' or ours— replete with streamlined chromium fixtures and dials and machines whose complexity is indicated by the number of colored lights they flash and strange noises they emit. There is the laboratory crowded with formidable boxes and scientific apparatus. There is a comparatively old-fashioned-looking conference room, where the scientists unfurl charts to explain the desperate state of things to the military. And each of these standard locales or backgrounds is subject to two modalities—intact and destroyed. We may, if we are lucky, be treated to a panorama of melting tanks, flying bodies, crashing walls, awesome craters and fissures in the earth, plummeting spacecraft, colorful deadly rays; and to a symphony of screams, weird electronic signals, the noisiest military hardware going, and the leaden tones of the laconic denizens of alien planets and their subjugated earthlings.

Certain of the primitive gratifications of science fiction films—for instance, the depiction of urban disaster on a colossally magnified scale—are shared with other types of films. Visually there is little difference between mass havoc as represented in the old horror and monster films and what we find in science fiction films, except (again) scale. In the old monster films, the monster always headed for the great city, where he had to do a fair bit of rampaging, hurling busses off bridges, crumpling trains in his bare hands, toppling buildings, and so forth. The archetype is King Kong, in Schoedsack and Cooper's great film of 1933, running amok, first in the native village (trampling babies, a bit of footage excised from most prints), then in New York. This is really no different in spirit from the scene in Inoshiro Honda's *Rodan* (1957) in which two giant reptiles—with a wingspan of 500 feet and supersonic speeds—by flapping their wings whip up a cyclone that blows most of Tokyo to smithereens. Or the destruction of half of Japan by the gigantic robot with the great incinerating ray that shoots forth from his eyes, at the beginning of Honda's *The Mysterians* (1959). Or, the devastation by the rays from a fleet of flying saucers of New York, Paris, and Tokyo, in *Battle in Outer Space* (1960). Or, the inundation of New York in *When Worlds Collide* (1951). Or, the end of London in 1966 depicted in George Pal's *The Time Machine* (1960). Neither do these sequences differ in aesthetic intention from the destruction scenes in the big sword, sandal, and orgy color spectaculars set in Biblical and Roman times—the end of Sodom in Aldrich's *Sodom and Gomorrah,* of Gaza in De Mille's *Samson and Delilah,* of Rhodes in *The Colossus of Rhodes,* and of Rome in a dozen Nero movies. Griffith began it with the Babylon sequence in *Intolerance,* and to this day there is nothing like the thrill of watching all those expensive sets come tumbling down.

In other respects as well, the science fiction films of the 1950s take up familiar themes. The famous 1930s movie serials and comics of the adventures of Flash Gordon and Buck Rogers, as well as the more recent spate of comic book super-heroes with extraterrestrial origins (the most famous is Superman, a foundling from the planet Krypton, currently described as having been exploded by a nuclear blast), share motifs with more recent science fiction movies. But there is an important difference. The old science fiction films, and most of the comics, still have an essentially innocent relation to disaster. Mainly they offer new versions of the oldest romance of all—of the strong invulnerable hero with a mysterious lineage come to do battle on behalf of good and against evil. Recent science fiction films have a decided grimness, bolstered by their much greater degree of visual credibility, which contrasts strongly with the older films. Modern historical reality has greatly enlarged the imagination of disaster, and the protagonists—perhaps by the very nature of what is visited upon them— no longer seem wholly innocent.

The lure of such generalized disaster as a fantasy is that it releases one from normal obligations. The trump card of the end-of-the-world movies—like *The Day the Earth Caught Fire* (1962)—is that great scene with New York or London or Tokyo discovered empty, its entire population annihilated. Or, as in *The World, the Flesh, and the Devil* (1957), the whole movie can be devoted to the fantasy of occupying the deserted metropolis and starting all over again, a world Robinson Crusoe.

Another kind of satisfaction these films supply is extreme moral simplification—that is to say, a morally acceptable fantasy where one can give outlet to cruel or at least amoral feelings. In this respect, science fiction films partly overlap with horror films. This is the undeniable pleasure we derive from looking at freaks, beings excluded from the category of the human. The sense of superiority over the freak conjoined in varying proportions with the titillation of fear and aversion makes it possible for moral scruples to be lifted, for cruelty to be enjoyed. The same thing happens in science fiction films. In the figure of the monster from outer space, the freakish, the ugly, and the predatory all converge— and provide a fantasy target for righteous bellicosity to discharge itself, and for the aesthetic enjoyment of suffering and disaster. Science fiction films are one of the purest forms of spectacle; that is, we are rarely inside anyone's feelings. (An exception is Jack Arnold's *The Incredible Shrinking Man* [1957].) We are merely spectators; we watch.

But in science fiction films, unlike horror films, there is not much horror. Suspense, shocks, surprises are mostly abjured in favor of a steady, inexorable plot. Science fiction films invite a dispassionate, aesthetic view of destruction and violence—a *technological* view. Things, objects, machinery play a major role in these films. A greater range of ethical values is embodied in the décor of these films than in the people. Things, rather than the helpless humans, are the locus of values because we experience them, rather than people, as the sources of power. According to science fiction films, man is naked without his artifacts. *They* stand for different values, they are potent, they are what get destroyed, and they are the indispensable tools for the repulse of the alien invaders or the repair of the damaged environment.

. . . .

The science fiction films are strongly moralistic. The standard message is the one about the proper, or humane, use of science, versus the mad, obsessional use of science. This message the science fiction films share in common with the classic horror films of the 1930s, like *Frankenstein, The Mummy, Island of Lost Souls, Dr. Jekyll and Mr. Hyde.* (George Franju's brilliant *Les Yeux sans Visage* [1959], called here *The Horror Chamber of Doctor Faustus,* is a more recent example.) In the horror films, we have the mad or obsessed or misguided scientist who pursues his experiments against good advice to the contrary, creates a monster or monsters, and is himself destroyed—often recognizing his folly himself, and dying in the successful effort to destroy his own creation. One science fiction equivalent of this is the scientist, usually a member of a team, who defects to the planetary invaders because "their" science is more advanced than "ours."

This is the case in *The Mysterians,* and, true to form, the renegade sees his error in the end, and from within the Mysterian space ship destroys it and himself. In *This Island Earth* (1955), the inhabitants of the beleaguered planet Metaluna propose to conquer earth, but their project is foiled by a Metalunan scientist named Exeter who, having lived on earth a while and learned to love Mozart, cannot abide such viciousness. Exeter plunges his spaceship into the ocean after returning a glamorous pair (male and female) of American physicists to earth. Metaluna dies. In *The Fly* (1958), the hero, engrossed in his basement-laboratory experiments on a matter-transmitting machine, uses himself as a subject, exchanges head and one arm with a housefly which had accidentally gotten into the machine, becomes a monster, and with his last shred of human will destroys his laboratory and orders his wife to kill him. His discovery, for the good of mankind, is lost.

Being a clearly labeled species of intellectual, scientists in science fiction films are always liable to crack up or go off the deep end. In *Conquest of Space* (1955), the scientist-commander of an international expedition to Mars suddenly acquires scruples about the blasphemy involved in the undertaking, and begins reading the Bible mid-journey instead of attending to his duties. The commander's son, who is his junior officer and always addresses his father as "General," is forced to kill the old man when he tries to prevent the ship from landing on

Mars. In this film, both sides of the ambivalence toward scientists are given voice. Generally, for a scientific enterprise to be treated entirely sympathetically in these films, it needs the certificate of utility. Science, viewed without ambivalence, means an efficacious response to danger. Disinterested intellectual curiosity rarely appears in any form other than caricature, as a maniacal dementia that cuts one off from normal human relations. But this suspicion is usually directed at the scientist rather than his work. The creative scientist may become a martyr to his own discovery, through an accident or by pushing things too far. But the implication remains that other men, less imaginative—in short, technicians—could have administered the same discovery better and more safely. The most ingrained contemporary mistrust of the intellect is visited, in these movies, upon the scientist-as-intellectual.

The message that the scientist is one who releases forces which, if not controlled for good, could destroy man himself seems innocuous enough. One of the oldest images of the scientist is Shakespeare's Prospero, the overdetached scholar forcibly retired from society to a desert island, only partly in control of the magic forces in which he dabbles. Equally classic is the figure of the scientist as satanist (*Doctor Faustus,* and stories of Poe and Hawthorne). Science is magic, and man has always known that there is black magic as well as white. But it is not enough to remark that contemporary attitudes—as reflected in science fiction films—remain ambivalent, that the scientist is treated as both satanist and savior. The proportions have changed, because of the new context in which the old admiration and fear of the scientist are located. For his sphere of influence is no longer local, himself or his immediate community. It is planetary, cosmic.

. . . .

One gets the feeling, particularly in the Japanese films but not only there, that a mass trauma exists over the use of nuclear weapons and the possibility of future nuclear wars. Most of the science fiction films bear witness to this trauma, and, in a way, attempt to exorcise it.

The accidental awakening of the super-destructive monster who has slept in the earth since prehistory is, often, an obvious metaphor for the Bomb. But there are many explicit references as well. In *The Mysterians,* a probe ship from the planet Mysteroid has landed on earth, near Tokyo. Nuclear warfare having been practiced on Mysteroid for centuries (their civilization is "more advanced than ours"), ninety percent of those now born on the planet have to be destroyed at birth, because of defects caused by the huge amounts of Strontium 90 in their diet. The Mysterians have come to earth to marry earth women, and possibly to take over our relatively uncontaminated planet. . . . In *The Incredible Shrinking Man,* the John Doe hero is the victim of a gust of radiation which blows over the water, while he is out boating with his wife; the radiation causes him to grow smaller and smaller, until at the end of the movie he steps through the fine mesh of a window screen to become "the infinitely small." . . . In *Rodan,* a horde of monstrous carnivorous prehistoric insects, and finally a pair of giant flying reptiles (the prehistoric Archeopteryx), are hatched from dormant eggs in the depths of a mine shaft by the impact of nuclear test explosions, and go on to destroy a good part of the world before they are felled by the molten lava of a volcanic eruption. . . . In the English film, *The Day the Earth Caught Fire,* two simultaneous hydrogen bomb tests by the United States and Russia change by 11 degrees the tilt of the earth on its axis and alter the earth's orbit so that it begins to approach the sun.

Radiation casualties—ultimately, the conception of the whole world as a casualty of nuclear testing and nuclear warfare—is the most ominous of all the notions with which science fiction films deal. Universes become expendable. Worlds become contaminated, burnt out, exhausted, obsolete. In *Rocketship X-M* (1950) explorers from the earth land on Mars, where they learn that atomic warfare has destroyed Martian civilization. In George Pal's *The War of the Worlds* (1953), reddish spindly alligator-skinned creatures from Mars invade the earth because their planet is becoming too cold to be inhabitable. In *This Island Earth,* also American, the planet Metaluna, whose population has long ago been driven underground by warfare, is dying under the missile attacks of an enemy planet. Stocks of uranium, which power the force field shielding Metaluna, have been used up; and an unsuccessful expedition is sent to earth to enlist earth scientists to devise new sources for nuclear power. In Joseph Losey's *The Damned* (1961), nine icy-cold radioactive children are being reared by a fanatical scientist in a dark cave on the English coast to be the only survivors of the inevitable nuclear Armageddon.

. . . .

There is a vast amount of wishful thinking in science fiction films, some of it touching, some of it depressing. Again and again, one detects the hunger for a "good war," which poses no moral problems, admits of no moral qualifications. The imagery of science fiction films will satisfy the most bellicose addict of war films, for a lot of the satisfactions of war films pass, untransformed, into science fiction films. Examples: the dogfights between earth "fighter rockets" and alien spacecraft in the *Battle in Outer Space* (1960); the escalating firepower in the successive assaults upon the invaders in *The Mysterians,* which Dan Talbot correctly described as a non-stop holocaust; the spectacular bombardment of the underground fortress of Metaluna in *This Island Earth.*

Yet at the same time the bellicosity of science fiction films is neatly channeled into the yearning for peace, or for at least peaceful coexistence. Some scientist generally takes sententious note of the fact that it took the planetary invasion to make the warring nations of the earth come to their senses and suspend their own conflicts. One of the main themes of many science fiction films—the color ones usually, because they have the budget and resources to develop the military spectacle—is this UN fantasy, a fantasy of united warfare. (The same wishful UN theme cropped up in a recent spectacular which is not science fiction, *Fifty-Five Days in Peking* [1963]. There, topically enough, the Chinese, the Boxers, play the role of Martian invaders who unite the earthmen, in this case the United States, England, Russia, France, Germany, Italy, and Japan.) A great enough disaster cancels all enmities and calls upon the utmost concentration of earth resources.

Science—technology—is conceived of as the great unifier. Thus the science fiction films also project a Utopian fantasy. In the classic models of Utopian thinking—Plato's Republic, Campanella's City of the Sun, More's Utopia, Swift's land of the Houyhnhnms, Voltaire's Eldorado—society had worked out a perfect consensus. In these societies reasonableness had achieved an unbreakable supremacy over the emotions. Since no disagreement or social conflict was intellectually plausible, none was possible. As in Melville's *Typee,* "they all think the same." The universal rule of reason meant universal agreement. It is interesting, too, that societies in which reason was pictured as totally ascendant were also traditionally pictured as having an ascetic or materially frugal and economically simple mode of life. But in the Utopian world community projected by science fiction films, totally pacified and ruled by scientific consensus, the demand for simplicity of material existence would be absurd.

·   ·

Yet alongside the hopeful fantasy of moral simplification and international unity embodied in the science fiction films lurk the deepest anxieties about contemporary existence. I don't mean only the very real trauma of the Bomb—that it has been used, that there are enough now to kill everyone on earth many times over, that those new bombs may very well be used. Besides these new anxieties about physical disaster, the prospect of universal mutilation and even annihilation, the science fiction films reflect powerful anxieties about the condition of the individual psyche.

For science fiction films may also be described as a popular mythology for the contemporary *negative* imagination about the impersonal. The other-world creatures that seek to take "us" over are an "it," not a "they." The planetary invaders are usually zombielike. Their movements are either cool, mechanical, or lumbering, blobby. But it amounts to the same thing. If they are non-human in form, they proceed with an absolutely regular, unalterable movement (unalterable save by destruction). If they are human in form—dressed in space suits, etc.—then they obey the most rigid military discipline, and display no personal characteristics whatsoever. And it is this regime of emotionlessness, of impersonality, of regimentation, which they will impose on the earth if they are successful. "No more love, no more beauty, no more pain," boasts a converted earthling in *The Invasion of the Body Snatchers* (1956). The half-earthling, half-alien children in *The Children of the Damned* (1960) are absolutely emotionless, move as a group and understand each others' thoughts, and are all prodigious intellects. They are the wave of the future, man in his next stage of development.

These alien invaders practice a crime which is worse than murder. They do not simply kill the person. They obliterate him. In *The War of the Worlds,* the ray which issues from the rocket ship disintegrates all persons and objects in its path, leaving no trace of them but a light ash. In Honda's *The H-Man* (1959), the creeping blob melts all flesh with which it comes in contact. If the blob, which looks like a huge hunk of red Jello and can crawl across floors and up and down walls, so much as touches your bare foot, all that is left of you is a heap of clothes on the floor. (A more articulated, size-multiplying blob is the villain in the English film *The Creeping Unknown* [1956].) In another version of this fantasy, the body is preserved but the person is entirely reconstituted as the automatized servant or agent of the alien powers. This is, of course, the vampire fantasy in new dress. The person is really dead, but he doesn't know it. He is "undead," he has become an "unperson." It happens to a whole California town in *The Invasion of the Body Snatchers,* to several earth scientists in *This Island Earth,* and to assorted innocents in *It Came from Outer Space, Attack of the Puppet People* (1958), and *The Brain Eaters* (1958). As the victim always backs away from the vampire's horrifying embrace, so in science fiction films the person always fights being "taken over"; he wants to retain his humanity. But once the deed has been done, the victim is eminently satisfied with his condition. He has not been converted from human amiability to monstrous "animal" bloodlust (a metaphoric exaggeration of sexual desire), as in the old vampire fantasy. No, he has simply become far more efficient—the very model of technocratic man, purged of emotions, volitionless, tranquil, obedient to all orders. (The dark secret behind human nature used to be the upsurge of the animal—as in *King Kong.* The threat to man, his availability to dehumanization, lay in his own animality. Now the danger is understood as residing in man's ability to be turned into a machine.)

The rule, of course, is that this horrible and irremediable form of murder can strike anyone in the film except the hero. The hero and his family, while greatly threatened, always escape this fate and by the end of the film the invaders have been repulsed or destroyed. I know of only one exception, *The Day That Mars Invaded Earth* (1963), in which after all the standard struggles the scientist-hero, his wife, and their two children are "taken over" by the alien invaders—and that's that. (The last minutes of the film show them being incinerated by the Martians' rays and their ash silhouettes flushed down their empty swimming pool, while their simulacra drive off in the family car.) Another variant but upbeat switch on the rule occurs in *The Creation of the Humanoids* (1964), where the hero discovers at the end of the film that he, too, has been turned into a metal robot, complete with highly efficient and virtually indestructible mechanical insides, although he didn't know it and detected no difference in himself. He learns, however, that he will shortly be upgraded into a "humanoid" having all the properties of a real man.

Of all the standard motifs of science fiction films, this theme of dehumanization is perhaps the most fascinating. For, as I have indicated, it is scarcely a black-and-white situation, as in the old vampire films. The attitude of the science fiction films toward depersonalization is mixed. On the one hand, they deplore it as the ultimate horror. On the other hand, certain characteristics of the dehumanized invaders, modulated and disguised—such as the ascendancy of reason over feelings, the idealization of teamwork and the consensus-creating activities of science, a marked degree of moral simplification—are precisely traits of the savior-scientist. It is interesting that when the scientist in these films is treated negatively, it is usually done through the portrayal of an individual scientist who holes up in his laboratory and neglects his fiancée or his loving wife and children, obsessed by his daring and dangerous experiments. The scientist as a loyal member of a team, and therefore considerably less individualized, is treated quite respectfully.

There is absolutely no social criticism, of even the most implicit kind, in science fiction films. No criticism, for example, of the conditions of our society which create the impersonality and dehumanization which science fiction fantasies displace onto the influence of an alien It. Also, the notion of science as a social activity, interlocking with social and political interests, is unacknowledged. Science is simply either adventure (for good or evil) or a technical response to danger. And, typically, when the fear of science is paramount—when science is conceived of as black magic rather than white—the evil has no attribution beyond that of the perverse will of an individual scientist. In science fiction films the antithesis of black magic and white is drawn as a split between technology, which is beneficent, and the errant individual will of a lone intellectual.

Thus, science fiction films can be looked at as thematically central allegory, replete with standard modern attitudes. The theme of depersonalization (being "taken over") which I have been talking about is a new allegory reflecting the age-old awareness of man that, sane, he is always perilously close to insanity and unreason. But there is something more here than just a recent, popular image which expresses man's perennial, but largely unconscious, anxiety about his sanity. The image derives most of its power from a supplementary and historical anxiety, also not experienced *consciously* by most people, about the depersonalizing conditions of modern urban life. Similarly, it is not enough to note that science fiction allegories are one of the new myths about—that is, one of the ways of accommodating to and negating—the perennial human anxiety about death. (Myths of heaven and hell, and of ghosts, had the same function.) For, again, there is a historically specifiable twist which intensifies the anxiety. I mean, the trauma suffered by everyone in the middle of the 20th century when it became clear that, from now on to the end of human history, every person would spend his individual life under the threat not only of individual death, which is certain, but of something almost insupportable psychologically—collective incineration and extinction which could come at any time, virtually without warning.

From a psychological point of view, the imagination of disaster does not greatly differ from one period in history to another. But from a political and moral point of view, it does. The expectation of the apocalypse may be the occasion for a radical disaffiliation from society, as when thousands of Eastern European Jews in the 17th century, hearing that Sabbatai Zevi had been proclaimed the Messiah and that the end of the world was imminent, gave up their homes and businesses and began the trek to Palestine. But people take the news of their doom in diverse ways. It is reported that in 1945 the populace of Berlin received without great agitation the news that Hitler had decided to kill them all, before the Allies arrived, because they had not been worthy enough to win the war. We are, alas, more in the position of the Berliners of 1945 than of the Jews of 17th century Eastern Europe; and our response is closer to theirs, too. What I am suggesting is that the imagery of disaster in science fiction is above all the emblem of an *inadequate response.* I don't mean to bear down on the films for this. They themselves are only a sampling, stripped of sophistication, of the inadequacy of most people's response to the unassimilable terrors that infect their consciousness. The interest of the films, aside from their considerable amount of cinematic charm, consists in this intersection between a naïve and largely debased commercial art product and the most profound dilemmas of the contemporary situation.

.   .   .   .

Ours is indeed an age of extremity. For we live under continual threat of two equally fearful, but seemingly opposed, destinies: unremitting banality and inconceivable terror. It is fantasy, served out in large rations by the popular arts, which allows most people to cope with these twin specters. For one job that fantasy can do is to lift us out of the unbearably humdrum and to distract us from terrors—real or anticipated—by an escape into exotic, dangerous situations which have last-minute happy endings. But another of the things that fantasy can do is to normalize what is psychologically unbearable, thereby inuring us to it. In one case, fantasy beautifies the world. In the other, it neutralizes it.

The fantasy in science fiction films does both jobs. The films reflect worldwide anxieties, and they serve to allay them. They inculcate a strange apathy concerning the processes of radiation, contamination, and destruction which I for one find haunting and depressing. The naïve level of the films neatly tempers the sense of otherness, of alien-ness, with the grossly familiar. In particular, the dialogue of most science fiction films, which is of a monumental but often touching banality, makes them wonderfully, unintentionally funny. Lines like "Come quickly, there's a monster in my bathtub," "We must do something about this," "Wait, Professor. There's someone on the telephone," "But that's incredible," and the old American stand-by, "I hope it works!" are hilarious in the context of picturesque and deafening holocaust. Yet the films also contain something that is painful and in deadly earnest.

There is a sense in which all these movies are in complicity with the abhorrent. They neutralize it, as I have said. It is no more, perhaps, than the way all art draws its audience into a circle of complicity with the thing represented. But in these films we have to do with things which are (quite literally) unthinkable. Here, "thinking about the unthinkable"—not in the way of Herman Kahn, as a subject for calculation, but as a subject for fantasy—becomes, however inadvertently, itself a somewhat questionable act from a moral point of view. The films perpetuate clichés about identity, volition, power, knowledge, happiness, social consensus, guilt, responsibility which are, to say the least, not serviceable in our present extremity. But collective nightmares cannot be banished by demonstrating that they are, intellectually and morally, fallacious. This nightmare—the one reflected, in various registers, in the science fiction films—is too close to our reality.

LIBBY GELMAN-WAXNER

Ms. Gelman-Waxner writes a monthly column in Premiere *magazine, and although she has been unmasked as the pseudonym of Paul Rudnick, she is, like England's Dame Edna Everage, such a powerful creation that she sweeps her creator under his own rug. Libby and Dame Edna have something else in common: They are not only very funny but proceed from a nugget of truth. In a column on "Dream Dates," Gelman-Waxner paused in her praise of Dennis Quaid long enough to survey the competition: "Bruce Willis, like Richard Gere, is his own Dream Date, and William Hurt, who had DD potential, now seems more like the weird, 40-year-old graduate student your aunt Rivka would fix you up with."*

"Libby 'Noir' "

As a cultivated student of the filmic medium, I have often heard the expression *"film noir";* after seeing several current examples of this genre, I now realize that the exact translation of *film noir* is "sexy and really, really boring." *Films noirs* explore the dark underbelly of America, which certainly beats Colonial Williamsburg as a weekend getaway, and they always feature the same characters: a hot, dangerous male drifter; a hot, dangerous, bored small-town slut; and at least one disgusting fat man who gets brutally killed, right after which the drifter and the slut have really great sex, usually near a ceiling fan and venetian blinds. Everybody in *film noir* sweats a lot, and deodorant and Irish Spring are never mentioned, so maybe *film noir* also means "unpleasant to stand behind at the cash machine."

The first *film noir* I saw this month was *Wild at Heart,* which was directed by David Lynch, who also co-created the TV show *Twin Peaks.* I saw *Wild at Heart* at a brand-new multiplex in SoHo, where there is a café that serves French pastries and at least ten different bottled waters, and where at least one of the theaters is always showing a blasphemous foreign film that portrays Jesus as either a cabdriver or a teenage girl. Everyone in the audience had asymmetrical haircuts, glasses with thick black frames, and clunky rubber-soled shoes. They looked like French opium addicts, but if you ask me, they were all probably assistants at public-relations firms uptown. All of these people loved *Wild at Heart,* and they all felt that David Lynch is a quirky visionary who deals in subconscious dream imagery, and after a while, I wished I was home watching a *Golden Girls* rerun. I have never been able to sit through a whole episode of *Twin Peaks;* it's a postmodern soap opera, which means that every time someone onscreen eats a piece of apple pie, you can hear a thousand grad students start typing their doctoral dissertations on *"Twin Peaks:* David Lynch and the Semiotics of Cobbler."

In *Wild at Heart,* Nicolas Cage is the studly drifter in a snakeskin jacket, and Laura Dern is the small-town sexpot; they hop into a flashy convertible and hightail it through the South, hoping to escape Laura's nasty mother and to discover surrealistic vignettes of American grotesquerie. Nicolas and Laura have lots of sex, and the screen turns different colors, just like it did for Mitzi Gaynor in *South Pacific.* The sex is really conventional, though; only Laura is naked, and the sheets are always awkwardly tucked around anything really interesting. Eventually, supporting actors die in car accidents, or get set on fire, or have their heads blown off with shotguns, and all the people in the theater thought it was visually arresting and a stunning treatment of classic American bloodshed, which is not what they'd say about the same sort of thing in a Rambo movie, where at least it's fun and there aren't any allusions to *The Wizard of Oz.*

After Dark, My Sweet was my next *film noir,* although I suspect it might actually be some sort of NASA stress test; they could show it continually to astronauts to see how long humans can exist in space without entertainment. This movie was not just boring, it was like a two-week sleep-over visit from my aunt Frieda, my uncle Morty, who has to keep his right leg elevated so the blood clots won't reach his brain, and their son, Heshy, who has started an international computer call-board for other 42-year-olds who still live at home and are interested in cyborg comics and the Talmud. *After Dark, My Sweet* is like the fulfillment of some ancient curse; it's as if God had said, By 1990, if people are still going to the movies and not getting enough fresh air, I will send down a punishment.

Jason Patric is the hunky drifter in this movie. He's an ex-boxer with beard stubble and a crumpled brown paper bag that he carries everywhere; after a while, I started to look for the matching shoes. Jason is gorgeous beyond belief, but this is *film noir,* so he's innocent yet troubled and violent, which means a lot of squinting, as if he's trying to duplicate Patrick Swayze's EKG. How do people become drifters, anyway? Do they take an aptitude test that says, You excel at stumbling along the highway, not changing your underwear, and getting hooked up with small-time criminals? Jason joins forces with Bruce Dern, who looks like Big Bird on methadone, and Rachel Ward, who plays the local slutty alcoholic widow; between the three of them, it's like the Olympics of terrible acting, but believe me, Rachel breezes off with the gold. I don't think Rachel could believably scream for water if her hair was on fire; it's like she was put on the planet to make Ali MacGraw feel better.

Rachel, Jason, and Bruce plot to kidnap a rich little boy, and they do it and then sort of forget about the kid; it's like watching a suspenseful crime movie in which everyone has Alzheimer's. I must confess that I didn't stay to see the end of *After Dark, My Sweet,* because I felt like I was dying, and I didn't want my children to remember me as a segment on *A Current Affair* entitled "Death without Butter: Movies That Kill."

My last *film noir* was *The Hot Spot,* and like the other *noirs,* it takes place somewhere really arid, in a sort of bleached-out town completely populated by animal skulls and art directors. In this movie, Don Johnson plays the drifter, and he lives in a cheap motel room with a flashing neon sign right outside the window; sexy drifters always request that room. Don is broke, but his '40s-style wardrobe is always impeccably dry-cleaned; he gets a job as a used-car salesman and messes around with Virginia Madsen, who plays the steamy slut married to Don's boss, and also with Jennifer Connelly, who plays a beautiful, innocent girl working as an accountant. Eventually, Don robs a bank, Virginia gives her husband a heart attack by tying him to the bed and wearing lingerie, and Jennifer snatches the Olympic honors from Rachel Ward without even trying. I read that Jennifer is currently enrolled at Yale, in the tradition of Jennifer Beals and of Brooke Shields, who went to Princeton. Jennifer, you're a knockout, but get that degree.

Virginia is naked a lot in this movie; at one point, she and Don are tussling in the moonlight out at a sawmill, and she jumps into a huge hill of wood chips. Then she climbs the hill while the camera shoots her from underneath and behind; she grabs Don, and they fall into the sawdust and make churning, passionate love. Doing it in sawdust does not strike me as particularly erotic; it would be like having sex in the salad bar at Sizzler—everything would stick to you and itch. Don keeps unveiling his naked behind, as if it were an engagement ring from Fortunoff's; after about the fourth rear display, I began to wonder if Don even *had* a penis. Then I remembered that Pamela Des Barres, a famous groupie, wrote in her autobiography about how well endowed Don is—Don, she didn't write about how pink and hefty your tush is, if you catch my drift. If Virginia is going to risk a sawdust infection, or even Dutch elm disease, the least you can do is swivel.

Since I couldn't figure out why people like *film noir,* I tried to put myself, Libby, in a *film noir* situation. I pictured myself lounging between my Wamsutta percales while my husband, Josh, was out correcting overbites; I imagined that I was listless and in heat. If a drifter came to my door, I decided that the first thing I would do would be to send him out to wait on line for tickets to *Miss Saigon.* Then I would make him finish college or get some sort of vocational training, since I couldn't very well introduce him to people by saying, This is so-and-so, you'll love him, he's a drifter. Then, if he still tried to entice me into killing my husband or pulling a bank job, I would say, Excuse me, do you have any idea what it's like for a woman in prison? Listening to Jean Harris whine all day about her royalties? Discussing a possible appeal with Joel Steinberg at the prison mixer? Then, if by some mad chance the drifter did convince me to kill my husband, I'd just say, Let's wait a few years; Josh is an overweight Jewish man from a family with a history of prostate trouble—time is on our side. If the drifter wanted to have sweaty, wild sex with me while we waited, I would tell him just what I tell my adorable seven-year-old daughter, Jennifer, whenever she wants the latest thing from L.A. Gear: if you still want it a year from now, then we'll see.

Maybe I'm just not a *noir* type of person; I think that lust and destiny and doom sound like home-shopping-club colognes. *Film noir* is like Jerry Lewis: it's something French people only pretend to like in order to upset Americans. Maybe to get back at them, we should all pretend to like Isabelle Huppert movies and that new glass pyramid in front of the Louvre. That'll fix 'em, if you ask me.

DIRECTORS

Luis Buñuel

Luis Buñuel (1900–1983) has one of the most distinctive styles of all directors; it is difficult to watch even a minute or two from any of his pictures without suspecting, or being sure, that it is by him. Yet he works with a strange bluntness; he tells the story simply, as if it is a task rather than an exercise, and the characters, approached so directly, denied the usual evasions of manners and personal styles, are splayed on the screen like specimens. Buñuel regards them as ridiculous above all else, and as they parade their greeds and lusts, he is chortling at their transparency. His autobiography, which was written in close collaboration with his longtime writer Jean-Claude Carrière, ends with a beautiful notion: He fears dying because he will be forever denied the contents of tomorrow's newspaper. Here he tells of early days in Paris, when he and Salvador Dali, heady with the founding of surrealism, made one of the few short films that anyone who cares at all about the movies will sooner or later see.

from *My Last Sigh*

A few months later, I made *Un Chien andalou,* which came from an encounter between two dreams. When I arrived to spend a few days at Dali's house in Figueras, I told him about a dream I'd had in which a long, tapering cloud sliced the moon in half, like a razor blade slicing through an eye. Dali immediately told me that he'd seen a hand crawling with ants in a dream he'd had the previous night.

"And what if we started right there and made a film?" he wondered aloud.

Despite my hesitation, we soon found ourselves hard at work, and in less than a week we had a script. Our only rule was very simple: No idea or image that might lend itself to a rational explanation of any kind would be accepted. We had to open all doors to the irrational and keep only those images that surprised us, without trying to explain why. The amazing thing was that we never had the slightest disagreement; we spent a week of total identification.

"A man fires a double bass," one of us would say.

"No," replied the other, and the one who'd proposed the idea accepted the veto and felt it justified. On the other hand, when the image proposed by one was accepted by the other, it immediately seemed luminously right and absolutely necessary to the scenario.

When the script was finished, I realized that we had such an original and provocative movie that no ordinary production company would touch it. So once again I found myself asking my mother for backing, which, thanks to our sympathetic attorney, she consented to provide. I wound up taking the money back to Paris and spending half of it in my usual nightclubs; ultimately, however, I settled down and contacted the actors Pierre Batcheff and Simone Mareuil, Duverger the cameraman, and made a deal to use the Billancourt studios.

The filming took two weeks; there were only five or six of us involved, and most of the time no one quite knew what he was doing.

"Stare out the window and look as if you're listening to Wagner," I remember telling Batcheff. "No, no—not like that. Sadder. Much sadder."

Batcheff never even knew what he was supposed to be looking at, but given the technical knowledge I'd managed to pick up, Duverger and I got along famously. Dali arrived on the set a few days before the end and spent most of his time pouring wax into the eyes of stuffed donkeys. He played one of the two Marist brothers who in one scene are painfully dragged about by Batcheff. For some reason, we wound up cutting the scene. You can see Dali in the distance, however, running with my fiancée, Jeanne, after the hero's fatal fall.

Once the film was edited, we had no idea what to do with it. I'd kept it fairly secret from the Montparnasse contingent, but one day at the Dôme, Thériade, from the *Cahiers d'Art,* who'd heard rumors about it, introduced me to Man Ray. Ray had just finished shooting *Les Mystères du château de Dé,* a documentary on the de Noailles and their friends, and was looking for a second film to round out the program. Man Ray and I got together a few days later at La Coupole, where he introduced me to a fellow surrealist, Louis Aragon, who had the most elegant French manners I'd ever seen. When I told them that *Un Chien andalou* was in many ways a surrealist film, they agreed to go to a screening the following day at the Studio des Ursulines and to start planning the premiere.

More than anything else, surrealism was a kind of call heard by certain people everywhere—in the United States, in Germany, Spain, Yugoslavia—who, unknown to one another, were already practicing instinctive forms of irrational expression. Even the poems I'd published in Spain before I'd heard of the surrealist movement were responses to that call which eventually brought all of us together in Paris. While Dali and I were making *Un Chien andalou* we used a kind of automatic writing. There was indeed something in the air, and my connection with the surrealists in many ways determined the course of my life.

My first meeting with the group took place at their regular café, the Cyrano, on the place Blanche, where I was introduced to Max Ernst, André Breton, Paul Eluard, Tristan Tzara, René Char, Pierre Unik, Yves Tanguy, Jean Arp, Maxime Alexandre, and Magritte—everyone, in other words, except Benjamin Péret, who was in Brazil. We all shook hands, and they bought me a drink, promising not to miss the premiere of the film that Aragon and Man Ray had already spoken of so highly.

The opening of *Un Chien andalou* took place at the Ursulines, and was attended by the *tout*-Paris—some aristocrats, a sprinkling of well-established artists (among them Picasso, Le Corbusier, Cocteau, Christian Bérard, and the composer Georges Auric), and the surrealist group in toto. I was a nervous wreck. In fact, I hid behind the screen with the record player, alternating Argentinian tangos with *Tristan and Isolde.* Before the show, I'd put some stones in my pocket to throw at the audience in case of disaster, remembering that a short time before, the surrealists had hissed Germaine Dulac's *La Coquille et le clergyman,* based on a script by Antonin Artaud, which I'd rather liked. I expected the worst; but, happily, the stones weren't necessary. After the film ended, I listened to the prolonged applause and dropped my projectiles discreetly, one by one, on the floor behind the screen.

My entry into the surrealist group took place very naturally. I was simply admitted to the daily meetings at the Cyrano or at André Breton's at 42, rue Fontaine. The Cyrano was an authentic Pigalle café, frequented by the working class, prostitutes, and pimps. People drank Pernod, or aperitifs like *picon*-beer with a hint of grenadine (Yves Tanguy's favorite; he'd swallow one, then a second, and by the third he had to hold his nose!).

The daily gathering was very much like a Spanish peña. We read and discussed certain articles, talked about the surrealist journal, debated any critical action we felt might be needed, letters to be written, demonstrations attended. When we discussed confidential issues, we met in Breton's studio, which was close by. I remember one amusing misunderstanding that arose because, since I was usually one of the last to arrive, I shook hands only with those people nearest me, then waved to Breton, who was always too far away to reach. "Does Buñuel have something against me?" he asked one day, very out of sorts. Finally, someone explained that I hated the French custom of shaking hands all around every time anyone went anywhere; it seemed so silly to me that I outlawed the custom on the set when we were filming *Cela s'appelle l'aurore.*

INGMAR BERGMAN

I was lucky enough to spend a day once in Stockholm's Film House, on the set of Ingmar Bergman's Face to Face. *It was as comfortable as a family reunion, and indeed many of the crew members—from the carpenter to the woman who served the tea every afternoon— had been with Bergman for more than twenty years. At noon he let me join him in his office, a monk's cell furnished with two straight chairs, a simple table, and an army cot. On the table were a box of Dutch chocolates, two apples, a banana, and a copy of the script. He told me that he found the human face the most fascinating possible subject for the camera. A few days earlier, he said, he had been watching Antonioni's* The Passenger *on TV, and it was followed by an interview with the director. Said Bergman: "I didn't hear a word of what he was saying, because I was looking so closely at his face, his eyes. The ten minutes he was on the screen were more fascinating than any of his, or my, work." For Bergman, the process of making a film often involved such journeys into the nature of being human. Here he describes a day on the set of* Fanny and Alexander *(1982), the last film he directed.*

from *The Magic Lantern*

I have chosen a day's filming in 1982. According to my notes, it was cold— twenty degrees Celsius below zero. I woke up as usual at five o'clock, which means I was woken, drawn as if in a spiral by some evil spirit out of my deepest sleep, and I was wide awake. To combat hysteria and the sabotage of my bowels, I got out of bed immediately and for a few moments stood quite still on the floor with my eyes closed. I went over my actual situation. How was my body, how was my soul and, most of all, what had got to be done today? I established that my nose was blocked (the dry air), my left testicle hurt (probably cancer), my hip ached (the same old pain), and there was a ringing in my bad ear (unpleasant but not worth bothering about). I also registered that my hysteria was under control, my fear of stomach cramp not too intensive. The day's work consisted of the scene between Ismael and Alexander, in *Fanny and Alexander,* and I was worried because the scene in question might be beyond the capacity of my brave young actor in the title rôle, Bertil Guve. But the coming collaboration with Stina Ekblad as Ismael gave me a jolt of happy expectation. The first inspection of the day was thus completed and had produced a small but nevertheless positive profit: if Stina is as good as I think, I can manage Bertil-Alexander. I had already thought out two strategies: one with equally good actors, the other with a principal actor and a secondary actor.

Now it was a question of taking things calmly, of being calm.

At seven o'clock, my wife Ingrid and I had breakfast together in friendly silence. My stomach was acquiescent and had forty-five minutes in which to create hell. While I was waiting for it to decide on its attitude, I read the morning papers. At a quarter to eight, I was fetched and driven to the studio, which at that particular time was in Sundbyberg and was owned by Europafilm Ltd.

Those once so reputable studios were decaying. They produced mainly videos, and any staff left from the days of film were disorientated and downhearted. The actual film studio was dirty, not sound-proof, and badly maintained. The editing room, at first sight comically luxurious, turned out to be useless. The projectors were wretched, incapable of keeping either definition or stills. The sound was bad, the ventilation did not function and the carpet was filthy.

At exactly nine o'clock, the day's filming started. It was important that our collective start was punctual. Discussions and uncertainties had to take place *outside* this innermost circle of concentration. From this moment on, we were a complicated but uniformly functioning machine, the aim of which was to produce living pictures.

The work quickly settled into a calm rhythm, and intimacy was uncomplicated. The only thing to disturb this day was the lack of sound-proofing and the lack of respect for the red lamps outside in the corridor and elsewhere. Otherwise it was a day of modest delight. From the very first moment, we all felt Stina Ekblad's remarkable empathy with the ill-fated Ismael and, best of all, Bertil-Alexander had at once accepted the situation. In that strange way children have, he gave expression to a complicated mixture of curiosity and fear with touching genuineness.

The rehearsals moved on smoothly and a quiet cheerfulness reigned, our creativity dancing along. Anna Asp had created a stimulating set for us. Sven Nykvist had done the lighting with that intuition which is difficult to describe, but which is his hallmark and makes him one of the leading lighting camera men in the world, perhaps the best. If you asked him how he did it, he would point out some simple ground rules (which have been of great use to me in my work in the theatre). He could not—or had no wish to—describe the actual secret. If for some reason he was disturbed, pressurized or ill at ease, everything went wrong and he would have to start all over again from the beginning. Confidence and total security prevailed in our collaboration. Occasionally I grieve over the fact that we shall never work together again. I grieve when I think back to a day such as the one I have depicted. There's a sensual satisfaction in working in close union with strong, independent and creative people: actors, assistants, electricians, production staff, props people, make-up staff, costume designers, all those personalities who populate the day and make it possible to get through.

Sometimes I really feel the loss of everything and everyone concerned. I understand what Fellini means when he says filming to him is a way of life and I also understand his little story about Anita Ekberg. Her last scene in *La Dolce Vita* took place in a car erected in the studio. When the scene had been taken and filming was over as far as she was concerned, she started crying and refused to leave the car, gripping firmly onto the wheel. She had to be carried out of the studio with gentle force.

Sometimes there is a special happiness in being a film director. An unrehearsed expression is born just like that, and the camera registers that expression. That was exactly what happened that day. Unprepared and unrehearsed, Alexander turned very pale, a look of sheer agony appearing on his face. The camera registered the moment. The agony, the intangible, was there for a few seconds and never returned. Neither was it there earlier, but the strip of film caught the moment. That is when I think days and months of predictable routine have paid off. It is possible I live for those brief moments.

Like a pearl fisher.

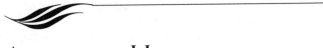

ALFRED HITCHCOCK

Sir Alfred Hitchcock (1899–1980) devised a certain number of things to say about his movies, and he said them over and over again all his life. I interviewed him twice, and I was never able to get him to say anything I had not already read, in one form or another, in books about him. Even his fellow director François Truffaut, in the wonderful book-length Hitchcock/Truffaut, *is able to pry revelations out of him only after great pains, and most of the interesting things said about Hitchcock movies in that book are said by*

Truffaut, with Hitchcock responding in surprise or gratification. What I cannot decide is whether Hitchcock really did believe in his oft-repeated methods and formulas or whether they were designed to throw us off the track—since in Hitchcock's work there is always that sinister sense that something else is going on beneath the surface. Here is an article printed in Sight & Sound *in 1937, with Hitchcock already polished as he reels off his familiar assertion that the real work on his films is all in the preparation, with the actual filming an anticlimax. His mistrust of long takes is revealing; they give the actor too much freedom, we can guess, from the control Hitchcock maintains with his story-boarded scripts that define every shot.*

"My Own Methods"

Many people think a film director does all his work in the studio, drilling the actors, making them do what he wants. That is not at all true of my own methods, and I can write only of my own methods. I like to have a film complete in my mind before I go on the floor. Sometimes the first idea one has of a film is of a vague pattern, a sort of haze with a certain shape. There is possibly a colourful opening developing into something more intimate; then, perhaps in the middle, a progression to a chase or some other adventure; and sometimes at the end the big shape of a climax, or maybe some twist or surprise. You see this hazy pattern, and then you have to find a narrative idea to suit it. Or a story may give you an idea first and you have to develop it into a pattern.

Imagine an example of a standard plot—let us say a conflict between love and duty. This idea was the origin of my first talkie, *Blackmail*. The hazy pattern one saw beforehand was duty—love—love versus duty—and finally either duty or love, one or the other. The whole middle section was built up on the theme of love versus duty, after duty and love had been introduced separately in turn. So I had first to put on the screen an episode expressing duty.

I showed the arrest of a criminal by Scotland Yard detectives, and tried to make it as concrete and detailed as I could. You even saw the detectives take the man to the lavatory to wash his hands—nothing exciting, just the routine of duty. Then the young detective says he's going out that evening with his girl, and the sequence ends, pointing on from duty to love. Then you start showing the relationship between the detective and his girl: they are middle-class people. The love theme doesn't run smoothly; there is a quarrel and the girl goes off by herself, just because the young man has kept her waiting a few minutes. So your story starts; the girl falls in with the villain—he tries to seduce her and she kills him. Now you've got your problem prepared. Next morning, as soon as the detective is put on to the murder case, you have your conflict—love versus duty. The audience know that he will be trying to track down his own girl, who has done the murder, so you sustain their interest: they wonder what will happen next.

The blackmailer was really a subsidiary theme. I wanted him to go through and expose the girl. That was my idea of how the story ought to end. I wanted the pursuit to be after the girl, not after the blackmailer. That would have brought the conflict on to a climax, with the young detective, ahead of the others, trying to push the girl out through a window to get her away, and the girl turning round and saying: "You can't do that—I must give myself up." Then the rest of the police arrive, misinterpret what he is doing, and say, "Good man, you've got her," not knowing the relationship between them. Now the reason for the opening comes to light. You repeat every shot used first to illustrate the duty theme, only now it is the girl who is the criminal. The young man is there ostensibly as a detective, but of course the audience know he is in love with the girl. The girl is locked up in her cell and the two detectives walk away, and the older one says, "Going out with your girl tonight?" The younger one shakes his head. "No. Not tonight."

That was the ending I wanted for *Blackmail,* but I had to change it for commercial reasons. The girl couldn't be left to face her fate. And that shows you how the films suffer from their own power of appealing to millions. They could often be subtler than they are, but their own popularity won't let them.

But to get back to the early work on a film. With the help of my wife, who does the technical continuity, I plan out a script very carefully, hoping to follow it exactly, all the way through, when shooting starts. In fact, this working on the script is the real making of the film, for me. When I've done it, the film is finished already in my mind. Usually, too, I don't find it necessary to do more than supervise the editing myself.

Settings, of course, come into the preliminary plan, and usually I have fairly clear ideas about them; I was an art student before I took up with films. Sometimes I even think of backgrounds first. *The Man Who Knew Too Much* started like that; I looked in my mind's eye at snowy Alps and dingy London alleys, and threw my characters into the middle of the contrast. Studio settings, however, are often a problem; one difficulty is that extreme effects—extremes of luxury or extremes of squalor—are much the easiest to register on the screen. If you try to reproduce the average sitting-room in Golders Green or Streatham it is apt to come out looking like nothing in particular, just nondescript. It is true that I have tried lately to get interiors giving a real lower-middle-class atmosphere—for instance, the Verlocs' living room in *Sabotage*—but there's always a certain risk in giving your audience humdrum truth.

However, in time the script and the sets are finished somehow and we are ready to start shooting. One great problem that occurs at once, and keeps on occurring, is to get the players to adapt themselves to film technique. Many of them, of course, come from the stage; they are not cinema-minded at all. So, quite naturally, they like to play long scenes straight ahead. But if I have to shoot a long scene continuously I always feel I am losing grip on it, from a cinematic point of view. The camera, I feel, is simply standing there, *hoping* to catch something with a visual point to it. I want to put my film together on the screen, not simply to photograph something that has been put together already in the form of a long piece of stage acting. This is what gives an effect of life to a picture—the feeling that when you see it on the screen you are watching something that has been conceived and brought to birth directly in visual terms.

You can see an example of what I mean in *Sabotage*. Just before Verloc is killed there is a scene made up entirely of short pieces of film, separately photographed. This scene has to show how Verloc comes to be killed—how the thought of killing him arises in Sylvia Sidney's mind and connects itself with the carving knife she uses when they sit down to dinner. But the sympathy of the audience has to be kept with Sylvia Sidney; it must be clear that Verloc's death, finally, is an accident. So, as she serves at the table, you see her unconsciously serving vegetables with the carving knife, as though her hand were keeping hold of the knife of its own accord. The camera cuts from her hand to her eyes and back to her hand; then back to her eyes as she suddenly becomes aware of the knife, making its error. Then to a normal shot—the man unconcernedly eating; then back to the hand holding the knife. In an older style of acting Sylvia would have had to show the audience what was passing in her mind by exaggerated facial expression. But people today in real life often don't show their feelings in their faces: so the film treatment showed the audience her mind through her hand, through its unconscious grasp on the knife. Now the camera moves again to Verloc—back to the knife—back again to his face. You see him seeing the knife, realising its implication. The tension between the two is built up with the knife as its focus.

Now when the camera has immersed the audience so closely in a scene such as this, it can't instantly become objective again. It must broaden the movement of the scene without loosening the tension. Verloc gets up and walks round the table, coming so close to the camera that you feel, if you are sitting in the audience, almost as though you must move back to make room for him. Then the camera moves to Sylvia Sidney again, then returns to the subject—the knife.

So you gradually build up the psychological situation, piece by piece, using the camera to emphasise first one detail, then another. The point is to draw the audience right inside the situation instead of leaving them to watch it from outside, from a distance. And you can do this only by breaking the action up into details and cutting from one to the other, so that each detail is forced in turn on the attention of the audience and reveals its psychological meaning. If you played the whole scene straight through, and simply made a photographic record of it with the camera always in one position, you would lose your power over the audience. They would watch the scene without becoming really involved in it, and you would have no means of concentrating their attention on those particular visual details which make them feel what the characters are feeling.

One way of using the camera to give emphasis is the reaction shot. By the reaction shot I mean any close-up which illustrates an event by showing instantly the reaction to it of a person or a group. The door opens for someone to come in, and before showing who it is you cut to the expressions of the persons already in the room. Or, while one person is talking, you keep your camera on someone else who is listening. This over-running of one person's image with another person's voice is a method peculiar to the talkies; it is one of the devices which help the talkies to tell a story faster than a silent film could tell it, and faster than it could be told on the stage.

Or, again, you can use the camera to give emphasis whenever the attention of the audience has to be focused for a moment on a certain player. There is no need for him to raise his voice or move to the centre of the stage or do anything dramatic. A close-up will do it all for him—will give him, so to speak, the stage all to himself.

I must say that in recent years I have come to make much less use of obvious camera devices. I have become more commercially-minded; afraid that anything at all subtle may be missed. I have learnt from experience how easily small touches are overlooked.

The film always has to deal in exaggerations. Its methods reflect the simple contrasts of black and white photography. One advantage of colour is that it would give you more intermediate shades. I should never want to fill the screen with colour: it ought to be used economically—to put new words into the screen's visual language when there's a need for them. You could start a colour film with a boardroom scene: sombre panelling and furniture, the directors all in dark clothes and white collars. Then the chairman's wife comes in, wearing a red hat. She takes the attention of the audience at once, just because of that one note of colour.

A journalist once asked me about distorted sound—a device I tried in *Black-mail* when the word "knife" hammers on the consciousness of the girl at breakfast on the morning after the murder. Again, I think this kind of effect may be justified. There have always been occasions when we have needed to show a phantasmagoria of the mind in terms of visual imagery. So we may want to show someone's mental state by letting him listen to some sound—let us say church bells—and making them clang with distorted insistence in his head. But on the whole nowadays I try to tell a story in the simplest possible way, so that I can feel sure it will hold the attention of any audience and won't puzzle them.

I know there are critics who ask why lately I have made only thrillers. Am I satisfied, they say, with putting on the screen the equivalent merely of popular novelettes? Part of the answer is that I am out to get the best stories I can which will suit the film medium, and I have usually found it necessary to take a hand in writing them myself. There is a shortage of good writing for the screen. In this country we can't usually afford to employ large writing staffs, so I have had to join in and become a writer myself. I choose crime stories because that is the kind of story I can write, or help to write, myself—the kind of story I can turn most easily into a successful film. It is the same with Charles Bennett, who has so often worked with me; he is essentially a writer of melodrama. I am ready to use other stories, but I can't find writers who will give them to me in a suitable form.

Sometimes I have been asked what films I should make if I were free to do exactly as I liked without having to think about the box-office. There are several examples I can give very easily. For one thing, I should like to make travel films with a personal element in them. Or I should like to do a verbatim of a celebrated trial. The Thompson-Bywaters case, for instance. The cinema could reconstruct the whole story. Or there is the fire at sea possibility—that has never been tackled seriously on the screen. It might be too terrifying for some audiences, but it would make a great subject worthwhile.

British producers are often urged to make more films about characteristic phases of English life.

Why, they are asked, do we see so little of the English farmer or the English seaman? Or is there not plenty of good material in the great British industries—in mining or shipbuilding or steel? One difficulty here is that English audiences seem to take more interest in American life—I suppose because it has a novelty value. They are rather easily bored by everyday scenes in their own country. But I certainly should like to make a film of the Derby, only it might not be quite in the popular class. It would be hard to invent a Derby story that wasn't hackneyed, conventional. I would rather do it more as a documentary—a sort of pageant, an animated modern version of Frith's "Derby Day." I would show everything that goes on all round the course, but without a story.

Perhaps the average audience isn't ready for that, yet. Popular taste, all the same, does move; today you can put over scenes that would have been ruled out a few years ago. Particularly towards comedy, nowadays, there is a different attitude. You can get comedy out of your stars, and you used not to be allowed to do anything which might knock the glamour off them.

In 1926 I made a film called *Downhill,* from a play by Ivor Novello, who acted in the film himself, with Ian Hunter and Isabel Jeans. There was a sequence showing a quarrel between Hunter and Novello. It started as an ordinary fight; then they began throwing things at one another. They tried to pick up heavy pedestals to throw and the pedestals bowled them over. In other words I made it comic.

I even put Hunter into a morning coat and striped trousers because I felt that a man never looks so ridiculous as when he is well dressed and fighting. This whole scene was cut out; they said I was guying Ivor Novello. It was ten years before its time.

I think public taste is turning to like comedy and drama more mixed up; and this is another move away from the conventions of the stage. In a play your divisions are much more rigid; you have a scene in one key—then curtain, and after an interval another scene starts. In a film you keep your whole action flowing; you can have comedy and drama running together and weave them in and out. Audiences are much readier now than they used to be for sudden changes of mood; and this means more freedom for a director. The art of directing for the commercial market is to know just how far you can go. In many ways I am freer now to do what I want to do than I was a few years ago. I hope in time to have more freedom still—if audiences will give it to me.

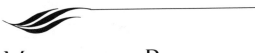

MICHAEL POWELL

The British director Michael Powell had a career of dazzling success, followed by puzzling failure and then by the scandal of his 1950 film Peeping Tom, *which received some of the most scathing reviews in London history. Then there was a period in which his films (made in partnership with the writer Emeric Pressburger, as the Archers) seemed all but forgotten, save for the durable classics* The Red Shoes *and* Black Narcissus. *Powell was rescued from obscurity and relative poverty first by the film critic David Thomson, whose* Biographical Dictionary of Film *contained a glowing entry about the director. Powell wrote thanking Thomson, who invited him to teach at Dartmouth College. The trip to America led to Powell's meeting Martin Scorsese, a devotee of the Archers films since he was eleven or twelve years old, and Scorsese's editor, Thelma Schoonmaker, who eventually became Powell's wife. The two directors made laser disc versions of several Powell films, discussing them on a parallel sound track in intriguing and detailed analyses. Powell's life in the cinema began in the silent era and included a stretch as the stills man for Alfred Hitchcock. Hitchcock left England to work in Hollywood in the late 1930s; Powell found he was not suited to the climate of big studios and powerful producers, as his memories of David O. Selznick illustrate.*

from *A Life in Movies*

There was nothing invisible about David O. Selznick. He came to meet the audience beaming, with hands outstretched, like Elmer Gantry. He was certain of his mission, which was to make great films. For him, Great was Big, and this confusion of the two adjectives was to haunt him all his life and prevent him ever becoming Great, although he was certainly Big. He achieved the ultimate in Bigness with his production of Margaret Mitchell's *Gone with the Wind,* but before that he had left his father-in-law's stables and set up for himself down the road as an independent producer. There he had surprised everybody by producing some excellent hard-hitting comedies like *Nothing Sacred,* starring Fredric March and Carole Lombard, and by signing up Alfred Hitchcock and bringing him over from England to direct Daphne du Maurier's *Rebecca,* starring Joan Fontaine and Laurence Olivier. Vivien Leigh accompanied Larry on this trip to Hollywood and in this way met Selznick, which resulted in her being cast as Scarlett O'Hara in *Gone with the Wind. Rebecca* was a great success and, as I have already related, Hitchcock stayed with Selznick through the war, learning the Hollywood game and assembling his forces around him, including stars like Cary Grant, James Stewart and Ingrid Bergman.

Somewhere about 1943 or 1944 Henry King, one of the great old-timers, directed a film for Fox about Saint Bernadette of Lourdes, from a book entitled *The Song of Bernadette.* The part of the peasant girl who has a vision of the Virgin Mary was played by an actress hitherto unknown, Jennifer Jones. It made her a star overnight. She was one of the most beautiful and talented young creatures that I have ever seen. She had the grace, strength and agility of an untamed animal, and I never tired of watching her. At the time she rocketed to stardom she appeared to be a teenager, but she had actually been married for four years to an actor, Robert Walker, and had two sons by him. He was a sensitive and intelligent young man in steady demand, and had already been spotted by Hitchcock who played him in one of his more popular melodramas, *Strangers on a Train.* That film, like *Bernadette,* was in black and white. It must be remembered that at this period most films were in black and white, but Dr. Kalmus and his wife, Nathalie, had given us a long lead in England by establishing a Technicolor lab at Heathrow just before the war and were anxious to help us in any way they could to make big films in colour. If you are a film-maker, you think in black and white or you think in colour. The Archers thought in colour from *The Thief of Bagdad* onwards.

Selznick had also experimented in colour with his comedies and, of course, the monumental *Gone with the Wind* had to be in colour. Scarlett O'Hara and

Rhett Butler were unthinkable in black and white. But big films like the Hitchcock productions of *Rebecca* or *Spellbound* were still being made in black and white, particularly since Hitch thought his stories out in terms of black and white images and was uncomfortable in colour. His later films never showed a flair for colour, and his most commercial film, *Psycho,* was shot in black and white with a television crew.

When David O. first met Jennifer Jones, he went off the deep end. The effect upon this megalomaniac was terrible. Her name was Phyllis Walker at that time, and he had created the name of Jennifer Jones for her and then badgered Henry King and Twentieth Century-Fox to cast her in *The Song of Bernadette*[,] for which she had won an Oscar. She triumphed again in *Since You Went Away* and Selznick started to plan a new production around her. It had to have his greatest male star in it, Gregory Peck. It had to have a great director . . . it had to have *three* great directors. He told her that he would make her the greatest star of the world. His intentions were obvious, but she refused to have anything to do with him. She told him she was happily married and had a family, and I don't suppose he heard a word of it. She was under contract to him, and completely at his mercy as far as work was concerned. Whether she liked it or not, she had to be in this film that he was preparing for her. There was no escape.

It was a tiny story, not much more than an anecdote, but he blew it up until it became almost another *Gone with the Wind*. She was to play a part-Indian girl and Greg the young rancher. It was set in the Southwest, and was a story of lust and dust and rape, and was to be in Technicolor. King Vidor, one of the greatest of early directors, was to direct it. Later, Josef von Sternberg, the one and only Josef von Sternberg, was brought in to advise on the production. After Vidor left the film William Dieterle was brought in to complete it.

It was the most outrageous courtship. Caught in the Hollywood net, the girl struggled desperately to escape the huntsman, but her struggles and appeals for mercy were greeted by an avalanche of presents and another million dollars on the budget of the film. I really believe that David O. added a train wreck to the picture because she had refused him the night before. In the end, of course, he triumphed, and by the time the film stopped rolling his wife, Irene, had left him and the actress's husband was no longer on the scene.

You might have thought that these Aeschylean results of his passion would have given him pause, but not a bit of it. He had spent millions to put her on a throne of blood for everybody to see. He had made her his mistress. Now she must be his wife. This man was capable of a genuine grand passion. He had possessed her body, now she must possess him, body and soul.

She refused. He insisted. He couldn't understand that he was an object of horror in her eyes. For the next four years, wherever they went, whatever they were doing, he continued to pester her to marry him. He thought of little else day and night. He never let it drop. What a candidate for *La Comédie Humaine*!

The film, of course, was *Duel in the Sun.* I have described how Emeric and I, visiting Hollywood for the first time in 1945 in search of an American girl who turned out to be Kim Hunter, visited Hitchcock at the Selznick Studios and met David O., who insisted on showing us his favourite sequences from *Duel in the Sun,* which was then in production. It had been an interesting experience to sit with this big boyish man while he acted out his fantasies with the two people on the screen. First he showed us the rape sequence. The young rancher comes into the room where the part-Indian girl is scrubbing the floor. He does the cigarette bit, smoke through the nostrils, the lot, and stands watching her. Conscious of his glance[,] she turns away from him and the swing of her hips as she works gives him other ideas. He throws away his cigarette, grabs her, and they struggle. I glanced at David O. He was watching the screen intently. He wasn't in the least interested in my reaction. When the rape was over he rang the projectionist and said, "OK, run the duel sequence." He sat back. This was his favourite bit. We sat, stunned with boredom, while mile after mile of film was unrolled of Jennifer Jones crawling up a mountain with a Winchester rifle, and Gregory Peck crawling down the mountain with another Winchester rife. When they finally opened fire on each other, Emeric whispered to me, "What a pity they didn't shoot the screenwriter."

I thought of the hot splintered rocks under the Arizona sun, Jennifer Jones's bleeding hands, knees, elbows, her face as she dragged herself up the mountain, trying to act, desperately hoping for the director to say, "Cut!" The reel finished abruptly. I said chattily, "Poor girl. You certainly made her work for her living."

The great David O. took a long draw on his cigarette, nodded and drawled, "Yeah, the poor kid took quite a beating."

Duel in the Sun would have disgraced any B-movie. David O. thought he could disguise this by hiring the best director and throwing in a perfectly gratuitous train wreck, which got a roar of laughter at the Press Show in London, together with a sunset sequence which must have emptied the Technicolor dye vats for several months. Not content with that, he added a line of dialogue to the sequence: "There's a strange glow in the sky tonight," which brought the house down. All through the film we felt that the producer was trying to pin the word "epic" on to a plot that even Richard Wagner would have scorned to have cluttering up his studio. The final film was a piece of pulp bound in morocco.

All through his life David O. was dogged by this confusion between Bigness and Greatness. He wasn't content to have made a success with Jennifer. Now he wanted to make an epic. Eventually he settled upon a story which could have been told in ten lines, about a girl all of whose problems were solved by a tidal wave. Christopher Miles's beautiful film, *The Virgin and the Gypsy,* from the story by D. H. Lawrence, has a similar construction; so has my own *I Know Where I'm Going!* In the one a dam burst comes roaring down the valley, washing the virgin into bed with the gypsies, in the other the principals get involved in a giant whirlpool. Both these films were loved by audiences, and I am sure David O. wanted audiences to love *Portrait of Jennie*. But his passion for Bigness, as opposed to Greatness, was too strong for him. He forgot his original intention—of creating a great film which would make Jennifer the biggest star in the Hollywood heavens—and spent all his money on the tidal wave, which was very fine in its way but which crashed down into empty cinemas because the audience, who liked stories and didn't get one, had gone home.

On the evidence, I think we must come to the surprising conclusion that the great David O. Selznick was a big fraud. He was a producer like other Hollywood producers: a packager, a memo-writer, a picker of other men's brains—not a creative person at all. When he worked with good craftsmen—Victor Fleming, Alfred Hitchcock, Howard Hawks, Ben Hecht, George Cukor, Carol Reed, Powell and Pressburger—he made good pictures. When he didn't, he didn't. He was a great director of other directors. After seeing their dailies he would send them page after page of criticisms until they threatened to walk out, and frequently did. Actors and actresses refused to perform if he appeared on the set, so he had to sneak in unobserved and hide behind the flats if he wanted to know what was going on. He was a pain in the neck.

JOHN HOUSEMAN

Orson Welles's Citizen Kane *routinely places first on lists of the greatest films of all time. It would also place high on any list of the best-documented films ever made because most of Welles's associates (Robert Wise, Richard Wilson, and John Houseman among them) had long and deep memories. Houseman (1902–1988) was Welles's associate in the Mercury Theater's stage and radio productions and had joined him in Hollywood, where the Mercury group was preparing a new movie. As this selection opens, Houseman is recalling how the idea for* Kane *occurred to Herman Mankiewicz (who was to share the screenplay credit with Welles) and how it was shaped into the film. Mankiewicz's inspiration was the newspaper tycoon William Randolph Hearst. Mankiewicz was a close friend of Hearst's mistress, Marion Davies, and it is Hollywood lore that during a formal dinner at Hearst's San Simeon estate, Mankiewicz, who had drunk too much, threw up and then observed optimistically, "Well, at least I brought up the white wine with the fish."*

from *Run-through*

In one of its earlier versions, the subject of this prismatic revelation had been a celebrated criminal like John Dillinger, whose personality and motivations were to be discovered successively, though not necessarily chronologically, through the eyes of his doting mother, the brother who hated him, a member of his gang, his childhood sweetheart, the FBI man who trailed him on his final flight and the woman who had lived with him for the last month of his life before turning him in for the reward. Then, while talking with Orson one day, an infinitely better idea had come to him. As a former newspaperman and an avid reader of contemporary history, he had long been fascinated by the American phenomenon of William Randolph Hearst. Unlike my friends of the Left to whom Hearst was now the archenemy, fascist isolationist and labor baiter, Mankiewicz remembered the years when Hearst had announced himself as the working man's friend and a political progressive. He had also observed him as a member of the film colony—grandiose, aging and vulnerable in the immensity of his reconstructed palace at San Simeon. By applying his "prism" notion to a figure of such complexity and stature and adding to it the charisma inherent in the public and private personality of Orson Welles, the possibility of a rich and unusual movie became apparent.

Welles, in his desperate search for a film subject, had snapped at it instantly. So did I when I heard it. After Mank and I had talked for several hours and Sarah had sent dinner up to the room, I phoned Orson from his bedside and told him I was ready to try. He arrived with a magnum of champagne, and we talked on until Sarah threw us out. The next day—no longer as president but as a writer—I made a deal with Mercury Productions for a period of twelve weeks. At Mank's insistence and remembering how badly I myself had worked with Orson peering over my shoulder, it was clearly stated in the agreement that we would do our work without interference. Welles would be shown what there was of the script after six weeks; the rest of it, if he decided he wanted to continue, when we were finished. It was felt by everyone, especially Sarah, that our only hope of getting such a difficult script done in such a limited time* was to move Mankiewicz out of his natural habitat—away from distractions and temptations of all sorts. The retreat chosen for us was a guest ranch in the Mesa country near Victorville at the top of the Cajon Pass.

Two days later, we set out for the San Bernardino Mountains in a small car-

---

*Under the luxurious, highly organized studio system of the day it was not uncommon for a script to be prepared over a period of from nine to eighteen months by five or six different writers.

avan that consisted of a studio limousine containing Mankiewicz, prone and protesting in the back seat, with a trained nurse and two pairs of crutches in the front, and a convertible driven by myself, containing a secretary, a typewriter and three cases of stationery and research material. That night the limousine departed and the next day we went to work.

The Campbell Ranch was owned and run by an intellectual couple, both lawyers, from Los Angeles. Our life was austere but comfortable; the food monotonous but adequate; the climate temperate, dry and perfect for work, with no distractions for a hundred miles around. Since we were there between seasons we had the place almost to ourselves during the week: weekends were crowded and there were musicales, symposia and folk dancing at night, from which we were excused on account of Mank's leg. He and I shared a bungalow with two bedrooms and a living room which we used as a study. His nurse was a long-suffering German body whom Mankiewicz summoned at all hours of the day and night for unnecessary services. The secretary, discovered and briefed by Sarah, was a patient, efficient, nice-looking English girl named Rita Alexander, married to a refugee recently arrived from Europe. No pair of internal revenue agents could have been more diligent in their daily inspection of Mank's room for intoxicants. This precaution proved unnecessary. With no family to make him feel guilty, no employer to hate and no one to compete with except an incomprehensible, cultivated, half-gentile hybrid with a British upper-class accent, the mental and emotional energy which had been squandered for years in self-generated conflicts and neurotic disorders was now concentrated on the single task of creating our script. After so many fallow years his fertility was amazing.

We started with the image of a man—a giant, a tycoon, a glamor figure, a controller of public opinion, a legend in his own lifetime—who had entered the world with all possible advantages, exploited them to the full, yet failed to achieve most of what he really wanted from life—including love. As we talked we asked each other how this man had got to be the way he was, made the choices he did. In the process we discovered what persons were associated with him; we learned what brought them together and what he did with them and to them over the years. In deciding who was qualified, personally and historically, to tell his story and reflect his image, in selecting the "prisms" which would most clearly reveal the parts from which we must finally create a whole, we found the dramatic structure of the film gradually asserting itself.

By trial and error we reduced the number of principal witnesses to five— each with different attitudes and subjective versions of the events of this man's life: the lawyer-guardian, who had observed him with exasperated and impotent disapproval in childhood, at the height of his fortunes and in his final, predictable collapse; his manager, who followed him with slavish and admiring devotion from the beginning of his career through his greatest triumphs and down again; the friend who understood him better than anyone else and who, for that reason, finally split with him; his mistress, whom he came closest to loving and who, through no fault of her own, helped to destroy him and finally left him; the servant, who saw only the ruin and the folly and the lonely end.

In the brouhaha that preceded and followed the first Hollywood press showings of *Citizen Kane*, amid the accusations and denials, the massive pressures and the truculent refutations, the whole question of Kane's identification with Hearst became wildly confused. The truth is simple: for the basic concept of Charles Foster Kane and for the main lines and significant events of his public life, Mankiewicz used as his model the figure of William Randolph Hearst. To this were added incidents and details invented or derived from other sources.

The main parallels are obvious. Both Kane and Hearst, as young men, entered the newspaper field by taking over a dying metropolitan daily into which each poured his inherited treasure at the rate of one million dollars a year. The calculated sensationalism, the use of patriotism as a circulation builder—these form part of the Hearst legend to which were grafted anecdotes from other giants of journalism, including Pulitzer, Northcliffe and Mank's first boss, Herbert Bayard Swope. Kane's political career and Hearst's are similar: Hearst ran on a reform ticket for mayor and then for governor of New York. (According to journalistic legend he had two special editions of the *Journal* ready to go to press on election night—one headed HEARST WINS, the other FRAUD AT POLLS.) He was defeated (not, like Kane, following a sex scandal) as proof of the American political axiom that money and power cannot, by themselves, win the people's vote. Both Hearst and Kane had unsuccessful first marriages; both took up in middle age with blonde young women whose professional careers (in different fields) they obstinately and vainly promoted in a tradition of American tycoons that includes McCormick, Brulatour and Samuel Insull. Both Hearst and Kane saw their empires collapse in the Depression. Both ended their days in extravagant and tedious retirement. Xanadu, the ultimate American vision of heaven on earth, was directly modeled after Hearst's San Simeon, which Mank had personally observed and which he now recreated in all its exorbitant folly, complete with private zoo, motorcade picnics, oversize Renaissance fireplaces and jigsaw puzzles.*

---

*This is where the film ran into trouble. It is unlikely that anyone would have bothered about the obvious parallels in the public lives of Hearst and Kane, but with the invasion of Xanadu a particularly sensitive nerve was touched. Not only Mankiewicz but every male and female columnist in Hollywood, not to mention actors, directors and film executives by the dozens had been entertained at San Simeon and had witnessed the embarrassing boredom of their aging unmarried hosts. To expose this in a movie seemed unethical, ungrateful and dangerous. Hearst, even in his decline, remained a powerful national figure: by uttering shrill cries of hypocritical indignation, the industry and the press were protecting themselves from the wrath to come.

With the single exception of Susan Alexander whose situation, though not her personality, clearly resembled that of Marion Davies, our "witnesses" had no individual equivalents in the life of William Randolph Hearst. Bernstein (to whom we gave some of the characteristics of Everett Sloane, who would be playing the part, and the surname of Orson's guardian, a music-loving doctor from Chicago) was the prototype of the shrewd, unquestioningly loyal business manager. Jed Leland, Kane's best friend, was superficially modeled after Ashton Stevens, the drama critic, a long-time friend of Hearst and, incidentally, of Orson's father. Thatcher, the guardian-lawyer-banker, was a wholly fictitious personage, to whom Mank added, mainly for his own amusement, overtones of J. P. Morgan, including a recent newsreel in which the haughty financier had been subjected, during a Congressional investigation, to the humiliation of being photographed with a midget on his knee.

This seemingly irrelevant clip was typical of the use he made throughout the script of newsreel material—real, reconstructed and imagined.* Assembled in staccato *March of Time* style and first shown as a summary of the fabulous career of Charles Foster Kane immediately after his death, many of those clips were repeated later in the body of the film, no longer as newsreels but as part of Kane's personal story. From this constant cross-fertilization between myth, fact and fiction the film acquired much of its vitality and dimension.

Throughout our work on the screenplay of what later came to be called *Citizen Kane,* we had one special advantage: we were not working in a vacuum, developing a script for some absent producer; we were—and we never for one instant forgot it—creating a vehicle suited to the personality and creative energy of a man who, at twenty-four, was himself only slightly less fabulous than the mythical hero he would be portraying. And the deeper we penetrated beyond the public events into the heart of Charles Foster Kane, the closer we seemed to come to the identity of Orson Welles.

Orson was aware of this. Far from resisting the resemblance, he pushed it even further when he came to shoot the film. Between young Kane and young Welles there is more than a surface likeness: in the dramatized person of Charles Foster Kane, "Champagne Charley" was finally able to realize extravagances that far exceeded anything achieved in life by Richard Welles and his precocious son. Kane's fury, too, was of a special and recognizable kind. A vague aura of violence surrounded the Hearst legend: there was the persistent rumor of the fatal shooting, in a jealous rage, of a well-known Hollywood director on a yacht off the Malibu coast. We made no reference to that episode in our script. We did

*In our search for related material we became veritable magpies: the *Reporter*'s first interview with Susan Kane in a sleazy bar in Atlantic City was based on a recent interview with Evelyn Nesbitt Thaw in the run-down nightclub where she was performing.

not need it. The wanton, wordless, destructive fury which Kane wreaks upon the inanimate objects in his wife's room when he realizes that she has left him was taken directly from our recent scene in the upper room at Chasen's. During its filming, Orson reproduced with frightening fidelity the physical gestures and the blind agony of rage with which he had hurled those flaming Sternos against the wall. The cuts he received on his hands on both occasions were, I was told, almost identical.

. . . .

Our days and nights on the Campbell Ranch followed a reassuring routine. Mankiewicz wrote and read half the night and slept in the morning. I got up early, had my breakfast in the main house so as not to disturb him, then went riding for an hour—my first contact with a horse since the Estancia Santa Maria. After that, while I waited for him to come to life, I would edit the pages Mank had dictated the night before, which the secretary had typed at dawn. At nine-thirty Mank received his breakfast in bed. An hour later, having made an enormous production of shaving, washing, and dressing himself on one leg, he was ready for work. This consisted of going over yesterday's material, arguing over changes and seeing how the new scenes fitted into the structure of the whole and affected the scenes to come.

The wranglers' daughters who served us our meals were frightened by our shouting, but we enjoyed our collaboration. Once Mank had come to trust me, my editing, for all our disagreements, gave him more creative freedom than his own neurotic self-censorship. We argued without competitiveness or embarrassment till the middle of the afternoon. At that time Mank, who suffered great pain from the knitting bones in his leg, would retire for his siesta while the secretary and I went over her notes on the day's talk. At six Mankiewicz rose, ready and eager for the great adventure of the day, when I would drive him and his crutches to a railroad bar known as The Green Spot, where we slowly drank one scotch apiece and watched the locals playing the pinball machines and dancing to the Western music of a jukebox. Once a week we visited the only movie, then returned to The Green Spot for dinner. Other evenings we worked until around ten, when I became sleepy from the mountain air. From my bed, through the closed door, I could hear Mank's voice as he continued his dictation, interrupted by games of cribbage which he had taught our devoted secretary.

We were not entirely incommunicado. Sarah drove up every other week to satisfy herself that all was well, and seemed astounded to discover that it was. Orson telephoned at odd hours to inquire after our progress. On the appointed day, at the end of six weeks, he arrived in a limousine driven by Alfalfa, read a hundred pages of script, listened to our outline of the rest, dined with us at The Green Spot, thanked us and returned to Los Angeles. The next day he informed the studio that he would start shooting early in July on a film which, at the time, was entitled *American*.

The script grew harder to write as it went along. We had started with a clear, objective outline of the Kane story—a linear record of the significant public and private events in his life, from the cradle to the grave. In the screenplay these events were briefly reviewed in the introductory March of Time, then revealed through the testimony of successive witnesses delving into memories that were shaped and colored by the bias of their own personal relations with Kane. Their testimonies followed each other in vaguely chronological order; they also criss-crossed, overlapped, anticipated and bled into each other. This gave the film its particular quality; it also created a structural problem that grew more serious with each new day's work. The richer and the more varied the sum of the testimonies became, the harder it got to keep them in manageable order. After each testimony it became necessary to go back into the script and make changes to conform to the new and sometimes seemingly contradictory events and situations that had just been revealed. Since our witnesses frequently appeared in scenes that took place before their own testimony began and stayed in the action long after their own story had ended, these multiple adjustments became increasingly delicate and complicated as the script developed.

Finally, after ten weeks, we were done. Raymond, the butler, had spoken his last snide word, and ROSEBUD had been reduced to ashes in the incinerator at Xanadu. The script was more than four hundred pages long—overrich, repetitious, loaded with irrelevant, fascinating detail and private jokes, of which we loved every one. We spent two more weeks going through the pages with machetes—hacking away, trimming, simplifying, clarifying its main dramatic lines and yelling at each other all the time. Above all, we worked on the connective tissue, substituting sharp cinematic cuts and visual transitions for what, in the first version, had too often been leisurely verbal and literary expositions. And, for the twentieth time, I reorganized the March of Time, which had become my special domain, to conform to what now appeared to be significant facts in the life of Charles Foster Kane.

Our peace was disturbed, during that last fortnight, by the news that was coming in night and day over the radio. The "phony war" was over: Hitler's invasion of Belgium and France had begun. Mank could not bear to be away from the half-dozen newspapers he was in the habit of reading each day. We extended our working hours. Then one evening, from The Green Spot, I called the studio and ordered the limousine for the next day. Mank's leg was almost healed, but he clung to his invalid's privileges. He lay alone, groaning, in the rear seat of the limousine and I followed in the convertible as we made the reverse journey through the Cajon Pass, down the steep curves of the San Bernardino Mountains, between the vineyards and orange groves of Azusa, through the slums of

Los Angeles to the RKO studio in Hollywood, where, before returning Mankiewicz to Poor Sarah, we solemnly presented Orson with a screenplay whose blue title page read:

AMERICAN

by

Herman Mankiewicz

PRESTON STURGES

Preston Sturges (1898–1959) blazed across Hollywood in the 1940s with one hit after another: The Lady Eve, Palm Beach Story, Unfaithfully Yours, Sullivan's Travels, *and all the others, written and directed in a style that combined glitter, wit, and a sharp, cynical intelligence. Then he lost his touch, partly because by the late 1940s he was drinking too much, and although he lived on and made more films, he never regained it. His youth was spent as a playboy and man-about-town, and in his glory years he liked to make it appear that filmmaking was something he had stumbled into and did in his spare time. Something of that tone is found here, along with his sardonic view of human nature, in this account of his early days as a writer.*

from *Preston Sturges on Preston Sturges*

In Hollywood I started at the bottom: a bum by the name of Sturgeon who had once written a hit called *Strictly Something-or-Other*. Carl Laemmle of Universal offered me a contract, with unilateral options exercisable by the studio, to join his team as a writer. My wife had decamped, my fortune was depleted, and even though I was living on coffee and moonlight, my costs of living continued to cost. I did not have to wrestle with any principles to leap on Laemmle's offer. On September 9, 1932, I arrived in Hollywood with my secretary, Bianca Gilchrist.

I was to write, offer suggestions and make myself generally useful, and for this I was to get a nominal or beginning writer's salary of a thousand dollars a week. Junior writers got less, of course, but I *had* written *Strictly Something-or-Other,* and that made me a kind of senior beginner. I was charmed; it vindicated my contention that writing was my profession, and the money proved it.

There were a great many writers on the lot, and the reason for this was that at the time, writers worked in teams, like piano movers. It was generally believed by the powers down in front that a man who could write comedy could not write tragedy, that a man who could write forceful, virile stuff could not handle the tender passages, and that if the picture was not to taste all of the same cook, a multiplicity of writers was essential. Four writers were considered the rock-bottom minimum required. Six writers, with the sixth member a woman to puff up the lighter parts, was considered ideal. Many, many more writers have been used on a picture, of course; several writers have even been assigned the same story unbeknownst to each other. The Screen Writers Guild of the day had even worked out some rather shameful rules governing the conduct and approach of one writer toward another when he has secretly been given the other's job: he was not in honor bound to volunteer any information, but if asked directly, he must not deny the sad truth.

.   .   .   .

A man in possession of many bolts of woolen cloth, quantities of lining and interlining, buttons, thread, needles, and padding is not, of necessity, a tailor. A man in possession of many characters, many situations, many startling and dramatic events, and many gags is not, of necessity, a storyteller.

The crafts of the tailor and the storyteller are not dissimilar, however, for out of a mass of unrelated material, each contrives to fashion a complete and well-balanced unit. Many stories are too heavy in the shoulders and too short in the pants, with the design of the material running upside-down.

In constructing a talking-picture play, the basic story to be filmed passes through many hands. Some writer turns out the first manuscript, which, being the first, is condemned even before it is written.

Another writer is called in and the second treatment is made. The second writer is no better than the first writer, but his treatment is vastly different, for the simple reason that every single person in the world will tell the same story differently: see the testimony of various bystanders at the scene of any street accident.

A third writer is now engaged, on the grounds that three are better than one, ignoring the rule that a chain is only as strong as its weakest link. Just as the fourth writer is about to be engaged, with the fifth and sixth creeping over the horizon, word comes from the front office that shooting will begin three days hence.

The script, which is by now voluminous, is carried posthaste to a Funny Man, who believes that only policemen are funny. In two strokes of a pencil, he changes all the male characters to policemen, thus making the script funny.

The script, now funny, requires only a slight tightening up by a Construction Expert in order to be in prime A1 condition. One glance is enough for this expert to detect what is wrong: the end should come first, obviously; the middle should come last; and the beginning should be thrown out. This is accomplished in less time than it takes to tell about it, and the polished script is laid on the desk of the production manager, who takes it home to peruse it. This last, of course, is only a technicality, as the script must surely be right by now.

The production manager, who is not such a sap, returns to the office in the morning, haggard, bulbous-eyed with worry. There seems to be something the matter with the script. It is not that all the material is not there. The proper number of smashed motorcars, the stupendous living rooms, the modernistic bedrooms, the pompous matrons, the sterling workmen, and comic butlers, comic Englishmen, all, all are there. But what in Nick's name are they supposed to be doing?

There is only one thing to be done, and the production manager does it. He calls in another writer. There is no haggling over the fee because time is precious. The story is disentangled and put in proper sequences again. That is to say, it begins at the beginning and ends at the end, passing through the middle. It is now ready for shooting, except for one or two technicalities. First, another Funny Man takes a whack at it and changes the policemen to soldiers. Only one more technicality to clear up and all will be set. Another Construction Expert changes the beginning to the middle; the middle to the beginning; and, now that the play is about soldiers, adds a good rousing battle scene to the end.

Zero hour being at hand, the screenplay is now given to the director, who shoots the script as it stands, excepting only that the locale is changed to the Middle Ages and the lovers meet on bicycles, achieving thus a very comical effect.

The customer walking home in his new suit is razzed by small boys as he passes.

.   .   .   .

I thought I knew how to put a story together, but it might turn out that I was meant to be a tailor.

Bianca and I were assigned beautiful offices in a little bungalow on the Universal lot affectionately known as the Bull Pen. Its only inconvenience was its location next to the gents' room. All the other distinguished authors who inhabited the Bull Pen had to pass through my office to reach the facilities and on the way out, they always dropped their paper towels on my desk. But at a thousand dollars a week, this was a small matter. I brushed off my desk and counted my money.

I liked the people at the studio and made a lot of new friends. Within a month,

I was elected to membership in the Writers' Club. In addition to quarters on Sunset Boulevard housing a bar and a little food where the members could congregate at will, the club had regular Wednesday luncheon meetings of the Corned Beef, Cabbage, and Culture Circle, which I much enjoyed. It was a club for men only, of course, with invitations extended to the ladies on special occasions. Among the active members who became my friends were Rupert Hughes, Doug Fairbanks, Charlie Chaplin, Harold Lloyd, Irving Thalberg, Ernst Lubitsch, John Gilbert, and Will Rogers.

It took me exactly two days on the job as a hired writer, or until I met my first director, to find out that I was in the wrong racket. I had expected my producer to be peculiar, of course, because the facts about Hollywood producers had been well publicized throughout the land. On meeting him, I was not disappointed. About directors, though, I knew very little, and it took me a few minutes to get the point.

It was not so much what the director said, it was the way he said it, especially the way he looked at me (a writer): coolly, confidently, courteously, but with a curious condescension, the way an Englishman looks at an American and an American looks at an Indian. He was a perfectly polite and affable little man and did his best to put me at my ease, but one of my knees kept twitching and I had the uneasy feeling that instead of standing on my feet looking down at him, I should have been on one knee looking up at him. The man was obviously a prince of the blood.

The more directors I met, the more I realized that this was not an isolated case. They were all princes of the blood. Nobody ever had them directing pictures in teams with one of them handling the horseback scenes and another handling the bedroom interludes: nobody ever put them in the Bull Pen or threw paper towels on their desks. The bungalows they lived in on the lot had open fireplaces and private bathrooms and big soft couches. Nobody ever assigned them to pictures they didn't like: they were timidly *offered* pictures. Sometimes they graciously condescended to direct them, but if they said no, a story was a piece of cheese, it was a piece of cheese.

This ennoblement, of course, had been conferred upon directors during the silent days, when the directors truly were the storytellers and the princes of the business. By the time I got to Hollywood, this aristocracy was merely a leftover from an earlier day. The reasons for it were no longer apparent, like the reasons for so many other aristocracies. Years later when I became a writer-director, actually the storyteller again, people said I was doing something new, but I was not; I was doing something old.

As I had never written anything but comedies, my producer assigned me the job of writing the ninth script of a horror picture: an adaptation of H. G. Wells' book, *The Invisible Man*. Hardly any of Wells' story was suited to a motion picture, so it actually meant coming up with an original story. Eight well-known writers had already been paid for adaptations which the studio said could not be used, and I thought that if mine were used, my future at Universal would be assured.

I hurried into the Bull Pen and came out ten weeks later with 180 pages of stuff so chilling that it would cause the hair of a statue to stand on end and cold sweat to stream down its sculptured back. The studio did not pick up its option on my services and I was fired without further ceremony. The director said it was a piece of cheese.

I had just been assigned a rewrite of a continuity for Slim Summerville and ZaSu Pitts when my contract was up, but I stayed on at the studio to finish the job and made them a present of a couple of weeks' work. For this they pronounced themselves grateful, and my hope was that this bread cast upon the waters would return as ham sandwiches.

Although off salary, I was not idle. Thoroughly displeased with the abysmal status of a Hollywood team writer, I considered the benefits of free-lancing, writing scripts on my own time and selling them to a studio later. I could then write anywhere I liked, spend the spring in Paris, for instance, the summer on my boat, the fall in New York and the winter in Palm Beach, coming to California for a couple of days a year to sign contracts for the sale of the scripts.

Free-lancing to me was also a stab at raising the writer's status, if not to the level of prince of the blood, at least to the level of tender of the royal shaving paper or something of equal dignity; anything to get out of the cellar to which custom had assigned the Hollywood team writer.

Bianca got behind the typewriter and I got to work on *The Power and the Glory,* a story inspired by some incidents Eleanor had told me about her mother's father, C. W. Post, founder of the Postum Cereal Company, known today as the General Foods Corporation. The fruits of inspiration bore no resemblance to the actual life and times of Eleanor's grandfather, of course, but I chose the nonchronological structure of the screenplay because I noticed that when Eleanor would recount adventures, the lack of chronology interfered not at all with one's pleasure in the stories and that, in fact, its absence often sharpened the impact of the tale.

The screenplay for *The Power and the Glory* had one thing that distinguished it from other scripts of the time. So far as I know, it was the first story conceived and written directly as a shooting script by its author on his own time and then sold to a moving picture company on a royalty basis, exactly as plays or novels are sold. It established a couple of other "firsts," too. It was the first script shot by a director almost exactly as written. It was also the first story to use what the publicity department dubbed *narratage,* that is, the narrator's, or author's, voice spoke the dialogue while the actors only moved their lips. Strangely enough, this was highly effective and the illusion was complete.

It was neither a silent film nor a talking film, but rather a combination of the two. It embodied the visual action of a silent picture, the sound of the narrator's voice, and the storytelling economy and the richness of characterization of a novel.

The reason for trying this method was to see if some way could be devised to carry American films into foreign countries. It would be extremely easy to put a narrator's voice on the sound track in any language, because the narrator for the most part is heard, but not seen. The further advantage of a narrator is that, like the author of a novel, he may describe not only what people do and say but also what they feel and what they think.

I sold the screenplay to Jesse Lasky at Fox in February 1933 for a large down payment and a percentage of the gross, cast it and directed the dialogue. Shooting started in March.

At that time, very few successful writers had ever watched the whole process of making a picture from beginning to end, including the rushes and the cutting, because they were usually on salary and busy writing something else while their last scripts were being filmed. I, however, was not a successful writer busy writing something else and could do as I liked. I spent six weeks on the set, at my own expense, helping to stage the dialogue and acting as sort of a general handyman, what one might call speculative directing. The director, Mr. William K. Howard, had a nice chair in front of the camera and a property man to take care of his hat and coat. He told everybody what to do and, in general, he had a nice time. Most of my time on the set was spent on top of a green stepladder in the back, watching and learning. Occasionally I would hurry down the stepladder to explain to Mr. Spencer Tracy or to Miss Colleen Moore what I meant by a line and how I thought it should be read, then hurry back up the stepladder and watch it being shot.

And there, on top of the green stepladder, watching Mr. William K. Howard direct *The Power and the Glory,* I got a tremendous yen to direct, coupled with the absolutely positive hunch that I could. I had never felt anything quite like it before. Never while watching a heavyweight title match had I had the desire to change places with one of the gentlemen in the ring. Nor at the six-day bicycle races, while a fallen rider was picking splinters out of his rear, had I felt impelled to swipe his vehicle and lap the field. Never at the fairgrounds did I envy the man who dove into a barrel of feathers from atop a hundred-foot pole. I am not an envious man. But from the top of the green stepladder, I ached to change places with Mr. William K. Howard, who was doing such an excellent job transferring my screenplay to film.

I did not wish Mr. Howard any hard luck like a bad automobile accident or a seriously broken back or anything like that. I merely wished that some temporary fever would assail him, something not too harmful that would lay him flat for the rest of the shooting schedule, so that the company would implore me, as the only other person thoroughly conversant with the script, to take over the direction in his stead. I have seen that same hopeful look on the faces of my young assistants, and it causes me to watch my step. I watched Mr. Howard with glittering eyes as he nearly tripped over cables, nearly fell off high parallels and sat in countless drafts, which I tested with a wet finger. He unfortunately remained disgustingly healthy, one of the prime requisites of a good director, and I unfortunately remained a writer.

When the picture was released, I naturally received sole credit as the writer, and found my name in the advertisements the same size as the director's.

This, coupled with the deal I made selling the screenplay for large monies up front and a percentage of the gross, made nothing but enemies for me. The directors said, "Who is this bum getting his name the same size as ours?" The producers said, "This sets a very bad precedent: you give these upstarts an inch and they'll want their names up in lights!" The heads of the studios said, "What is this rubbish about giving writers a percentage of the gross which shakes the very foundations of the industry?" The trade press said, "What is this business of shooting a picture by a single writer when we are accustomed to getting ads from six or eight of them per picture?" And the writers, yea, even my brethren, viewed with alarm the whittling down of jobs that would ensue if only one writer, God forbid, worked on each script. I was as popular as a polecat and, with all that money in the bank, as independent.

It is true that I was voted that year's equivalent of an Academy Oscar for the best original screenplay, but it is also true that I didn't get any work for a long, long time. So long that I had to go out and borrow.

Before I got to that stage though, I bought the hull of a seagoing schooner, fifty-two foot overall, which gave me something to live for, filling my mind with repairs and refittings and ropes and chains and teak and mahogany and brass fittings and diesel engines.

It was during this period that I decided to change my profession once more and become a director instead of a team writer. It seemed easier for one man to change his profession than for hundreds of men to so improve theirs that I would be proud to be a screenwriter.

WOODY ALLEN

It's a peculiar thing about Woody Allen that although he has written more than twenty-five movies and many plays and articles, he has apparently never written anything about the movies. The closest he came was this fantasy about a stage production of Disney's Snow White and the Seven Dwarfs. *It is so clearly inspired by the Disney cartoon that I think it qualifies for a movie anthology—particularly after Disney realized Woody's fantasy by converting* Beauty and the Beast *into a Broadway musical.*

"Snow White and the Seven Dwarfs"

Last night, the Lincoln Center theater opened the new season with the Elia Kazan all-star production of *Snow White,* starring Marlon Brando, Lee J. Cobb, Anthony Quinn, Jason Robards, Jr., Rod Steiger, George C. Scott and Sidney Poitier as the seven dwarfs, with Kim Stanley as the queen and Mildred Dunnock in the title role.

First, let me say that the show is the best *Snow White* ever done, including the Gielgud production that played a limited run on Broadway some years back; and while Sir Ralph Richardson's Dopey was deemed a masterpiece of technical virtuosity at the time, Lee Cobb's is infinitely more moving. But I will get to that. I think what distinguishes this *Snow White* from any other is its success in coming to grips with issues. What is the meaning of life? Why does man feel alienated? And wherein lies his salvation? At the end of act two, Bashful kills himself upon learning that his brother Sneezy has gone insane. He echoes the words of the philosopher Nietzsche, who wrote, "God is dead. Everything is now possible." Coming from a shy dwarf, the impact is staggering. But on to the performances.

Rod Steiger has always been an actor of unusual sensitivity and, in Doc, he at last has a challenge equal to his abilities. Frustrated, alcoholic, impotent, Doc is unable to "whistle while he works." Haunted by the image of the surgeon he could have become were he just a few feet taller, he is reduced to podiatry, a branch of medicine he hates but which is within his grasp. "What he could never understand," Snow White sobs at one point, "is that there's as much poetry in a bunion as a ventricle. But how many of us realize that?"

Unable to stop sneezing, Robards' Sneezy—the victim of a morbid neurosis—is racked with guilt over complicity with the Nazis during World War Two. Faced with a firing squad, he chose to inform on Happy, leader of the dwarf resistance, who, posing as a gnome, successfully harassed the Germans. Gnomes—and Mr. Kazan makes a very telling point here—were highly instrumental in sabotaging the German infantry by deepening their trenches as they slept, making it impossible for them to see over the tops. There is also some allusion to an eighth dwarf, Weepy, who was executed by the Gestapo as a result of Sneezy's treason. And while other forest creatures have forgiven Sneezy, it is just this forgiveness that adds further torment to his guilty soul. Robards chooses to play him with an objective, nonjudging quality that makes it all the more agonizing when his mind rejects reality and, in a burst of vein-throbbing hysteria, he accuses Grumpy of taking his porridge.

Anthony Quinn's Bashful is electrifying and will probably be the definitive Bashful for years to come. Shy, inarticulate, except for sudden explosions of rage, Bashful finds solace in morphine, a habit he acquired years ago, as a result of having it prescribed for him to kill the pain after he had been run over by a beaver. He finds now that life is unbearable without a drug of some kind and is forced to steal twigs in an effort to support his addiction. His "connection," a troll (Fredric March), meets him beneath a bridge each night and, for a price, supplies him with the necessary fix. As his dependency grows, the troll increases the price of morphine to several twigs. Bashful is forced to roll elves and when he is caught shooting up behind a bunch of daffodils, he takes an overdose and dies. He is laid to rest on a bed of leaves and throughout all the forest there is a hush. His eulogy is brief but remarkably moving, considering it is delivered by a frog (Pat Hingle).

In Cobb's Dopey, we have the single greatest tragedy of the dwarfs. Dopey has been a success in the past. Living in Hollywood and earning wealth and adulation as a film star who specialized in playing the hero's wisecracking friend, he delighted audiences of all ages with his deadpan whimsy. He is embittered now because of a black-listing before a vague and sinister group, referred to only as "the committee," that claims that all dwarfs are Communist inspired. Panicky over threats of exposure, Dopey had gone before the committee and lied, claiming to be a midget. Destroyed as a perjurer, he finally returns to the forest and marries a squirrel. Bewildered at life's cruelties, he says movingly, "I, who once had my pick of any bimbo in Hollywood, am now reduced to matrimony with a furry rodent. Go figure."

Yawning constantly as an expression of man's boredom with an apparently meaningless universe, Mr. Brando's Sleepy reels and drifts into slumber again and again, choosing to mount his tiny little bed with cap and nightgown, rather than face the harsh realities of a crumbling existence. In a moment of true poignancy, he turns to his brother Doc and says, "Y'know, Doc—sometimes when I'm alone in bed at night and everything's pitch black, I have these thoughts. Terrible thoughts. Like, I'm not really as cute and cuddly as I think I am. Oh, sure, I'm tiny as could be and I got a little pointed hat. But I don't know—I just wish I was . . . more adorable." Convinced that there is more to life than living in the forest and gathering nectar and dewdrops, Sleepy runs away to the city but returns, scorned and disillusioned. Here, Mr. Kazan tells us that all men have their own private forests. For some it's the office; others, the marriage bed or analyst's couch. I am certain that is his point. Either that or some men are named Forest. This is the one section of the play that becomes obscure, although the audience seemed to love it.

Sidney Poitier's Happy is a study in racial tension so agonizingly real yet restrained that it recalls the unadorned brilliance of Paul Robeson's Jiminy Cricket some seasons back. Poitier has extracted every last drop of emotion from Happy and the scene in which Snow White rejects him, "not because you are a Negro but because I could never love a man whose head came up to my kneecap," is unbearably moving. Happy cannot believe he is being turned down for any reason other than the color of his skin, a misconception that infuriates him. In an effort to elicit a human response from anyone, he talks increasingly of suicide and then threatens to throw himself off the stump of a tree. Snow White pleads with him to reconsider, but it is too late. He jumps. Instead of dying, he lands on a tulip and is crippled for life.

Despite the virtuoso performance of George C. Scott, and there can be no doubt that he is one of the great American actors, this reviewer felt he missed the point of Grumpy entirely. Grumpy is psychotic when the play begins. He is fiercely anti-Semitic and feels the forest is assuming an ever-increasing "Jewish essence," which he deplores. There is an incident where several chipmunks are storing nuts in their cheeks. This tends to give them what Grumpy feels is a "Hasidic look." It leads to quarreling and finally, to Grumpy's master plan to restrict the forest to pure-blooded Aryan types: tall, blond, blue-eyed. This is in direct conflict with the fact that he himself has Jewish blood. (His mother, we learn, was seduced by a water sprite named Ben Fleagel, who promised her stockings.) Grumpy becomes more and more schizophrenic as he speaks of the final solution of the Jewish problem while studying the Torah. He is taken away to a dwarf asylum and given shock therapy with a joy buzzer.

Finally, Mildred Dunnock plays the frigid Snow White with a brooding intensity and Kim Stanley is broadly hilarious as the wicked queen. Credit must also be given to the prince (Christopher Plummer) who awakens Snow White with a kiss and, with nothing more than a raised eyebrow, makes his part into a delightful cameo. The sets by Jo Mielziner are ingenious. I particularly like the clever way in which he has made the forest on a bright spring morning look like Auschwitz. Mr. Kazan has directed the entire production with a gossamer touch. One last note on a brilliant "inside" bit of stage business: Although he is not credited in the program, the voice of the mirror in the "Mirror, mirror on the wall" sequence is unmistakably Walter Winchell's.

JOHN HUSTON

John Huston (1906–1987) titled his autobiography An Open Book, *but it was closed for all it reveals about the man himself. That's consistent with the impression I got during several meetings with him: He spoke with great courtesy and attentiveness, agreeing with almost everything one said, elaborating, embroidering, choosing his words with a certain ornate formality, yet when the conversation was over, it was difficult to determine what he had actually said. I think it was a verbal strategy for keeping the world at arm's length; revelations were reserved for his friends and lovers. The book too is at arm's length: a record but not a confessional. Only when he talks about his craft, as he does here in a discussion of his style, do you feel he is really leveling with you.*

from *An Open Book*

I'm not aware of myself as a director having a style. I'm told that I do, but I don't recognize it. I see no remote similarity, for example, between *The Red Badge of Courage* and *Moulin Rouge*. However observant the critic, I don't think he'd be able to tell that the same director made them both. Bergman has a style that's unmistakably his. He is a prime example of the *auteur* approach to making pictures. I suppose it is the best approach: the director conceives the idea, writes it, puts it on film. Because he is creating out of himself, controlling all aspects of the work, his films assume a unity and a direction. I admire directors like Bergman, Fellini, Buñuel, whose every picture is in some way connected with their private lives, but that's never been my approach. I'm eclectic. I like to draw on sources other than myself; further, I don't think of myself as simply, uniquely and forever a director of motion pictures. It is something for which I have a certain talent, and a profession the disciplines of which I have mastered over the years, but I also have a certain talent for other things, and I have worked at those disciplines as well. The idea of devoting myself to a single pursuit in life is unthinkable to me. My interests in boxing, writing, painting, horses have at certain periods in my life been every bit as important as that in directing films.

I have been speaking of style, but before there can be style, there must be grammar. There is, in fact, a grammar to picture-making. The laws are as inexorable as they are in language, and are to be found in the shots themselves. When do we fade-in or fade-out with a camera? When do we dissolve, pan, dolly, cut? The rules governing these techniques are well grounded. They must, of course, be disavowed and disobeyed from time to time, but one must be aware of their existence, for motion pictures have a great deal in common with our own physiological and psychological processes—more so than any other medium. It is almost as if there were a reel of film behind our eyes . . . as though our very thoughts were projected onto the screen.

Motion pictures, however, are governed by a time sense different from that of real life; different from the theater, too. That rectangle of light up there with the shadows on it *demands* one's whole attention. And what it furnishes must satisfy that demand. When we are sitting in a room in a house, there is no single claim on our awareness. Our attention jumps from object to object, drifts in and out of the room. We listen to sounds coming from various points; we may even smell something cooking. In a motion-picture theater, where our undivided attention is given to the screen, time actually moves more slowly, and action has to be speeded up. Furthermore, whatever action takes place on that screen must not violate our sense of the appropriate. We accomplish this by adhering to the proper grammar of film-making.

For example, a fade-in or a fade-out is akin to waking up or going to sleep. The dissolve indicates either a lapse of time or a change of place. Or it can, in certain instances, indicate that things in different places are happening at the same time. In any case, the images impinge . . . the way dreams proceed, or like the faces you can see when you close your eyes. When we pan, the camera turns from right to left, or vice versa, and serves one of two purposes: it follows an individual, or it informs the viewer of the geography of the scene. You pan from one object to another in order to establish their spatial relationship; thereafter you cut. We are forever cutting in real life. Look from one object to another across the room. Notice how you involuntarily blink. *That's a cut.* You know what the spatial relationship is, there's nothing to discover about the geography, so you cut with your eyelids. The dolly is when the camera doesn't simply turn on its axis but moves horizontally or backward and forward. It may move closer to intensify interest and pull away to come to a tableau, thereby putting a finish—or a period—to a scene. A more common purpose is simply to include another figure in the frame.

The camera usually identifies itself with one of the actors in a scene, and it sees the others through his eyes. The nature of the scene determines how close the actors are to each other. If it's an intimate scene, obviously you don't show the other individual as a full-length figure. The image on the screen should correspond to what we experience in real life. Seated a few feet apart, the upper body of one or the other would fill the screen. Inches apart would be a big-head close-up. The size of their images must be in accordance with the proper spatial relationship. Unless there's a reason: when actors are some distance apart and the effect of what one is saying has a significant impact upon the person he's talking to, you might go into a close-up of the listener. But still his distance, as he views the person who is speaking, must remain the same. Going into a big-head close-up with dialogue that is neither intimate nor significant serves only to over-emphasize the physiognomy of the actor.

Usually the camera is in one of two positions: "standing up" or "sitting down." When we vary this, it should be to serve a purpose. Shooting up at an individual ennobles him. As children we looked up to our parents, or we look up at a monumental sculpture. On the other hand, when we look down, it's at someone weaker than we are, someone to laugh at, pity or feel superior to. As the camera goes higher and higher looking downward, it becomes God-like.

The conventional film-maker usually shoots a scene in full shot—a master scene—followed by medium shots, close shots and close-ups . . . at various angles . . . then decides in the cutting room what to use. The opposite way is to find the one shot that serves as an introduction to a scene; the rest will follow naturally. Again there's a grammar to it. Once you write your first declarative sentence, the narration flows. Understanding the syntax of a scene implies that you already know the way the scene will be cut together, so you shoot only what's required. That's called "cutting with the camera."

I work closely with the cameraman and with the operator, the man who actually manipulates the camera. He looks through the lens, executing what you've specified. At the end of a shot you look to him to see if he's brought it off. The camera is sometimes required to take part in a sort of a dance with the artists, and its movements timed as if they were to music, and I've noticed that most good operators have a natural sense of rhythm. They usually dance well, play drums, juggle or do something that requires good timing and balance.

Cameramen—most of them ex-operators—are really lighting experts. They like to be known not as cameramen but as directors of lighting. Young directors are, as a rule, somewhat frightened of their cameramen. This is understandable, for cameramen often proceed in an independent fashion to light each scene precisely as they please. Lighting is their first interest, since other cameramen will judge them by it.

As an actor, it's been my opportunity to observe the working methods of other directors. For the most part, they go by the book. Inexperienced directors put great stock in the master scene—which is shot as though all the actors were on a stage; you see everybody at once, and all the action. Their idea is that if they've missed something in the closer work with the camera that they should see, they can always fall back to the master shot. They think of it as a way of protecting themselves. I've often heard cameramen advise such a procedure, but a cameraman is not a cutter. The tact that falling back to the master scene interrupts the flow of the whole scene and breaks whatever spell has been evoked through good close-up work is of no concern to him. Obviously I am not speaking about all cameramen. There are any number of outstanding professionals who are just as concerned with getting that ideal sequence of shots—whatever the cost—as any director.

So many things can go wrong while filming a scene. If only everything bad that's going to happen would happen at once and be over with! You're seldom that fortunate. Instead, it's the camera, or an actor forgetting his lines, or the sound of an airplane, or a car backfiring, or an arc light that flickers. When things of this kind occur, you simply have to start again. It can drive a director up the wall. I recall an incident involving one especially volatile director who was making a film in Africa. During one take a native baby began crying, and that stopped the scene. He started over, and a lion began roaring when it wasn't supposed to. The director shouted: "Cut! I can see that there's only one way to get this God-damned scene! Throw the fucking baby to the fucking lion!"

Now, if you can make use of two or even three set-ups—going from one balanced, framed picture to another without cutting—a sense of richness, grace and fluency is evoked. For example, one set-up might be a long shot of a wagon train moving slowly across the screen. The camera moves with it and comes to two men standing together, talking. Then one of the men walks toward the camera, and the camera pulls back to the point where he encounters a third individual, who stands back to the camera until the other man has passed on out of the scene. Then he turns and looks after him, in close-up. Three complete set-ups—without cutting. Of course, the set-ups must be carefully laid out and perfectly framed, and this multiplies the chances of something going wrong. But

I've discovered that, even with the increased possibility of error, the time spent is not much more than would be spent on three separate set-ups.

Such linked shots are the mark of a good director. The scenes I have put together in this fashion have scarcely—if ever—been remarked on by an audience or a critic. But the fact that they have gone unnoticed is, in a sense, the best praise they could receive. They are so natural that the audience is caught up in the flow. This is the exact opposite of the kind of thing people tend to think of as clever—somebody's distorted reflection in a doorknob, for instance, a stunt that distracts one's attention from the scene. It is important to say things on the screen with ingenuity, but never to belabor the audience with images that say, "Look at this!" The work of the camera with the actors, as I mentioned before, often amounts to a dance—panning, dollying, following the movement of the actors with grace, not cutting. There's a choreography to it. Not many picture-makers are up to this. I'd say a dozen or so.

It is best to shoot chronologically. In this way you can benefit by accidents, and you don't paint yourself into corners. However, if the picture begins in India and ends in India, with other countries in between, it is economically impractical not to shoot all the Indian material at one time. When you are on a distant location, you do everything that calls for that location. That is a compromise, but making a picture is a series of compromises. It is when you feel that the compromise will affect—or risks affecting—the overall quality of the picture that you must decide whether or not to go along with it.

Plain, ordinary judgment plays a big part. For instance, you may well get what seems to be the ideal scene on your first take. Then you must question whether you have been sufficiently critical. Is the scene truly as good as you first thought? Inexperienced directors are inclined to shoot almost every scene at least twice, in the fear that something may have escaped them. They may be blessed and not realize it—and, in trying to improve upon something that doesn't need improving, may run into these technical problems that I mentioned earlier. If the action is right and the artists have been everything you desire, then a second take will do you no good. If something is wrong with the film or the lighting, it will be wrong on the second or third take, too, so that's no kind of insurance. A director has to learn to trust his judgment.

Each time you get a good scene is a kind of miracle. Usually there is something wrong, however slight, and you must consider the importance of the error. As you repeat a scene, your demands in terms of quality tend to increase proportionately. You've got to watch this, and not become a fanatic.

I've come onto sets where a director has prepared all the lighting and designated all the action before bringing in any of the performers. In some cases it was an inexperienced director following the advice of his cameraman—in others, a matter of such a tight schedule that every second counted. But simply to light a set and say, "Now you sit here. You stand there," without any preliminaries, is only to embalm the scene: The actors are put into strait-jackets. The best way, the only way, is to search out that first shot—that first declarative sentence which I mentioned earlier—and the rest will follow naturally. It's not easy to come by, especially when there are a number of people in the scene. But until you get that shot you're at sea. The answer is not simply to pull back for a full shot. Instead, look for something that has style and visual energy, something in keeping with your ideas for the picture as a whole. You have the actors go through their paces and you still don't see it. Now, don't panic. Don't worry about what the actors and the crew may think (that the director doesn't know what the hell he's doing!). This anxiety may force you into something false. And if you get off to a false start, there's no correcting it. Given time and freedom, the actors will fall naturally into their places, discover when and where to move, and you will have your shot. And given all those shots, cut together, you will have your microcosm: the past on the winding reel; the present on the screen; the future on the unwinding reel . . . inevitable . . . unless the power goes off.

These observations are seldom remarked upon by picture-makers. They are so true, I suppose, that they are simply accepted without question as conventions. But they are conventions that have meaning—even for mavericks.

JEAN RENOIR

No one except Orson Welles has ever scored higher than Jean Renoir (1894–1979) in Sight & Sound's *ten-yearly polls of the world's greatest films. Usually two are mentioned:* The Rules of the Game *and* The Grand Illusion. *Renoir was a sunny man, somehow reflecting the jolly view of life that his father's paintings reflected, and in his last decades he lived in Southern California, where after directing his last film, he lived on as a friend, adviser, confidant, and wit, making friends of everyone he met. Here he discusses the genesis of* La Règle du Jeu *(*The Rules of the Game*), which remains one of the glories of the cinema.*

from *My Life and My Films*

You spend an evening listening to records and the result is a film. I cannot say that it was French baroque music that inspired me to make *La Règle du Jeu,* but certainly it played a part in making me wish to film the sort of people who danced to that music. I based my thought on it only at the beginning. It does not accompany the film except generically. I was entering a period of my life when my daily companions were Couperin, Rameau and every composer from Lulli to Grétry. By degrees my idea took shape and the subject became simplified, and after a few days, while I lived to baroque rhythms, it became more and more clearly defined.

I thought of certain of my friends whose amorous intrigues seemed to be their only object in life. As Lestringuez said: "If you want to write the truth you must get it well into your head that the world is one large knocking-shop. Men only think of one thing, and that is laying women; and the ones who think of anything else are played out—drowned in the muddy waters of sentimentality." Lestringuez was, of course, speaking for himself, but his words impressed me and I decided to transpose the characters, enacting that hitherto non-existent theme into our own period. Then I began to see the outline of the story, but not to the point where I had decided on any definite style.

I needed a background: it was the Sologne which provided me with the setting in which the actors were to discover the truth about the characters they were playing. Its mists took me back to the happy days of my childhood when Gabrielle and I went to the Théâtre Montmartre to be enthralled by *Jack Sheppard, ou les Chevaliers du Brouillard.* Nothing is more mysterious than a countryside emerging from fog. In that cotton-wool atmosphere the sound of gunshots is deadened. It is a perfect setting for a tale by Andersen. One expects to see will-o'-the-wisps emerging from every pool, or even the King of the Marshes himself. The Sologne is a region of marshes entirely devoted to hunting, a sport which I detest. I consider it an abominable exercise in cruelty. By situating my story amid those vapours I gave myself the chance to depict a shooting-party. These various elements crowded through my mind, compelling me to find a story in which they could be used.

My first idea was to produce an up-to-date version of *Les Caprices de Marianne.* This is the tale of a tragic misunderstanding: Marianne's lover is mistaken for someone else and killed in an ambush. I need not go into details; I introduced so much else into it that the story itself was reduced to a thread. An important element is the emotional honesty of Christine, the heroine. Since the authors of films and books are generally men, they tell stories about men. I like to describe women. Another important element is the purity of Jurieu, the victim, who, trying to fit into a world to which he does not belong, fails to respect the rules of the game. During the shooting of the film I was torn between my desire to make a comedy of it and the wish to tell a tragic story. The result of this ambivalence was the film as it is. I had moments of profound discouragement; but then, when I saw the way the actors were interpreting my ideas, I became wildly enthusiastic. My uncertainties are apparent in the development of the story and the acting of its protagonists. I recall the hesitations of Christine. The part was played by Nora Grégor, who was none other than Princess Stahremberg. Her husband, Prince Stahremberg, was an Austrian landowner who had founded an anti-Hitler peasant party. In his own domain the peasants voted for him, but the wave of Hitlerism was to sweep them aside.

I had got to know him shortly before *La Règle du Jeu*. He and his wife were in a state of great disarray. Everything they believed in was collapsing. One could write a novel about the state of mind of those exiles. But I was content to use the appearance of Nora Grégor, her look of "birdlike" sincerity, to shape the character of Christine. Once again I started from externals to arrive at the creation of a character or a plot. I must ask forgiveness for dwelling upon this point, but, having reached the time of life when I must face the fact that I shall make no more films, I am more than ever attached to that principle. One starts with the environment to arrive at the self. I respect and admire artists who proceed in the opposite direction. Abstract art corresponds to the necessities of our time. But personally I remain a man of the nineteenth-century and I need observation as a point of departure. My father, who mistrusted imagination, said: "If you paint the leaf on a tree without using a model you risk becoming stereotyped, because your imagination will only supply you with a few leaves whereas Nature offers you millions, all on the same tree. No two leaves are exactly the same. The artist who paints only what is in his mind must very soon repeat himself."

One does not really know what a film is until it has been edited. The first showings of *La Règle du Jeu* filled me with misgiving. It is a war film, and yet there is no reference to the war. Beneath its seemingly innocuous appearance the story attacks the very structure of our society. Yet all I thought about at the beginning was nothing avant-garde but a good little orthodox film. People go to the cinema in the hope of forgetting their everyday problems, and it was precisely their own worries that I plunged them into. The imminence of war made them even more thin-skinned. I depicted pleasant, sympathetic characters, but showed them in a society in process of disintegration, so that they were defeated at the outset, like Stahremberg and his peasants. The audience recognized this. The truth is that they recognized themselves. People who commit suicide do not care to do it in front of witnesses.

I was utterly dumbfounded when it became apparent that the film, which I wanted to be a pleasant one, rubbed most people up the wrong way. It was a resounding flop, to which the reaction was a kind of loathing. Despite a few favourable notices, the public as a whole regarded it as a personal insult. There was no question of contrivance; my enemies had nothing to do with its failure. At every session I attended I could feel the unanimous disapproval of the audience. I tried to save the film by shortening it, and to start with I cut the scenes in which I myself played too large a part, as though I were ashamed, after this rebuff, of showing myself on the screen. But it was useless. The film was dropped, having been judged to be "too demoralizing."

Many explanations of this attitude have been propounded. For my own part, I think the audience's reaction was due to my candour. The film had been shaped in response to influences in my personal life, the most powerful being those of my childhood. But that part of my life had been lived with my parents and Gabrielle, people incapable of not perceiving the truth behind the mask. To use a word that crops up frequently in the modern vocabulary, life with my family had been a "de-mystification." We are all "mystified"—that is to say, fooled, duped, treated as of no account. I had the good fortune to have been taught to see through the trickery in my youth. In *La Règle du Jeu,* I passed on what I knew to the public. But this is something that people do not like; the truth makes them feel uncomfortable. A quarter of a century later I gave a lecture at Harvard University. *La Règle du Jeu* was showing at a nearby cinema. There was a burst of cheering when I appeared on the platform. The students were applauding the film. Since then its reputation has steadily grown. What seemed an insult to society in 1939 has become clear-sightedness.

But the fact remains that the failure of *La Règle du Jeu* so depressed me that I resolved either to give up the cinema or to leave France.

AKIRA KUROSAWA

If the Japanese thought Ozu's films were too Japanese to travel to the West, they had the opposite problem with Akira Kurosawa: He was often criticized for making films that were too Western, with non-Japanese music on the sound track and stories that might as often have originated with Shakespeare, Maxim Gorky, or Ed McBain as with a Japanese au-

thor. Yet Kurosawa was responsible for creating images of medieval Japan that have since been reflected in countless other films and TV programs. Consider Seven Samurai, Yojimbo, The Hidden Fortress—*or his masterpiece* Rashōmon, *which he writes about here in his autobiography.*

from *Something Like an Autobiography*

During that time the gate was growing larger and larger in my mind's eye. I was location-scouting in the ancient capital of Kyōto for *Rashōmon,* my eleventh-century period film. The Daiei management was not very happy with the project. They said the content was difficult and the title had no appeal. They were reluctant to let the shooting begin. Day by day, as I waited, I walked around Kyōto and the still more ancient capital of Nara a few miles away, studying the classical architecture. The more I saw, the larger the image of the Rashōmon gate became in my mind.

At first I thought my gate should be about the size of the entrance gate to Tōji Temple in Kyōto. Then it became as large as the Tengaimon gate in Nara, and finally as big as the main two-story gates of the Ninnaji and Tōdaiji temples in Nara. This image enlargement occurred not just because I had the opportunity to see real gates dating from that period, but because of what I was learning, from documents and relics, about the long-since-destroyed Rashōmon gate itself.

"Rashōmon" actually refers to the Rajōmon gate; the name was changed in a Noh play written by Kanze Nobumitsu. "Rajō" indicates the outer precincts of the castle, so "Rajōmon" means the main gate to the castle's outer grounds. The gate for my film *Rashōmon* was the main gate to the outer precincts of the ancient capital—Kyōto was at that time called "Heian-Kyō." If one entered the capital through the Rajōmon gate and continued due north along the main thoroughfare of the metropolis, one came to the Shujakumon gate at the end of it, and the Tōji and Saiji temples to the east and west, respectively. Considering this city plan, it would have been strange had the outer main gate not been the biggest gate of all. There is tangible evidence that it in fact was: The blue roof tiles that survive from the original Rajōmon gate show that it was large. But, no matter how much research we did, we couldn't discover the actual dimensions of the vanished structure.

As a result, we had to construct the *Rashōmon* gate to the city based on what we could learn from looking at extant temple gates, knowing that the original was probably different. What we built as a set was gigantic. It was so immense that a complete roof would have buckled the support pillars. Using the artistic device of dilapidation as an excuse, we constructed only half a roof and were able to get away with our measurements. To be historically accurate, the imperial palace and the Shujakumon gate should have been visible looking north through our gate. But on the Daiei back lot such distances were out of the question, and even if we had been able to find the space, the budget would have made it impossible. We made do with a cut-out mountain to be seen through the gate. Even so, what we built was extraordinarily large for an open set.

When I took this project to Daiei, I told them the only sets I would need were the gate and the tribunal courtyard wall where all the survivors, participants and witnesses of the rape and murder that form the story of the film are questioned. Everything else, I promised them, would be shot on location. Based on this low-budget set estimate, Daiei happily took on the project.

Later Kawaguchi Matsutarō, at that time a Daiei executive, complained that they had really been fed a line. To be sure, only the gate set had to be built, but for the price of that one mammoth set they could have had over a hundred ordinary sets. But, to tell the truth, I hadn't intended so big a set to begin with. It was while I was kept waiting all that time that my research deepened and my image of the gate swelled to its startling proportions.

When I had finished *Scandal* for the Shōchiku studios, Daiei asked if I wouldn't direct one more film for them. As I cast about for what to film, I suddenly remembered a script based on the short story "Yabu no naka" ("In a Grove") by Akutagawa Ryūnosuke. It had been written by Hashimoto Shinobu, who had been studying under director Itami Mansaku. It was a very well-written piece, but not long enough to make into a feature film. This Hashimoto had visited my home, and I talked with him for hours. He seemed to have substance, and I took a liking to him. He later wrote the screenplays for *Ikiru* (1952) and *Shichinin no samurai* (*Seven Samurai*, 1954) with me. The script I remembered was his Akutagawa adaptation called "Male-Female."

Probably my subconscious told me it was not right to have put that script aside; probably I was—without being aware of it—wondering all the while if I couldn't do something with it. At that moment the memory of it jumped out of one of those creases in my brain and told me to give it a chance. At the same time I recalled that "In a Grove" is made up of three stories, and realized that if I added one more, the whole would be just the right length for a feature film. Then I remembered the Akutagawa story "Rashōmon." Like "In a Grove," it was set in the Heian period (794–1184). The film *Rashōmon* took shape in my mind.

Since the advent of the talkies in the 1930's, I felt, we had misplaced and forgotten what was so wonderful about the old silent movies. I was aware of the esthetic loss as a constant irritation. I sensed a need to go back to the origins of the motion picture to find this peculiar beauty again; I had to go back into the past.

In particular, I believed that there was something to be learned from the spirit of the French avant-garde films of the 1920's. Yet in Japan at this time we had no film library. I had to forage for old films, and try to remember the structure of those I had seen as a boy, ruminating over the esthetics that had made them special.

Rashōmon would be my testing ground, the place where I could apply the ideas and wishes growing out of my silent-film research. To provide the symbolic background atmosphere, I decided to use the Akutagawa "In a Grove" story, which goes into the depths of the human heart as if with a surgeon's scalpel, laying bare its dark complexities and bizarre twists. These strange impulses of the human heart would be expressed through the use of an elaborately fashioned play of light and shadow. In the film, people going astray in the thicket of their hearts would wander into a wider wilderness, so I moved the setting to a large forest. I selected the virgin forest of the mountains surrounding Nara, and the forest belonging to the Kōmyōji temple outside Kyōto.

There were only eight characters, but the story was both complex and deep. The script was done as straightforwardly and briefly as possible, so I felt I should be able to create a rich and expansive visual image in turning it into a film. Fortunately, I had as cinematographer a man I had long wanted to work with, Miyagawa Kazuo; I had Hayasaka to compose the music and Matsuyama as art director. The cast was Mifune Toshirō, Mori Masayuki, Kyō Machiko, Shimura Takashi, Chiaki Minoru, Ueda Kichijirō, Katō Daisuke and Honma Fumiko; all were actors whose temperaments I knew, and I could not have wished for a better line-up. Moreover, the story was supposed to take place in summer, and we had, ready to hand, the scintillating midsummer heat of Kyōto and Nara. With all these conditions so neatly met, I could ask nothing more. All that was left was to begin the film.

However, one day just before the shooting was to start, the three assistant directors Daiei had assigned me came to see me at the inn where I was staying. I wondered what the problem could be. It turned out that they found the script baffling and wanted me to explain it to them. "Please read it again more carefully," I told them. "If you read it diligently, you should be able to understand it because it was written with the intention of being comprehensible." But they wouldn't leave. "We believe we have read it carefully, and we still don't understand it at all; that's why we want you to explain it to us." For their persistence I gave them this simple explanation:

Human beings are unable to be honest with themselves about themselves. They cannot talk about themselves without embellishing. This script portrays such human beings—the kind who cannot survive without lies to make them feel they are better people than they really are. It even shows this sinful need for flattering falsehood going beyond the grave—even the character who dies cannot give up his lies when he speaks to the living through a medium. Egoism is a sin the human being carries with him from birth; it is the most difficult to redeem. This film is like a strange picture scroll that is unrolled and displayed by the ego. You say that you can't understand this script at all, but that is because the human heart itself is impossible to understand. If you focus on the impossibility of truly understanding human psychology and read the script one more time, I think you will grasp the point of it.

After I finished, two of the three assistant directors nodded and said they would try reading the script again. They got up to leave, but the third, who was the chief, remained unconvinced. He left with an angry look on his face. (As it turned out, this chief assistant director and I never did get along. I still regret that in the end I had to ask for his resignation. But, aside from this, the work went well.)

During the rehearsals before the shooting I was left virtually speechless by Kyō Machiko's dedication. She came in to where I was still sleeping in the morning and sat down with the script in her hand. "Please teach me what to do," she requested, and I lay there amazed. The other actors, too, were all in their prime. Their spirit and enthusiasm was obvious in their work, and equally manifest in their eating and drinking habits.

They invented a dish called Sanzoku-yaki, or "Mountain Bandit Broil," and ate it frequently. It consisted of beef strips sautéed in oil and then dipped in a sauce made of curry powder in melted butter. But while they held their chopsticks in one hand, in the other they'd hold a raw onion. From time to time they'd put a strip of meat on the onion and take a bite out of it. Thoroughly barbaric.

The shooting began at the Nara virgin forest. This forest was infested with mountain leeches. They dropped out of the trees onto us, they crawled up our legs from the ground to suck our blood. Even when they had had their fill, it was no easy task to pull them off, and once you managed to rip a glutted leech out of your flesh, the open sore seemed never to stop bleeding. Our solution was to put a tub of salt in the entry of the inn. Before we left for the location in the morning we would cover our necks, arms and socks with salt. Leeches are like slugs—they avoid salt.

In those days the virgin forest around Nara harbored great numbers of massive cryptomerias and Japanese cypresses, and vines of lush ivy twined from tree to tree like pythons. It had the air of the deepest mountains and hidden glens. Every day I walked in this forest, partly to scout for shooting locations and partly for pleasure. Once a black shadow suddenly darted in front of me: a deer from the Nara park that had returned to the wild. Looking up, I saw a pack of monkeys in the big trees above my head.

The inn we were housed in lay at the foot of Mount Wakakusa. Once a big monkey who seemed to be the leader of the pack came and sat on the roof of the inn to stare at us studiously throughout our boisterous evening meal. Another time the moon rose from behind Mount Wakakusa, and for an instant we saw the silhouette of a deer framed distinctly against its full brightness. Often after supper we climbed up Mount Wakakusa and formed a circle to dance in the moonlight. I was still young and the cast members were even younger and bursting with energy. We carried out our work with enthusiasm.

When the location moved from the Nara Mountains to the Kōmyōji temple forest in Kyōto, it was Gīon Festival time. The sultry summer sun hit with full force, but even though some members of my crew succumbed to heat stroke, our work pace never flagged. Every afternoon we pushed through without even stopping for a single swallow of water. When work was over, on the way back to the inn we stopped at a beer hall in Kyōto's downtown Shijō-Kawaramachi district. There each of us downed about four of the biggest mugs of draft beer they had. But we ate dinner without any alcohol and, upon finishing, split up to go about our private affairs. Then at ten o'clock we'd gather again and pour whiskey down our throats with a vengeance. Every morning we were up bright and clear-headed to do our sweat-drenched work.

Where the Kōmyōji temple forest was too thick to give us the light we needed for shooting, we cut down trees without a moment's hesitation or explanation. The abbot of Kōmyōji glared fearfully as he watched us. But as the days went on, he began to take the initiative, showing us where he thought trees should be felled.

When our shoot was finished at the Kōmyōji location, I went to pay my respects to the abbot. He looked at me with grave seriousness and spoke with deep feeling. "To be honest with you, at the outset we were very disturbed when you went about cutting down the temple trees as if they belonged to you. But in the end we were won over by your wholehearted enthusiasm. 'Show the audience something good.' This was the focus of all your energies, and you forgot yourselves. Until I had the chance to watch you, I had no idea that the making of a movie was a crystallization of such effort. I was very deeply impressed."

The abbot finished and set a folding fan before me. In commemoration of our filming, he had written on the fan three characters forming a Chinese poem: "Benefit All Mankind." I was left speechless.

We set up a parallel schedule for the use of the Kōmyōji location and open set of the Rashōmon gate. On sunny days we filmed at Kōmyōji; on cloudy days we filmed the rain scenes at the gate set. Because the gate set was so huge, the job of creating rainfall on it was a major operation. We borrowed fire engines and turned on the studio's fire hoses to full capacity. But when the camera was aimed upward at the cloudy sky over the gate, the sprinkle of the rain couldn't be seen against it, so we made rainfall with black ink on it. Every day we worked in temperatures of more than $85°$ Fahrenheit, but when the wind blew through the wide-open gate with the terrific rainfall pouring down over it, it was enough to chill the skin.

I had to be sure that this huge gate looked huge to the camera. And I had to figure out how to use the sun itself. This was a major concern because of the decision to use the light and shadows of the forest as the keynote of the whole film. I determined to solve the problem by actually filming the sun. These days it is not uncommon to point the camera directly at the sun, but at the time *Rashōmon* was being made it was still one of the taboos of cinematography. It was even thought that the sun's rays shining directly into your lens would burn the film in your camera. But my cameraman, Miyagawa Kazuo, boldly defied this convention and created superb images. The introductory section in particular, which leads the viewer through the light and shadow of the forest into a world where the human heart loses its way, was truly magnificent camera work. I feel that this scene, later praised at the Venice International Film Festival as the first instance of a camera entering the heart of a forest, was not only one of Miyagawa's masterpieces but a world-class masterpiece of black-and-white cinematography.

And yet, I don't know what happened to me. Delighted as I was with Miyagawa's work, it seems I forgot to tell him. When I said to myself, "Wonderful," I guess I thought I had said "Wonderful" to him at the same time. I didn't realize I hadn't until one day Miyagawa's old friend Shimura Takashi (who was playing the woodcutter in *Rashōmon*) came to me and said, "Miyagawa's very concerned about whether his camera work is satisfactory to you." Recognizing my oversight for the first time, I hurriedly shouted "One hundred percent! One hundred for camera work! One hundred plus!"

There is no end to my recollections of *Rashōmon*. If I tried to write about all of them, I'd never finish, so I'd like to end with one incident that left an indelible impression on me. It has to do with the music.

As I was writing the script, I heard the rhythms of a bolero in my head over the episode of the woman's side of the story. I asked Hayasaka to write a bolero kind of music for the scene. When we came to the dubbing of that scene, Hayasaka sat down next to me and said, "I'll try it with the music." In his face I saw uneasiness and anticipation. My own nervousness and expectancy gave me a painful sensation in my chest. The screen lit up with the beginning of the scene, and the strains of the bolero music softly counted out the rhythm. As the scene progressed, the music rose, but the image and the sound failed to coincide and seemed to be at odds with each other. "Damn it," I thought. The multiplication of sound and image that I had calculated in my head had failed, it seemed. It was enough to make me break out in a cold sweat.

We kept going. The bolero music rose yet again, and suddenly picture and sound fell into perfect unison. The mood created was positively eerie. I felt an icy chill run down my spine, and unwittingly I turned to Hayasaka. He was looking at me. His face was pale, and I saw that he was shuddering with the same eerie emotion I felt. From that point on, sound and image proceeded with incredible speed to surpass even the calculations I had made in my head. The effect was strange and overwhelming.

And that is how *Rashōmon* was made. During the shooting there were two fires at the Daiei studios. But because we had mobilized the fire engines for our filming, they were already primed and drilled, so the studios escaped with very minor damage.

After *Rashōmon* I made a film of Dostoevsky's *The Idiot* (*Hakuchi,* 1951) for the Shōchiku studios. This *Idiot* was ruinous. I clashed directly with the studio heads, and then when the reviews on the completed film came out, it was as if they were a mirror reflection of the studio's attitude toward me. Without exception, they were scathing. On the heels of this disaster, Daiei rescinded its offer for me to do another film with them.

I listened to this cold announcement at the Chōfu studios of Daiei in the Tokyo suburbs. I walked out through the gate in a gloomy daze, and, not having the will even to get on the train, I ruminated over my bleak situation as I walked all the way home to Komae. I concluded that for some time I would have to "eat cold rice" and resigned myself to this fact. Deciding that it would serve no purpose to get excited about it, I set out to go fishing at the Tamagawa River. I cast my line into the river. It immediately caught on something and snapped in two. Having no replacement with me, I hurriedly put my equipment away. Thinking this was what it was like when bad luck catches up with you, I headed back home.

I arrived home depressed, with barely enough strength to slide open the door to the entry. Suddenly my wife came bounding out. "Congratulations!" I was unwittingly indignant: "For what?" "*Rashōmon* has the Grand Prix." *Rashōmon* had won the Grand Prix at the Venice International Film Festival, and I was spared from having to eat cold rice.

Once again an angel had appeared out of nowhere. I did not even know that *Rashōmon* had been submitted to the Venice Film Festival. The Japan representative of Italiafilm, Giuliana Stramigioli, had seen it and recommended it to Venice. It was like pouring water into the sleeping ears of the Japanese film industry.

Later *Rashōmon* won the American Academy Award for Best Foreign Language Film. Japanese critics insisted that these two prizes were simply reflections of Westerners' curiosity and taste for Oriental exoticism, which struck me then, and now, as terrible. Why is it that Japanese people have no confidence in the worth of Japan? Why do they elevate everything foreign and denigrate everything Japanese? Even the woodblock prints of Utamaro, Hokusai and Sharaku were not appreciated by Japanese until they were first discovered by the West. I don't know how to explain this lack of discernment. I can only despair of the character of my own people.

JEREMY BERNSTEIN

The New Yorker *writer Jeremy Bernstein was one of the few outsiders allowed to watch the shooting of Stanley Kubrick's* 2001: A Space Odyssey *(1968), and he visited the set at a time when the giant centrifuge (which allowed the illusion of weightlessness in the space voyage scenes) was used. Although Kubrick as usual filmed in secrecy, the production attracted enormous curiosity, and I remember the anticipation at the film's first public screening, which was held in Los Angeles on the night before the "official" world premiere in Washington. The audience was first intrigued and then restless; at the intermission Rock Hudson stalked out, loudly complaining, "Will someone tell me what this movie is about?" The early reviews were mixed. Then word of mouth set in,* 2001 *developed a following, the film ran for months in many theaters, and it is now enshrined on the* Sight & Sound *list of the greatest films of all time.*

Stanley Kubrick

On December 29, 1965, shooting of the film began, and in early March the company reached the most intricate part of the camerawork, which was to be done in the interior of a giant centrifuge. One of the problems in space travel will be weightlessness. While weightlessness has, because of its novelty, a certain glamour and amusement, it would be an extreme nuisance on a long trip, and probably a health hazard as well. Our physical systems have evolved to work against the pull of gravity, and it is highly probable that all sorts of unfortunate things, such as softening of the bones, would result from exposure to weightlessness for months at a time. In addition, of course, nothing stays in place without gravity, and no normal activity is possible unless great care is exercised; the slightest jar can send you hurtling across the cabin. Therefore, many spacecraft designers figure that some sort of artificial gravity will have to be supplied for space travelers. In principle, this is very easy to do. An object on the rim of a wheel rotating at a uniform speed is subjected to a constant force pushing it away from the center, and by adjusting the size of the wheel and the speed of its rotation this centrifugal force can be made to resemble the force of gravity. Having accepted this notion, Kubrick went one step further and commissioned the Vickers Engineering Group to make an actual centrifuge, large enough for the astronauts to live in full time. It took six months to build and cost about three hundred thousand dollars. The finished product looks from the outside like a Ferris wheel thirty-eight feet in diameter and can be rotated at a maximum speed of about three miles an hour. This is not enough to parallel the force of gravity—the equipment inside the centrifuge has to be bolted to the floor—but it has enabled Kubrick to achieve some remarkable photographic effects. The interior, eight feet wide, is fitted out with an enormous computer console, an electronically operated medical dispensary, a shower, a device for taking an artificial sunbath, a recreation area, with a Ping-Pong table and an electronic piano, and five beds with movable plastic domes—hibernacula, where astronauts who are not on duty can, literally, hibernate for months at a time. (The trip to Jupiter will take two hundred and fifty-seven days.)

I had seen the centrifuge in the early stages of its construction and very much wanted to observe it in action, so I was delighted when chance sent me back to England in the early spring. When I walked through the door of the *2001* set one morning in March, I must say that the scene that presented itself to me was overwhelming. In the middle of the hangarlike stage stood the centrifuge, with cables and lights hanging from every available inch of its steel-girdered superstructure. On the floor to one side of its frame was an immense electronic console (not a prop), and, in various places, six microphones and three television receivers. I learned later that Kubrick had arranged a closed-circuit-television system so that he could watch what was going on inside the centrifuge during scenes being filmed when he could not be inside himself. Next to the microphone was an empty canvas chair with "Stanley Kubrick" painted on its back in fading black letters. Kubrick himself was nowhere to be seen, but everywhere I looked there were people, some hammering and sawing, some carrying scripts, some carrying lights. In one corner I saw a woman applying makeup to what appeared to be an astronaut wearing blue coveralls and leather boots. Over a loudspeaker, a pleasantly authoritative English voice—belonging, I learned shortly, to Derek Cracknell, Kubrick's first assistant director—was saying, "Will someone bring the Governor's Polaroid on the double?" A man came up to me and asked how I would like my tea and whom I was looking for, and almost before I could reply "One lump with lemon" and "Stanley Kubrick," led me, in a semi-daze, to an opening at the bottom of the centrifuge. Peering up into the dazzlingly illuminated interior, I spotted Kubrick lying flat on his back on the floor of the machine and staring up through the viewfinder of an enormous camera, in complete concentration. Keir Dullea, dressed in shorts and a white T shirt, and covered by a blue blanket, was lying in an open hibernaculum on the rising curve of the floor. He was apparently comfortably asleep, and Kubrick was telling him to wake up as simply as possible. "Just open your eyes," he said. "Let's not have any stirring, yawning, and rubbing."

One of the lights burned out, and while it was being fixed, Kubrick unwound himself from the camera, spotted me staring openmouthed at the top of the centrifuge, where the furniture of the crew's dining quarters was fastened to the ceiling, and said, "Don't worry—that stuff is bolted down." Then he motioned to me to come up and join him.

No sooner had I climbed into the centrifuge than Cracknell, who turned out to be a cheerful and all but imperturbable youthful-looking man in tennis shoes (all the crew working in the centrifuge were wearing tennis shoes, not only to keep from slipping but to help them climb the steeply curving sides; indeed, some of them were working while clinging to the bolted-down furniture halfway up the wall), said, "Here's your Polaroid, Guv," and handed Kubrick the camera. I asked Kubrick what he needed the Polaroid for, and he explained that he used it for checking subtle lighting effects for color film. He and the director of photography, Geoffrey Unsworth, had worked out a correlation between how the lighting appeared on the instantly developed Polaroid film and the settings on the movie camera. I asked Kubrick if it was customary for movie directors to participate so actively in the photographing of a movie, and he said succinctly that he had never watched any other movie director work.

The light was fixed, and Kubrick went back to work behind the camera. Keir Dullea was reinstalled in his hibernaculum and the cover rolled shut. "You better take your hands from under the blanket," Kubrick said. Kelvin Pike, the camera operator, took Kubrick's place behind the camera, and Cracknell called for quiet. The camera began to turn, and Kubrick said, "Open the hatch." The top of the hibernaculum slid back with a whirring sound, and Keir Dullea woke up, without any stirring, yawning, or rubbing. Kubrick, playing the part of the solicitous computer, started feeding him lines.

"Good morning," said Kubrick. "What do you want for breakfast?"

"Some bacon and eggs would be fine," Dullea answered simply.

Later, Kubrick told me that he had engaged an English actor to read the computer's lines in the serious dramatic scenes, in order to give Dullea and Lockwood something more professional to play against, and that in the finished film he would dub in an American-accented voice. He and Dullea went through the sequence four or five times, and finally Kubrick was satisfied with what he had. Dullea bounced out of his hibernaculum, and I asked him whether he was having a good time. He said he was getting a great kick out of all the tricks and gadgets, and added, "This is a happy set, and that's something."

When Kubrick emerged from the centrifuge, he was immediately surrounded by people. "Stanley, there's a black pig outside for you to look at," Victor Lyndon was saying. He led the way outside, and, sure enough, in a large truck belonging to an animal trainer was an enormous jet-black pig. Kubrick poked it, and it gave a suspicious grunt.

"The pig looks good," Kubrick said to the trainer.

"I can knock it out with a tranquilizer for the scenes when it's supposed to be dead," the trainer said.

"Can you get any tapirs or anteaters?" Kubrick asked.

The trainer said that this would not be an insuperable problem, and Kubrick explained to me, "We're going to use them in some scenes about prehistoric man."

At this point, a man carrying a stuffed lion's head approached and asked Kubrick whether it would be all right to use.

"The tongue looks phony, and the eyes are only marginal," Kubrick said, heading for the set. "Can somebody fix the tongue?"

Back on the set, he climbed into his blue trailer. "Maybe the company can get back some of its investment selling guided tours of the centrifuge," he said. "They might even feature a ride on it." He added that the work in the machine was incredibly slow, because it took hours to rearrange all the lights and cameras for each new sequence. Originally, he said, he had planned on a hundred and thirty days of shooting for the main scenes, but the centrifuge sequences had slowed them down by perhaps a week. "I take advantage of every delay and breakdown to go off by myself and think," he said. "Something like playing chess when your opponent takes a long time over his next move."

At one o'clock, just before lunch, many of the crew went with Kubrick to a small projection room near the set to see the results of the previous day's shooting. The most prominent scene was a brief one that showed Gary Lockwood exercising in the centrifuge, jogging around its interior and shadow-boxing to the accompaniment of a Chopin waltz—picked by Kubrick because he felt that an intelligent man in 2001 might choose Chopin for doing exercise to music. As the film appeared on the screen, Lockwood was shown jogging around the complete interior circumference of the centrifuge, which appeared to me to defy logic as well as physics, since when he was at the top he would have needed suction cups on his feet to stay glued to the floor. I asked Kubrick how he had achieved this effect, and he said he was definitely, absolutely not going to tell me. As the scene went on, Kubrick's voice could be heard on the sound track, rising over the Chopin: "Gain a little on the camera, Gary! . . . Now a flurry of lefts and rights! . . . A little more vicious!" After the film had run its course Kubrick appeared quite pleased with the results, remarking, "It's nice to get two minutes of usable film after two days of shooting."

SATYAJIT RAY

Satyajit Ray's Pather Panchali, *the first part of the Apu Trilogy, is often listed as one of the best films of all time. As Ray (1921–1992) makes clear here, the first day of filming was also the first day he ever directed. At the Hawaii Film Festival a few years ago I met Subatra Mitra, Ray's cinematographer on this and other great films. He told me it was also his first day as a cinematographer; he had never shot a foot of film before and was quietly terrified. At the festival Mitra was given the Eastman Kodak Award for Excellence in Cinematography, and in his acceptance speech he thanked not Satyajit Ray—that went without saying—but his camera and his film.*

"A Long Time on the Little Road"

I remember the first day's shooting of *Pather Panchali* very well. It was in the festive season, in October, and the last of the big *pujas* was taking place that day. Our location was seventy-five miles away from Calcutta. As our taxi sped along the Grand Trunk Road, we passed through several suburban towns and villages and heard the drums and even had fleeting glimpses of some images. Someone said it would bring us luck. I had my doubts, but I wished to believe it. All who set about making films need luck as much as they need the other things: talent, money, perseverance and so on. We needed a little more of it than most.

I knew this first day was really a sort of rehearsal for us, to break us in, as it were. For most of us it was a start from scratch. There were eight on our unit of whom only one—Bansi, the art director—had previous professional experience. We had a new cameraman, Subroto, and an old, much-used Wall camera which happened to be the only one available for hire on that particular day. Its one discernible advantage seemed to be a device to ensure smoothness of panning. We had no sound equipment, as the scene was to be a silent one.

It was an episode in the screenplay where the two children of the story, brother and sister, stray from their village and chance upon a field of *kaash* flowers. The two have had a quarrel, and here in this enchanted setting they are reconciled and their long journey is rewarded by their first sight of a railway train. I chose to begin with this scene because on paper it seemed both effective and simple. I considered this important, because the whole idea behind launching the production with only 8,000 rupees in the bank was to produce quickly and cheaply a reasonable length of rough cut which we hoped would establish our bonafides, the lack of which had so far stood in the way of our getting a financier.

At the end of the first day's shooting we had eight shots. The children behaved naturally, which was a bit of luck because I had not tested them. As for myself, I remember feeling a bit strung up in the beginning; but as work progressed my nerves relaxed and in the end I even felt a kind of elation. However, the scene was only half finished, and on the following Sunday we were back on the same location. But was it the same location? It was hard to believe it. What was on the previous occasion a sea of fluffy whiteness was now a mere expanse of uninspiring brownish grass. We knew *kaash* was a seasonal flower, but surely they were not that short-lived? A local peasant provided the explanation. The flowers, he said, were food to the cattle. The cows and buffaloes had come to graze the day before and had literally chewed up the scenery.

This was a big setback. We knew of no other *kaash* field that would provide the long shots that I needed. This meant staging the action in a different setting, and the very thought was heart-breaking. Who would have known then that we would be back on the identical location exactly two years later and indulge in the luxury of reshooting the entire scene with the same cast and the same unit but with money provided by the Government of West Bengal.

When I look back on the making of *Pather Panchali,* I cannot be sure whether it has meant more pain to me than pleasure. It is difficult to describe the peculiar torments of a production held up for lack of funds. The long periods of enforced idleness (there were two gaps totalling a year and a half) produce nothing but the deepest gloom. The very sight of the scenario is sickening, let alone thoughts of embellishing it with details, or brushing up the dialogue.

But work—even a day's work—has rewards, not the least of which is the gradual comprehension of the complex and fascinating nature of film making itself. The edicts of the theorists learnt assiduously over the years doubtless perform some useful function at the back of your mind, but grappling with the medium in a practical way for the first time, you realise (*a*) that you know rather less about it than you thought you did; (*b*) that the theorists do not provide all the answers, and (*c*) that your approach should derive not from Dovzhenko's *Earth*, however much you may love that dance in the moonlight, but from the earth, the soil, of your own country—assuming, of course, that your story has its roots in it.

Bibhutibhusan Banerji's *Pather Panchali* was serialised in a popular Bengali magazine in the early 1930s. The author had been brought up in a village and the book contained much that was autobiographical. The manuscript had been turned down by the publishers on the ground that it lacked a story. The magazine, too, was initially reluctant to accept it, but later did so on condition that it would be discontinued if the readers so wished. But the story of Apu and Durga was a hit from the first instalment. The book, published a year or so later, was an outstanding critical and popular success and has remained on the best-seller list ever since.

I chose *Pather Panchali* for the qualities that made it a great book: its humanism, its lyricism, and its ring of truth. I knew I would have to do a lot of pruning and reshaping—I certainly could not go beyond the first half, which ended with the family's departure for Banaras—but at the same time I felt that to cast the thing into a mould of cut-and-dried narrative would be wrong. The script had to retain some of the rambling quality of the novel because that in itself contained a clue to the feel of authenticity: life in a poor Bengali village does ramble.

Considerations of form, rhythm or movement did not worry me much at this stage. I had my nucleus: the family, consisting of husband and wife, the two children, and the old aunt. The characters had been so conceived by the author that there was a constant and subtle interplay between them. I had my time span of one year. I had my contrasts—pictorial as well as emotional: the rich and the poor, the laughter and the tears, the beauty of the countryside and the grimness of poverty existing in it. Finally, I had the two natural halves of the story culminating in two poignant deaths. What more could a scenarist want?

What I lacked was firsthand acquaintance with the *milieu* of the story. I could, of course, draw upon the book itself, which was a kind of encyclopaedia of Bengali rural life, but I knew that this was not enough. In any case, one had only to drive six miles out of the city to get to the heart of the authentic village.

While far from being an adventure in the physical sense, these explorations into the village nevertheless opened up a new and fascinating world. To one born and bred in the city, it had a new flavour, a new texture: you wanted to observe and probe, to catch the revealing details, the telling gestures, the particular turns of speech. You wanted to fathom the mysteries of "atmosphere." Does it consist in the sights, or in the sounds? How to catch the subtle difference between dawn and dusk, or convey the grey humid stillness that precedes the first monsoon shower? Is sunlight in spring the same as sunlight in autumn? . . .

The more you probed the more was revealed, and familiarity bred not contempt but love, understanding, tolerance. Problems of film making began to recede into the background and you found yourself belittling the importance of the camera. After all, you said, it is only a recording instrument. The important thing is Truth. Get at it and you've got your great humanist masterpiece.

But how wrong you were! The moment you are on the set the three-legged instrument takes charge. Problems come thick and fast. Where to place the camera? High or low? Near or far? On the dolly or on the ground? Is the thirty-five O.K. or would you rather move back and use the fifty? Get too close to the action and the emotion of the scene spills over; get too far back and the thing becomes cold and remote. To each problem that arises you must find a quick answer. If you delay, the sun shifts and makes nonsense of your light continuity.

Sound is a problem too. Dialogue has been reduced to a minimum, but you want to cut down further. Are those three words really necessary, or can you find a telling gesture to take their place? The critics may well talk of a laudable attempt at a rediscovery of the fundamentals of silent cinema, but you know within your heart that while there may be some truth in that, equally true was your anxiety to avoid the uninspiring business of dubbing and save on the cost of sound film.

Cost, indeed, was a dominant factor at all times, influencing the very style of the film. Another important factor—and I would not want to generalise on this—was the human one. In handling my actors I found it impossible to get to the stage of impersonal detachment where I could equate them with so much raw material to be moulded and remoulded at will. How can you make a woman of eighty stand in the hot midday sun and go through the same speech and the same actions over and over again while you stand by and watch with half-closed eyes and wait for that precise gesture and tone of voice that will mean perfection for you? This meant, inevitably, fewer rehearsals and fewer takes.

Sometimes you are lucky and everything goes right in the first take. Sometimes it does not and you feel you will never get what you are aiming at. The number of takes increases, the cost goes up, the qualms of conscience become stronger than the urge for perfection and you give up, hoping that the critics will forgive and the audience will overlook. You even wonder whether perhaps you were not being too finicky and the thing was not as bad or as wrong as you thought it was.

And so on and on it goes, this preposterous balancing act, and you keep hoping that out of all this will somehow emerge Art. At times when the strain is too much you want to give up. You feel it is going to kill you, or at least kill the artist in you. But you carry on, mainly because so much and so many are involved, and the day comes when the last shot is in the can and you are surprised to find yourself feeling not happy and relieved, but sad. And you are not alone in this.

Everybody, from "Auntie," for whom it has been an exciting if strenuous come-back after thirty years of oblivion, down to the little urchin who brought the live spiders and the dead toad, shares this feeling.

To me it is the inexorable rhythm of its creative process that makes film mak-ing so exciting in spite of the hardships and the frustrations. Consider this process: you have conceived a scene, any scene. Take the one where a young girl, frail of body but full of some elemental zest, gives herself up to the first monsoon shower. She dances in joy while the big drops pelt her and drench her. The scene excites you not only for its visual possibilities but for its deeper im-plications as well: that rain will be the cause of her death.

You break down the scene into shots, make notes and sketches. Then the time comes to bring the scene to life. You go out into the open, scan the vista, choose your setting. The rain clouds approach. You set up your camera, have a last quick rehearsal. Then the "take." But one is not enough. This is a key scene. You must have another while the shower lasts. The camera turns, and presently your scene is on celluloid.

Off to the lab. You wait, sweating—this is September—while the ghostly negative takes its own time to emerge. There is no hurrying this process. Then the print, the "rushes." This looks good, you say to yourself. But wait. This is only the content, in its bits and pieces, and not the form. How is it going to join up? You grab your editor and rush off to the cutting room. There is a gruelling couple of hours, filled with aching suspense, while the patient process of cut-ting and joining goes on. At the end you watch the thing on the moviola. Even the rickety old machine cannot conceal the effectiveness of the scene. Does this need music, or is the incidental sound enough? But that is another stage in the creative process, and must wait until all the shots have been joined up into scenes and all the scenes into sequences and the film can be comprehended in its to-tality. Then, and only then, can you tell—if you can bring to bear on it that de-tachment and objectivity—if your dance in the rain has really come off.

But is this detachment, this objectivity, possible? You know you worked honestly and hard, and so did everybody else. But you also know that you had to make changes, compromises—not without the best of reasons—on the set and in the cutting room. Is it better for them or worse? Is your own satisfaction the final test or must you bow to the verdict of the majority? You cannot be sure. But you can be sure of one thing: you are a better man for having made it.

FEDERICO FELLINI

*Federico Fellini (1920–1993) was not born in Rome—his childhood in Rimini is well
documented in his films and writings—but he loved it and knew it as well as anyone, and
in* La Dolce Vita *(1960) he made the Via Veneto, its notorious street of nightlife, world-
famous. It was a street he knew well for many years, as a café artist who supported himself in his early days in Rome by sketching the patrons in restaurants. He was thrown out
of so many of them, he recalls, that after he became a successful director, he stayed away
from the street for a while, afraid of being recognized. But eventually a film about the
street and its denizens began to take shape in his imagination.*

from *Fellini on Fellini*

For a while I steered clear of Via Veneto and its surroundings, afraid of being
recognised as the painter of shop windows. Besides, my partner was not particularly successful at it either, so we decided to make a change. The "Marc Au-
relio" had accepted a few of my short articles in the meantime, and suddenly all
was set fair, when the war intervened. Even the declaration of war is linked, in
my mind, with a memory of Via Veneto. I had heard Mussolini's voice ("People of Italy, to arms . . .") on the wireless in the porter's room at the "Marc Au-
relio" and had been wandering about the streets on my own, worried and shaken.
Rome was empty: in the whole of Via Veneto, with its trees fully in leaf since
it was June, there wasn't a soul to be seen. Then a man came riding down on a
bicycle towards Piazza Barberini without touching the pedals. He raised a hand
from the handle-bars to greet me and shouted: "Hey, war's been declared!"

The years went by and my feeling of inferiority about Via Veneto went away
too. Throughout the war, the liberation and the postwar years, the intellectuals continued to gather at Rosati's, as if they were its guardians. The only difference now, was that one of them occasionally greeted me. And I myself was

entering their circle more casually, through meetings with script writers and directors like Pinelli, Lattuada and Germi. We would often spend hours discussing the psychology of some character or the possible variants on some dramatic situation, sunk deep in the armchairs of a café; and meantime Rome was gradually changing outside, becoming the navel of a world sated with living in a new jazz age, waiting for a third world war, or for a miracle, or for the Martians. The cinema exploded, the Americans came, café society prospered, the women became marvellous, the sack dress came into fashion, and cars began to look like legendary monsters. One evening I sat enthralled for a long time, gazing at a fat man with a black moustache drinking mineral water at a table in the Café de Paris, enjoying the cool sunset with a girl like some fruitful goddess: it was the ex-king of Egypt, Farouk. I watched the photographers prowling round his table and realise that they were pushing their bulbs closer and closer to him, just to annoy. In the end Farouk leapt furiously to his feet, the table was overturned, people rushed up and the cameras flashed more than ever.

I spent many evenings with the photographer-reporters of Via Veneto, chatting with Tazio Secchiaroli and the others, and getting them to tell me about the tricks of their trade. How they fixed on their victim, how they behaved to make him nervous, how they prepared their pieces, exactly as required, for the various papers. They had amusing tales to tell: waiting in ambush for hours, thrilling escapes, dramatic chases. One evening I actually took them all out to dinner, and I must admit they thought up all kinds of tall stories for my benefit. In the end Secchiaroli said: "Stop inventing, you idiots, you're talking to an old hand at the game," and I didn't know whether to take it as a compliment or an insult.

I started planning scenes and having ideas for characters based on the style of life which was now so precisely characteristic of the place. One evening I gave a lift to a blond young man wearing eye-shadow whom everyone called Chierichetta, as I was determined to discover what such a person was like. He told me he lived at Borgo San Pio, near St. Peter's; and that he was very Catholic, loving only his mother and Jesus—so much so that he would have liked to wear his hair in a Jesus style. While we were wandering aimlessly around the Appia Antica district he burst out with his troubles, saying he wanted to change his life, that he could hear the voice of conscience, exactly as if there was someone inside him saying: "Mind what you're doing." He wanted to set up with a lawyer, a serious person, and let all the rest go, all the more so because there was going to be an apocalypse within the next few years and all the wicked would be swept away in a new deluge. He had a way of giving form to his fears which, though it never quite ceased to be grotesque, nevertheless had a sincerely religious note about it. What he said struck me profoundly.

With Flaiano, Pinelli and Brunello Rondi I checked my impressions of the material I had been gathering and went ahead in the vague direction of a film which would deal with the life of those years. And thus, through the warm summer evenings of 1958, along Via Veneto, *La dolce vita* was born, and with it all my arduous trek from producer to producer, from office to office, determined to fight for a film which, in professional circles, was said to be a failure before it had been started.

When we came to start work, Via Veneto became a problem. The city authorities allowed us to film in the street only from two till six in the morning and hedged this permission with all kinds of reservations. For the scene in which Marcello Mastroianni took Anita home, after her bathe in the Trevi Fountain, there were no difficulties. We started off in the middle of the night and managed to "capture" a really lovely dawn, with Anita's teeth chattering with cold, Marcello worried over the punches he was to get from the athletic Lex Barker, and the photo-reporters, the *paparazzi,* jumping around the set like a lot of devils. The scene in the car between Marcello and Anouk Aimée was more complicated, because I didn't want to use any tricks in directing it. There were endless discussions with the police and in the end we got permission to film the scene in movement so long as we didn't ever stop and snarl up the traffic. Clemente Fracassi organised a line of cars that looked like a procession of the Three Wise Men. I started it in my car, driving half twisted backwards to see what was happening. Marcello and Anouk followed me in an open Cadillac. Anouk could hardly drive but the scene made it necessary for her to do so: she was pale, tense and frightened. Beside her, Mastroianni, who prides himself on being an experienced driver, was suffering horribly. They were followed by the car carrying the camera and then by the row of production cars, while little Fiats and mopeds carrying the assistants bustled about at the sides of the long column.

As the scene required several takes, we made the same trip by turning off round the blocks of buildings and reassembling the procession in Via Ludovisi. A large number of people had gathered on the pavements to watch this triumphal procession go by; a scene that was both swanky and slightly sordid, as it always is when you're filming in the midst of ordinary people. I remember particularly the face of a curious onlooker outside the "Excelsior," a man wearing a beret, with a face of dark leather, like a saracen. This young fellow was waiting anxiously for me to pass and, knowing perfectly well that I couldn't stop without the skies falling, when I was just a yard or so away yelled one of those Roman words at me that cannot be printed in a newspaper. This happened four, five, six times: as soon as I arrived at the traffic lights the saracen would stare at me, grinning from a distance, savouring the prospect of insulting me. Then when I came close to him—bang, every time he would fling that word at me, always the same word but spoken each time with mounting enthusiasm. When I went by the seventh time I was fed up with him and would have stopped the car and got out and hit him if I hadn't been afraid of ruining a night's work. So I merely answered him in kind, using words and gestures that only my impotent fury at the time could justify. As soon as the filming was finished and the column of cars had broken up in Via Sardegna, I asked a couple of the toughest drivers to follow me and ran back to the "Excelsior" to settle accounts. But the man who had sworn at me had vanished, melted away. Even today I have his image stamped on my mind, with his beret and everything else, and I still haven't given up hope of meeting him some day.

It was the shock of this incident that made me force the producers to let me build a reconstruction of Via Veneto. I had to film a number of scenes at café tables, among them the one in which Marcello meets his father, and it just wasn't possible to film them late at night or using hidden cameras. So Piero Gherardi, the designer, started taking measurements and built me a large slice of Via Veneto on Number 5 stage at Cinecittà. We even had a party there, inviting people from the other Via Veneto, and the illusion was perfect. All the stars of the film were at it: Anita, Anouk, Yvonne Furneaux, Luise Rainer, who was to appear in a scene we dropped later on. Their presence caused very delicate problems of precedence, which amused me a great deal at the party. Only towards the end of it, as an answer to the voices of gloom criticising the cost of it all and the time it was taking, did I say to a journalist: "We've decided to have a party like this every three months while we're working on the film." Angelo Rizzoli heard me and merely waved a threatening fist at me from the opposite pavement of our imaginary street.

The Via Veneto which Gherardi rebuilt was exact down to the smallest detail, but it had one thing peculiar to it: it was flat instead of sloping. As I worked on it I got so used to this perspective that my annoyance with the real Via Veneto grew even greater and now, I think, it will never disappear. When I pass the Café de Paris, I cannot help feeling that the real Via Veneto was the one on Stage 5, and that the dimensions of the rebuilt street were more accurate or at any rate more agreeable. I even feel an invisible temptation to exercise over the real street the despotic authority I had over the fake one. This is all a complicated business which I ought to talk about to someone who understands psychoanalysis.

ANTHONY QUINN

Anthony Quinn is one of the great exuberant presences in the movies, remembered for Viva
Zapata!, La Strada, Lawrence of Arabia, *and* Zorba the Greek, *but he has also been
present in countless other movies for half a century, some good, some bad, some priceless
(see his Aristotle Onassis in* The Greek Tycoon). *At eighty he wrote his autobiography,*
One Man Tango, *and here he writes about meeting a young Italian named Federico Fellini
who wanted to make a movie in a way that the visiting star from Hollywood could only
have misgivings about. Quinn's book is one of the rare star autobiographies worth reading; it's not that he always tells the truth (who knows?) but that he re-creates his memories so vividly. The Rome he portrays in this book is the same city that Fellini himself was
to record in* La Dolce Vita, *a film that essentially brought an end to the era it was about.*

from *One Man Tango*

NEO-REALIST COWBOYS

It is a funny thing, that I am here, now, in this restaurant. I have been returning to this place for years, but I have come today for a reason. It is only now that
I puzzle together the realization.

This, after all, is the same place an exciting young director took me to discuss a script, back in 1953, over lunch. He wore a quizzical smile and an outlandish cowboy hat, each of which he refused to take off during the meal. It was
not much of a script—only a few pages—and yet it held the rough edges of a
masterpiece. The director had sent it to me the night before, but it was in Italian, and I pushed it back across the table, unread, asking my host to tell me the
story instead.

The story he told would change my life completely, and immediately, and it
is a wonder that I have returned to the very spot of its unfolding. How is it that

in a moment of impulsive rediscovery a man manages to retrace his steps so precisely? Is there some path that has been predetermined for me? Is God pulling my strings and moving me along by design? I had no idea where I was headed, when I set out from Vigna S. Antonio this morning, and yet at every turn I stumble across a telling reminder of my past. Either I have lived too much of a life to avoid such coincidence, or I have entrusted myself so thoroughly to the whims of memory that coincidence cannot help but find me.

Indeed, as the headwaiter returns with my second bottle of wine, I realize that even he fits in the correlation. He is the same man who served that fateful lunch, all those years ago. What are the odds of this? It is not his restaurant—he is just a hired hand—and yet he is still here. He approaches, and seems to make the same connection. The director has become our mutual acquaintance, our secret. We talk of him often. He is the one thing we share.

"Our friend," the waiter says, filling my glass, "he was something, no?"

He was something, yes. Federico Fellini had only made two full-length pictures at the time of our first meeting—*The White Sheik* and *I Vitelloni*—and I had not seen either one, but his reputation was already enormous. He was one of the leading neo-realists, and the talk of the Italian cinema. I did not know what a neo-realist was, but figured I would find out. The ridiculous cowboy hat did nothing to diminish his standing, and he held forth underneath its wide brim as if he had worn one all his life.

I had gone to Rome earlier that year, as the axis of the motion picture industry tilted toward Europe. Italian pictures such as *Open City, Shoeshine, Paisan,* and *The Bicycle Thief* were having a tremendous impact in Hollywood, and signaled a renaissance in movie making. In contrast, American pictures seemed locked in an industrial and creative crisis, and hopelessly stale. Now that I was enjoying some sudden success, I wanted to act on the richest possible stage, surrounded by the biggest talents. The only audience I craved was an audience of my peers. I needed to be where it mattered most, so I packed up my family and followed the wave.

It was an enchanted time. I fell in love with Rome the moment I set foot in the city. Six hours later, I was in a hospital with food poisoning—it might have been the fava, the pecuno, or the wine—but that was part of Rome's charm. It gave as good as it took. Right away I felt the inventive energy that Hemingway, Fitzgerald, Picasso, and Joyce had created in Montparnasse. Rome had its own Gertrude Steins, but its literary explosion was fueled by images. The artists of this renaissance were not producing paintings for churches, or manuscripts for the ages, but pictures for movie houses. What the hell did I care? To me, one artist was much like another. All expression is the same. What difference did it make if we worked in a modern medium, as long as we worked well and remained true to our calling?

The city was seething with moviemakers from all over the world. It was like Hollywood, New York, and Cannes, all rolled into one. Most deals were made on Via Veneto, over Campari or espresso. Every player had to make an appearance. On Sunday mornings, sidewalk cafes on both sides of the street were filled to overflowing. An actor's popularity was measured by how many scripts he was offered as he traversed the street. Kirk Douglas, with whom I worked in *Ulysses,* my first Italian picture (produced by Dino De Laurentiis and Carlo Ponti), used to engage me in a singular game of one-upmanship. One Sunday, he ran the gauntlet from the Excelsior Hotel to the Porta Pinciana and back again, returning with nineteen legitimate offers.

He topped my best by two.

I had no frame of reference for such a spectacle. In Hollywood, the stars would only assemble at premieres or awards ceremonies, but along the Via Veneto it was common to see Greg Peck, Ingrid Bergman, Bill Holden, Anna Magnani, Gene Kelly, Silvana Mangano, Clark Gable, Audrey Hepburn, Gary Cooper, Jennifer Jones, or Errol Flynn turn out for the sidewalk show, often on the same afternoon. The six blocks between the Excelsior and the Porta Pinciana were the center of the motion picture industry, and we were drawn to it as if by suction.

To walk those six blocks with aplomb became quite an accomplishment, and a test of confidence. Ingrid Bergman strolled with a stately Nordic gait, like a conquering Viking. Coop refused to run the obstacle course; he saved his showmanship for the screen, but his refraining was itself a powerful statement. Kirk Douglas was probably the most successful at it—he overwhelmed everyone with his infectious enthusiasm—but I preferred Anna Magnani's majestic style. She paraded down the street with her two black German shepherds, while all other activity came to a halt. She walked that road just as Calpurnia must have walked through ancient Rome, the empress of all she surveyed.

I arrived during springtime and felt a part of things from the first. Rome is like that, I have come to realize, and in this it is like no other city in the world. All the great places sneak up on you—Paris has to be discovered: Athens takes its time—but only Rome grabs you at the outset, and never lets go. I was immediately drunk with its beauty, and felt the city had something to say to me, just. We shared a secret, Rome and I, and for the longest time I was not telling a soul.

The steps of the Piazza di Spagna were awash in color, limned by huge potted azaleas advertising the change in season. The entire city seemed to be on a festive kick. It was just eight years since the end of the war, and the energy that had been capped during the German occupation was still in release. And no people are more eager to release their energy, I learned, than the Italians. There was a famous line about Italians—"Forty million great actors, and only the bad ones make movies!"—and its root was on every face, on every corner. It was a place that breathed life, and gave life in return.

It was wonderful.

I ran the Via Veneto gauntlet immediately, and went to work. From *Ulysses,* I moved to a dramatic version of *Cavelleria Rusticana* (in 3-D, no less!), and a convoluted Giuseppe Amato picture called *Donne Proibite,* with Linda Darnell, who no longer thought I was a fairy. When one picture wrapped, I went straight to another.

Katherine and I lived in the city, in a house rented from Eduardo De Filippo's brother, and I took to the lifestyle right away. My wife was less sure of the change, and less sure of me. She was beginning to think I was crazy—talking to myself, and my father; stalking the demons that still prowled our bed—and I was beginning to think she might be right. I could find no happiness in our marriage, no peace. I walked around looking for answers to questions that had not yet occurred to me. Katherine was also searching. She had become a deeply religious person, and was by now extremely active in the Moral Rearmament movement, dedicated to the moral awakening of mankind, through faith and purity. (These evangelists had a hold on her I could never understand!) Our daughter Valentina was born just the year before, and I think we both recognized the child's birth as the beginning of our last act. We might stay together for the rest of our lives—for the sake of the children, for appearances, perhaps even for ourselves—but the marriage was dying. After more than fifteen years, it was clear that neither one of us had the power (or the inclination) to revive it.

Work was my release, my escape. I took a part in another Ponti–De Laurentiis production, *Attila, Flagello di Dio*—as Attila the Hum, opposite Sophia Loren and Irene Papas. It was to mark the beginning of a long association with the fiery Greek actress, who at the time preferred to be called "Ereenee." She had an intensity about her that was difficult to ignore, but her frailty was what I found most appealing. We were too much alike to ever truly get along. She seemed to be of my blood. She could have been my sister or my grandmother. My feelings for her were mixed with incestuous guilt, but I could not look away from them.

Irene was the kind of girl who walked into your room and held up her hand. She would not talk to you until she looked under your bed, through your bookcases and your collection of records and photographs. Then she would know who you were. I remarked that her cataloging would be useless with me—I was living with rented furnishings!—but she was determined. I had no idea what the bad hotel paintings told her about me, but she did not go away.

The *Attila* production was notable for a comic disaster that might have shut down the entire picture. If it was up to me, it would have.

We shot a great many scenes on Monte Cavo, in Rocca di Papa, just south of

Rome. One afternoon, at the beginning of a rare snowstorm, the director left to shoot a few scenes that did not involve Irene or me. He took the entire crew with him, and left the two of us in a hotel up on a hill. We welcomed the short break. There was a bar and a restaurant. It would just be a few hours. We would be fine.

I had spent hours in makeup and wardrobe that morning, and it made no sense to take everything off just to put it back on again in the afternoon, so I walked around the hotel in a suit of armor. My eyes were pinched back with a powerful glue, to leave me looking properly Asian and barbaric. I was preparing to attack Rome in my next scene, and this was what you looked like when you attacked Rome. Irene too was dressed in a wild outfit, and we lounged around like two beasts from another century.

Actually, for a while, it was rather fun, noodling around the old hotel with Irene in period costume, but the novelty wore off soon enough when we noticed the snowstorm getting worse. There were no wristwatches in the Dark Ages, and we lost all track of time. Irene walked over to the window and gasped. "Tony, look," she said. "The snow. It's blocking the door."

I went over to see for myself. The snow was about three feet deep. There were drifts reaching up to the windows. The wind and fog made it difficult to see for more than a few feet.

"What the hell time is it?" I wondered.

Irene had no idea. We went down to the front desk to use the hotel telephone. It was four o'clock. Four o'clock! Jesus, where the hell did everybody go? We could not get an outside line at first, but eventually we reached the studio in Rome. I got one of De Laurentiis's assistants on the other end. "Where the fuck are you people?" I railed. "Are you gonna use us today or what?"

"You're still up there?" the kid said. He explained that shooting broke several hours ago, when the snows threatened the roads. Everyone had been sent home.

"Yes, we're still up here. Where are we gonna go?"

The kid was scared for his job, but it was not his fault. "Mr. Quinn," he said. "I'm terribly sorry. Would you mind staying in the hotel tonight?"

"You're fuckin' right, I mind. I can't stay with Irene in the hotel. Jesus, all of Rome will be talking about it. You get a car up here."

"We can't get a car," the kid tried to reason. "The roads are closed. And that hill, leading up to the hotel, that hill must be treacherous."

The manager could not help but overhear my tirade, and he offered one of the hotel trucks to take us back down Monte Cavo and into Rome. "It's just a bread truck, Mr. Quinn," he cautioned, "and there's no room in the cab, but you should make it down the hill. The driver needs to get back down to the bakery, so he's going anyway."

So Irene and I piled into the back of the truck, dressed like barbarians and surrounded by sacks filled with fresh-baked bread. Jesus, we must have been a sight! We slipped down that hill like it was an amusement park ride. I was certain we would fly off the side of the road and tumble to our deaths in the valley below.

What a way to go!—crushed by a bakery truck, smelling of blood and flour, dressed as Attila the Hun. I imagined the headlines.

By this time, the snow had stopped and the skies cleared. The countryside was absolutely magnificent, like a winter wonderland, but I did not care about the scenery. I was cold, and tired, and hungry. I wanted to go home.

The driver made to let us out at the bottom of the hill, but I was not moving. "We can't get out here," I shouted. "Look how we're dressed! We're in costume, goddamn it!" Outside I could see children playing in the streets. It was like a mid-afternoon holiday. The entire town was out to romp in the snow. The last thing I needed was to step from the truck as Attila the Hun, into the middle of that scene.

I ripped the glue-mask from my temples in anger—I still have the scars!— and then I gave the driver about two hundred dollars in U.S. money to take us back to Rome.

The next day, I refused to go to work. I was furious at the director. What kind of asshole maroons his two stars in the middle of one of the worst storms in memory? What was he thinking?

"Fuck you," I said, when someone at the studio called to see where I was. "I'm not coming in."

The day after that, it was the same. I stayed home for a week. Every day they called, and every day I told them to go to hell. Finally, I thought I had punished them enough. A week was enough time for a proper tantrum. Anything more would have been unprofessional. I had wanted to shut down the picture, but I thought it was enough that I crippled it.

I got into my car and drove to the studio, but they were no longer expecting me. "What the fuck are you doing here?" De Laurentiis said, when I reported for work.

"I'm here to finish the picture," I said. "I was too mad to come back to work, but I'm not mad anymore. I've held out long enough. I know I've been costing you a lot of money."

Dino flashed a villainous smile. "Not exactly," he said. "We're collecting insurance. Your little protest is actually making us a profit."

"You bastard," I laughed. "I'm stewing at home, teaching you a lesson, and you're making money?" It was a fitting irony.

"Go back home," Dino said, conspiratorially. "Go back to bed. The insurance company is sending someone to check you out. You must tell them you've had a horrible experience. Tell them you don't know when you'll be able to come back to work." He hurried me back to my car, giggling like a boy caught with his hand in the cookie jar.

The making of *Attila* was also notable as counterpoint, for it was in the middle of my self-imposed exile that I first met Fellini. I had played opposite his wife, the actress Giulietta Masina, and she was forever touting her brilliant husband. It seemed that everyone was singing the man's praises. For all its grandeur, the Italian film community was rather intimate; it did not take long to recognize the players, and to know everybody's business. Fellini's name was all over the place. He was like an exciting storm on the horizon, and all we could do was secure ourselves against him.

Giulietta tried to arrange a meeting while we were shooting *Donne Proibite,* but for some reason we did not get together until I had begun work on *Attila.* She was anxious for me to work with her husband, she said, because it was meant to be. I was the man Fellini was looking for to make his next picture.

Well, I did not know about that, but I did want to meet him. My friends Ingrid Bergman and Roberto Rossellini told me to take absolutely any part he offered me, at any price. "You must work with him," urged Rossellini, who had given Fellini his first break as a screenwriter. "It will mean everything."

I liked Fellini immediately, even with the silly cowboy hat. He gave me the most marvelous piece of advice. He had seen me interviewed by some Italian journalists, and thought that I had been too forthcoming in my response. "Why do you tell these people the truth?" he wondered from behind his crooked smile. "I do not understand it. Are you psychoanalyzing yourself? Are you using your confessions so that you may fight your way out of them? Is that why you do it?"

He did not wait for a reply, but continued talking. "Me," he said, "I never tell the truth to a journalist. I always lie. It is like an exercise to me, because when I lie I have to use my imagination, I have to think. Tell them whatever you want and they will believe you. Tell them you are making a million dollars a picture. Tell them you have an identical twin who works in a fish hatchery. Tell them and you will read it in the papers the next day."

I looked at him with deep admiration. It had never occurred to me to bullshit my way through the trappings of celebrity. "It is a remarkable philosophy," I allowed.

"What philosophy?" he dismissed. "It is just a game. I make up stories, then I make a picture out of it. You, you tell the truth and you're stuck with it. You don't move anywhere. Creatively, you don't move."

Perhaps he was right. The story he had made up and had now come to tell me was about a miserable minstrel who travels the back roads of Italy, staging cheesy roadside attractions for the locals. He is part showman, part strongman, part no man at all. He lives in a tiny shack of a trailer, hitched to the back of a beat-up motorcycle. He collects a simple girl from a small village and works her into his act. He treats her like a slave. They set off together on separate missions; to the girl, it is an adventure, and the chance to serve the man who has come to claim her; to the man, it is another leg of his long escape, and the chance to squeeze a few extra pennies from the townspeople along the way.

Fellini was calling his picture *La Strada*—The Road—and to him it was all about one man's bitter loneliness, and his rejection of the love and devotion of the one woman who would have him. I listened to Fellini's tale and for a moment thought he was talking about me.

I still did not know from neo-realism, but I liked the story well enough, and I was anxious to learn what all the fuss was about surrounding this looming giant of the Italian cinema. Fellini did not look like any giant, but he was an interesting fellow and he seemed to care about pictures. I told him I would gladly play the part of Zampano, the wandering strongman.

He asked me what my salary was and I told him.

"That's the budget for the whole picture!" he choked.

He was in no position to haggle, and neither was I. *Viva Zapata!* had made me a star, and my stock was rising. Who knew how long I would be in demand? The trick, in pictures, was to get your price while you could, and take whatever you could get after that. It would be some time before I could make a picture just for the hell of it.

"Tell you what," he finally said. "I'll give you twenty-five percent of the picture."

I looked across the table at Fellini and smiled. He must have really wanted me for the role. No one had ever wanted me enough to give me a piece of the picture. Plus, I liked him, and I liked the story.

"Fine," I said, extending my hand. "Let's make a picture."

We very nearly had a deal, but for Dino De Laurentiis. I had not counted on him, but he surfaced soon enough. I was under contract to Dino at the time, and smack in the middle of the *Attila* shoot. Fellini wanted to begin production right away. The only way around the conflict, I thought, was to get De Laurentiis to bend a bit on his exclusivity clause, and to break my ass in the bargain.

I had it all figured out. In those days, Italian studios functioned under so-called French hours, which meant we worked from noon to seven o'clock in the evening, without breaking for lunch. Of course, the hours were sometimes shifted to accommodate an exterior shot requiring morning light, or a tight deadline, but the producers were usually good about sticking to the later schedule. It was quite a civil change for the American actors accustomed to arriving on the set by seven or eight in the morning, but the Europeans—bless them all!—preferred to work later in the evening in exchange for a good night's rest.

What the French hours meant for me, and Fellini, was that I would be able to play the part of Zampano if he could arrange to shoot *La Strada* in the mornings. It was not an ideal situation for him—the picture was to be shot almost entirely outdoors, and he hated to give up all those daylight hours—but it was better than nothing. And it would not be ideal for me, working virtually around the clock for a stretch of several weeks, but I wanted to see if I was up to it.

It fell to me to extract De Laurentiis's approval.

"Dino," I explained, visiting him in his office the next morning. "I met a guy named Fellini, and he wants to make a picture with me."

"Fellini?" he said. "That no-talent? He's so full of shit I can't understand what he's saying. He wanted me to finance a picture of his, some nonsense about a circus, or a strongman."

"That's it," I said. "That's the picture. That's the one he wants me to make."

"Don't be an idiot, Tony. The man likes to put his wife in his pictures."

I chose not to remind Dino that his own wife, Silvana Mangano, was a fixture in several De Laurentiis productions. "What's wrong with that?" I asked instead. "I've worked with Giulietta before. She's quite good."

"She's wrong for the part. I'd rather use Gina Lollobrigida in that part."

He was talking like a producer. Gina Lollobrigida was wrong for Fellini's picture. "Look, Dino," I said, "I want to make the picture. I'll shoot that picture in the mornings and come to work for you in the afternoons."

"You can't do that!" he blustered. "We have a contract!"

"We do. That's why I'm here. I was hoping we could work something out."

What we worked out was that De Laurentiis and Ponti would finance Fellini's picture, in order to keep a tight rein on my schedule. It cost them $250,000, which was nothing next to the money they had already dropped on *Attila*. Plus, I convinced them it was a good investment. And it was. Dino and Carlo made millions on *La Strada*, and the picture established them as two of the most powerful producers on the international scene. Hell, it won them an Academy Award, as best foreign language film, when it was finally released in the United States in 1956, and as far as I know they never once thanked the director for his vision, or any of the actors for their performances—or me, for persuading them to invest in the picture in the first place.

But all of that was unimportant next to everything else. *La Strada* placed Federico Fellini at the vanguard of the motion picture industry, and laid the groundwork for his extraordinary career. I squired him around Hollywood, after the American release, helping him to shop for a studio deal. The studio heads were leapfrogging each other to sign up the Italian auteur, offering him as much as a million dollars for his next picture—a phenomenal sum in those days. I translated for my friend.

"A million dollars," Fellini said, incredulous. "What for?"

"For a picture. Just to direct a picture."

"No," he finally said. "I can't. I can't direct an American picture. I would not know how to tell an American actor how to hold his cigarette."

La Strada vaulted me from respect as a supporting player to international recognition. It might have made me a rich man too—if I had held on to my piece of the picture. I had no idea the movie would have such an impact, even after it was in the can. I arranged a special showing for my agent and several friends, and when the lights came on in the screening room, everyone was scratching his head. No one could understand it, and I was so convinced the picture would be a flop that I let my agent sell my twenty-five percent stake for a lousy twelve thousand dollars, turning one of the best deals of my life into one of the worst.

Even when the dice rolled my way, I crapped out.

KENNETH TYNAN

Mel Brooks once came to my film class to speak. The students had just seen his great comedy The Producers, *and one of them told him he thought it was vulgar. "I would like to explain something to you," Brooks said. "This movie, it rises below vulgarity." Brooks himself is such a funny man, so warm and engaging, that a documentary of his average day might be more entertaining than some of his movies. Kenneth Tynan, with Harold Hobson one of the two most influential British drama critics from the 1950s through the flowering of the Angry Young Men, wrote a series of show business profiles for* The New Yorker. *Here he records Brooks on just such an average day.*

Mel Brooks

I draw on my journal for the following impressions of the Once and Future Five at work (and play) on *High Anxiety*, a quintuple-threat Brooks movie in which he functioned as producer, director, co-author, title-song composer, and star:

July 14, 1977: Arrive in Pasadena for the last day of shooting. By pure but pleasing coincidence, location is named Brookside Park. Temperature ninety degrees, atmosphere smog-laden. Only performers present are Brooks, leaping around in well-cut charcoal-gray suit with vest, and large flock of trained pigeons. As at Mamma Leone's, he is playing a psychiatrist. Sequence in rehearsal is parody of *The Birds*, stressing aspect of avian behavior primly ignored by Hitchcock: Pigeons pursue fleeing Brooks across park, subjecting him to bombardment of bird droppings. Spattered star seeks refuge in gardener's hut, slams door, sinks exhausted onto upturned garbage can. After momentary respite, lone white plop hits lapel, harbinger of redoubled aerial assault through hole in roof. Brooks's hundred-yard dash is covered by tracking camera, while gray-haired technicians atop motorized crane mounted on truck squirt bird excreta (simulated by mayonnaise and chopped spinach) from height of thirty feet. Barry Levinson, one of four collaborators on screenplay, observes to me, "We have enough equipment here to put a man on the moon, and it's all being used to put bird droppings on Brooks." After each of numerous trial runs and takes, pigeons obediently return to their cages, putty in the hands of their trainer—"the same bird wrangler," publicity man tells me, "who was employed by Hitchcock himself." Find manic energy of Brooks, now fifty-one years old, awesome: by the time shot is satisfactorily in can, he will have sprinted, in this depleting heat, at least a mile, without loss of breath, ebullience, or directorial objectivity, and without taking a moment's break.

Each take is simultaneously recorded on videotape and instantly played back on TV screen—a technique pioneered by Jerry Lewis—to be scrutinized by Brooks, along with his fellow authors, Levinson, Rudy DeLuca, and Ron Clark, who make comments ranging from condign approval to barbed derision. Dispelling myth that he is megalomaniac, Brooks listens persuadably to their suggestions, many of which he carries out. The writers, receiving extra pay as consultants, have been with him throughout shooting, except for three weeks when they went on strike for more money. Brooks coaxed them back by giving up part of his own share of profits not only of *High Anxiety* but of *Silent Movie*, on which he worked with same three authors. Main purpose of their presence is not to rewrite—hardly a line has been changed or cut—but to offer pragmatic advice. In addition, they all play supporting roles in picture. Later, as also happened on *Silent Movie*, they will view first assembly of footage and help Brooks with process of reducing it to rough-cut form. "Having us around keeps Mel on his toes," Levinson explains to me. "He likes to have constant feedback, and he knows we won't flatter him." All of which deals telling blow to already obsolescent *auteur* theory, whereby film is seen as springing fully armed from mind of director. Good to find Brooks, who reveres writers, giving them place in sun: he has often said that he became a director primarily in self-defense, to "protect my vision"—i.e., the script as written. "There's been no interference from the front office," Levinson continues, as Brooks trudges back to his mark for yet another charge through cloudburst of salad dressing. "Nobody from Fox has even come to see us. Mel has free rein. Jerry Lewis once had that kind of liberty, but who has it now? Only Mel and, I guess, Woody Allen."

Am reminded of remark made to me by Allen a few days earlier: "In America, people who do comedy are traditionally left alone. The studios feel we're on a wavelength that's alien to them. They believe we have access to some secret formula that they don't. With drama, it's different. Everybody thinks he's an expert."

Writers and camera crew gather round tree-shaded monitor to watch replay of latest take. Smothered in synthetic ordure, star bustles over to join them:

BROOKS: I stare at life through fields of mayonnaise. (*Wipes eyes with towel.*) Was it for this that I went into movies? Did I say to my mother, "I'm going to be a big star, momma, and have birds shit on me"? I knew that in show business *people* shit on you—but *birds*! Some of this stuff is not mayonnaise, you know. Those are real pigeons up there.

The take (last of twenty) is generally approved, and Brooks orders it printed. Welcoming me to location, he expresses pleasure at hearing British accent, adding, "I love the Old World. I love the courteous sound of the engines of English cabs. I also love France and good wine and good food and good homosexual production designers. I believe all production designers should have a brush stroke, a scintilla, of homosexuality, because they have to hang out with smart people." (Brooks once declared, in an interview with *Playboy*, that he loved Europe so much that he always carried a photograph of it in his wallet. "Of course," he went on, "Europe was a lot younger then. It's really not a very good picture. Europe looks much better in person." He lamented the fact that his beloved continent was forever fighting: "I'll be so happy when it finally settles down and gets married.")

Brooks's version of shower scene from *Psycho*, shot several days before, now appears on monitor. An unlikely stand-in for Janet Leigh, Brooks is seen in bathrobe approaching fatal tub. Cut to closeup of feet as he daintily sheds sandals, around which robe falls to floor. Next comes rear view of Brooks, naked from head to hips, stepping into bath. Star watches himself entranced.

BROOKS (*passionately*): When people see this, I want them to say, "He may be just a small Jew, but I love him. A short little Hebrew man, but I'd follow him to the ends of the earth." I want every fag in L.A. to see it and say, "Willya *look* at that *back*?"

Before lunch break, he takes opportunity to deliver speech of thanks to assembled crew, whose reactions show that they have relished working with him.

Recall another apposite quote from Woody Allen, who said to me in tones of stunned unbelief, "I hear there's a sense of enjoyment on Mel's set. I hear the people on his movies love the experience so much that they wish it could go on forever. On my movies, they're *thrilled* when it's over."

"As you all know," Brooks begins, "you'll never get an Academy Award with me, because I make comedies." This is a recurrent gripe. Brooks feels that film comedy has never received, either from industry or from audience, respect it deserves, and he is fond of pointing out that Chaplin got his 1971 Academy Award "just for surviving," not for *The Gold Rush* or *City Lights*.

BROOKS (*continuing*): I want to say from my heart that you're the best crew I ever found. Of course, I didn't look that hard. But you have been the most fun, and the costliest. I wish to express my sincere hope that the next job you get is—*work*.

Over lunch, consumed at long trestle tables under trees, he recounts—between and sometimes during mouthfuls—how he visited Hitchcock to get his blessings on *High Anxiety*.

BROOKS: He's a very emotional man. I told him that where other people take saunas to relax, I run *The Lady Vanishes*, for the sheer pleasure of it. He had tears in his eyes. I think he understood that I wasn't going to make fun of him. If the picture is a sendup, it's also an act of homage to a great artist. I'm glad I met him, because I love him. I love a lot of people that I want to meet so I can tell them about it before they get too old. Fred Astaire, for instance. And Chaplin. I've got to go to Switzerland and tell him—just a simple "Thank you," you know? [Chaplin died five months later, before this pilgrimage could be made.]

More Brooksian table talk, in response to student writing dissertation on his work:

STUDENT: What's the best way to become a director?

BROOKS: The royal road to direction used to be through the editing room. Today my advice would be: write a few successful screenplays. Anybody can direct. There are only eleven good writers. In all of Hollywood. I can name you many, many screenwriters who have gone on to become directors. In any movie, they are the prime movers.

STUDENT: Have you any ambition to make a straight dramatic film?

BROOKS (*vehemently*): No! Why should I waste my good time making a straight dramatic film? Sydney Pollack can do that. The people who can't make you laugh can do that. Suppose I became the Jean Renoir of America. What the hell would be left for the other guys to do? I would take all their jobs away. It would be very unfair of me.

STUDENT: In other words, "Shoemaker, stick to your last"?

BROOKS: Yes. And in Hollywood you're only as good as your last last.

STUDENT: But don't you want to surprise your audience?

BROOKS: Sure. Every time. I gave them *Blazing Saddles*, a Jewish Western with a black hero, and that was a megahit. Then I gave them a delicate and private film, *Young Frankenstein*, and that was a hit. Then I made *Silent Movie*, which I thought was a brave and experimental departure. It turned out to be another Mel Brooks hit. *High Anxiety* is the ultimate Mel Brooks movie. It has lunatic class.

STUDENT: But what if you had a serious dramatic idea that really appealed to you? Would you—

BROOKS: Listen, there are one hundred and thirty-one viable directors of drama in this country. There are only two viable directors of comedy. Because in comedy you have to do everything the people who make drama do—create plot and character and motive and so forth—and *then,* on top of *that,* be funny.

UNIDENTIFIED BEARDED MAN: Have you ever thought of being funny onstage?

BROOKS: No, because I might become this white-belted, white-shoed, maroon-mohair-jacketed type who goes to Vegas and sprays Jew-jokes all over the audience. A few years of that and I might end up going to England, like George Raft or Dane Clark, wearing trench coats in B movies.

Debate ensues about differences (in style and personality) between Brooks and the other "viable director of comedy," Woody Allen. Both are New York Jewish, both wrote for Sid Caesar, both are hypochondriacs, much influenced by time spent in analysis. There is general agreement at table on obvious distinction—that Brooks is extrovert and Allen introvert.

BARRY LEVINSON: They're total opposites. Mel is a peasant type. His films deal with basic wants and greeds, like power and money. Woody's films are about inadequacies—especially sexual inadequacy—and frailty and vulnerability. Also, like Chaplin, Woody is his own vehicle. His movies are like episodes from an autobiography. You couldn't say that about Mel.

HOWARD ROTHBERG (*slim, dark-haired young man who has been Brooks's personal manager since 1975*): The big difference is that Mel's appeal is more universal. *Blazing Saddles* grossed thirty-five million domestically and *Silent Movie* is already up to twenty million. Woody, on the other hand, appeals to a cult. I love his pictures, but they have a box-office ceiling. They don't go through the roof.

BROOKS (*who has been wolfing cannelloni, followed by ice cream*): No matter how much *High Anxiety* grosses, it won't give me one more iota of freedom. I have the freedom right now to do anything I want. My contract is with the public—to entertain them, not just to make money out of them. I went into show business to make a noise, to *pronounce myself.* I want to go on making the loudest noise to the most people. If I can't do that, I'm not going to make a quiet, exquisite noise for a cabal of cognoscenti.

This is Brooks the blusterer speaking, the unabashed attention-craver who started out as a teenage timpanist and is still metaphorically beating his drum. Can testify that drummer has alter ego, frequently silenced by the din: Brooks the secret connoisseur, worshipper of good writing, and expert on the Russian classics, with special reference to Gogol, Turgenev, Dostoevski, and Tolstoy. Is it possible that—to adapt famous aphorism by Cyril Connolly—inside every Mel Brooks a Woody Allen is wildly signalling to be let out?

STUDENT: I think your films are somehow more benevolent and affirmative than Woody Allen's.

BROOKS: Let's say I'm beneficent. I produce beneficial things. A psychiatrist once told me he thought my psyche was basically very healthy, because it led to *product*. He said I was like a great creature that gave beef or milk. I'm munificent. I definitely feel kingly. Same kind of Jew as Napoleon.

STUDENT: Napoleon was Jewish?

BROOKS: Could have been. He was short enough. Also, he was very nervous and couldn't keep his hands steady. That's why he always kept them under his lapels. I put him in one of my records. [Fans will remember how the Two-Thousand-Year-Old Man took a summer cottage on Elba, where he met the exiled Emperor on the beach—"a shrimp, used to go down by the water and cry"—without at first realizing who he was: "The guy was in a bathing suit, how did I know? There was no place to put his hands."] Anyway, there's something disgustingly egotistical about me. I never truly felt inferior. I never developed small defenses. I never ran scared. Even in comedy, you don't want your hero to be a coward. You want him to go forth and give combat, which is what I do in *High Anxiety*. Now, Woody makes Fellini-ish, Truffaut-ish films. He starts out with the idea of making art. He feels that his art is his life. And more power to him. The difference is that if someone wants to call my movies art or crap, I don't mind.

Detect, once more, sound of obsessive drumbeating; last sentence, in particular, seems intended to convince drummer himself as much as anyone else. Conversation breaks off as Brooks returns to work. Hear him in distance inviting youthful assistant to take over direction of brief scene in gardener's hut, already rehearsed, where star is deluged anew with bird droppings—"a job," he graciously declares to the grinning apprentice, "fully commensurate with your latent talents."

Finishing my coffee, I mull over recent conversations with Gene Wilder, who has been directed thrice by Brooks (in *The Producers, Blazing Saddles,* and *Young Frankenstein*) and once by Allen (in *Everything You Always Wanted to Know about Sex but Were Afraid to Ask*). According to Wilder: "Working with Woody is what it must be like to work with Ingmar Bergman. It's all very hushed. You and I were talking quietly now, but if we were on Woody's set someone would already have told us to keep our voices down. He said three things to me while we were shooting—'You know where to get tea and coffee?' and 'You know where to get lunch?' and 'Shall I see you tomorrow?' Oh, and there was one other thing: 'If you don't like any of these lines, change them.' Mel would never say that. The way Woody makes a movie, it's as if he was lighting ten thousand safety matches to illuminate a city. Each one of them is a little epiphany, topical, ethnic, or political. What Mel wants to do is set off atom bombs of laughter. Woody will take a bow and arrow or a hunting rifle and aim it at small, precise targets. Mel

grabs a shotgun, loads it with fifty pellets, and points it in the general direction
of one enormous target. Out of fifty, he'll score at least six or seven huge bull's-
eyes, and those are what people always remember about his films. He can syn-
thesize what audiences all over the world are feeling, and suddenly, at the right
moment, blurt it out. He'll take a universal and crystallize it. Sometimes he's
vulgar and unbalanced, but when those seven shots hit that target, I know that
little maniac is a genius. A loud kind of Jewish genius—maybe that's as close as
you can get to defining him."

This reminds me of something written in 1974 by the critic Andrew Sarris:

> Allen's filmmaking is more cerebral, and Brooks's more intuitive. In a strange
> way, Brooks is more likable than Allen. Thus, even when Allen tries to do the
> right thing, he seems very narrowly self-centered, whereas even when Mel Brooks
> surrenders to the most cynical calculations—as he does so often in *Blazing Sad-
> dles*—he still spills over with emotional generosity. . . . What Allen lacks is the
> reckless abandon and careless rapture of Brooks.

Reflect that this positive judgment is not necessarily incompatible with negative opinion I have lately heard from former colleague of Brooks; viz., "Woody
has become a professional, whereas Mel is still a brilliant amateur. Amateurs are
people putting on parties with multimillion-dollar budgets."

Return to set, where, after nearly twelve weeks' shooting, current party is
over. Brooks has brought in picture—budgeted at four million dollars—four
days ahead of schedule. Though in buoyant mood, he expresses horror at rock-
eting cost of filmmaking: "One actor and a few birds, but I'll bet you this has
been a twenty-thousand-dollar day." (Studio accounting department afterward
confirms that he would have won his bet.) I take my leave. Brooks clicks heels
and bows, saying, "Your obedient Jew." He misses no opportunity to brandish
his Jewishness, which he uses less as a weapon than as a shield. Remember (he
seems to be pleading) that I must be liked, because it is nowadays forbidden to
dislike a Jew.

Manager Rothberg accompanies me to parking lot, explaining how much success of movie means to Brooks. I suggest that surely he can afford to make a flop.
"Financially, he can," Rothberg says. "Psychologically, he can't."

August 31, 1977: "My beloved, you are guinea pigs." It is a balmy evening
seven weeks later, and Brooks is introducing first showing of rough-cut to audience of two hundred (including workers on picture, their friends and relations,
and minor studio employees such as waiters, cleaners, and parking attendants)
who have crowded into private theatre at Fox. He continues, "There are children present. Some of them may be mine, so I'm not going to do the filthy speech
that is customary on these occasions. For the nonce, by which I mean no offense,
this movie is called *High Anxiety*, a phrase that I hope will enter common par-

lance and become part of the argot of Americana. But what you will see tonight has no music, no sound effects, and no titles. You won't even see our swirling artwork. You will, however, see a lot of crayon lines, which I will explain for the benefit of the editor. They indicate something called opticals. This picture has one hundred and six dissolves, of which you will see *not one*. There are some other very fancy opticals that I am having processed in Cairo right now. There is also one crayon mark that should be on a men's room wall, but we couldn't get it out in time. As you know, it's incumbent on us all to be killed in a Hitchcock movie, and you will see several people being very tastefully slaughtered. I regret to tell you that in casting four crucial roles we ran out of money, so the people who *wrote* the picture are *in* it. Finally, let me say that I wish you well, but I wish myself better."

ANDY WARHOL AND PAUL HACKETT

It is amazing to recall, in these days of meticulously marketed big-budget blockbusters, that there was once a time when not only did Andy Warhol make films, but they played all over the country and ordinary moviegoers bought tickets to see them. Sex was the key; at the moment in the 1960s when Warhol's best-known films began to appear, people would sit all the way through Chelsea Girls *for even the promise of nudity, although what was much more intriguing was the milieu itself. What Warhol was really making were cinema verité documentaries about people who thought they were making a movie.*

from *POPism*

The only thing "underground" about American underground movies—I mean, in the strict political sense of having to hide from some authority—was that in the early sixties there was the big censorship problem with nudity. The fifties had been *Lolita*-scandal time—even as late as '59 there was the big deal about Grove Press publishing *Lady Chatterley's Lover* and later on about Henry Miller's

Tropic of Cancer. The censorship policies in this country have always completely baffled me because there was never a time when you couldn't walk into any 42nd Street peep show and see all the cocks and cunts and tits and asses you wanted, then suddenly out of the blue the courts would single out one popular movie with a few racy scenes in it for "obscenity."

Some underground filmmakers actually kind of hoped the police would seize their movies so they'd get in all the papers for being persecuted for "freedom of expression," and that was always considered a worthy cause. But it was pretty much a fluke who the police arrested and who they didn't and after a certain point it all got boring for everyone.

The first movie of mine that was seized was a two-minute-forty-five-second one-reeler that I'd shot out in Old Lyme of everybody during the filming of Jack Smith's *Normal Love*—the one where the cast made a room-size cake and got on top of it. Actually, it was seized by mistake—what the police were out to get was Jack's *Flaming Creatures.*

Jonas's Coop had moved from the Gramercy Arts Theater to the building Diane di Prima and some of the other poets used on St. Mark's Place on the southeast corner of the Bowery. After *Flaming Creatures* was seized, the screenings were stopped for a little while. Then Jonas rented the Writers Stage on 4th Street between Second Avenue and the Bowery and he screened Genet's *Un Chant d'amour* there. "I knew that Jack's would be a difficult case to fight," Jonas told me, "with nobody really knowing who he was, and I felt that Genet—for the right or wrong reasons—would be a better case because he was a famous writer. And I was right—when they clubbed us that time for obscenity, we won."

After all the court cases Jonas realized that he needed some type of umbrella nonprofit organization, so he created the Film Culture Non-Profit Organization, which published *Film Culture* magazine and sponsored screenings and other things. During that period they had screenings in "respectable" places—like that Washington Square art gallery of Ruth Kligman's—so they wouldn't be closed down again by the police. Ruth's was where Jonas showed a lot of Marie Menken's films and in the fall we showed *Blow Job* there publicly for the first time.

All through '64 we filmed movies without sound. Movies, movies, and more movies. We were shooting so many, we never even bothered to give titles to a lot of them. Friends would stop by and they'd wind up in front of the camera, the star of that afternoon's reel.

. . . .

Once [Emile De Antonio] started making movies, he never went back to the art scene. In the past year we'd only seen each other a couple of times, at parties. But then I bumped into him one afternoon on the street and we went to the Russian Tea Room for a drink. We sat there gabbing about what we'd been doing, and I offered that since we were both doing movies now, wouldn't it be great to do one together. Now, with people who know me, I'm famous for this sort of thing—proposing collaborations. (I'm also famous for not spelling out what the collaboration will consist of—who'll do what—and lots of people have told me how frustrating that can be. But the thing is, I never know exactly what I want to do, and the way I see it, why worry about things like specifics beforehand, since nothing may ever come of the project? Do it first, then look at what you've got, and *then* worry about who did what. But most people would disagree with me, saying it's better to have an understanding at the outset.) When I suggested doing some sort of a joint production to De, I was just being impulsive. But De was always so practical, he squelched my suggestion right away, saying that our lives and styles and politics (I can't remember if he was calling himself a Marxist yet) and philosophies were just too different.

I must have looked very disappointed, because he held up his drink and said, "Okay, Andy, I'll do something for you that I'm sure nobody's ever offered to do for you and you can film it: I'll drink an entire quart of Scotch whiskey in twenty minutes."

We went right over to 47th Street and made a seventy-minute film. De finished the bottle before I reloaded at the halfway point, but he wasn't showing the liquor yet. However, in just the little while it took to put more film in the camera, he was suddenly on the floor—singing and swearing and scratching at the wall, the whole time trying to pull himself up and not being able to.

Now, the thing was, I didn't really know what he'd meant when he told me, "I'll risk my life for you." Even when I saw him crawling around on all fours, I just thought of it simply as someone being really drunk. Then Rotten Rita, who was hanging around, said, "Marine Corps sergeants keel over dead from that. Your liver can't take it."

But De didn't die, and I called the movie *Drink* so it could be a trilogy with my *Eat* and *Sleep*. When the little old lady we used as a go-between brought it back from the lab, I called De to come over and see it. He said, "I'm bringing my woman and an English friend and I hope no one else will be there." There was no one at the Factory right then anyway, except for Billy and Gerard and me and a couple of people who looked like they were on their way out. But as soon as I hung up, a gang of Gerard's friends happened to walk in, and by the time De got there, there were around forty people all over the place. We ran the film and after it was over, De said to me, "I'll probably sue you if you ever screen it publicly again." I knew he'd never sue me, of course, but that was his way of telling me not to have a print made of it.

.   .   .   .

At the end of '64 we made *Harlot*, our first sound movie *with* sound—*Empire*, the eight-hour shot of the Empire State Building, had been our first "sound" movie with*out* sound. Now that we had the technology to have sound in our movies, I realized that we were going to be needing a lot of dialogue. It's funny how you get the solution to things. Gerard and I were down at the Café Le Metro for one of the Wednesday night poetry readings when a writer named Ronnie Tavel was reading passages from his novel and some poems. He seemed to have reams of paper around; I was really impressed with the sheer amount of stuff he'd evidently written. While he was reading, I was thinking how wonderful it was to find someone so prolific just at the point when we were going to need "sounds" for our sound movies. Immediately after the reading I asked Ronnie if he'd come by the Factory and just sit in a lounge chair off-camera and talk while we shot Mario Montez in *Harlot*, and he said fine. As we left Le Metro, Gerard sneered, "Your standards are really ridiculous sometimes." I guess he thought I was too impressed with the quantity of stuff Ronnie turned out. But the thing was, I liked the content, too, I thought he was really talented.

. . . .

Mario Montez, the star of *Harlot*, was in a lot of off-off-Broadway plays and doing a lot of underground acting for Jack Smith and Ron Rice and Jose Rodriguez-Soltero and Bill Vehr. And this was all in addition, he told me, to his regular job: working for the post office. Mario was one of the best natural comedians I'd ever met; he knew instinctively how to get a laugh every time. He had a natural blend of sincerity and distraction, which has to be one of the great comedy combinations.

A lot of Mario's humor came from the fact that he adored dressing up like a female glamour queen, yet at the same time he was painfully embarrassed about being in drag (he got offended if you used that word—he called it "going into costume"). He used to always say that he knew it was a sin to be in drag—he was Puerto Rican and a very religious Roman Catholic. The only spiritual comfort he allowed himself was the logic that even though God surely didn't *like* him for going into drag, that still, if He really hated him, He would have struck him dead.

Mario was a very sympathetic person, very benign, although he did get furious at me once. We were watching a scene of his in a movie we called *The Fourteen-Year-Old Girl*, and when he saw that I'd zoomed in and gotten a close-up of his arm with all the thick, dark masculine hair and veins showing, he got very upset and hurt and accused me in a proud Latin way, "I can see you were trying to bring out the worst in me."

. . . .

Ronnie Tavel appeared for the *Harlot* shooting and he and a couple of other people just talked normally off-camera. Sometimes the talk was about what we were shooting and other times it wasn't—I loved the effect of having unrelated dialogue. After that Ronnie did quite a few scenarios for us—*The Life of Juanita Castro*, *Horse*, *Vinyl*, *The Fourteen-Year-Old Girl*, *Hedy (The Shoplifter)*, *Lupe*, *Kitchen*, and others. I enjoyed working with him because he understood instantly when I'd say things like "I want it simple and plastic and white." Not everyone can think in an abstract way, but Ronnie could.

.   .   .   .

We filmed a lot of movies over at Edie's place on 63rd Street near Madison. Things like the *Beauty* series that was just Edie with a series of beautiful boys, sort of romping around her apartment, talking to each other—the idea was for her to have her old boyfriends there while she interviewed new ones. All the movies with Edie were so innocent when I think back on them, they had more of a pajama-party atmosphere than anything else.

Edie was incredible on camera—just the way she moved. And she never stopped moving for a second—even when she was sleeping, her hands were wide awake. She was all energy—she didn't know what to do with it when it came to living her life, but it was wonderful to film. The great stars are the ones who are doing something you can watch every second, even if it's just a movement inside their eye.

Whenever you went over to Edie's, you felt like you were about to be arrested or something—there were always a lot of cops patrolling her block (they were guarding some consulate across the street). When I first knew her, she had a limousine and driver parked out front at all times, but after a little while, the limo was gone. Then she stopped buying couture clothes. Someone told me that she'd finally used up her whole trust fund and that from now on she was going to have to live on five hundred dollars a month allowance from home.

But I still couldn't figure out whether she really had money or not. She was wearing dime-store T-shirts instead of designer clothes, but still it was a fabulous look that anyone would have wanted to have. And she was still picking up the checks every night for everybody—she'd sign for everything every place we went. But again, I couldn't figure out if she knew the management or if somebody was paying all her bills or what. I mean, I couldn't figure out if she was the richest person I knew or the poorest. All I knew was that she never had any cash on her, but then that's a sign of being *really* rich.

I filmed a movie—*Poor Little Rich Girl*—of Edie talking about being a debutante who'd just spent her inheritance—talking on the phone, walking back to her bed, showing off the white mink coat that was her trademark.

I always wanted to do a movie of a whole day in Edie's life. But then, that was what I wanted to do with most people. I never liked the idea of picking out certain scenes and pieces of time and putting them together, because then it ends up being different from what really happened—it's just not like life, it seems so corny. What I liked was chunks of time all together, every real moment. Somebody once asked Mario Montez what working with me was like, did I "rehearse" the actors, etc., and Mario told them that since rehearsing was related to editing, naturally someone who wouldn't edit his movies wouldn't rehearse them either. That was exactly right. I only wanted to find great people and let them be themselves and talk about what they usually talked about and I'd film them for a certain length of time and that would be the movie. In those days we were using Ronnie Tavel scripts for some of the movies, and for others we just had an idea or a theme that we gave people to work with. To play the poor little rich girl in the movie, Edie didn't need a script—if she'd needed a script, she wouldn't have been right for the part.

. . . .

During the summer and fall, Edie started saying she was unhappy being in underground movies. One night she asked Mel and me to meet her at the Russian Tea Room for a "conference." She wanted him to arbitrate while she explained to me how she felt about her career. That was one of her standard ploys—getting everyone involved in whether she should do this or that. And you really did get involved. That night she said she'd decided that she definitely was going to quit doing movies for the Factory.

Jonas Mekas had just offered us a lot of consecutive nights' screenings at the Cinemathèque to do whatever we wanted with, and we thought it would be fabulous to have an Edie Sedgwick Retrospective—meaning, all of her films from the last eight months. When we'd first thought of it, we all thought it was hilarious, including Edie. In fact, I think Edie was the one who thought of it. But now, this night at dinner, she was claiming that we only wanted to make a fool out of her. The waiter moved the Moscow Mules aside and put our dinners down, but Edie pushed the plate aside and lit up a cigarette.

"Everybody in New York is laughing at me," she said. "I'm too embarrassed to even leave my apartment. These movies are making a complete fool out of me! Everybody knows I just stand around in them doing nothing and you film it and what kind of talent is that? Try to imagine how I feel!" Mel reminded her that she was the envy of every girl in New York at that moment, which she absolutely was—I mean, everybody was copying her look and her style.

Then she attacked the idea of the Edie Retrospective specifically, saying that it was just another way for us to make a fool out of her. By now I was getting red in the face; she was making me so upset I could hardly talk.

I told her, "But don't you *understand*? These movies are art!" (Mel told me later that he was floored when he heard me say that: "Because your usual position was to let other people say that your movies were works of art," he said, "but not to say it yourself.") I tried to make her understand that if she acted in enough of these underground movies, a Hollywood person might see her and put her in a big movie—that the important thing was just to be up there on the screen and let everybody see how good she was. But she wouldn't accept that. She insisted we were out to make a fool of her.

The funny thing about all this was that the whole idea behind making those movies in the first place was to be ridiculous. I mean, Edie and I both knew they were a joke—that was why we were doing them! But now she was saying that if they really were ridiculous, she didn't want to be in them. She was driving me nuts. I kept reminding her that *any* publicity was good publicity. Then, around midnight, I was so crazy from all the dumb arguing that I walked out.

Mel and Edie stayed up talking until dawn, and finally she made some sort of "decision." "But you could never expect anything too systematic from Edie's thinking," Mel told me later, "because the next afternoon when I called her, everything she'd 'decided' was all changed around."

That was essentially the problem with Edie: the mood shifts and the mind changes. Of course, all the drugs she was taking by now had a lot to do with that.

Anyway, she did make some more movies with us.

.   .   .   .

All that summer we were shooting the short interior sequences that we later combined to make up *Chelsea Girls,* using all the people who were around. A lot of them were staying at the Hotel Chelsea, so we were spending a lot of time over there. Often, we'd have dinner and sangría at the El Quixote Restaurant downstairs and everybody would be coming and going back and forth from their own rooms or somebody else's. I got the idea to unify all the pieces of these people's lives by stringing them together as if they lived in different rooms in the same hotel. We didn't actually film all the sequences at the Chelsea; some we shot down where the Velvets were staying on West 3rd, and some in other friends' apartments, and some at the Factory—but the idea was they were all characters that were around and *could* have been staying in the same hotel.

Everybody went right on doing what they'd always done—being themselves (or doing one of their routines, which was usually the same thing) in front of the camera. I once heard Eric telling someone about the direction I gave him for his first scene. "Andy just told me to tell the story of my life and to somewhere along the line take off all my clothes." After thinking for a second, he added, "And that's what I've been doing ever since." Their lives became part of my movies, and of course the movies became part of their lives; they'd get so into them that pretty soon you couldn't really separate the two, you couldn't tell the difference—and sometimes neither could they. During the filming of *Chelsea Girls,* when Ondine slapped Pepper in his sequence as the Pope, it was so for real that I got upset and had to leave the room—but I made sure I left the camera running. This was something new. Up until this, when people had gotten violent during any of the filmings, I'd always turned the camera off and told them to stop, because physical violence is something I just hate to see happen, unless, of course, both people like it that way. But now I decided to get it *all* down on film, even if I had to leave the room.

Poor Mario Montez got his feelings hurt for real in his scene where he found two boys in bed together and sang "They Say That Falling in Love Is Wonderful" for them. He was supposed to stay there in the room with them for ten minutes, but the boys on the bed insulted him so badly that he ran out in six and we couldn't persuade him to go back in to finish up. I kept directing him, "You were terrific, Mario. Get back in there—just pretend you forgot something, don't let *them* steal the scene, it's no good without you," etc., etc. But he just wouldn't go back in, he was too upset.

Jack Smith always said that Mario was his favorite underground actor because he could instantly capture the sympathy of the audience. And that was certainly true. He lived in constant fear that his family or the people in the civil service job where he worked would discover that he dressed up in drag. He told me that every night he prayed in his little apartment on the Lower East Side for himself and his parents and for all the dead celebrities that he loved, like "Linda Darnell and James Dean and Eleanor Roosevelt and Dorothy Dandridge."

Mario had that classic comedy combination of seeming dumb but being able to say the right things with perfect timing; just when you thought you were laughing at him, he'd turn it all around. (A lot of the superstars had that special quality.)

For her reel in *Chelsea Girls,* Brigid played the Duchess. She got so into the role that she started to think she really was a big dope dealer: she took a dirty hypodermic needle and jabbed Ingrid in the fanny. (The Duchess wouldn't have done it any better herself.) Then, as we filmed, she picked up the phone and called a lot of real people up (who had no idea they were part of her movie scene) telling them about all the drugs she had for sale. She was so believable that the hotel operators, who were always listening in, called the police. They arrived at the room while we were still filming and searched everyone, but all they could come up with was two Desoxyn pills. Still, after people saw Brigid in the movie, they were as scared of her as they were of the Duchess.

. . . .

While I was in the hospital [after being shot by Valerie Solanas], Paul gave me reports on the local filming of John Schlesinger's *Midnight Cowboy.* Before I was shot, they'd asked me to play the Underground Filmmaker in the big party scene, and I'd suggested Viva for the part instead. They liked the idea of that. And then

John Schlesinger had asked Paul to make an "underground movie" to be shown during the "underground party" scene, so Paul went and filmed Ultra for that. Then the casting agent had asked Paul to round up a lot of people we knew—the kids around Max's—to be day players and extras. I felt like I was missing a big party, lying there in the hospital like that, but everybody kept me up to the minute on what was happening, they were all so excited about being in a Hollywood movie.

. . . .

I had the same jealous feeling thinking about *Midnight Cowboy* that I had had when I saw *Hair* and realized that people with money were taking the subject matter of the underground, counterculture life and giving it a good, slick, commercial treatment. What we'd had to offer—originally, I mean—was a new, freer content and a look at real people, and even though our films weren't technically polished, right up through '67 the underground was one of the only places people could hear about forbidden subjects and see realistic scenes of modern life. But now that Hollywood—and Broadway, too—was dealing with those same subjects, things were getting a little confused: before, the choice had been like between black and white, and now it was like between black and gray. I realized that with both Hollywood and the underground making films about male hustlers—even though the two treatments couldn't have been more different—it took away a real drawing card from the underground, because people would rather go see the treatment that *looked* better. It was much less threatening. (People do tend to avoid new realities; they'd rather just add details to the old ones. It's as simple as that.) I kept feeling, "They're moving into our territory." It made me more than ever want to get money from Hollywood to do a beautiful-looking and -sounding movie with our own attitude, so at last we could compete equally. I was so jealous: I thought, "Why didn't they give *us* the money to do, say, *Midnight Cowboy?* We would have done it so *real* for them." I didn't understand then that when they said they wanted real life, they meant real movie life!

"Isn't it amazing?" Paul said on the phone one night while I was still in the hospital. "Hollywood's just gotten around to doing a movie about a 42nd Street male hustler, and we did ours in '65. And there are all *our* great New York people sitting on *their* set all day—Geraldine, Joe, Ondine, Pat Ast, Taylor, Candy, Jackie, Geri Miller, Patti D'Arbanville—and they never even get around to using them. . . ."

"What's Dustin like?" I asked.

"Oh, he's very nice."

"And Jon Voight?"

"He's very nice, too. . . . So's Brenda Vaccaro," he said, absently. "They're all very nice." Then he laughed, remembering Sylvia Miles. "And Sylvia's absolutely indomitable. A force of nature."

I got the feeling that making that little film of Ultra and then just hanging around a movie set watching the production had been pretty frustrating for Paul—he thought he should be out there doing a film himself. After all, he'd done his own films before he came to the Factory.

"Well, you know," I said, "maybe we did our film too early. Maybe now *is* the smart time to do a film about a male hustler. Why don't you do another one—this time it can be in color."

"That's what I was sort of thinking," Paul admitted.

ANDREI TARKOVSKY

Tarkovsky's movies come as close as the cinema probably can come to providing transcendent experiences. The bell-casting sequence in Andrei Rublev *is one of the greatest sustained pieces of film I have ever seen, and his* Solaris, Nostalgia, *and* The Sacrifice *are visionary works. But he was a very serious man. A few years before he died, Tarkovsky (1932–1986) was honored at the Telluride Film Festival. I will never forget his speech after he had been presented with the Telluride Medal. Rugged in the new Levi's and western shirt he'd purchased in Las Vegas, on the drive to Colorado, he stepped to the front of the stage, and as he spoke, his Russian was translated by the Polish director Krzyzstof Zanussi: "The cinema, she is a whore. First she charge a nickel, now she charge five dollars. Until she learn to give it away free, she will always be a whore." Wild applause. The next night the Telluride Medal was presented to Richard Widmark, who stepped to the front of the stage, cocked an eye at the audience, and said, "I'd like to name some pimps. Griffith, Chaplin, Hitchcock, Welles. . . ."*

from *Sculpting in Time*

I should not want to impose my views on cinema on anybody else. All I hope is that everyone I am addressing (in other words, people who know and love the cinema) has his own ideas, his particular view of the artistic principles of film-making and film criticism.

A mass of preconceptions exists in and around the profession. And I do mean preconceptions, not traditions: those hackneyed ways of thinking, clichés, that grow up around traditions and gradually take them over. And you can achieve nothing in art unless you are free from received ideas. You have to work out your own position, your individual point of view—subject always, of course, to common sense—and keep this before you, like the apple of your eye, all the time you are working.

Directing starts not when the script is being discussed with the writer, nor during work with the actor, or with the composer, but at the time when, before the interior gaze of the person making the film and known as the director, there emerges an image of the film: this might be a series of episodes worked out in detail, or perhaps the consciousness of an aesthetic texture and emotional atmosphere, to be materialised on the screen. The director must have a clear idea of his objectives and work through with his camera team to achieve their total, precise realisation. However, all this is no more than technical expertise. Although it involves many of the conditions necessary to art, in itself it is not sufficient to earn for the director the name of artist.

He starts to be an artist at the moment when, in his mind or even on film, his own distinctive system of images starts to take shape—his own pattern of thoughts about the external world—and the audience are invited to judge it, to share with the director in his most precious and secret dreams. Only when his personal viewpoint is brought in, when he becomes a kind of philosopher, does he emerge as an artist, and cinema—as an art. (Of course he is a philosopher only in a relative sense. As Paul Valéry observed, "Poets are philosophers. You might equally well compare the painter of sea-scapes to a ship's captain.")

Every art form, however, is born and lives according to its particular laws. When people talk about the specific norms of cinema, it is usually in juxtaposition with literature. In my view it is all-important that the interaction between cinema and literature should be explored and exposed as completely as possible, so that the two can at last be separated, never to be confused again. In what ways are literature and cinema similar and related? What links them?

Above all the unique freedom enjoyed by practitioners in both fields to take what they want of what is offered by the real world, and to arrange it in sequence. This definition may appear too wide and general, but it seems to me to take in all that cinema and literature have in common. Beyond it lie irreconcilable differences, stemming from the essential disparity between word and screened image: for the basic difference is that literature uses words to describe the world, whereas film does not have to use words: it manifests itself to us directly.

In all these years no single binding definition has been found for the specific character of cinema. A great many views exist, either in conflict with each other, or worse—overlapping in a kind of eclectic confusion. Every artist in the film world will see, pose and solve the problem in his own way. In any case there has to be a clear specification if one is to work in the full consciousness of what one is doing, for it is not possible to work without recognising the laws of one's own art form.

What are the determining factors of cinema, and what emerges from them? What are its potential, means, images—not only formally, but even spiritually? And in what material does the director work?

I still cannot forget that work of genius, shown in the last century, the film with which it all started—*L'Arrivée d'un Train en Gare de La Ciotat*. That film made by Auguste Lumière was simply the result of the invention of the camera, the film and the projector. The spectacle, which only lasts half a minute, shows a section of railway platform, bathed in sunlight, ladies and gentlemen walking about, and the train coming from the depths of the frame and heading straight for the camera. As the train approached panic started in the theatre: people jumped up and ran away. That was the moment when cinema was born; it was not simply a question of technique, or just a new way of reproducing the world. What came into being was a new aesthetic principle.

For the first time in the history of the arts, in the history of culture, man found the means *to take an impression of time*. And simultaneously the possibility of reproducing that time on screen as often as he wanted, to repeat it and go back to it. He acquired a matrix for *actual time*. Once seen and recorded, time could now be preserved in metal boxes over a long period (theoretically for ever).

That is the sense in which the Lumière films were the first to contain the seed of a new aesthetic principle. But immediately afterwards cinema turned aside from art, forced down the path that was safest from the point of view of philistine interest and profit. In the course of the following two decades almost the whole of world literature was screened, together with a huge number of theatrical plots. Cinema was exploited for the straightforward and seductive purpose of recording theatrical performance. Film took a wrong turn; and we have to accept the fact that the unfortunate results of that move are still with us. The worst of it was not, in my view, the reduction of cinema to mere illustration: far worse was the failure to exploit artistically the one precious potential of the cinema—the possibility of printing on celluloid the actuality of time.

In what form does cinema print time? Let us define it as *factual*. And fact can consist of an event, or a person moving, or any material object; and furthermore the object can be presented as motionless and unchanging, in so far as that immobility exists within the actual course of time.

That is where the roots are to be sought of the specific character of cinema. Of course in music too the problem of time is central. Here, however, its solution is quite different: the life force of music is materialised on the brink of its own total disappearance. But the virtue of cinema is that it appropriates time, complete with that material reality to which it is indissolubly bound, and which surrounds us day by day and hour by hour.

Time, printed in its factual forms and manifestations: such is the supreme idea of cinema as an art, leading us to think about the wealth of untapped resources in film, about its colossal future. On that idea I build my working hypotheses, both practical and theoretical.

Why do people go to the cinema? What takes them into a darkened room where, for two hours, they watch the play of shadows on a sheet? The search for entertainment? The need for a kind of drug? All over the world there are, indeed, entertainment firms and organisations which exploit cinema and television and spectacles of many other kinds. Our starting-point, however, should not be there, but in the essential principles of cinema, which have to do with the human need to master and know the world. I think that what a person normally goes to the cinema for is *time*: for time lost or spent or not yet had. He goes there for living experience; for cinema, like no other art, widens, enhances and concentrates a person's experience—and not only enhances it but makes it longer, significantly longer. That is the power of cinema: "stars," story-lines and entertainment have nothing to do with it.

MARTIN SCORSESE

Martin Scorsese was the greatest of the American directors who came out of the exciting late 1960s, and in the high level of his work and the persistence of his personal vision he remains in the lead. No one else can point to such an astonishing filmography. Mean Streets, Taxi Driver, Raging Bull, *and* Goodfellas *will be treasured as long as film exists, and he has never, in my opinion, made a bad film (although* Boxcar Bertha *is good primarily in the way it transcends or eludes the conditions of its making). Yet his career has not been easy, and on one occasion he told me he thought it was over: "No one will finance another one of my films." His most fruitful collaborations have been with the actor Robert De Niro, the editor Thelma Schoonmaker (whose husband, the British director Michael Powell, was Scorsese's hero), and the writer Paul Schrader (*Taxi Driver,*

Raging Bull, The Last Temptation of Christ). *Here Scorsese describes the conditions under which he collaborated with De Niro and Schrader on* Taxi Driver, *which was the best film of the 1970s, just as* Raging Bull *was the best film of the 1980s.*

from *Scorsese on Scorsese*

Brian De Palma introduced me to Paul Schrader. We made a pilgrimage out to see Manny Farber, the critic, in San Diego. I wanted Paul to do a script of *The Gambler* by Dostoevsky for me. But Brian took Paul out for dinner, and they contrived it so that I couldn't find them. By the time I tracked them down, three hours later, they'd cooked up the idea of *Obsession*. But Brian told me that Paul had this script, *Taxi Driver,* that he didn't want to do or couldn't do at that time, and wondered if I'd be interested in reading it. So I read it and my friend read it and she said it was fantastic: we agreed that this was the kind of picture we should be making.

That year, 1971, De Niro was about to win the Academy Award for *The God-father Part II,* Ellen Burstyn won the Award for *Alice Doesn't Live Here Anymore,* and Paul had sold *The Yakuza* to Warner Brothers, so it was all coming together. Michael and Julia Phillips, who owned the script, had won an Award for *The Sting* and figured there was enough power to get the film made, though in the end we barely raised the very low budget of $1.3 million. In fact, for a while we even thought of doing it on black and white videotape! Certainly we felt it would be a labour of love rather than any kind of commercial success—shoot very quickly in New York, finish it in Los Angeles, release it and then bounce back into *New York, New York,* on which we'd already begun pre-production. De Niro's schedule had to be rearranged anyway, because he was due to film *1900* with Bertolucci.

Much of *Taxi Driver* arose from my feeling that movies are really a kind of dream-state, or like taking dope. And the shock of walking out of the theatre into broad daylight can be terrifying. I watch movies all the time and I am also very bad at waking up. The film was like that for me—that sense of being almost awake. There's a shot in *Taxi Driver* where Travis Bickle is talking on the phone to Betsy and the camera tracks away from him down the long hallway and there's nobody there. That was the first shot I thought of in the film, and it was the last I filmed. I like it because I sensed that it added to the loneliness of the whole thing, but I guess you can see the hand behind the camera there.

The whole film is very much based on the impressions I have as a result of growing up in New York and living in the city. There's a shot where the camera is mounted on the hood of the taxi and it drives past the sign "Fascination," which is just down from my office. It's that idea of being fascinated, of this avenging angel floating through the streets of the city, that represents all cities for me. Because of the low budget, the whole film was drawn out on storyboards, even down to medium close-ups of people talking, so that everything would connect. I had to create this dream-like quality in those drawings. Sometimes the character himself is on a dolly, so that we look over his shoulder as he moves towards another character, and for a split second the audience would wonder what was happening. The overall idea was to make it like a cross between a Gothic horror and the New York *Daily News*.

There is something about the summertime in New York that is extraordinary. We shot the film during a very hot summer and there's an atmosphere at night that's like a seeping kind of virus. You can smell it in the air and taste it in your mouth. It reminds me of the scene in *The Ten Commandments* portraying the killing of the first-born, where a cloud of green smoke seeps along the palace floor and touches the foot of a first-born son, who falls dead. That's almost what it's like: a strange disease creeps along the streets of the city and, while we were shooting the film, we would slide along after it. Many times people threatened us and we had to take off quickly. One night, while we were shooting in the garment district, my father came out of work and walked by the set. The press of bodies on the pavement was so thick that, in the moment I turned away from the camera to talk to him, it was impossible to get back. That was typical.

As in my other films, there was some improvisation in *Taxi Driver*. The scene between De Niro and Cybill Shepherd in the coffee-shop is a good example. I didn't want the dialogue as it appeared in the script, so we improvised for about twelve minutes, then wrote it down and shot it. It was about three minutes in the end. Many of the best scenes, like the one in which De Niro says, "Suck on this," and blasts Keitel, were designed to be shot in one take. Although every shot in the picture had been drawn beforehand, with the difficulties we encountered, including losing four days of shooting because of rain, a lot of the stuff taken from the car had to be shot as documentary.

We looked at Hitchcock's *The Wrong Man* for the moves when Henry Fonda goes into the insurance office and the shifting points of view of the people behind the counter. That was the kind of paranoia that I wanted to employ. And the way Francesco Rosi used black and white in *Salvatore Giuliano* was the way I wanted *Taxi Driver* to look in colour. We also studied Jack Hazan's *A Bigger Splash* for the head-on framing, such as the shot of the grocery store before Travis Bickle shoots the black guy. Each sequence begins with a shot like that, so before any moves you're presented with an image like a painting.

I don't think there is any difference between fantasy and reality in the way these should be approached in a film. Of course, if you live that way you are clinically insane. But I can ignore the boundary on film. In *Taxi Driver* Travis Bickle lives it out, he goes right to the edge and explodes. When I read Paul's script, I realized that was exactly the way I felt, that we all have those feelings, so this was a way of embracing and admitting them, while saying I wasn't happy about them. When you live in a city, there's a constant sense that the buildings are getting old, things are breaking down, the bridges and the subway need repairing. At the same time society is in a state of decay; the police force are not doing their job in allowing prostitution on the streets, and who knows if they're feeding off it and making money out of it. So that sense of frustration goes in swings of the pendulum, only Travis thinks it's not going to swing back unless he does something about it. It was a way of exorcizing those feelings, and I have the impression that De Niro felt that too.

I never read any of Paul's source materials—I believe one was Arthur Bremer's diary. But I had read Dostoevsky's *Notes from Underground* some years before and I'd wanted to make a film of it; and *Taxi Driver* was the closest thing to it I'd come across. De Niro had tried his hand at scriptwriting on the subject of a political assassin, and he'd told me the story. We weren't very close at this time, I'd just worked with him on *Mean Streets,* but he read the script and said it was very similar to his idea, which he therefore might as well drop. So we all connected with this subject.

Travis really has the best of intentions; he believes he's doing right, just like St. Paul. He wants to clean up life, clean up the mind, clean up the soul. He is very spiritual, but in a sense Charles Manson was spiritual, which doesn't mean that it's good. It's the power of the spirit on the wrong road. The key to the picture is the idea of being brave enough to admit having these feelings, and then act them out. I instinctively showed that the acting out was not the way to go, and this created even more ironic twists to what was going on.

It was crucial to Travis Bickle's character that he had experienced life and death around him every second he was in south-east Asia. That way it becomes more heightened when he comes back; the image of the street at night reflected in the dirty gutter becomes more threatening. I think that's something a guy going through a war, any war, would experience when he comes back to what is supposedly "civilization." He'd be more paranoid. I'll never forget a story my father told me about one of my uncles coming back from the Second World War and walking in the street. A car backfired and the guy just instinctively ran two blocks! So Travis Bickle was affected by Vietnam: it's held in him and then it explodes. And although at the end of the film he seems to be in control again, we give the impression that any second the time bomb might go off again.

It wasn't easy getting Bernard Herrmann to compose the music for *Taxi Driver*. He was a marvellous, but crotchety old man. I remember the first time I called him to do the picture. He said it was impossible, he was very busy, and then asked what it was called. I told him and he said, "Oh, no, that's not my kind of picture title. No, no, no." I said, "Well, maybe we can meet and talk about it." He said, "No, I can't. What's it about?" So I described it and he said, "No, no, no. I can't. Who's in it?" So I told him and he said, "No, no, no. Well, I suppose we could have a quick talk." Working with him was so satisfying that when he died, the night he had finished the score, on Christmas Eve in Los Angeles, I said there was no one who could come near him. You get to know what you like if you see enough films, and I thought his music would create the perfect atmosphere for *Taxi Driver*.

I was shocked by the way audiences took the violence. Previously I'd been surprised by audience reaction to *The Wild Bunch,* which I first saw in a Warner Brothers screening room with a friend and loved. But a week later I took some friends to see it in a theatre and it was as if the violence became an extension of the audience and vice versa. I don't think it was all approval, some of it must have been revulsion. I saw *Taxi Driver* once in a theatre, on the opening night, I think, and everyone was yelling and screaming at the shoot-out. When I made it, I didn't intend to have the audience react with that feeling. "Yes, do it! Let's go out and kill." The idea was to create a violent catharsis, so that they'd find themselves saying, "Yes, kill"; and then afterwards realize, "My God, no"—like some strange Californian therapy session. That was the instinct I went with, but it's scary to hear what happens with the audience.

All around the world people have told me this, even in China. I was there for a three-week seminar and there was a young Mongolian student who spoke some English following me around Peking; and he would talk about *Taxi Driver* all the time. He said, "You know, I'm very lonely," and I'd say, "Yes, basically we all are." Then he said, "You dealt with loneliness very well," and I thanked him. Then he'd come round again and ask me, "What do I do with the loneliness?" He wasn't just weird, he was a film student who was really interested. I said, "Very often I try to put it into the work." So a few days later he came back and said, "I tried putting it into the work, but it doesn't go away." I replied, "No, it doesn't go away, there's no magic cure."

People related to the film very strongly in terms of loneliness. I never realized what that image on the poster did for the film—a shot of De Niro walking down the street with the line, "In every city there's one man." And we had thought that audiences would reject the film, feeling that it was too unpleasant and no one would want to see it!

I wanted the violence at the end to be as if Travis had to keep killing all these people in order to stop them once and for all. Paul saw it as a kind of Samurai "death with honour"—that's why De Niro attempts suicide—and he felt that if he'd directed the scene, there would have been tons of blood all over the walls, a more surrealistic effect. What I wanted was a *Daily News* situation, the sort you read about every day: "Three men killed by lone man who saves young girl from them." Bickle chooses to drive his taxi anywhere in the city, even the worst places, because it feeds his hate.

I was thinking about the John Wayne character in *The Searchers*. He doesn't say much, except "That'll be the day" (from which Buddy Holly did the song). He doesn't belong anywhere, since he's just fought in a war he believed in and lost, but he has a great love within him that's been stamped out. He gets carried away, so that during the long search for the young girl, he kills more buffalo than necessary because it's less food for the Comanche—but, throughout, he's determined that they'll find her, as he says, "as sure as the turning of the Earth."

Paul was also very influenced by Robert Bresson's *Pickpocket*. I admire his films greatly, but I find them difficult to watch. In *Pickpocket* there's a wonderful sequence of the pickpockets removing wallets with their hands, a lot of movement in and out, and it's the same with Travis, alone in the room practising with his guns. I felt he should talk to himself while doing this, and it was one of the last things we shot, in a disused building in one of the roughest and noisiest areas of New York. I didn't want it to be like other mirror sequences we'd seen, so while Bob kept saying, "Are you talking to me?" I just kept telling him, "Say it again." I was on the floor wearing headphones and I could hear a lot of street noise, so I thought we wouldn't get anything, but the track came out just fine.

I was also very much influenced by a film called *Murder by Contract* (1958), directed by Irving Lerner, who worked on *New York, New York* as an editor and to whom the film was dedicated following his death. I saw *Murder by Contract* on the bottom half of a double bill with *The Journey,* and the neighbourhood guys constantly talked about it. It had a piece of music that was like a theme, patterned rather like *The Third Man,* which came round and round again. But above all, it gave us an inside look into the mind of a man who kills for a living, and it was pretty frightening. I had even wanted to put a clip of it into *Mean Streets,* the sequence in a car when the main character describes what different sizes of bullet do to people, but the point had really been made. Of course, you find that scene done by me in *Taxi Driver*.

SPIKE LEE

Few films have ever shaken me as much as Do the Right Thing *did when I saw it in May 1989 at the Cannes Film Festival. In its portrait of a summer day on a single big city block, it evoked so many of the prejudices, misunderstandings, old wounds, and recent hurts that contribute to the lack of communication between the races in America. What struck me most about Lee's film was its fairness; it was not an antiwhite film, a knee-jerk attack on racism, but a carefully developed, considered, brilliantly written portrait of the people who lived on that city street and the forces that built up in them on that day. It is possible, I believe, for a viewer of any race to identify with any of the film's characters. Spike Lee's work as a whole has been more perceptive and useful than any other single cinematic source in helping us understand the situation of the races in modern America. Here, in entries from notebooks he kept during the development of* Do the Right Thing, *he writes about how some of his ideas developed.*

from *Do the Right Thing*

DECEMBER 25, 1987

It's nine in the morning and I'm sitting down to get started on my next project, *Do the Right Thing.* I hope to start shooting next August. I want the film to take place over the course of one day, the hottest day of the year, in Brooklyn, New York. The film has to look hot, too. The audience should feel like it's suffocating, like *In the Heat of the Night.*

I'll have to kick butt to pull things together by August. If I'm not happy with the script, I'll hold off until the following summer. It's better to go at it right away, though, like Oliver Stone did by following *Platoon* with *Wall Street.*

I want most of the film to take place on one block. So, I need to scout a block in Brooklyn with vicious brownstones. We can build sets for the interiors, but most scenes will take place in the street and on stoops and fire escapes.

It's been my observation that when the temperature rises beyond a certain point, people lose it. Little incidents can spark major conflicts. Bump into someone on the street and you're liable to get shot. A petty argument between husband and wife can launch a divorce proceeding. The heat makes everything explosive, including the racial climate of the city. Racial tensions in the city are high as it is, but when the weather is hot, forget about it. This might be the core of a vicious climax for the film.

This block is in a Black neighborhood in Brooklyn. On one corner is a pizza parlor run by an Italian family who have refused to leave the neighborhood. One of the young Black characters will have a job at the pizzeria.

Although the Black and Puerto Rican block residents seem to get along with the Italian family, there is still an undercurrent of hostility. Of course this tension explodes in the finale. There should be a full-scale riot—all hell should break loose. Something provocative must set it off, like a cop shoots a kid and brothers go off. Then the rains come. I know, I know, sounds corny. But goddamn, this is only the first page.

I'm making an allusion to the Howard Beach incident by using a pizza parlor. The white kids in this case could be the sons of the owner of the pizzeria. Danny Aiello would be good for the role of the owner. But depending on how big the role is, I could ask Bob De Niro. He'd do it if he likes the script. One of the sons could be Richard Edson from *Stranger than Paradise.*

The pizza parlor will have red, white, and green signs all over it like "Italian Americans #1"—the kind of banners you see at the Feast of San Gennaro in Little Italy.

Throughout the film we hear a DJ's voice over the radio, broadcasting from some fictional station. This device has been used to death, but we might be able to rework it.

The station's call name is WE LOVE RADIO. It broadcasts from a storefront on the block. The DJ looks directly out onto the street and observes all the comings and goings. Passersby can watch him as he rocks the mike. This is gonna be very stylized.

The DJ's name is Mister Señor Love Daddy, the world's only 7-24-365 DJ. That's 7 days a week, 24 hours a day, 365 days a year. He never goes to sleep. "I work overtime for your love," he says.

Playing on the final words of *School Daze,* "Please wake up," the first words of *Do the Right Thing* could be the DJ's: "Hello Nueva York. It's time to wake up. It's gonna be hot as a motherfucker." Vicious. Maybe this is where we could bring in Ossie Davis, our storyteller. Periodically he could come on camera and narrate.

OSSIE: That's right. Hot as a motherfucker. Of course y'can't use that kind of language on the radio, but if you could, that's what Mister Señor Love Daddy would say. It was so hot . . .

Then we cut to various things and characters he's describing.

OSSIE: . . . I mean hot. Hot as two dogs in heat. Okay, okay, y'get the picture.

I'm not sure about this running narration by a storyteller. Even if I don't do it, Ruby Dee and Ossie Davis are still gonna be down.

Something is happening. It's not of my will, but something is happening. I'm being singled out for my acting as much as for my writing and directing. It started with *She's Gotta Have It.* I never expected such a response to Mars Blackmon.

I had a chance to forecast on my appeal as an actor at the five recruited screenings we've had to date for *School Daze.* The minute I appear on screen, the audience got excited. Every recruited audience gave my character, Half-Pint, the highest rating. I'm not trying to say I did the strongest acting in the film, but folks identified with me. I have something with people, and I think at this stage it would be a mistake not to take this into consideration as I write *Do the Right Thing.*

I do realize my limits as an actor. I could never carry an entire movie, nor would I want to. But I know the things I can do. In this film I might want to play a crazy, crazy kid, a psychopath, a madman. But he's funny. The kind who would kill somebody for stepping on his new sneakers—Air Jordans, no doubt.

I see a Black couple as being important characters in the film. The woman will be pregnant. This will make for some good dialogue since pregnant women are naturally cranky and the summertime is the worst time in the world to be pregnant.

WOMAN: I wish I wasn't pregnant, goddamnit. This is the last one.
HUSBAND: Honey, relax you're just irritable now.
WOMAN: Irritable, my ass, I'm miserable. It's hot as shit.

As usual I gotta have a vicious sex scene. For this one it's gonna be a naked female body with ice cubes. We should shoot it similar to the scenes in *She's Gotta Have It,* with extreme closeups. You'll see these clear ice cubes melting fast on a beautiful Black body. Smoke would be even better—smoke emitting from the body. This female is literally on fire. The guy wants to love her, but she says it's too hot and sticky. "I don't want to be bothered. It's too hot for you to be humping on me." The guy, not to be outdone, goes to the refrigerator and pulls out an ice tray. FREAKY DEAKY.

Certain characters in this joint will have nicknames of jazz musicians and athletes.

NICKNAMES

ML	Jade	True Mathematics
Cannonball	E-Man	Moe
Count	Love Daddy	Deek
Duke	Kid	Mo-Freek
Sassy Sarah	Money	Sweto
Divine Dinah	Black	Cee
Tain	Lightskin	C
J-Master	Veets	Magic
Steep	Punchie	Enos
Puddin' Head	Red	West Indian Willie
Lockjaw	Flatbush Phil	Coconut Sid
Ready Freddy	Black Jesus	Bleek
Dizzy	Ella	Brother
Mookie	Monk	Indestructible
Sally Boy	Theolopilus	Four Eyes
Sweet Feet	Ahmad	Milk Man
Bushwhack	Peace God	Sweet Dick Willie
Nighttrane	Born Knowledge	Joe Radio
Too Tall	Gooders	Corn Bread
Shorty	Fila	Jambone
Twinkie	Satchel	Macho
Smiley	Satchmo	Cool Papa Bell
Re-Re	Big Bethel	Josh
Clean Head	Knock Knock	Be So Mighty

I have to include a fire hydrant scene in the film. Someone opens a johnny pump (in closeup). The water gushes out, then they put a can over the stream of water, making the water spray clear across the street. Kids are thrown into the water. Motorists drive by without closing their windows and their cars get drenched.

A man drives down the street in a convertible. He pleads with the kids not to wet him and they promise not to; one kid even stands in front of the hydrant. The kid moves and the convertible is instantly soaked. The driver gets out and chases after the kid, only to be hit by a blast of water from the hydrant. We hear a siren. The cops show up and listen to the driver's complaint. The driver wants an arrest made. The people in the neighborhood stand around watching, but no one points a finger to the kid who did it. The cops turn the hydrant off and promise to bust some heads if they're called again. When the kids grumble about the heat, the cops tell them to watch out or they'll be telling it to the judge.

We see the two cops in this scene throughout the film. They are corrupt, probably crack dealers themselves.

The neighborhood will have a feel of the different cultures that make up the city, specifically Black American, Puerto Rican, West Indian, Korean, and Italian American. Unlike Woody Allen's portraits of New York.

There ought to be an old lady who sits in her window, minding the block's business. She never leaves the window, or so it seems. And she doesn't miss a thing, either. Ruby Dee would be a great choice for this role.

Fellini's *Roma* is a good model for this film. I remember seeing it years ago. It's a day in the life of Rome. In *Do the Right Thing,* it's the hottest day of summer in Brooklyn, New York.

Everybody is outside on hot summer nights. No one stays in their apartments. Much of the action and dialogue should take place on the stoops. The stoops should play a very important role in this film. Of course, it would be a crime if we left out rooftops. Roofs are great locations.

We should see kids running in the streets. Kids on dirt bikes, skateboards, jumping double dutch, and playing pattycake. When I was a kid and the johnny pump was open we would use ice cream sticks as boats and race them along the gutter. There should be a feeling that the people on this block have lived as neighbors for a long time.

The block where the bulk of the film takes place should be a character in its own right. I need to remember my early years for this. We gotta have a Mr. Softee Ice Cream truck playing its theme song. When I was a kid, I ran after an ice cream truck and was almost hit by a speeding car. A neighbor ran into the street and snatched me from in front of the car in the nick of time. I ran home as fast as I could, crying up a storm. That might be an episode, who knows?

The look of the film should be bright. The light in daytime should be an intense white light, almost blinding, and the colors, bright. I mean Puerto Rican bright. AFROCENTRIC bright. Everybody will be wearing shorts and cutoff jeans. Men will be shirtless, women in tube tops.

The image of this pizzeria keeps coming into my mind. It's gonna be important in the end. It's gonna be important. I see my character working there. He hates it there, but he's gotta have a job.

Sometime soon the characters will start talking to me very specifically. I will hear their individual voices and put their words down on paper.

With the release of *School Daze,* there will be another slew of actors that I've worked with before who will want roles in this new film. That's fine, but I want to keep *Do the Right Thing* fresh with new faces. It's always exciting to see a new face give a good performance.

Not everyone who worked on *School Daze* is gonna be down on this one. Some actors truly showed their ass. I have to watch that I don't get too friendly with the actors. Some take our friendship as a guarantee of a job for them.

The acting in *School Daze* is great. I will definitely use Bill Nunn, Kadeem Hardison, Branford Marsalis, Eric Payne, Giancarlo Esposito, Larry Fishburne, Leonard Thomas, Sam Jackson, and Tisha Campbell (provided her mother isn't her manager anymore). These people are a joy to work with.

Bill Nunn would be perfect as Mister Señor Love Daddy. At this stage, I shouldn't get caught up in who's playing who. It will all come soon enough. Robi Reed will be the casting director for this picture.

I would like to use some cast members from *Sarafina!* in this film. I'll make a point of inviting the entire cast to the premiere of *School Daze*.

Whenever I'm in L.A. I go to see Robin Harris at the Comedy Act Theatre. He's the MC there and he's funny as shit. Don't let Robin see somebody who looks funny or is wearing some ill-fitting, ill-colored clothes, he goes off on them. The guy has me in stitches. I have to suggest to Robi that we find a role for him. He's talented and deserves a shot.

I don't know if I want to cast in L.A. this time. The best actors, for me, are in Nueva York. There is a difference in attitude. Most L.A. actors are on a Hollywood trip. They're into being stars and that's it. The actors from New York are more about work, which is the way it should be. Later for the star types. Give me actors like Bill Nunn and Sam Jackson anytime.

I would like my main man, Monty Ross, vice-president of production at Forty Acres, to play a small role in this film. He's concentrating on producing now but he's still a good actor. At most it would be a day's work. He can play someone from the South. Who, I don't know yet.

I definitely want Raye Dowell to have a substantial role in *Do the Right Thing*. I still feel bad I had to cut her part in *School Daze*. But the entire scene had to go. She's a good actress and she gets better all the time.

I've agreed to write another short film for *Saturday Night Live*. It's gonna be a parody commercial featuring Slick Mahoney selling blue and green contact lenses to Black people and introducing a new color, sapphire. It'll take one day to shoot. We can do it in the office in Brooklyn with a skeleton crew.

I'm trying to make the best film I can. I know there will be a million comparisons made between this film and *School Daze*, but I can't let that worry me. *Do the Right Thing* isn't as big in scope as *School Daze*. And hopefully it won't have as many characters. I do want it to be humorous. The story won't be as linear as *School Daze*. I would like to stop, tell a story within a story, and move on.

In this script I want to show the Black working class. Contrary to popular belief, we work. No welfare rolls here, pal, just hardworking people trying to make a decent living. Earlier I wanted to get into the whole gentrification issue, but I'm less enthusiastic about it now.

For the entire month of January I'm gonna put my ideas down on legal pads. I think I'll have enough material to start writing the actual script on or around the first of February. Now mind you, February is also the month *School Daze* opens. But I'll try to be disciplined and not miss a day.

God willing, I'll finish my first draft around the beginning of March. That would give me five months before the first of August, when I want to start shooting. I can shoot all my exterior scenes in August and save my interiors for cover sets. That would be ideal. I would like the luxury of a ten-week shoot—at least.

I'm definitely not going back to Columbia Pictures with this project. It was ideal under David Puttnam and David Picker, but with Dawn Steel (Steely Dawn), forget about it. We both went at it from the start. I don't like her tastes, don't like her movies.

Two of my first choices are Paramount Pictures and Touchstone. Jeffrey Katzenberg at Touchstone is persistently pursuing my next film. I met with the big cheeses at Paramount, Ned Tannen, Sid Ganis, and Gary Luchiesi, the last time I was out in L.A. Paramount told me that they are interested. And since Paramount Communications Inc. owns the Knicks, I might finally get the season tickets to games I need and deserve. Regardless, I'm looking for a place, a home, where I can make the films I want to make without outside or inside interference.

I must reserve the right to approve final cut of this film in my contract. *School Daze* was such a learning experience for me. Monty, who coproduced the film, and I weren't aware of the many details—especially relating to contracts—that must be seen to when you make a film on the scale of *School Daze*. That's why we hired an executive producer to hold our hands. Getting our executive producer to share this knowledge was like pulling teeth. Monty and I found out what we needed to know in the end. But on the next project we will be better prepared for all matters relating to producing the film.

After *Do the Right Thing,* I might do *The Autobiography of Malcolm X.* The project is at Warner Brothers and Denzel Washington, who played Malcolm in an off-Broadway play, is interested in the film role. We both agree that our involvement is contingent on absolute artistic control. If you think I'm gonna let some white people determine the outcome of a project like the Malcolm X piece with my name attached, you're crazy. If that film is not done truthfully and righteously, Black folks are gonna want to hang the guy behind it. Hell no. I'm not having no *Color Purple* fiasco on my conscience.

Dialogue

We were so poor, we ate the hole out of a doughnut.

Idea

When we see people drinking beer, they'll be sipping it through straws, ghetto style.

DECEMBER 27, 1987

I would like this script to be circular. Every character should have a function. If a character is introduced, he or she should appear again and advance the script in some way.

I may use an image that reappears throughout the film. In *The Last Emperor* it was the cricket. Seeing the cricket at the end of the film made it magical for me.

After the climax of the film, I would like to have a coda. This scene could take place the morning after the riot. We see the aftermath from the night before. It's not so hot on this day, and folks seem to have regained their senses. I'll have to think of a way to convey this.

It's early, but I don't want anyone to die in the riot. Some people will get hurt. Some will definitely get fucked up, but as of now, no one will be killed.

While I was in the grocery today I heard a radio newscast that two Black youths had been beaten up by a gang of white youths in Bensonhurst. The two Black kids were hospitalized. They were collecting bottles and cans when they got jumped. This happened on Christmas night. Just the other day some Black kids fired up a white cab driver in Harlem. New York City is tense with racial hatred. Can you imagine if these incidents had taken place in the summer, on the hottest day of the year? I'd be a fool not to work the subject of racism into *Do the Right Thing*.

The way I see it, we'll introduce the subject very lightly. People will expect another humorous film from Spike Lee, but I'll catch them off guard. Then I'll drop the bomb on them, they won't be prepared for it.

If a riot is the climax of the film, what will cause the riot? Take your pick: an unarmed Black child shot, the cops say he was reaching for a gun; a grandmother shot to death by cops with a shotgun; a young woman, charged with nothing but a parking violation, dies in police custody; a male chased by a white mob onto a freeway is hit by a car.

It's funny how the script is evolving into a film about race relations. This is America's biggest problem, always has been (since we got off the boat), always will be. I've touched upon it in my earlier works, but I haven't yet dealt with it head on as a primary subject.

I need to use my juice to get the testimony of Cedric Sandiford and other key witnesses in the Howard Beach case. We're not only talking Howard Beach: It's Eleanor Bumpers, Michael Stewart, Yvonne Smallwood, etc.

If I go ahead in this vein, it might be in conflict with the way I want to tell the story. It can't be just a diatribe, WHITE MAN THIS, WHITE MAN THAT. The treatment of racism will have to be carried in the subtext until the end of the film. Then again, being too avant-garde, too indirect, might trivialize the subject matter. Any approach I take must be done carefully and realistically. I won't be making any apologies. Truth and righteousness is on our side. Black folks are tired of being killed.

This is a hot one. The studios might not want to touch this film. I know I'll come up against some static from the white press. They'll say I'm trying to incite a race riot.

The entire story is starting to happen in my mind. "The hottest day of the summer" is a good starting point, but I need more. I'll be examining racial tensions and how the hot weather only makes them worse. These tensions mount, then something happens outside or inside of the pizza parlor that triggers a major incident.

Now I'm grounded. I know what I'm doing. It will be told from a Black point of view. I've been blessed with the opportunity to express the views of Black people who otherwise don't have access to power and the media. I have to take advantage of this while I'm still bankable.

The character I play in *Do the Right Thing* is from the Malcolm X school of thought: "An eye for an eye." Fuck the turn-the-other-cheek shit. If we keep up that madness we'll be dead. YO, IT'S AN EYE FOR AN EYE.

It's my character who sees a great injustice take place and starts the riot. He turns a garbage can upside down, emptying the trash in the street. Then he goes up to the pizza parlor screaming, "An eye for an eye, Howard Beach," and hurls the garbage can. It flies through the air in slow motion, shattering the pizza parlor's glass windows. All hell breaks loose. Everyone takes part in the riot, even the old woman who sits in her window watching the block. This is random violence. But before this, the cops do something that escalates the conflict to violence. They might even kill someone. The riot takes off, and it's the Italians in the pizza parlor who have to pay.

In the riot scene, it might be vicious if no words were spoken until my character throws the garbage can in the window and screams "Howard Beach."

The subject matter is so volatile, it must be on the QT. No way are people gonna read the script, especially agents. I'm not giving out information on the film until it's about to be released. Mum's da word.

My sister Joie will be the female lead in this film. With each film she's gotten bigger and better roles. Joie has been studying acting with Alice Spivak, who taught me while I was at NYU. Joie has a natural thing with a camera. Either you have it or you don't, and Joie does. Now it's up to me to write the right role for her. She'll definitely be a star in this one. Joie will play my character's sister. We live together in an apartment on the block. For the most part, I'm shiftless and lazy and have no ambition. My sister always pushes me to do better, to expect more from myself. She works and goes to school at night.

One of the sons of the pizza parlor owner has an eye for her. I know this and I tell him "no haps." After the pizza parlor is burnt to the ground in the riot, Sal's sons want the big payback. They happen to run into my sister on her way from night school. What they do to her, I don't know yet.

Dialogue

Those who tell don't know.
Those who know won't tell.

DECEMBER 28, 1987

Of course we must have one of those Uncle Tom Handkerchief Niggers on the block. He's one of those people who love the white man more than he loves himself. He tries to stop the riot. He's in front of the pizzeria urging folks not to tear it down. The folks pull him to the side and give him a few good licks upside the head.

There might be a fruit and vegetable stand on the block, owned by a Korean family. During the riot scene, the entire family is outside the store pleading ME BLACK, ME BLACK, ME NO WHITE, ME BLACK TOO. The folks are more amused than anything else. They leave the store untouched.

The Italian family that owns and runs the pizzeria does not live in the neighborhood. They might live in Canarsie or Bensonhurst.

There's static between my character and the sons of the pizzeria owner. We go at it all the time, exchanging insults. "You junglebunny—nigger motherfucker!" "You dago—wop—spaghetti bender—fake Don Corleone asshole!" Their father has to break it up and threatens to fire all of us.

When the sons are alone with the father, they want to know why he hired me. They ask him if he's a nigger lover. The father tells them that having my character around makes for good business. "This is a Black neighborhood, we're a minority. Look, I've never had no trouble with Blacks, don't want none either. So don't you start. Isn't it hot enough already without you starting up? Listen to your old man. Relax or I'm gonna kick your I'm-a-man-know-it-all ass. Now all of youse, go and work. Let your old man take a breather."

When the pizzeria is being burnt to the ground, the owner asks one of the old people, maybe Ruby Dee's character, why his store was hit. The woman answers: "You were there. The first white folks they saw. You was there. That's all."

Somewhere in the script there should be a dialogue about how the Black man in America owns very little. The character points to the Korean fruit and vegetable stand across the street:

MAN #1: Look at those Korean motherfuckers across the street. I betcha they hadn't been a month off the boat before they opened up their place. A motherfucking month off the boat and they're in business in our neighborhood, occupying a storefront that had been boarded up for longer than I care to remember, and I've been here a long time. Now for the life of me, I haven't been able to figger this out. Either dem Koreans are geniuses or we Blacks are dumb.

MAN #2: But wait a minute, it's not just the Koreans. Don't pick on them. Everyone else has a business and supports their own but us. I'll be one happy fellow to see us have our own businesses. I'd be the first one in line to spend my hard-earned money. Yep, that's right. I'd be the first in line.

Somebody in his audience says: "Aw shut up nigger and sit down."

I can't have too many of these speeches. This is cinema, not the stage.

My goal as a filmmaker is to get better with each outing. I have to pinpoint the areas I need to work on. What are my weaknesses? The first thing that comes to mind is better communication with actors. I need to give them a clearer idea of my vision, my understanding of the script, and of the characters. I might have a picture in my head, but I have to take it further than that. I would also like to enhance my visual sense. In the past I've leaned too heavily on my cinematographer Ernest Dickerson, who I've worked with since film school. But I'm gonna assert myself more in that area.

I want the camera moving all the time, more than it did in *School Daze*. I see a shot where the camera tracks down a row of stoops filled with people. On each stoop there's a different conversation happening. The camera moves slowly from stoop to stoop. Vicious. Also, I want to use long choreographed shots for most of this film. I do not want a lot of cutting.

It might be possible to use a sky-cam given that we'll be shooting on one block. Since a sky-cam camera is controlled by remote, it could float effortlessly from rooftops down to the sidewalk and vice versa.

We definitely have to use a sky-cam on the shot where I scream "Howard Beach" and throw the garbage can. The sky cam has to descend from the heavens into a closeup of me screaming "Howard Beach." Vicious.

It's of utmost importance that this film be shot in summer. The earliest we could do it is August. We're talking the dog days of summer. There would be no need to fake the heat. This means I've got work ahead of me. But if it's film work, that's okay.

I want to have fun writing this script. I never want it to be a chore or a burden. It doesn't have to be. Any day shit isn't flowing, I'll just stop and continue the next day. Whenever I force myself to write, I don't produce anything worth while anyway.

Wouldn't it be interesting if I brought a character or two back from *She's Gotta Have It* or *School Daze*? I think I'm gonna do it. Reprising Mars Blackmon would be a big mistake. Should Tracy Camilia Johns come back as Nola Darling? Nah, bad idea. Maybe shouldn't bring anyone back.

SIMON GLEAVE AND JASON FOREST

Quentin Tarantino's first two features had an impact in film circles not unlike the early performances of Robert Altman, Martin Scorsese, and Spike Lee. Tarantino himself quickly became a high-profile celebrity by appearing on talk shows and in an endless stream of cameos in his friends' films. He was talented, he was articulate, he was exhibitionist, and his films attacked the tired formulas of conventional screenplays. Generation X embraced him like a savior. By coincidence, his Pulp Fiction *(1994) became a hit at about the same time the Internet and World Wide Web were exploding, and Tarantino became the Net's favorite director. At one point there was even a "Church of Tarantino," not to mention countless discussion groups and Web pages. Here is a "FAQ File" from a Tarantino net site in Great Britain; the initials stand for "Frequently Asked Questions" that the proprietors are tired of handling one at a time. It's the detail here that's astonishing: QT's fans seem to have gone over his films with a fine-toothed cinematic comb. All original punctuation, spelling, and language have been preserved.*

"Frequently Asked Questions about Quentin Tarentino"

PULP FICTION

The film opens in a diner as a couple of thieves discuss the possibility of holding up restaurants. This leads us into three distinct strands; a date between a hit man and the wife of his boss, the boxer who is supposed to throw a fight and the cleaning up of a hit man's mistake. The stories are told in non chronological order and we finally return to the diner for the final scene.

1. What is contained in the briefcase?

There is no real answer to this and Tarantino has actually said that he didn't know what to put in the case so he decided to leave it to the viewers to decide. However, it has been suggested that it contains 'the evil that men do' and as the combination of the briefcase is 666, I'm prepared to go with this. Another great suggestion is that it contains the diamonds from 'Reservoir Dogs'.

2. What films have influenced Tarantino in the making of 'Pulp Fiction'?

The dance competition is clearly influenced by Jean Luc Godard's 1964 film 'Bande A Parte' which Tarantino has named his production company after.

The unknown contents of the briefcase are a homage to Robert Aldrich's film 'Kiss Me Deadly', made in 1955.

When Butch stops at the lights and sees Marsellus crossing the road, we are reminded of Alfred Hitchcock's film 'Psycho' when Janet Leigh stops at a set of lights to see her boss crossing the road.

The pawn shop rape is clearly reminiscent of 'Deliverance', made in 1972 by John Boorman.

'The Bonnie Situation' contains Jules and his friend Jimmy, clearly a reference to Francois Truffaut's film, 'Jules et Jim'.

The character of Wolf in this story is taken from Jean Reno's portrayal of a 'cleaner' in Luc Besson's 'La Femme Nikita', a role reprised by Keitel himself in the American remake 'Point of No Return'.

In addition, the films of John Woo, Sam Peckinpah, Brian De Palma and Don Siegel are all important.

3. Why did Mia overdose at her house?

She thought that she was snorting cocaine whereas she was taking Vince's extremely pure heroin. His heroin had been packaged as cocaine would normally be because his dealer had run out of the standard heroin packaging.

4. *Why did Butch return to the pawn shop to save Marsellus?*

Redemption is one of the central themes of this film and this scene along with Jules' saving of Honey Bunny and Pumpkin in the diner are the best examples of this. Butch's conscience made him go back to save Marsellus and this acted as his redemption for killing Wilson in the previous night's boxing match.

5. *Why did Vince leave his gun on the counter at Butch's apartment when he went to the bathroom?*

Quite simply, he didn't, the gun belonged to Marsellus. Vince was clearly with somebody else at the apartment as he didn't react when Butch came in, thinking it was his partner. Jules had given up 'the life' by this point and Marsellus was probably filling in on this job. For further evidence look at the scene where Butch runs Marsellus over; the 'big man' is carrying two cups and as he is near to Butch's apartment, we can assume that he is Vince's partner.

6. *Why are Honey Bunny's lines different from the beginning of the film and at the end?*

A lot of people seem to think this is a mistake. My opinion is that Tarantino was showing us the difference between perceptions of different people in the diner, the second time being Jules' perception. It makes little sense for Tarantino to shoot the scene twice, unless there was a reason.

7. *What was Winston Wolf doing in a tuxedo at 8:30 in the morning? Where was he?*

The script explains that Winston was in a hotel suite where people were gambling. If you listen closely, you can hear someone in the room telling the gamblers to 'place their bets'.

8. *What was the book that Vince was reading on the toilet?*

"Modesty Blaise", a pulpy novel written by Peter O'Donnell in 1965 which is very much in keeping with the film's title.

9. *How does a guy like Jimmy know a gangster like Jules? Why does Jules refer to him as 'his partner'?*

Quentin has said in an interview (Denver Post) that Jimmy used to work for Marsellus, but when he married Bonnie she made him quit, and Jules respects that.

10. *Who was Marvin and why did Jules and Vince take him with them?*
I think we can assume that Marvin also works for Marsellus as Vince refers to 'our guy' before they go up to the apartment.

11. *Why is there a band-aid on Marsellus' neck?*
The actor Ving Rhames simply had a rather ugly looking scar on the back of his neck and so the make-up artist covered this up with a band-aid so that the scar didn't distract the audience too much.

12. *There's bullet holes in the wall behind Jules and Vince before 'The Fourth Man' (a.k.a. Seinfeld) empties his gun. Was this an editing error?*
It seems to be possible that the holes might have been there for other reasons, it's not a great apartment, but it could be a mistake in editing.

13. *Red Apple cigarettes appear throughout the film, what are they?*
Tarantino seems to have invented this brand presumably to minimise the amount of product placement in the film. This is also done by using other brands which were around in the 1970's but are no longer available (ie Fruite Brute cereal).

14. *What happened to the Gimp? Did Butch kill him, or was he just knocked out?*
The script explains that Butch hitting the Gimp caused him to hang himself to death on his leash.

15. *Trivia*
a) During the opening scene, you can see the bottom half of Vince as he makes his way to the bathroom. Look out for his book, shorts, t-shirt and 'strut'.

b) The Buddy Holly waiter in Jack Rabbit Slims is played by Steve Buscemi who as Mr Pink in Reservoir Dogs, refused to tip waitresses.

c) The room in Lance's apartment where Mia receives the injection of adrenalin contains two board games, Operation and Life.

d) The cabdriver, Esmeralda Villa Lobos (Angela Jones) appeared in a 30 minute short called 'Curdled' in which she played a character who cleaned up after murders. This makes her fascinated by the idea of murder. Tarantino saw this film and decided to include this character in Pulp Fiction but as a cabdriver.

e) When Butch is sneaking up to his apartment, there is an advert for Jack Rabbit Slims on the radio.

f) Butch's great-grandfather bought the gold watch in Knoxville, Tennessee and this is also where Butch is meeting his connection. Knoxville is Quentin Tarantino's birthplace.

g) The undercard for Butch's fight is Vossler vs Martinez; Russell Vossler and

Jerry Martinez are two friends of Tarantino's from Video Archives who use to live together and their constant fighting was the butt of jokes around the store.

h) Lawrence Bender plays the 'long haired yuppy scum' in the restaurant hold up.

i) The guy who comes out of the bathroom is played by Alexis Arquette who is the brother of Rosanna and Patricia.

j) The cartoon being watched by the young Butch was 'Clutch Cargo', a kid's show from the sixties. The film playing in the motel room was 'The Losers' directed by Jack Starrett in 1970; it's about five Hell's Angels sent to Cambodia by the CIA to rescue a presidential adviser who has been captured by communists.

Soundtrack and Location in the Film:

Misirlou – Dick Dale Opening credits.

Jungle Boogie – Kool and the Gang Opening credits.

Let's Stay Together – Al Green While Jules and Vincent are at Marsellus' club.

Bustin' Surfboards – The Tornadoes Playing when Rosanna Arquette is talking about her body piercing.

Lonesome Town – Ricky Nelson Sung by the Ricky Nelson impersonator at Jack Rabbit Slims.

Son of a Preacherman – Dusty Springfield While Vincent is waiting for Mia at her house.

Bullwinkle Pt. II – Centurians As Vincent is driving to Mia's house after leaving Lance's place.

You Never Can Tell – Chuck Berry The Twist Contest at Jack Rabbit Slims.

Girl, You'll Be A Woman Soon – Urge Overkill Mia dancing by herself while Vince is in the bathroom at her house.

If Love Is a Red Dress – Maria McKee Maynard's store when Butch and Marsellus first come in fighting. Comanche – The Revels Butch and Zed "bonding" in the pawn shop.

Flowers on the Wall – Statler Brothers Playing when Butch is leaving his apartment having killed Vincent.

Surf Rider – The Lively Ones End credits.

TARANTINO MISCELLANY

Jules' speech from Ezekiel 25:17:

'The path of the righteous man is beset on all sides with the iniquities of the selfish and the tyranny of evil men. Blessed is he who in the name of charity and good will shepherds the weak through the valley of darkness, for he is truly his brother's keeper and the finder of lost children. And I will strike down upon those with great vengeance and with furious anger those who attempt to poison and destroy my brothers. And you will know that my name is the Lord when I lay my vengeance upon thee.'

This is actually not directly from Ezekiel 25:17 and in fact, only the last sentence and part of the second last sentence will be found there.

THE RACISM QUESTION

I've decided not to tackle this subject because whatever I write is not going to change anybody's viewpoint. However, Tarantino has said, ". . . that's the way my characters talk in the movies I've made so far. I also feel that the word 'nigger' is one of the most volatile words in the English language and anytime anyone gives a word that much power, I think everybody should be shouting it from the rooftops to take the power away. I grew up around blacks and have no fear of it, I grew up saying it as an expression." Movieline, Aug 1994

THE 'TARANTINOVERSE'

There has been a lot of discussion about the fact that the same character names appear in different Tarantino scripts and whether these people are either related or one in the same. The common names so far are as follows:

Alabama – White has worked with someone of this name in RD [*Reservoir Dogs*] and she is one of the main protagonists in TR [*True Romance*].

Spivey – Marsellus is mentioned in RD and Drexl appears in TR.

Marsellus – as above and 'the big man' in PF [*Pulp Fiction*].

Vega – Vic (Mr. Blonde) in RD and Vincent in PF.

Marvin – the cop in RD and the inside man in PF.

Scagnetti – Seymour in RD and Jack in NBK [*Natural Born Killers*].

Nash – Marvin the cop in RD, and Gerald the cop in NBK.

The best explanation is that the names reflect Tarantino's ideas so the name Vega is used for a killer, the name Marvin is a fall guy and Scagnetti is an authority figure. I don't hold with the view that Vincent and Blonde are brothers and this seems to be a much more satisfactory explanation.

WRITERS

BEN HECHT

In 1925 the screenwriter Herman Mankiewicz cabled his old newspaper pal Ben Hecht: "Will you accept three hundred per week to work for Paramount Pictures. All expenses paid. The three hundred is peanuts. Millions are to be grabbed out here and your only competition is idiots. Don't let this get around." Hecht (1893–1964) answered the call and stayed to become one of the most prolific screenwriters in Hollywood history, often in collaboration with his friends Gene Fowler and Charles MacArthur. Hecht was a legendary drinker, bon vivant, and storyteller, whose autobiography, A Child of the Century, *documents the raffish side of Hollywood in the 1930s. Here he tells about rewriting* Gone with the Wind, *explaining to Al Capone's lieutenants why* Scarface *was not about Scarface, and witnessing the last days of the has-been silent star Jack Gilbert.*

from *A Child of the Century*

APULEIUS' GOLDEN STOOGE

I have taken part in at least a thousand story conferences. I was present always as the writer. Others present were the "producer," the director and sometimes the head of the studio and a small tense group of his admirers.

The producer's place in movie making is a matter that, in Hollywood, has not yet been cleared up. I shall try to bring some clarity to it.

The big factory where movies are made is run by a superproducer called Head of the Studio who sits in the Front Office and is as difficult of access as the Grand Lama. He is the boss, appointed by the studio Owner himself. Thus, despite the veneration in which he is held by the thousand studio underlings, he is actually the greatest of the movieland stooges. He must bend his entire spirit to the philosophy of the movie Owner—"make money." He must translate this greedy cry of the Owner into a program for his studio. He must examine every idea, plot or venture submitted to him from the single point of view of whether it is trite enough to appeal to the masses.

If he fails in this task, he is summoned from his always teetering studio throne to the movie Owner's New York Office, in which nothing ever teeters. Here he receives a drubbing which the lowest of his slaves would not tolerate. He is shown pages of box-office returns. He is shoved into the presence of homicidal theater Owners snarling of empty seats. Proof is hurled at his head that he has betrayed his great trust, that he is ruining the movie industry, and that he is either an idiot or a scoundrel.

Shaken and traumatized, he returns to his throne in the studio. Here he must wiggle himself into the Purple again and be ready to flash his eyes and terrorize his underlings with his Olympian whims.

His immediate underlings are the producers. He has hired them to do the actual movie making for him. After all, no one man can weigh, discuss and manipulate fifty movie plots at one time. He has to have lieutenants, men who will keep their heads in the noisy presence of writers and directors and not be carried away by art in any of its subversive guises.

ILLUSTRATIONS BY DORÉ (GUSTAVE)

There are different kinds of producers in the studios, ranging from out-and-out illiterates to philosophers and aesthetes. But all of them have the same function. Their task is to guard against the unusual. They are the trusted loyalists of cliché. Writers and directors can be carried away by a "strange" characterization or a new point of view; a producer, never. The producer is the shadow cast by the studio's Owner. It falls across the entire studio product.

I discovered early in my movie work that a movie is never any better than the stupidest man connected with it. There are times when this distinction may be given to the writer or director. Most often it belongs to the producer.

The job of turning good writers into movie hacks is the producer's chief task. These sinister fellows were always my bosses. Though I was paid often five and ten times more money than they for my working time, they were my judges. It was their minds I had to please.

I can recall a few bright ones among them, and fifty nitwits. The pain of having to collaborate with such dullards and to submit myself to their approvals was always acute. Years of experience failed to help. I never became reconciled to taking literary orders from them. I often prepared myself for a producer conference by swallowing two sleeping pills in advance.

I have always considered that half of the large sum paid me for writing a movie script was in payment for listening to the producer and obeying him. I am not being facetious. The movies pay as much for obedience as for creative work. An able writer is paid a larger sum than a man of small talent. But he is paid this added money *not* to use his superior talents.

I often won my battle with producers. I was able to convince them that their suggestions were too stale or too infantile. But I won such battles only as long as I remained on the grounds. The minute I left the studio my victory vanished. Every sour syllable of producer invention went back into the script and every limping foot of it appeared on the screen.

Months later, watching "my" movie in a theater, I realized that not much damage actually had been done. A movie is basically so trite and glib that the addition of a half dozen miserable inanities does not cripple it. It blares along barking out its inevitable clichés, and only its writer can know that it is a shade worse than it had to be.

DIAVOLO, AGAIN—

Such is half of my story of Hollywood. The other half is the fun I had—during the heyday of the movies—1925 to 1945. There was never a more marzipan kingdom than this land of celluloid.

There was only one factory rule. Make a movie that went over big at the preview, and the town was yours. You could be as daft as you wanted, as drunk and irreverent as Panurge, and, still, the bosses bowed as you passed. The bosses were all earthy fellows with the smell of junk yards, tire exchanges, and other murky business pasts clinging to their sport ensembles. Though we wore their yoke, we were nevertheless literary royalty, men of grammar.

In the time when I first arrived in it, the movie world was still young. Jhinns and ogres, odalisques, Sindbads and earth shakers were still around in wholesale lots, especially the ogres. And whatever the weather elsewhere in the world, it rained only gold in Hollywood.

Mankiewicz's telegram had told the truth. Hollywood, 1925, was another boom town, and my nerves were alive to its hawker's cry an hour after I had left the train. It reminded me happily of that other Eldorado—Miami. Miami had run up the price of its real estate. Hollywood was doing the same thing for talent, any kind of talent from geese trainers to writers and actors.

Hungry actors leaped from hall bedrooms to terraced mansions. Writers and newspapermen who had hoboed their way West began hiring butlers and laying down wine cellars. Talent, talent, who had talent for anything—for beating a drum, diving off a roof, writing a joke, walking on his hands? Who could think up a story, any kind of story? Who knew how to write it down? And who had Ego? That was the leading hot cake—Ego or a pair of jiggling boobies under morning-glory eyes. Prosperity chased them all. New stars were being hatched daily, and new world-famous directors and producers were popping daily out of shoe boxes.

I went to work for Paramount Pictures, Inc., over which the Messrs. Zukor, Lasky and Schulberg presided. They occupied the three Vatican suites on the main floor of a long, plaster building that looked like a Bavarian bathhouse. It still stands, empty of almost everything but ghosts.

Most of the important people got drunk after one o'clock, sobered up around three-thirty and got drunk again at nine. Fist fights began around eleven. Seduction had no stated hours. The skimpy offices shook with passion. The mingled sound of plotting and sexual moans came through the transoms. It was a town of braggadocio and youth. Leading ladies still suffered from baby fat (rather than budding wattles as today) and the film heroes had trouble growing mustaches.

Nor was the industry yet captive. There were as many wildcatters around as bankers. And the movies, God bless 'em, were silent. The talkies had not yet come to make headaches for the half-illiterate viziers of the Front Office. In fact, to the best of my recollection, there were no headaches. There were no unions, no censor boards, no empty theater seats. It was Round Three and everybody looked like a champion.

Movies were seldom written. They were yelled into existence in conferences that kept going in saloons, brothels and all-night poker games. Movie sets roared with arguments and organ music. Sometimes little string orchestras played to help stir up the emotions of the great performers—*"Träumerei"* for Clara Bow and the "Meditation" from *Thaïs* for Adolphe Menjou, the screen's most sophisticated lover.

I was given an office at Paramount. A bit of cardboard with my name inked on it was tacked on the door. A soiree started at once in my office and lasted for several days. Men of letters, bearing gin bottles, arrived. Bob Benchley, hallooing with laughter as if he had come on the land of Punch and Judy, was there; and the owlish-eyed satirist Donald Ogden Stewart, beaming as at a convention of March Hares. One night at a flossy party Don appeared on the dance floor in a long overcoat. "That's silly and showing off to dance in an overcoat," said the great lady of the films in his arms. "Please take it off." Don did. He had nothing on underneath. F. Scott Fitzgerald was there, already pensive and inquiring if there were any sense to life, and muttering, at thirty, about the cruelty of growing aged.

Listening to Mankiewicz, Edwin Justice Mayer, Scott Fitzgerald, Ted Shayne and other litterateurs roosting in my office, I learned that the Studio Bosses (circa 1925) still held writers in great contempt and considered them a waste of money. I learned, also, that Manky had gotten me my job by a desperate coup.

The studio chieftain, the mighty B. P. Schulberg, smarting from experience with literary imports, had vowed never to hitch another onto the pay roll. Manky had invaded the Front Office, his own two-year contract in his hand. He had announced that if his friend Hecht failed to write a successful movie they could tear up his contract and fire us both.

I was pleased to hear this tale of loyalty and assured Manky *The New York Times* would be happy to take him back on its staff if things went awry.

On my fourth day, I was summoned and given an assignment. Producer Bernard Fineman, under Schulberg, presented me with the first "idea" for a movie to smite my ears.

An important industrialist, said he, was shaving one morning. His razor slipped and he cut his chin. He thereupon sent out his butler to buy an alum stick to stop the flow of blood. The butler was slowed up by a traffic jam and the great industrialist, fuming in his onyx bathroom, had to wait fifteen minutes for the alum stick. The movie I was to make up was to show all the things that were affected in the world by this fifteen-minute delay. I recall of the details only that something went wrong with the pearl fisheries. The whole thing ended up with the great industrialist's mistress deserting him, his vast enterprises crashing, and his wife returning to his side to help him build a new life.

I relate this plot because my distaste for it started me as a successful scenario writer. I had seen no more than a dozen movies but I had heard in my four days in Hollywood all that was to be known about the flickers.

"I want to point out to you," said Manky, "that in a novel a hero can lay ten girls and marry a virgin for a finish. In a movie this is not allowed. The hero, as well as the heroine, has to be a virgin. The villain can lay anybody he wants, have as much fun as he wants cheating and stealing, getting rich and whipping the servants. But you have to shoot him in the end. When he falls with a bullet in his forehead, it is advisable that he clutch at the Gobelin tapestry on the library wall and bring it down over his head like a symbolic shroud. Also, covered by such a tapestry, the actor does not have to hold his breath while he is being photographed as a dead man."

An idea came to me. The thing to do was to skip the heroes and heroines, to write a movie containing only villains and bawds. I would not have to tell any lies then.

Thus, instead of a movie about an industrialist cutting his chin, I made up a movie about a Chicago gunman and his moll called Feathers McCoy. As a newspaperman I had learned that nice people—the audience—loved criminals, doted on reading about their love problems as well as their sadism. My movie, grounded on this simple truth, was produced with the title of *Underworld*. It was the first gangster movie to bedazzle the movie fans and there were no lies in it— except for a half-dozen sentimental touches introduced by its director, Joe von

Sternberg. I still shudder remembering one of them. My head villain, Bull Weed, after robbing a bank, emerged with a suitcase full of money and paused in the crowded street to notice a blind beggar and give him a coin—before making his getaway.

It was not von Sternberg who helped me put the script together but another director, Arthur Rossen. Art Rossen was the first of these bonny directorial gentlemen with whom I was for many years to spend happy days locked away in fancy hotel rooms sawing away at plots. Art was one of the best of them, but, with a few nightmarish exceptions, they were all good. They were the new sort of storyteller produced by the movies, and, to this day, they remain the only authentic talent that has come out of Hollywood.

The Paramount Viziers, all four of them including the ex-prize fighter Mr. Zukor, listened to my reading of *Underworld*. It was eighteen pages long and it was full of moody Sandburgian sentences. The viziers were greatly stirred. I was given a ten-thousand-dollar check as a bonus for the week's work, a check which my sponsor Mankiewicz snatched out of my hand as I was bowing my thanks.

"You'll have it back in a week," Manky said. "I just want it for a few days to get me out of a little hole."

My return to New York was held up for several weeks while Manky struggled to raise another ten thousand to pay me back. He gambled valiantly, tossing a coin in the air with Eddie Cantor and calling heads or tails for a thousand dollars. He lost constantly. He tried to get himself secretly insured behind his good wife Sarah's back, planning to hock the policy and thus meet his obligation. This plan collapsed when the insurance company doctor refused to accept him as a risk.

I finally solved the situation by taking Manky into the Front Office and informing the studio bosses of our joint dilemma. I asked that my talented friend be given a five-hundred-dollar-a-week raise. The studio could then deduct this raise from his salary and give it to me. Thus in twenty weeks I would be repaid.

I left the Vatican suite with another full bonus check in my hand; and Manky, with his new raise, became the highest paid writer for Paramount Pictures, Inc.

THE CLOWNS: PINK PERIOD

Making movies is a game played by a few thousand toy-minded folk. It is obsessive, exhausting and jolly, as a good game should be. Played intently, it divorces you from life, as a good game will do. For many years I was one of the intent, though part-time, players. I paid some twenty visits to Hollywood and remained there each time only long enough to earn enough money to live on for the rest of the year. This required from two weeks to three or four months of work. With my bank balance restored, I would seize my hat and fly. Nearing penury again, I would turn again to Hollywood. There went with me, usually, Rose, a relative or two, two or three servants, many trunks and suitcases, all my oil paintings and whatever animals we possessed.

I remember, along with my indignation, the sunny streets of Hollywood, full of amiable and antic destinations. I remember studios humming with intrigue and happy-go-lucky excitements. I remember fine homes with handsome butlers and masterpieces on the walls; vivid people, long and noisy luncheons, nights of gaiety and gambling, hotel suites and rented palaces overrun with friends, partners, secretaries and happy servants. I remember thousands of important phone calls, yelling matches in the lairs of the caliphs, baseball, badminton and card games; beach and ocean on diamond-sparkling days, rainstorms out of Joseph Conrad and a picnic of money-making. More than all these pleasant things, I remember the camaraderie of collaboration.

Although I wrote most of my sixty movies alone, all my movie writing was a collaboration of one sort or another. The most satisfactory of these were my actual literary collaborations with MacArthur, Lederer or Fowler. The Hollywood party grew happier at such times.

But even without collaborators, the loneliness of literary creation was seldom part of movie work. You wrote with the phone ringing like a firehouse bell, with the boss charging in and out of your atelier, with the director grimacing and grunting in an adjoining armchair. Conferences interrupted you, agents with dream jobs flirted with you, and friends with unsolved plots came in hourly. Disasters circled your pencil. The star for whom you were writing fell ill or refused to play in the movie for reasons that stood your hair on end. ("I won't do this movie," said Ingrid Bergman of *Spellbound*, "because I don't believe the love story. The heroine is an intellectual woman, and an intellectual woman simply can't fall in love so deeply." She played the part very convincingly.) The studio for which you were working suddenly changed hands and was being reorganized. This meant usually no more than the firing of ten or twenty stenographers, but the excitement was unnerving. Or the studio head decided it would be better to change the locale of your movie from Brooklyn to Peking. You listened to these alarms, debated them like a juggler spinning hoops on his ankles, and kept on writing.

Of the bosses with whom I collaborated, Selznick and Zanuck and Goldwyn were the brightest. David, in the days he loved movie making, was a brilliant plotter. He could think of twenty different permutations of any given scene without stopping to catch his breath. Darryl was also quick and sharp and plotted at the top of his voice, like a man hollering for help. Goldwyn as a collaborator was inarticulate but stimulating. He filled the room with wonderful panic and beat at your mind like a man in front of a slot machine, shaking it for a jackpot.

Of the directors with whom I collaborated, most were sane and able fellows. I remember them happily—the young, piano-playing Leo McCarey, with a comedy fuse sputtering in his soul; the ex–clog dancer Ernst Lubitsch, who loved rhythm and precision in his scripts; the drawling fashion plate Howard Hawks, a-purr with melodrama; the moody and elegant Harry D'Arrast; the gentlemanly Alfred Hitchcock, who gave off plot turns like a Roman candle; the witty and Boccaccian Otto Preminger; the antic Jack Conway; the hysterical Gregory Ratoff; the chuckling, wild-hearted Willie Wellman; the soft-spoken, world-hopping Henry Hathaway; the aloof and poetical Victor Fleming. These and many others were all men of talent with salty personalities. Working with them was like playing a game—"Gimmick, Gimmick, Who's Got the Gimmick?"

There were directors, however, who added some depressing rules to the game and made collaboration a messy affair. These were the humorless ones to whose heads fame had gone like sewer gas. They resented a scenario writer as if he were an enemy hired by the Front Office to rob them of their greatness. They scowled at dialogue, shuddered at jokes, and wrestled with a script until they had shaken out of it all its verbal glitter and bright plotting. Thus they were able to bring to the screen evidence only of their own "genius." This consisted of making great psychological or dramatic points by using props, scenic effects or eye-rolling close-ups instead of speech. Knowing these pretenders well and the foolish egomania that animated their work, I managed to avoid most of them. A few, however, fell like rain into my life and darkened some of my days.

This sickly "greatness" is, however, rare in Hollywood. I remember little of it. At dinner parties where all the guests were famous movie stars and directors, none acted famous or even felt famous. Their world-known faces were full of shyness or sociability. The enormous publicity that flared around stars and directors seldom touched their inner personalities, which were as modest and eager as those of factory workers on a picnic. The only strut I remember was the strut of power. A few of the studio caliphs were inclined to make lordly entrances and to relish a bit of homage.

My favorite collaborator in Hollywood was neither writer, director nor boss, but the cameraman Lee Garmes. It was with Lee as a partner that I made all my own pictures, starting with *Crime without Passion* and *The Scoundrel, Specter of the Rose* and *Actors and Sin*. Lee introduced me to the real magic of the movie world—its technical talents. He was not only one of the finest camera artists in Hollywood but more learned about movie making than anyone I met in movieland. The camera was a brush with which he painted, but in his painting was the knowledge of the hundred hazards of a movie set. Nothing I ever encountered in the movies was as uniquely talented as the eyes of Lee Garmes. I prided myself on being an acute observer, but beside Lee I was almost a blind man. Driving his car at fifty miles an hour he would inquire if I had noticed the girl in the back seat of a car that had passed us, speeding in the opposite direction. What about her, I would ask. Lee would beam, "We ought to put that in a picture sometime. She was using daisies for cuff links, real daisies."

Standing on a set, Lee saw a hundred more things than I did. He saw shadows around mouths and eyes invisible to me, high lights on desk tops, ink stands and trouser legs. He spotted wrong reflections and mysterious obstructions— shoulders that blocked faces in the background, hands that masked distant and vital objects. These were all hazards that no look of mine could detect. He corrected them with a constant murmur of instructions. While ridding the set of its wrong nuances of light and shade, Lee also watched the grouping of figures and carried the cutting of the picture in his head. He knew the moods of space, the value of planes, the dynamics of symmetry as well as any painting master. And all this wisdom went into his pointing of the camera.

Working with Lee, I became aware of the other fine talents that are part of movie making. The gaffer, or head electrician, taking his orders from Garmes was a fellow as fond of his work and as full of technical skill. Carpenters, prop men, painters, special-effects men all moved about with quick and economic gestures. They were as removed from laborers as the master craftsmen working beside Cellini in his silver smithy. As director of the movie being shot, I was the final word on all matters. But I would sit by silent and full of admiration as Lee and his overalled magicians prepared the set for my "direction." My job seemed to me little more than putting a frame on a finished canvas.

A Visit from Scarface

My first dealing with Myron involved going to work for Howard Hughes. I told Myron I didn't trust Mr. Hughes as an employer. I would work for him only if he paid me a thousand dollars every day at six o'clock. In that way I stood to waste only a day's labor if Mr. Hughes turned out to be insolvent.

Myron was pleased by my attitude and put the deal over with dispatch. The work I did for Hughes was a movie called *Scarface*. News that it was a biographical study of Al Capone brought two Capone henchmen to Hollywood to make certain that nothing derogatory about the great gangster reached the screen. The two henchmen called on me at my hotel. It was after midnight. They entered the room as ominously as any pair of movie gangsters, their faces set in scowls and guns bulging their coats. They had a copy of my *Scarface* script in their hands. Their dialogue belonged in it.

"You the guy who wrote this?" I said I was.

"We read it." I inquired how they had liked it.

"We wanna ask you some questions." I invited them to go ahead.

"Is this stuff about Al Capone?"

"God, no," I said. "I don't even know Al."

"Never met him, huh?"

I pointed out I had left Chicago just as Al was coming into prominence.

"I knew Jim Colisimo pretty well," I said.

"That so?"

"I also knew Mossy Enright and Pete Gentleman."

"That so? Did you know Deanie?"

"Deanie O'Banion? Sure. I used to ride around with him in his flivver. I also knew Barney."

"Which Barney?"

"Barney Grogan—Eighteenth Ward," I said.

A pause.

"O.K., then. We'll tell Al this stuff you wrote is about them other guys."

They started out and halted in the doorway, worried again.

"If this stuff ain't about Al Capone, why are you callin' it *Scarface*? Everybody'll think it's him."

"That's the reason," I said. "Al is one of the most famous and fascinating men of our time. If we call the movie *Scarface,* everybody will want to see it, figuring it's about Al. That's part of the racket we call showmanship."

My visitors pondered this, and one of them finally said, "I'll tell Al." A pause. "Who's this fella Howard Hughes?"

"He's got nothing to do with anything," I said, speaking truthfully at last. "He's the sucker with the money."

"O.K. The hell with him."

My visitors left.

SOME GILDED ASSIGNMENTS

Writing under handicaps of one sort or another—deadlines to be met, censors to be outwitted, stars to be unruffled—was normal procedure. Writing to please a producer who a few years ago had been a garage owner or a necktie salesman was another of the handicaps. But given a producer literate as Anatole France, there was still the ugly handicap of having to write something that would miraculously please forty million people and gross four million dollars. The handicaps, including this last Liverpool Jump, only added bounce to the job. They made it always a half-desperate performance. If there was little excitement in the script, there was more than enough in its preparation to keep me stimulated.

Goldwyn, Selznick and Eddie Mannix of Metro were my favorite handicap makers. I wrote million-dollar movies for Mannix in a week each. They had to be rushed to the camera to catch release dates set long in advance. For Goldwyn I rewrote an entire script in two days. It was called *Hurricane. Nothing Sacred,* done for Selznick in two weeks, had to be written on trains between New York and Hollywood.

One of my favorite memories of quickie movie writing is the doing of half the *Gone with the Wind* movie. Selznick and Vic Fleming appeared at my bedside one Sunday morning at dawn. I was employed by Metro at the time, but David had arranged to borrow me for a week.

After three weeks' shooting of *Gone with the Wind,* David had decided his script was no good and that he needed a new story and a new director. The shooting had been stopped and the million-dollar cast was now sitting by collecting its wages in idleness.

The three of us arrived at the Selznick studio a little after sunrise. We had settled on my wages on the way over. I was to receive fifteen thousand dollars for the week's work, and no matter what happened I was not to work longer than a week. I knew in advance that two weeks of such toil as lay ahead might be fatal.

Four Selznick secretaries who had not yet been to sleep that night staggered in with typewriters, paper and a gross of pencils. Twenty-four-hour work shifts were quite common under David's baton. David himself sometimes failed to go to bed for several nights in a row. He preferred to wait till he collapsed on his office couch. Medication was often necessary to revive him.

David was outraged to learn I had not read *Gone with the Wind,* but decided there was no time for me to read the long novel. The Selznick overhead on the idle *Wind* stages was around fifty thousand dollars a day. David announced that he knew the book by heart and that he would brief me on it. For the next hour I listened to David recite its story. I had seldom heard a more involved plot. My verdict was that nobody could make a remotely sensible movie out of it. Fleming, who was reputed to be part Indian, sat brooding at his own council fires. I asked him if he had been able to follow the story David had told. He said no. I suggested then that we make up a new story, to which David replied with violence that every literate human in the United States except me had read Miss Mitchell's book, and we would have to stick to it. I argued that surely in two years of preparation someone must have wangled a workable plot out of Miss Mitchell's Ouïdalike flight into the Civil War. David suddenly remembered the first "treatment," discarded three years before. It had been written by Sidney Howard, since dead. After an hour of searching, a lone copy of Howard's work was run down in an old safe. David read it aloud. We listened to a precise and telling narrative of *Gone with the Wind.*

We toasted the dead craftsman and fell to work. Being privy to the book, Selznick and Fleming discussed each of Howard's scenes and informed me of the habits and general psychology of the characters. They also acted out the scenes, David specializing in the parts of Scarlett and her drunken father and Vic playing Rhett Butler and a curious fellow I could never understand called Ashley. He was always forgiving his beloved Scarlett for betraying him with another of his rivals. David insisted that he was a typical Southern gentleman and refused flatly to drop him out of the movie.

After each scene had been discussed and performed, I sat down at the typewriter and wrote it out. Selznick and Fleming, eager to continue with their acting, kept hurrying me. We worked in this fashion for seven days, putting in eighteen to twenty hours a day. Selznick refused to let us each lunch, arguing that food would slow us up. He provided bananas and salted peanuts. On the fourth day a blood vessel in Fleming's right eye broke, giving him more of an Indian look than ever. On the fifth day Selznick toppled into a torpor while chewing on a banana. The wear and tear on me was less, for I had been able to lie on the couch and half doze while the two darted about acting. Thus on the seventh day I had completed, unscathed, the first nine reels of the Civil War epic.

Many of the handicaps attending script writing I invented without anyone's aid. I often undertook to do two or more movies at the same time. Once I did four simultaneously, writing two of them with Lederer, one with Quentin Reynolds and one by myself. The house in Oceanside where this mass composition went on swarmed with secretaries, and producers motored down from Beverly Hills to spy on me. Lederer and I had small time for our favorite diversions, which were Klabiash, badminton, horseshoes on the beach and cooking up Napoleonic schemes for getting rich without effort.

FAREWELL, SOLDIER

I knew few actors and actresses well in Hollywood. Adventures and work shared with actors are not enough to make friendships. Actors are modest and warmhearted but they remain stubbornly in their own world. One of the few exceptions was Jack Gilbert. He became a friend, suddenly. We met at a dinner party and Jack came home with me and talked all night.

In the time of Hollywood's most glittering days, he glittered the most. He received ten thousand dollars a week and could keep most of it. He lived in a castle on top of a hill. Thousands of letters poured in daily telling him how wonderful he was. The caliphs for whom he worked bowed before him as before a reigning prince. They built him a "dressing room" such as no actor ever had. It was a small Italian palace. There were no enemies in his life. He was as unsnobbish as a happy child. He went wherever he was invited. He needed no greatness around him to make him feel distinguished. He drank with carpenters, danced with waitresses and made love to whores and movie queens alike. He swaggered and posed but it was never to impress anyone. He was being Jack Gilbert, prince, butterfly, Japanese lantern and the spirit of romance.

One night Jack sat in a movie theater and heard the audience laugh at him in a picture. It was his first talkie. His squeaky boy's voice accompanying his derring-do gestures turned him into a clown.

After the preview the Metro caliphs decided not to use him again. His contract for ten thousand a week still had many years to run. He would draw his salary and remain idle.

Jack called in three vocal coaches. He worked two hours a day with each of them. He started breaking into the front offices crying out, "Listen to me now. I can talk." And he recited passages from Shakespeare and the poets. The caliphs remembered the laughter in the theater and waved him away.

One day he entered Walter Wanger's office, fell on his knees and pleaded for the male lead in *Queen Christina*. Garbo, one of his former leading ladies, was being starred in it.

"Listen to me talk," said Jack. "It's a real voice, a man's voice." Tears fell from his eyes.

Wanger gave him the lead. Gilbert played it well, but the movie failed to bring him back to fame. The Gilbert voice no longer made audiences laugh. It left them, however, unimpressed. Jack played in no more pictures. He became a ten-thousand-dollar-a-week beachcomber. He strutted around the movie lot and gave drinking parties in his Italian-palace dressing room. There was no gloom visible in him. He played Jack Gilbert to a small audience of masseurs, fencing and boxing instructors, vocal coaches, barkers, whores, hangers-on and a few friends.

One rainy afternoon I called on him in his dressing room. He was lying down on one of his five-thousand-dollar beds reading one of my books. He asked me to autograph it. I wrote in it, "To Jack Gilbert—Dumas loaned him a mustache." I regretted the sentence as soon as I put it down. Jack grinned as he looked at it. "So true," he said. "Can you have dinner with me tonight?"

The rain became a tropic storm. Four of us drove out to Gilbert's house on Malibu Beach. MacArthur was one of the guests. Another was one of Jack's staunchest friends, Dick Hyland, the athlete and sports writer.

We drank and told stories after dinner. The wind howled in the night and the dark sea came crashing almost up to the windows. Gilbert was silent. He sat drinking and smiling at us. At eleven o'clock he sprang to his feet.

"I've got a date," he said. "I'm swimming out and returning a mustache to Dumas. Good-by—everybody—sweethearts and sonsobitches, all."

He waved a bottle of liquor at us and was gone. We saw him for a moment racing in the storm toward the roaring ocean. No one moved.

"For God's sake!" young Hyland said. "He's gone to drown himself!"

Hyland watched the storm for a few minutes and then left to find Jack. He returned in an hour, drenched and wearied. We were still drinking and talking.

"I couldn't find him," Hyland said. "He's gone."

I looked at MacArthur and asked, "What do you think, Charlie?"

"I don't know," said my friend, "but if a man wants to kill himself that's his privilege. Everybody destroys himself sooner or later."

MacArthur stood up unsteadily. He had remembered a phrase out of the Bible, which was always half-open in his head.

"A man fell in Israel," he quoted, and resumed his drinking.

The noises of the storm filled the room. The door opened suddenly. Rain and wind rushed in. A dripping Jack Gilbert stood weaving in the doorway. He grinned and tried to speak. Instead he vomited, and fell on the floor.

"Always the silent star," said MacArthur.

I thought of the Hans Christian Andersen tale of the Steadfast Tin Soldier. He had been swept away to sea in a paper boat, and in his ears as he was drowning had sounded the voice of one he loved.

> Farewell, soldier, true and brave,
> Nothing now thy life can save.

A few months later Gilbert went to a gay Hollywood party. While he was dancing with a movie queen, his toupee fell off. Amid shouts of laugher he retrieved it from under the dancers' feet. He was found dead the next morning in bed—in his castle on the hill.

GORE VIDAL

The auteur theory has not found many fans among writers, who believe that the director is at best the coauthor of a film. Gore Vidal, who has worked more in Hollywood, both credited and uncredited, than almost any other serious writer, has made a point of insisting that he, not director Franklin J. Schaffner, was the primary author of the film The Best Man. *Here he provides a tour of the rise of the auteur theory, explains its shortcomings, prepares the ground for a reevaluation of the writer's role, and tells many won-*

derful anecdotes. *(He can be seen retelling the most memorable, about his quick fix for the Ben-Hur screenplay, in* The Celluloid Closet, *a 1995 documentary about hidden and implied homosexuality in Hollywood movies during the Production Code days and after.)*

"Who Makes the Movies?"

Forty-nine years ago last October Al Jolson not only filled with hideous song the sound track of a film called *The Jazz Singer,* he also spoke. With the words "You ain't heard nothin' yet" (surely the most menacing line in the history of world drama), the age of the screen director came to an end and the age of the screenwriter began.

Until 1927, the director was king, turning out by the mile his "molds of light" (André Bazin's nice phrase). But once the movies talked, the director as creator became secondary to the writer. Even now, except for an occasional director-writer like Ingmar Bergman,* the director tends to be the one interchangeable (if not entirely expendable) element in the making of a film. After all, there are thousands of movie technicians who can do what a director is supposed to do because, in fact, collectively (and sometimes individually) they actually do do his work behind the camera and in the cutter's room. On the other hand, there is no film without a written script.

In the Fifties when I came to MGM as a contract writer and took my place at the Writers' Table in the commissary, the Wise Hack used to tell us newcomers, "The director is the brother-in-law." Apparently the ambitious man became a producer (that's where the power was). The talented man became a writer (that's where the creation was). The pretty man became a star.

Even before Jolson spoke, the director had begun to give way to the producer, Director Lewis Milestone saw the writing on the screen as early as 1923 when "baby producer" Irving Thalberg fired the legendary director Erich von Stroheim from his film *Merry Go Round.* "That," wrote Milestone somberly in *New Theater and Film* (March 1937), "was the beginning of the storm and the end of the reign of the director. . . ." Even as late as 1950 the star Dick Powell assured the film cutter Robert Parrish that "anybody can direct a movie, even I could do it. I'd rather not because it would take too much time. I can make more money acting, selling real estate and playing the market." That was pretty much the way

---

*Questions I am advised to anticipate: What about such true *auteurs du cinéma* as Truffaut? Well, *Jules et Jim* was a novel by Henri-Pierre Roché. Did Truffaut adapt the screenplay by himself? No, he worked with Jean Gruault. Did Buñuel create *The Exterminating Angel*? No, it was "suggested" by an unpublished play by José Bergamin. Did Buñuel take it from there? No, he had as co-author Luis Alcorisa. So it goes.

the director was viewed in the Thirties and Forties, the so-called classic age of the talking movie.

Although the essential creator of the classic Hollywood film was the writer, the actual master of the film was the producer, as Scott Fitzgerald recognized when he took as protagonist for his last novel Irving Thalberg. Although Thalberg himself was a lousy movie-maker, he was the head of production at MGM; and in those days MGM was a kind of Vatican where the chief of production was Pope, holding in his fists the golden keys of Schenck. The staff producers were the College of Cardinals. The movie stars were holy and valuable objects to be bought, borrowed, stolen. Like icons, they were moved from sound stage to sound stage, studio to studio, film to film, bringing in their wake good fortune and gold.

With certain exceptions (Alfred Hitchcock, for one), the directors were, at worst, brothers-in-law; at best, bright technicians. All in all, they were a cheery, unpretentious lot, and if anyone had told them that they were *auteurs du cinéma,* few could have coped with the concept, much less the French. They were technicians; proud commercialities, happy to serve what was optimistically known as The Industry.

This state of affairs lasted until television replaced the movies as America's principal dispenser of mass entertainment. Overnight the producers lost control of what was left of The Industry and, unexpectedly, the icons took charge. Apparently, during all those years when we thought the icons nothing more than beautiful painted images of all our dreams and lusts, they had been not only alive but secretly greedy for power and gold.

"The lunatics are running the asylum," moaned the Wise Hack at the Writers' Table, but soldiered on. Meanwhile, the icons started to produce, direct, even write. For a time, they were able to ignore the fact that with television on the rise, no movie star could outdraw the "$64,000 Question." During this transitional decade, the director was still the brother-in-law. But instead of marrying himself off to a producer, he shacked up, as it were, with an icon. For a time each icon had his or her favorite director and The Industry was soon on the rocks.

Then out of France came the dreadful news: all those brothers-in-law of the classic era were really autonomous and original artists. Apparently each had his own style that impressed itself on every frame of any film he worked on. Proof? Since the director was the same person from film to film, each image of his *oeuvre* must then be stamped with his authorship. The argument was circular but no less overwhelming in its implications. Much quoted was Giraudoux's solemn inanity: "There are no works, there are only *auteurs.*"

The often wise André Bazin eventually ridiculed this notion in *La Politique des Auteurs,* but the damage was done in the pages of the magazine he founded, *Cahiers du cinéma.* The fact that, regardless of director, every Warner Brothers film during the classic age had a dark look owing to the Brothers' passion for saving money in electricity and set-dressing cut no ice with ambitious critics on the prowl for high art in a field once thought entirely low.

In 1948, Bazin's disciple Alexandre Astruc wrote the challenging *"La Camé-ra-stylo."* This manifesto advanced the notion that the director is—or should be—the true and solitary creator of a movie, "penning" his film on celluloid. Astruc thought that *caméra-stylo* could

> tackle any subject any genre. . . . I will even go so far as to say that contemporary ideas and philosophies of life are such that only the cinema can do justice to them. Maurice Nadeau wrote in an article in the newspaper *Combat*: "If Descartes lived today, he would write novels." With all due respect to Nadeau, a Descartes of today would already have shut himself up in his bedroom with a 16mm camera and some film, and would be writing his philosophy on film: for his *Discours de la Méthode* would today be of such a kind that only the cinema could express it satisfactorily.

With all due respect to Astruc, the cinema has many charming possibilities but it cannot convey complex ideas through words or even, paradoxically, dialogue in the Socratic sense. *Le Genou de Claire* is about as close as we shall ever come to dialectic in a film and though Rohmer's work has its delights, the ghost of Descartes is not very apt to abandon the marshaling of words on a page for the flickering shadows of talking heads. In any case, the Descartes of Astruc's period did not make a film; he wrote the novel *La Nausée*.

But the would-be camera-writers are not interested in philosophy or history or literature. They want only to acquire for the cinema the prestige of ancient forms without having first to crack the code. "Let's face it," writes Astruc:

> between the pure cinema of the 1920s and filmed theater, there is plenty of room for a different and individual kind of film-making.
>
> This of course implies that the scriptwriter directs his own scripts; or rather, that the scriptwriter ceases to exist, for in this kind of film-making the distinction between author and director loses all meaning. Direction is no longer a means of illustrating or presenting a scene, but a true act of writing.

It is curious that despite Astruc's fierce will to eliminate the scriptwriter (and perhaps literature itself), he is forced to use terms from the art form he would like to supersede. For him the film director uses a *pen* with which he *writes* in order to become—highest praise—an *author.*

As the French theories made their way across the Atlantic, bemused brothers-in-law found themselves being courted by odd-looking French youths with tape recorders. Details of long-forgotten Westerns were recalled and explicated.

Every halting word from the *auteur*'s lips was taken down and reverently examined. The despised brothers-in-law of the Thirties were now Artists. With newfound confidence, directors started inking major pacts to meg superstar thesps whom the meggers could control as hyphenates: that is, as director-producers or even as writer-director-producers. Although the icons continued to be worshiped and overpaid, the truly big deals were now made by directors. To them, also, went the glory. For all practical purposes the producer has either vanished from the scene (the "package" is now put together by a "talent" agency) or merged with the director. Meanwhile, the screenwriter continues to be the prime creator of the talking film, and though he is generally paid very well and his name is listed right after that of the director in the movie reviews of *Time,* he is entirely in the shadow of the director just as the director was once in the shadow of the producer and the star.

What do directors actually do? What do screenwriters do? This is difficult to explain to those who have never been involved in the making of a film. It is particularly difficult when French theoreticians add to the confusion by devising false hypotheses (studio director as *auteur* in the Thirties) on which to build irrelevant and misleading theories. Actually, if Astruc and Bazin had wanted to be truly perverse (and almost accurate), they would have declared that the cameraman is the *auteur* of any film. They could then have ranked James Wong Howe with Dante, Braque, and Gandhi. Cameramen do tend to have styles in a way that the best writers do but most directors don't—style as opposed to preoccupation. Gregg Toland's camera work is a vivid fact from film to film, linking *Citizen Kane* to Wyler's *The Best Years of Our Lives* in a way that one cannot link *Citizen Kane* to, say, Welles's *Confidential Report.* Certainly the cameraman is usually more important than the director in the day-to-day making of a film as opposed to the preparation of a film. Once the film is shot the editor becomes the principal interpreter of the writer's invention.

Since there are few reliable accounts of the making of any of the classic talking movies, Pauline Kael's book on the making of *Citizen Kane* is a valuable document. In considerable detail she establishes the primacy in that enterprise of the screenwriter Herman Mankiewicz. The story of how Orson Welles saw to it that Mankiewicz became, officially, the noncreator of his own film is grimly fascinating and highly typical of the way so many director-hustlers acquire for themselves the writer's creation.* Few directors in this area possess the modesty of Kurosawa, who said, recently, "With a very good script, even a second-class director may make a first-class film. But with a bad script even a first-class director cannot make a really first-class film."

---

*Peter Bogdanovich maintains that Kael's version of the making of *Citizen Kane* is not only inaccurate but highly unfair to Orson Welles, a master whom I revere.

·   ·

A useful if necessarily superficial look at the way movies were written in the classic era can be found in the pages of *Some Time in the Sun*. The author, Mr. Tom Dardis, examines the movie careers of five celebrated writers who took jobs as movie-writers. They are Scott Fitzgerald, Aldous Huxley, William Faulkner, Nathanael West, and James Agee.

Mr. Dardis' approach to his writers and to the movies is that of a deeply serious and highly concerned lowbrow, a type now heavily tenured in American Academe. He writes of "literate" dialogue, "massive" biographies. Magisterially, he misquotes Henry James on the subject of gold. More seriously, *he misquotes Joan Crawford*. She did not say to Fitzgerald, "Work hard, Mr. Fitzgerald, work hard!" when he was preparing a film for her. She said *"Write hard. . . ."* There are many small inaccuracies that set on edge the film buff's teeth. For instance, Mr. Dardis thinks that the hotel on Sunset Boulevard known, gorgeously, as The Garden of Allah is "now demolished and reduced to the status of a large parking lot. . . ." Well, it is not a parking lot. Hollywood has its own peculiar reverence for the past. The Garden of Allah was replaced by a bank that subtly suggests in glass and metal the mock-Saracen façade of the hotel that once housed Scott Fitzgerald. Mr. Dardis also thinks that the hotel was "demolished" during World War II. I stayed there in the late Fifties, right next door to fun-loving, bibulous Errol Flynn.

Errors and starry-eyed vulgarity to one side, Mr. Dardis has done a good deal of interesting research on how films were written and made in those days. For one thing, he catches the ambivalence felt by the writers who had descended (but only temporarily) from literature's Parnassus to the swampy marketplace of the movies. There was a tendency to play Lucifer. One was thought to have sold out. "Better to reign in hell than to serve in heaven," was more than once quoted—well, paraphrased—at the Writers' Table. We knew we smelled of sulphur. Needless to say, most of the time it was a lot of fun if the booze didn't get you.

For the Parnassian writer the movies were not just a means of making easy money; even under the worst conditions, movies were genuinely interesting to write. Mr. Dardis is at his best when he shows his writers taking seriously their various "assignments." The instinct to do good work is hard to eradicate.

Faulkner was the luckiest (and the most cynical) of Mr. Dardis' five. For one thing, he usually worked with Howard Hawks, a director who might actually qualify as an *auteur*. Hawks was himself a writer and he had a strong sense of how to manipulate those clichés that he could handle best. Together Faulkner and Hawks created a pair of satisfying movies, *To Have and Have Not* and *The Big Sleep*. But who did what? Apparently there is not enough remaining evidence (at least available to Mr. Dardis) to sort out authorship. Also, Faulkner's public line was pretty much: I'm just a hired hand who does what he's told.

Nunnally Johnson (as quoted by Mr. Dardis) found Hawks's professional relationship with Faulkner mysterious. "It may be that he simply wanted his name attached to Faulkner's. Or since Hawks liked to write it was easy to do it with Faulkner, for Bill didn't care much one way or the other. . . . We shall probably never know just how much Bill cared about any of the scripts he worked on with Hawks." Yet it is interesting to note that Johnson takes it entirely for granted that the director wants—and must get—*all* credit for a film.

Problem for the director: how to get a script without its author? Partial solution: of all writers, the one who does not mind anonymity is the one most apt to appeal to an ambitious director. When the studio producer was king, he used to minimize the writer's role by assigning a dozen writers to a script. No director today has the resources of the old studios. But he can hire a writer who doesn't "care much one way or the other." He can also put his name on the screen as co-author (standard procedure in Italy and France). Even the noble Jean Renoir played this game when he came to direct *The Southerner.* Faulkner not only wrote the script, he liked the project. The picture's star Zachary Scott has said that the script was entirely Faulkner's. But then, other hands were engaged and "the whole problem," according to Mr. Dardis, "of who did what was nearly solved by Renoir's giving himself sole credit for the screenplay—the best way possible for an *auteur* director to label his films."

Unlike Faulkner, Scott Fitzgerald cared deeply about movies; he wanted to make a success of movie-writing and, all in all, if Mr. Dardis is to be believed (and for what it may be worth, his account of Fitzgerald's time in the sun tallies with what one used to hear), he had a far better and more healthy time of it in Hollywood than is generally suspected.

Of a methodical nature, Fitzgerald ran a lot of films at the studio. (Unlike Faulkner, who affected to respond only to Mickey Mouse and Pathé News). Fitzgerald made notes. He also did what an ambitious writer must do if he wants to write the sort of movie he himself might want to see: he made friends with the producers. Rather censoriously, Mr. Dardis notes Fitzgerald's "clearly stated intention to work with film producers rather than with film directors, here downgraded to the rank of 'collaborators.' Actually, Fitzgerald seems to have had no use whatsoever for directors as such." But neither did anyone else.

During much of this time Howard Hawks, say, was a low-budget director known for the neatness and efficiency of his work. Not until the French beatified him twenty years later did he appear to anyone as an original artist instead of just another hired technician. It is true that Hawks was allowed to work with writers, but then, he was at Warner Brothers, a frontier outpost facing upon barbarous Burbank. At MGM, the holy capital, writers and directors did not get much chance to work together. It was the producer who worked with the writer, and Scott Fitzgerald was an MGM writer. Even as late as my own years at MGM (1956–1958), the final script was the writer's creation (under the producer's supervision). The writer even pre-empted the director's most important function by describing each camera shot: Long, Medium, Close, and the director was expected faithfully to follow the writer's score.

One of the most successful directors at MGM during this period was George Cukor. In an essay on "The Director" (1938), Cukor reveals the game as it used to be played. "In most case," he writes, "the director makes his appearance very early in the life story of a motion picture." I am sure that this was often the case with Cukor but the fact that he thinks it necessary to mention "early" participation is significant.

> There are times when the whole idea for a film may come from [the director], but in a more usual case he makes his entry when he is summoned by a producer and it is suggested that he should be the director of a proposed story.

Not only was this the most usual way but, very often, the director left the producer's presence with the finished script under his arm. Cukor does describe his own experience working with writers but Cukor was something of a star at the studio. Most directors were "summoned" by the producer and told what to do. It is curious, incidentally, how entirely the idea of the working producer has vanished. He is no longer remembered except as the butt of familiar stories: fragile artist treated cruelly by insensitive cigar-smoking producer—or Fitzgerald savaged yet again by Joe Mankiewicz.

Of Mr. Dardis' five writers, James Agee is, to say the least, the lightest in literary weight. But he was a passionate film-goer and critic. He was a child of the movies just as Huxley was a child of Meredith and Peacock. Given a different temperament, luck, birthdate, Agee might have been the first American cinema *auteur*: a writer who wrote screenplays in such a way that, like the score of a symphony, they needed nothing more than a conductor's interpretation, . . . an interpretation he could have provided himself and perhaps would have provided if he had lived.

Agee's screenplays were remarkably detailed. "All the shots," writes Mr. Dardis, "were set down with extreme precision in a way that no other screenwriter had ever set things down before. . . ." This is exaggerated. Most screenwriters of the classic period wrote highly detailed scripts in order to direct the director but, certainly, the examples Mr. Dardis gives of Agee's screenplays show them to be remarkably visual. Most of us hear stories. He saw them, too. But I am not so sure that what he saw was the reflection of a living reality in his head. As with many of today's young directors, Agee's memory was crowded with memories not of life but of old films. For Agee, rain falling was not a memory of April at Exeter but a scene recalled from Eisenstein. This is particularly noticeable in the adaptation Agee made of Stephen Crane's *The Blue Hotel,* which, Mr. Dardis tells us, no "film director has yet taken on, although it has been televised twice, each time with a different director and cast and with the Agee script cut to the bone, being used only as a guidepost to the story." This is nonsense. In 1954, CBS hired me to adapt *The Blue Hotel.* I worked directly from Stephen Crane and did not know that James Agee had never adapted it until I read *Some Time in the Sun.*

At the mention of any director's name, the Wise Hack at the Writers' Table would bark out a percentage, representing how much, in his estimate, a given director would subtract from the potential 100 percent of the script he was directing. The thought that a director might *add* something worthwhile never crossed the good gray Hack's mind. Certainly he would have found hilarious David Thomson's *A Biographical Dictionary of Film,* whose haphazard pages are studded with tributes to directors.

Mr. Thomson has his own pleasantly eccentric pantheon in which writers figure hardly at all. A column is devoted to the dim Micheline Presle but the finest of all screenwriters, Jacques Prévert, is ignored. There is a long silly tribute to Arthur Penn; yet there is no biography of Penn's contemporary at NBC television, Paddy Chayefsky, whose films in the Fifties and early Sixties were far more interesting than anything Penn has done. Possibly Chayefsky was excluded because not only did he write his own films, he would then hire a director rather the way one would employ a plumber—or a cameraman. For a time, Chayefsky was the only American *auteur,* and his pencil was the director. Certainly Chayefsky's early career in films perfectly disproves Nicholas Ray's dictum (approvingly quoted by Mr. Thomson): "If it were all in the script, why make the film?" If it is not all in the script, there is no film to make.

Twenty years ago at the Writers' Table we all agreed with the Wise Hack that William Wyler subtracted no more than 10 percent from a script. Some of the most attractive and sensible of Bazin's pages are devoted to Wyler's work in the Forties. On the other hand, Mr. Thomson does not like him at all (because Wyler lacks those redundant faults that create the illusion of a Style?). Yet whatever was in a script, Wyler rendered faithfully: when he was given a bad script, he would make not only a bad movie, but the script's particular kind of badness would be revealed in a way that could altogether too easily boomerang on the too skillful director. But when the script was good (of its kind, *of its kind!*), *The Letter,* say, or *The Little Foxes,* there was no better interpreter.

At MGM, I worked exclusively with the producer Sam Zimbalist. He was a remarkably good and decent man in a business where such qualities are rare. He was also a producer of the old-fashioned sort. This meant that the script was prepared for him and with him. Once the script was ready, the director was summoned; he would then have the chance to say, yes, he would direct the script or, no, he wouldn't. Few changes were made in the script after the director was assigned. But this was not to be the case in Zimbalist's last film.

For several years MGM had been planning a remake of *Ben-Hur,* the studio's most successful silent film. A Contract Writer wrote a script; it was discarded. Then Zimbalist offered me the job. I said no, and went on suspension. During the next year or two S. N. Behrman and Maxwell Anderson, among others, added many yards of portentous dialogue to a script which kept growing and changing. The result was not happy. By 1958 MGM was going bust. Suddenly the remake of *Ben-Hur* seemed like a last chance to regain the mass audience lost to television. Zimbalist again asked me if I would take on the job. I said that if the studio released me from the remainder of my contract, I would go to Rome for two or three months and rewrite the script. The studio agreed. Meanwhile, Wyler had been signed to direct.

On a chilly March day Wyler, Zimbalist, and I took an overnight flight from New York. On the plane Wyler read for the first time the latest of the many scripts. As we drove together into Rome from the airport, Wyler looked gray and rather frightened. "This is awful," he said, indicating the huge script that I had placed between us on the back seat. "I know," I said. "What are we going to do?"

Wyler groaned: "These Romans. . . . Do you know anything about them?" I said, yes, I had done my reading. Wyler stared at me. "Well," he said, "when a Roman sits down and relaxes, what does he unbuckle?"

That spring I rewrote more than half the script (and Wyler studied every "Roman" film ever made). When I was finished with a scene, I would give it to Zimbalist. We would go over it. Then the scene would be passed on to Wyler. Normally, Wyler is slow and deliberately indecisive; but first-century Jerusalem had been built at enormous expense; the first day of shooting was approaching; the studio was nervous. As a result, I did not often hear Wyler's famous cry, as he would hand you back your script, "If I knew what was wrong with it, I'd fix it myself."

The plot of *Ben-Hur* is, basically, absurd and any attempt to make sense of it would destroy the story's awful integrity. But for a film to be watchable the characters must make some kind of psychological sense. We were stuck with the following: the Jew Ben-Hur and the Roman Messala were friends in childhood. Then they were separated. Now the adult Messala returns to Jerusalem; meets Ben-Hur; asks him to help with the Romanization of Judea. Ben-Hur refuses; there is a quarrel; they part and vengeance is sworn. This one scene is the sole motor that must propel a very long story until Jesus Christ suddenly and pointlessly drifts onto the scene, automatically untying some of the cruder knots in the plot. Wyler and I agreed that a single political quarrel would not turn into a lifelong vendetta.

I thought of a solution, which I delivered into Wyler's good ear. "As boys they were lovers. Now Messala wants to continue the affair. Ben-Hur rejects him. Messala is furious. *Chagrin d'amour,* the classic motivation for murder."

Wyler looked at me as if I had gone mad. "But we can't do *that!* I mean this is Ben-Hur! My God. . . ."

"We won't really do it. We just suggest it. I'll write the scenes so that they will make sense to those who are tuned in. Those who aren't will still feel that Messala's rage is somehow emotionally logical."

I don't think Wyler particularly liked my solution but he agreed that "anything is better than what we've got. So let's try it."

I broke the original scene into two parts. Charlton Heston (Ben-Hur) and Stephen Boyd (Messala) read them for us in Zimbalist's office. Wyler knew his actors. He warned me: "Don't ever tell Chuck what it's all about, or he'll fall apart."* I suspect that Heston does not know to this day what luridness we managed to contrive around him. But Boyd knew: every time he looked at Ben-Hur it was like a starving man getting a glimpse of dinner through a pane of glass. And so, among the thundering hooves and clichés of the last (to date) *Ben-Hur,* there is something odd and authentic in one unstated relationship.

As agreed, I left in early summer and Christopher Fry wrote the rest of the script. Before the picture ended, Zimbalist died of a heart attack. Later, when it came time to credit the writers of the film, Wyler proposed that Fry be given screen credit. Then Fry insisted that I be given credit with him, since I had written the first half of the picture. Wyler was in a quandary. Only Zimbalist (and Fry and myself—two interested parties) knew who had written what, and Zimbalist was dead. The matter was given to the Screenwriters Guild for arbitration and they, mysteriously, awarded the credit to the Contract Writer whose script was separated from ours by at least two other discarded scripts. The film was released in 1959 (not 1959–1960, as my edition of *The Filmgoer's Companion* by Leslie Halliwell states) and saved MGM from financial collapse.

I have recorded in some detail this unimportant business to show the near-impossibility of determining how a movie is actually created. Had *Ben-Hur* been taken seriously by, let us say, those French critics who admire *Johnny Guitar,* then Wyler would have been credited with the unusually subtle relationship between Ben-Hur and Messala. No credit would ever have gone to me because my name was not on the screen, nor would credit have gone to the official scriptwriter because, according to the *auteur* theory, every aspect of a film is the creation of the director.

---

*Wyler now denies that I ever told him what I was up to. It is possible that these conversations took place with Zimbalist but I doubt it. Anyway, the proof is on the screen.

The twenty-year interregnum when the producer was supreme is now a memory. The ascendancy of the movie stars was brief. The directors have now regained their original primacy, and Milestone's storm is only an echo. Today the marquees of movie houses feature the names of directors and journalists ("*A work of art*," J. Crist); the other collaborators are in fine print.

This situation might be more acceptable if the film directors had become true *auteurs*. But most of them are further than ever away from art—not to mention life. The majority are simply technicians. A few have come from the theatre; many began as editors, cameramen, makers of television series, and commercials; in recent years, ominously, a majority have been graduates of film schools. In principle, there is nothing wrong with a profound understanding of the technical means by which an image is impressed upon celluloid. But movies are not just molds of light any more than a novel is just inked-over paper. A movie is a response to reality in a certain way and that way must first be found by a writer. Unfortunately, no contemporary film director can bear to be thought a mere interpreter. He must be sole creator. As a result, he is more often than not a plagiarist, telling stories that are not his.

Over the years a number of writers have become directors, but except for such rare figures as Cocteau and Bergman, the writers who have gone in for directing were generally not much better at writing than they proved to be at directing. Even in commercial terms, for every Joe Mankiewicz or Preston Sturges there are a dozen Xs and Ys, not to mention the depressing Z.

Today's films are more than ever artifacts of light. Cars chase one another mindlessly along irrelevant freeways. Violence seems rooted in a notion about what ought to happen next on the screen to help the images move rather than in any human situation anterior to those images. In fact, the human situation has been eliminated not through any intentional philosophic design but because those who have spent too much time with cameras and machines seldom have much apprehension of that living world without whose presence there is no art.

I suspect that the time has now come to take Astruc seriously . . . after first rearranging his thesis. Astruc's *caméra-stylo* requires that "the script writer ceases to exist. . . . The filmmaker/author writes with his camera as a writer writes with his pen." Good. But let us eliminate not the screenwriter but that technician-hustler—the director (a.k.a. *auteur du cinéma*). Not until he has been replaced by those who can use a pen to write from life for the screen is there going to be much of anything worth seeing. Nor does it take a genius of a writer to achieve great effects in film. Compared to the works of his nineteenth-century mentors, the writing of Ingmar Bergman is second-rate. But when he writes straight through the page and onto the screen itself his talent is transformed and the result is often first-rate.

As a poet, Jacques Prévert is not in the same literary class as Valéry, but Prévert's films *Les Enfants du Paradis* and *Lumière d'été* are extraordinary achievements. They were also disdained by the French theoreticians of the Forties who knew perfectly well that the directors Carné and Grémillon were inferior to their scriptwriter; but since the Theory requires that only a director can create a film, any film that is plainly a writer's work cannot be true cinema. This attitude has given rise to some highly comic critical musings. Recently a movie critic could not figure out why there had been such a dramatic change in the quality of the work of the director Joseph Losey after he moved to England. Was it a difference in the culture? the light? the water? Or could it—and the critic faltered— could it be that perhaps Losey's films changed when he . . . when he—oh, dear!—got Harold Pinter to write screenplays for him? The critic promptly dismissed the notion. Mr. Thomson prints no biography of Pinter in his *Dictionary*.

I have never much liked the films of Pier Paolo Pasolini, but I find most interesting the ease with which he turned to film after some twenty years as poet and novelist. He could not have been a filmmaker in America because the costs are too high; also, the technician-hustlers are in total charge. But in Italy, during the Fifties, it was possible for an actual *auteur* to use for a pen the camera (having first composed rather than stolen the narrative to be illuminated).

Since the talking movie is closest in form to the novel ("the novel is a narrative that organizes itself in the world, while the cinema is a world that organizes itself into a narrative"—Jean Mitry), it strikes me that the rising literary generation might think of the movies as, peculiarly, their kind of novel, to be created by them in collaboration with technicians but without the interference of The Director, that hustler-plagiarist who has for twenty years dominated and exploited and (occasionally) enhanced an art form still in search of its true authors.

CHRISTOPHER ISHERWOOD

Written in 1945, Christopher Isherwood's Prater Violet *is one of his less-known novels, about a writer named Christopher Isherwood who finds himself working in London with a director who is a refugee from Austria, in 1936, as Hitler's shadow lengthens. It is interesting how "Isherwood," who has a reputation as a serious writer, finds the requirements of a movie potboiler to be daunting and gains a new respect for the skills of those who can make one work. The real Isherwood (1904–1986) was a British writer who settled in California in 1939 and often used thinly or not disguised versions of himself in his fiction. His* Berlin Stories *inspired the movie* Cabaret.

from *Prater Violet*

One of Chatsworth's underlings had installed Bergmann in a service flat in Knightsbridge, not far from Hyde Park Corner. I found him there next morning, at the top of several steep flights of stairs. Even before we could see each other, he began to hail me from above. "Come up! Higher! Higher! Courage! Not yet! Where are you? Don't weaken! Aha! At last! *Servus,* my friend!"

"Well?" I asked, as we shook hands. "How do you like it here?"

"Terrible!" Bergmann twinkled at me comically from under his black bush of eyebrow. "It's an inferno! You have made the *as*-cent to hell."

This morning, he was no longer an emperor but an old clown, shock-headed, in his gaudy silk dressing gown. Tragicomic, like all clowns, when you see them resting backstage after the show.

He laid his hand on my arm. "First, tell me one thing, please. Is your whole city as horrible as this?"

"Horrible? Why, this is the best part of it! Wait till you see our slums, and the suburbs."

Bergmann grinned. "You console me enormously."

He led the way into the flat. The small living room was tropically hot, under a heavy cloud of cigarette smoke. It reeked of fresh paint. The whole place was littered with clothes, papers and books, in explosive disorder, like the debris around a volcano.

Bergmann called, "Mademoiselle!" and a girl came out of the inner room. She had fair smooth hair, brushed plainly back from her temples, and a quiet oval face, which would have looked pretty, if her chin hadn't been too pointed. She wore rimless glasses and the wrong shade of lipstick. She was dressed in the neat jacket and skirt of a stenographer.

"Dorothy, I introduce you to Mr. Isherwood. Dorothy is my secretary, the most beautiful of all the gifts given me by the munificent Mr. Chatsworth. You see, Dorothy, Mr. Isherwood is the good Virgil who has come to guide me through this Anglo-Saxon comedy."

Dorothy smiled the smile of a new secretary—a bit bewildered still, but prepared for anything in the way of lunatic employers.

"And please suppress that fire," Bergmann added. "It definitely kills me."

Dorothy knelt down and turned off the gas fire, which had been roaring away in a corner. "Do you want me now," she asked, very businesslike, "or shall I be getting on with the letters?"

"We always want you, my darling. Without you, we could not exist for one moment. You are our Beatrice. But first, Mr. Virgil and I have to become acquainted. Or rather, he must become acquainted with me. For, you see," Bergmann continued, as Dorothy left the room, "I know everything about you already."

"You do?"

"Certainly. Everything that is important. Wait. I shall show you something."

Raising his forefinger, smilingly, to indicate that I must be patient, he began to rummage among the clothes and scattered papers. I watched with growing curiosity, as Bergmann's search became increasingly furious. Now and then, he would discover some object, evidently not the right one, hold it up before him for a moment, like a nasty-smelling dead rat, and toss it aside again with a snort of disgust or some exclamation such as "Abominable!" "*Scheusslich!*" "Too silly for words!" I watched him unearth, in this way, a fat black notebook, a shaving mirror, a bottle of hair tonic and an abdominal belt. Finally, under a pile of shirts, he found a copy of *Mein Kampf* which he kissed, before throwing it into the wastepaper basket. "I love him!" he told me, making a wry, comical face.

The search spread into the bedroom. I could hear him plunging about, snorting and breathing hard, as I stood by the mantelpiece, looking at the photographs of a large, blonde, humorous woman and a thin, dark, rather frightened girl. Next, the bathroom was explored. A couple of wet towels were flung out into the passage. Then Bergmann uttered a triumphant "Aha!" He strode back into the living room, waving a book above his head. It was my novel, *The Memorial*.

"So! Here we are! You see? I read it at midnight. And again this morning, in my bath."

I was absurdly pleased and flattered. "Well," I tried to sound casual, "how did you like it?"

"I found it grandiose."

"It ought to have been much better. I'm afraid I . . ."

"You are wrong," Bergmann told me, quite severely. He began to turn the pages. "This scene—he tries to make a suicide. It is genial." He frowned solemnly, as if daring me to contradict him. "This I find clearly genial."

I laughed and blushed. Bergmann watched me, smiling, like a proud parent who listens to his son being praised by the headmaster. Then he patted me on the shoulder.

"Look, if you do not believe me. I will show you. This I wrote this morning, after reading your book." He began to fumble in his pockets. As there were only seven of them, it didn't take him long. He pulled out a crumpled sheet of paper. "My first poem in English. To an English poet."

I took it and read:

> When I am a boy, my mother tells to me
> It is lucky to wake up when the morning is bright
> And first of all hear a lark sing.
>
> Now I am not longer a boy, and I wake. The morning is dark.
> I hear a bird singing with unknown name
> In a strange country language, but it is luck, I think.
>
> Who is he, this singer, who does not fear the gray city?
> Will they drown him soon, the poor Shelley?
> Will Byron's hangmen teach him how one limps?
> I hope they will not, because he makes me happy.

"Why," I said, "it's beautiful!"

"You like it?" Bergmann was so delighted that he began rubbing his hands. "But you must correct the English, please."

"Certainly not. I like it the way it is."

"Already I think I have a feeling for the language," said Bergmann, with modest satisfaction. "I shall write many English poems."

"May I keep this one?"

"Really? "You want it?" he beamed. "Then I shall inscribe it for you."

He took out his fountain pen and wrote: "For Christopher, from Friedrich, his fellow prisoner."

I laid the poem carefully on the mantelpiece. It seemed to be the only safe place in the room. "Is this your wife?" I asked, looking at the photographs.

"Yes. And that is Inge, my daughter. You like her?"

"She has beautiful eyes."

"She is a pianist. Very talented."

"Are they in Vienna?"

"Unfortunately. Yes. I am most anxious for them. Austria is no longer safe. The plague is spreading. I wished them to come with me, but my wife has to look after her mother. It's not so easy." Bergmann sighed deeply. Then, with a sharp glance at me, "You are not married." It sounded like an accusation.

"How did you know?"

"I know these things. . . . You live with your parents?"

"With my mother and brother. My father's dead."

Bergmann grunted and nodded. He was like a doctor who finds his most pessimistic diagnosis is confirmed. "You are a typical mother's son. It is the English tragedy."

I laughed. "Quite a lot of Englishmen do get married, you know."

"They marry their mothers. It is a disaster. It will lead to the destruction of Europe."

"I must say, I don't quite see . . ."

"It will lead definitely to the destruction of Europe. I have written the first chapters of a novel about this. It is called *The Diary of an Etonian Oedipus.*" Bergmann suddenly gave me a charming smile. "But do not worry. We shall change all that."

"All right," I grinned. "I won't worry."

Bergmann lit a cigarette, and blew a cloud of smoke into which he almost disappeared.

"And now," he announced, "the horrible but unavoidable moment has come when we have to talk about this crime we are about to commit: this public outrage, this enormous nuisance, this scandal, this blasphemy. . . . You have read the original script?"

"They sent a messenger round with it, last night."

"And . . . ?" Bergmann watched me keenly, waiting for my answer.

"It's even worse than I expected."

"Marvelous! Excellent! You see, I am such a horrible old sinner that nothing is ever as *bad* as I expect. But you are surprised. You are shocked. That is because you are innocent. It is this innocence which I need absolutely to help me, the innocence of Alyosha Karamazov. I shall proceed to corrupt you. I shall teach you everything from the very beginning. . . . Do you know what the film is?" Bergmann cupped his hands, lovingly, as if around an exquisite flower. "The film is an infernal machine. Once it is ignited and set in motion, it revolves with an enormous dynamism. It cannot pause. It cannot apologize. It cannot retract anything. It cannot wait for you to understand it. It cannot explain itself. It simply ripens to its inevitable explosion. This explosion we have to prepare, like anarchists, with the utmost ingenuity and malice. . . . While you were in Germany did you ever see *Frau Nussbaum's letzter Tag?*"

"Indeed I did. Three or four times."

Bergmann beamed. "I directed it."

"No? Really?"

"You didn't know?"

"I'm afraid I never read the credits. . . . Why, that was one of the best German pictures!"

Bergmann nodded, delighted, accepting this as a matter of course. "You must tell that to Umbrella."

"Umbrella?"

"The Beau Brummel who appeared to us yesterday at lunch."

"Oh, Ashmeade . . ."

Bergmann looked concerned. "He is a great friend of yours?"

"No," I grinned. "Not exactly."

"You see, this umbrella of his I find extremely symbolic. It is the British respectability which thinks: 'I have my traditions, and they will protect me. Nothing unpleasant, nothing ungentlemanly can possibly happen within my private park.' This respectable umbrella is the Englishman's magic wand, with which he will try to wave Hitler out of existence. When Hitler declines rudely to disappear, the Englishman will open his umbrella and say, 'After all, what do I care for a little rain?' But the rain will be a rain of bombs and blood. The umbrella is not bomb-proof."

"Don't underrate the umbrella," I said. "It has often been used successfully, by governesses against bulls. It has a very sharp point."

"You are wrong. The umbrella is useless. . . . Do you know Goethe?"

"Only a little."

"Wait. I shall read you something. Wait. Wait."

.   .   .   .

"The whole *beauty* of the film," I announced to my mother and Richard next morning at breakfast, "is that it has a certain fixed *speed*. The way you see it is mechanically conditioned. I mean, take a painting—you can just glance at it, or you can stare at the left-hand top corner for half an hour. Same thing with a book. The author can't stop you from skimming it, or starting at the last chapter and reading backwards. The point is, you choose your approach. When you go into a cinema, it's different. There's the film, and you have to look at it as the director wants you to look at it. He makes his points, one after another, and he allows you a certain number of seconds or minutes to grasp each one. If you miss anything, he won't repeat himself, and he won't stop to explain. He can't. He's started something, and he has to go through with it. . . . You see, the film is really like a sort of infernal machine . . ."

I stopped abruptly, with my hands in the air. I had caught myself in the middle of one of Bergmann's most characteristic gestures.

.   .   .   .

I had always had a pretty good opinion of myself as a writer. But, during those first days with Bergmann, it was lowered considerably. I had flattered myself that I had imagination, that I could invent dialogue, that I could develop a character. I had believed that I could describe almost anything, just as a competent artist can draw you an old man's face, or a table, or a tree.

Well, it seemed that I was wrong.

The period is early twentieth century, some time before the 1914 war. It is a warm spring evening in the Vienna Prater. The dancehalls are lighted up. The coffee houses are full. The bands blare. Fireworks are bursting above the trees. The swings are swinging. The roundabouts are revolving. There are freak shows, gypsies telling fortunes, boys playing the concertina. Crowds of people are eating, drinking beer, wandering along the paths beside the river. The drunks sing noisily. The lovers, arm in arm, stroll whispering in the shadow of the elms and the silver poplars.

There is a girl named Toni, who sells violets. Everybody knows her, and she has a word for everybody. She laughs and jokes as she offers the flowers. An officer tries to kiss her; she slips away from him goodhumoredly. An old lady has lost her dog; she is sympathetic. An indignant, tyrannical gentleman is looking for his daughter; Toni knows where she is, and with whom, but she won't tell.

Then, as she wanders down the alleys carrying her basket, light-hearted and fancy-free, she comes face to face with a handsome boy in the dress of a student. He tells her, truthfully, that his name is Rudolf. But he is not what he seems. He is really the Crown Prince of Borodania.

All this I was to describe. "Do not concern yourself with the shots," Bergmann had told me. "Just write dialogue. Create atmosphere. Give the camera something to listen to and look at."

I couldn't. I couldn't. My impotence nearly reduced me to tears. It was all so simple, surely? There is Toni's father, for instance. He is fat and jolly, and he has a stall where he sells *Wiener Wuerstchen*. He talks to his customers. He talks to Toni. Toni talks to the customers. They reply. It is all very gay, amusing, delightful. But what the hell do they actually say?

I didn't know. I couldn't write it. That was the brutal truth—I couldn't draw a table. I tried to take refuge in my pride. After all, this was movie work, hack work. It was something essentially false, cheap, vulgar. It was beneath me. I ought never to have become involved in it, under the influence of Bergmann's dangerous charm, and for the sake of the almost incredible twenty pounds a week which Imperial Bulldog was prepared, quite as a matter of course, to pay me. I was betraying my art. No wonder it was so difficult.

Nonsense. I didn't really believe that, either. It isn't vulgar to be able to make people talk. An old man selling sausages isn't vulgar, except in the original meaning of the word, "belonging to the common people." Shakespeare would have known how he spoke. Tolstoy would have known. I didn't know because, for all my parlor socialism, I was a snob. I didn't know how anybody spoke, except public-school boys and neurotic bohemians.

I fell back, in my despair, upon memories of other movies. I tried to be smart, facetious. I made involved, wordy jokes. I wrote a page of dialogue which led nowhere and only succeeded in establishing the fact that an anonymous minor character was having an affair with somebody else's wife. As for Rudolf, the incognito Prince, he talked like the lowest common denominator of all the worst musical comedies I had ever seen. I hardly dared to show my wretched attempts to Bergmann at all.

He read them through with furrowed brows and a short profound grunt; but he didn't seem either dismayed or surprised. "Let me tell you something, Master," he began, as he dropped my manuscript casually into the wastepaper basket, "the film is a symphony. Each movement is written in a certain key. There is a note which has to be chosen and struck immediately. It is characteristic of the whole. It commands the attention."

Sitting very close to me, and pausing only to draw long breaths from his cigarette, he started to describe the opening sequence. It was astounding. Everything came to life. The trees began to tremble in the evening breeze, the music was heard, the roundabouts were set in motion. And the people talked. Bergmann improvised their conversation, partly in German, partly in ridiculous English; and it was vivid and real. His eyes sparkled, his gestures grew more exaggerated, he mimicked, he clowned. I began to laugh. Bergmann smiled delightedly at his own invention. It was all so simple, so effective, so obvious. Why hadn't I thought of it myself?

Bergmann gave me a little pat on the shoulder. "It's nice, isn't it?"

"It's wonderful! I'll note that down before I forget."

Immediately, he was very serious. "No, no. It is wrong. All wrong. I only wanted to give you some idea . . . No, that won't do. Wait. We must consider . . ."

Clouds followed the sunshine. Bergmann scowled grimly as he passed into philosophical analysis. He gave me ten excellent reasons why the whole thing was impossible. They, too, were obvious. Why hadn't I thought of them? Bergmann sighed. "It's not so easy . . ." He lit another cigarette. "Not so easy," he muttered. "Wait. Wait. Let us see . . ."

He rose and paced the carpet, breathing hard, his hands folded severely behind his back, his face shut against the outside world, implacably, like a prison door. Then a thought struck him. He stopped, amused by it. He smiled.

"You know what my wife tells me when I have these difficulties? 'Friedrich,' she says, 'Go and write your poems. When I have cooked the dinner, I will invent this idiotic story for you. After all, prostitution is a woman's business.' "

.   .   .   .

We started shooting the picture in the final week of January. I give this approximate date because it is almost the last I shall be able to remember. What followed is so confused in my memory, so transposed and foreshortened, that I can only describe it synthetically. My recollection of it has no sequence. It is all of a piece.

Within the great barnlike sound-stage, with its high bare padded walls, big enough to enclose an airship, there is neither day nor night: only irregular alternations of activity and silence. Beneath a firmament of girders and catwalks, out of which the cowled lamps shine coldly down like planets, stands the inconsequent, half-dismantled architecture of the sets; archways, sections of houses, wood and canvas hills, huge photographic backdrops, the frontages of streets; a kind of Pompeii, but more desolate, more uncanny, because this is, literally, a half-world, a limbo of mirror-images, a town which has lost its third dimension. Only the tangle of heavy power cables is solid, and apt to trip you as you cross the floor. Your footsteps sound unnaturally loud; you find yourself walking on tiptoe.

In one corner, amidst these ruins, there is life. A single set is brilliantly illuminated. From the distance, it looks like a shrine, and the figures standing around it might be worshippers. But it is merely the living room of Toni's home, complete with period furniture, gaily colored curtains, a canary cage and a cuckoo clock. The men who are putting the finishing touches to this charming, life-size doll's house go about their work with the same matter-of-fact, unsmiling efficiency which any carpenters and electricians might show in building a garage.

In the middle of the set, patient and anonymous as tailor's dummies, are the actor and actress who are standing in for Arthur Cromwell and Anita Hayden. Mr. Watts, a thin bald man with gold-rimmed spectacles, walks restlessly back and forth, regarding them from various angles. A blue-glass monocle hangs from a ribbon around his neck. He raises it repeatedly to observe the general effect of the lighting; and the gesture is incongruously like that of a Regency fop. Beside him is Fred Murray, red-haired and wearing rubber shoes. Fred is what is called "the Gaffer," in studio slang. According to our etiquette, Mr. Watts cannot condescend to give orders directly. He murmurs them to Fred; and Fred, as if translating into a foreign language, shouts up to the men who work the lamps on the catwalk, high above.

"Put a silk on that rifle. . . . Take a couple of turns on number four. . . . Kill that baby."

"I'm ready," says Mr. Watts, at length.

"All right," Fred Murray shouts to his assistants. "Save them." The arcs are switched off and the house lights go on. The set loses its shrinelike glamour. The stand-ins leave their positions. There is an atmosphere of anti-climax, as though we were about to start all over again from the beginning.

"Now then, are we nearly ready?" This is Eliot, the assistant-director. He has a long pointed nose and a public-school accent. He carries a copy of the script, like an emblem of office, in his hand. His manner is bossy, but self-conscious and unsure. I feel sorry for him. His job makes him unpopular. He has to fuss and keep things moving; and he doesn't know how to do it without being aggressive. He doesn't know how to talk to the older men, or the stagehands. He is conscious of his own high-pitched, cultured voice. His shirt collar has too much starch in it.

"What's the hold-up?" Eliot plaintively addresses the world in general. "What about you, Roger?"

Roger, the sound-recordist, curses under his breath. He hates being rushed. "There's a baffle on this mike," he explains, with acid patience. "It's a bloody lively set. . . . Shift your boom a bit more round to the left, Teddy. We'll have to use a flower pot."

The boom moves over, dangling the microphone, like a fishing rod. Teddy, who works it, crosses the set and conceals a second microphone behind a china figure on the table.

Meanwhile, somewhere in the background, I hear Arthur Cromwell calling, "Where's the invaluable Isherwood?" Arthur plays Toni's father. He is a big handsome man who used to be a matinee idol—a real fine old ham. He wants me to hear him his part. When he forgets a line, he snaps his fingers, without impatience.

"What's the matter, Toni? Isn't it time to go to the Prater?"

"Aren't you going to the Prater today?" I prompt.

"Aren't you going to the Prater today?" But Arthur has some mysterious actor's inhibition about this. "Bit of a mouthful, isn't it? I can't hear myself saying that, somehow. . . . How about 'Why aren't you at the Prater?' "

"All right."

Bergmann calls, "Isherwood!" (Since we have been working in the studio, he always addresses me by my surname in public.) He marches away from the set with his hands behind his back, not even glancing around to see if I am following. We go through the double doors and out onto the fire-escape. Everybody retires to the fire-escape when they want to talk and smoke, because smoking isn't allowed inside the building. I nod to the doorman, who is reading the *Daily Herald* through his pince-nez. He is a great admirer of Soviet Russia.

Standing on the little iron platform, we can see a glimpse of the chilly gray river beyond the rooftops. The air smells damp and fresh, after being indoors, and there is a breeze which ruffles Bergmann's bushy hair.

"How is the scene? Is it all right like this?"

"Yes, I think so." I try to sound convincing. I feel lazy, this morning, and don't want any trouble. We both examine our copies of the script; or, at least, I pretend to. I have read it so often that the words have lost their meaning.

Bergmann frowns and grunts. "I thought, maybe, if we could find something. It seems so bare, so poor. . . . Couldn't perhaps Tony say, 'I cannot sell the violets of yesterday; they are unfresh?' "

" 'I can't sell yesterday's violets; they wither so quickly.' "

"Good. Good . . . Write that down."

I write it into the script. Eliot appears at the door. "Ready to rehearse now, sir."

"Let us go." Bergmann leads the way back to the set, with Eliot and myself following—a general attended by his staff. Everybody watches us, wondering if anything important has been decided. There is a childish satisfaction in having kept so many people waiting.

Eliot goes over to the door of Anita Hayden's portable dressing room. "Miss Hayden," he says, very self-consciously, "would you come now, please? We're ready."

Anita, looking like a petulant little girl in her short flowered dress, apron and frilly petticoats, emerges and walks onto the set. Like nearly all famous people, she seems a size smaller than her photographs.

I approach her, afraid that this is going to be unpleasant. I try to grin. "Sorry! We've changed a line again."

But Anita, for some reason, is in a good mood.

"Brute!" she exclaims, coquettishly. "Well, come on, let's hear the worst."

Eliot blows his whistle. "Quiet there! Dead quiet! Full rehearsal! Green light!" This last order is for the doorman, who will switch on the sign over the sound-stage door: "Rehearsal. Enter quietly."

At last we are ready. The rehearsal begins.

Toni is standing alone, looking pensively out of the window. It is the day after her meeting with Rudolf. And now she has just received a letter of love and farewell, cryptically worded, because he cannot tell her the whole truth: that he is the Prince and that he has been summoned to Borodania. So Toni is heartbroken and bewildered. Her eyes are full of tears. (This part of the scene is covered by a close-up.)

The door opens. Toni's father comes in.

Father: "What's the matter, Toni? Why aren't you at the Prater?"

Toni (inventing an excuse): "I—I haven't any flowers."

Father: "Did you sell all you had yesterday?"

Toni (with a faraway look in her eyes, which shows that her answer is symbolic): "I can't sell yesterday's violets. They wither so quickly."

She begins to sob, and runs out of the room, banging the door. Her father stands looking after her, in blank surprise. Then he shrugs his shoulders and grimaces, as much as to say that woman's whims are beyond his understanding.

"Cut." Bergmann rises quickly from his chair and goes over to Anita. "Let me tell you something, Madame. The way you throw open that door is great. It is altogether much too great. You give to the movement a theatrical importance beside which the slaughter of Rasputin is just a quick breakfast."

Anita smiles graciously. "Sorry, Friedrich. I *felt* it wasn't right." She *is* in a good mood.

"Let me show you, once . . ." Bergmann stands by the table. His lips tremble, his eyes glisten; he is a beautiful young girl on the verge of tears. "I cannot sell violets of yesterday . . . They wither . . ." He runs, with face averted, from the room. There is a bump, behind the scenes, and a muttered, *"Verflucht!"* He must have tripped over one of the cables. An instant later, Bergmann reappears, grinning, a little out of breath. "You see how I mean? With a certain lightness. Do not hit it too hard."

"Yes," Anita nods seriously, playing up to him. "I *think* I see."

"All right, my darling," Bergmann pats her arm. "We shoot it once."

"Where's Timmy?" Anita demands, in a bored, melodious voice. The make-up man hurries forward. "Timmy darling, is my face all right?"

She submits it to him, as impersonally as one extends a shoe to the bootblack; this anxiously pretty mask which is her job, her source of income, the tool of her trade. Timmy dabs at it expertly. She glances at herself coldly, without vanity, in his pocket mirror. The camera operator's assistant measures the distance from the lens to her nose, with a tape.

A boy named George asks the continuity girl for the number of the scene. It has to be chalked on the board which he will hold in front of the camera, before the take.

Roger calls from the sound booth, "Come in for this one, Chris. I need an alibi." He often says this, jokingly, but with a certain veiled resentment, which is directed chiefly against Eliot. Roger resents any criticism of the sound recording. He is very conscientious about his job.

I go into the sound booth, which is like a telephone box. Eliot begins to shout bossily, "Right! Ready, sir? Ready, Mr. Watts? Bell, please. Doors! Red light!" Then, because some people are still moving about, "Quiet! This is a take!"

Roger picks up the headphones and plugs in to the sound-camera room, which is in a gallery, overlooking the floor. "Ready to go, Jack?" he asks. Two buzzes: the okay signal.

"Are we all set?" asks Eliot. Then, after a moment, "Turn them over."

"Running," the boy at the switchboard tells him.

George steps forward and holds the board up before the camera.

Roger buzzes twice to the sound camera. Two buzzes in reply. Roger buzzes twice to signal Bergmann that Sound is ready.

Clark, the boy who works the clappers, says in a loud voice, "104, take one." He claps the clappers.

Bergmann, sitting grim in his chair, hisses between shut teeth, "Camera!"

I watch him, throughout the take. It isn't necessary to look at the set; the whole scene is reflected in his face. He never shifts his eyes from the actors for an instant. He seems to control every gesture, every intonation, by a sheer effort of hypnotic power. His lips move, his face relaxes and contracts, his body is thrust forward or drawn back in its seat, his hands rise and fall to mark the phases of the action. Now he is coaxing Toni from the window, now warning against too much haste, now encouraging her father, now calling for more expression, now afraid the pause will be missed, now delighted with the tempo, now anxious again, now really alarmed, now reassured, now touched, now pleased, now very pleased, now cautious, now disturbed, now amused. Bergmann's concentration is marvelous in its singleness of purpose. It is the act of creation.

When it is all over, he sighs, as if awaking from sleep. Softly, lovingly, he breaths the word, "Cut."

He turns to the camera operator. "How was it?"

"All right, sir, but I'd like to go again."

Roger gives two buzzes.

"Okay for sound, sir," says Teddy.

Joyce, the continuity girl, checks the footage with the operator. Roger puts his head out of the booth. "Teddy, will you favor round toward Miss Hayden a bit? I'm afraid of that bloody camera."

This problem of camera noise is perpetual. To guard against it, the camera is muffled in a quilt, which makes it look like a pet poodle wearing its winter jacket. Nevertheless, the noise persists. Bergmann never fails to react to it. Sometimes he curses, sometimes he sulks. This morning, however, he is in a clowning mood. He goes over to the camera and throws his arms around it.

"My dear old friend, we make you work so hard! It's too cruel! Mr. Chatsworth should give you a pension, and send you to the meadow to eat grass with the retired racehorses."

Everybody laughs. Bergmann is quite popular on the floor. "He's what I call a regular comedian," the doorman tells me. "This picture will be good, if it's half as funny as he is."

Mr. Watts and the camera operator are discussing how to avoid the mike shadow. Bergmann calls it "the Original Sin of the Talking Pictures." On rare occasions, the microphone itself somehow manages to get into the shot, without anybody noticing it. There is something sinister about it, like Poe's Raven. It is always there, silently listening.

A long buzz from the sound-camera room. Roger puts on the headphones and reports, "Sound-camera reloading, sir." Bergmann gives a grunt and goes off into a corner to dictate a poem to Dorothy. Amidst all this turmoil, he still finds time to compose one, nearly every day. Fred Murray is shouting directions for the readjustment of various lamps on the spot-rail and gantry; the tweets, the snooks and the baby spots. Joyce is typing the continuity report, which contains the exact text of each scene, as acted, with details of footage, screen-time, hours of work and so forth.

"Come on," shouts Eliot. "Aren't we ready, yet?"

Roger calls up to the camera room, "Going again, Jack."

Teddy notices that Eliot is inadvertently standing in front of Roger's window, blocking our view of the set. He grins maliciously, and says, in an obvious parody of Eliot's most officious tone, "Clear the booth, please!" Eliot blushes and moves aside, murmuring, "Sorry." Roger winks at me. Teddy, very pleased with himself, swings the microphone-boom, over whistling, and warning his crew, "Mind your heads, my braves!"

Roger generally lets me ring the bell for silence and make the two-buzz signal. It is one of the few opportunities I get of earning my salary. But, this time, I am mooning. I watch Bergmann telling something funny to Fred Murray, and wonder what it is. Roger has to make the signals himself. "I'm sorry to see a falling off in your wonted efficiency, Chris," he tells me. And he adds, to Teddy, "I was thinking of giving Chris his ticket, but now I shall have to reconsider it."

Roger's nautical expressions date back to the time when he was a radio operator on a merchant ship. He still has something of the ship's officer about him, in his brisk movements, his conscientiousness, his alert, pink, open-air face. He studies yachting magazines in the booth, between takes.

"Quiet! Get settled down. Ready? Turn them over."

"Running."

"104, take two."

"Camera . . ."

"Cut."

"Okay, sir."

"Okay for sound, Mr. Bergmann."

"All right. We print this one."

"Are you going again, sir?"

"We shoot it once more, quickly."

"Right. Come on, now. Let's get this in the can."

But the third take is N.G. Anita fluffs a line. In the middle of the fourth take, the camera jams. The fifth take is all right, and will be printed. My long, idle, tiring morning is over, and it is time for lunch.

RAYMOND CHANDLER

Moviegoers often refer to characters by the name of the actors who play them: "John Wayne walks into the saloon and starts shooting." What is amusing in the letter from Raymond Chandler (1888–1959) to his publisher, Hamish Hamilton, is that even though he created the character of Philip Marlowe, he sometimes refers to the character as Bogart. The plot of The Big Sleep *became legendary for its confusion, and there is a story that William Faulkner, who worked on the screenplay, called Chandler for guidance on a puzzling detail, and Chandler was unable to explain it either. Reading this letter makes it clear that the movie was assembled out of elements of the various screenplay drafts and the original novel by Howard Hawks, in response to a series of studio demands and that the film, wonderful as it is, was never entirely thought through.*

from *Selected Letters*

To Hamish Hamilton

May 30th, 1946

Dear Jamie:

When and if you see *The Big Sleep* (the first half of it anyhow), you will realize what can be done with this sort of story by a director with the gift of atmosphere and the requisite touch of hidden sadism. Bogart, of course, is also so much better than any other tough-guy actor that he makes bums of the Ladds and the Powells. As we say here, Bogart can be tough without a gun. Also he has a sense of humor that contains that grating undertone of contempt. Ladd is hard, bitter and occasionally charming, but he is after all a small boy's idea of a tough guy. Bogart is the genuine article.

Like Edward G. Robinson when he was younger all he has to do to dominate a scene is to enter it. *The Big Sleep* has had an unfortunate history. The girl who played the nymphy sister[1] was so good she shattered Miss Bacall completely. So they cut the picture in such a way that all her best scenes were left out except one. The result made nonsense and Howard Hawks threatened to sue to restrain Warners from releasing the picture. After long argument, as I hear it, he went back and did a lot of re-shooting. I have not seen the result of this. The picture has not even been trade-shown. But if Hawks got his way, the picture will be the best of its kind. Since I had nothing to do with it, I say this with some faint regret. Well, that's not exactly true because Hawks time after time got dissatisfied with his script and would go back to the book and shoot scenes straight out of it. There was also a wonderful scene he and I planned together in talk. At the end of the picture Bogart and Carmen were caught in Geiger's house by the Eddie Mars and his lifetakers. That is Bogart (Marlowe) was trapped there and the girl came along and they let her go in. Bogart knew she was a murderess and he also knew that the first person out of that door would walk into a hail of machine gun bullets. The girl didn't know this. Marlowe also knew that if he sent the girl out to be killed, the gang would take it on the lam, thus saving his own life for the time being. He didn't feel like playing God or saving his skin by letting Carmen leave. Neither did he feel like playing Sir Philip Sidney to save a worthless life. So he put it up to God by tossing a coin. Before he tossed the coin he prayed out loud, in a sort of way. The gist of his prayer was that he, Marlowe, had done the best he knew how and through no fault of his own was put in a position of making a decision God had no right to force him to make. He wanted that decision made by the authority who allowed all this mess to happen. If the coin came down heads, he would let the girl go. He tossed and it came down heads. The girl thought this was some kind of a game to hold her there for the police. She started to leave. At the last moment, as she had her hand on the doorknob, Marlowe weakened and started for her to stop her. She laughed in his face and pulled a gun on him. Then she opened the door an inch or two and you could see she was going to shoot and was thoroughly delighted with the situation. At that moment a burst of machine gun fire walked across the panel of the door and tore her to pieces. The gunmen outside had heard a siren in the distance and panicked and thrown a casual burst through the door just for a visiting card—without expecting to hit anyone. I don't know what happened to this scene. Perhaps the boys wouldn't write it or couldn't. Perhaps Mr. Bogart wouldn't

[1] Martha Vickers.

play it. You never know in Hollywood. All I know is it would have been a hair-raising thing if well done. I think I'll try it myself sometime.

All the best,

Ray

To Ray Stark

October 1948

Dear Ray:

The point about Marlowe to remember is that he is a first person character, whether he shows up that way in a radio script or not. A first person character is under the disadvantage that he must be a better man to the reader than he is to himself. Too many first person characters give an offensively cocky impression. That's bad. To avoid that you must not always give him the punch line or the exit line. Not even often. Let the other characters have the toppers. Leave him without a gag. Insofar as it is possible. Howard Hawks, a very wise hombre, remarked to me when he was doing *The Big Sleep* that he thought one of Marlowe's most effective tricks was just giving the other man the trick and not saying anything at all. That puts the other man on the spot. A devastating crack loses a lot of its force when it doesn't provoke any answer, when the other man just rides with the punch. Then you either have to top it yourself or give ground.

Don't have Marlowe say things merely to score off the other characters. When he comes out with a smash wisecrack it should be jerked out of him emotionally, so that he is discharging an emotion and not even thinking about laying anyone out with a sharp retort. If you use similes, try and make them both extravagant and original. And there is a question of how the retort discourteous is delivered. The sharper the wisecrack, the less forcible should be the way it is said. There should not be any effect of gloating. All this is a question of taste. If you haven't got it, you can't get it by rules. There are a lot of clever people in Hollywood who overreach themselves because they don't know where to stop. It's bad enough in pictures; but on the radio it is worse, because the voice is everything and you can't have an expression on the face that offsets the words. You can't really throw away a line as if it was something that tasted bad when you said it.

Oh well, I'm not so smart either.

Yours,

Ray

CHARLES BUKOWSKI

I spent a long day and night on the set of Barfly, *the Barbet Schroeder movie that was written by Charles Bukowski (1920–1995).* Hollywood *is Bukowski's novel based on that production, and on the basis of how he transformed what I witnessed into fiction, his strategy was to keep everything that was entertaining and add dialogue. The movie is a very thinly disguised roman à clef; in this selection Francine Bowers represents Faye Dunaway, Jon Pinchot is Schroeder, and Jack Bledsoe is Mickey Rourke. Henry Chinaski of course is always Bukowski.*

from *Hollywood*

I said to one of the men as we walked along, "God damn it, we left our wine bottle in the car! We are going to need a couple of bottles of wine for the movie!"

"I'll get them for you, Mr. Chinaski," the man said. I had no idea who he was. He broke away from the group.

"And don't forget a corkscrew!" I yelled after him.

We moved further into the mall. Far over to our left I could see flashbulbs popping. Then I saw Francine Bowers. She was posing, looking first this way, then that. She was regal. The best of the last.

We followed the men. Then there was a tv camera. More flashbulbs. I recognized the lady as one of the interviewers on an entertainment station.

"Henry Chinaski," she greeted me.

"How do you do," I bowed.

Then before she could ask any questions, I said, "We are worried. We left our wine in the limo. The chauffeur is probably drinking it right now. We need more wine."

"As the screenwriter, do you like the way the movie turned out?"

"The director handled two difficult actors, the leads, without any problem at all. We used real barflies, none of whom are able to make it out here tonight. The camera work is great and the screenplay is well written."

"Is this the story of your life?"

"A few days out of a ten year period . . ."

"Thank you, Mr. Chinaski, for speaking to us . . ."

"Sure . . ."

Then John Pinchot was there. "Hello, Sarah, hello, Hank . . . Follow me . . ."

There was a small group with cassette recorders. Some flashbulbs went off. I didn't know who they were. They began asking questions.

"Do you think drinking should be glorified?"

"No more than anything else . . ."

"Isn't drinking a disease?"

"Breathing is a disease."

"Don't you find drunks obnoxious?"

"Yes, most of them are. So are most teetotalers."

"But who would be interested in the life of a drunk?"

"Another drunk."

"Do you consider heavy drinking to be socially acceptable?"

"In Beverly Hills, yes. On skid row, no."

"Have you 'gone Hollywood'?"

"I don't think so."

"Why did you write this movie?"

"When I write something I never think about why."

"Who is your favorite male actor?"

"Don't have any."

"Female."

"Same answer."

Jon Pinchot tugged at my sleeve.

"We'd better go. I think the movie is about to begin . . ."

Sarah and I followed him. We were rushed along. Then we were at the theatre. Everybody seemed to be inside.

Then there was the voice behind us: "WAIT!"

It was the man who had gone for the wine. He had a large paper bag. He ran up and thrust it into my arms.

"You are one of the world's great men!" I told him.

He just turned and ran off.

"Who was that?" I asked Jon. "Does he work for Firepower?"

"I don't know . . ."

"Come on," said Sarah, "we better go in."

We followed Jon into the lobby. The doors were already closed. Jon pushed them open. It was dark and we followed him down the aisle. The movie had already begun.

"Shit," I said, "couldn't they have waited for us? We are the writers!"

"Follow me," said Jon, "I saved you two seats."

We followed him all the way down to the first row, side aisle. There were two seats up against the wall.

"I'll see you later," said Jon.

There were two girls seated in our same aisle. One of them said to the other, "I don't know what we are doing here. I really hate Henry Chinaski. He's a disgusting human being!"

I fumbled in the dark for one of the wine bottles and an opener. The screen went from dark to light.

"Henry Chinaski," the girl went on, "hates women, he hates children, he's a creepy bitter old fuck, I don't see what people see in him!"

The other girl saw me in the light of the screen and dug her friend in the ribs with her elbow.

"Shhhh . . . I think that's him!"

I opened one bottle for Sarah and one for me. We each lifted them high. Then Sarah said, "I ought to beat up those cunts!"

"Don't," I said, "my enemies are the source of half my income. They hate me so much that it becomes a subliminal love affair."

We were in a terrible position to view the movie. From where we sat, all the bodies were tall, elongated and thin, and the heads were the worst. Large and misshapen, big foreheads, and yet as big as the foreheads were there seemed to be almost no eyes or mouths or chins to the heads. Also the sound was too loud and badly distorted. The dialog sounded like, "WHOOO, WOOOO, WULD WAFT TA KRISTOL, YO TO YO . . ."

The premiere of my first and only movie and I couldn't make anything out of it.

I was later to find out that there was another theatre right next door showing our movie at exactly the same time and that it was only half-full.

"Jon didn't plan this very well," Sarah suggested.

"Well, we'll see it on video cassette some day," I told her.

"Yeah," she said.

And we lifted our bottles in unison.

The girls watched us in total fascination and disgust.

The oversized heads with big foreheads kept moving around on the screen.

And the heads spoke loudly to each other.

"FLAM FLAM WOOL WO, TAKA BRAK VO SO . . ."

"YA DOL YA, TEK TA TAM, YA VO DO . . ."

"Preebers . . ."

"Braka dam . . ."

"They fucked over my dialogue, Sarah."

"Uh . . . yeah . . ."

But it was best when the big tall foreheads went for the very tall thin drinks, the drink filled half the screen, and then the drink went somewhere in, under the forehead, and then it was gone, and then there were just undulating empty glasses, changing shape, stretching and contracting, glistening empty glasses from hades. What hangovers those foreheads would have.

Finally, Sarah and I stopped watching the screen and just worked on our wine bottles.

And, with time, the movie ended.

There was some applause and then we waited for the audience to file out. We waited for a good while. Then we got up and went out.

There were more flashbulbs in the lobby. Handshakes. We ducked that.

We needed the restrooms.

"See you by the potted plant across from the ladies room," I told Sarah.

I made it to the men's room. In the urinal next to me was a swaying drunk. He looked over.

"Hey, you're Henry Chinaski, aren't ya?"

"No, I'm his brother, Donny."

The drunk swayed some more, pissing away.

"Chinaski never wrote about no brother."

"He hates me, that's why."

"How come?"

"Because I've kicked his ass about 60 or 70 times."

The drunk didn't know what to think about that. He just kept pissing and swaying. I went over, washed up, got out of there.

I waited by the potted plant. The chauffeur stepped out from behind it.

"I've been instructed to take you to the celebration party."

"Great," I said, "as soon as Sarah . . ."

And there was Sarah. "You know, baby, most chauffeurs wait outside but our man, Frank, he came inside and found us. But he took off his cap so as not to look like a chauffeur."

"It's been a strange night," she said.

We followed Frank through the mall. He was about two steps ahead.

"You didn't drink our wine, did you, Frank?"

"No, sir . . ."

"Frank, isn't the first rule for a chauffeur never to leave his limo? Suppose somebody stole the limo, for instance?"

"Sir, nobody would ever steal that piece of crap."

"You're right."

As soon as we stepped outside of the mall, Frank put his cap back on. The limo was parked right at the curb.

He helped us into the back seat and we were off.

. . . .

The post premiere party was at Copperfield's on La Brea Avenue. Frank pulled up in front, let us out and we moved toward the entrance to more flashbulbs. I got the idea that they didn't know who they were photographing. As long as you got out of a limo you qualified.

We were recognized at the entrance and were let inside to a crowd of people, closely packed in and all holding glasses of red wine in their hands. They stood in groups of 3 or 4 or more, talking or not talking. There was no air conditioning and although it was cool outside, it was hot in there, very hot. There were just too many people sucking in the oxygen.

Sarah and I got our wine and stood there, trying to get it down. The wine was very abrasive. There is nothing worse than cheap red wine unless it's cheap white wine that has been allowed to get warm.

"Who are all these people, Sarah? What do they want here?"

"Some are in the business, some are on the edge of the business and some are just here because they can't think of anyplace else to be."

"What are they doing?"

"Some are trying to make contacts, others are trying to stay in contact. Some go to every function like this that they are able to. Also there's a smattering of the press."

The feeling in the air was not good. It was joyless. These were the survivors, the scramblers, the sharks, the cheapies. The lost souls chatted away and it was hot, hot, hot.

Then a man in an expensive suit came up. "Aren't you Mr. and Mrs. Chinaski?"

"Yes," I said.

"You don't belong down here. You belong upstairs. Follow me."

We followed him.

We followed him up a stairway and to the second floor. It was not quite as crowded. The man in the expensive suit turned and faced us.

"You mustn't drink the wine they are serving here. I will get you your own bottle."

"Thanks. Make it two."

"Of course. I'll be right back . . ."

"Hank, what does all this mean?"

"Accept it. It will never happen again."

I looked at the crowd. I got the same feeling from them as I got from the crowd downstairs.

"I wonder who that guy is?" I asked.

Then he was back with two bottles of good wine and a corkscrew, plus fresh wine glasses.

"Thank you much," I said.

"You're welcome," he said. "I used to read your column in the *L.A. Free Press*."

"You don't look that old."

"I'm not. My dad was a hippie. I read the paper after he was done with it."

"Can I ask your name?"

"Carl Wilson. I own this place."

"Oh, I see. Well, thank you again for the good wine."

"You're welcome. Let me know if you need more."

"Sure."

Then he was gone. I opened a bottle and poured two glasses. We gave it a try. Really good wine.

"Now," I asked Sarah, "who are these people up here? How are they different than the ones downstairs?"

"They are the same. They just have more pull, better luck. Money, politics, family. Those in the industry bring in their family and friends. Ability and talent are secondary. I know I sound like I'm on a soapbox but that's the way it is."

"It adds up. Even the so-called best movies seem very bad to me."

"You'd rather watch a horse race."

"Of course . . ."

Then Jon Pinchot walked up.

"My god! These people! I feel like I've been covered with shit!" I laughed.

Then Francine Bowers came over. She was elated. She had made her comeback.

"You were good, Francine," I said.

"Yes," said Jon.

"You let your hair down," said Sarah.

"Maybe too much?"

"Not at all," I said.

"Hey," said Francine, "what's that wine you're drinking? It looks like good stuff."

"Have some," I tilted the bottle into her glass.

"Me too," said Jon.

"How come you get his good stuff?" Francine asked.

"The owner's father was a hippie. They both read the *L.A. Free Press*. I used to write a column, 'Notes of a Neanderthal Man.' "

Then we all stood there not saying anything. There was nothing more to say. The movie was finished.

"Where's Jack Bledsoe?" I asked.

"Oh," said Jon, "he doesn't come to these things."

"Well, I do," said Francine.

"We do too," Sarah admitted.

Then there was some beckoning from another group.

"A magazine wants to interview you, Francine. *Movie Mirror*."

"Of course," said Francine. "Forgive me," she said to us.

"Sure."

She walked over, stately and proud. I felt good for her. I felt good for anybody who made a comeback after being relegated to the hinterlands.

"You go over there with her, Jon," said Sarah. "She'll feel better . . ."

"Should I go too, Sarah?"

"No, Hank, you'll only try to hog the interview. And remember, you charge $1,000 now."

"That's right . . ."

"All right," said Jon, "I'll go over there."

Then he was gone, over there.

A young man walked up with a tape recorder. "I'm from the *Herald-Examiner*. I do the 'Talk and Tell' column. How did you like the way the movie came out?"

"Do you have a thousand dollars?" Sarah asked.

"Sarah, this is just chit-chat, it's all right."

"Well, how did you like the way the movie turned out?"

"It's a better than average movie. Long after this year's Academy Award movies are forgotten, *The Dance of Jim Beam* will be showing up now and then in the Art houses. And it will pop up on tv from time to time, if the world lasts."

"You really think so?"

"Yes. And as it's viewed again and again special meanings will be found in the lines and scenes that weren't intended by anyone. Overpraise and underpraise is the norm in our society."

"Do barflies talk like that?"

"Some of them do until somebody kills them."

"You seem to rate this movie pretty high."

"It's not that good. It's only that the others are so bad."

"What do you consider to be the greatest movie that you have ever seen?"

"*Eraserhead*."

"*Eraserhead?*"

"Yes."

"And what's next on your list?"

"Who's Afraid of Virginia Woolf?"

Then Carl Wilson was back. "Chinaski, there's a guy downstairs who claims he knows you. He wants to come up. One John Galt."

"Let him up here, please."

"Well, thank you, Chinaski," said the *Herald-Examiner* man.

"You're welcome."

I uncorked the second bottle and poured us a couple more. Sarah held her booze remarkably well. She only became talkative when we were alone together. And then she talked good sense, mostly.

Then, there he was John Galt. Big John Galt. He walked up.

"Hank and I never shake hands," he smiled. "Hello, Sarah," he said, "got this guy under control?"

"Yes, John."

Damn, I thought, I know so many guys named John.

The biblical names hung on. John, Mark, Peter, Paul.

Big John Galt looked good. His eyes had gotten kinder. Kindness came finally to the better ones. There was less self-interest. Less fear. Less competitive gamesmanship.

"You're looking good, baby," I told him.

"You look better now than you did 25 years ago," he said.

"Better booze, John."

"It's the vitamins and health foods," said Sarah. "No red meat, no salt, no sugar."

"If this ever gets out my book sales are going to plummet, John."

"Your stuff will always sell, Hank. A child can read it."

Big John Galt. God damn, what a life-saver he had been. Working for the post office, I had gone over to his place instead of eating or sleeping or doing all the other things. Big John was always there. A lady supported him. The ladies always supported Big John. "Hank, when I work, I'm not happy. I want to be happy," he would say.

There was always this big bowl of speed sitting on the coffeetable between us. It was usually filled to the brim with pills and capsules. "Have some."

I would dip in and eat them like candy. "John, this shit is going to destroy your brain." "Each man is different, Hank, what destroys one doesn't affect another."

Marvelous nights of bullshit. I brought my own beer and popped the pills. John was the best-read man I had ever met, but not pedantic. But he was odd. Maybe it was the speed.

Sometimes at 3 or 4 A.M. he'd get the urge to raid garbage cans and backyards. I'd go with him. "I want *this.*" "Shit, John, it's just an old left boot somebody threw away." "I want it."

His whole house was filled with trash. Piles of it everywhere. When you wanted to sit on the couch you'd have to push a mound of trash to one side. And his walls were pasted over with mottos and odd newspaper headlines. All the stuff was way off key. Like the last words of the earth's last maniac. In the cellar of his house were thousands of books stacked up and they were swollen and wet and rotted with the damp. He had read them all and come away quite well. All he needed to survive was a shoestring and you'd better not get in a chess game with him, or a struggle to the death. He was a marvel. I do suppose in those days I had a fair amount of self-pity and he made me aware of that. Mainly, those times and those hours were *entertaining*. I fed off of Big John Galt when there was nothing else around. He was a writer too. And later I got lucky with the word and he didn't. He could write a very powerful poem but in between times there were spaces where he just seemed vacant. He explained it to me, "I don't want to be famous, I just want to feel good." He was one of the best readers of poetry, his or anybody else's, that I had ever heard. He was a beautiful man. And later, after my luck, when I'd mention Big John Galt here and there, I'd get the same feedback, "I don't see what Chinaski sees in that old blow-hard." Those who had accepted me and my work wouldn't accept him and his work and I wondered if maybe my writing was made for fools? Which I couldn't help. A bird flies, a snake crawls, I change typewriter ribbons.

Anyhow, it felt good seeing John Galt once again. He had a new lady with him.

"This is Lisa," he said. "She writes poetry too."

Lisa jumped right in and began talking. She talked up a storm and John just stood there. Maybe it was an off night for her but she sounded like an old time Female Libber. Which is all right, for them, except they tend to eat up the oxygen and it was already too hot in there for lack of fresh air. She went on and on, telling us everything. John and she often read together. Did I ever hear of Babs Danish? "No," I told her. Well, Babs Danish was *black* and she was *female* and when she read she wore big earrings and she was very passionate and the earrings jumped up and down and her brother Tip provided a musical backdrop for her readings. I should hear her.

"Hank doesn't go to poetry readings," Sarah said, "but I've heard Babs Danish and I like her very much."

"John and I and Babs are reading at Beyond Baroque next Wednesday night, will you come?"

"I probably will," said Sarah. And she probably would.

I took a long look at John Galt then. He looked gentle and good but I saw a deep pain in his eyes that I had never seen before. For a man who had wanted to be happy he looked like a man who had lost two pawns in the early rounds of a chess match without gaining an advantage.

Then the *Herald-Examiner* man was back.

"Mr. Chinaski," he said, "I wanted to ask you another question."

I introduced him to John Galt and Lisa.

"John Galt," I said, "is the great undiscovered poet in America. This man helped me to go on when all else said stop. I want you to interview John Galt."

"Well, Mr. Galt?"

"Hank and I knew each other maybe 20 years ago . . ."

Sarah and I drifted off.

"Looks like with Lisa John's got a full nine innings on his hands," I said.

"Maybe it's good for him."

"Maybe."

.   .   .   .

More people had come upstairs. It seemed that nobody had left. What was there? Contacts? Opportunities? Was it worth it? Wasn't it better not to be in show business? No, no. Who wants to be a gardener or a taxi driver? Who wants to be a tax accountant? Weren't we all artists? Weren't our minds better than that? Better to suffer this way rather than the other. At least it looks better.

Our second bottle was almost empty.

Then Jon Pinchot returned.

"Jack Bledsoe is here. He wants to see you."

"Where is he?"

"He's over there, by the doorway."

And sure enough, there was Jack Bledsoe, just leaning in the doorway with his famous and sensitive smile.

Sarah and I walked over. I reached out and Jack and I shook hands.

I thought of John Galt's saying, "Hank and I never shake hands."

"Good show, Jack, great acting. I'm really glad you were aboard."

"Did I put it over?"

"I think you did."

"I didn't want to get too much of your voice in there or too much of your slouch . . ."

"You didn't."

"I just wanted to come by to say hello to you."

That one struck me. I didn't know how to react.

"Well, hell, baby, we can get drunk together anytime."

"I don't drink."

"Oh, yeah . . . Well, thank you, Jack, glad you came by. How about one for the road anyhow?"

"No, I'm going . . ."

Then he turned and walked down the stairway.

He was alone. No bodyguards, no bikers. Nice kid, nice smile. Goodbye, Jack Bledsoe.

.   .   .   .

I wormed another bottle out of Carl Wilson and Sarah and I stood around with the other people but actually nothing was occurring. Just people standing around. Maybe they were waiting for me to get drunk and insane and abusive like I sometimes did at parties. But I doubted that. They were just dull inside. There was nothing for them to do but stay within the self that was not quite there. That wasn't too painful. It was a soft place to be.

With me, my main vision for life was to avoid as many people as possible. The less people I saw the better I felt. I met one other man, once, who shared my philosophy, Sam the Whorehouse Man. He lived in the court behind mine in East Hollywood. He was on ATD.

"Hank," he told me, "when I was doing time, I was always in trouble. The warden kept throwing me in the hole. But I *liked* the hole. The warden would come around and lift the lid and look in, and he asked me one time, 'HAVE YOU HAD ENOUGH? ARE YOU READY TO COME OUT OF THERE?' I took a piece of my shit and threw it up and hit him in the face. He closed the lid and left me down there. I just stayed in there. When the warden came back he didn't lift the lid all the way. 'WELL, HAVE YOU HAD ENOUGH YET?' 'NOT AT ALL,' I yelled back. Finally the warden had me pulled out of there. 'HE EN-JOYS IT TOO MUCH,' he told the guards. 'GET HIS ASS OUT OF THERE!' "

Sam was a great guy, then he got to gambling. He couldn't pay his rent, he was always in Gardena, he slept in the crappers there and began gambling again as soon as he woke up. Finally Sam got tossed out of his apartment. I traced him to a tiny room down in the Korean district. He was sitting in a corner.

"Hank, all I can do is drink milk but it comes right up. But the doctors say there is nothing wrong with me."

Two weeks later he was dead. This man who shared my philosophy about people.

"Listen," I said to Sarah, "there's nothing happening here. This is death. Let's leave."

"We have all the free drinks we want . . ."

"It's not worth it."

"But the night is young, maybe something will happen."

"Not unless I make it happen and I'm not in the mood."

"Let's wait just a little while . . ."

I knew what she meant. For us it was the end of Hollywood. All in all, she cared more for that world than I did. Not much, but some. She had begun studying to be an actor.

Still it was just people standing, that's all. The women weren't beautiful and the men weren't interesting. It was duller than dull. The dullness actually hurt.

"I'm going to crack unless we get out of here," I told Sarah.

"All right," she said, "let's leave."

.   .   .   .

Good old Frank was downstairs with the limo.

"You're leaving early," he said.

"Uh huh," I said.

Frank placed us in the back and we found a new bottle of wine in the limo. We uncorked it as our trusty man found the Harbor Freeway south.

"Hey, Frank, want a drink?"

"Sure as shit, man!"

He hit a button and the little glass partition dropped. I slipped the bottle through.

As Frank drove the limo along he took a hit from the wine bottle. I don't know but somehow it all looked very strange and funny and Sarah and I started laughing.

At last, the night was alive.

CRITICS

GRAHAM GREENE

Reviewing a spy movie, I once described the job of being a professional Cold War wire-tapper: "You sit for long hours in a dark, cold room, with people you don't like, listening to strangers making love, and waiting for something to happen. Not unlike being a film critic." While the profession of film criticism has been ennobled by some of its practitioners, the job itself is a very strange one. You attend one, two, or three movies a day (more during film festivals), taking notes or not, emerging for five minutes or an hour in between to blink in the daylight, and then you try to describe what happened to you. The British novelist Graham Greene (1904–1991) did this job for nearly five years, succeeding in the process in libeling Shirley Temple.

"Memories of a Film Critic"

Four and a half years of watching films several times a week . . . I can hardly believe in that life of the distant thirties now, a way of life which I adopted quite voluntarily from a sense of fun. More than four hundred films—and I suppose there would have been many, many more if I had not suffered during the same period from other obsessions—four novels had to be written, not to speak of a travel book which took me away for months to Mexico, far from the Pleasure Dome—all those Empires and Odeons of a luxury and an extravagance which we shall never see again. How, I find myself wondering, could I possibly have written all those film reviews? And yet I remember opening the envelopes, which contained the gilded cards of invitation for the morning press performances (mornings when I should have been struggling with other work), with a sense of curiosity and anticipation. Those films were an escape—escape from that hellish problem of construction in Chapter Six, from the secondary character who obstinately refused to come alive, escape for an hour and a half from the melancholy which falls inexorably round the novelist when he has lived for too many months on end in his private world.

The idea of reviewing films came to me at a cocktail party after the dangerous third martini. I was talking to Derek Verschoyle, the Literary Editor of the *Spectator*. The *Spectator* had hitherto neglected films and I suggested to him I should fill the gap—I thought in the unlikely event of his accepting my offer it might be fun for two or three weeks. I never imagined it would remain fun for four and a half years and only end in a different world, a world at war. Until I came to reread the notices the other day I thought they abruptly ended with my review of *Young Mr. Lincoln*. If there is something a little absentminded about that review, it is because, just as I began to write it on the morning of 3 September 1939, the first air-raid siren of the war sounded and I laid the review aside so as to make notes from my high Hampstead lodging on the destruction of London below. "Woman passes with dog on lead," I noted, "and pauses by lamp-post." Then the all-clear sounded and I returned to Henry Fonda.

My first script—about 1937—was a terrible affair and typical in one way of the cinema world. I had to adapt a story of John Galsworthy—a traditional tale of a murderer who killed himself and an innocent man who was hanged for the suicide's crime. If the story had any force in it at all it lay in its extreme sensationalism, but as the sensation was impossible under the British Board of Film Censors, who forbade suicide and forbade a failure of English justice, there was little of Galsworthy's plot left when I had finished. This unfortunate first effort was suffered with good-humoured nonchalance by Laurence Olivier and Vivien Leigh. I decided after that never to adapt another man's work and I have only broken that rule once in the case of *Saint Joan*—the critics will say another deplorable adaptation, though I myself would defend the script for retaining, however rearranged, Shaw's epilogue and for keeping a sense of responsibility to another while reducing a play of three-and-a-half hours to a film of less than two.

I have a more deplorable confession—a film story directed by Mr. William Cameron Menzies called *The Green Cockatoo* starring Mr. John Mills—perhaps it preceded the Galsworthy (the Freudian Censor is at work here). The script of *Brighton Rock* I am ready to defend. There were good scenes, but the Boulting Brothers were too generous in giving an apprentice his rope, and the film-censor as usual was absurd—the script was slashed to pieces by the Mr. Watkyn of his day. There followed two halcyon years with Carol Reed, and I began to believe that I was learning the craft with *The Fallen Idol* and *The Third Man,* but it was an illusion. No craft had been learnt, there had only been the luck of working with a fine director who could control his actors and his production.

If you sell a novel outright you accept no responsibility: but write your own script and you will observe what can happen on the floor to your words, your continuity, your idea, the extra dialogue inserted during production (for which you bear the critics' blame), the influence of an actor who is only concerned with the appearance he wants to create before his fans. . . . Perhaps you will come to think, there may be a solution if the author takes his hand in its production.

Those were not the first film reviews I wrote. At Oxford I had appointed myself film critic of the *Oxford Outlook,* a literary magazine which appeared once a term and which I edited. *Warning Shadows, Brumes d'Automne, The Student of Prague*—these are the silent films of the twenties of which I can remember whole scenes still. I was a passionate reader of *Close-Up* which was edited by Kenneth Macpherson and Bryher and published from a *chateau* in Switzerland. Marc Allégret was the Paris Correspondent and Pudovkin contributed articles on montage. I was horrified by the arrival of "talkies" (it seemed the end of film as an art form), just as later I regarded colour with justifiable suspicion. "Technicolor," I wrote in 1935, "plays havoc with the women's faces; they all, young and old, have the same healthy weather-beaten skins." Curiously enough it was a detective story with Chester Morris which converted me to the talkies—for the first time in that picture I was aware of *selected* sounds: until then every shoe had squeaked and every door handle had creaked. I notice that the forgotten film *Becky Sharp* gave me even a certain hope for colour.

Re-reading those reviews of more than forty years ago I find many prejudices which are modified now only by the sense of nostalgia. I had distinct reservations about Greta Garbo whom I compared to a beautiful Arab mare, and Hitchcock's "inadequate sense of reality" irritated me and still does—how inexcusibly he spoilt *The Thirty-Nine Steps.* I still believe I was right (whatever Monsieur Truffaut may say) when I wrote: "His films consist of a series of small 'amusing' melodramatic situations: the murderer's button dropped on the baccarat board; the strangled organist's hands prolonging the notes in the empty church . . . very perfunctorily he builds up to these tricky situations (paying no attention on the way to inconsistencies, loose ends, psychological absurdities) and then drops them: they mean nothing: they lead to nothing."

The thirties too were a period of "respectable" film biographies—Rhodes, Zola, Pasteur, Parnell and the like—and of historical romances which only came to a certain comic life in the hands of Cecil B. de Mille (Richard Coeur de Lion was married to Berengaria according to the rites of the Anglican Church). I preferred the Westerns, the crime films, the farces, the frankly commercial, and I am glad to see that in reviewing one of these forgotten commercial films I gave a warm welcome to a new star, Ingrid Bergman—"What star before has made her first appearance on the international screen with a highlight gleaming on her nose-tip?"

There were dangers, I was to discover, in film-reviewing. On one occasion

I opened a letter to find a piece of shit enclosed. I have always—though probably incorrectly—believed that it was a piece of aristocratic shit, for I had made cruel fun a little while before of a certain French marquis who had made a documentary film in which he played a rather heroic role. Thirty years later in Paris at a dinner of the *haute bourgeoisie* I sat opposite him and was charmed by his conversation. I longed to ask him the truth, but I was daunted by the furniture. Then, of course, there was the Shirley Temple libel action. The review of *Wee Willie Winkie* which set Twentieth-Century Fox alight cannot be found here for obvious reasons. I kept on my bathroom wall, until a bomb removed the wall, the statement of claim—that I had accused Twentieth-Century Fox of "procuring" Miss Temple for "immoral purposes" (I had suggested that she had a certain adroit coquetry which appealed to middle-aged men). Lord Hewart, the Lord Chief Justice, sent the papers in the case to the Director of Public Prosecutions, so that ever since that time I have been traceable on the files of Scotland Yard. The case appeared before the King's Bench on 22 March 1938, with myself *in absentia,* and on 23 May 1938, the following account of the hearing appeared among the Law Reports of *The Times.* I was at the time in Mexico on a writing assignment. It is perhaps worth mentioning in connection with the "beastly publication" that *Night and Day* boasted Elizabeth Bowen as theatre critic, Evelyn Waugh as chief book reviewer, Osbert Lancaster as art critic, and Hugh Casson as architectural critic, not to speak of such regular contributors as Herbert Read, Hugh Kingsmill and Malcolm Muggeridge.

The case appeared as follows in *The Times* Law Reports:

HIGH COURT OF JUSTICE
King's Bench Division
Libel on Miss Shirley Temple: 'A Gross Outrage'
Temple and Others v. Night and Day Magazine.
Limited, and Others
Before the Lord Chief Justice

A settlement was announced of this libel action which was brought by Miss Shirley Jane Temple, the child actress (by Mr Roy Simmonds, her next friend), Twentieth-Century Fox Film Corporation, of New York, and Twentieth-Century Fox Film Company Limited, of Berners Street, W., against Night and Day Magazines, Limited, and Mr Graham Greene, of St Martin's Lane, W.C., and Messrs Chatto and Windus, publishers, of Chandos Street, W.C., in respect of an article written by Mr Greene and published in the issue of the magazine *Night and Day* dated October 28, 1937.

Sir Patrick Hastings, KC, and Mr G.O. Slade appeared for the plaintiffs; Mr Valentine Holmes for all the defendants except Hazell, Watson, and Viney, Limited, who were represented by Mr Theobald Mathew.

Sir Patrick Hastings, in announcing the settlement, by which it was agreed that Miss Shirley Temple was to receive £2,000, the film corporation £1,000 and the film company £500, stated that the first defendants were the proprietors of the magazine *Night and Day,* which was published in London. It was only right to say that the two last defendants, the printers and publishers, were firms of the utmost respectability and highest reputation, and were innocently responsible in the matter.

The plaintiff, Miss Shirley Temple, a child of nine years, has a world-wide reputation as an artist in films. The two plaintiff companies produced her in a film called *Wee Willie Winkie,* based on Rudyard Kipling's story.

On October 28 last year Night and Day Magazines, Limited, published an article written by Mr Graham Greene. In his (counsel's) view it was one of the most horrible libels that one could well imagine. Obviously he would not read it all— it was better that he should not—but a glance at the statement of claim, where a poster was set out, was quite sufficient to show the nature of the libel written about this child.

This beastly publication, said counsel, was written, and it was right to say that every respectable distributor in London refused to be a party to selling it. Notwithstanding that, the magazine company, with the object no doubt of increasing the sale, proceeded to advertise the fact that it had been banned.

Shirley Temple was an American and lived in America. If she had been in England and the publication in America it would have been right for the American Courts to have taken notice of it. It was equally right that, the position being reversed, her friends in America should know that the Courts here took notice of such a publication.

SHOULD NOT BE TREATED LIGHTLY

Money was no object in this case. The child had a very large income and the two film companies were wealthy concerns. It was realised, however, that the matter should not be treated lightly. The defendants had paid the film companies £1,000 and £500 respectively, and that money would be disposed of in a charitable way. With regard to the child, she would be paid £2,000. There would also be an order for the taxation of costs.

In any view, said counsel, it was such a beastly libel to have written that if it had been a question of money it would have been difficult to say what would be an appropriate amount to arrive at.

Miss Shirley Temple probably knew nothing of the article, and it was undesirable that she should be brought to England to fight the action. In his (counsel's) opinion the settlement was a proper one in the circumstances.

Mr Valentine Holmes informed his Lordship that the magazine *Night and Day* had ceased publication. He desired, on behalf of his clients, to express the deepest apology to Miss Temple for the pain which certainly would have been caused to her by the article if she had read it. He also apologized to the two film companies for the suggestion that they would produce and distribute a film of the character indicated by the article. There was no justification for the criticism of the film, which, his clients instructed him, was one which anybody could take their children to see. He also apologized on behalf of Mr Graham Greene. So far as the publishers of the magazine were concerned, they did not see the article before publication.

His Lordship—Who is the author of this article?

Mr Holmes—Mr Graham Greene.

His Lordship—Is he within the jurisdiction?

Mr Holmes—I am afraid I do not know, my Lord.

Mr Theobald Mathew, on behalf of the printers, said that they recognized that the article was one which ought never to have been published. The fact that the film had already been licensed for universal exhibition refuted the charges which had been made in the article. The printers welcomed the opportunity of making any amends in their power.

His Lordship—Can you tell me where Mr Greene is?

Mr Mathew—I have no information on the subject.

His Lordship—This libel is simply a gross outrage, and I will take care to see that suitable attention is directed to it. In the meantime I assent to the settlement on the terms which have been disclosed, and the record will be withdrawn.

From film-reviewing it was only a small step to scriptwriting. That also was a danger, but a necessary one as I now had a wife and two children to support and I remained in debt to my publishers until the war came. I had persistently attacked the films made by Mr. Alexander Korda and perhaps he became curious to meet his enemy. He asked my agent to bring me to Denham Film Studios and when we were alone he asked if I had any film story in mind. I had none, so I began to improvise a thriller—early morning on Platform 1 at Paddington, the platform empty, except for one man who is waiting for the last train from Wales. From below his raincoat a trickle of blood forms a pool on the platform.

"Yes? And then?"

"It would take too long to tell you the whole plot—and the idea needs a lot more working out."

I left Denham half an hour later to work for eight weeks on what seemed an extravagant salary, and the worst and least successful of Korda's productions thus began (all I can remember is the title, *The Green Cockatoo*). So too began our friendship which endured and deepened till his death, in spite of my reviews which remained unfavourable. There was never a man who bore less malice, and I think of him with affection—even love—as the only film producer I have ever known with whom I could spend days and nights of conversation without so much as mentioning the cinema. Years later, after the war was over, I wrote two screenplays for Korda and Carol Reed, *The Fallen Idol* and *The Third Man,* and I hope they atoned a little for the prentice scripts.

If I had remained a film critic, the brief comic experience which I had then of Hollywood might have been of lasting value to me, for I learned at first hand what a director may have to endure at the hands of a producer. (One of the difficult tasks of a critic is to assign his praise or blame to the right corner.)

David Selznick, famous for having produced one of the world's top-grossing films, *Gone with the Wind,* held the American rights in *The Third Man* and, by the terms of the contract with Korda, the director was bound to consult him about the script sixty days before shooting began. So Carol Reed, who was directing the film, and I journeyed west. Our first meeting with Selznick at La Jolla in California promised badly, and the dialogue remains as fresh in my mind as the day when it was spoken. After a brief greeting he got down to serious discussion. He said, "I don't like the title."

"No? We thought . . ."

"Listen, boys, who the hell is going to a film called *The Third Man?*"

"Well," I said, "it's a simple title. It's easily remembered."

Selznick shook his head reproachfully. "You can do better than that, Graham," he said, using my Christian name with a readiness I was not prepared for. "You are a writer. A good writer. I'm no writer, but you are. Now what we want— it's not right, mind you, of course, it's not right, I'm not saying it's right, but then I'm no writer and you are, what we want is something like *Night in Vienna,* a title which will bring them in."

"Graham and I will think about it," Carol Reed interrupted with haste. It was a phrase I was to hear Reed frequently repeat, for the Korda contract had omitted to state that the director was under any obligation to accept Selznick's advice. Reed during the days that followed, like an admirable stonewaller, blocked every ball.

We passed on to Selznick's view of the story.

"It won't do boys," he said, "it won't do. It's sheer buggery."

"Buggery?"

"It's what you learn in your English schools."

"I don't understand."

"This guy comes to Vienna looking for his friend. He finds his friend's dead. Right? Why doesn't he go home then?"

After all the months of writing, his destructive view of the whole venture left me speechless. He shook his grey head at me. "It's just buggery, boys."

I began weakly to argue. I said, "But this character—he has a motive of revenge. He has been beaten up by a military policeman." I played a last card. "Within twenty-four hours he's in love with Harry Lime's girl."

Selznick shook his head sadly. "Why didn't he go home before that?"

That, I think, was the end of the first day's conference. Selznick removed to Hollywood and we followed him—to a luxurious suite in Santa Monica, once the home of Hearst's film-star mistress. During the conference which followed I remember there were times when there seemed to be a kind of grim reason in Selznick's criticisms—surely here perhaps there *was* a fault in "continuity." I hadn't properly "established" this or that. (I would forget momentarily the lesson which I had learned as a film critic—that to "establish" something is almost invariably wrong and that "continuity" is often the enemy of life. Jean Cocteau has even argued that the mistakes of continuity belong to the unconscious poetry of a film.) A secretary sat by Selznick's side with her pencil poised. When I was on the point of agreement Carol Reed would quickly interrupt—"Graham and I will think about it."

There was one conference which I remember in particular because it was the last before we were due to return to England. The secretary had made forty pages of notes by this time, but she had been unable to record one definite concession on our side. The conference began as usual about 10.30 P.M. and finished after 4 A.M. Always by the time we reached Santa Monica dawn would be touching the Pacific.

"There's something I don't understand in this script, Graham. Why the hell does Harry Lime . . . ?" He described some extraordinary action on Lime's part.

"But he doesn't," I said.

Selznick looked at me for a moment in silent amazement.

"Christ, boys," he said, "I'm thinking of a different script."

He lay down on his sofa and crunched a benzedrine. In ten minutes he was as fresh as ever, unlike ourselves.

I look back on David Selznick now with affection. The forty pages of notes remained unopened in Reed's files, and since the film has proved a success, I suspect Selznick forgot that the criticisms had ever been made. Indeed, when next I was in New York he invited me to lunch to discuss a project. He said, "Graham, I've got a great idea for a film. It's just made for you."

I had been careful on this occasion not to take a third martini.

"The life of St. Mary Magdalene," he said.

"I'm sorry," I said, "no. It's not really in my line."

He didn't try to argue. "I have another idea," he said. "It will appeal to you as a Catholic. You know how next year they have what's called the Holy Year in Rome. Well, I want to make a picture called *The Unholy Year*. It will show all the commercial rackets that go on, the crooks . . ."

"An interesting notion," I said.

"We'll shoot it in the Vatican."

"I doubt if they will give you permission for that."

"Oh sure they will," he said. "You see, we'll write in one Good Character."

(I am reminded by this story of another memorable lunch in a suite at the Dorchester when Sam Zimbalist asked me if I would revise the last part of a script which had been prepared for a remake of *Ben Hur*. "You see," he said, "we find a kind of anti-climax after the Crucifixion.")

Those indeed were the days. I little knew that the reign of Kubla Khan was nearly over and that the Pleasure Dome would soon be converted into an enormous bingo hall, which would provide other dreams to housewives than had the Odeons and the Empires. I had regretted the silent films when the talkies moved in and I had regretted black and white when Technicolor washed across the screen. So today, watching the latest soft-porn film, I sometimes long for those dead thirties, for Cecil B. de Mille and his Crusaders, for the days when almost anything was likely to happen.

DWIGHT MACDONALD

It was Dwight Macdonald (1906–1982), writing every month in Esquire *in the 1950s and early 1960s, who first led me to begin thinking about movies in the way a critic might. His criticism, month after month, was some of the best ever written in America, and a lot of it is collected in* On Movies, *a book now out of print but worth searching for. In his introduction he discusses in a general way what a critic should, and should not, look for in a movie. When I began writing reviews for the* Chicago Sun-Times, *I read this essay about once a month.*

from *On Movies*

I know something about cinema after forty years, and being a congenital critic, I know what I like and why. But I can't explain the *why* except in terms of the specific work under consideration, on which I'm copious enough. The general theory, the larger view, the gestalt—these have always eluded me. Whether this gap in my critical armor be called an idiosyncrasy or, less charitably, a personal failing, it has always been most definitely there.

But people, especially undergraduates hot for certainty, keep asking me what rules, principles or standards I judge movies by—a fair question to which I can never think of an answer. Years ago, some forgotten but evidently sharp stimulus spurred me to put some guidelines down on paper. The result, hitherto unprinted for reason which will become clear, was:

1. Are the characters consistent, and in fact are there characters at all?

2. Is it true to life?

3. Is the photography cliché, or is it adapted to the particular film and therefore original?

4. Do the parts go together; do they add up to something; is there a rhythm established so that there is form, shape, climax, building up tension and exploding it?

5. Is there a mind behind it; is there a feeling that a single intelligence has imposed his own view on the material?

The last two questions rough out some vague sort of meaning, and the third is sound, if truistic. But I can't account for the first two being there at all, let alone in the lead-off place. Many films I admire are not "true to life" unless that stretchable term is strained beyond normal usage: *Broken Blossoms, Children of Paradise, Zéro de Conduite, Caligari, On Approval,* Eisenstein's *Ivan the Terrible.* And some have no "characters" at all, consistent or no: *Potemkin, Arsenal, October, Intolerance, Marienbad, Orpheus, Olympia.* The comedies of Kenton, Chaplin, Lubitsch, the Marx Brothers and W. C. Fields occupy a middle ground. They have "consistent" characters all right, and they are also "true to life." But the consistency is always extreme and sometimes positively compulsive and obsessed (W. C., Groucho, Buster), and the truth is abstract. In short, they are so highly stylized (cf. "the Lubitsch touch") that they are constantly floating up from *terra firma* into the empyrean of art, right before my astonished and delighted eyes.

. . . .

The first half of Keaton's *Sherlock Junior,* for example, is one of those genre comedies of calf love that the more earthbound Harold Lloyd specialized in. It's set in a small town whose streets, houses, and interiors are photographed with that sharp realism common in our silent comedies (what an accurate, detailed family album of how America used to look!). It is populated by the commonplace types of the period (given the usual comic twist that exaggerates them into folk-mythical grotesques, just as the prosaic policeman was metamorphosed into the Mack Sennett cop). But the second half of *Sherlock Junior* cuts loose from these mooring strings and drifts free across magical country. By a great stroke of invention, the lovesick Buster is a movie projectionist, so that the medium becomes the artist's material—an advanced approach Keaton undoubtedly never heard of and wouldn't have understood if he had. He falls asleep in his projection booth, dreaming about his girl and his frustrated love. His *doppelganger* extracts itself from his sleeping body, takes off its hook the ghost of the Keaton pancake hat, literally a "lid" (the real lid still hanging there: a nice touch), claps it on his head, and walks down the aisle of the darkened theatre to climb up on the stage and step into the society-crook melodrama being projected on the screen. The characters become transformed into his girl, her parents, his rival, and himself, all of them dressed to the nines. As the great detective, Buster sports a soup-and-fish outfit, slightly baggy in the seat and gaping in the wing collar, but including a magnificently draped watch chain he twirls with uneasy insouciance.

The rest of the film—except for a brief and funny real-life coda—chronically violates every natural law except that of optics (movie optics, that is). In one sequence, the background keeps shifting arbitrarily, crossing up Buster who jumps into a ravine and lands on a rock in the midst of a choppy sea, into which he dives, only to sprawl on his face in the sands of a desert. In another, he escapes from gangsters who have him trapped in a dead-end street by taking a running dive through a large square aperture which, by raising her tray, a motherly old lady selling pencils opens up not only in her own midriff but also in the wall behind her. There's no explanation of this or any other *lapsus naturalis* in this 1924 film which makes later efforts by Dali, Buñuel, and Cocteau look pedestrian and a bit timid. They felt obliged to clarify matters by a symbolistic apparatus. Keaton never rose—or sunk—to that.

T. S. Eliot summed it all up long ago with his usual laconic authority: "The egregious merit of Chaplin is that he has escaped in his own way from the realm of the cinema and invented a *rhythm*. Of course, the unexplored possibilities of the cinema for eluding realism must be very great." (I especially like that offhand "of course.") This prophetic *aperçu* is one that recent explorations by Bergman, Fellini, Resnais, and other contemporary masters into the "possibilities for eluding realism" are beginning to illustrate two generations later.

. . . .

Getting back to general principles, I can think offhand (the only way I seem able to think about general principles) of two ways to judge the quality of a movie. They are mere rules of thumb, but they work—for me anyway:

A. Did it change the way you look at things?

B. Did you find more (or less) in it the second, third, *n*th time? (Also, how did it stand up over the years, after one or more "periods" of cinematic history?)

Both rules are *post facto* and so, while they may be helpful to critics and audiences, they aren't of the slightest use to those who make movies. This is as it should be. The critic's job doesn't include second-guessing the director by giving him helpful suggestions as to how he might have made a better film. If the director knows his business, such "constructive criticism" (as it's called by sincere philistines in the boondocks and by insincere philistines on Madison Avenue—which might be called a metropolitan boondock) is an impertinence.* If a director *doesn't* know his business, which is not uncommon, it's an irrelevance. Of all the sources from which he might get wised up—agents, girl friends, colleagues, observant cutters, perceptive grips, Mom, Dad, Billy Graham, Christian Science—the least likely is by reading the reviews of his stillborn creations. The intelligent ones will mystify and depress him, and the dumb ones will tell him he's doing just fine.

Shifting the focus from the director to the critic (and paraphrasing Groucho), I wouldn't want to see a movie by a director who had to learn to make movies from my reviews. They say it's easy enough to be critical, or negative, or destructive, but it isn't really. To stick to serious, negative, unconstructive criticism takes a lot of thought and effort. In this country today, the undertow pulling the critic into the dangerous waters of positive, responsible thinking seems to be getting stronger every year. In forty years I can't recall anything I've written that has had a specific, definable effect on anybody connected with the making of movies. I've encouraged some directors to persist, but since all directors appear to persist unto death (and sometimes afterward, it seems) there's no way to tell. The only hard evidence would be the opposite: my success in encouraging directors and actors to get out of movies and into something better suited to their talents, like selling insurance or becoming the bursar of a small denominational college in upper Michigan.

---

*The director's business, of course, may not coincide with the critic's business. William Wyler, to take the first Hollywood veteran that comes to mind, knows by now (as he should) just how to make a slickly-machined, chromium-plated Hollywood movie. But his business has never come close to mine. Looking over the two inches of his film credits in Leslie Halliwell's useful reference book *The Filmgoer's Companion* I find many pretentious middlebrow duds like *Wuthering Heights, Dead End, The Best Years of Our Lives, The Children's Hour,* and many films like *Ben-Hur* and *The Friendly Persuasion* that are unpretentious lowbrow duds. In all this industrious manufacture, there's nothing except *Detective Story,* a sound melodrama, that I recall with even the mild pleasure evoked by four or five of the almost-as-many films of Billy Wilder—another old Hollywood hand (or hack) often confused with William Wilder, but more lively and talented. Not very much more—only enough to be visible on the Hollywood scale, where the local Doctor Johnsons don't disdain to settle the precedence between a flea and a louse. Quite the contrary, it's their main occupation.

ANDREW SARRIS

Andrew Sarris is one of the high priests of American film criticism, best known for having introduced the French auteur theory of film criticism to this country in his influential weekly column for the Village Voice. *His* The American Cinema *went so far as to rank American directors in various categories of importance and relevance, beginning with* The Pantheon *(Hawks, Hitchcock, etc.) and moving on to* The Far Side of Paradise *and* Less than Meets the Eye. *Understandably this hierarchy, which was compiled with at least the tip of his tongue in his cheek, inspired outrage. But both Sarris's supporters and opponents tended to focus on the auteur component in his work, overlooking the countless reviews in which he was applying no theory and was simply an intelligent man writing well about a movie he had just seen. Here he looks back in wonder at the furor he stirred.*

from *Confessions of a Cultist*

My career as a cultist began unobtrusively, if not inadvertently, in a dingy railroad flat on New York's Lower East Side back in the unlamented Eisenhower era. It was there and then that I first met Jonas and Adolfas Mekas, the genially bohemian (actually Lithuanian) editors of a new magazine called *Film Culture,* an unfortunately pompous title that always made me think of microbic movies under glass. I had been taking an evening course in film appreciation at Columbia between meandering through graduate English and malingering in Teachers College. The movie mentor was Roger Tilton, a film-maker (*Jazz Dance*) himself and one of *Film Culture*'s first sponsors, whatever that meant. (Among other "sponsors" listed on a back page were James Agee, Shirley Clarke, David and Francis Flaherty, Lewis Jacobs, Arthur Knight, Helen Levitt, Len Lye, Hans Richter, Willard Van Dyke and Amos Vogel.) Tilton sent me to the Mekas brothers, and the rest is cult history.

The brothers Mekas were generally buried under a pile of manuscripts ranging from the illegible to the unreadable, and I am afraid I only added to the confusion. The entire operation seemed hopelessly impractical to a congenital pessimist like me. I took the satirical view that we were not poor because we were pure, but pure because we were poor, and our integrity was directly proportional to our obscurity. Still, I suppose we represented a new breed of film critic. The cultural rationale for our worthier predecessors—Agee, Ferguson, Levin, Murphy, Sherwood, *et al.*—was that they were too good to be reviewing movies. We, on the contrary, were not considered much good for anything else. Like one-eyed lemmings, we plunged headlong into the murky depths of specialization. No back pages of literary and political pulps for us. We may have lived in a ramshackle house, but we always came in the front door.

Somehow, the first issue of *Film Culture*—January 1955, Volume I, Number 1—had already materialized without my assistance. I was enlisted as a reviewer and editor for Number 2. I recall that I was not enchanted by the prospect of writing and editing for no money at all. It seemed almost as demeaning as paying to be published, an act of vanity I vowed never to perform even at the cost of immortality. However, my bargaining position was not enhanced by the fact that all my previous professional writing credits added up to seven movie columns in the Fort Devens *Dispatch,* within the period of my tour of duty through the Army's movie houses during the Korean war.

At the time I started writing in *Film Culture* I was not quite twenty-seven years old, a dangerously advanced age for a writer *manqué* if not *maudit,* a dreadfully uncomfortable age for a middle-class cultural guerrilla without any base, contacts, or reliable lines of supply. I was of the same generation as Norman Podhoretz, but while he had been "making it" as an undergraduate at Columbia I had drifted, like Jack Kerouac, down from Morningside Heights ever deeper into the darkness of movie houses, not so much in search of a vocation as in flight from the laborious realities of careerism. Nonetheless I agree with Podhoretz that failure is more banal and more boring than success. Indeed, I have always been impatient as a critic with characters (like Ginger Coffey) who manage to mess up every job. The trouble with failure as a subject is that it is not instructive in any way and only contributes to an audience's false sense of superiority. Unfortunately, success stories lack "charm" unless they are leavened with audience-pleasing intimations of futility. The trick of the stand-up comic and the syndicated columnist is to ingratiate himself with his audience by groveling in his own weaknesses and misfortunes, real and fabricated, while withholding all the evidence of his manipulative personality. This strategy evolves from a conspiracy of the successful to delude the unsuccessful into thinking that worldly success doesn't really matter. But as I look back upon my own failures I am appalled by my unoriginal reactions of self-hatred and meanspirited paranoia. Every block and hang-up known to the disenfranchised intellect seemed at the time uniquely personal and chock-full of anecdotal fascination. My biggest problem was focusing my general knowledge on a specific intellectual target. Novels, short stories, plays, screenplays, poems slithered off my typewriter in haphazard spasms of abortive creation. Far from filling up trunks, I could barely jam up a drawer, and yet if I had been knowledgeable enough to understand the fantastic odds against me, I might never have invested in a typewriter. As it was, I was not even sophisticated enough to realize what a stroke of luck my meeting with the Mekas brothers turned out to be. I was always looking beyond *Film Culture* (and later the *Village Voice*) for more lucrative opportunities elsewhere. There was never a time that I would not have given up being a cultist to be a careerist. And then one day—I don't remember exactly when—I realized that if I had not yet indeed succeeded, I had at least stopped failing. I had managed at long last to function in a role I had improvised with my left hand while my right hand was knocking at all the doors of the Establishment. I had written and published a million words under my own name, and I had made contact with thousands of people, and in the process I had managed to locate myself while mediating between my readers and the screen.

In the realm of role-playing, I stopped lowering my head at the epithet "cultist" as soon as I realized that the quasi-religious connotation of the term was somewhat justified for those of us who loved movies beyond all reason. No less a cultist than the late André Bazin had once likened film festivals to religious revivals, and a long sojourn in Paris in 1961 reassured me that film not only demanded but deserved as much faith as did any other cultural discipline. (Cultists and buffs in other areas are generally described as scholars and specialists, but interdisciplinary intolerance seems to be the eternal reaction of the old against the new.) As I remember that fateful year in Paris, deliriously prolonged conversations at sidewalk cafés still assault my ears with what in Paris passed for profundity and in New York for peculiarity. I have never really recovered from the Parisian heresy (in New York eyes) concerning the sacred importance of the cinema. Hence I returned to New York not merely a cultist but a subversive cultist with a foreign ideology.

Thereafter I could see more clearly that the main difference between a cultist and a careerist is that the cultist does not require the justification of a career to pursue his passion, and the careerist does. Indeed, passion is too strong a word to apply to journalistic reviewers who would be equally happy in the Real Estate departments of their publications, or to high-brow humanists who admire the late Siegfried Kracauer's *From Caligari to Hitler* simply because they, like Kracauer, are more interested in Hitler than in *Caligari*. Of course, lacking intellectual discipline, the passion of a cultist could be perverted into mindless mysticism and infantile irrationality. (I must admit that I had qualms about the title of this book after glancing at the lurid *Daily News* headline shortly after the

Sharon Tate murders: "Police Seek Cultists.") Still, film scholarship was in such a shambles by the early sixties that the risks of passion were preferable to the rigidities of professionalism.

As I look back on the past I have very mixed feelings about all the slights I have suffered and all the furors I have caused. People were always telling me that I was lucky to be attacked in print and that the only thing that really mattered was the correct spelling of my name. However, it has been my observation that no one enjoys being attacked in print or in person no matter what publicity may accrue from the aggression. Indeed, I have been struck by the inability of critics who love dishing out abuse to take the mildest reproof in return. For myself, I can't really complain in terms of any Kantian categorical imperative. He who lives by the sword of criticism must expect counterthrusts as a matter of course. All that is required of the embattled critic as a test of his courage is that he never lose faith in his own judgment. And all the slings and arrows of outraged opponents never led me to doubt the direction I had chosen as a critic. Part of my intransigence may be attributed to the relative ignorance that my generally bookish attackers displayed in the movie medium. Not that I believe (as do the maxi-McLuhanists) that books have become culturally irrelevant. On the contrary, every aspect of culture is relevant to every other aspect, and the best criticism, like the best poetry, is that which is richest in associations. Unfortunately, too many bookish film critics have perverted the notion of ecumenical erudition by snobbishly subordinating film to every other art. Whereas the late James Agee discovered cinema through his love for movies, too many of his self-proclaimed successors chose to abuse movies in the name of *Kultur.*

Hence I was the beneficiary as well as the victim of the intellectual vacuum that occurred in movie reviewing with the death of Agee in 1955. For reasons that I still do not fully understand, serious film reviewing on a steady basis had fallen into cultural disrepute when I started breaking into print. My very existence was generally ignored for almost eight years, a period in which I was occasionally quoted without credit. Then in 1963 I rose from obscurity to notoriety by being quoted out of context. Even so, I was treated as a relatively unique phenomenon, however invidious to the cultural establishment. The late New York *Herald Tribune* even listed me as one of the phrase-makers of the avant-garde, a distinction that helped keep me unemployable as far as the Establishment was concerned. I didn't realize at the time that slowly but surely was gathering professional seniority in a discipline that was about to explode. I didn't even have to maneuver or manipulate. All I had to do was stand my ground, and suddenly I would find myself in the center of the cultural landscape, returning in triumph to Columbia University, a scholar more prodigal than prodigious.

Even at the time of my most painfully polemical agonies I realized that most controversies in the intellectual world are determined by the first principle of Euclidean egeometry: *Two egos cannot occupy the same position of power at the same time.* It follows that the first inkling that I had acquired a position of power came when I was attacked by other critics. Ironically, my enemies were the first to alert me to the fact that I had followers. And with followers came increased responsibilities to clarify and develop my position as a critic and historian.

Still, I shall not pretend at this late date that my career as a cultist has followed a preconceived pattern. Nor shall I define the role of the film critic in self-congratulatory terms applicable only to me. My response to my role as a critic has generally been intuitive, and nothing is to be gained by institutionalizing my intuitions. Every would-be critic must seek his or her own role in terms of his or her own personality and outlook. I am grateful to film for allowing me to focus my intellectual insights and world views within a manageable frame. I believe the subject of film is larger than any one critic or indeed the entire corps of critics. What follows is my personal view of the films that have helped mold my consciousness. At this climactic moment of self-revelation all I can do is commend my critical soul to your mercy and understanding.

STANLEY KAUFFMANN

Stanley Kauffmann has been writing film reviews for the New Republic *since 1958, and I have been reading them since about 1962. He is the sanest of critics and the one most likely to place any film within its wider context of literature, philosophy, art, or politics. I read other critics for their insights, their writing, or simply to see what they think; I don't much care whether I agree with them or not. But when I read Kauffmann, who became a regular weekly destination for me five years before I wrote my own first reviews, more is at stake; on important films, if we agree, I am gratified, and if we disagree, I am likely to go back to my own review and have another uneasy look at it. It's not that I assume he is right and I am wrong; it's that after Kauffmann disagrees, I wonder if he was perhaps more right. There is another thing about his work: his economy of expression. It's not that his column is particularly short but that he seems able to say more in fewer words than anyone else.*

"Why I'm Not Bored"

The two most frequent questions are: "How many films do you see a week?" "Don't you get bored with going to films?" I've been writing about them in *The New Republic* since 1958, with one intermission of a year and a half, have heard each of these questions at least once a week in that time, and am always pleased by them. As for the first, the number has varied sharply from none to twelve—usually it's about three—but the point is that most weeks it wouldn't have been less even if I weren't a critic. (And, grown gray in the ranks, I still get a thrill out of getting in free.) Once in a great while there have been too many. On two separate occasions there were two successive days in which I had to see four films each day—no kind of record but sickening to me. After each of those pairs of days it was a week before I could see another picture. But most of the time when I'm asked the question, I can't really remember how many times I've gone in the previous week or two, it all seems so natural. And therefore pleasant.

As to the second and more interesting question, the answer is a firm no. A happy no. To salute the obvious, this doesn't mean that I never see boring films or that I am unborable. On the contrary, I'm somewhat more acutely borable—by reason, I tell myself, of professional acuteness—than most of my friends. But the *idea* of going to films is never boring. The former editor of *The New Republic* once generously suggested that I also write about television from time to time. The prospect of merely crossing the living room to switch on television dramas was numbing. But even when I have to leave the house to see the most unpromising of films (and I limit myself to those with at least some sort of promise), there is something beyond the specifics of the film that tingles and attracts.

To begin with, there is the elemental kinetic aspect. As with billions of people throughout the world since 1900, the mere physical act of filmgoing is part of the kinesis of my life—the getting up and going out and the feeling of coming home, which is a somewhat different homecoming feeling from anything else except the theater (and which is totally unavailable from television). When I am not going out, rather frequently, to films (as a New Yorker this is also true for me of the theater), it's because I'm ill or sore beset with work or isolated somewhere in the country. To have my life unpunctuated by the physical act of filmgoing is almost like walking with a limp, out of my natural rhythm.

Past that there is the community, also known to billions, of being in a group dream, a group reality. This is true of the theater as well, but with films there is a paradox: because of the greater darkness there is, even in the middle of a group, the sense of private ownership of the occasion. That ownership has attachments. No one goes to a film theater—or a press screening-room—without taking with him all of his filmgoing past, including his initial fear. (For years students have been writing papers for me on their recollections of their very first film experiences, and more often than not, that first experience had included a feeling of fear.) That fear is never quite lost, perhaps, though gradually it is understood, is used to underpin and nourish other responses. No one can go to a film theater without taking with him his parents and childhood friends and the first grapplings of romance in the balcony. And no one can sit in a film theater without acknowledging, however secretly, that this is where some part of his psyche originated. Messenger boy or mogul, peasant or Pope, there can hardly be anyone alive whose secret fantasies, controlled and uncontrolled, have not in some measure been made by film. This has never been so widely true of any other art. My guess is that it is not yet true of television, may never be true in quite the same way. The size of the film screen in itself plays a part in its sacerdotal function; it ministers down to us while the television screen paws upward, smaller than we are, vulnerable to dials and switches. (If films ever really become principally available through television cassettes, as has been prophesied sporadically for years, whole psychic orders will have to be redeployed.)

All this exercise and enjoyment before we even touch matters of art, discrimination, esthetics! Once we get to the question of specific films rather than generic experience, the specter of boredom raises its threat. Some films turn out to be just as boring as feared, though not so many as the fulfilled dreads in the theater and not many more than with new fiction. No one assumes that a literary critic gets bored, yet, having worked in both kinds of criticism, I know that the rewards of poor films are more savorable, more certain, than those of poor novels.

In Westerns, however feeble, there are horses, the creak of leather, the reach of landscape. In any film there are likely to be attractive women or, if you prefer, attractive men. For myself, heterosexually straitened though I am, I get a kick out of seeing O'Toole and Newman and Redford, just as I did with Cooper and Grant and March. Then there are syntactical rewards. Richard Lester's maritime thriller *Juggernaut* missed the boat, but its editing and photography were in themselves thrilling. Visconti's *Ludwig* was drear, but the costumes were sumptuous. The music in *Once upon a Time in the West* was like a Puccini sauna. I don't suggest that anyone go to see those films for those reasons: I'm just answering the once-a-week question.

There are other, greater things. Direction, for instance. Joseph Sargent, out of television, has done a really crisp job with *The Taking of Pelham One Two Three*. I enjoyed the way he used the subway tunnels and the racing through the streets and the compact arena of the hijacked subway car in a picture that, as a whole, was fading before it finished. (I couldn't read the novel.)

And in some dismal pictures one can often find bright spots of acting. A thriller called *11 Harrowhouse* is laden with Charles Grodin and Candice Bergen and a finale that was apparently devised by a moron on LSD; but James Mason plays an aging diamond expert, dying of cancer, who revenges himself on his niggardly employers by collaborating with thieves, and he creates a whole man, quietly, in the middle of roaring nonsense. Jon Voight has the leading role in a more seriously inane thriller, *The Odessa File,* and presents the young German journalist he is supposed to be, even to a beautifully precise accent. (Obeying that hilarious convention under which Germans in Germany, speaking English to one another in English-language films, have German accents.)

It would be easy to put together a large bouquet, a garden, several hothouses of flowers culled from poor pictures. They don't quite compensate for those pictures, not even for the waste of themselves in those pictures, still they are rewards not easily accessible in poor examples of other arts. Theater performances, yes, when they stand out from a bad script and/or a bad company. As for other matters, although the theater's symbolic systems are just as "real" as film's, they are less intensely packed to the square millimeter, and when one is forced away from the foreground by tedium, the theater's supportive symbols are less varied, less continuingly interesting. Boris Aronson's beautiful setting for *Company* didn't *continue* to make up for a dullish evening as Tonino delli Colli's cinematography almost did for Pasolini's *Decameron.*

But that's enough of scrounging, of beggarly gratitude for edible scraps amidst the swill. The chief reason for never being bored with the idea of film is that boredom is incompatible with hope, and hope is more of a constant in film than in virtually any other art in America. Fiction and poetry and dance and theater performance (as against playwriting) are in good estate, with good prospects; but (say the experts I've met) this is not true of painting or sculpture or musical composition or architecture. And no art is more persistently, almost irritatingly, pulsing with prospects than the film.

Distribution of films is in difficulties, but it always was: only the type of trouble changes. The vulgar and the violent are more popular than the good; so what else is new? Nothing rotten that happens in film—and most of what does happen is rotten—can negate the fact that it is still an avenue of possibilities, an expanding nebula of esthetic mysteries, a treasury of aptness for our time.

In 1966 I published an essay called "The Film Generation" that is now sometimes knocked because the size of the audience has not much increased, has not returned to anything like the size of the mid-1940s, and, worse, because some of the best pictures that come along—works by Bresson and Bellocchio, for instance—have short first-run lives. But I wouldn't alter much in that essay today. (Except for one addition: I've learned since writing it, by a lot of travel around the country and through four years' service on the Theater Panel of the National Endowment for the Arts, that theater appetite among young people is lesser only in size, not in urgency, to film appetite.) The film audience is smaller than it used to be because, obviously, free movies are available at home, as well as free vaudeville; but the fact that the film audience has not completely disappeared in the face of that situation is itself proof of that audience's vitality. Far from disappearing, that audience is now increasing. And if the television-threat argument were valid, there ought now to be no film theaters at all.

Blacks flocking to cheap "blaxploitation" films, yes. Kung-fu kooks, yes. Hard and soft porno for hard and soft fans, yes. But if statistics prove that those types account for a lot, statistics prove other things as well. *Somebody* is taking those thousands of film courses in those 1000-plus universities and colleges that offer them; *somebody* is buying those film books and magazines that continue to flood out, attending those festivals that continue to spring up and those film societies and campus and community series. It's not quite a nation of Bazins and Agees as yet, but to argue that the smaller audience has not improved qualitatively is either a confusion of cynicism with taste or a fear of improvement, a nostalgia for Hedda Hopper's Hollywood. The fact that Ozu doesn't run very long in the nation's biggest city doesn't prove any more about the status of the art and its audience than the fact that *Boesman and Lena* didn't break the *Hello, Dolly!* record or that Berryman's *Dream Songs* doesn't outsell Rod McKuen.

Film is in money trouble these days because of inflation, but so is everything, including book publishing. Relatively, money doesn't control the making of films much more than it does the publication of poetry and fiction: if film investments are higher, so are possible profits. The money squeeze is not new: finance has always worked cruelly in the film world even when money seemed to be more free (true of publishing, too), distribution has always been tyrannical, you've always been just as successful as your last picture, the putrid ones have always seemed to be surging up to our nostrils, and still the good ones have been made here and abroad—where the difficulties are different only in nomenclature or proportion—and the lesser ones have had their compensations.

To me this combination of views is hard-headed, with no touch of Pollyanna—unless there is also a touch of Pollyanna in the human race's general insistence on survival. Concurrent with our lives runs this muddied, quasi-strangulated, prostituted art, so life-crammed and responsive and variegated and embracing, so indefinable no matter how far one strings out phrases like these, that to deny it seems to me to deny the worst and the best in ourselves, a chance to help clarify which is which, and which is in the ascendant on any particular day. No matter how much I know about a film's makers or its subject before I go, I never *really* know what it's going to do to me: depress me with its vileness, or just roll past, or change my life in some degree, or some combination of all three, or affect me in some new way that I cannot imagine. So I like being asked whether filmgoing gets boring: it makes me think of what I don't know about the next film I'm going to see.

QUENTIN CRISP

Quentin Crisp's autobiography, The Naked Civil Servant, *describes a lifetime during which he persisted in presenting himself exactly as he preferred—as a flamboyantly effeminate homosexual—regardless of the consequences. It was his conviction that he was providing a valuable duty to society. For many years he scraped by in poverty, until the book brought fame, film and TV roles, speaking tours, and a measure of financial security. Although he was played by John Hurt in the film of his book, Crisp played an even more characteristic role, Queen Elizabeth I, in* Orlando *[1993]. During a stay in New York, Crisp agreed to write film reviews for the gay magazine* Christopher Street *and found the experience unsettling.*

from *How to Go to the Movies*

In his wonderful novel *The Child Buyer,* Mr. Hersey makes an anxious citizen inquire what will happen to the little boy who is being purchased by a vast business concern. The kindly reply is that he will be well treated. Then this disturbing phrase is added: "Of course, he will have to go into the forgetting chamber."

For me, this was the story's moment of true poetry.

At the very end of the book, as he is being led away from his home forever, the victim asks, "What will happen to my dreams?" This is the question that all of us might well ask ourselves.

Apparently, it has been scientifically established that to forget real life for a few hours every night is not enough—that people become more psychotic when forced to go without their dreams than when deprived of sleep. I seldom remember my dreams, but I recall every frame of every movie I see and my fantasy life used to be lived chiefly in the cinema. However, a regular diet of celluloid is fast becoming difficult to obtain.

In the 1950s, it was prophesied that television would kill the movies; it didn't, but it helped to drive the industry mad. I am not an economist and cannot account for what has gone wrong, but, like the rest of the world, I have no difficulty in seeing that the trend has been away from a steady flow of seldom first rate but very acceptable pictures to a few productions upon which so much money has been squandered and on which so many expectations ride that a kind of financial hysteria has set in. The producers, the actors, and the audiences have all been led to believe that each new release will be the greatest ever. It is as though every sexual union between a husband and his wife must be the most shattering experience ever or the marriage will fail. As Dr. Westheimer would be the first to point out, it is the accumulated understanding by each partner of the other's needs that is the foundation of a successful relationship; and it is the continuous appreciation of a director's work or an actress's performances that are the deepest joy of moviegoing.

As a child, I was totally absorbed in each picture I saw and so was everybody I knew. In factories, laundries, kitchens where the faithful were gathered together, the conversation was about nothing except the week's releases. Every sentence began with the words "Didn't you love the bit where . . . ?" Between the years 1926 and 1930, all the women in England looked like Miss Garbo (or wished they did). Then *The Blue Angel* burst upon their group consciousness; they ran home to curl their hair and shave off their eyebrows in order to redraw them wantonly across their foreheads and look like Miss Dietrich.

In spite of the intensity of her interest, the average movie maniac knew little about the mechanics of filmmaking. Only a highbrow critic would have spoken of a powerful sequence in *Anna Karenina* in which, though the count forbade his wife to leave their house, she defied him. The rest would have said, ". . . and that Basil Rathbone, he shouted at her, but you know our Greta; she didn't take a blind bit of notice." It didn't matter that in one picture an actress might be wearing an Empire dress and in the next, a preruined raincoat; each movie was seen as another day in the life of its star. These great ladies were not exactly our friends, because friends are people with whom you get stuck; they were what the word *star* implies—distant, permanent, dazzling icons who evoked from us a loyalty and an adoration that only a fool would have lavished upon a lover or a member of her family.

The cinema—at least the American cinema—was then a phantasmagoric realm in which feelings ran higher than elsewhere, sentiments were purer, human beings were capable of greater nobility or degradation, and yet we took this other world completely for granted, like daylight. Reciprocally, the big film companies felt equally sure of their audiences. They even gave us serial films of which each episode ended with the words "Come next week and see another installment of this exciting adventure." Such pictures counted on our fidelity; they assumed we would never leave our hometown. They fulfilled exactly the same function as the soap operas of modern television, except that now the whole world is everybody's hometown.

At that time, movies, some of which are not the subjects of scholarly theses, were deemed to be entertainment for the masses. My mother did not consider herself to be a mass, and only accompanied me to the cinema in that spirit of ostentatious condescension with which the British middle classes now treat television. If questioned closely, they say, "Well, yes, we do have a television set but, of course, we never watch it."

The early moviemakers were fully aware of the lowliness of their audiences; they catered to it; they wallowed in it and, accordingly, kept cinema seats well within the financial reach of almost everybody.

When I lived in London, a woman who occupied the room behind mine nagged me into consenting to read a book entitled *The Children of Sanchez*. She was excruciatingly Russian and wished to rub my powdered nose in the excrement of the world. This vast tome described in monotonous and squalid detail the tribulations of one poor Mexican family. In my cotenant's presence, I opened the book at random. Immediately, my disdainful gaze fell on the sentence "My mother went to the movies almost every afternoon." Thus was confirmed my conviction that people—especially women—are prepared to make do without the barest necessities but not without the cinema.

This law does not only prevail in Mexico. By the time I was as adult as I am ever likely to be, there were three movie "circuits" in Britain. They were the Odeon, the Gaumont, and the A.B.C. Throughout the length and breadth of the land, in throbbing cities, in smug towns, in marooned villages, each of these cinema chains exhibited a different double feature every week of the year, come rain or come shine, as Miss Garland would have said. This meant that with a little luck, a lot of ingenuity, and a total disregard for domestic duties, it was possible for everyone to spend three and a half hours on three nights a week away from the inclement world. Almost all the films shown in those days were American, until a "quota" system came into force, which compelled each cinema manager to foist upon his clientele a certain number of English pictures as part of their weekly fare of illusion. As Mr. Korda says in his fascinating book about his famous uncle, *Charmed Lives*: "when this law came into effect the British public went mad as though it had been asked to do without bread." This extreme reaction was due not only to the self-evident inferiority of the home product; it was also occasioned by the fact that to the British, British films did not constitute a visit to the forgetting chamber; they were as boring as life in England really is. Serious crime, which is the staple diet of scriptwriters, seemed to be a daily occurrence in Chicago and New York but was almost unknown in Manchester or Wigan. There, if he played his cards right, a murderer could stay on the front page of the *Daily Telegraph* for weeks. Who wants art to reflect his own humdrum existence?

The years of the double feature were the happiest days of their lives not only for audiences; they were also the golden age of actresses.

Today, when people speak of the seven-year contract, they do so with curled lips. Now that everyone thinks he has rights, that arrangement is considered to have been too heavily loaded in favor of the employer. It has become yet another area in which the unions have raised their ugly heads; but, as Miss Kerr has pointed out, in fact it provided a stable atmosphere in which an actress could perfect her skills with at least some assurance that they would be used. Her studio would carry her through at least one flop, and by the time her contract was well under way, she had usually acquired her own secretary, her own makeup artist—in some cases, her own cameraman. (Mr. Daniels photographed almost all of Miss Garbo's movies.) In other words, a leading lady became a kind of queen bee attended by five or six drones who had no other function than to enhance her assets and conceal her defects. No wonder so many of them became permanent stars. What keeps a woman young and beautiful is not repeated surgery but perpetual praise. They were the eternal mistresses of their public. In deference to the art directors of their films, they changed their costumes occasionally, but only as ballerinas wear tights and tutus to remind us that they are first and foremost classical dancers but, if spoken to nicely, will don a turban to show that for the moment they are the playthings of cruel Turks. A movie star never deprived her public of the thrill of instant recognition at her first appearance on the screen.

This happy predictability no longer prevails. Now, every new picture is a desperate gamble, deafeningly publicized, with its mounting costs broadcast like news of a forest fire. If a film fails, even though its star may have been judged by the critics to have been the only good thing in it, when her name is mentioned, some movie mogul will growl, "Isn't that the broad that cost us thirty-four million dollars?" In these circumstances, actresses have decided to be different people in different roles; they have taken to acting—a desperate measure indeed.

Though television has wrought all this havoc in Hollywood, it is no real substitute for the movies. It has its star; it has Miss Collins, who remains through all vicissitudes of plot the last of the "vamps." If she ever appeared on any screen, large or small, as a nice home girl, the world would come to an abrupt and ignominious end. In general, however, the effect of television upon our lives has been pernicious. Big was beautiful. Television diminishes the scale of our fantasies, but it does worse than that; it domesticates them. It does not compel us to give it our whole attention. We can sip our instant decaffeinated coffee while being thrown out of the fortieth-floor windows of an expensive hotel; we can file our nails while being raped by hooded intruders. We see television on our own mundane turf. It is as injurious to the soul as fast food is to the body.

We should vacate our homes and go to a movie for the very reason that this exodus will force us to take the occasion seriously, to abandon everyday life, to place ourselves for a while where there are fewer distractions, where the telephone bell cannot toll for us. We ought to visit a cinema as we would go to church. Those of us who wait for films to be made available for television are as deeply under suspicion as lost souls who claim to be religious but who boast that they never go to church. As Mr. Godard has said, such people are as wholly to be condemned as the Philistines who say they are art lovers but who never step inside a gallery, preferring instead merely to buy picture postcards of famous paintings.

The way to go to the movies is incessantly. The more often we visit the cinema, the more exciting the experience becomes, not the more boring, as one might have expected. Films teach us how to see them; they are written in a language that we must learn. If, some fifty years ago, the average audience had been shown a film as complicated as *Charade* or *Arabesque,* it would have tottered out into the light of day completely bewildered. Now, in a carefully constructed, well-told movie, we can perceive and interpret the slightest tremor of the camera, the most fleeting glance of an actor. We must go to the movies so often that, while remaining distant, the stars become calculable to us, allowing us to recognize and dote upon their gestures, the tones of their voices, their every idiosyncrasy. After a while, even the unseen presence of our favorite directors will become traceable.

The way to go to the movies is reverently. We must be prepared to believe in the most improbable hypothesis, provided that it is presented to us with sufficient conviction, enough passion. We must surrender our whole beings to whatever reaction the story demands—gasping, laughing, weeping, wincing, sighing with utter abandonment. Thus we shall be spared the appalling likelihood of giving way to indecorous emotion in real life. Audiences who consider themselves sophisticated do not always understand this. When *Last Tango in Paris* was first shown in London, journalists, their microphones erect, lurked outside the cinema like rapists, waiting to pounce upon the female members of the clientele. "What did you think of it?" they inquired. "We liked it," the girls replied somewhat nonplussed. Never known for their delicacy in such matters, the reporters then asked, "What did you think of the sexy bits?" To this onslaught on their maidenly modesty, the girls then answered, "Oh, we just laughed"—not, you will note, "we laughed" but "we *just* laughed," meaning that they felt no more involving emotion. Why? If we are prepared—nay, eager—to be shot by Mr. Robinson or to be driven at breakneck speed through busy narrow streets by Mr. McQueen, why do we not long to be defiled by Mr. Brando? This thin-lipped response is typically English and must be cured.

The way to go to the movies is critically. That is to say, we must take to each cinema two pairs of spectacles. While we plunge into each picture as though it were happening to us, we must also watch it from a distance, judging it as a work of art. Thus, to seeing a film will be added an extra pleasure that can never be derived from real life, which has no plot and is so badly acted. This dual vision is especially beneficial when watching a movie made in a different era. In these productions, their old-fashioned clothes and morality render them superficially ludicrous, but their quaintness must not blind us to the skill with which they have been made.

If we go to the movies often enough and in a sufficiently reverent spirit, they will become more absorbing than the outer world, and the problems of reality will cease to burden us.

This is the state of affairs toward which so many of us unsuccessfully strive. Opium is the religion of the people, or it was until very recently when cocaine came back into fashion, but we are told by heaps of teenagers that the ecstasies of crack only last about a quarter of an hour—hardly as long as a travelogue or an animated cartoon. A first feature lasts eight times as long. No toxic substance is a real answer. Comrade Dostoyevsky said that without tobacco and alcohol, life for most men would be intolerable, but he had never been to a double feature. It is true that movies are as addictive as dope, but they are far less injurious to health and they ought not to be as expensive.

Clearly, the salvation of the Western world is in the hands of the film industry.

In order that the poorest among us may once again go to the movies several times a week, someone must find a way to lower the price of cinema seats. The unions must be crushed and there must be a return to the making of low-budget pictures so as to provide us with longer programs.

The world is pining for a steady diet of celluloid; it desperately needs an alternative life to that through which it drags itself at the office or, worse, at home. This other existence need not be prettier, but it must be richer; it must have the power to use those capacities for love and courage for which we can find no worthy object in real life.

For me, it was in middle age that mundane activities claimed so much of my time. For my own sake and for the sake of other people's survival, I tried to take part in real life. In old age, as in childhood, I have been lucky; I have felt less need to keep my feet on the ground; I have begun to float into other realms. For some people, this higher plane is mysticism or reincarnation or worse; for me, it has been the cinema.

For the chance to indulge this passion, I have to thank *Christopher Street* magazine and especially its editor, Mr. Steele. I would like to think that the reviews in this book show that, even when I have found fault with some particular film, I have enjoyed watching it. I also hope that I have been able to impart to my readers a little of the pleasure that I have experienced in the forgetting chamber.

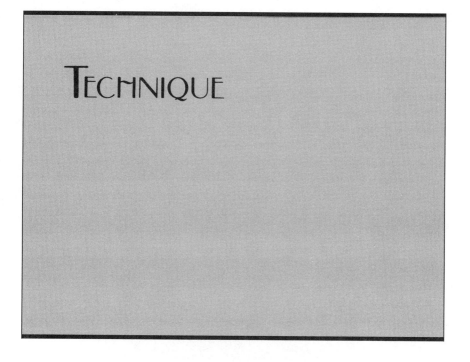

TECHNIQUE

NESTOR ALMENDROS

In this article, written for John Boorman's Projections *magazine, the gifted Cuban cinematographer Nestor Almendros (1930–1992) writes lovingly of the great screen beauties he has photographed—and then, not missing a beat, reveals every secret he can think of about the lighting, camera angles, makeup secrets, and even hair removal that contributed to their images. The result is one of the most objective discussions I've come across about why a few people look like movie stars and most do not.*

"Matters of Photogenics"

Throughout my career I have been privileged to photograph some of the most beautiful and interesting women in the world, in many countries, on two continents. Photographing actresses past their prime represents something of a problem for the cinematographer, who is forced to use diffusion filters in front of the lens to diminish the wrinkles (though in reality they don't hide much), but I have filmed most of these women at the best time of their lives. Isabelle Adjani, for example, was almost an adolescent in *The Story of Adèle H.* Her alabaster complexion had a marvellous transparency. Meryl Streep, whom I have filmed several times, is another actress with a wonderful face, whose skin has an almost marble-like quality.

I have also photographed mature stars like Catherine Deneuve, who, like good wine, has improved with the passage of time. Looking now at one of Ms. Deneuve's first pictures, it is clear that when she was very young she was only a pretty girl, not the sensational beauty she is now. Without a doubt, the years have been kind, giving her style and class, turning her into a real goddess. There is a kind of woman who is at her best between the ages of thirty and forty. When I filmed her in *The Last Metro,* she was at the height of her beauty.

Photographing Simone Signoret in *Madame Rosa,* at the end of her life and career, I did not have to worry about covering wrinkles, or hiding her age, since the role did not require it. On the contrary, she had to be made to look older. This great actress took the procedure in her stride and asked that wrinkles be added to her make-up, so as to give the impression of an elderly and defeated woman. Simone Signoret was once very beautiful. Who could forget her in *Casque d'Or* or *Dédée d'Anvers?*

More recently, I have had the privilege of photographing that new French actress, the tall and beautiful Fanny Ardant. I was fortunate to film her in black and white, which is especially good for portraits. When taking close-ups in a colour picture, there is too much visual information in the background, which tends to draw attention away from the face. That is why the faces of the actresses in the old black and white pictures are so vividly remembered. Even now, movie fans nostalgically recall Dietrich . . . Garbo . . . Lamarr . . . Why? Filmed in black and white, those figures looked as if they were lit from within. When a face appeared on the screen over-exposed—the high-key technique, which also erased imperfections—it was as if a bright object was emerging from the screen.

But today we almost always have to work in colour. This makes good features even more important. I photographed Brooke Shields in *The Blue Lagoon,* when she was very young. She was only fourteen years old, really a child, although she portrayed a sixteen-year-old. Her face comes close to absolute perfection. But surface beauty is not everything. We could say that Sally Fields is a woman whose beauty comes from within. In *Places in the Heart,* she played a provincial woman, and her modesty was most appropriate for the role. She wanted to appear almost without make-up, dressed in well-worn clothes, as a simple American country woman—something which has its own beauty.

At the time of writing, I am in the midst of shooting a film, *Nadine,* directed by Robert Benton, with one of the most attractive young stars of the new American cinema, Kim Basinger. Kim's career has just started, but she is making her presence felt. Both her face and her figure are perfect—it is rare for one person to have both. Her face is completely symmetrical, which is quite unique. Her perfection might even seem excessive, almost as inhuman as a mannequin's, a problem sometimes experienced by models (which Ms. Basinger once was). However, she is also an excellent actress, with a fiery look, and that saves her. In *Nadine,* which is set in the 1950s, the dresses are of bright solid colours, and the lipstick and nail polish are of a violent red, which was the fashion at that time. This was a challenge for me, and I can't predict how well the photography will turn out, because it is the first time I have been faced with such a range of colours.

It is impossible to say which is the most beautiful of all these women, because each in her own way is extraordinary: Deneuve, as a great lady, is splendid, a classic beauty for all times; personifying the freshness of youth, Brooke Shields is unique; Meryl Streep, whose face looks as if it has been sculpted by Brancusi, is the most expressive and intelligent. But there is something common to all of them, something that makes them photograph well. The truth is that the camera lenses love some women more than others. The mystery of being photogenic has to do with bones. A person who "has no bones" is very difficult to light. The great beauties of the screen such as Garbo, Crawford and Mangano all have a well-structured face. The nose was sufficient and well defined, not a cute little one; they had high cheekbones, well-drawn eyebrows, splendid jaws. A good bone structure in the face gives the light something to hold on to and allows it to create an interplay of shadows. If the face is flat, the light has nowhere to fall.

Of course, the eyes are very important, and I believe that dark-haired people with light-coloured eyes have a great advantage in the movies, because of the effect of contrasts on the face. Blondes with very light eyes are difficult to photograph, because there is a certain visual monotony. It is not by chance that Gene Tierney and Hedy Lamarr, two women with dark hair and very light eyes, were such a sensation on the screen. This asymmetry might also be said to apply to Deneuve, who is a blonde with dark eyes—an eye-catching contrast.

Most of these beautiful stars have had a fair complexion, without any tan. The problem with suntan is that it makes the skin appear monochrome on the screen. A face which has not been excessively exposed to the sun will have rosy cheeks, white forehead and natural red lips; different shades of the skin will show through. With a bronzed complexion, however, it all comes together and appears uniform. In any case the woman with a suntan has been over-exploited by commercial advertising, to the point where it has become rather a vulgar image. Yet until the 1920s women used umbrellas as protection against the sun. It is true that sometimes an actor's role requires bronzed skin, yet having a tan has often become an obsession to the extent of defying all logic. Male actors today are especially inclined to fall victim to the suntan craze. Roy Scheider, an excellent actor, always has a tan because he believes it is becoming. But when we were filming *Still of the Night,* in which he portrayed a New York psychiatrist, that suntan was not appropriate to the role. Robert Benton, the director, and I had to insist that he stop sunbathing at weekends. The same thing happened with Jack Nicholson in *Heartburn.*

Certain movie stars, international celebrities, turn out to be, in person, less interesting than you expected, and can even seem unattractive. Is there a secret to that improved image we see on the screen? I believe that the lens captures their inner personality. Thanks to the close-up, the camera almost acts as a microscope, revealing their hidden beauty.

But one should remember that even the most beautiful person in the world has some defects. The important thing is to pinpoint such flaws and try to minimize them, so that they will not show on the screen. For example, a very young actress (I shan't name her) whom I had to photograph had overgrown gums. When she laughed or smiled, they were revealed in their abundance, giving her an almost horsy look. I became aware of this before the filming started, so I informed the director, and the actress, since a good actress is always ready to cooperate with the director of photography. Our job is similar to a doctor's, who diagnoses an illness and prescribes a remedy. We spot the defects and must do our best to hide them. In fact, most actresses are aware of their flaws, because they know themselves well, and are grateful to us for helping them hide such imperfections. Consequently, once they know we know, they put themselves in our hands with confidence and let us guide them. In this case, we advised the actress not to laugh or smile openly during the film, but merely to smile with her eyes, Mona Lisa style. Having followed these suggestions, she appeared incredibly beautiful on film, and in no time at all was a star.

There are other ways of hiding imperfections. One is by use of corrective make-up, a technique that is not that well known to lay people. For example, an actress with whom I worked some years ago had a very low and narrow hairline, which reduced her forehead, unbalancing the face and making her jaw look very prominent. I suggested lifting the hairline about an inch by means of hair removal. This procedure had been undergone many years before by Rita Hayworth, who had a similar problem. Her image was changed with the hair-lift and from a third-rate starlet she became the "sex symbol" of the age. Another example of camouflage through make-up, lights and angles is Marlene Dietrich. When she started in the movies she had a rather round face, like a German peasant's. It is said that when she moved to Hollywood she asked her dentist to extract some molars; this operation served to emphasize her cheekbones. She also lost weight, as she had been asked to do. One should compare the German film *The Blue Angel* of 1930 with *The Shangai Express,* filmed in America two years later. Another method of hiding an actress's flaws is to photograph only her best angles. Some people have one profile which is better than the other; that is to say, their faces are uneven, one side quite different from the other, or the nose is not straight. If this is the case, the photographer should place the main light opposite the side towards which the nose leans, making it look straight.

But let's go back to Marlene Dietrich, who knew herself so well. Marlene thought, not without reason, that her profile was inferior to the frontal view of her face, that she had a duck nose. In love scenes, which show the profiles of the man and woman looking at each other, she always managed to face the camera, and always with a light placed in such a way as to emphasize her famous cheekbones. Since the man was in profile and she was facing the camera, she had to look at him sideways, something that later became Marlene's trademark in the movies. This sideways glance developed into her famous *femme fatale* look. This is how Dietrich, very intelligently, turned a defect into an advantage. Perhaps von Sternberg was instrumental in this. Another strategy well known by men and women in the movies, especially older ones, is to smile. A smile stretches the skin and so thus lifts the face. This is why many actors and actresses smile all the time at the cameras, even where the scene calls for no such thing.

In some cases what might be considered a flaw turns out to be an advantage. Richard Gere's eyes are quite small. I realized this right away when looking through my view-finder, during the filming of *Days of Heaven*. But I decided that, far from being a drawback, they gave him a certain animal look, penetrating and alive, that has become part of his sex appeal and has contributed to his success. Actors with enviably big eyes often project a beefy, boring and expressionless look, a false beauty.

It is true that the movies make people look taller than they really are. The explanation is very simple: it is because of the enlargement of dimensions as the film is projected on to the screen. Since comparisons cannot easily be made, everyone looks the same height. But if the leading man happens to be shorter than his partner, we raise him on a platform to add some inches; on the whole, feet don't show, so there is no problem. Perceived height is also linked with personality: stars with a strong personality seem taller. When I filmed my second picture with Meryl Streep, as usual there was a stand-in for the actress. Stand-ins should be at least the same height and should project a similar general demeanour, to facilitate our work in lining up the shots in the actors' absence. I began to think that Meryl's stand-in was shorter than the actress, yet after measuring her we found that she was in fact slightly taller.

It is often said that people look slightly heavier on the screen, but I believe that the notion that the camera adds 10 pounds is an exaggeration. I have no doubt that in order to be photogenic an actress doesn't have to be thin. The diet craze is misconceived. Women of yesteryear, with their curvy shapes, had a very special beauty. The advertising media have done much to promote this modern preoccupation with being almost emaciated, an image which is now all but played out. In the movie *Witness,* Kelly McGillis is a slightly plump woman by movie standards. When she appears in the nude, she looks attractively like the Venus de Milo. I believe that women should have curves. But that does not mean I approve of the present tendency towards developing muscles.

Any worthwhile director of photography will work closely with the hairstylist, costume designer and make-up expert to create that elusive image of the woman whose beauty is admired by all. In any film with a substantial budget, tests are made for the hairstyles, wardrobe and make-up. During pre-production all possibilities are explored; tests are filmed, shown in a projection room, discussed and submitted to the director and producer for approval. The tests include, of course, variations of lighting. One might find out then, for example, that an actress who has a rather round face should never have both sides of her face lighted

Marlene Dietrich as Lola-Lola in *The Blue Angel* (1930)

Emil Jannings and Marlene Dietrich in *The Blue Angel*

Studio portrait of Marlene Dietrich

with the same intensity, since this will make it seem wider. We will illuminate half of the face and leave the other side in semi-darkness. We might discover too, if a person has a longish face, that lighting one side only will accentuate the length; so a frontal light will have to be used. We will see that, if the actor or actress has deep-set eyes, the lights should be placed low, because if they are high the shadow of the eyebrows will not let the eyes show. This was the case with an exceptional French actor, Jean-Pierre Léaud, with whom I have filmed four pictures. Lit properly, his eyes were his greatest asset.

One of the actresses with whom I have worked had a gorgeous face and a marvellous torso and arms, but the lower part of her body was not too well shaped. The strategy was to dress her in long, dark skirts that covered her legs, and to avoid showing her body full length. Obviously, these decisions should be taken after the tests are made. It should be stressed that in our efforts to beautify the actresses, there is no magic, no mystery—just common sense and hard work.

As director of photography I have to walk away from what a woman wants us to believe and, instead, analyse her just as she is. Many women have personalities which make men think they are beautiful, without actually being so. In my profession I have to be totally objective, going to great lengths, when I am working, to become an asexual human being, analysing people in a dispassionate manner. Very often the director, full of enthusiasm for an actor or actress, is not aware of their physical shortcomings. It is my job to point them out so that something can be done to help minimize these flaws. I am paid to do this, not just to light a scene.

There is a law which may be applied to nature, as well as to the movies, and it is that no woman's face can stand the light that comes from high above. That is why in the tropics many girls of marriageable age would go out only in the late afternoon, when the sun is low and the light has a warmer tone and is less harsh, which improves their looks. The midday light forms a shadow under the eyes, which clouds the look, and another under the nose, giving the impression of a moustache. In movie sets, as well as at home, a light that comes from the top should illuminate a plant or a painting, never a face. The most flattering lights are those from lamps set at the sides—lights that are not harsh, but soft, diffused. That is why the invention of the lampshade was so important! The spotlights or track lights that became fashionable in the 1960s are a disaster, because they emphasize all the flaws on the skin. Another classic trick is that used by the character of Blanche Dubois in *A Streetcar Named Desire*: low-key lighting to camouflage imperfections. Also effective is the use of warm-coloured lampshades like rose or amber. This unifies and hides sun blemishes and ageing and may be used in real life as well as in cinema. Candlelight is very flattering too, a fact well-known even by decorators of second-rate restaurants and nightclubs.

Which actresses from the past do I wish I could have photographed? In first place is the great Marlene Dietrich. After her I would place Louise Brooks, Hedy Lamarr, Ava Gardner, Maria Felix, Gene Tierney, Joan Crawford, Silvana Mangano, Danielle Darieux, Alida Valli and Dolores del Rio. Unfortunately, when I started working in the movies, these exquisite actresses were on their way out.

ROBERT BENCHLEY

*The movie magazines today feature monthly columns collecting anachronisms and conti-nuity errors: Look how Sean Connery's top button is open in the close-up but closed in the over-the-shoulder shot and how when Michael Caine climbs out of the water, his shirt is dry! This genre, if such it is, was satirized before it was invented, by Robert Benchley (1889–1945), a humorist whose own short subjects (*The Treasurer's Report, The Sex Life of the Newt*) were favorites of audiences in the 1930s and 1940s.*

"Movie Boners"

One of the most popular pastimes among movie fans is picking out mistakes in the details of a picture. It is a good game, because it takes your mind off the picture.

For example (Fr. *par example*) in the picture called "One Night Alone—for a Change," the Prince enters the door of the poolroom in the full regalia of an of-ficer in the Hussars. As we pick him up coming in the door, in the next shot, he has on chaps and a sombrero. Somewhere on the threshold he must have changed. This is just sheer carelessness on the part of the director.

. . . .

In "We Need a New Title for This," we have seen Jim, when he came to the farm, fall in love with Elsie, although what Elsie does not know is that Jim is re-ally a character from another picture. The old Squire, however, knows all about it and is holding it over Jim, threatening to expose him and have him sent back to the other picture, which is an independent, costing only a hundred thousand dollars.

Now, when Jim tells Elsie that he loves her (and, before this, we have already been told that Elsie has been in New York, working as secretary to a chorus girl who was just about to get the star's part on the opening night) he says that he is a full-blooded Indian, because he knows that Elsie likes Indians. So far, so good.

But in a later sequence, when they strike oil in Elsie's father (in a previous shot we have seen Elsie's father and have learned that he has given an option on himself to a big oil company which is competing with the old Squire, but what the old Squire does not know is that his house is afire) and when Elsie comes to Jim to tell him that she can't marry him, the clock in the sitting room says ten-thirty. When she leaves it says ten-twenty. That would make her interview minus ten minutes long.

.   .   .   .

In "Throw Me Away!" the street car conductor is seen haggling with the Morelli gang over the disposition of the body of Artie ("Muskrat") Weeler. In the next shot we see Artie haggling with the street-car conductor over the disposition of the bodies of the Morelli gang. This is sloppy cutting.

In "Dr. Tanner Can't Eat" there is a scene laid in Budapest. There is no such place as Budapest.

What the general public does not know is that these mistakes in detail come from the practice of "block-booking" in the moving picture industry. In "block-booking" a girl, known as the "script-girl," holds the book of the picture and is supposed to check up, at the beginning of each "take" (or "baby-broad"), to see that the actors are the same ones as those in the previous "take."

The confusion comes when the "script-girl" goes out to lunch and goes back to the wrong "set." Thus, we might have one scene in *The Little Minister* where everybody was dressed in the costumes of *The Scarlet Empress,* only *The Little Minister* and *The Scarlet Empress* were made on different "lots" and at different times.

It might happen, even at that.

JOE BONOMO

Not a year goes by without a story of a stuntman or woman killed or critically injured on a film set. I find the stories so sad: the careful preparations, the anticipation of success, the stunt person striding off with bravado, and then a miscalculation and death. "You always hold your breath for a moment after the stunt," an actress said after an accident she witnessed, "because the stuntwoman doesn't move until the director says 'cut.' Then she jumps up and waves, and everybody claps. But when she didn't jump up, there was a terrible silence." The following description of an early stunt gone wrong is from a rare and curious book, The Strongman, *by a stuntman, muscleman, and sometime B movie star named Joe Bonomo, who published it himself in 1968. What is evocative is that Bonomo doesn't boast about his own stunts (he performed hundreds) but writes about one he had a feeling wouldn't work: "I'll never forget that look in his eyes. It seemed to tell me he knew that I was right."*

from *The Strongman*

In one picture there was a sequence in which a stuntman was to double for the hero when he changed from an airplane to a speeding freight train. Now, I had already done so much of that kind of work that the director naturally chose me for the job. It didn't sound especially difficult when we talked about it, and I agreed to do it. Just another stunt, I thought.

However, the next morning, when we were all on location, that warning voice inside me told me not to go up. I didn't like the flyer who was to pilot the plane. Somehow, I didn't have confidence in him. The regular pilots that we usually worked with were nowhere around, and believe me, the life of a stuntman depends so much on the skill of his pilot in this sort of stunt. So I told the director I wouldn't do the stunt unless Al Wilson—another of the Black Cats— piloted the plane. Al was the pilot I usually worked with, and I was sure he knew his job. Al, incidentally, was the last of the Cats to go—killed in 1933 stunting at an air carnival. But he was a heck of a good man and we were close friends. On this particular day, Al was working another job. I was sorry, I said, but I just didn't like the looks of the guy who was to pilot for this stunt.

The director became angry, and refused to change pilots, muttering something about "temperamental stuntmen with no guts." He insisted that this pilot was thoroughly competent.

"What's the matter with you, Bonomo," he said. "Running out of gas?" (This was a common movie expression for losing your nerve.)

"I'm sorry," I said. "But maybe that's it. You do the stunt if you want to, and I'll direct the cameras."

This other stuntman (I'll just call him "Lefty" here) was a close friend of mine. We had worked together, on and off, for several years. He was a specialist in this kind of stunt, too. When it came to coolness under fire, and courage at all times, well, Lefty had no master. A great guy.

After about an hour, Lefty arrived, and the director told him what had happened. I was standing some distance away, and I couldn't hear what they were saying, but the director occasionally glanced at me with scorn. Pretty soon Lefty nodded his head and grinned, and I knew he had agreed to do the stunt. The director went back to his camera crew, and I approached Lefty. He was getting into his belts and other straps, the natural protection all stuntmen wear.

"You going up, huh?" I said.

"Sure, Joe. Why not?"

What could I tell him? I had no logical reason why not. Just a feeling. "I've just got a bum hunch about this pilot," I said.

"What's he got to do? Just fly the plane, that's all," he replied.

"Lefty," I said, "Don't go up."

I'll never forget that look in his eyes. It seemed to tell me that he knew I was right. It's a funny thing, but he understood the way I felt. Since the fight with the director I had been left alone on the lot like I had leprosy. But here was a guy who understood. He seemed to hesitate a moment, but then he broke out in his usual grin, tightening his protective chest belt.

"What the hell, it's a job," he laughed. "I'll see ya later." He jabbed me playfully in the gut and walked off to talk to the pilot.

They took off a few minutes later and the train was started way down to the left, coming up toward us. The thing was to be timed so that the transfer to the train happened just in front of us. The plane circled as the train picked up speed. Instead of overtaking and settling down on the train from the rear, can you imagine our horror on the ground when this pilot who was supposed to be so competent, approached the train from the side! There was no radio in the plane; our only communication with the plane was by hand signals. And the dummy in the cockpit probably had all he could do to fly the plane, probably didn't even look down.

There was nothing we could do but wave at him, and that having no effect, stand by and watch the tragedy. Lefty was down at the end of the rope ladder. The plane was coming in too low, and at right angles to the train. At the last minute, we saw Lefty try to climb back up the ladder. He managed to get back up a few rungs on the swaying, free-hanging ladder, but it was not enough. The plane, doing probably seventy miles an hour, slapped him up against the side of the moving freight train, dragged and bounced him over the top, and he was lost to view on the other side.

When the train had passed, we could see the plane rise a little, with Lefty still hanging on to the ladder. We were all screaming our lungs out, trying to wave the pilot off, but he misunderstood the signal, I guess, and thought the director wanted another try.

By this time the train was some distance down the track, and we saw the approach from sort of behind. The plane approached again, and again too low. Lefty, battered and probably broken in a dozen places, couldn't climb up and he couldn't let go to fall to the ground. It was probably only on sheer guts that he hung on at all. We all stood looking with a helpless sick feeling, as into the side of the train he was swung again, bounced and dragged over the top again. He hung on for maybe fifty yards on the other side, then slipped off the ladder and fell to the ground. He hit and bounced almost as high as the low-flying plane, then hit again, rolled a few more yards, and lay there.

When we reached him, Lefty was still conscious. Instead of blaming the stupidity of the pilot, he apologized to the director for ruining the picture.

"I'm sorry I missed, Bill," were the last words he said. He became unconscious, and about a minute later he died, almost every bone in his body sticking out through his flesh in jagged splinters. The first of the Black Cats had been kissed.

The pilot responsible for this boy's death didn't do any more work in films, you can bet on that. The plane had circled the scene of the accident a couple of times, and the pilot must have looked down and seen what had happened. He wasn't too bright, but I'm sure he must have known whose fault it was, because the plane just flew away. The guy never even showed up to collect his pay.

JANET LEIGH

I once shared a ski lift with Janet Leigh at the Telluride Film Festival. We hung high in the air, utterly alone, for twenty minutes, and our conversation was inhibited by my uncertainty: I was a journalist, and she was a star, so should there be small talk or an interview? I was determined not to be so banal as to bring up the shower scene in Psycho, *which is not only her most famous scene but high on the list of anyone's favorite scenes, but somehow it did come up, and she laughed and said she has been asked so many times about so many of the details of the scene that she thought she had become, almost out of self-protection, one of the leading experts on it. A few years later she published a book that proved her point. She leaves out, however (perhaps because it is apocryphal), the famous story about Hitchcock's receiving a letter from a man who complains that after Di-*abolique *his daughter was afraid to take a bath and now, after* Psycho, *was afraid to take a shower. "What should I do with her?" he asked, and Hitchcock replied: "Send her to the dry cleaners."*

from *Behind the Scenes of "Psycho"*

THE SHOWER

The bathroom scenes were scheduled to be shot December 17 through December 23, 1959. It's ironic when you think of it: During the day I was in the throes of being stabbed to death, and at night I was wrapping presents from Santa Claus for the children. And hubby. And family. And friends. Christmas was always a big celebration for me; the spirit of the holiday itself meant so much. When I was a young girl in Stockton, California, and we didn't have very much, it was a festive occasion nonetheless. The choirs I belonged to in church and school would go all over the city singing Christmas carols for different groups and clubs. We usually traveled to Merced, California, to visit Grandma and

Grandpa Morrison. And I still joyfully anticipated whatever little gifts we could scrape together. So finally, when I was earning a good living, I was able to really make a point of going all out for everybody.

Evening was the time for me to be the wife as well as the mother, the two identities that have always had priority over everything else in my life. As I worked on *Psycho,* my husband, Tony Curtis, was making *Rat Race* with our friend Debbie Reynolds. So, between the two of us, there was always a great deal to discuss at dinner. Aside from comparing notes about our respective films, we were concerned about Debbie, who had been through a difficult time the year before with her divorce from Eddie Fisher. The public only sees the actor's screen persona and rarely understands what a toll personal tragedies can take on a creative individual.

Fortunately, Mr. Hitchcock did not like to work late. Some directors never seemed to want to go home and kept slave hours. But not Hitch!

> Hilton Green: "Our crew, coming from television, was used to a shorter shooting schedule, doing more setups in a day. Mr. Hitchcock never wanted to work past six P.M. And he had one standing engagement: Every Thursday, Mr. Hitchcock and madame would have a quiet dinner at Chasen's. So on Thursdays we finished even earlier than usual."

As Christmas approached, the question consuming me during the day was: what to wear in the shower? Rita Riggs and I pored over magazines that showed wardrobe suggestions for strippers. Every guy on the set was eager to look and give his opinion on what would work. The pictures were entertaining—we all laughed for hours—but hardly practical. There was an impressive display of pinwheels, feathers, sequins, toy propellers, balloons, etc., but nothing suitable for our needs. Rita solved the puzzle. Nude-colored moleskin! Over the vital parts! Perfect!

> Neither of us ever thought about negative consequences. But there were a few. Water had the tendency to melt the adhesive, for one. Plus wearing the moleskin for any length of time made my skin raw when we peeled it off. So we would remove it between shots to give my skin some relief, which, of course, was time-consuming.

Before the actual filming began, Mr. Hitchcock showed me the storyboards, drawn for the shower montage by the brilliant artist Saul Bass, who also did the titles for the movie. There were anywhere from seventy-one to seventy-eight angles planned for the series, each one lasting for two to three seconds on the screen. But whether an image appeared on screen for two seconds or two minutes or twenty minutes, it took just as long to prepare for a camera setup; the groundwork was the same.

Years later, at the American Film Institute tribute to Mr. Hitchcock, Tony and I presented one segment. In the dialogue prepared by George Stevens, Jr., who is meticulous in his research, it is said there were seventy-one setups; however, in another book on Psycho, *it was stated there were seventy-eight. In all the interviews Chris and I conducted for this book and in all the searching we did at Universal, Paramount, and the Academy, we found no verification of the exact number. Therefore the number remains vague to this day.*

The shower sequence was the exception to Hitchcock's attitude toward film editing. This next series of shots *depended* on the cutting to startle and terrify, which is why he was so careful about following the storyboard. The word "cutting" is appropriate here, because the quick flashes were meant to be indicative of the continuous slashing, plunging knife.

Now is an appropriate time to address another popular question:

Did Saul Bass direct the shower scene, as he claims?

This is an easy one—a definite "absolutely not!" I have emphatically said this in any interview I've ever given. I've said it to his face in front of other people. For the life of me, I cannot understand what possessed Saul Bass to make that statement. He is a celebrated designer of titles, a three-time Academy Award nominee as a producer of animated short films, and so forth and so on. Why would he say that? Why would he need to do that? Mr. Hitchcock and everyone else associated with Psycho *acknowledged Mr. Bass for his contributions. The movie credits read: Titles Designed by Saul Bass, Pictorial Consultant—Saul Bass.*

I was in that shower for seven days, and, believe you me, Alfred Hitchcock was right next to his camera for every one of those seventy-odd shots.

Lillian Burns Sidney gave me some prudent advice after the successful release of my first film. The studio was buzzing about its newest star. "One film does not a star make," she told me. "Come back in twenty years, then maybe you'll be a star." I never forgot it. Now I have some advice for Mr. Bass: "Drawing some pictures does not a director make."

I am not the only one who has been incensed by Bass's assertion. Joseph Stefano and Rita Riggs have voiced their dismay at Mr. Bass's claims as well. And listen to Hilton.

Hilton Green: "Saul might have visited the set, but I don't recall him there that much, maybe a half day in all. There is not a shot in that movie that I didn't roll the camera for. And I can tell you I never rolled the camera for Mr. Bass.

"I have been quoted before, and you can quote me again, because I am very outspoken on this matter."

I hope this puts that rumor to bed once and for all.

For Marion, going into the shower was more than just a need to wash away the day's grime. Hitch and I discussed the implications at great length. Marion had decided to go back to Phoenix, come clean, and take the consequences, so when she stepped into the tub it was as if she were stepping into the baptismal waters. The spray beating down on her was purifying the corruption from her mind, purging the evil from her soul. She was like a virgin again, tranquil, at peace.

If I could convey this to the audience, the attack would become even more horrifying and appalling.

The seven days in the water were trying for everyone. There were many repeats of the same action, taken from different angles. Then there were the delays due to moleskin problems or camera technicalities. We were fortunate that the cast and crew were patient and had a sense of humor, because these circumstances could have caused some flare-ups.

> *By the way, contrary to what is said on the* Psycho *tour at Universal Studios, Mr. Hitchcock did not turn on the cold water to get a shocked reaction from me when Mother came in. I was able to do that all by myself, thank you very much. In fact, he was adamant about the water temperature being very comfortable.*

Security was a constant source of trouble. Even though I wore the moleskin, I was still pretty much . . . on display, so to speak. I didn't want strangers lurking around, hoping to get a peek in case of any accidental mishap. If anything did slip up, at least only my friends would get a look.

Hitch didn't want extra people around either—for my sake, of course, but also I'm sure to keep the hype going about what was *really* happening on that crazy set!

When I was in the tub looking up toward the showerhead, I was surprised at how many gaffers (electricians) were on the overhead scaffolding. I hadn't seen that many technicians up there even during elaborate scenes on the huge stages, let alone for one person in a tiny bathroom. And each one must have had two or three "assistants." I have a hunch they worked dirt cheap on those days.

One of the toughest shots in the entire film—for me anyway—was at the end of the murder scene. The camera started on a close-up of the dead eye, then gradually pulled back to include more and more of the tub, the shower, the bathroom, until it was very high (as from a bird's-eye view? A *stuffed* bird's-eye view?).

As I mentioned earlier, I could not wear the special contact lenses the scene seemed to require and "going it alone" was not easy. I would blink involuntarily, or swallow, or breathe. On my slide down the tiled wall and collapse over the edge, I had landed in the most awkward position—my mouth and nose were squished against the side of the tub. And drops from the splashing water settled upon my eyelashes and brows and face, and they tickled. It was a formidable task not to react.

The camera didn't have the automatic focus in 1959, so the operator had to do it manually, changing it as the camera moved. Very demanding. So—again the exception to the Hitchcock rule—there were many takes on this shot. Somewhere in the twenties—Hilton Green and I both agreed between twenty-two and twenty-six. Everyone was keeping their fingers crossed. We were almost near the end and nothing had gone wrong. Hallelujah!

At that moment (thanks to Hitch's compassionate insistence on warm water), I could feel the damn moleskin pulling away from my left breast. I knew the lens would not pick it up—that part was below the top of the tub. But I also knew the guys in the balcony would get an eyeful. By that time, I was sore where I was pressed against the ungiving porcelain—my body ached—and I didn't want to shoot this again if we didn't have to. So I decided not to say anything—the hell with it, I said to myself; let 'em look!

Time to deal with another question:

Did Hitchcock try to persuade you to be nude in the shower?

> *Mr. Hitchcock never asked me to do the scene nude. I would like to explain something at this point. This book was intended to set the record straight about* Psycho *by sharing unknown stories, incidents, and memories. So when we reread most of what has been written and said about* Psycho, *and spoke with so many of the actual participants, we felt even more compelled to correct the blatant inaccuracies and lingering tall tales.*
>
> *There would have been no point in Hitch suggesting that I play the scene nude, because the industry operated under the scrutiny of a censor's office. Every script and finished product had to be approved by this board. And nudity was not allowed to be shown. And you know what else? Doing the scene nude would have cheated Hitch and millions of movie fans, because all would have missed his mastery of insinuating situations and conditions.*
>
> *If you had looked at the storyboard, you would have noticed that there was no need to see the whole body nude: One angle would show an arm here, a tummy there, shoulders down to the great divide, legs, back.*
>
> *(The back—one of the sexiest parts of the body. For a scene in* The Vikings, *Kirk Douglas ripped my gown down the back, exposing the whole length of skin to the lowest hollow. He has always believed the back is a real turn-on.)*
>
> *Joseph Stefano cleared up a couple of other points. Mr. Hitchcock did* not *say to him, "I'm going to have a problem with Janet; she thinks her breasts are too big!" (I would have had to be pretty stupid to worry about my boobs being too big. Actually I often say, "Thank you, God.")*
>
> *Stefano also told me about another erroneously printed statement: "I never said anything to anyone about a trembling actress." (This refers to a remark Hitchcock allegedly made to Stefano about the possibility of me appearing nude in the shower: "I don't want to deal with a trembling actress.")*

Another question:

Were you really in the shower?

I am amazed that I am still asked that question. You look at that sequence closely and you see—me! Unquestionably, without a doubt, unequivocally, I was in that shower for seven drenching days. I was in that shower so much that my skin was beginning to look like a wrinkled prune.

Every player has a stand-in. And on most dangerous stunts, the movie's insurance coverage insists on stunt doubles as well. Although sometimes we fudge a bit and do more of the stunts than we really should—it can be fun! (Of course, you have to be a mite zany to think that way. But we all have some of that daredevil craziness in us.)

On Psycho, *Mr. Hitchcock hired a body double, a professional artist's model who was accustomed to being nude, it being all in a day's work. Her name was Marli Renfro, and she was paid $400 a week, one week guaranteed. He used Ms. Renfro to see how much of the body outline the camera would pick up behind the shower curtain, and to test the density of the water—what level of water force would read well and yet not obscure Marion. But she was* not *on camera during the shower scene.*

At the end of the murder, Norman wrapped the corpse in the shower curtain and dragged it out to the car. That was the only *shot I was not in. Hitch showed me that no one could see who it was, so there was no need for me to be bounced around. I totally agreed.*

However, my naughty friend Mr. Hitchcock did try to slip one shot by the inspectors.

Joseph Stefano: "He [Hitchcock] knew he would never get away with frontal nudity, but he thought he might squeak by with a high overhead shot of Marion lying over the tub. For this shot he used the model. But her buttocks were seen. The incredible thing was that the scene right before this one was when he went to your [Janet's] eye and it was heartbreaking. There was no sex connected to it at all. There was this beautiful person whom I had cared about all through the movie up to this point, and she was lying there dead. But no deal. It was the only angle from the shower sequence that was cut."

The day they were filming that long shot, John Gavin had quite an awakening.

John Gavin: "I had rooms at the studio [Universal]; I used one as an office. I noticed on the call sheet that the shower montage was still being shot, so I came by to say hello. [He didn't realize I, Janet, was finished with my part.] The sign read Closed Set, and I thought, 'Well, it's not closed to me, I belong to this company.' So I opened the door and went in. And indeed, no one said a boo. I walked around and all of a sudden I noticed this girl just wandering about absolutely stark naked. My eyes almost fell out of my head, like a great lout. But no one else was paying any attention to her; I guess they had become quite used to her."

Every person we spoke with who had been involved with the movie was dumbfounded that anyone could think it wasn't me in the shower. But once people got wind that there was a nude model on the set at all, it was fireworks for trivia.

You know what I think? I think Hitch deliberately hired the model partly to plant the seed in people's minds that this picture had nudity. He had started to manipulate the audiences before the film was even in a theater. He teased the pros, the nonpros, the sophisticated, and the naive. He knew the rumor would eventually become the gospel truth. The seed would blossom to such an extent that when the viewers came out of the movie houses, they would swear on the Bible that they had seen nudity. And gushing blood. And weapon penetration. Such was Alfred Hitchcock's gift.

Mark O'Donnell

I have always vaguely grasped that the laws of physics in cartoons, while different from those proposed by Newton, have a consistency of their own. Mark O'Donnell is the Newton of the art form.

"The Laws of Cartoon Motion"

(1). Any body suspended in space will remain in space until made aware of its situation. Daffy Duck steps off a cliff, expecting further pastureland. He loiters in midair, soliloquizing flippantly, until he chances to look down. At this point, the familiar principle of thirty-two feet per second per second takes over.

(2). Any body in motion will tend to remain in motion until solid matter intervenes suddenly. Whether shot from a cannon or in hot pursuit on foot, cartoon characters are so absolute in their momentum that only a telephone pole or an outsize boulder retards their forward motion absolutely. Sir Isaac Newton called this sudden termination of motion the stooge's surcease.

(3). Any body passing through solid matter will leave a perforation conforming to its perimeter. Also called the silhouette of passage, this phenomenon is the specialty of victims of directed-pressure explosions and of reckless cowards who are so eager to escape that they exit directly through the wall of a house, leaving a cookie-cutout-perfect hole. The threat of skunks or matrimony often catalyzes this reaction.

(4). The time required for an object to fall twenty stories is greater than or equal to the time it takes for whoever knocked it off the ledge to spiral down twenty flights to attempt to capture it unbroken. Such an object is inevitably priceless, the attempt to capture it inevitably unsuccessful.

(5). All principles of gravity are negated by fear. Psychic forces are sufficient in most bodies for a shock to propel them directly away from the earth's surface. A spooky noise or an adversary's signature sound will induce motion upward, usually to the cradle of a chandelier, a treetop, or the crest of a flagpole. The feet of a character who is running or the wheels of a speeding auto need never touch the ground, especially when in flight.

(6). As speed increases, objects can be in several places at once. This is particularly true of tooth-and-claw fights, in which a character's head may be glimpsed emerging from the cloud of altercation at several places simultaneously. This effect is common as well among bodies that are spinning or being throttled. A "wacky" character has the option of self-replication only at manic high speeds and may ricochet off walls to achieve the velocity required.

(7.) Certain bodies can pass through solid walls painted to resemble tunnel entrances; others cannot. This trompe l'oeil inconsistency has baffled generations, but at least it is known that whoever paints an entrance on a wall's surface to trick an opponent will be unable to pursue him into this theoretical space. The painter is flattened against the wall when he attempts to follow into the painting. This is ultimately a problem of art, not of science.

(8). Any violent rearrangement of feline matter is impermanent. Cartoon cats possess even more deaths than the traditional nine lives might comfortably afford. They can be decimated, spliced, splayed, accordion-pleated, spindled, or disassembled, but they cannot be destroyed. After a few moments of blinking self pity, they reinflate, elongate, snap back, or solidify. Corollary: A cat will assume the shape of its container.

(9). For every vengeance there is an equal and opposite revengeance. This is the one law of animated cartoon motion that also applies to the physical world at large. For that reason, we need the relief of watching it happen to a duck instead.

AKIRA KUROSAWA

Great directors are notoriously shy about revealing or discussing their methods, often preferring, like Hitchcock, to use indirection or, like John Ford, to claim that they are simply doing a job of work and have no notions of any larger meaning. In Japan it is not quite the same because the idea of artistic individualism has not been, until recently, part of the artist's idea of himself. Instead artists in many media deliberately built upon the work of their predecessors, continuing within the same tradition and then passing on their methods to the next generation. There is something of that feeling in these notes by Kurosawa; they were written as advice to young filmmakers and read as if they were written by a man who has learned his craft, knows it, and has confidence that he can pass it on.

from *Something Like an Autobiography*

SOME RANDOM NOTES ON FILMMAKING

. . . .

What is cinema? The answer to this question is no easy matter. Long ago the Japanese novelist Shiga Naoya presented an essay written by his grandchild as one of the most remarkable prose pieces of his time. He had it published in a literary magazine. It was entitled "My Dog," and ran as follows: "My dog resembles a bear; he also resembles a badger; he also resembles a fox. . . ." It proceeded to enumerate the dog's special characteristics, comparing each one to yet another animal, developing into a full list of the animal kingdom. However, the essay closed with, "But since he's a dog, he most resembles a dog."

I remember bursting out laughing when I read this essay, but it makes a serious point. Cinema resembles so many other arts. If cinema has very literary characteristics, it also has theatrical qualities, a philosophical side, attributes of painting and sculpture and musical elements. But cinema is, in the final analysis, cinema.

. . . .

There is something that might be called cinematic beauty. It can only be expressed in a film, and it must be present in a film for that film to be a moving work. When it is very well expressed, one experiences a particularly deep emotion while watching that film. I believe it is this quality that draws people to come and see a film, and that it is the hope of attaining this quality that inspires the filmmaker to make his film in the first place. In other words, I believe that the essence of the cinema lies in cinematic beauty.

. . . .

When I begin to consider a film project, I always have in mind a number of ideas that feel as if they would be the sort of thing I'd like to film. From among these one will suddenly germinate and begin to sprout; this will be the one I grasp and develop. I have never taken on a project offered to me by a producer or a production company. My films emerge from my own desire to say a particular thing at a particular time. The root of any film project for me is this inner need to express something. What nurtures this root and makes it grow into a tree is the script. What makes the tree bear flowers and fruit is the directing.

. . . .

The role of director encompasses the coaching of the actors, the cinematography, the sound recording, the art direction, the music, the editing and the dubbing and sound-mixing. Although these can be thought of as separate occupations, I do not regard them as independent. I see them all melting together under the heading of direction.

. . . .

A film director has to convince a great number of people to follow him and work with him. I often say, although I am certainly not a militarist, that if you compare the production unit to an army, the script is the battle flag and the director is the commander of the front line. From the moment production begins to the moment it ends, there is no telling what will happen. The director must be able to respond to any situation, and he must have the leadership ability to make the whole unit go along with his responses.

. . . .

Although the continuity for a film is all worked out in advance, that sequence may not necessarily be the most interesting way to shoot the picture. Things can happen without warning that produce a startling effect. When these can be incorporated in the film without upsetting the balance, the whole becomes much more interesting. This process is similar to that of a pot being fired in a kiln. Ashes and other particles can fall onto the melted glaze during the firing and cause unpredictable but beautiful results. Similarly unplanned but interesting effects arise in the course of directing a movie, so I call them "kiln changes."

. . . .

With a good script a good director can produce a masterpiece; with the same script a mediocre director can make a passable film. But with a bad script even a good director can't possibly make a good film. For truly cinematic expression, the camera and the microphone must be able to cross both fire and water. That is what makes a real movie. The script must be something that has the power to do this.

. . . .

A good structure for a screenplay is that of the symphony, with its three or four movements and differing tempos. Or one can use the Noh play with its three-part structure: jo (introduction), ha (destruction) and kyū (haste). If you devote yourself fully to Noh and gain something good from this, it will emerge naturally in your films. The Noh is a truly unique art form that exists nowhere else in the world. I think the Kabuki, which imitates it, is a sterile flower. But in a screenplay, I think the symphonic structure is the easiest for people of today to understand.

.   .   .   .

In order to write scripts, you must first study the great novels and dramas of the world. You must consider why they are great. Where does the emotion come from that you feel as you read them? What degree of passion did the author have to have, what level of meticulousness did he have to command, in order to portray the characters and events as he did? You must read thoroughly, to the point where you can grasp all these things. You must also see the great films. You must read the great screenplays and study the film theories of the great directors. If your goal is to become a film director, you must master screenwriting.

.   .   .   .

I've forgotten who it was that said creation is memory. My own experiences and the various things I have read remain in my memory and become the basis upon which I create something new. I couldn't do it out of nothing. For this reason, since the time I was a young man I have always kept a notebook handy when I read a book. I write down my reactions and what particularly moves me. I have stacks and stacks of these college notebooks, and when I go off to write a script, these are what I read. Somewhere they always provide me with a point of breakthrough. Even for single lines of dialogue I have taken hints from these notebooks. So what I want to say is, don't read books while lying down in bed.

.   .   .   .

I began writing scripts with two other people around 1940. Up until then I wrote alone, and found that I had no difficulties. But in writing alone there is a danger that your interpretation of another human being will suffer from one-sidedness. If you write with two other people about that human being, you get at least three different viewpoints on him, and you can discuss the points on which you disagree. Also, the director has a natural tendency to nudge the hero and the plot along into a pattern that is the easiest one for him to direct. By writing with about two other people, you can avoid this danger also.

.   .   .   .

Something that you should take particular notice of is the fact that the best scripts have very few explanatory passages. Adding explanation to the descriptive passages of a screenplay is the most dangerous trap you can fall into. It's easy to explain the psychological state of a character at a particular moment, but it's very difficult to describe it through the delicate nuances of action and dialogue. Yet it is not impossible. A great deal about this can be learned from the study of the great plays, and I believe the "hard-boiled" detective novels can also be very instructive.

· · · · · · · · · · · · · · · · · · ·

I begin rehearsals in the actors' dressing room. First I have them repeat their lines, and gradually proceed to the movements. But this is done with costumes and makeup on from the beginning; then we repeat everything on the set. The thoroughness of these rehearsals makes the actual shooting time very short. We don't rehearse just the actors, but every part of every scene—the camera movements, the lighting, everything.

· · · · · · · · · · · · · · · · · · ·

The worst thing an actor can do is show his awareness of the camera. Often when an actor hears the call "Roll 'em" he will tense up, alter his sight lines and present himself very unnaturally. This self-consciousness shows very clearly to the camera's eye. I always say, "Just talk to the actor playing opposite. This isn't like the stage, where you have to speak your lines to the audience. There's no need to look at the camera." But when he knows where the camera is, the actor invariably, without knowing it, turns one-third to halfway in its direction. With multiple moving cameras, however, the actor has no time to figure out which one is shooting him.

· · · · · · · · · · · · · · · · · · ·

During the shooting of a scene the director's eye has to catch even the minutest detail. But this does not mean glaring concentratedly at the set. While the cameras are rolling, I rarely look directly at the actors, but focus my gaze somewhere else. By doing this I sense instantly when something isn't right. Watching something does not mean fixing your gaze on it, but being aware of it in a natural way. I believe this is what the medieval Noh playwright and theorist Zeami meant by "watching with a detached gaze."

· · · · · · · · · · · · · · · · · · ·

Many people choose to follow the actors' movements with a zoom lens. Although the most natural way to approach the actor with the camera is to move it at the same speed he moves, many people wait until he stops moving and then zoom in on him. I think this is very wrong. The camera should follow the actor as he moves; it should stop when he stops. If this rule is not followed, the audience will become conscious of the camera.

.   .   .   .

Much is often made of the fact that I use more than one camera to shoot a scene. This began when I was making *Seven Samurai,* because it was impossible to predict exactly what would happen in the scene where the bandits attack the peasants' village in a heavy rainstorm. If I had filmed it in the traditional shot-by-shot method, there was no guarantee that any action could be repeated in exactly the same way twice. So I used three cameras rolling simultaneously. The result was extremely effective, so I decided to exploit this technique fully in less action-filled drama as well, and I next used it for *Ikimono no kiroku (Record of a Living Being).* By the time I made *The Lower Depths* I was using largely a one-shot-per-scene method.

.   .   .   .

Working with three cameras simultaneously is not so easy as it may sound. It is extremely difficult to determine how to move them. For example, if a scene has three actors in it, all three are talking and moving about freely and naturally. In order to show how the A, B and C cameras move to cover this action, even complete picture continuity is insufficient. Nor can the average camera operator understand a diagram of the camera movements. I think in Japan the only cinematographers who can are Nakai Asakazu and Saitō Takao. The three camera positions are completely different for the beginning and end of each shot, and they go through several transformations in between. As a general system, I put the A camera in the most orthodox positions, use the B camera for quick, decisive shots and the C camera as a kind of guerilla unit.

.   .   .   .

The task of the lighting technicians is an extremely creative one. A really good lighting man has his own plan, though he of course still needs to discuss it with the cameraman and the director. But if he does not put forth his own concept, his job becomes nothing more than lighting up the whole frame. I think, for example, that the current method of lighting for color film is wrong. In order to bring out the colors, the entire frame is flooded with light. I always say the lighting should be treated as it is for black-and-white film, whether the colors are strong or not, so that the shadows come out right.

.   .   .   .

I am often accused of being too exacting with sets and properties, of having things made, just for the sake of authenticity, that will never appear on camera. Even if I don't request this, my crew does it for me anyway. The first Japanese director to demand authentic sets and props was Mizoguchi Kenji, and the sets in his films are truly superb. I learned a great deal about filmmaking from him, and the making of sets is among the most important. The quality of the set influences the quality of the actors' performances. If the plan of a house and the design of the rooms are done properly, the actors can move about in them naturally. If I have to tell an actor, "Don't think about where this room is in relation to the rest of the house," that natural ease cannot be achieved. For this reason, I have the sets made exactly like the real thing. It restricts the shooting, but encourages that feeling of authenticity.

. . . .

From the moment I begin directing a film, I am thinking about not only the music but the sound effects as well. Even before the camera rolls, along with all the other things I consider, I decide what kind of sound I want. In some of my films, such as *Seven Samurai* and *Yojimbo,* I use different theme music for each main character or for different groups of characters.

. . . .

I changed my thinking about musical accompaniment from the time Hayasaka Fumio began working with me as composer of my film scores. Up until that time film music was nothing more than accompaniment—for a sad scene there was always sad music. This is the way most people use music, and it is ineffective. But from *Drunken Angel* onward, I have used light music for some key sad scenes, and my way of using music has differed from the norm—I don't put it in where most people do. Working with Hayasaka, I began to think in terms of the counterpoint of sound and image as opposed to the union of sound and image.

. . . .

The most important requirement for editing is objectivity. No matter how much difficulty you had in obtaining a particular shot, the audience will never know. If it is not interesting, it simply isn't interesting. You may have been full of enthusiasm during the filming of a particular shot, but if that enthusiasm doesn't show on the screen, you must be objective enough to cut it.

. . . .

Editing is truly interesting work. When the rushes come up, I rarely show them to my crew exactly as they are. Instead I go to the editing room when shooting is over that day and with the editor spend about three hours editing the rushes together. Only then do I show them to the crew. It is necessary to show them this edited footage for the sake of arousing their interest. Sometimes they don't understand what it is they are filming, or why they had to spend ten days to get a particular shot. When they see the edited footage with the results of their labor, they become enthusiastic again. And by editing as I go along, I have only the fine cut to complete when the shooting is finished.

. . . .

I am often asked why I don't pass on to young people what I have accomplished over the years. Actually, I would like very much to do so. Ninety-nine percent of those who worked as my assistant directors have now become directors in their own right. But I don't think any of them took the trouble to learn the most important things.

David Mamet

Many directors may have thought it, but David Mamet is one of the few brave directors to say it: "Most actors are, unfortunately, not good actors." His prescription for good act-ing is typical of the Chicago School also espoused by the Steppenwolf actors: No theory, no thinking, just prepare yourself, and do it. "The acting should be a performance of the simple physical action. Period." Mamet's greatest success has come as a playwright and screenwriter, but for me his films are a bracing experience because they contain so much rigor and intelligence. House of Games *in particular is an unfolding Chinese box of plot, character, and motivation. And look what he does to the crime genre in* Homicide. *He wrote* On Directing Film *after having directed only two of them, but that helps the book, I think, because he was still fresh, still aware of theory, and what he was doing had not yet become habit.*

from *On Directing Film*

What to Tell the Actors and Where to Put the Camera

I've seen directors do as many as sixty takes of a shot. Now, any director who's watched dailies knows that after the third or fourth take he can't remember the first; and on the set, when shooting the tenth take, you can't remember the purpose of the scene. And after shooting the twelfth, you can't remember why you were born. Why do directors, then, shoot this many takes? Because they don't know what they want to take a picture of. And they're frightened. If you don't know what you want, how do you know when you're done? If you know what you want, shoot it and sit down. Suppose you are directing the "get a retraction" movie. What are you going to tell the actor who does that first beat for you? What do we refer to; what is our compass here? What is a simple tool to which we may refer to answer this question?

To give direction to the actor, you do the same thing you do when you give direction to the cameraman. You refer to *the objective of the scene*, which in this case is *to get a retraction;* and to the meaning of this beat, which here is *to arrive early.*

Based on this, you tell the actor to do those things, and only those things, he needs to do for you to shoot the beat, *to arrive early.* You tell him to go to the door, try the door, and sit down. That is literally what you tell him. Nothing more.

Just as the shot doesn't have to be inflected, the acting doesn't have to be inflected, nor should it be. The acting should be a performance of the simple physical action. Period. Go to the door, try the door, sit down. He doesn't have to walk down the hall respectfully. This is the greatest lesson anyone can ever teach you about acting. Perform the physical motions called for by the script as simply as possible. Do *not* "help the play along."

He doesn't have to sit down respectfully. He doesn't have to turn the door respectfully. The script is doing that work. The more the actor tries to make each physical action carry the meaning of the "scene" or the "play," the more that actor is ruining your movie. The nail doesn't have to look like a house; it is not a house. It is a *nail.* If the house is going to stand, the nail must do the work of a nail. To do the work of the nail, it has to *look* like a nail.

The more the actor is giving him or herself over to the specific uninflected physical action, the better off your movie is, which is why we like those old-time movie stars so much. They were awfully damn simple. "What do I do in this scene?" was their question. Walk down the hall. How? Fairly quickly. Fairly slowly. Determinedly. Listen to those simple adverbs—the choice of actions and adverbs constitutes the craft of directing actors.

What's the scene? *To get a retraction.* What's the meaning of the beat? *To arrive early.* What are the specific shots? Guy walking down the hall, guy tries the doorknob, guy sits down. Good luck will be the residue of good design. When the actor says, "how do I walk down the hall?" you say, "I don't know . . . quickly." Why do you say that? Because your subconscious is working on the problem. Because you've paid your dues at this point and you're entitled to make what may seem to be an arbitrary decision but may also be a subconscious solution to a problem; and you have honored the subconscious by referring the problem to it long enough for it to cough up the answer.

Just as it's in the nature of the audience to want to help the story along, to help along good work, that is to say work which is respectful of its inner nature, just so it's in the nature of your subconscious to want to help this task along. A lot of decisions that you think are going to be made arbitrarily are arrived at through the simple and dedicated workings of your subconscious. When you look back at them, you will say, "well, I got lucky there, didn't I?" and the answer will be "yes" because you paid for it. You paid for that subconscious help when you agonized over the structure of the film. The shot list.

Actors will ask you a lot of questions. "What am I thinking here?" "What's my motivation?" "Where did I just come from?" The answer to all of these questions is *it doesn't matter*. It doesn't matter because you can't act on those things. I defy anyone to act where he just came from. If you can't act on it, why think about it? Instead, your best bet is to ask the actor to do his simple physical actions as simply as possible.

"Please walk down the hall, try the doorknob." You don't have to say "try the doorknob and it's locked." Just try the doorknob and sit down. Movies are made out of very simple ideas. The good actor will perform each small piece as completely and as simply as possible.

Most actors are, unfortunately, not good actors. There are many reasons for this, the prime reason being that theater has fallen apart in our lifetime. When I was young, most actors, by the time they got to be thirty, had spent ten years on the stage, earning their living.

Actors don't do that anymore, so they never get a chance to learn how to act well. Virtually all of our actors in this country are badly trained. They're trained to take responsibility for the scene, to be emotional, to use each role to audition for the next. To make each small and precious moment on the stage or screen both "mean" the whole play and display their wares, to act, in effect, "sit down because I'm the king of France." It's not that actors are dumb people. To the contrary, the job, in my experience, attracts folk of high intelligence, and most of them are dedicated people; bad actors and good actors are in the main dedicated and hardworking people. Unfortunately, most actors don't accomplish much, because they're badly trained, underemployed, and anxious both to advance their career and to "do good."

Also, most actors try to use their intellectuality to portray the idea of the movie. Well, that's not their job. Their job is to accomplish, *beat by beat,* as simply as possible, the specific action set out for them by the script and the director.

The purpose of rehearsal is to tell the actors *exactly* the actions called for, beat by beat.

When you get on the set, the good actors who took careful notes will show up, *do* those actions—not *emote,* not *discover,* but do what they're getting paid to do, which is to perform, as simply as possible, exactly the thing they rehearsed.

If you, the director, understand the theory of montage, you don't have to strive to bring the actors to a real or pretended state of frenzy or love or hate or anything emotional. It's not the actor's job to be emotional—it is the actor's job to be *direct.*

Acting and dialogue fall into the same boat. Just as with the acting, the purpose of the dialogue is not to pick up the slack in the shot list. The purpose of dialogue is not to carry information about the "character." The only reason people speak is to get what they want. In film or on the street, people who describe themselves to you are lying. Here is the difference: In the bad film, the fellow says, "hello, Jack, I'm coming over to your home this evening because I need to get the money you borrowed from me." In the good film, he says, "where the hell were you yesterday?"

You don't have to narrate with the dialogue any more than you have to narrate with the pictures or the acting. The less you narrate, the more the audience is going to say, "wow. What the *heck* is happening here? What the *heck* is going to happen next . . . ?" Now, if you're telling the story with the pictures, then the dialogue is the sprinkles on top of the ice cream cone. It's a gloss on what's happening. The story is being carried by the shots. Basically, the perfect movie doesn't have any dialogue. So you should always be striving to make a silent movie. If you don't, what will happen to you is the same thing that happened to the American film industry. Instead of writing the shot list, you'll have the student rise and say, "isn't that Mr. Smith? I think I'll get a retraction from him." Which is what happened to American films when sound came in, and they've gotten worse ever since.

If you can learn to tell a story, to break down a movie according to the shots and tell the story according to the theory of montage, then the dialogue, if it's good, will make the movie somewhat better; and if it's bad, will make the movie somewhat worse; but you'll still be telling the story *with the shots,* and they can take the brilliant dialogue out, if need be—as, in fact, they do when a film is subtitled or dubbed—and a great film, so treated, is injured hardly at all.

Now that we know what to tell the actors, we need an answer to the one question the crew will ask you again and again—"where do we put the camera?" The answer to this question is, "over there."

There are some directors who are visual masters—who bring to moviemaking a great visual acuity, a brilliant visual sense. I am not one of those people. So the answer I'm giving is the only answer I know. I happen to know a certain amount about the construction of a script, so that's what I'm telling you. The question is, "where do I put the camera?" That's the simple question, and the answer is, "over there in that place in which it will capture the uninflected shot necessary to move the story along."

"Yes, but," a lot of you are saying, "I know that the shot should be uninflected, but really since it's a scene about *respect* shouldn't we put the camera at a respectful angle?"

No; there is no such thing as "a respectful angle." Even if there *were,* you wouldn't want to put the camera there—if you did so, you wouldn't be letting the story *evolve.* It's like saying: "a naked man is walking down the street copulating with a whore while going to a whorehouse." Let him *get* to the whorehouse. Let each shot stand by itself. The answer to the question "where do you put the camera?" is the question "what's the shot of?"

That's my philosophy. I don't know better. If I knew a better answer to it, I would give it to you. If I knew a better answer to the shot, I would give it to you, but because I don't, I have to go back to step number one, which is "keep it simple, stupid, and don't violate those rules that you *do* know. If you don't know which rule applies, just don't muck up the more general rules."

I know it's a shot of *a guy walking down a hall.* I'm going to put the camera *somewhere.* Is one place better than another? Probably. Do I know which place is better than another? No? Then I'll let my subconscious pick one, and put the camera there.

Is there a better answer to the question? There may be, and the better answer may be this: in the storyboard for a movie or a scene, you may see a certain pattern developing, which might tell you something. Perhaps your task as a designer of shots is, after a point, that of a "decorator," quite frankly.

"What are the 'qualities' of the shot?" I don't happen to think that's the most important question in making a movie. I think it's an important question, but I don't think it's the most important question. When faced with the necessity of a particular election, I'm going to answer what I think is the most important question first, and then reason backward and answer the smaller question as best I can.

Where do you put the camera? We did our first movie and we had a bunch of shots with a hall here and a door there and a staircase there.

"Wouldn't it be nice," one might say, "if we could get this hall *here,* really around the corner from that door *there;* or to get that door *here* to *really be* the door that opens on the staircase to that door *there?*" So we could just move the camera from one to the next?

It took me a great deal of effort and still takes me a great deal and will continue to take me a great deal of effort to answer the question thusly: no, not only is it not important to have those objects literally contiguous; it is important to fight against this desire, because fighting it reinforces an understanding of the essential nature of film, which is that it is made of disparate shots, cut to-

gether. It's a *door,* it's a *hall,* it's a *blah-blah. Put* the camera "there" and photograph, *as simply as possible,* that object. If we don't understand that we both can
and *must* cut the shots together, we are sneakily falling victim to the mistaken
theory of the Steadicam. It might be nice to have these objects next to each other
so as to avoid having to move the crew, but you don't get any sneaky artistic
good out of literally having them next to each other. *You can cut the shots together.*

This relates to what I said about acting: if you can cut different pieces,
different scenes together, different lines together, you don't have to have somebody in every shot with the same "continuous intention." The same "commitment to and understanding of the character." You don't need it.

The actor has to be performing a simple physical action for the space of ten
seconds. It does not have to be part of the "performance of the film." Actors talk
about the "arc of the film" or the "arc of the performance." It doesn't exist on
stage. It's not there. The performance takes care of both. The "arc of the performance," the act of controlling, of doling out emotion here and withholding
emotion there, just doesn't exist. It's like a passenger sticking his arms out of
the airplane window and flapping them to make the plane more aerodynamic.
This commitment to the arc of the film—it's ignorance on the part of the actor,
ignorance of the essential nature of acting in film, which is that the performance
will be created by the juxtaposition of simple, for the most part uninflected shots,
and simple, uninflected physical actions.

The way to shoot the car crash is not to stick a guy in the middle of the street
and run over him and keep the camera on. The way to shoot the car crash is to
shoot the pedestrian walking across the street, shoot the shot of the onlooker
whose head turns, shoot the shot of a man inside the car who looks up, shoot
the shot of the guy's foot coming down on the brake pedal, and shoot the shot
underneath the car with the set of legs lying at a strange angle (with thanks to
Pudovkin, for the above). Cut them together, and the audience gets the idea:
accident.

If that's the nature of film for the director, that's the nature of film for the
actor too. Great actors understand this.

Humphrey Bogart told this story: When they were shooting *Casablanca* and
S. Z. (Cuddles) Sakall or someone comes to him and says, "they want to play
the 'Marseillaise,' what should we do?—the Nazis are here and we shouldn't
be playing the 'Marseillaise,' " Humphrey Bogart just nods to the band, we cut
to the band, and they start playing "bah-bah-bah-*bah.*"

Someone asked what he did to make that beautiful scene work. He says, "they
called me in one day, Michael Curtiz, the director, said, 'stand on the balcony
over there, and when I say "action" take a beat and nod,' " which he did. That's
great acting. Why? What more could he possibly have done? He was required
to nod, he nodded. There you have it. The audience is terribly moved by his

simple *restraint* in an emotional situation—and this is the essence of good the-ater: good theater is people doing extraordinarily moving tasks as simply as pos-sible. Contemporary playwriting, filmmaking, and acting tend to offer us the reverse—people performing mundane and predictable actions in an overblown way. The good actor performs his tasks as simply and *as unemotionally* as possi-ble. This lets the audience "get the idea"—just as the juxtaposition of uninflected images in service of a third idea creates the play in the mind of the audience.

Learn this, and go out and make the movie. You'll get someone who knows how to take a picture, or *you* learn how to take a picture; you get someone who knows how to light, or *you* learn how to light. There's no magic to it. Some peo-ple will be able to do some tasks better than others—depending upon the de-gree of their technical mastery and their aptitude for the task. Just like playing the piano. Anybody can learn how to play the piano. For some people it will be very, very difficult—but they can learn it. There's almost no one who can't learn to play the piano. There's a wide range in the middle, of people who can play the piano with various degrees of skill; a very, very narrow band at the top, of people who can play brilliantly and build upon a simple technical skill to create great art. The same thing is true of cinematography and sound mixing. Just tech-nical skills. Directing is just a technical skill. Make your shot list.

HOLLYWOOD

F. Scott Fitzgerald

Scott Fitzgerald (1896–1940) went to work in Hollywood at a time when his alcoholism had impaired his productivity and the quality of his writing. But Hollywood, which has destroyed so many writers, was not all bad for him; it was there he finally stopped drinking and began The Last Tycoon *which contains some of his best writing. And his experiences led to a lot of short stories, including this one, in which the character of Joel Coles might not be a million miles removed from Fitzgerald himself. It is interesting the way he prepares the ground for Coles in the third paragraph, with the sentence "Ordinarily he did not go out on Sundays but stayed sober and took work home with him." Only an alcoholic would take note of having stayed sober. But the story is about much more—is about, in a sense, Miles Calman, seen through the eyes of the supporting players in his life.*

"Crazy Sunday"

It was Sunday—not a day, but rather a gap between two other days. Behind, for all of them, lay sets and sequences, the long waits under the crane that swung the microphone, the hundred miles a day by automobiles to and fro across a county, the struggles of rival ingenuities in the conference rooms, the ceaseless compromise, the clash and strain of many personalities fighting for their lives. And now Sunday, with individual life starting up again, with a glow kindling in eyes that had been glazed with monotony the afternoon before. Slowly as the hours waned they came awake like "Puppenfeen" in a toy shop: an intense colloquy in a corner, lovers disappearing to neck in a hall. And the feeling of "Hurry, it's not too late, but for God's sake hurry before the blessed forty hours of leisure are over."

Joel Coles was writing continuity. He was twenty-eight and not yet broken by Hollywood. He had had what were considered nice assignments since his arrival six months before and he submitted his scenes and sequences with enthusiasm. He referred to himself modestly as a hack but really did not think of it that way. His mother had been a successful actress; Joel had spent his childhood between London and New York trying to separate the real from the unreal, or at least to keep one guess ahead. He was a handsome man with the pleasant cow-brown eyes that in 1913 had gazed out at Broadway audiences from his mother's face.

When the invitation came it made him sure that he was getting somewhere. Ordinarily he did not go out on Sundays but stayed sober and took work home with him. Recently they had given him a Eugene O'Neill play destined for a very important lady indeed. Everything he had done so far had pleased Miles Calman, and Miles Calman was the only director on the lot who did not work under a supervisor and was responsible to the money men alone. Everything was clicking into place in Joel's career. ("This is Mr. Calman's secretary. Will you come to tea from four to six Sunday—he lives in Beverly Hills, number———.")

Joel was flattered. It would be a party out of the top-drawer. It was a tribute to himself as a young man of promise. The Marion Davies crowd, the high-hats, the big currency numbers, perhaps even Dietrich and Garbo and the Marquis, people who were not seen everywhere, would probably be at Calman's.

"I won't take anything to drink," he assured himself. Calman was audibly tired of rummies, and thought it was a pity the industry could not get along without them.

Joel agreed that writers drank too much—he did himself, but he wouldn't this afternoon. He wished Miles would be within hearing when the cocktails were passed to hear his succinct, unobtrusive, "No, thank you."

Miles Calman's house was built for great emotional moments—there was an air of listening, as if the far silences of its vistas hid an audience, but this afternoon it was thronged, as though people had been bidden rather than asked. Joel noted with pride that only two other writers from the studio were in the crowd, an ennobled limey and, somewhat to his surprise, Nat Keogh, who had evoked Calman's impatient comment on drunks.

Stella Calman (Stella Walker, of course) did not move on to her other guests after she spoke to Joel. She lingered—she looked at him with the sort of beautiful look that demands some sort of acknowledgment and Joel drew quickly on the dramatic adequacy inherited from his mother:

"Well, you look about sixteen! Where's your kiddy car?"

She was visibly pleased; she lingered. He felt that he should say something more, something confident and easy—he had first met her when she was struggling for bits in New York. At the moment a tray slid up and Stella put a cocktail glass into his hand.

"Everybody's afraid, aren't they?" he said, looking at it absently. "Everybody watches for everybody else's blunders, or tries to make sure they're with people that'll do them credit. Of course that's not true in your house," he covered himself hastily. "I just meant generally in Hollywood."

Stella agreed. She presented several people to Joel as if he were very important. Reassuring himself that Miles was at the other side of the room, Joel drank the cocktail.

"So you have a baby?" he said. "That's the time to look out. After a pretty woman has had her first child, she's very vulnerable, because she wants to be reassured about her own charm. She's got to have some new man's unqualified devotion to prove to herself she hasn't lost anything."

"I never get anybody's unqualified devotion," Stella said rather resentfully.

"They're afraid of your husband."

"You think that's it?" She wrinkled her brow over the idea; then the conversation was interrupted at the exact moment Joel would have chosen.

Her attentions had given him confidence. Not for him to join safe groups, to slink to refuge under the wings of such acquaintances as he saw about the room. He walked to the window and looked out towards the Pacific, colourless under its sluggish sunset. It was good here—the American Riviera and all that, if there were ever time to enjoy it. The handsome, well-dressed people in the room, the lovely girls, and the—well, the lovely girls. You couldn't have everything.

He saw Stella's fresh boyish face, with the tired eyelid that always drooped a little over one eye, moving about among her guests and he wanted to sit with her and talk a long time as if she were a girl instead of a name; he followed her to see if she paid anyone as much attention as she had paid him. He took another cocktail—not because he needed confidence but because she had given him so much of it. Then he sat down beside the director's mother.

"Your son's gotten to be a legend, Mrs. Calman—Oracle and a Man of Destiny and all that. Personally, I'm against him but I'm in a minority. What do you think of him? Are you impressed? Are you surprised how far he's gone?"

"No, I'm not surprised," she said calmly. "We always expected a lot from Miles."

"Well now, that's unusual," remarked Joel. "I always think all mothers are like Napoleon's mother. My mother didn't want me to have anything to do with the entertainment business. She wanted me to go to West Point and be safe."

"We always had every confidence in Miles." . . .

He stood by the built-in bar of the dining-room with the good-humoured, heavy-drinking, highly paid Nat Keogh.

"—I made a hundred grand during the year and lost forty grand gambling, so now I've hired a manager."

"You mean an agent," suggested Joel.

"No, I've got that too. I mean a manager. I make over everything to my wife and then he and my wife get together and hand me out the money. I pay him five thousand a year to hand me out my money."

"You mean your agent."

"No, I mean my manager, and I'm not the only one—a lot of other irresponsible people have him."

"Well, if you're irresponsible why are you responsible enough to hire a manager?"

"I'm just irresponsible about gambling. Look here—"

A singer performed; Joel and Nat went forward with the others to listen.

II

The singing reached Joel vaguely; he felt happy and friendly towards all the people gathered there, people of bravery and industry, superior to bourgeoisie that outdid them in ignorance and loose living, risen to a position of the highest prominence in a nation that for a decade had wanted only to be entertained. He liked them—he loved them. Great waves of good feeling flowed through him.

As the singer finished his number and there was a drift towards the hostess to say good-bye, Joel had an idea. He would give them "Building It Up," his own composition. It was his only parlour trick, it had amused several parties and it might please Stella Walker. Possessed by the hunch, his blood throbbing with the scarlet corpuscles of exhibitionism, he sought her.

"Of course," she cried. "Please! Do you need anything?"

"Someone has to be the secretary that I'm supposed to be dictating to."

"I'll be her."

As the word spread, the guests in the hall, already putting on their coats to leave, drifted back and Joel faced the eyes of many strangers. He had a dim foreboding, realizing that the man who had just performed was a famous radio entertainer. Then someone said "Sh!" and he was alone with Stella, the centre of a sinister Indian-like half-circle. Stella smiled up at him expectantly—he began.

His burlesque was based upon the cultural limitations of Mr. Dave Silverstein, an independent producer; Silverstein was presumed to be dictating a letter outlining a treatment of a story he had bought.

"—a story of divorce, the younger generators and the Foreign Legion," he heard his voice saying, with the intonations of Mr. Silverstein. "But we got to build it up, see?"

A sharp pang of doubt struck through him. The faces surrounding him in the gently moulded light were intent and curious, but there was no ghost of a smile anywhere; directly in front the Great Lover of the screen glared at him with an eye as keen as the eye of a potato. Only Stella Walker looked up at him with a radiant, never faltering smile.

"If we make him a Menjou type, then we get a sort of Michael Arlen only with a Honolulu atmosphere."

Still not a ripple in front, but in the rear a rustling, a perceptible shift towards the left, towards the front door.

"—then she says she feels this sex appeal for him and he burns out and says, 'Oh, go on destroy yourself—' "

At some point he heard Nat Keogh snicker and here and there were a few encouraging faces, but as he finished he had the sickening realization that he had made a fool of himself in view of an important section of the picture world, upon whose favour depended his career.

For a moment he existed in the midst of a confused silence, broken by a general trek for the door. He felt the undercurrent of derision that rolled through the gossip; then—all this was in the space of ten seconds—the Great Lover, his eye hard and empty as the eye of a needle, shouted "Boo! Boo!" voicing in an overtone what he felt was the mood of the crowd. It was the resentment of the professional towards the amateur, of the community towards the stranger, the thumbs-down of the clan.

Only Stella Walker was still standing near and thanking him as if he had been an unparalleled success, as if it hadn't occurred to her that anyone hadn't liked it. As Nat Keogh helped him into his overcoat, a great wave of self-disgust swept over him and he clung desperately to his rule of never betraying an inferior emotion until he no longer felt it.

"I was a flop," he said lightly, to Stella. "Never mind, it's a good number when appreciated. Thanks for your co-operation."

The smile did not leave her face—he bowed rather drunkenly and Nat drew him towards the door. . . .

The arrival of his breakfast awakened him into a broken and ruined world. Yesterday he was himself, a point of fire against an industry, to-day he felt that he was pitted under an enormous disadvantage, against those faces, against individual contempt and collective sneer. Worse than that, to Miles Calman he was to become one of those rummies, stripped of dignity, whom Calman regretted he was compelled to use. To Stella Walker on whom he had forced a martyrdom to preserve the courtesy of her house—her opinion he did not dare to guess. His gastric juices ceased to flow and he set his poached eggs back on the telephone table. He wrote:

Dear Miles:

You can imagine my profound self-disgust. I confess to a taint of exhibitionism, but at six o'clock in the afternoon, in broad daylight! Good God! My apologies to your wife.

Yours ever,

Joel Coles

Joel emerged from his office on the lot only to slink like a malefactor to the tobacco store. So suspicious was his manner that one of the studio police asked to see his admission card. He had decided to eat lunch outside when Nat Keogh, confident and cheerful, overtook him.

"What do you mean you're in permanent retirement? What if that Three-Piece Suit did boo you?

"Why, listen," he continued, drawing Joel into the studio restaurant. "The night of one of his premières at Grauman's, Joe Squires kicked his tail while he was bowing to the crowd. The ham said Joe'd hear from him later but when Joe called him up at eight o'clock next day and said, 'I thought I was going to hear from you,' he hung up the phone."

The preposterous story cheered Joel, and he found a gloomy consolation in staring at the group at the next table, the sad, lovely Siamese twins, the mean dwarfs, the proud giant from the circus picture. But looking beyond at the yellow-stained faces of pretty women, their eyes all melancholy and startling with mascara, their ball gowns garish in full day, he saw a group who had been at Calman's and winced.

"Never again," he exclaimed aloud, "absolutely my last social appearance in Hollywood!"

The following morning a telegram was waiting for him at his office:

> You were one of the most agreeable people at our party. Expect you at my sister June's buffet supper next Sunday.
>
> Stella Walker Calman

The blood rushed fast through his veins for a feverish minute. Incredulously he read the telegram over.

"Well, that's the sweetest thing I ever heard of in my life!"

III

Crazy Sunday again. Joel slept until eleven, then he read a newspaper to catch up with the past week. He lunched in his room on trout, avocado salad and a pint of California wine. Dressing for the tea, he selected a pin-check suit, a blue shirt, a burnt orange tie. There were dark circles of fatigue under his eyes. In his second-hand car he drove to the Riviera apartments. As he was introducing himself to Stella's sister, Miles and Stella arrived in riding clothes—they had been quarrelling fiercely most of the afternoon on all the dirt roads back of Beverly Hills.

Miles Calman, tall, nervous, with a desperate humour and the unhappiest eyes Joel ever saw, was an artist from the top of his curiously shaped head to his nig-

gerish feet. Upon these last he stood firmly—he had never made a cheap picture though he had sometimes paid heavily for the luxury of making experimental
flops. In spite of his excellent company, one could not be with him long without realizing that he was not a well man.

From the moment of their entrance Joel's day bound itself up inextricably
with theirs. As he joined the group around them Stella turned away from it with
an impatient little tongue click—and Miles Calman said to the man who happened to be next to him:

"Go easy on Eva Goebel. There's hell to pay about her at home." Miles
turned to Joel, "I'm sorry I missed you at the office yesterday. I spent the afternoon at the analyst's."

"You being psychoanalysed?"

"I have been for months. First I went for claustrophobia, now I'm trying to
get my whole life cleared up. They say it'll take over a year."

"There's nothing the matter with your life," Joel assured him.

"Oh, no? Well, Stella seems to think so. Ask anybody—they can all tell you
about it," he said bitterly.

A girl perched herself on the arm of Miles's chair; Joel crossed to Stella, who
stood disconsolately by the fire.

"Thank you for your telegram," he said. "It was darn sweet. I can't imagine
anybody as good-looking as you are being so good-humoured."

She was a little lovelier than he had ever seen her and perhaps the unstinted
admiration in his eyes prompted her to unload on him—it did not take long, for
she was obviously at the emotional bursting point.

"—and Miles has been carrying on this thing for two years, and I never knew.
Why, she was one of my best friends, always in the house. Finally when people
began to come to me, Miles had to admit it."

She sat down vehemently on the arm of Joel's chair. Her riding breeches were
the colour of the chair and Joel saw that the mass of her hair was made up of
some strands of red gold and some of pale gold, so that it could not be dyed,
and that she had on no make-up. She was that good-looking—

Still quivering with the shock of her discovery, Stella found unbearable the
spectacle of a new girl hovering over Miles; she led Joel into a bedroom, and
seated at either end of a big bed they went on talking. People on their way to
the washroom glanced in and made wisecracks, but Stella, emptying out her
story, paid no attention. After a while Miles stuck his head in the door and said,
"There's no use trying to explain something to Joel in half an hour that I don't
understand myself and the psychoanalyst says will take a whole year to understand."

She talked on as if Miles were not there. She loved Miles, she said—under
considerable difficulties she had always been faithful to him.

"The psychoanalyst told Miles that he had a mother complex. In his first marriage he transferred his mother complex to his wife, you see—and then his sex turned to me. But when we married the thing repeated itself—he transferred his mother complex to me and all his libido turned towards this other woman."

Joel knew that this probably wasn't gibberish—yet it sounded like gibberish. He knew Eva Goebel; she was a motherly person, older and probably wiser than Stella, who was a golden child.

Miles now suggested impatiently that Joel come back with them since Stella had so much to say, so they drove out to the mansion in Beverly Hills. Under the high ceilings the situation seemed more dignified and tragic. It was an eerie bright night with the dark very clear outside of all the windows and Stella all rose-gold raging and crying around the room. Joel did not quite believe in picture actresses' grief. They have other preoccupations—they are beautiful rose-gold figures blown full of life by writers and directors, and after hours they sit around and talk in whispers and giggle innuendoes, and the ends of many adventures flow through them.

Sometimes he pretended to listen and instead thought how well she was got up—sleek breeches with a matched set of legs in them, an Italian-coloured sweater with a little high neck, and a short brown chamois coat. He couldn't decide whether she was an imitation of an English lady or an English lady was an imitation of her. She hovered somewhere between the realest of realities and the most blatant of impersonations.

"Miles is so jealous of me that he questions everything I do," she cried scornfully. "When I was in New York I wrote him that I'd been to the theatre with Eddie Baker. Miles was so jealous he phoned me ten times in one day."

"I was wild," Miles snuffled sharply, a habit he had in times of stress. "The analyst couldn't get any results for a week."

Stella shook her head despairingly. "Did you expect me just to sit in the hotel for three weeks?"

"I don't expect anything. I admit that I'm jealous. I try not to be. I worked on that with Dr. Bridgebane, but it didn't do any good. I was jealous of Joel this afternoon when you sat on the arm of his chair."

"You were?" She started up. "You were! Wasn't there somebody on the arm of your chair? And did you speak to me for two hours?"

"You were telling your troubles to Joel in the bedroom."

"When I think that that woman"—she seemed to believe that to omit Eva Goebel's name would be to lessen her reality—"used to come here—"

"All right—all right," said Miles wearily. "I've admitted everything and I feel as bad about it as you do." Turning to Joel he began talking about pictures, while Stella moved restlessly along the far walls, her hands in her breeches pockets.

"They've treated Miles terribly," she said, coming suddenly back into the conversation as if they'd never discussed her personal affairs. "Dear, tell him about old Beltzer trying to change your picture."

As she stood hovering protectively over Miles, her eyes flashing with indignation in his behalf, Joel realized that he was in love with her. Stifled with excitement he got up to say good night.

With Monday the week resumed its workaday rhythm, in sharp contrast to the theoretical discussions, the gossip and scandal of Sunday; there was the endless detail of script revision—"Instead of a lousy dissolve, we can leave her voice on the sound track and cut to a medium shot of the taxi from Bell's angle or we can simply pull the camera back to include the station, hold it a minute and then pan to the row of taxis"—by Monday afternoon Joel had again forgotten that people whose business was to provide entertainment were ever privileged to be entertained. In the evening he phoned Miles's house. He asked for Miles but Stella came to the phone.

"Do things seem better?"

"Not particularly. What are you doing next Saturday evening?"

"Nothing."

"The Perrys are giving a dinner and theatre party and Miles won't be here— he's flying to South Bend to see the Notre Dame-California game. I thought you might go with me in his place."

After a long moment Joel said, "Why—surely. If there's a conference I can't make dinner but I can get to the theatre."

"Then I'll say we can come."

Joel walked to his office. In view of the strained relations of the Calmans, would Miles be pleased, or did she intend that Miles shouldn't know of it? That would be out of the question—if Miles didn't mention it Joel would. But it was an hour or more before he could get down to work again.

Wednesday there was a four-hour wrangle in a conference room crowded with planets and nebulæ of cigarette smoke. Three men and a woman paced the carpet in turn, suggesting or condemning, speaking sharply or persuasively, confidently or despairingly. At the end Joel lingered to talk to Miles.

The man was tired—not with the exaltation of fatigue but life-tired, with his lids sagging and his beard prominent over the blue shadows near his mouth.

"I hear you're flying to the Notre Dame game."

Miles looked beyond him and shook his head.

"I've given up the idea."

"Why?"

"On account of you." Still he did not look at Joel.

"What the hell, Miles?"

"That's why I've given it up." He broke into a perfunctory laugh at himself.

"I can't tell what Stella might do just out of spite—she's invited you to take her to the Perrys', hasn't she? I wouldn't enjoy the game."

The fine instinct that moved swiftly and confidently on the set muddled so weakly and helplessly through his personal life.

"Look, Miles," Joel said frowning. "I've never made any passes whatsoever at Stella. If you're really seriously cancelling your trip on account of me, I won't go to the Perrys' with her. I won't see her. You can trust me absolutely."

Miles looked at him, carefully now.

"Maybe." He shrugged his shoulders. "Anyhow there'd just be somebody else. I wouldn't have any fun."

"You don't seem to have much confidence in Stella. She told me she'd always been true to you."

"Maybe she has." In the last few minutes several more muscles had sagged around Miles's mouth. "But how can I ask anything of her after what's happened? How can I expect her—" He broke off and his face grew harder as he said, "I'll tell you one thing, right or wrong and no matter what I've done, if I ever had anything on her I'd divorce her. I can't have my pride hurt—that would be the last straw."

His tone annoyed Joel, but he said:

"Hasn't she calmed down about the Eva Goebel thing?"

"No." Miles snuffled pessimistically. "I can't get over it either."

"I thought it was finished."

"I'm trying not to see Eva again, but you know it isn't easy just to drop something like that—it isn't some girl I kissed last night in a taxi. The psychoanalyst says—"

"I know," Joel interrupted. "Stella told me." This was depressing. "Well, as far as I'm concerned if you go to the game I won't see Stella. And I'm sure Stella has nothing on her conscience about anybody."

"Maybe not," Miles repeated listlessly. "Anyhow I'll stay and take her to the party. Say," he said suddenly, "I wish you'd come too. I've got to have somebody sympathetic to talk to. That's the trouble—I've influenced Stella in everything. Especially I've influenced her so that she likes all the men I like—it's very difficult."

"It must be," Joel agreed.

IV

Joel could not get to the dinner. Self-conscious in his silk hat against the unemployment, he waited for the others in front of the Hollywood Theatre and watched the evening parade: obscure replicas of bright, particular picture stars, spavined men in polo coats, a stomping dervish with the beard and staff of an apostle, a pair of chic Filipinos in collegiate clothes, reminder that this corner of the Republic opened to the seven seas, a long fantastic carnival of young shouts which proved to be a fraternity initiation. The line split to pass two smart limousines that stopped at the curb.

There she was, in a dress like ice-water, made in a thousand pale-blue pieces, with icicles trickling at the throat. He started forward.

"So you like my dress?"

"Where's Miles?"

"He flew to the game after all. He left yesterday morning—at least I think—" She broke off. "I just got a telegram from South Bend saying that he's starting back. I forgot—you know all these people?"

The party of eight moved into the theatre.

Miles had gone after all and Joel wondered if he should have come. But during the performance, with Stella a profile under the pure grain of light hair, he thought no more about Miles. Once he turned and looked at her and she looked back at him, smiling and meeting his eyes for as long as he wanted. Between the acts they smoked in the lobby and she whispered:

"They're all going to the opening of Jack Johnson's night club—I don't want to go, do you?"

"Do we have to?"

"I suppose not." She hesitated. "I'd like to talk to you. I suppose we could go to our house—if I were only sure—"

Again she hesitated and Joel asked:

"Sure of what?"

"Sure that—oh, I'm haywire I know, but how can I be sure Miles went to the game?"

"You mean you think he's with Eva Goebel?"

"No, not so much that—but supposing he was here watching everything I do. You know Miles does odd things sometimes. Once he wanted a man with a long beard to drink tea with him and he sent down to the casting agency for one, and drank tea with him all afternoon."

"That's different. He sent you a wire from South Bend—that proves he's at the game."

After the play they said good night to the others at the curb and were answered by looks of amusement. They slid off along the golden garish thoroughfare through the crowd that had gathered around Stella.

"You see he could arrange the telegrams," Stella said, "very easily."

That was true. And with the idea that perhaps her uneasiness was justified, Joel grew angry: if Miles had trained a camera on them he felt no obligations towards Miles. Aloud he said:

"That's nonsense."

There were Christmas trees already in the shop windows and the full moon over the boulevard was only a prop, as scenic as the giant boudoir lamps of the corners. On into the dark foliage of Beverly Hills that flamed as eucalyptus by day, Joel saw only the flash of a white face under his own, the arc of her shoulder. She pulled away suddenly and looked up at him.

"Your eyes are like your mother's," she said. "I used to have a scrap book full of pictures of her."

"Your eyes are like your own and not a bit like any other eyes," he answered.

Something made Joel look out into the grounds as they went into the house, as if Miles were lurking in the shubbery. A telegram waited on the hall table. She read aloud:

Chicago

Home tomorrow night. Thinking of you. Love.

Miles

"You see," she said, throwing the slip back on the table, "he could easily have faked that." She asked the butler for drinks and sandwiches and ran upstairs, while Joel walked into the empty receptions rooms. Strolling about he wandered to the piano where he had stood in disgrace two Sundays before.

"Then we could put over," he said aloud, "a story of divorce, the younger generation and the Foreign Legion."

His thoughts jumped to another telegram.

"You were one of the most agreeable people at our party—"

An idea occurred to him. If Stella's telegram had been purely a gesture of courtesy then it was likely that Miles had inspired it, for it was Miles who had invited him. Probably Miles had said:

"Send him a wire—he's miserable—he thinks he's queered himself."

It fitted in with "I've influenced Stella in everything. Especially I've influenced her so that she likes all the men I like." A woman would do a thing like that because she felt sympathetic—only a man would do it because he felt responsible.

When Stella came back into the room he took both her hands.

"I have a strange feeling that I'm a sort of pawn in a spite game you're playing against Miles," he said.

"Help yourself to a drink."

"And the odd thing is that I'm in love with you anyhow."

The telephone rang and she freed herself to answer it.

"Another wire from Miles," she announced. "He dropped it, or it says he dropped it, from the aeroplane at Kansas City."

"I suppose he asked to be remembered to me."

"No, he just said he loved me. I believe he does. He's so very weak."

"Come sit beside me," Joel urged her.

It was early. And it was still a few minutes short of midnight a half-hour later, when Joel walked to the cold hearth, and said tersely:

"Meaning that you haven't any curiosity about me?"

"Not at all. You attract me a lot and you know it. The point is that I suppose I really do love Miles."

"Obviously."

"And to-night I feel uneasy about everything."

He wasn't angry—he was even faintly relieved that a possible entanglement was avoided. Still as he looked at her, the warmth and softness of her body thawing her cold blue costume, he knew she was one of the things he would always regret.

"I've got to go," he said. "I'll phone a taxi."

"Nonsense—there's a chauffeur on duty."

He winced at her readiness to have him go, and seeing this she kissed him lightly and said, "You're sweet, Joel." Then suddenly three things happened: he took down his drink at a gulp, the phone rang loud through the house and a clock in the hall struck in trumpet notes.

Nine—ten—eleven—twelve—

V

It was Sunday again. Joel realized that he had come to the theatre this evening with the work of the week still hanging about him like cerements. He had made love to Stella as he might attack some matter to be cleaned up hurriedly before the day's end. But this was Sunday—the lovely, lazy perspective of the next twenty-four hours unrolled before him—every minute was something to be approached with lulling indirection, every moment held the germ of innumerable possibilities. Nothing was impossible—everything was just beginning. He poured himself another drink.

With a sharp moan, Stella slipped forward inertly by the telephone. Joel picked her up and laid her on the sofa. He squirted soda-water on a handkerchief and slapped it over her face. The telephone mouthpiece was still grinding and he put it to his ear.

"—the plane fell just this side of Kansas City. The body of Miles Calman has been identified and—"

He hung up the receiver.

"Lie still," he said, stalling, as Stella opened her eyes.

"Oh, what's happened?" she whispered. "Call them back. Oh, what's happened?"

"I'll call them right away. What's your doctor's name?"

"Did they say Miles was dead?"

"Lie quiet—is there a servant still up?"

"Hold me—I'm frightened."

He put his arm around her.

"I want the name of your doctor," he said sternly. "It may be a mistake but I want someone here."

"It's Doctor—Oh, God, is Miles dead?"

Joel ran upstairs and searched through strange medicine cabinets for spirits of ammonia. When he came down Stella cried:

"He isn't dead—I know he isn't. This is part of his scheme. He's torturing me. I know he's alive. I can feel he's alive."

"I want to get hold of some close friend of yours, Stella. You can't stay here alone to-night."

"Oh, no," she cried. "I can't see anybody. You stay, I haven't got any friend." She got up, tears streaming down her face. "Oh, Miles is my only friend. He's not dead—he can't be dead. I'm going there right away and see. Get a train. You'll have to come with me."

"You can't. There's nothing to do to-night. I want you to tell me the name of some woman I can call: Lois? Joan? Carmel? Isn't there somebody?"

Stella stared at him blindly.

"Eva Goebel was my best friend," she said.

Joel thought of Miles, his sad and desperate face in the office two days before. In the awful silence of his death all was clear about him. He was the only American-born director with both an interesting temperament and an artistic conscience. Meshed in an industry, he had paid with his ruined nerves for having no resilience, no healthy cynicism, no refuge—only a pitiful and precarious escape.

There was a sound at the outer door—it opened suddenly, and there were footsteps in the hall.

"Miles!" Stella screamed. "Is it you, Miles? Oh, it's Miles."

A telegraph boy appeared in the doorway.

"I couldn't find the bell. I heard you talking inside."

The telegram was a duplicate of the one that had been phoned. While Stella read it over and over, as though it were a black lie, Joel telephoned. It was still early and he had difficulty getting anyone; when finally he succeeded in finding some friends he made Stella take a stiff drink.

"You'll stay here, Joel," she whispered, as though she were half-asleep. "You won't go away. Miles liked you—he said you—" She shivered violently, "Oh, my God, you don't know how alone I feel!" Her eyes closed. "Put your arms around me. Miles had a suit like that." She started bolt upright. "Think of what he must have felt. He was afraid of almost everything, anyhow."

She shook her head dazedly. Suddenly she seized Joel's face and held it close to hers.

"You won't go. You like me—you love me, don't you? Don't call up anybody. To-morrow's time enough. You stay here with me to-night."

He stared at her, at first incredulously, and then with shocked understanding. In her dark groping Stella was trying to keep Miles alive by sustaining a situation in which he had figured—as if Miles's mind could not die so long as the possibilities that had worried him still existed. It was a distraught and tortured effort to stave off the realization that he was dead.

Resolutely Joel went to the phone and called a doctor.

"Don't, oh, don't call anybody!" Stella cried. "Come back here and put your arms around me."

"Is Doctor Bales in?"

"Joel," Stella cried. "I thought I could count on you. Miles liked you. He was jealous of you—Joel, come here."

Ah then—if he betrayed Miles she would be keeping him alive—for if he were really dead how could he be betrayed?

"—has just had a very severe shock. Can you come at once, and get hold of a nurse?"

"Joel!"

Now the door-bell and the telephone began to ring intermittently, and automobiles were stopping in front of the door.

"But you're not going," Stella begged him. "You're going to stay, aren't you?"

"No," he answered. "But I'll be back, if you need me."

Standing on the steps of the house which now hummed and palpitated with the life that flutters around death like protective leaves, he began to sob a little in his throat.

"Everything he touched he did something magical to," he thought. "He even brought that little gamine alive and made her a sort of masterpiece."

And then:

"What a hell of a hole he leaves in this damn wilderness—already!"

And then with a certain bitterness, "Oh, yes, I'll be back—I'll be back!"

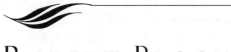

ROBERT BLOCH

Robert Bloch (1917–1994) won film immortality for providing Hitchcock with the materials for Psycho. *But he was a prolific author of novels, screenplays, and short stories, and in this little-known tale he uses the freedom of fantasy in order to explain the curious lure that draws extras back day after day to work long hours and be treated like cattle, for a few dollars and the promise of proximity to cinematic glory. This story strikes a chord in me because I have often met people so obsessed with the movies that they scrutinize them deeply, trying to extract hidden signs and messages.*

"The Movie People"

Two thousand stars.

Two thousand stars, maybe more, set in the sidewalks along Hollywood Boulevard, each metal slab inscribed with the name of someone in the movie industry. They go way back, those names; from Broncho Billy Anderson to Adolph Zukor, everybody's there.

Everybody but Jimmy Rogers.

You won't find Jimmy's name because he wasn't a star, not even a bit player—just an extra.

"But I deserve it," he told me. "I'm entitled, if anybody is. Started out here in 1920 when I was just a punk kid. You look close, you'll spot me in the crowd shots in *The Mark of Zorro*. Been in over 450 pictures since, and still going strong. Ain't many left who can beat that record. You'd think it would entitle a fella to something."

Maybe it did, but there was no star for Jimmy Rogers, and that bit about still going strong was just a crock. Nowadays Jimmy was lucky if he got a casting call once or twice a year; there just isn't any spot for an old-timer with a white muff except in a western barroom scene.

Most of the time Jimmy just strolled the boulevard; a tall, soldierly-erect incongruity in the crowd of tourists, fags and freakouts. His home address was on Las Palmas, somewhere south of Sunset. I'd never been there but I could guess what it was—one of those old frame bungalow-court sweatboxes put up about the time he crashed the movies and still standing somehow by the grace of God and the disgrace of the housing authorities. That's the sort of place Jimmy stayed at, but he didn't really *live* there.

Jimmy Rogers lived at the Silent Movie.

The Silent Movie is over on Fairfax, and it's the only place in town where you can still go and see *The Mark of Zorro.* There's always a Chaplin comedy, and usually Laurel and Hardy, along with a serial starring Pearl White, Elmo Lincoln, or Houdini. And the features are great—early Griffith and DeMille, Barrymore in *Dr. Jekyll and Mr. Hyde,* Lon Chaney in *The Hunchback of Notre Dame,* Valentino in *Blood and Sand,* and a hundred more.

The bill changes every Wednesday, and every Wednesday night Jimmy Rogers was there, plunking down his ninety cents at the box office to watch *The Black Pirate* or *Son of the Shiek* or *Orphans of the Storm.*

To live again.

Because Jimmy didn't go there to see Doug and Mary or Rudy or Clara or Gloria or the Gish sisters. He went there to see himself, in the crowd shots.

At least that's the way I figured it, the first time I met him. They were playing *The Phantom of the Opera* that night, and afterward I spent the intermission with a cigarette outside the theatre, studying the display of stills.

If you asked me under oath, I couldn't tell you how our conversation started, but that's where I first heard Jimmy's routine about the 450 pictures and still going strong.

"Did you see me in there tonight?" he asked.

I stared at him and shook my head; even with the shabby hand-me-down suit and the white beard, Jimmy Rogers wasn't the kind you'd spot in an audience.

"Guess it was too dark for me to notice," I said.

"But there were torches," Jimmy told me. "I carried one."

Then I got the message. He was in the picture.

Jimmy smiled and shrugged. "Hell, I keep forgetting. You wouldn't recognize me. We did *The Phantom* way back in 'twenty-five. I looked so young they slapped a mustache on me in Make-up and a black wig. Hard to spot me in the catacombs scenes—all long shots. But there at the end, where Chaney is holding back the mob, I show up pretty good in the background, just left of Charley Zimmer. He's the one shaking his fist. I'm waving my torch. Had a lot of trouble with that picture, but we did this shot in one take."

In weeks to come I saw more of Jimmy Rogers. Sometimes he was up there on the screen, though truth to tell, I never did recognize him: he was a young man in those films of the twenties, and his appearances were limited to a flickering flash, a blurred face glimpsed in a crowd.

But always Jimmy was in the audience, even though he hadn't played in the picture. And one night I found out why.

Again it was intermission time and we were standing outside. By now Jimmy had gotten into the habit of talking to me and tonight we'd been seated together during the showing of *The Covered Wagon*.

We stood outside and Jimmy blinked at me. "Wasn't she beautiful?" he asked. "They don't look like that any more."

I nodded. "Lois Wilson? Very attractive."

"I'm talking about June."

I stared at Jimmy and then I realized he wasn't blinking. He was crying.

"June Logan. My girl. This was her first bit, the Indian attack scene. Must have been seventeen—I didn't know her then, it was two years later we met over at First National. But you must have noticed her. She was the one with the long blond curls."

"Oh, *that* one." I nodded again. "You're right. She was lovely."

And I was a liar, because I didn't remember seeing her at all, but I wanted to make the old man feel good.

"Junie's in a lot of the pictures they show here. And from 'twenty-five on, we played in a flock of 'em together. For a while we talked about getting hitched, but she started working her way up, doing bits—maids and such—and I never broke out of extra work. Both of us had been in the business long enough to know it was no go, not when one of you stays small and the other is headed for a big career."

Jimmy managed a grin as he wiped his eyes with something which might once have been a handkerchief. "You think I'm kidding, don't you? About the career, I mean. But she was going great, she would have been playing second leads pretty soon."

"What happened?" I asked.

The grin dissolved and the blinking returned. "Sound killed her."

"She didn't have a voice for talkies?"

Jimmy shook his head. "She had a great voice. I told you she was all set for second leads—by nineteen thirty she'd been in a dozen talkies. Then sound killed her."

I'd heard the expression a thousand times, but never like this. Because the way Jimmy told the story, that's exactly what had happened. June Logan, his girl Junie, was on the set during the shooting of one of those early ALL TALKING—ALL SINGING—ALL DANCING epics. The director and camera crew, seeking to break away from the tyranny of the stationary microphone, rigged up one of the first traveling mikes on a boom. Such items weren't standard equipment yet, and this was an experiment. Somehow, during a take, it broke loose and the boom crashed, crushing June Logan's skull.

It never made the papers, not even the trades; the studio hushed it up and June Logan had a quiet funeral.

"Damn near forty years ago," Jimmy said. "And here I am, crying like it was yesterday. But she was my girl—"

And that was the other reason why Jimmy Rogers went to the Silent Movie. To visit his girl.

"Don't you see?" he told me. "She's still alive up there on the screen, in all those pictures. Just the way she was when we were together. Five years we had, the best years for me."

I could see that. The two of them in love, with each other and with the movies. Because in those days, people *did* love the movies. And to actually be *in* them, even in tiny roles, was the average person's idea of seventh heaven.

Seventh Heaven, that's another film we saw with June Logan playing a crowd scene. In the following weeks, with Jimmy's help, I got so I could spot his girl. And he'd told the truth—she was a beauty. Once you noticed her, really saw her, you wouldn't forget. Those blond ringlets, that smile, identified her immediately.

One Wednesday night Jimmy and I were sitting together watching *The Birth of a Nation.* During a street shot Jimmy nudged my shoulder. "Look, there's June."

I peered up at the screen, then shook my head. "I don't see her."

"Wait a second—there she is again. See, off to the left, behind Walthall's shoulder?"

There was a blurred image and then the camera followed Henry B. Walthall as he moved away.

I glanced at Jimmy. He was rising from his seat.

"Where you going?"

He didn't answer me, just marched outside.

When I followed I found him leaning against the wall under the marquee and breathing hard; his skin was the color of his whiskers.

"Junie," he murmured. "I saw her—"

I took a deep breath. "Listen to me. You told me her first picture was *The Covered Wagon.* That was made in 1923. And Griffith shot *The Birth of a Nation* in 1914."

Jimmy didn't say anything. There was nothing to say. We both knew what we were going to do—march back into the theatre and see the second show.

When the scene screened again we were watching and waiting. I looked at the screen, then glanced at Jimmy.

"She's gone," he whispered. "She's not in the picture."

"She never was," I told him. "You know that."

"Yeah." Jimmy got up and drifted out into the night, and I didn't see him again until the following week.

That's when they showed the short feature with Charles Ray—I've forgotten the title, but he played his usual country-boy role, and there was a baseball game in the climax with Ray coming through to win.

The camera panned across the crowd sitting in the bleachers and I caught a momentary glimpse of a smiling girl with long blond curls.

"Did you see her?" Jimmy grabbed my arm.

"That girl—"

"It was Junie. She winked at me!"

This time I was the one who got up and walked out. He followed, and I was waiting in front of the theatre, right next to the display poster.

"See for yourself." I nodded at the poster. "This picture was made in 1917." I forced a smile. "You forget, there were thousands of pretty blond extras in pictures and most of them wore curls."

He stood there shaking, not listening to me at all, and I put my hand on his shoulder. "Now look here—"

"I *been* looking here," Jimmy said. "Week after week, year after year. And you might as well know the truth. This ain't the first time it's happened. Junie keeps turning up in picture after picture I know she never made. Not just the early ones, before her time, but later, during the twenties when I knew her, when I knew exactly what she was playing in. Sometimes it's only a quick flash, but I see her—then she's gone again. And the next running, she doesn't come back.

"It got so that for a while I was almost afraid to go see a show—figured I was cracking up. But now you've seen her too—"

I shook my head slowly. "Sorry, Jimmy. I never said that." I glanced at him, then gestured toward my car at the curb. "You look tired. Come on, I'll drive you home."

He looked worse than tired; he looked lost and lonely and infinitely old. But there was a stubborn glint in his eyes, and he stood his ground.

"No, thanks. I'm gonna stick around for the second show."

As I slid behind the wheel I saw him turn and move into the theatre, into the place where the present becomes the past and the past becomes the present. Up above in the booth they call it a projection machine, but it's really a time machine; it can take you back, play tricks with your imagination and your memory. A girl dead forty years comes alive again, and an old man relives his vanished youth—

But I belonged in the real world, and that's where I stayed. I didn't go to the Silent Movie the next week or the week following.

And the next time I saw Jimmy was almost a month later, on the set.

They were shooting a western, one of my scripts, and the director wanted some additional dialogue to stretch a sequence. So they called me in, and I drove all the way out to location, at the ranch.

Most of the studios have a ranch spread for western action sequences, and this was one of the oldest: it had been in use since the silent days. What fascinated me was the wooden fort where they were doing the crowd scene—I could swear I remembered it from one of the first Tim McCoy pictures. So after I huddled with the director and scribbled a few extra lines for the principals, I began nosing around behind the fort, just out of curiosity, while they set up for the new shots.

Out front was the usual organized confusion; cast and crew milling around the trailers, extras sprawled on the grass drinking coffee. But here in the back I was all alone, prowling around in musty, log-lined rooms built for use in forgotten features. Hoot Gibson had stood at this bar, and Jack Hoxie had swung from this dance-hall chandelier. Here was a dust-covered table where Fred Thomson sat, and around the corner, in the cut-away bunkhouse—

Around the corner, in the cut-away bunkhouse, Jimmy Rogers sat on the edge of a mildewed mattress and stared up at me, startled, as I moved forward.

"You—?"

Quickly I explained my presence. There was no need for him to explain his; casting had called and given him a day's work here in the crowd shots.

"They been stalling all day, and it's hot out there. I figured maybe I could sneak back here and catch me a little nap in the shade."

"How'd you know where to go?" I asked. "Ever been here before?"

"Sure. Forty years ago in this very bunkhouse. Junie and I, we used to come here during lunch break and—"

He stopped.

"What's wrong?"

Something *was* wrong. On the pan make-up face of it, Jimmy Rogers was the perfect picture of the grizzled western old-timer: buckskin britches, fringed shirt, white whiskers and all. But under the make-up was pallor, and the hands holding the envelope were trembling.

The envelope—

He held it out to me. "Here. Mebbe you better read this."

The envelope was unsealed, unstamped, unaddressed. It contained four folded pages covered with fine handwriting. I removed them slowly. Jimmy stared at me.

"Found it lying here on the mattress when I came in," he murmured. "Just waiting for me."

"But what is it? Where'd it come from?"

"Read it and see."

As I started to unfold the pages the whistle blew. We both knew the signal: the scene was set up, they were ready to roll, principals and extras were wanted out there before the cameras.

Jimmy Rogers stood up and moved off, a tired old man shuffling out into the hot sun. I waved at him, then sat down on the moldering mattress and opened the letter. The handwriting was faded, and there was a thin film of dust on the pages. But I could still read it, every word. . . ,

Darling:

I've been trying to reach you so long and in so many ways. Of course I've seen you, but it's so dark out there I can't always be sure, and then too you've changed a lot through the years.

But I *do* see you, quite often, even though it's only for a moment. And I hope you've seen me, because I always try to wink or make some kind of motion to attract your attention.

The only thing is, I can't do too much or show myself too long or it would make trouble. That's the big secret—keeping in the background, so the others won't notice me. It wouldn't do to frighten anybody, or even to get anyone wondering why there are more people in the background of a shot than there should be.

That's something for you to remember, darling, just in case. You're always safe, as long as you stay clear of closeups. Costume pictures are the best—about all you have to do is wave your arms once in a while and shout, "On to the Bastille," or something like that. It really doesn't matter except to lip-readers, because it's silent, of course.

Oh, there's a lot to watch out for. Being a dress extra has its points, but not in ballroom sequences—too much dancing. That goes for parties, too, particularly in a DeMille production where they're "making whoopee" or one of von Stroheim's orgies. Besides, von Stroheim's scenes are always cut.

It doesn't hurt to be cut, don't misunderstand about that. It's no different than an ordinary fadeout at the end of a scene, and then you're free to go into another picture. Anything that was ever made, as long as there's still a print available for running somewhere. It's like falling asleep and then having one dream after another. The dreams are the scenes, of course, but while the scenes are playing, they're real.

I'm not the only one, either. There's no telling how many others do the same thing; maybe hundreds for all I know, but I've recognized a few I'm sure of and I think some of them have recognized me. We never let on to each other that we know, because it wouldn't do to make anybody suspicious.

Sometimes I think that if we could talk it over, we might come up with a better understanding of just how it happens, and why. But the point is, you *can't* talk, everything is silent; all you do is move your lips and if you tried to communicate such a difficult thing in pantomime you'd surely attract attention.

I guess the closest I can come to explaining it is to say it's like reincarnation—you can play a thousand roles, take or reject any part you want, as long as you don't make yourself conspicuous or do something that would change the plot.

Naturally you get used to certain things. The silence, of course. And if you're in a bad print there's flickering; sometimes even the air seems grainy, and for a few frames you may be faded or out of focus.

Which reminds me—another thing to stay away from, the slapstick comedies. Sennett's early stuff is the worst, but Larry Semon and some of the others are just as bad; all that speeded-up camera action makes you dizzy.

Once, you can learn to adjust, it's all right, even when you're looking off the screen into the audience. At first the darkness is a little frightening—you have to remind yourself it's only a theatre and there are just people out there, ordinary people watching a show. They don't know you can see them. They don't know that as long as your scene runs, you're just as real as they are, only in a different way. You walk, run, smile, frown, drink, eat—

That's another thing to remember, about the eating. Stay out of those Poverty Row quickies where everything is cheap and faked. Go where there's real set-dressing, big productions with banquet scenes and real food. If you work fast you can grab enough in a few minutes, while you're off-camera, to last you.

The big rule is, always be careful. Don't get caught. There's so little time, and you seldom get an opportunity to do anything on your own, even in a long sequence. It's taken me forever to get this chance to write you—I've planned it for so long, my darling, but it just wasn't possible until now.

This scene is playing outside the fort, but there's quite a large crowd of settlers and wagon-train people, and I had a chance to slip away inside here to the rooms in back—they're on camera in the background all during the action. I found this stationery and a pen, and I'm scribbling just as fast as I can. Hope you can read it. That is, if you ever get the chance!

Naturally, I can't mail it—but I have a funny hunch. You see, I noticed that standing set back here, the bunkhouse, where you and I used to come in the old days. I'm going to leave this letter under the mattress, and pray.

Yes, darling, I pray. Someone or something *knows* about us, and about how we feel. How we felt about being in the movies. That's why I'm here, I'm sure of that: because I've always loved pictures so. Someone who knows *that* must also know how I loved you. And still do.

I think there must be many heavens and many hells, each of us making his own, and—

The letter broke off there.

No signature, but of course I didn't need one. And it wouldn't have proved anything. A lonely old man, nursing his love for forty years, keeping her alive inside himself somewhere until she broke out in the form of a visual hallucination up there on the screen—such a man could conceivably go all the way into a schizoid split, even to the point where he could imitate a woman's handwriting as he set down the rationalization of his obsession.

I started to fold the letter, then dropped it on the mattress as the shrill scream of an ambulance siren startled me into sudden movement.

Even as I ran out the doorway I seemed to know what I'd find: the crowd huddling around the figure sprawled in the dust under the hot sun. Old men tire easily in such heat, and once the heart goes—

Jimmy Rogers looked very much as though he were smiling in his sleep as they lifted him into the ambulance. And I was glad of that; at least he'd died with his illusions intact.

"Just keeled over during the scene—one minute he was standing there, and the next—"

They were still chattering and gabbling when I walked away, walked back behind the fort and into the bunkhouse.

The letter was gone.

I'd dropped it on the mattress, and it was gone. That's all I can say about it. Maybe somebody else happened by while I was out front, watching them take Jimmy away. Maybe a gust of wind carried it through the doorway, blew it across the desert in a hot Santa Ana gust. Maybe there *was* no letter. You can take your choice—all I can do is state the facts.

And there aren't very many more facts to state.

I didn't go to Jimmy Rogers' funeral, if indeed he had one. I don't even know where he was buried: probably the Motion Picture Fund took care of him. Whatever *those* facts may be, they aren't important.

For a few days I wasn't too interested in facts. I was trying to answer a few abstract questions about metaphysics—reincarnation, heaven and hell, the difference between real life and reel life. I kept thinking about those images of actual people indulging in make-believe. But even after they die, the make-believe goes on, and that's a form of reality too. I mean, where's the borderline? And if there *is* a borderline—is it possible to cross over? *Life's but a walking shadow*—

Shakespeare said that, but I wasn't sure what he meant.

I'm still not sure, but there's just one more fact I must state.

The other night, for the first time in all the months since Jimmy Rogers died, I went back to the Silent Movie.

They were playing *Intolerance,* one of Griffith's greatest. Way back in 1916 he built the biggest set ever shown on the screen—the huge temple in the Babylonian sequence.

One shot never fails to impress me, and it did so now; a wide angle on the towering temple, with thousands of people moving antlike amid the gigantic carvings and colossal statues. In the distance, beyond the steps guarded by rows of stone elephants, looms a mighty wall, its top covered with tiny figures. You really have to look closely to make them out. But I did look closely, and this time I can swear to what I saw.

One of the extras, way up there on the wall in the background, was a smiling girl with long blond curls. And standing right beside her, one arm around her shoulder, was a tall old man with white whiskers. I wouldn't have noticed either of them, except for one thing.

They were waving at me . . .

BLAISE CENDRARS

Blaise Cendrars (1887–1961) was a French poet and writer who came to live in Los Angeles and wrote fetchingly about it in the 1930s. His charming book Hollywood: Mecca of the Movies, *with Bemelmanesque drawings by Jean Guérin, regarded the scene with a bemused enthusiasm. Here he conducts a tour of the main gates to the major studios, succeeding at the same time in describing how each studio has its own personality and aura.*

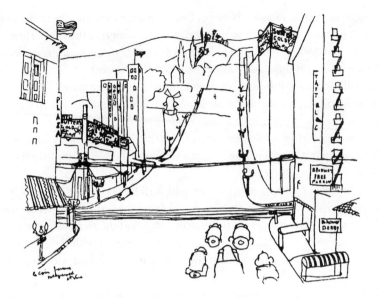

The Famous Corner of
Hollywood & Vine

"If You Want to Make Movies . . ."

IF YOU WANT TO MAKE MOVIES, COME TO HOLLYWOOD:
BUT UNLESS YOU PAY THE PRICE, YOU WON'T SUCCEED!

When you get off the train in Los Angeles, you're practically thrown into the street!

Los Angeles has many beautiful skyscrapers, but the big city's train station is plainly insufficient. The long transcontinental trains slow to a stop and shove off again in the street. Thus, from the second you step out of your coach, you enter at ground level into the jumbled racket of trams, buses, and taxis.

Grab whichever one of these passing vehicles, toss the driver an address, race off, or head out on foot; from that moment on I defy you not to feel lost in the streets, above all if, like so many others, you've made your way to Hollywood with the hope of some day making movies.

In Hollywood, all roads lead . . . to a studio! So, at whatever pace you want to walk and no matter which direction you choose or how much time you take to get your bearings, any one of these streets intersecting in front of you and taking off in straight lines to the East, to the West, to the South, to the North, ends fatally at a wall.

This wall is the famous Great Wall of China that surrounds every studio and that makes Hollywood, already a difficult city to conquer, a true forbidden city—actually, either better or worse than that, since Hollywood is comprised of many interior barriers encircling numerous kremlins and defending access to dozens of seraglios, and I believe it is not only because of the radiance of the stars and the attraction they exert the world over that we have baptized Hollywood (where the advertising *slogan* is: *Hollywood, where the stars shine day and night*) Mecca of the Movies, but, strictly speaking, above all because the entrances to these studios are nearly impassable for the noninitiate, as if, really, to wish to make your way into a studio is to want to force entry into the Holy of Holies.

So, if you want to make movies in Hollywood, come on! . . . but announce it with a maximum of publicity, create a sensation, otherwise, unless you're willing to pay the price, you'll never get through, for there is the wall.

THE BREAK IN THE WALL

This wall, which surrounds every studio, is pierced by one small opening where, without fail, there is a crowd, since all other outlets in the enclosure are barricaded, grilled over, bolted, closed.

This tiny opening, this narrow, half-open door leads into a corridor or antechamber where you will find the blessed studio entrance through which so many long to slip.

But before being allowed to step across the threshold and push, heart pounding, through the turnstile that lets you in and chimes wickedly behind your back upon registering your entry, you are required, no matter who you are, to stand in a long line at a window open in the back wall, into which is embedded the anonymous head of a Pharisee, a head that belongs to the Cerberus of the place.

Head? What am I saying! This gatekeeper, now barking, now whispering into the telephone, no matter how many copies of him have been turned out, no matter what his type—brutal, a killjoy, sad, impassive, breezy, crafty, ill-tempered, cold, exaggeratedly polite, bewildered, a dimwit, narrow-minded, mean, dreamy or smiling—this monster of hypocrisy always made me think, every time, of what I would like to have done to him (which is why I had to watch myself), to this guardian of pagan hell, who, as everyone knows, was a

Entrance to the Studios (Universal) —
Helen Westey

dog with three heads: the first always raised to the sky, howling at the moon, the second, with glowering eyes, slavering, foaming at the mouth, and snarling ceaselessly, the third, whom no one trusts because she's always cringing and pretending to be asleep, given to sudden lunges so as to bite from behind the ankles of the damned as they pass by. . . . And, actually, it was the damned that these passersby standing around at the studio gates made me think about, waiting patiently without ever losing heart for a message from inside or the goodwill of a lying gatekeeper who just wants to be rid of them, all of these common folk of humble means, but enthusiasts of the cinema keeping the faith; men, women, boys, girls, little children flocked from every city in the world to wait in attendance at the gates to the underworld of this artificial paradise of the movies!

The Pharisees

Dante placed above the gate that descends into the regions of hell the famous inscription: *"Abandon all hope, ye who enter here . . ."*

In Hollywood they're a lot more brief, a lot more direct, a lot more cynical. They're not hampered by having to come up with a beautiful phrase. They tell people exactly what they feel the need to tell them, and not being able to tell them brutally enough in four letters, they let them know it in three words. They post above the door, for the benefit of those who insist on wanting to come in, a placard: *Do not enter.* That's it, period. So much the worse for those who don't understand, so much the worse for those who end up cracking their noses or breaking bones, and so much the worse, or so much the better, for those who finally succeed in getting through. We'll see soon enough what will happen to them then!

At Universal

So it is that at the entrance to Universal Films, beneath the window occupied by a dummy representative of Cerberus, whose head my friend Jean Guérin knew how to draw so well (it's a fairly prevalent type among the common herd in America), a sign is nailed up that reads: *It's useless to wait.—It's useless to insist.—You're wasting your time.—Recommendations won't get you anywhere.—This place was not meant for you.—Do not enter.*

With that, you've been warned.

But as Carl Laemmle, the president of this company, had in any case launched a frenzied publicity campaign in the newspapers, printing notices signed in his name in which he personally asks the public to please be so kind as to collaborate with him by sending in observations, comments, suggestions, promising to pay from $50 to $100 in *cash* if one of the submitted ideas was accepted, it was perhaps at the gate of Universal that the most suckers were cooling their heels.

These poor folks may not have understood anything of the gatekeeper's ostracizing them, but I'll swear between us that this sort of shriveled chameleon playing dumb always feigned not to know who we were talking about when we gave him one of the names of the company's bosses, and even when we handed him an urgent, signed notice, he played the innocent and claimed not to know where it came from!

The Window (Universal)

At Paramount

At Paramount, the whole team that works the window is of the boxing kind. They're young, beefy fellows, quick on their feet, and very determined. And they're not in "sports" for nothing! If your name is Durand, they announce Mr. Dupont, and if you ask to be put in contact with a Mr. Adam, they coolly address you to a Mr. Cook.

One day, one of these young swashbucklers who had made me spell three times not "Constantinople," but my name, and who had noted it correctly right in front of me, *C-e-n-d-r-a-r-s,* had the effrontery to announce to a starlet who was waiting for me, thinking I wouldn't catch the name he was conjuring on the telephone, "*that a certain Mr. Wilson wanted to see her*"!

You have to believe that such con games are in wide use at this firm, and that this chamber of lunatic concierges had the run of the place, because every time a Paramount department head makes an appointment with you he's obliged to come down himself or to send his secretary to fill out an entrance pass in advance, a simple phone call from him not being enough to cut through the temperamental moods of the boxers. Anyway, this piece of paper is often found having gone astray by the time you present yourself at the window at the appropriate hour, which is exactly what happened to me on another day when Charles Boyer, who could spare but one short hour for lunch, died of both boredom and hunger while waiting for me in the studio commissary, as a young preoccupied athlete who had misplaced my entrance permit suggested I apply myself to the instructions he had from Cerberus, who wasn't about to permit anyone to enter! I had to parley for three-quarters of an hour and unsettle twenty people before winning my case, which was just to get in . . . and go about finding Charles Boyer, who ended up taking off without eating, since he had run out of time.

AT UNITED ARTISTS

At United Artists, the window clerk is not only a completely different type from the young boxers in training at Paramount, he is also from another generation and even of an entirely different social extraction, as befits this right-minded firm, the most distinguished in the world of cinema and the only one in Hollywood to dabble in refinement and civility.

It is, accordingly, a gracious man who assists me when I show up, a distinguished gentleman with grand, patronizing gestures, and this dear man is in such a hurry to accommodate me that he can't even wait for me to form a thought or pronounce a name before he has already pushed a button and the door opens in front of me. As I begin to move forward, this gentleman-Cerberus rises and accompanies me three steps, the better to clarify the directions he gives me. I am overwhelmed, beside myself with thank yous.

There's no doubt about it, I follow his instructions to the letter: South Courtyard, Building 39, Corridor B, Stairway 111, 1st Floor, Office 13 . . . and when I arrive at my destination, I enter an office, heated of course, with a red rose in a vase, cigarettes, matches, a ream of white paper, exquisitely sharpened pencils, the day's newspapers, an office without one particle of dust, but an office in which there is absolutely no one and in which the telephone is deaf-mute!

Restaurant (Universal) — Lunch with Cendrars: Ed Arnold, Pinki Tomkin, Helen Westey, etc.

I went back three times to this imperturbable straight-faced joker from United Artists, and each time he spun me onto the same outrageous course. Now that I think of it, this didn't really surprise me that much because at first sight I had thought there was something fishy about this gentleman, with his head like some old saint in an almanac which ought to have been bearded and covered with hair but which had in fact just been sheared with an electric razor and then polished, something that was stupefying, comic, inconceivable, even for an alien, but it Americanized him in a way that was somehow extremely suspect.

The third time, realizing that all of this blasted wag's directions were false, I thought it was hilarious and took advantage of the situation by going on an adventure through these vast studios that house a dozen or so enterprises, among them Mary Pickford's company.

The offices pertaining to this latter, into which I glanced indiscreetly in passing, were composed of a series of daintily furnished rooms draped in Liberty print cloth, with spinsters leaning over their typewriters as if over sewing machines (Mary Pickford is now Hollywood's lady patroness) and a darling little white doggie, no bigger than a ball of wool, splashed onto the carpet like a cream puff from a tea table.

It was also on that day that I encountered, coming around the corner of a building and slipping furtively into a courtyard, Douglas Fairbanks, whom the newspapers had announced was still in Cannes and whom I surprised returning incognito to this establishment, which was his at one time and perhaps still is, half of it anyway. The two of us, buttoned into our raincoats, collars up, hats cocked over our eyes on account of the rain, we had the air of a couple of thieves. Having passed by quickly without really noticing me, he turned around to see who I was, but didn't recognize me . . . and as for me, I didn't run after him to shake his hand, figuring that Doug didn't want to have been sighted. . . .

AT M.G.M.

At Metro-Goldwyn-Mayer, the first time I went there, hundreds of Japanese sailors were blocking the corridor. Clearing a path for myself among them, I thought I was plowing through a bunch of uniformed extras. But I was wrong, that's how you'll get fooled every step of the way in the free-for-all of the Hollywood studios, because you never really know if the person whose feet you have just stepped on is a real or a phoney character, least of all when that person is wearing a uniform or is decorated.

.   .   .   .

But sure enough, my Japanese mariners were the real thing, bona fide sailors. They were on shore leave from a battle cruiser of the Imperial Navy and had come to make a tour of Hollywood, and they all wanted to see—I heard this with my own ears when it was almost my turn to approach the window—"*the Missus Roma and the Mista Djuliet!*" M.G.M. having been filming just then Shakespeare's *Romeo and Juliet,* with the blazing Norma Shearer in the starring role.

Now, everyone knows that this star is a capricious creature who can't stand the presence of the least stranger on the set when she's filming because it makes her nervous and drains her of all her powers.

Which is to say that the Japanese were getting very upset and that the Cerberus at hand ought to have had a hundred reasons to be frazzled that morning. Absolutely not! This extraordinarily cool and prodigiously dextrous man, a veritable Cerberus-virtuoso, astounded me, for he certainly had a lot more guts than Napoléon, and the number of people he was in the midst of executing when it came my turn to meet him flooded me with admiration.

It's said that Napoléon dictated his mail to ten secretaries at once; the gatekeeper at M.G.M., he spoke into and answered eleven telephoned at once. He had a thicket of receivers in each hand, Japanese harassing him in gibberish, and if he was patched in to Norma Shearer or to someone on her general staff, they were saying god only knows what on the other end, and surely things that were none too pleasant for him—none of which kept him from asking me (he had a very strong German accent) what it was I wanted and, what rapture! from putting me immediately in touch with Mr. Vogel, Mr. Robert M. W. Vogel himself, chief of international publicity and the man I actually wanted to see, and not some Mr. Levy, a name they spell *Lavee* over there, not for camouflage but in accordance with local pronunciation.

As it was the only time I was received right away in Hollywood, I have often asked myself since whether or not it was due to an error or to some happy coincidence, or if, in this powerful German-American trust,* good practical sense and German order weren't in the process—since a solid native accent cuts through the fluent English of most of this company's employees—of exerting pressure, of reducing the complications, the nonsense, the red tape of a meddlesome and bureaucratic administration, and of setting a famous example of efficiency and energy for the American organization, so often frivolous, wanton, or full of gaps, or else which runs in neutral, is an inhuman luxury, pure technicality, an art for art's sake.

And if I tell you that I asked around and discovered that this Cerberus-virtuoso was a young Nazi fresh off the boat from Germany, would we be able to draw certain conclusions?

Maybe so . . .

---

*Since M.G.M. does not seem to have been owned even in part by a German concern, one can only presume that this was yet another tongue-in-cheek embellishment.

GORE VIDAL

For Hollywood royalty in the 1930s, one of the perks was an invitation to ride on William Randolph Hearst's private train from Los Angeles up to a siding near Hearst's San Simeon, the vast architectural curiosity that inspired Welles's Xanadu. The train remained parked while the guests finished their night's sleep, and then a breakfast buffet was served before cars ferried them to San Simeon for a weekend's entertainment. Gore Vidal re-creates some of that life in Hollywood, *a historical novel that seems more based on fact than most books in the genre and that here re-creates a time when San Simeon was still on the drawing boards.*

from *Hollywood*

I

Caroline lay tied to the railroad track, the hot sun in her face while in her ears the ominous sound of an approaching steam engine. A high male voice called out, "Look frightened."

"I am frightened."

"Don't talk. Look more to the left."

"But, Chief, she's got too much shadow on her face. You can't see the eyes."

"Look straight ahead." The slow-moving steam engine was now within a yard of her. She could see it out of the corner of her right eye. The engineer stared down at her, hand on—what?—the brake she prayed. A stone pressed into her back, just below the left shoulder blade. She wanted to scream.

"Scream!" shouted William Randolph Hearst; and Caroline obliged. As she filled the air with terrified exhalation, a man on horseback rode up to the railroad engine and leapt into the engine room, where he pulled a cord, releasing a quantity of ill-smelling steam from the engine's smoke-stack. As the train ground to a halt, he ran toward Caroline and knelt beside her.

"Cut!" said the Chief. "Stay right where you are, Mrs. Sanford."

"I have no choice," said Caroline. The sweaty young man—a cowboy belonging to Hearst's ranch—smiled down at her reassuringly. "It won't take a minute, ma'am," he said. "He's got to change the camera so he can get a real close look at me untying you."

"Why doesn't he just show a card on the screen, with the information that two weeks after Lady Belinda's eleventh-hour rescue she was home again in London, pouring tea. I think I can do that rather well."

Hearst was now standing over her, his vast bulk mercifully blocking the sun. "That was swell. Really," he said. "Joe's rolling up the camera now. It won't take a minute. I never knew you were such a pro."

"Neither," said Caroline, "did I."

"Actually, there's nothing easier than movies," said Millicent Hearst, whom

Caroline had known since she was the younger partner of a vaudeville sister act. "Either you look nice on the screen or you don't. If you do, they'll love you. If you don't you can act your butt off and nothing's going to happen."

"You're certainly very effective on the screen." Caroline spoke brightly, still flat on her back, with the dusty cowboy to one side of her while, to the other, Mr. and Mrs. Hearst gazed down on her, observing the social amenities with a flow of good talk.

"Actually if Millicent weren't so old, I could make a star out of her." Hearst was his usual kindly, tactless self.

"I'm not all that much older than Mary Pickford." Millicent's voice had never ceased to be Hell's Kitchen New York Irish. "But it's a mug's game, acting, and the hours they keep here in the movies you wouldn't believe."

"But I do. In fact, one of those hours has passed," said Caroline, "since I was tied up."

"We're ready," said Joe Hubbell, the cameraman, just out of Caroline's range.

"All right. Let's get started." The Hearsts withdrew. The cowboy and Caroline waited, patiently, to be told what to do. As they did, Caroline admired, yet again, Hearst's instinct, which had now drawn him to the most exciting of all the games that their country had yet devised. As he had invented "yellow journalism," which obliged reality to mirror not itself but Hearst's version of it, now he had plunged into movie-making, both amateur like this film and professional like the Hearst-produced *The Perils of Pauline,* the most successful serial of 1913. Now in summer residence at San Simeon, a quarter-million-acre ranch to the north of Hollywood, the Chief was amusing himself with a feature-length film in which he had gallantly starred his houseguest, Caroline, who was several years older than Millicent, and by no means as conventionally pretty. Once Caroline had accepted George Creel's assignment to be the Administration's emissary to the moving-picture business, she had started her embassy by paying a call on her old friend Hearst, who disapproved of the war in general and Wilson in particular. Nevertheless, he was most lavishly a host not to mention meticulously a director.

An hour later, Caroline, no longer Lady Belinda, was freed from her track by the cowboy, whom she was directed to kiss full on the lips. He had blushed furiously, and she had been intrigued to find how soft a young man's lips could be, not that she had had much experience with young men or, for that matter, old, she also noted that he smelled, powerfully, of sweating horse.

Caroline and her maid, Héloise, shared a tent close to the wooden house of the Hearsts atop Camp Hill. Since there were always a dozen houseguests as well as an army of servants, gardeners, ranchhands, the hill was now a city of temporary tents, surrounding the elaborate wooden house, which was taken down in winter and put up in summer.

"And here, right here," said Hearst, "I'm going to build a castle, just like the one you and Blaise have at Saint-Cloud-le-Duc."

They were seated in the Chief's principal sitting room, with its rough-hewn beams and unfinished pine walls on which were hung perhaps the largest collection of false old masters that any American millionaire had ever accumulated. But then it was always said of Hearst that after thirty years of the wholesale buying of art, he could always tell a good fake from a bad one; and of the world's forgeries, he chose, invariably, the ones with the most accurate brushwork. "He has," the art merchant Duveen was supposed to have said, "an excellent cocked-eye."

While Caroline drank sherry, Hearst stood over a round table on which was placed what looked to be a wedding cake covered with velvet. Like a matador, he removed the covering to reveal the model of a castle with two towers, all meticulously detailed in plaster. "This is it," he said. "What I'm going to build up here."

"It is," Caroline was guarded, "like nothing else."

"Nothing else in California, anyway. Can't wait to get started." Hearst's major-domo of twenty years, George Thompson, was now as round as an owl and as rosy as a piglet; for more than twenty years he had appeared at the same hour with Coca-Cola in a silver-embossed mug for the Chief; and now sherry for Caroline. "Good evening, Mrs. Sanford." She smiled upon him. After all, it was George who encouraged the Chief to traffic with fashionables like herself in addition to the Chief's own preference, politicians and theater folk, while the friendly Millicent tended to keep her distance from her husband's friends. She preferred New York to California; motherhood to glamour; respectability to Hearstian fame; and Roman Catholic strictness to Protestant easiness. She was said to be quite aware that she had been superseded in the Chief's affections by a showgirl, who was either twenty years old or seventeen; if the latter, she was the same age that Millicent had been when she and her sister had danced their way off the stage of the Herald Square Theater, where they had been two of the many maidens in *The Girl from Paris,* and into Hearst's great heart. Now history was repeating itself with Miss Marion Davies, the daughter of a Brooklyn politician named Bernard Douras. Blaise had approved the *Tribune* story of the romance, which Caroline had read with delight and promptly spiked as a Matter of Taste, all important for the *Tribune* as the war-time President's favorite Washington newspaper now that Ned McLean's *Post* was known as "the court circular." Actually, the vaudeville-loving President would probably have enjoyed very much the highly suggestive but never absolutely libellous story of the young showgirl for whom the fifty-year-old Hearst had, if not forsaken his wife, abandoned her to the rigors of respectable domesticity while he squired, without cigarettes, alcohol or bad language, his chorus girl through the only slightly subdued night life of wartime New York. Miss Davies had left her convent—

always a convent, Blaise had decreed—when a mere girl to join the chorus of
Chu Chin Chow, Oh, Boy! and now her apotheosis in the *Ziegfeld Follies of 1917.*
There were whispers at San Simeon that when the Missis left, the Miss would
arrive. But Hearst was silent on all personal matters; and Millicent seemed un-
perturbed.

"So George Creel wants you to organize the movie business." Hearst sat in a
throne opposite Caroline while George lit the kerosene lamps. The electricity
at San Simeon was home-made and unreliable. "Stories about Huns raping Belgian nuns?"

"Surely your papers have told us all that we want to hear on that subject."
Caroline was smooth, relaxed by sherry. "I thought, perhaps, Huns raped by Belgian nuns, to encourage women to resist the beast."

"I always said," Hearst did not even smile, "that *you* were the newspaperman,
not Blaise."

"Well, I did buy the *Tribune,* and I made it popular by copying faithfully your
Journal."

"No. You've got a better paper. Better town, too. Particularly now. I'm
thinking. . . . You know, Creel worked for me on the *Journal.* Ambitious.
Movies." Hearst stared at a Mantegna whose wooden frame sported wormholes
only down one side; thanks to Hearst's usual haste, there had been no time for
the forger to drill holes in the rest of the frame. "I think movies are the answer."

"To what?"

"The world." Hearst's glaring eagle eyes were fixed on Caroline and the hair
that had been blond when they first met was now gray. "I always thought it was
going to be the press. So simple to print. So simple to transmit with telegraph.
But there's the language problem. By the time Jamie Bennett's stolen all our
stories for his Paris *Herald,* the news is old hat. The beauty of the movies is they
don't talk. Just a few cards in different languages to tell you what the plot is,
what they're saying. Everyone in China watches my *Perils of Pauline,* but they
can't read any of my papers there."

"You're going in?"

Hearst nodded. "I do this for fun, what we did today. Though if it looks okay,
I'll distribute it. I've got my own company. You don't mind?"

"I'd be thrilled, of course." Of all professions that Caroline had ever day-
dreamed of for herself that of actress had not been one. As a girl, she had been
taken by her father back-stage to see Sarah Bernhardt; and the sweat, the dirt,
the terror had impressed itself upon her in a way that the splendor of what the
public saw from the front of the stage had not. As for movie-acting, Millicent,
an old showgirl, had grasped it all. Either the camera favored you or it did not.
At forty, Caroline assumed that she would look just that; after all, there were,
officially at least, no leading ladies of forty. She herself was interested only in

the business end of the movies; she had also been commissioned to investigate the propaganda possibilities of this unexpected popular novelty. It had not been until such movie favorites as Charlie Chaplin and Douglas Fairbanks had taken to the market-place and sold Liberty Bonds to millions of their fans that the government had realized how potent were the inventors of Hollywood; and Creel had agreed.

But Hearst, as usual, was idiosyncratic. "Distribution companies, theater chains, those are what matter. The rest is a bit like the theater, a gamble. Except you almost can't lose money on a film unless somebody like the director—what's his name—the two girls, the initials?"

"D. W. Griffith." Caroline knew all the names from her own paper.

"Decides he wants to make the biggest movie in the world by spending the most money, building things like all of Babylon. I hear he's broke. And Triangle wants to sell out. I've made a bid. But Zukor and Lasky have got more cash than I do—in hand, that is. This business is like a cornucopia, like Alaska in '49. A million dollars just for Mary Pickford. Incredible. Only danger is these Griffith types. Stage-door johnnies who start to think big once you give them a camera to play with. Though," the thin lips widened into a smile, "it is the best fun there is, making a movie. Sort of like a printer's block, the way you can keep rearranging all the pieces. But without a paper's deadline. You can keep at it until you get all the pieces in the right order. They call that part—just like we do—editing. Then it just doesn't lie there dead on the page, it moves."

"Let's sell our papers and go to Southern California." Caroline was always easily fired by Hearst.

"If I were younger I would. But," Hearst frowned, "there's New York."

"That's right. Didn't we endorse you for mayor, this fall?"

Hearst's face was blank. "The *Tribune,* on orders from Wilson I expect, has told me to tend to my papers, and support the incumbent, the hopeless John Purroy Mitchel."

Caroline was all mock wide-eyed innocence. "That must be our new editorial writer . . ."

"*That* was my old friend Blaise. You must've missed the issue. Anyway, I've got Murphy. I've got Tammany. So if I win . . ."

"You'll be the Democratic candidate for president in 1920."

"And the president in 1921, when I take the oath of office. It's about time, don't you think?"

Caroline had never understood Hearst's ambition other than to suspect that there was, simply, nothing more to it than sheer energy. "I have never known an election when there were so many candidates so early, and so—so unashamed."

"Nothing to be ashamed of." He rinsed his teeth noisily in Coca-Cola. "The people don't like third terms. They also don't like Wilson. Roosevelt's a wreck and a spoiler and the people are tired of him. McAdoo . . ." He paused.

"James Burden Day?" Loyally, Caroline said the name, which did not interest Hearst. "Champ Clark?" The Speaker of the House was the leading Bryanite; and already at work. "And those are just the Democrats."

"The Republicans will nominate Roosevelt, who's done for, or Leonard Wood, who I can do in any day of the week. He's a general," Hearst added with disdain.

"So is Pershing, and when we win . . ."

"There won't be a general on any ballot. Remember what I say. This war's too big. The ordinary man hates officers, West Pointers particularly. Every man who's gone through training will want to get back at the men who gave him such a hard time."

"Why wasn't this true in the other wars?"

"Well, it was true in my little war against Spain. I don't count Roosevelt, who was already a politician when he rode up that hill with my best reporters covering him. The true war candidate—back then—should've been Dewey. Dewey of Manila. Dewey the conquering hero. So what happened? Nothing."

"He was stupid."

"That's usually no drawback. Anyway, *this* time something called selective service is going to crowd the military out. These boys aren't volunteers for this war. They're being taken captive to go fight alongside people they hate, like the English, or against their own people."

"Your Irish and German supporters?"

"You bet. Or if they're just ordinary buckwheat Americans they won't know where they are once they're in Europe, or why they're supposed to be mad at something called the Kaiser. That means when they get back, if they get back, they're going to blame Wilson and their officers for the whole mess. You know, you ought to put some flags on your front page. There's this new color process. Good red. Pretty good blue. Looks nice and cheery. Patriotic. People like it."

Caroline had always regarded Hearst as a mindless genius; or an idiot savant; or something simply not calculable by the ordinary criteria of intelligence. Yet there was no getting round the preciseness and practicality of his instincts, including his occasional odd forays into socialism. Recently he had convinced Tammany Hall of the necessity of municipal ownership of public utilities. If such a thing were to come to pass and if Hearst were to become president, the entire Senate, at his inauguration, would converge upon him and strike him down, like Caesar, in the name of those sacred trusts that had paid for their togas.

Twenty sat down to dinner in a long timbered room hung with Aubusson tapestries. On the table huge crystal girandoles alternated with bottles of tomato ketchup and Worcestershire sauce. Caroline sat on the Chief's right in deference to her high place as a fellow publisher. Seated on Caroline's right, at her request, was Timothy X. Farrell, the successful director of ten—or was it twenty—photoplays in the last two years. Farrell had come to see Hearst on secret business, which Caroline had quickly discovered involved a screen career for Marion Davies and a new production company for Hearst, who had also just acquired, he told Caroline, casually, the Pathé Company from its war-beleaguered French owners.

Farrell was thin and dark and nearer thirty than forty; spoke with a Boston Irish brogue; had been to Holy Cross when he had got the call to make movies at Flushing, New York. He had moved on to Santa Monica, California, where he had worked as a carpenter and general handyman for Thomas Ince. Now he was a successful director, noted for his use of light. Caroline was in a new world of jargon, not unlike—but then again not very like—journalism. Farrell was touchingly eager to make films celebrating the United States, freedom, democracy, while attacking, of course, the bestial Hun, monarchy and the latest horror, Bolshevism, now emerging from the ruins of czarist Russia and connected closely, Creel maintained, with various American labor unions, particularly those that sought to reduce the work day from twelve to eight hours.

"What we need is a story," said Farrell. "You can't just start shooting away, like the Chief. He's old-fashioned. He thinks *Perils of Pauline is* the latest in the movies. But it isn't. That serial's four years old. Four years is like a century in the movies. Everything's different now. The audience won't pay their dollars— or even nickels—to see just anything that moves on a sheet. But they'll pay as much as two dollars for a real story, and a real spectacle. Griffith changed everything."

"You, too," Caroline remembered to flatter. A film director was no different from a senator.

"Well, I got lucky last year. *Missy Drugget* had the biggest gross of any film for the year, in the States." Farrell frowned. "That's another problem with this war. Our overseas distributors—crooks all of them to begin with, but now there's a war they can really cheat us, and they do. Goldstein was going to do something about it. But now I guess he's going to jail."

"Who's Goldstein, and why jail?"

"*Spirit of '76.* Remember? About the American Revolution? Came out just before April, before we were in the war. Well, your friends in Washington thought," there seemed to be no sarcasm in Farrell's naturally urgent voice, "that any mention of our own revolution was an insult to our ally, England. You know it might confuse our simple folks to be told how we once had this war with England so that we could be a free country. Anyway, under one of the new laws, the government went and indicted Bob Goldstein, the producer, and they say he's going to get ten years in prison."

"Just for making a movie about how we became a free country?"

Farrell seemed without irony, but his voice was hard. "Free to put anyone—everyone—in jail. Yes."

"Why hasn't the press taken this up?"

"Ask Mr. Hearst. Ask yourself." The eyes were arctic blue with black lashes and brows.

"What is the exact charge against Goldstein?"

"I don't know. But it's all covered by the . . . what's its name? Espionage Act, which didn't even exist when we made the picture."

"Your picture, too?"

Farrell flushed. "Yes. Me, too. I did the lighting and camera work as a favor. But they don't go after the small fry. Now, I'm working with Triangle. They're the group that Mr. Ince did *Civilization* with. He's a friend of Mr. Hearst, which is how I happen to be here, I guess."

"Will Mr. Ince be arrested, too?" Caroline remembered that Ince's *Civilization* had been a pacifist film. Since Hearst not only had been against the war but was considered pro-German, Caroline suspected a connection between the anti-war films of some of the best movie-makers and Hearst himself. In fact, Hearst had been so anti-Allies that the British and French governments had denied his newspapers the use of their international cables. In a fit of over-excitement, Canada had banned all of Hearst's newspapers and should a Canadian be caught reading so much as the Katzenjammer Kids comic pages, he could be imprisoned for five years.

"I doubt it. He has connections. He knows the President. But I'll bet he wishes he'd stuck to 'westerns.' "

After dinner, Hearst led them into a tent that served as a theater; and here he showed them a western of his own making, *Romance of the Rancho.* The hero was Hearst, looking rather bulkier than his giant horse; the heroine was Millicent, who sat next to Caroline during the performance, complaining bitterly about her appearance. "I look like a Pekingese. It's awful, seeing yourself like this."

"I wouldn't know," said Caroline, who was attracted to the idea of film not as an art or as light or as whatever one wanted to call so collective and vulgar a storytelling form but as a means of preserving time, netting the ephemeral and the fugitive—there it is! now, it's past, gone forever. Millicent, *now,* was seated beside her, face illuminated by the flickering light upon the screen while, on the screen, one saw Millicent *then,* weeks ago—whenever, unchanging and unchangeable forever.

As applause for *Romance of the Rancho* ended, Hearst stood up and gave a mock bow, and said, "I wrote the title cards, too. Couldn't be easier. Just like picture captions." He looked at Caroline. "Now we'll see something that's still in the works. A super western epic." The lights went out. A beam of light from the projector was aimed at the screen, which suddenly filled with a picture of Hearst's train-of-all-work coming to a halt. Caroline recognized the sweaty cowboy with whom she had worked that day. Obviously he was much used in Hearst's home movies. She was struck at how startlingly handsome his some-what—in life—square, crude face became on the screen. She noted, too, that his eyebrows grew together in a straight line, like those of an archaic Minoan athlete.

There was a murmur in the tent as a slender woman got off the train. She was received by the cowboy, hat in hand. A porter then gave him her suitcase. The camera was now very close on the woman's face: a widow's peak and a cleft chin emphasized the symmetry of her face, high cheekbones made flattering shadows below large eyes. Slowly, the woman smiled. There was a sigh from the audience.

"Jesus Christ," murmured Millicent, now all Hell's Kitchen Irish, "ain't you the looker!"

"I don't believe it." And Caroline did not. A title card said, "Welcome to Dodge City, Lady Belinda."

Then the cowboy and Lady Belinda walked toward a waiting buggy; and Caroline stared at herself, mesmerized. But this was no longer herself. This was herself of two weeks ago; hence, two weeks younger than she now was. Yet here she was, aged forty, forever, and she scrutinized the screen for lines and found them only at the edge of the eyes—mascara could hide the worst, she thought automatically. Then as she smiled what she always took to be her most transparently insincere smile of greeting, usually produced in honor of a foreign dignitary or the president of the moment, she noted that Lady Belinda—she regarded the woman on the screen as an entirely third person—looked ravishing and ravished, and the only lines discernible in the bright sunlight were two delicate brackets at the corners of her mouth. For twenty minutes the incomplete film ran.

When the lights came on, Caroline was given a standing ovation, led by Hearst. "We've got a brand-new star," he said, sounding exactly like a Hearst story from the entertainment page of the *Journal,* where a different chorus girl, at least a half-dozen times a year, went on stage in the place of a stricken star, and always triumphed and became the Toast of the Town.

Arthur Brisbane, Hearst's principal editor, shook Caroline's hand gravely. "Even without blue eyes, you hold the screen." Brisbane was notorious for his theory that all great men and presumably women, too, were blue-eyed.

"Perhaps my eyes will fade to blue in the sun." Caroline gave him her ravishing smile; and felt like someone possessed. She was two people. One who existed up there on the screen, a figure from the past but now and forever immutable, while the other stood in the center of a stuffy tent, rapidly aging with each finite heartbeat entirely in the present tense, as she accepted congratulations.

"It's a pity you aren't younger," said the merciless Millicent. "You could really do something in pictures."

"Lucky that I don't want to, and so I can enjoy my middle age."

The cameraman, Joe Hubbell, came up to her. "It was really my idea, sticking the film together like this. So you could see it."

Hearst nodded. "We've Joe to thank. I never look through the camera lens and I don't see rushes. So when Joe kept telling me that Mrs. Sanford is really something, I thought he was just being nice to the guests."

"He was," said Caroline. "He is." She was thoroughly bemused and alarmed, like one of those savages who believe that a photograph can steal away the soul.

After most of the guests had retired to their tents, Caroline and a chosen few went back to Hearst's wooden house, where George poured Coca-Cola, and Caroline talked to Farrell about the uses of film for propaganda purposes. "I don't think you—or Mr. Creel—will have to do much arm-twisting. Everybody in Hollywood does the same thing anyway, particularly now we're in the war, and you can go to jail if you criticize England or France or . . ."

"Our government. In order to make the world safe for democracy," Caroline parodied herself as an editorial writer, "we must extinguish freedom at home."

"That's about it." Farrell gave her a sharp look. "Personally, I don't see much choice between the Hun and the Espionage Act."

"You are Irish, and hate England, and wish we had stayed out." Caroline was direct.

"Yes. But since I don't want to join Bob Goldstein in the clink, I shall make patriotic films about gallant Tommies, and ever-cheerful doughboys or hayseeds or whatever we'll call our boys."

Caroline stared at Hearst across the room. He was in deep conversation with a number of editors from various Hearst newspapers; or rather the editors, led by Brisbane, were deeply conversing while their Chief listened enigmatically. For the first time in her life, Caroline was conscious of true danger. Something was shifting in this, to her, free and easy-going—too easy-going in some ways— republic. Although she and Blaise had contributed to the war spirit—the *Tribune* was the first for going to war on the Allied side—she had not thought through the consequences of what she had helped set in motion. She had learned from Hearst that truth was only one criterion by which a story could be judged, but at the same time she had taken it for granted that when her *Tribune* had played up the real or fictitious atrocities of the Germans, Hearst's many newspapers had been dispensing equally pro-German sentiments. Each was a creator of "facts" for the purpose of selling newspapers; each, also, had the odd bee in bonnet that could only be satisfied by an appearance in print. But now Hearst's bee was stilled. The great democracy had decreed that one could only have a single view of a most complex war; otherwise, the prison was there to receive those who chose not to conform to the government's line, which, in turn, reflected a spasm of national hysteria that she and the other publishers had so opportunistically created, with more than usual assistance from home-grown political demagogues and foreign-paid propagandists. Now the Administration had invited Caroline herself to bully the movie business into creating ever more simplistic rationales of what she had come, privately, despite her French bias, to think of as the pointless war. Nevertheless, she was astonished that someone had actually gone to prison for making a film. Where was the much-worshipped Constitution in all of this? Or was it never anything more than a document to be used by the country's rulers when it suited them and otherwise ignored? "Will your friend Mr. Goldstein go to the Supreme Court?"

"I don't think he has the money. Anyway, it's war-time so there's no freedom of speech, not that there ever has been much."

"You are too severe." Caroline rallied to what was, after all, her native land. "One can—or could—say—or write—almost anything."

"You remember that picture with Nazimova? *War Brides?* In 1916?"

"That was an exception." In 1916 a modernized version of *Lysistrata* had so enraged the pro-war lobby that it had been withdrawn.

"That was peace-time."

"Well, no one went to jail." Caroline's response was weak. How oddly, how gradually, things had gone wrong.

"It'll be interesting if they get Mr. Hearst."

"They've tried before. Remember when Colonel Roosevelt held him responsible for President McKinley's murder?"

"That was just peace-time politics. But now they can lock him up if he doesn't praise England and hit the Germans . . ."

"And the Irish?" Caroline had got Farrell's range. "For not coming to England's aid?"

"Well . . ." Farrell accepted Coca-Cola from George. "Your friend Mr. Creel's moving fast. I've been invited to join the moving-picture division of his committee, to work with the Army Signal Corps, to glorify our warriors."

"But they haven't done anything yet. Of course, when they do . . ."

"We'll be ready. You're very beautiful, you know." As no one had said such a thing to Caroline since she was nine years old, she had taken it for granted that whatever beauty she might ever have had was, literally, unremarkable and so unremarked.

"I think that you think," she was precise in her ecstasy, "that my picture projected a dozen times life-size on a bedsheet is beautiful, which is not the same thing as me."

"No. It's you, all right. I'm sorry. I have no manners." He laughed, then coughed. "My father kept a bar in Boston. In the South End."

"Your manners are very agreeable. It's your taste I question. But without zeal, as the French say. At my age, I can endure quite a few compliments without losing my head."

Caroline allowed Mr. Farrell to escort her to her tent, where, in the moonlight, to the howls of appreciative coyotes, a man not her lover kissed her. She noted that his lips were far less soft and alluring than those of the Minoan cowboy.

"Women are not destined to have everything," she observed to Héloise, who helped her undress. "Or, perhaps, anything." But this sounded too neat; as well as wrong. "I mean, anything that we really want."

BUDD SCHULBERG

Budd Schulberg's father was the pioneering movie producer B. P. Schulberg, and the son had a first-row seat as he was coming of age in the Hollywood of the 1930s. He got his first job at Paramount when he was seventeen, worked as a press agent and screenwriter, and published his first novel in 1941. It became an enduring Hollywood classic, a merciless portrayal of an ambitious executive on the rise; the hero's name, Sammy Glick, became shorthand for a type.

from *What Makes Sammy Run?*

You could see the beams of the giant searchlights ballyhooing Sammy's preview plowing broad white furrows through the sky. "There it is," Sammy said as we turned off Sunset toward the Village. The words came out of his mouth like hard, sharp-sided pebbles. "Jesus."

He meant those lights up there were spelling Sammy Glick. There was no other word for the sound of pride mouthed with apprehension. There wasn't much talking, Sammy's mood always provided the backdrop for the rest of us, and he was nervous. Even when he tried to cover it with wisecracks, they were nervous wisecracks.

"What kind of a house is this?" he said.

"A tough one," Kit said. "They only laugh when it's funny, not when it's supposed to be funny. And they never cry when it's maudlin. Only when it's pathetic."

"Jesus," Sammy said.

"And they're preview wise," she warned. "They've had so many previews out here that they all sound like little DeMilles. They complain about the angles, and the smoothness of the dissolves, and they even tell you what to cut."

"The bastards," Sammy said, "they better think my picture is funny. I know it's funny. I counted the laughs myself. One hundred and seventeen."

The theater entrance was full of excitement that came mostly from women who were attracted to the leading man, and men resentful or regretful that they would never go to bed with anybody like the star, and unimportant people who idealized their envy into admiration and kids who wanted to have more autographs than anybody else in the world.

All the lights were on in the theater and everybody in the audience had his head turned toward the entrance. It looked crazy, as if the screen had suddenly been set up behind their backs. They were all watching for the celebrities to fill up the loge section that had been roped off for them. I realized why Sammy had rushed us through dinner. He wanted to be sure and get there before the lights went out.

The three of us started down the aisle together but we had only gone a couple of rows when we lost Sammy. When I looked around, Sammy was practically in the lap of a dignified, gray-haired man, with a pink, gentle face, which was a little too soft around the mouth.

"That's his producer," Kit said as I was about to ask. "Sidney Fineman." I looked again. Fineman was one of the magic names like Goldwyn and Mayer.

As we waited for the lights to fade, we talked about Fineman. He was one of the few real old-timers still on top. He had written scenarios for people who have become myths or names of streets like Griffith and Ince. He was supposed to have one of the finest collections of rare books in the country.

"And it isn't just conspicuous consumption," she said. "His idea of how to spend one hell of an evening is to lock himself in his library alone. He built a special house for his books at the back of his estate."

The more she told me the more curious I was that a man like Sidney Fineman should want to work with Sammy.

"Fineman isn't the man he was fifteen years ago," she said. "He has just as much taste as Thalberg and more guts. Hollywood was his girl. He loved her all the time. He had ideas for making something out of her . . ."

I could see Sammy out of the corner of my eye. He had finally worked his way down to our aisle. He was leaning over two or three people to shake hands with Junior Laemmle.

"But that's all gone," Kit was saying. "The depression killed something in him. Not only losing his own dough, but the big bank boys like Chase and Atlas moving in on his company. He began to get an obsession about the Wall Street bunch working behind his back. He started playing safe. Now he's just one of the top dozen around town, making his old hits over and over again because he's scared to death that the minute he starts losing money they'll take his name off the door. He's convinced Sammy is a money writer. And I have a sneaking suspicion who convinced him."

Sammy ducked into the seat beside me as the credit titles came on. I watched his face as his name filled the screen:

ORIGINAL SCREEN PLAY

by

SAMMY GLICK

There is no word in English to describe it. You could say gloat, smile, leer, grin, smirk, but it was all of those and something more, a look of deep sensual pleasure. The expression held me fascinated because I felt it was something I should not be allowed to see, like the face of the boy who roomed across the hall from me in prep school when I had made the sordid mistake of entering without knocking.

Then Sammy leaned over and whispered something in my ear that will always seem more perverse than anything in Krafft-Ebing.

"Just for a gag," he said, "clap for me."

The most perverse part of the story is that I did. There were my hands clapping foolishly like seal flappers. The applause was taken up and spread through the house, not what you would call a thunderous ovation, just enough of a sprinkle to make my hands feel like blushing. It wasn't bad enough that I had become Sammy's drinking companion. I had to be his one-man claque. My applause couldn't have been more automatic if Sammy had previously hypnotized me and led me into the theater.

As I stared at that credit title I had a feeling that something was missing. But it wasn't until the screen was telling us who designed the wardrobe and assisted the director that I remembered what it was. Julian. Julian Blumberg, the kid who made the little snowball that Sammy was rolling down the Alps. Granting that Sammy had written, God knows how, the screen play alone, the worst it should have been was original story by Samuel Glick and Julian Blumberg preceding the screen play credit. But there it was, all Sammy Glick, no Julian Blumberg.

On impulse, but a better one than before, I leaned over and asked Sammy whether he noticed anything funny about that screen credit and when he didn't, I enlightened him. It was like lighting a candle in Mammoth Cave.

"That first story we did all went in the ashcan, Al," he said in a thick whisper. "I had to start from scratch. I know it's a tough break for the kid, but that's Hollywood."

"The hell it is," I said. "That's Sammy Glick."

Kit said a sharp *shhhhh*.

As the picture was opening I was wondering whether I would have agreed with Sammy about Hollywood before I met her.

The picture wasn't anything that would come back to you as you were climbing into bed, or even remember as you were reaching under the seat for your hat; it was a good example of the comedy romance formula that Hollywood has down cold, with emphasis not on content but on the facility with which it is told. It was right in the groove that Hollywood has been geared for, slick, swift and clever. What Kit calls the Golden Rut.

But in spite of the entertainment on the screen I preferred the show going on in the adjoining seat. I never saw a man work so hard at seeing a picture. "Eleven already," he said to me a couple of minutes after the picture started, and I realized he had a clocker in his hand and was counting the laughs. And each time they laughed he jotted down feverishly the line or the bit of business. And every time they didn't he'd mumble, "It's that goddam ham—he's murdering my line," or "That's a dead spot they can kill when they trim it."

I just sat there watching him learn the motion-picture business. He was an apt student all right. He learned something about pictures in five months that I'm just beginning to understand after five years. Hollywood always has its bumper crop of phonies, but believe it or not, Sammy was one of the less obvious ones. He was smart enough to know that the crook who cracks his jobs too consistently is sure to be caught. His secret was to be just as conscientious about the real work he did as about the filching and finagling.

The picture got a good hand as the lights came on again. I turned to follow Sammy up the aisle but Kit grabbed my arm.

"Out this way," she said. "It's better."

She indicated the emergency exit on the side. It led us to an alley that ran around the theater. As we walked through the darkness toward the street, Kit said:

"I always like to duck out before anybody asks me how I liked the picture."

"Even if you did?"

"It isn't that simple. Hollywood has a regular ritual for preview reactions. When they know they've got a turkey they want to be reassured. And when they have one that's okay they expect superlatives."

She illustrated her point by telling the old Hollywood story about the three yes-men who are asked what they think of the preview. The first says it is without a doubt the greatest picture ever made. The second says it is absolutely colossal and stupendous. The third one is fired for shaking his head and saying, "I don't know, I only think it's great."

"Just the same," I said, "I'm impressed. To tell the truth I didn't know Sammy had it in him."

"Don't misunderstand," she said. "I think it's a damn good movie. The only thing I have against those guys is that they're like the old Roman Caesars—every piddling little success becomes an excuse for staging a triumph. And I just don't happen to enjoy being dragged along behind the chariot."

When we reached the street Sammy was standing with half a dozen men bunched on the curb in front of the theater. They all seemed to be talking at once, though Sammy was doing his best to drown them out. Kit pointed out the others besides Sammy and Fineman, the director, the cutter, several other executives and the cameraman. A couple of others were hovering around the edge, mostly listening and reacting. Fineman and the director seemed to be having an argument. The director was yelling that if they yanked his favorite scene they could take his name off the picture. Sammy was supporting Fineman.

We watched a boy bring out a ladder and climb up efficiently to change the lettering on the marquee, and then Kit said, "These sidewalk conferences are liable to last all night. Let's go and have a drink. He can meet us there."

My mind kept remembering the way she had made herself at home at Sammy's as we left that night. It was crazy to let it annoy me because I hadn't even made up my mind yet whether I liked her or not. I liked the way her mind drove at things but there was something disconcerting about the way she kept you from getting too close to her.

As we started for the parking station, she turned around and called to Sammy briskly. "The Cellar."

An anemic young man in a shabby overcoat was waiting at the car. I knew him, but I couldn't place him until he began to talk. Of course it was Julian Blumberg.

He was unable to hide the terrible effort it was for him to approach me. You could see it was an act of desperation.

"Mr. Manheim; I don't think you remember me . . ."

His eyes seemed to be forever crying. He kept cracking his knuckles, shifting his balance and looking everywhere but at me. The Jewish language has the best word I have ever heard for people like Julian: *nebbish*. A *nebbish* person is not exactly an incompetent, a dope or a weakling. He is simply the one in the crowd that you always forget to introduce. "Of course I do," I said. "Glad to see you."

I tried to make it sound hearty. He extended his hand as if he expected me to crack it with a ruler. I could feel the perspiration in his palm.

When I introduced him to Kit he gave her a preoccupied nod and then, as if he had been sucking in his breath for it a long time, he blurted out what he wanted to say to me. As with so many timorous people, when it finally came out it sounded brusque and overbold.

"Mr. Manheim, I've got to see you right away."

"Sure, Julian," I said, "can you tell me what it's about?"

He looked at Kit suspiciously. "Alone," he said. "I want to talk to you alone."

His voice begged and demanded at the same time. I suppose I should have been sore, but it was hard to miss the undertones in Julian's rudeness.

"All right," I said, "will it take very long?"

The determination valve suddenly seemed to loosen and the bluster leaked out of him. "Gosh, Mr. Manheim, I know I'm being a nuisance but I wouldn't think of bothering you like this unless . . ."

"How long would you say it would take?" I interrupted impatiently.

"It's—there's quite a lot to tell. I'd say a couple of hours."

I looked at Kit. "Why don't you two go ahead?" she said. "I don't mind being alone."

That was the trouble, I knew she didn't mind being alone.

"I'll tell you what you do, Julian. It'll keep until lunch tomorrow, won't it? How about dropping around at the studio? Twelve-thirty okay?"

He was so grateful it was painful. He backed away like an awkward courtier, hoping he wasn't being too much trouble and thanking me again.

"Who is that damp little fellow?" Kit asked as she pressed her foot on the starter.

I still didn't feel I knew her well enough to tell her the story of *Girl Steals Boy*. So I just said he was a writer Sammy and I knew in New York who was out here looking for a job.

"No wonder he looked worried," she said. "There were exactly two hundred and fifty of us working today. The Guild keeps a daily check-up. And do you know how many screen writers there are? Nearly a thousand. With carloads of bright-eyed college kids arriving every week—willing to do or die for dear old World-Wide at thirty-five a week."

HOWARD KOCH

The time of the blacklist was a dark age for Hollywood, as anti-Communist witch-hunters went on the prowl in the late 1940s and early 1950s, encouraging industry figures to denounce one another. Those who did not found themselves unemployable and went into exile, left the industry, or worked at cut rates under pseudonyms. One of the dirty little secrets of the congressional Red hunters was that you could get off the blacklist if you paid off the right guy and were willing to make a "confession." This plot detail was used in Irwin Winkler's Guilty by Suspicion *(1991), a film about the blacklist, and here is testimony that the practice actually existed. Howard Koch, the coauthor of* Casablanca, *was one of the blacklist victims and along with other suspects was subpoenaed to testify in Washington.*

from *As Time Goes By*

Before appearing in Washington, those of us who had been served subpoenas gathered in Edward G. Robinson's home in Beverly Hills to discuss how to deal collectively with the situation confronting nineteen of us, the opening move in a campaign that was going to affect the entire film community and, eventually, the country at large. John Huston and Philip Dunne had organized what was termed the "Committee of a Hundred" to support us and defend our rights. Present at the meeting were many of Hollywood's celebrated figures, including Katharine Hepburn, Humphrey Bogart, Lauren Bacall, and John Garfield. After much discussion it was decided that as many of their committee as could get away would appear at the hearings on our behalf.

That nightmarish week in Washington will remain with me the rest of my life. We were in our own capital, yet no foreign city could have been more alien and hostile. All our hotel rooms were bugged. When we, the nineteen "unfriendly witnesses," wanted to talk with each other or with our attorneys, we had either to keep twirling a metal key to jam the circuit or to go out of doors. It became clear from the outset of the hearings that this was no impartial investigation or trial, but an inquisition, impure and simple, designed to break down, expose, and vilify the political and social beliefs of those who dissented from the now-established Cold War policies.

Although I was one of the nineteen, I was in one sense an outsider from my own group since I disagreed with the stand taken by the majority.

Led by members of what later became known as the "Hollywood Ten" and approved by all three of our lawyers, they decided not to answer any of the committee's questions relating to their political associations and beliefs. Their position was based on a literal interpretation of the First Amendment protecting an individual's freedom of belief and expression. I had every respect for their principled position and still have. My disagreement was purely tactical. I contended that in a period of public hysteria induced by the widely publicized "Red menace," the Bill of Rights would be disregarded or circumvented one way or another. My counterproposal was for all of us to speak out and defend affirmatively our own and each other's political beliefs and associations.

Several of the ten and one of our lawyers tried hard to persuade me that theirs was the right course and that my stand would disrupt the unity of the "unfriendly nineteen." I argued that our refusal to answer would be interpreted by the press and the public as an admission of guilt, as proof of our having something to hide. Actually, there was nothing hidden from the committee. They knew who was and who wasn't a party member and, in fact, everything about us and our associations. For the past months they had planted informers to infiltrate and report on our activities. And any gap was filled in by the "friendly witnesses" who testified against us at the start of the hearings.

Since most of the ten and the lawyers were solidly against my proposal, I had misgivings: perhaps I was wrong, perhaps I was taking the easier way out since I was not a party member, although at that time there was no law making membership a crime. To test my position I met several times with John Huston at night on the street where our conversation couldn't be bugged. He listened to both sides of the argument, then talked it over with the Committee of a Hundred. He reported back to me that they agreed with my proposal and were willing to back it with full support of everyone under attack, whether a party member or not.

This failed to sway the ten, who confronted the Congressional committee with their refusals to answer, often eloquently. The First Amendment was brushed aside by the committee and later by the courts; the ten men eventually went to prison. Nine of the ten held steadfastly to their political beliefs and today, two decades later, receptions are held in their honor, books and plays are written, based on the transcripts of the hearings, in which they appear, deservedly, in the role of heroes.

One evening when it had become clear we were losing whatever public and industry support we once had, several of us were gathered in our hotel room talking over our plight. The mood was anything but cheerful. Paul Draper, the dancer and a long-time friend, dropped in, took a look at us, and made a suggestion. Paul stuttered in ordinary conversation but never on the stage.

"L-look, you guys. When you're as d-down as you are tonight, there's only one th-thing to do."

We all turned and looked at him. What was he going to propose—suicide?

"You order the b-best champagne you can get and d-drink it up. It never f-fails."

Anne thought it was a great idea; the rest of us went along. Paul did the ordering. He knew the right vineyard and the best vintage year, directing the wine steward to find what was wanted even if he had to dig it out of the vaults. And it worked its bubbling magic. As the wine went down, our spirits rose. We became almost euphoric, casting out all inhibitions. If the committee played back on their recording machine what was said that night, they must have heard some astonishing things.

This little spree was a much-needed antidote to what was going on in the committee room. The "friendly witnesses" such as Jack Warner, John Wayne, and Adolphe Menjou were cataloguing our "political sins" in great detail and getting full coverage by the press. Warner testified that in his opinion I was a "Communist"; the studio had had to get rid of me because I was "slipping Communist propaganda in their films." This had a special irony since it was at his urgent request that I wrote the screenplay for *Mission to Moscow,* which had brought him kudos at the time but was now obviously an embarrassment. I had no opportunity to point this out at the hearings, as the committee canceled my subpoena by a last-minute telegram, apparently not eager to have me testify. Later Warner lamely admitted to a friend that he had "made a mistake." However that might be, I am still listed in the *Congressional Record* as Warner described me, which shows that lies are preserved in these official volumes as carefully as the truth.

The heads of the Hollywood studios, frightened by threats of boycotts of their films by the American Legion and like-minded groups, capitulated and began a wholesale purge of anyone suspected of Communist membership or leftist leanings.

Contracts were broken at will. The morals clause, equating nonconformity with immorality, provided a legal excuse. Caution dictated the pictures now being made. Any idea with the slightest social implication was taboo. Using the threat of boycott, the various committees and their adherents had captured a powerful communications medium which, for a time, had dared to question what had become official policy.

In social gatherings one had to be careful what subjects were discussed, and with whom. One even had to watch which movie houses one attended. (Avoid Russian films. Self-appointed spies could be lurking to record the identifying numbers on car license plates.) And this shadowed world had its physical counterpart. Smog had seeped in from the open storage tanks of the oil refineries and, fed by the increasing motor traffic, was casting its pall over Los Angeles and its environs.

. . . .

Not because of sentiment, but because my pictures had made the studios a great deal of money, a powerful agent who shall be nameless asked me to come to his office; he had a proposition to make. He would arrange a meeting for me with the attorney who was the liaison to the House Un-American Activities Committee. All I had to do was spend a half-hour with this party, renouncing some of my unpopular political views and associates, and pay the attorney seventy-five hundred dollars. I told him that was a pretty expensive half-hour, both in money and in conscience.

He said, "Don't worry about the money. A studio will advance it as a down payment on a writing assignment."

"That isn't what I'm worried about. It's the other."

He brushed that concern aside. "What do you care what you tell those bastards? Keep your fingers crossed."

"I'd have to keep them crossed the rest of my life." I was curious. "Tell me, who gets the seventy-five hundred dollars? That's a pretty stiff fee for a half-hour of anyone's time."

"That's their business, not ours."

"Well, thanks for trying, but the answer is 'no.' "

"Don't decide now. This is your last chance to stay in pictures. Talk it over with your wife."

"Her answer wouldn't be any different."

He shook his head. "Too bad. You're throwing away a fine career."

I went back to Palm Springs. There was a black telephone in an alcove off the living room. I had never been conscious of how silent a phone could be until it stops ringing.

NATHANAEL WEST

The Day of the Locust, by Nathanael West (1903–1940), published in 1939, was an apocalyptic vision of a Hollywood ruled by the mob; perhaps its buried subject was fascism. Its hero, a lowly studio employee and would-be painter named Tod Hackett, shares with several other men (and no doubt with millions more in the darkness of theaters) a passion for Faye Greener, a starlet whose friendly contempt for his feelings only inflames them. In this chapter Faye has been avoiding Tod, and as he pursues her on a studio back lot, West makes a hallucinatory nightmare out of the back lot jumble.

from *The Day of the Locust*

Faye moved out of the San Berdoo the day after the funeral. Tod didn't know where she had gone and was getting up the courage to call Mrs. Jenning when he saw her from the window of his office. She was dressed in the costume of a Napoleonic vivandiere. By the time he got the window open, she had almost turned the corner of the building. He shouted for her to wait. She waved, but when he got downstairs she was gone.

From her dress, he was sure that she was working in the picture called "Waterloo." He asked a studio policeman where the company was shooting and was told on the back lot. He started toward it at once. A platoon of cuirassiers, big men mounted on gigantic horses, went by. He knew that they must be headed for the same set and followed them. They broke into a gallop and he was soon outdistanced.

The sun was very hot. His eyes and throat were choked with the dust thrown up by the horses' hooves and his head throbbed. The only bit of shade he could find was under an ocean liner made of painted canvas with real life boats hanging from its davits. He stood in its narrow shadow for a while, then went on toward a great forty-foot papier mache sphinx that loomed up in the distance. He had to cross a desert to reach it, a desert that was continually being made larger by a fleet of trucks dumping white sand. He had gone only a few feet when a man with a megaphone ordered him off.

He skirted the desert, making a wide turn to the right, and came to a Western street with a plank sidewalk. On the porch of the "Last Chance Saloon" was a rocking chair. He sat down on it and lit a cigarette.

From there he could see a jungle compound with a water buffalo tethered to the side of a conical grass hut. Every few seconds the animal groaned musically. Suddenly an Arab charged by on a white stallion. He shouted at the man, but got no answer. A little while later he saw a truck with a load of snow and several malamute dogs. He shouted again. The driver shouted something back, but didn't stop.

Throwing away his cigarette, he went through the swinging doors of the saloon. There was no back to the building and he found himself in a Paris street. He followed it to its end, coming out in a Romanesque courtyard. He heard voices a short distance away and went toward them. On a lawn of fiber, a group of men and women in riding costume were picnicking. They were eating cardboard food in front of a cellophane waterfall. He started toward them to ask his way, but was stopped by a man who scowled and held up a sign—"Quite, Please, We're Shooting." When Tod took another step forward, the man shook his fist threateningly.

Next he came to a small pond with large celluloid swans floating on it. Across one end was a bridge with a sign that read, "To Kamp Komfit." He crossed the bridge and followed a little path that ended at a Greek temple dedicated to Eros. The god himself lay face downward in a pile of old newspapers and bottles.

From the steps of the temple, he could see in the distance a road lined with Lombardy poplars. It was the one on which he had lost the cuirassiers. He pushed his way through a tangle of briars, old flats and iron junk, skirting the skeleton of a Zeppelin, a bamboo stockade, an adobe fort, the wooden horse of Troy, a flight of baroque palace stairs that started in a bed of weeds and ended against the branches of an oak, part of the Fourteenth Street elevated station, a Dutch windmill, the bones of a dinosaur, the upper half of the Merrimac, a corner of a Mayan temple, until he finally reached the road.

He was out of breath. He sat down under one of the poplars on a rock made of brown plaster and took off his jacket. There was a cool breeze blowing and he soon felt more comfortable.

He had lately begun to think not only of Goya and Daumier but also of certain Italian artists of the seventeenth and eighteenth centuries, of Salvator Rosa, Francesco Guardi and Monsu Desiderio, the painters of Decay and Mystery. Looking down hill now, he could see compositions that might have actually been arranged from the Calabrian work of Rosa. There were partially demolished buildings and broken monuments half hidden by great, tortured trees, whose exposed roots writhed dramatically in the arid ground, and by shrubs that carried, not flowers or berries, but armories of spikes, hooks and swords.

For Guardi and Desiderio there were bridges which bridged nothing, sculpture in trees, palaces that seemed of marble until a whole stone portico began to flap in the light breeze. And there were figures as well. A hundred yards from where Tod was sitting a man in a derby hat leaned drowsily against the gilded poop of a Venetian barque and peeled an apple. Still farther on, a charwoman on a stepladder was scrubbing with soap and water the face of a Buddha thirty feet high.

He left the road and climbed across the spine of the hill to look down on the other side. From there he could see a ten-acre field of cockleburs spotted with clumps of sunflowers and wild gum. In the center of the field was a gigantic pile of sets, flats and props. While he watched, a ten-ton truck added another load to it. This was the final dumping ground. He thought of Janvier's "Sargasso Sea." Just as that imaginary body of water was a history of civilization in the form of a marine junkyard, the studio lot was one in the form of a dream dump. A Sargasso of the imagination! And the dump grew continually, for there wasn't a dream afloat somewhere which wouldn't sooner or later turn up on it, having first been made photographic by plaster, canvas, lath and paint. Many boats sink and never reach the Sargasso, but no dream ever entirely disappears. Somewhere it troubles some unfortunate person and some day, when that person has been sufficiently troubled, it will be reproduced on the lot.

When he saw a red glare in the sky and heard the rumble of cannon, he knew it must be Waterloo. From around a bend in the road trotted several cavalry regiments. They wore casques and chest armor of black cardboard and carried long horse pistols in their saddle holsters. They were Victor Hugo's soldiers. He had worked on some of the drawings for their uniforms himself, following carefully the descriptions in "Les Miserables."

He went in the direction they took. Before long he was passed by the men of Lefebvre-Desnouttes, followed by a regiment of gendarmes d'elite, several companies of chasseurs of the guard and a flying detachment of Rimbaud's lancers.

They must be moving up for the disastrous attack on La Haite Santee. He hadn't read the scenario and wondered if it had rained yesterday. Would Grouchy or Blucher arrive? Grotenstein, the producer, might have changed it.

The sound of cannon was becoming louder all the time and the red fan in the sky more intense. He could smell the sweet, pungent odor of blank powder. It might be over before he could get there. He started to run. When he topped a rise after a sharp bend in the road, he found a great plain below him covered with early nineteenth-century troops, wearing all the gay and elaborate uniforms that used to please him so much when he was a child and spent long hours looking at the soldiers in an old dictionary. At the far end of the field, he could see an enormous hump around which the English and their allies were gathered. It was Mont St. Jean and they were getting ready to defend it gallantly. It wasn't quite finished, however, and swarmed with grips, property men, set dressers, carpenters and painters.

Tod stood near a eucalyptus tree to watch, concealing himself behind a sign that read, " 'Waterloo'—A Charles H. Grotenstein Production." Near by a youth in a carefully torn horse guard's uniform was being rehearsed in his lines by one of the assistant directors.

"Vive l'Empereur!" the young man shouted, then clutched his breast and fell forward dead. The assistant director was a hard man to please and made him do it over and over again.

In the center of the plain, the battle was going ahead briskly. Things looked tough for the British and their allies. The Prince of Orange commanding the center, Hill the right and Picton the left wing, were being pressed hard by the veteran French. The desperate and intrepid Prince was in an especially bad spot. Tod heard him cry hoarsely above the din of battle, shouting to the Hollande-Belgians, "Nassau! Brunswick! Never retreat!" Nevertheless, the retreat began. Hill, too, fell back. The French killed General Picton with a ball through the head and he returned to his dressing room. Alten was put to the sword and also retired. The colors of the Lunenberg battalion, borne by a prince of the family of Deux-Ponts, were captured by a famous child star in the uniform of a Parisian drummer boy. The Scotch Greys were destroyed and went to change into another uniform. Ponsonby's heavy dragoons were also cut to ribbons. Mr. Grotenstein would have a large bill to pay at the Western Costume Company.

Neither Napoleon nor Wellington was to be seen. In Wellington's absence, one of the assistant directors, a Mr. Crane, was in command of the allies. He reinforced his center with one of Chasse's brigades and one of Wincke's. He supported these with infantry from Brunswick, Welsh foot, Devon yeomanry and Hanoverian light horse with oblong leather caps and flowing plumes of horsehair.

For the French, a man in a checked cap ordered Milhaud's cuirassiers to carry Mont St. Jean. With their sabers in their teeth and their pistols in their hands, they charged. It was a fearful sight.

The man in the checked cap was making a fatal error. Mont St. Jean was unfinished. The paint was not yet dry and all the struts were not in place. Because of the thickness of the cannon smoke, he had failed to see that the hill was still being worked on by property men, grips and carpenters.

It was the classic mistake, Tod realized, the same one Napoleon had made. Then it had been wrong for a different reason. The Emperor had ordered the cuirassiers to charge Mont St. Jean not knowing that a deep ditch was hidden at its foot to trap his heavy cavalry. The result had been disaster for the French; the beginning of the end.

This time the same mistake had a different outcome. Waterloo, instead of being the end of the Grand Army, resulted in a draw. Neither side won, and it would have to be fought over again the next day. Big losses, however, were sustained by the insurance company in workmen's compensation. The man in the checked cap was sent to the dog house by Mr. Grotenstein just as Napoleon was sent to St. Helena.

When the front rank of Milhaud's heavy division started up the slope of Mont St. Jean, the hill collapsed. The noise was terrific. Nails screamed with agony as they pulled out of joists. The sound of ripping canvas was like that of little children whimpering. Lath and scantling snapped as though they were brittle bones. The whole hill folded like an enormous umbrella and covered Napoleon's army with painted cloth.

It turned into a route. The victors of Bersina, Leipsic, Austerlitz, fled like schoolboys who had broken a pane of glass. "Sauve qui peut!" they cried, or, rather, "Scram!"

The armies of England and her allies were too deep in scenery to flee. They had to wait for the carpenters and ambulances to come up. The men of the gallant Seventy-Fifth Highlanders were lifted out of the wreck with block and tackle. They were carted off by the stretcher-bearers, still clinging bravely to their claymores.

OSCAR LEVANT

In many of the musicals of the 1940s and 1950s Oscar Levant (1906–1972) was like the ghost at the banquet. What did audiences make of his dyspeptic cynicism in the midst of all that music and romance? Yet he was wildly popular, the costar of a radio program with Al Jolson. It was widely known that he was a neurotic pillhead—that was his persona, somewhat modified for general consumption—and a case can be made that he paved the way for Lenny Bruce and the other revolutionary comics of the 1950s. He was also a talented pianist and composer and probably one of the smartest men in Hollywood at the time, and perhaps his unlikely career as a movie star can be explained by the fact that so many powerful people enjoyed having him around. His Memoirs of an Amnesiac *reads like a guy recalling all his one-liners, but because they were great one-liners, that's okay.*

from *The Memoirs of an Amnesiac*

In 1940 I was asked to do a movie for Paramount Studios. When I informed them that I couldn't act, my modesty beguiled them and I was signed for three pictures.

The first was *Rhythm on the River* with Bing Crosby and for a Crosby picture it was quite good. I played an unsympathetic part—myself—in which I was relentlessly and irrepressibly audacious, supplying many of my own lines.

Basil Rathbone, a charming man, was the heavy in the picture. He played a stuffed shirt and, I may add, he was not miscast. At lunch the conversation was limited to the success or failure of his bowel movements.

I got along with everybody including Mary Martin and the director Victor Schertzinger, a good musician who had written the songs for *The Love Parade,* Ernst Lubitsch's first talking picture.

My second picture for Paramount was *Kiss the Boys Goodbye,* based loosely on a play by Clare Boothe Luce.

Mary Martin had made a big hit in a New York musical doing a charming striptease as she sang "My Heart Belongs to Daddy," but the mild strip number that she did in *Kiss the Boys Goodbye* was as sexy as hanging out the wash.

On my return to New York, after that picture, I was interviewed at Grand Central Station and when asked what kind of part I had played, I said, "It's the kind of part you get when the studio wants to break your contract." Actually it was a good part and I can't account for that remark except that it was said out of impudence.

. . . .

In 1944 I was signed by Warner Brothers to appear in *Rhapsody in Blue,* the alleged story of George Gershwin.

Igor Stravinsky visited the set when we were making that picture. Immediately before his visit I'd read the life of Ferruccio Busoni, who was a great pianist and a major figure in promulgating the ultimate contemporary music of his period. I learned that during World War I, all the great musicians were in neutral Switzerland and that Busoni and Stravinsky had met only once, though they lived a mere five miles apart. Stravinsky was of course a young man at that time.

"Why did you visit Busoni only once?" I asked Stravinsky.

His answer was cryptic. He said, "Because he represented the immediate past and I hate the immediate past."

Igor Stravinsky can be waspish, too. When someone called him for an appointment recently, he looked at his appointment book, then said, "Not Monday . . . not Tuesday . . . not Wednesday . . ." Then suddenly, in a burst of ecstasy, he slammed the book closed and cried, "Never!"

Rhapsody in Blue was a big hit and I was signed by Warners for two more pictures.

My next was *Humoresque,* which was based on a rejected script of *Rhapsody in Blue,* written by Clifford Odets. There was also another writer, but I wrote most of my own lines. I was let loose on this picture as though I were Franz Liszt giving a recital.

Jerry Wald produced *Humoresque* and drew upon my personal experiences as a concert artist to authenticate the role of the violinist, played by John Garfield.

John Garfield had made his first big movie hit in the picture *Four Daughters,* in which he based his characterization on me. The one person to recognize this and point it out was Hedda Hopper, whom I had met in my early days in Hollywood.

As technical adviser of *Humoresque* I insisted that when Garfield made his debut as a violinist in one scene, the hall be only half filled, with no tuxedoes worn and no formal attire. People don't go to concerts in white ties. That still goes on only in the movies.

I believe that this picture was the first attempt in a movie to reveal the true conditions of a struggling concert artist in the preparation and problems of a debut.

What made the picture seem slightly old-fashioned was the role of the personalized patron of the arts. The lower East Side boy (Garfield) launched in his career by a wealthy socialite (Joan Crawford) was indigenous to the time when Fannie Hurst wrote the novel *Humoresque.*

John Garfield, whom everyone called Julie, had to be photographed playing the violin, simulating the technique of the left hand fingering and the right hand bowing it. They had great difficulty with this scene. They couldn't arrive at a *modus operandi* until finally, in close shots, they had two violinists crouched out of camera range; one did the fingerwork and the other the bowing. The violin was attached to Garfield's neck. The real playing was pre-recorded by the great Isaac Stern, and I accompanied him on the piano. After a couple of takes, I suggested, "Why don't the five of us make a concert tour?"

One of the most astonishing musical crimes ever perpetrated in a serious picture was the arrangement for violin, piano and orchestra of all the salient climactic portions of *Tristan and Isolde* as background music for the final ten minutes of *Humoresque,* during which time Joan Crawford laboriously committed suicide. Isaac Stern didn't object but I did to no avail. However, it was very effective.

In one scene the director wanted my face to reflect deep concern. He tried several takes, then finally said, "Oscar, just imagine that your kids are sick—*very* sick." I got so mad that I almost punched him in the nose.

I said a line to Joan Crawford, who played the part of a married woman with multiple sexual activities, "Why don't you get a divorce and settle down?"

I had one line in the script which I refused to utter unless I gave due credit. It was originally said by Leopold Godowsky, a great pianist in his time, whose son is married to George Gershwin's sister Frankie. The line was: "I don't like to go to concerts because if they're good, I'm jealous; if they're bad, I'm bored."

Jerry Wald said, "Why don't you say it?"

"I'll say it if I can say, 'as Leopold Godowsky said . . .' " I replied.

"You can't do that," he insisted.

So I didn't say the line. But when I saw the picture, Garfield said it—without acknowledging the source.

Jerry would always come on the set with copious notes and he would keep asking me, "Can't you use this line: 'Don't think it hasn't been fun, because it hasn't'?" It was an archaic line even then, but he wouldn't give up.

With stoical resistance, I continued to refuse.

I recall suggesting a line to Jerry—"I love you is an inadequate way to say I love you"—which he used in his next picture, *Possessed*. *The New Yorker* critic singled the line out as being most peculiar.

Joan Crawford was the illustrious and glamorous star of *Humoresque*. She was always accompanied to lunch by her hairdresser, the equivalent of priest, psychoanalyst and lawyer. The hairdresser is the most important member of a star's family. It was right after the war and Crawford always had two raw steaks under her arm.

The queen of the Warner lot at that time was Bette Davis. One day at lunch she was sitting a table away and Joan Crawford went over and said some pleasantry. Bette Davis cut her dead. Joan was bathed in tears and didn't recover for quite a while.

Jerry Wald and I were very close friends, though we had occasional minor disagreements, and any close friend of mine—as I've often said—must be crazy.

Jerry was a man of infectious enthusiasm, and was warm, kind and generous in his private life.

He had an enormous library and I would borrow his books. They had voluminous notations on almost every page; not just significant or epithetical or epigrammatical notes, but line after line underlined in red ink. I borrowed a great number of them and I not only loathed, but often refused, to return them.

Once Jerry borrowed Kenneth Tynan's first book, *He Who Would Play King,* from me. I'd borrowed it from Vincente Minnelli. Jerry refused to return it.

After his death, his widow said to Vincente, "I'll return the book Jerry borrowed from you."

Vincente replied, "Oh, that was José Ferrer's book in the first place. I had to return it to him, so I sent to England for a copy."

Jerry's two favorite plays, which he manipulated mysteriously, were Robert Sherwood's *The Petrified Forest* and Somerset Maugham's *The Letter.* In a number of the pictures Jerry made, he had these counterplots disguised, and Warner Brothers also had a big backlog of dramatic properties which he constantly, and not too surreptitiously, drew upon.

As far as directors were concerned he was limited to those who were under contract to Warners, and when he signed John Huston to direct *Key Largo* it was considered a brilliant coup. However[,] Richard Brooks, who was the scriptwriter, told me that Jerry was only able to achieve this by promising Huston a great screen treatment. When it proved to be less than true, Huston was furious and barred Jerry from the set. Despite this antagonism Jerry had accomplished what he had wanted—to hire a director of stature. It did have quite a cast, with Edward G. Robinson and Humphrey Bogart; and I think it was very successful.

Claire Trevor was in it and had to sing a song without accompaniment. She told Huston that she'd take vocal lessons, but he wouldn't let her; he wanted the opposite result: a naked, barren, raw voice unadorned. Claire won an award for that picture.

The most critical comment about Jerry Wald that I can remember was made by Phil Yordan—a writer of mysterious origins.

Phil confided to me with a gentle sigh—it was like one elder statesman commenting on another—"You know, Jerry Wald never really knew how to steal."

When Yordan was on my television show, he was trying to plug *Anna Lucasta,* a picture based on his play.

It bore a marked resemblance to *Anna Christie* but ethnically it was about a Polish family and then changed to an all-Negro cast for the movie. The picture was done with Eartha Kitt and Sammy Davis, Jr.

At the end of my show, Yordan asked, "Do you want to hear about my failures?"

I said, "No, your successes are depressing enough."

Jerry Wald finally did *To Have and Have Not,* by Hemingway. It was the third time it had been done.

There was a robbery in Jerry's version. I looked at the script and the robbery looked foolproof. I said to Jerry, "The hell with the picture . . . let's do the robbery."

He took credit for this line and issued it to the newspapers—no one used self-advertisement more egregiously than he.

Jerry once quoted another producer as saying, "My comedies are not to be laughed at."

During his years as a producer at Warner Brothers, Jerry did two of Tennessee Williams' plays but when he went to 20th Century-Fox Tennessee's price became too prohibitive as far as Jerry was concerned.

He suddenly became involved with Faulkner. He'd buy a Faulkner property and that turgid, incomprehensible prose was on one occasion transformed into *The Long Hot Summer.* In that picture Orson Welles played a "big daddy" type of role. Sometimes he was inaudible—Those were his best moments.

Jerry took me to a televised theatre showing of the Marciano-Archie Moore fight. He was just about to make *The Harder They Fall,* by Budd Schulberg.

In the second round Moore hit Rocky Marciano, who went down quickly but got up at the count of five. Jerry made a note of that and incorporated it in *The Harder They Fall.*

Fortunately I never saw the picture, but it was about Primo Carnera. I saw Carnera's first fight with Big Boy Peterson. I was with Jean Arthur the night Carnera fought Ernie Schaaf; in the twelfth round Schaaf went down. Everyone stood up and booed, thinking it was a fixed fight. Ernie Schaaf died a short time later.

When Jerry was top independent producer at Columbia, Cecil B. De Mille's hot breath was down everyone's neck, so Jerry decided to do a Biblical picture. One of the only stories that hadn't been touched was *Joseph and His Brothers,* but in order to avoid paying for the rights to Thomas Mann's trilogy, Wald hired Clifford Odets to write a treatment. Odets had just written what was to be his last play, *The Flowering Peach,* about Noah.

Columbia had a contract with Rita Hayworth, then a glittering symbol of Hollywood and still beautiful. A starting date had been set, so they built sets without having a script, and Odets just wrote a few scenes for Rita, who was to play Potiphar's wife. Rita claimed the script was skeletal and refused to do it.

Odets worked at it and finally had a thousand-page script, but they never did the picture. I don't know what the final straw was, but I believe the costs were astronomical.

Rita was then married to Dick Haymes. June and I met them, and Haymes, a rather presumptuous fellow, proceeded to tell us about the size of Joseph Haydn's orchestra. Interestingly, he was in error on all counts.

For political or temperamental reasons, Harry Cohn, head of Columbia, liked people no one else wanted and always gave them jobs. In the early 30's, when I used to go with Jean Arthur, she was out of work and we were sitting in the Vine Street Brown Derby when Cohn was lunching there. He saw her, gave her a job on the spot, and she became a great star.

.   .   .   .

Clifford Odets wrote the script for a picture for Elvis Presley. In the story he had Presley commit suicide at the end of the picture, which was far from endearing to the audience at the preview. Never was such horror expressed by so many. He rewrote the finish, but only Odets would write a story for Elvis in which he committed suicide. Actually, it was humiliating that Odets had to write that kind of picture at all, but he needed the money. Everything he was against, in the beginning of his career, he wound up doing himself.

Clifford Odets first made his stunning presence felt on Broadway with *Awake and Sing* and *Waiting for Lefty*. He was invited to all the big parties; and Beatrice Lillie was quite taken with him for a while. There were other girls, one a famous picture star whom he brought to our apartment for dinner. I asked him why he didn't marry her.

"She has no bosom," he replied rather dejectedly.

I considered that a rather narrow and specious comment about love.

(In the early 40's, he and I had a great summit meeting at Lindy's with Dr. Karl Menninger, Moss Hart, Artie Shaw and all the leading Broadway neurotics. I told Dr. Menninger that we were wearing our sweaters with the letter F for Freud.)

When Clifford's play *Night Music* opened, Moss Hart and I had a date for dinner. Moss had a mildly hysterical case of jealousy about Odets, with his plays of social protest. I arrived at Dinty Moore's five minutes late and Moss carried on like a wounded stag. I said to Moss, "I'm not a dame. I'm only five minutes late!" But when *Night Music* had revealed itself as a rehashed rewrite of *Paradise Lost* and *Awake and Sing,* Moss was in a state of high elation.

In those days Clifford was the most arrogant man I'd ever met, but I was easily mesmerized by egomaniacs.

He once said to me, "The three greatest living playwrights are O'Neill, O'Casey and Odets."

The last time we saw Clifford, my wife reminded him of that remark.

"Did I say that?" he asked. He was shocked.

In the early 40's when I was on my way to the Pacific Coast to play some concerts, Odets and I were on the same train for three or four days. He was reading *The Storm,* a play by the Russian, Aleksandr Ostrovski. (Tschaikowsky in his diary wrote that Andrew Carnegie looked just like Ostrovski.)

At the end of the first act Clifford threw the play down with a tremendous bang and shouted, "This guy can't kiss my ass!" He peremptorily dismissed it and ranted at me, "You're supposed to be a friend of mine!"

"I am," I replied.

"Then did you like my play *Night Music?*" he asked.

"I liked it but you wrote it much better in *Paradise Lost,*" I said.

"You're a friend of mine?" he asked again.

"Yes," I repeated.

"If you were a friend of mine, you would have seen *Night Music* three times—four times!" he yelled, pounding the table.

And he kept reproaching me for not having seen the play more than once. Actually, I'd loathed it. It had that inescapable Communist ending: Let there be light, or Let there be air or what have you.

We stopped off in Chicago where Al Jolson was appearing in *Hold onto Your Hats.* We went to the Drake Hotel to see him, and found him in a terrible state. He'd been divorced from Ruby Keeler, his great love, and Al wanted her to let their adopted child see him in the show but Ruby had refused her permission. Jolson carried on in a harangue of profanity that surprised Clifford.

In Kansas City, the great stop in the hegira of the Super Chief, there was a superior bookstore in the station, but Clifford wouldn't get off the train. He pulled down the blinds and refused to move. I had a Kansas City paper which said that Martin Dies was in town that day. Dies was then Chairman of the House Un-American Activities Committee, and it was well known that Clifford was suspect. But I still thought it strange that he wouldn't at least stretch his legs for a few minutes.

We were shunted into a siding in some small town in Arizona and a freight train kept huffing and puffing on the other track.

"*Chug! Chug! Chug!*" Clifford shouted excitedly as he made rhythmic pumping movements with his feet in imitation of the train. "That's *power!*"

"That's corny," I replied, "they now have diesels that don't make a sound."

He glared at me.

When Odets was married to Luise Rainer, she gave a sour-cream dinner in my honor, but they fought during the first course and he left and went to a strikers' meeting.

When Luise won the Academy Award, Clifford said that she had not wanted to attend the ceremonies—she thought it would be fun to dress in old clothes and mingle anonymously with the crowds outside the theatre. It was only at the last minute that he was able to persuade her to go.

I used to talk to Clifford about the old days of *Golden Boy* and *Rocket to the Moon.* His plays were usually directed by Harold Clurman, but Odets resented the fact that Luther Adler (who is a wonderful actor) played the title role in *Golden Boy.* Clifford had wanted John Garfield and was always reluctant to forgive Clurman for that.

Frances Farmer, who played Lorna Moon in *Golden Boy,* was pursued by both

Odets and Clurman. The mention of her name by Clifford was usually accompanied by an enigmatic smile.

Clifford Odets had a tough time financially in his later years in Hollywood. He had two children and he would cook for them. He had a pressure cooker and was always cooking lamb shanks which were delicious.

A few years before he died I used to go over and ask for a few sleeping pills. He would give them to me along with some of his lamb shanks.

Once when I went over to beg some pills he said, "You're like my mother. Life was too tough for my mother and it's too tough for you."

He would occasionally give me a pill until my wife found out and asked him not to give me any more. He stopped even though I got desperate and called him and pleaded with him. One night he seemed to relent; he said he would drive over to my house. I waited as eagerly as Marcel Proust did for his mother's good night kiss. Then I got a call. Clifford said that in good conscience—because of June—he couldn't give me any pills.

. . . .

My last picture for Warners was *Romance on the High Seas*. It was Doris Day's first picture; that was before she became a virgin. She demonstrated her talents as a superb comedienne and song stylist in that picture and it was no surprise that she became one of the biggest Hollywood stars.

. . . .

When I was at Warner Brothers, I came to know Howard Hawks; an illustrious American director. I even did a lamentable picture with him.

Up until recently the man who was in charge of studio operations, story, casting, direction, and so forth, was called the Vice-President in Charge of Production.

Darryl Zanuck had that job most of his career. When June worked there, I told her that she seemed to think he was President of the United States.

Some years ago Darryl was at a café in Paris with Howard Hawks, and he expressed strong interest in a girl.

"I'm Darryl Zanuck, Vice-President in Charge of Production at 20th Century-Fox," he proclaimed.

It made quite an impression. He was doing very well when he suddenly had to retire to the men's room. While he was away the girl turned to Howard Hawks.

"Is he really Vice-President of 20th Century-Fox?" she asked.

Howard Hawks nodded.

"How do you know?" she pressed.

Howard Hawks kept his usual poker face.

"Because I'm President," he solemnly announced.

When Zanuck returned to the table, there was a marked diminution of ardor on the girl's part. The whole romance collapsed and the girl wound up with Hawks.

I told Howard Hawks that I thought it was surprising that Hemingway's *The Sun Also Rises* had never been sold to the movies. There was an obvious reason: the hero was impotent, though Hemingway had made him impotent physiologically rather than psychologically. Nobody would touch it. It was before the censors had relaxed.

Hawks bought the book for $7,500. He later sold it to Charlie Feldman, the agent, for an enormous profit. Then Feldman sold it to Darryl Zanuck for an even more enormous profit. But the grim irony remains—Hemingway got only $7,500.

I did a couple of uninspired pictures for 20th Century-Fox. It was the only studio that made me adhere rigidly to the script. There was one director whose name I won't mention—a grizzled old veteran, and a nice man. I once asked him how to read a certain line and he said helplessly: "Ask me anything but that!"

I met Marilyn Monroe while doing a picture at 20th. It was in the makeup department and Jean Peters was there. Jean—who had been a schoolteacher before becoming an actress—was much more attractive to me than Marilyn. The latter was quite young then and hadn't reached her notorious acclaim. She was undulating her lips, putting on lipstick, and she was very agreeable.

I said something to her and Jean Peters questioned my grammar. That was one of the nadir points of my career, to have my grammar corrected in front of Marilyn Monroe. Jean is now married to Howard Hughes, which amounts to total commitment.

Years ago my wife and I and some guests were in Chasen's restaurant when a slovenly attired man came in and said hello to me. I cut him dead.

Someone said, "That was Howard Hughes."

Just to reveal my lack of character, I got up, went to his table, and shook hands with him.

Howard Hughes' whims and indulgences make any other Hollywood character look like a pigmy.

When he had a bungalow at the Beverly Hills Hotel, he parked his car on the street overnight, which is against the police regulations. A friend of mine who lived in another bungalow there told me that he couldn't figure it out. He couldn't park his car overnight without getting a ticket and he wondered how Howard Hughes could. Then he discovered the answer. Every month Hughes would send a large check to the Beverly Hills police station, for the fines. He parked without worry for two years.

.   .   .   .

When July Garland had her weekly television shows in 1963, her voice became wobbly and she had depleted herself by taking off too much weight. But she's a vocal sorceress whose range—at its best—has a deep, interior vibrancy of great emotional urgency. Strangely enough, her medium and soft palates are not interesting. She has no great variety of expression; she's more Sarah Bernhardt than Eleonora Duse. Judy has become the living F. Scott Fitzgerald of song.

Arthur Freed is the best producer of musical pictures in the history of Hollywood, although he's eccentric and has his careless quirks. Arthur, a former songwriter, named two of his pictures after his songs. When he produced *Pagan Love Song,* he forgot to put the song he'd written into the picture. Louis B. Mayer had to remind him.

L.B. was a rather humorless man and I never saw him laugh. But if you had an idea and if he was back of the producer, he was a gambler and the money flowed.

Mayer had a private dining room off the commissary at M.G.M., where the feature was L.B. Mayer's matzoth-ball soup. He had a consuming passion for food.

Once, when he was courting a girl, he arrived at her door beaming with excitement, his hands behind his back.

"Guess what I've got!" he cried.

No doubt the lady expected furs or jewels.

"Give up?" he asked, then displayed his surprise. He had a plucked uncooked chicken in each hand.

In the 30's, George Kaufman used to sing a song called, "I'd rather have TB than LB." But L.B. was a rather formidable man physically and he had a terrible temper. (I think he even had fistfights with John Barrymore in the 20's.)

Betty Comden and Adolph Green were once ushered into his office and L.B. went into his favorite chant. He started singing "Ah! Sweet Mystery of Life" at the top of his voice. Then he said to Adolph and Betty, "Where are the songs of yesteryear?"

Adolph and Betty shrugged helplessly, then looked under the table. Adolph said, "Yeah, where are they?"

Mayer was always complaining about a picture that King Vidor made about 1929. He said that Vidor had had the gall to show a natural function. He was referring to the fact that Vidor had shown a toilet—a hideous idea to L.B. Indeed, it was so repellent that he'd bring it up every few weeks for years. "Don't show the natural functions!" he'd warn everyone.

.   .   .   .

Several years ago my friend Goddard Lieberson, President of Columbia Records, returned from Europe and raved to Freed about the great art galleries there.

Arthur listened, then rejoined, "If you really want to see paintings, you should see Bill Goetz' collection."

In 1951, Goddard, who had made a recording of *Porgy and Bess,* came out to California and June and I took him to visit the Freeds. Then we were going on to the Gershwins' to play the record for the first time. No one had heard it.

Arthur Freed, who has an obsessive compulsion to know everything first, asked, "How long does the record take?"

Goddard said, "Three hours."

Freed promptly replied, "Yes, I know"—which was mystifying.

Again, he came to my house one afternoon when I was watching a big football game on television.

"What are you watching?" he asked.

I replied, "A football game."

"I saw it," said Freed.

I was with Arthur and Bill Perlberg, another producer, late one night when Perlberg spoke of a certain property on which he claimed he had first refusal.

Freed whispered in my ear, "I have first refusal too."

.   .   .   .

As a producer, Freed dominates the scene always. At the beginning of *American in Paris* he announced, "We won't have any concert music. I don't want any lulls in this picture." This was directed at me.

I was heartbroken. Ten minutes later I came up with the idea of the ego fantasy where I play the Gershwin Piano Concerto, act as the conductor, play the other instruments and at the conclusion sit in a box and cheer myself.

But I was afraid to tell this to Freed, because of his decision.

However, I did tell the fantasy idea to Vincente Minnelli, who persuaded Arthur to use it; Raoul Dufy, the great painter, later told Freed that it was his favorite scene in the picture.

The Gershwin score for that picture was extraordinary and included some rather obscure songs that were little known or sung. One was called "By Strauss," and during rehearsal I played it for Gene Kelly, who was also the choreographer.

I did the Viennese afterbeat—I don't know how to describe it; the second beat precedes the real beat. I had learned my Strauss waltzes from Max Dreyfus.

Kelly asked, "Where is that in the music?"

We had quite a fight, but our differences were resolved and we finally achieved an agreeable relationship.

Gene did "I Got Rhythm" in a very unique and original way by using children. And the woman in the scene in which "By Strauss" was sung was an aged flowerwoman in a bistro whom Gene grabbed and swung into a rather tepid waltz that tore at your heartstrings. As talented as he is, Gene is not averse to a good dose of corn now and then.

I asked Jack Cole, the great dancer and choreographer, how he liked the choreography.

He said, rather bitterly, "With old women and children, how can you miss?"

American in Paris was Leslie Caron's first picture—Gene Kelly had discovered her in France and she was brought over with much publicity. After I had met her, June asked me what she looked like.

"She looks too much like me as far as I'm concerned," I replied.

My daughter Amanda looks a little like her.

After my heart attack in 1952, I worried about not getting well in time to do another picture, *Bandwagon,* for Arthur Freed. It featured Fred Astaire, Cyd Charisse, Jack Buchanan and me. Comden and Green had written the book, the music was comprised of old songs by Howard Dietz and Arthur Schwartz, except for one new number called "That's Entertainment." Michael Kidd was the choreographer.

The picture started six weeks after my heart attack, but I was able to work. It was the only picture I'd ever done in which I wasn't a bachelor; I was married to Nanette Fabray. I treated her atrociously—just as though she were indeed my real wife.

Jack Buchanan played the role of an actor-director-impresario. A scene in the script had him walking off-stage in the makeup of Oedipus Rex, gouged-out eyes, bloody face and all, and his line was "Get me a hot pastrami on rye." That was the extent of the scene.

Minnelli decided to embellish it by showing Buchanan onstage doing the role of Oedipus.

He became so carried away by the idea that he wrote to the widow of Yeats asking for Yeats' version of *Oedipus.* When he didn't receive a reply he hired Norman Corwin to adapt a few scenes. He also engaged Louis Calhern to coach Buchanan in the role of Oedipus. The shooting required many days.

Obviously it was folly to interrupt a musical show with a large portion of tragedy so the only part that remained in the finished picture was the original scene requesting a pastrami sandwich.

Oliver Smith, the great scenic designer, did the brilliant sets for *Bandwagon.* When he was very young, Oliver had been an usher at the Roxy Theatre in New York—a monstrous building with a complicated inside light system controlled from an airport-like tower that signaled the ushers about the availability of seats. On a certain Saturday night with the usual long line of people waiting to gain access, Oliver, choking with nausea about the militaristic regimentation of his job, decided to quit then and there. As a parting gesture he threw open the doors to the crowd, creating confusion and bedlam as the lights flashed wildly on and off in a dazzling concerto of meteors.

We were rehearsing the end of "That's Entertainment," a number where we had to walk down a long ramp, taking large strides at great speed. The physical effort involved worried me and when I told my doctor about this he said not to do it. At the next rehearsal I refused to do it, so in great disgust Fred Astaire said, "All right. I'll carry you down."

So I did it.

I have had the honor of playing with champions. One of the best of these is Fred Astaire. Several years ago when he was on the Jack Paar show, Fred demonstrated gentlemanliness beyond the call of duty.

Paar asked, "Who's older, you or your sister?"

Without hesitating a second, Fred said he was. The truth is that Adele is his senior. I thought that was gallant.

Fred and Adele Astaire were the toast of London in 1926, starring in *Lady Be Good*, which they'd done in New York previously. I remember how *soigné* he looked entering the Kit Kat Club. He was a favorite of the Prince of Wales.

In the early part of World War II, I did a radio show to help sell War Bonds. I was the moderator and Fred Astaire was a guest. I had him sing a very obscure song from *Lady Be Good* called "I Got the You-Don't-Know-the-Half-of-It, Dearie, Blues." That was the first time we ever worked together.

His sister Adele is a very zany character—really quite funny. George Gershwin wrote the score for *Funny Face*, a musical starring the Astaires, and George and Adele liked each other. George Jean Nathan was attracted to her also and it was suspected that that was the reason he gave Gershwin a bad review.

Once Adele and Fred and I had lunch at M.G.M. and I asked Fred, "When did you become a good dancer?"

"When Adele retired," he said.

Unlike Fred, Adele used to swear a lot. Fred would never use profanity. He's rather prudish—a very cautious fellow about everything. I think he probably drives slower than anyone in America. When he's making a picture, he's a great worrier, needs constant reassurance. However, he's not in the least temperamental and he's very considerate.

He talked about his youth: he told me of the time when he was about five years old and was first in vaudeville with Adele. He remembered the rooming-house in New York where his mother had locked him in. He even remembered the name of the street it was on.

We were reminiscing about girls and he spoke of Eleanor Holm. He was taken with her but couldn't get anywhere. There was a famous *Follies* girl whom he was mad about.

He told about Frank Fay tapping him on the shoulder and saying, "Lay off that one. She's Faysie's." Fred said he was so scared he never went near that girl again.

No one except possibly Ethel Merman has had more great songs written for him than Fred Astaire. It started with Vincent Youmans' *Flying Down to Rio*. Some of the people who wrote for him were: Con Conrad who wrote "The Continental"; Cole Porter, "Night and Day"; Jerome Kern and the Gershwin did the music for two pictures apiece; Irving Berlin the same for three pictures. Fred Astaire is the best singer of songs the movie world ever knew. His phrasing has individual sophistication that is utterly charming.

Presumably the runner-up would be Bing Crosby, a wonderful fellow, though he doesn't have the unstressed elegance of Astaire.

Dick Rodgers once told me that he had written for every great star but two— Fred Astaire and Ethel Merman. I don't understand how Fred Astaire missed Rodgers.

GROUCHO MARX

Groucho's letter to Warner Brothers is probably his most famous; he was a lifelong correspondent with the great (T. S. Eliot) and the obscure. I spent some days with him in his eighty-first year, interviewing him for Esquire, *and found him as advertised: funny, crotchety, filled with puns and wisecracks, literate, reflective about life. At the end of our final meeting, lunch at Le Bistro, I strolled with him down the street until he saw a theater playing a movie he wanted to see. He walked up to the ticket booth and said, "Good afternoon, I'm Groucho Marx—the living legend. Do you have the nerve to charge me for a ticket?" They didn't.*

from *The Groucho Letters*

When the Marx Brothers were about to make a movie called "A Night in Casablanca," there were threats of legal action from the Warner Brothers, who, five years before, had made a picture called, simply, "Casablanca" (with Humphrey Bogart and Ingrid Bergman as stars). Whereupon Groucho, speaking for his brothers and himself, immediately dispatched the following letters:

Dear Warner Brothers:

Apparently there is more than one way of conquering a city and holding it as your own. For example, up to the time that we contemplated making this picture, I had no idea that the city of Casablanca belonged exclusively to Warner Brothers. However, it was only a few days after our announcement appeared that we received your long, ominous legal document warning us not to use the name Casablanca.

It seems that in 1471, Ferdinand Balboa Warner, your great-great-grandfather, while looking for a shortcut to the city of Burbank, had stumbled on the shores of Africa and, raising his alpenstock (which he later turned in for a hundred shares of the common), named it Casablanca.

I just don't understand your attitude. Even if you plan on re-releasing your picture, I am sure that the average movie fan could learn in time to distinguish between Ingrid Bergman and Harpo. I don't know whether I could, but I certainly would like to try.

You claim you own Casablanca and that no one else can use that name without your permission. What about "Warner Brothers"? Do you own that, too? You probably have the right to use the name Warner, but what about Brothers? Professionally, we were brothers long before you were. We were touring the sticks as The Marx Brothers when Vitaphone was still a gleam in the inventor's eye, and even before us there had been other brothers—the Smith Brothers; the Brothers Karamazov; Dan Brothers, an outfielder with Detroit; and "Brother, Can You Spare a Dime?" (This was originally "Brothers, Can You Spare a Dime?" but this was spreading a dime pretty thin, so they threw out one brother, gave all the money to the other one and whittled it down to, "Brother, Can You Spare a Dime?")

Now Jack, how about you? Do you maintain that yours is an original name? Well, it's not. It was used long before you were born. Offhand, I can think of two Jacks—there was Jack of "Jack and the Beanstalk," and Jack the Ripper, who cut quite a figure in his day.

As for you, Harry, you probably sign your checks, sure in the belief that you are the first Harry of all time and that all other Harrys are imposters. I can think of two Harrys that preceded you. There was Lighthouse Harry of Revolutionary fame and a Harry Appelbaum who lived on the corner of 93rd Street and Lexington Avenue. Unfortunately, Appelbaum wasn't too well known. The last I heard of him, he was selling neckties at Weber and Heilbroner.

Now about the Burbank studio. I believe this is what you brothers call your place. Old man Burbank is gone. Perhaps you remember him. He was a great man in a garden. His wife often said Luther had ten green thumbs. What a witty woman she must have been! Burbank was the wizard who crossed all those fruits and vegetables until he had the poor plants in such a confused and jittery condition that they could never decide whether to enter the dining room on the meat platter or the dessert dish.

This is pure conjecture, of course, but who knows—perhaps Burbank's survivors aren't too happy with the fact that a plant that grinds out pictures on a quota settled in their town, appropriated Burbank's name and uses it as a front for their films. It is even possible that the Burbank family is prouder of the potato produced by the old man than they are of the fact that from your studio emerged "Casablanca" or even "Gold Diggers of 1931."

This all seems to add up to a pretty bitter tirade, but I assure you it's not meant to. I love Warners. Some of my best friends are Warner Brothers. It is even possible that I am doing you an injustice and that you, yourselves, know nothing at all about this dog-in-the-Wanger attitude. It wouldn't surprise me at all to discover that the heads of your legal department are unaware of this absurd dispute, for I am acquainted with many of them and they are fine fellows with curly black hair, double-breasted suits and a love of their fellow man that out-Saroyans Saroyan.

I have a hunch that this attempt to prevent us from using the title is the brainchild of some ferret-faced shyster, serving a brief apprenticeship in your legal department. I know the type well—hot out of law school, hungry for success and too ambitious to follow the natural laws of promotion. This bar sinister probably needled your attorneys, most of whom are fine fellows with curly black hair, double-breasted suits, etc., into attempting to enjoin us. Well, he won't get away with it! We'll fight him to the highest court! No pasty-faced legal adventurer is going to cause bad blood between the Warners and the Marxes. We are all brothers under the skin and we'll remain friends till the last reel of "A Night in Casablanca" goes tumbling over the spool.

Sincerely,

GROUCHO MARX

For some curious reason, this letter seemed to puzzle the Warner Brothers legal department. They wrote—in all seriousness—and asked if the Marxes could give them some idea of what their story was about. They felt that something might be worked out. So Groucho replied:

Dear Warners:

There isn't much I can tell you about the story. In it I play a Doctor of Divinity who ministers to the natives and, as a sideline, hawks can openers and pea jackets to the savages along the Gold Coast of Africa.

When I first meet Chico, he is working in a saloon, selling sponges to barflies who are unable to carry their liquor. Harpo is an Arabian caddie who lives in a small Grecian urn on the outskirts of the city.

As the picture opens, Porridge, a mealy-mouthed native girl, is sharpening some arrows for the hunt. Paul Hangover, our hero, is constantly lighting two cigarettes simultaneously. He apparently is unaware of the cigarette shortage.

There are many scenes of splendor and fierce antagonisms, and Color, an Abyssinian messenger boy, runs Riot. Riot, in case you have never been there, is a small night club on the edge of town.

There's a lot more I could tell you, but I don't want to spoil it for you. All this has been okayed by the Hays Office, Good Housekeeping and the survivors of the Haymarket Riots; and if the times are ripe, this picture can be the opening gun in a new worldwide disaster.

Cordially,

GROUCHO MARX

Instead of mollifying them, this note seemed to puzzle the attorneys even more; they wrote back and said they still didn't understand the story line and they would appreciate it if Mr. Marx would explain the plot in more detail. So Grouch obliged with the following:

Dear Brothers:

Since I last wrote you, I regret to say there have been some changes in the plot of our new picture, "A Night in Casablanca." In the new version I play Bordello, the sweetheart of Humphrey Bogart. Harp and Chico are itinerant rug peddlers who are weary of laying rugs and enter a monastery just for a lark. This is a good joke on them, as there hasn't been a lark in the place for fifteen years.

Across from this monastery, hard by a jetty, is a waterfront hotel, chockfull of apple-cheeked damsels, most of whom have been barred by the Hays Office for soliciting. In the fifth reel, Gladstone makes a speech that sets the House of Commons in a uproar and the King promptly asks for his resignation. Harpo marries a hotel detective; Chico operates an ostrich farm. Humphrey Bogart's girl, Bordello, spends her last years in a Bacall house.

This, as you can see, is a very skimpy outline. The only thing that can save us from extinction is a continuation of the film shortage.

Fondly,

Groucho Marx

After that, the Marxes heard no more from the Warner Brothers' legal department.

Julia Phillips

Julia Phillips rode high in the Hollywood of the 1970s as one of the producers of Taxi Driver *and* Close Encounters of the Third Kind. *Then she fell hard, into an extended period of drug abuse, alcoholism, and financial crisis. She is unforgiving toward herself in her memoir* You'll Never Eat Lunch in This Town Again *(1991), recalling a time when cocaine played an important role in many movies and deals and yesterday's wonder kids became today's washed-up losers. In the opening pages of her book she remembers Oscar night of 1974, when her success already contained the seeds of her failure.*

from *You'll Never Eat Lunch in This Town Again*

House Lights Dim Before Titles

The Sting *had been nominated, two months before, in ten categories, including Cinematography, Editing, Actor, Screenplay, Director, and Best Picture.* The Exorcist, *which had garnered an equal number of nominations, had been released the same day, two days before Christmas. It had received an enormous amount of initial publicity; even* The New York Times *carried pictures of people lined up in the cold to get in.*

Warners had been far too cautious in its release of The Exorcist. *It had opened in only twenty-four theaters. At 90/10 deals, Leo Greenfield kept reminding us. But then, he was the guy who told us, based on the first week's figures, that our picture would gross maybe fifteen mil. We had opened in 220 theaters, with 70/30 deals, and kept widening the release. Warners waited a good six weeks until they went wide. But The Exorcist was only a three-week picture; the audience lost interest before it was available.*

The Sting, on the other hand, had staying power. It had hung in, week after week, and it had opened in ten times the number of theaters. Not only was The Sting racking up some very impressive figures, but people had started to notice that it was an excellent movie. It certainly didn't send you out in the street unsure whether to hit a church or a bar, as The Exorcist did. And Warners had a crack at The Sting and turned us down.

We'd made damn sure John Calley and Dick Shepard came to the one screening Universal permitted us before the release of the picture. As they were walking out, I collared Calley, because I knew how much it annoyed him, and asked him how he liked the picture.

"I'm going home to slash my wrists," he said. Good. Supercilious motherfucker.

It would be them or us tonight at the Awards.

Michael and Tony had spent weeks aggravating over whether The Sting would win for Best Picture or not. They had practiced speeches, how they would stand up, their walks to the stage. I hadn't dared to contemplate the possibility of winning. I was not a big believer in the power of positive thinking, although I had gone to college with Norman Vincent Peale's daughter. Didn't wanna put a mojo on it; didn't wanna tempt the evil eye.

I translated all my anxiety into finding a dress. Joel Schumacher was my fashion consultant. We agreed I was a New York girl, most comfortable in black, and since so many Californians dressed in colors, that I would probably stand out. Where I got the chutzpah to think I might stand out at such a gathering I don't know. We traipsed from store to store and I would try something on and I would say, "Now if I win . . ." and then see if the dress was comfortable to walk in, and he would pull at a strap and say, "Now, when you win . . ." We finally settled on a black spaghetti-strap number by Halston at Giorgio's, a long strand of pearls, and a double feather boa made up of guinea hen and black ostrich feathers.

I was still, six months after Kate's birth, a little wide in the hip. Joel was adamant that I should wear beautiful black sandal-heels but I couldn't find any tall enough. I needed height. I ended up buying a pair of giant platform shoes from Fred Slatten. Black satin with rhinestones. They stayed hidden under the dress and they definitely gave me height. They also filled me with the quiescent fear that I might actually fall off them on global TV. A toss-up, looks or safety. The hips won out.

TRANCAS, CALIFORNIA
APRIL 2, 1974

I wake with a shudder at six thirty. The sun creates hot bounce on the sky/sea horizon. It is quite a sight, but I take this view for granted. Without pausing a moment in sincere appreciation, I automatically pop a diet pill. Bad move. Within twenty minutes, I'm dancing around the sandy living room, neatening up. I run along the beach, take a perfunctory dip in the freezing-cold Pacific, race indoors for a brief hot shower.

When I hit the bedroom, Michael is standing on his head, yoga-style, in the corner of the room. "I gotta pick up my tuxedo," Michael says, still upside down. The veins in his temples explode and contract on each syllable. Upstairs, I hear Kate's first baby-musings for the day. Sonya heats formula in the kitchen. I can smell it. I don't know how Kate can stand that shit.

"Good, that'll give me time to be nervous all by myself. Maybe Sonya could take Kate out for awhile." As in: I. NEED. MY. SPACE. . . .

Within the hour, they're toast. I lay out some coke on a small mirror. Secret stash. Mine. Michael doesn't even know I have it . . . that's how it's gotten. I chop it lightly with a razor. It falls apart like butter. This is good coke. Smooth. I do a hit, then another. I roll a joint and smoke it out on the deck. Less than a hundred yards from me, the ocean beats down in heavy waves against the sand. I pace, my heart beating in triple time to the waves.

I watch the postal van ease its way toward our mailbox, vault over the deck, and scramble down the hill to meet it. The mailman has a stack, bills mostly, junk mail addressed to Occupant. Sandwiched between the telephone bill and the latest issue of *Time* is a small blue envelope. The handwriting addressing Michael and Julia Phillips is familiar. I tear open the envelope as I return to the house, yelling "Thanks" over my shoulder to the mailman's wishes for our good luck that night. The letter is short and pithy, my favorites:

Dear Michael & Julia:

In a few days, you will be getting cards and letters and telegrams from everyone, so I wanted to get in what I had to say now. The important thing to remember is that you are nice sweet people. You are about to have a lot of temptation thrown your way, so try not to forget that.

Love,

John

Maybe too pithy. The letter upsets me; just now, Michael and I are nice sweet people to everybody but each other. Marriage . . . Here today, gone today. I pop half a Valium and look at my shaking hands. Shut up, I tell them.

When they do, I set about the arduous process of blow-drying my hair, then spicing it up with a curling iron. I swallow another three Valium halves and re-curl my hair as a chaser each time until it is time to get dressed. After I'm dressed, I have a little coke as a chaser for all that Val out of my secret stash. I don't offer Michael any. It would provoke a fight. I'm not into fighting with Michael tonight.

Universal has been kind enough to provide a limousine for us and Tony and Antoinette Bill, and David Ward and his wife, Chris. When I first met Antoinette Bill, everybody called her Mrs. Tony. Her given name was Antoinette, but she had gone under the name Toni all her life. Tony, who was in actual fact née Gerard Anthony Bill, was also called Tony. Somehow, Tony stayed and Toni became Mrs. Tony. I, of course, was outraged.

"You sound like his chattel," I told her at lunch at Ma Maison one day. I had just had my lip and legs painfully waxed by Charlotte at Elizabeth Arden's, which was making me bristle. The fact that Patrick had the restaurant wrapped in polyethylene, something my father participated in inventing, and that it was a hot day with too little air conditioning, might also have added to my dyspeptic worldview. "Isn't there something else I can call you?"

She smiled. "Well, my real name is Antoinette, but I always thought it was pretentious."

"Maybe when you were ten, but you're a grown-up married lady now with two kids and a husband named Gerard who likes to be called Tony, not that I blame him. I'm gonna call you Antoinette from now on. Okay?" I still asked permission in certain matters . . .

She grinned and flushed. "Why not? What the hell!" She laughed and toasted me with a glass of dry white wine.

I started calling her Antoinette; pretty soon some other people started calling her Antoinette; after awhile everyone but Tony called her Antoinette. One day she went out and had her checks, credit cards, license, passport—everything identifying her—changed to Antoinette Bill. I felt as good that day as I did the day Michael's mother, Sherry, started getting paid for finding the dresses that Michael's father, Larry, knocked off in his lower-priced dress line. I was a fucking one-woman consciousness-raising session . . .

.   .   .   .

Michael and I have to be the first to leave because we're in Trancas, which is as far away from the Dorothy Chandler Pavilion as you can be, and still live in the county of L.A. David and Chris live in Topanga Canyon, so we pick them up on the way into town. There is something very silly about being all duded up at three o'clock in the afternoon, sitting in the back of a stretch limo, but the door will be closed, the Academy has reminded us in numerous missives preceding the event, at six thirty promptly.

We have already split up Bill/Phillips Productions and there's bad blood between Tony and us. This isn't to become known until we are. Tony decides to drive himself and meet us there. He doesn't want to be Hollywood and arrive in a limo. If you really feel that way, I think, why go at all? Because we're going to win. This concept makes me as nervous as the thought of losing.

A limo provided by the studio for the producers and the writer is a truly grandiose gesture, given all previous behavior by Universal. Basically we have been treated as a nasty inconvenience to be just barely tolerated. By Zanuck and Brown. By George Roy Hill. Mostly by those who live in the Black Tower, sometimes referred to locally as the Black Mariah, the reflector-sunglass mausoleum that houses all the Universal Executives, both living and dead. To them, our youth, so chic at some of the other studios, is an impudence.

The day the nominations came out, and both those who had made *American Graffiti* and *The Sting,* a ubiquitously young group, had snagged an incredible number of honors for Universal, we received telegrams from the top two execs at Universal: Lew Wasserman and Sid Sheinberg.

SINCEREST CONGRATULATIONS AND BEST WISHES FROM ALL OF US AT UNIVERSAL FOR TEN ACADEMY AWARD NOMINATIONS, INCLUDING BEST PICTURE, FOR THE STING. LEW R. WASSERMAN

Not warm, but essentially correct.

CONGRATULATIONS FOR THE ACADEMY AWARD NOMINATION FOR AMERICAN GRAFFITI. THE FILM IN OUR JUDGEMENT IS AN AMERICAN CLASSIC AND DESERVING OF ALL OF ITS ACCOLADES. LET'S HOPE THERE ARE OTHER VENTURES THAT WE CAN SHARE WITH YOU IN THE FUTURE. SID SHEINBERG

Not warm, and incorrect in all its essentials.

I have this image of Sid's secretary: Well, all young people look alike, don't they? I've always wondered if the message Western Unioned to George Lucas congratulated him on the receipt of so many nominations for *The Sting.* I wonder if he kept his, too . . .

.   .   .   .

And now, here we are: Chris and David and Michael and Julia, flying along the Pacific Coast Highway, compliments of Universal Airlines, to the Dorothy Chandler Pavilion. I have nibbled another half a Valium at the Wards'. I've decided it's okay to carry Valium to the Academy Awards. Most of the people in the Academy are from the Valium-and-Alcohol Generation. I'm becoming a tad too relaxed behind it, though. Sleepy might be a better word.

Need a little hit, I think, as my head lolls around on my neck. Need a big hit, I amend. You have a big hit. *The Sting* . . . Not that kind of a hit . . . maybe coffee. If nothing else was around. I'm pissed at myself for leaving my secret stash behind. I focus on getting downtown, like that's going to make the drive quicker.

By the time we reach the exit to the Music Center, limousines are backed up onto the ramp. Behind us they stack up quickly. Limos to the left of me, limos to the right. A limo! A limo! My kingdom for a limo! It is a boiling-hot day and all the air conditioners are blasting. The hot and the cold mingles with the poisonous air; the exhaust makes a greenish brown cloud that hangs over us. I feel I am in line for the funeral of the most popular guy in Hollywood. Who could that be, I wonder . . .

The limousines, the cloud, the heat, make me think: We are all going to die. A thought I have two, maybe three hundred times a day anyway. I concentrate on Life and it makes me realize I have to pee semi-badly. At the rate we're moving, I won't get to check my makeup. I know the only part of my face that is glowing with health right now is my shiny forehead.

It's ridiculous to worry about how I look. There's a long red carpet; it is the only route to the door. The door that closes promptly at six thirty! There are barricades and cops and fans and photographers. Everywhere. We do not rate a flicker. There is nothing quite like being the only unknown in a bevy of luminaries. Unless it is to be the only name at a gathering of nobodies. If I had to vote for the lesser of two evils, as I do for my president, I'd go with anonymity. But I didn't know that then.

We walk along that red carpet, graced by Sally Kellerman in front of us and Paul and Linda McCartney behind us. Nobody reaches out to us. No Army Archerd interview. No hail-fellow-well-met interchange with milling celebs. An all-time Humbler. A year or two before, I'd have been amazed to be here. Now that I am, I can see that the only way to attend one of these events is as a star. We traverse the gauntlet in that casual way that says: I don't care to be noticed. I feel like a walk-on in a high-school play.

Of course, Tony and Antoinette are here already. We see Tony chatting up Steve Shagan, who's in competition with David Ward for Best Screenplay, and drinking, from the look around his mouth, his third glass of wine. He looks pretty cool in his tux. He looks like he belongs. Shagan insincerely wishes us luck. That's okay, I forgive him. He's insisted we hire Norman Garey, who acts as our lawyer and is truly our friend. I shift back and forth, no small feat on platforms four inches from the ground in the toe and probably six in the heel. It gives me the illusion that I am taking steps, presumably away, from a situation that makes me uncomfortable.

People are chatting, waving, drinking. Mostly they are checking their watches. I have felt the same palpable heat of anticipation on only two other occasions: The Band of Gypsies concert, New Year's Eve, 1968. Probably the last live Jimi Hendrix performance. The Rolling Stones at Madison Square Garden in 1972. The tour that ended at Altamont . . .

. . . .

People make their way to their seats. Apparently NBC or the Academy, whoever is running the show, expects *The Sting* and the *The Exorcist* to run neck and neck because nominated personnel for each film fill up the first three rows on opposite sides of the aisle. Gives me pause about Price-Waterhouse.

The very first production number features Liza. She's fabulous. Getting to be a real show stopper. Like Mama, which is what she always calls her famous mother. She's been Tony's friend for a long time, and Michael and I have met her a few times: once or twice, in fact, as a guest at our house at the beach. We introduced her to Redford out there. When she finishes, she winks at us. The ordeal we're about to endure for the longest hours of all my hours seems a bit more personal, more friendly.

To be perfectly fair, though, I had been partaking from a panoply of mood enhancers, stimulants, and depressants all day. Every once in awhile, I would strike upon the perfect chemical combination: for Oscar night it's been a diet pill, a small amount of coke, two joints, six halves of Valium, which makes three, and a glass-and-a-half of wine. So far. I have a warm and comfortable feeling of well-being.

This is greatly enhanced by *The Sting* picking up some awards. Best Editing. Best Music. Bill Reynolds and Marvin Hamlisch make nice acceptance speeches. They even thank us. Best Screenplay! David Ward, our pal, has won! My heart begins to samba in my chestal cavity. I hope it doesn't embarrass me by exploding. At least not before we win. *If* we win. I can barely hear David's acceptance speech over my internal din. Boomalacka Boomalacka . . .

One of the TV crew rushing around in front of me slips on some cable and steps on my foot. Hard. Just keeps going, too. Doesn't even apologize. He's with the team telecasting the event to one hundred million people or so, and he has more important things on his mind . . . he's only behaving the way everybody in The Business does: all is sacrificed on the altar of the show. Hey, whatever's good for the project. . . .

If you're fucking over your partner for the good of the project, that's different from just plain fucking him over. In fact, if you're fucking him over just for the hell of it, but you can make it seem like it's for the good of the project, you're applauded for being "professional." This poor son of a bitch is hurting my toes because they're in his way. He has to step on my feet for the good of the show. He does it to me several times during the course of the festivities; I'm finally forced to grab him by his bow tie and browbeat an apology and a promise from him that he won't do that anymore.

My mind is starting to wander and my mouth is getting dry and I have to take another nerve-pee. I know it's okay to get up and walk out because people have been doing it steadily throughout the night. The reason that we never see this on TV is that the second anybody vacates a seat, one of the staff working on the show, all of whom are dressed in formal attire, sits in the empty seat.

I clunk my way to the ladies' room in the Fred Slatten platforms. I promise,

Joel, I'll never go against you again. In the fashion department. The bar in the lounge holds Jack Lemmon up. Aloft. As it were. He waves as I pass. He doesn't know me at all. But he waves. Nice guy . . .

I pee, fix hair, remove shine from forehead, reapply lipstick. Have a hit of coke which I scrape from the inside of my purse. A little leftover from the last big occasion. Probably New Year's Eve. Swallow half a Valium dry. Check in the mirror. Perfect. I stop at the bar for a glass of water. On the loudspeaker I can hear the nominees for Best Actress being announced.

"We'd better go back in," Jack says merrily. "Our time's coming up." He takes my arm ceremoniously and walks me to the door. When we step through, we are engulfed in darkness.

"Someone's sitting in our seats," I whisper.

"No problem," he says vaguely and drops my arm. He ambles to his seat and sits on the NBC stand-in's lap. It gives me a giggle and the giggle gives me a rush. I edge my way back to my seat in the darkness. It is empty.

I study my program. It's just Best Actor, Best Director, and Best Picture. Redford's nominated for *The Sting,* but he doesn't win. Jack Lemmon does, for *Save the Tiger,* Shagan's picture. Based on our relationship at the bar, I feel personally involved, a tad miffed when he doesn't thank me. Redford doesn't attend and he's assigned Eileen Brennan, a featured player in the picture, to accept on his behalf; I think he should have assigned me, so deep down I'm glad he hasn't won. Even if he is in my movie. I am at the onset of what I think of as my Hollywood Period.

Everything about John Huston, presenter of the award for Best Director, is long: the tails of his jacket, his face, his vowels, his speech. He's drunk and hurls invective in a series of unfinished sentences at the audience for a good five minutes. This can be a v-e-e-r-y long time if you're just a category away from knowing if you've won an Oscar or not. Outside of president, or mondomondo rock 'n' roll star, it doesn't get much better for shallow capitalist American youth.

"And they tell the winners, Don't take too much time," Michael whispers. We laugh and squeeze clammy hands. Finally, Houston reads the nominees for the Best Director. And the winner is . . . George Roy Hill.

As George walks up the stairs to the stage, he winks at us. I look across the aisle and catch a brief glimpse of Billy Friedkin, nominated as Best Director for *The Exorcist.* His face seems a twisted portrait. Tentative title: Hatred and Loss. Not his fault. It's a guy thing.

During the course of the evening, the atmosphere of the Dorothy Chandler Pavilion has deteriorated to something fetid, not unlike the air in Tijuana. If you consider that a good portion of the audience is filled with nominees, you can imagine that the losing vibes become more and more profound as the ceremonies wear on. With each passing category, there are more and more—let us call them "nonwinners"—in the crowd. It's a wonder they can applaud at all, I think.

RE: the quintessential Hollywood gathering: incredible glamour—jewels, furs, limos—accompanied by the stench of loss.

David Niven comes out to introduce Elizabeth Taylor, who is presenting the award for Best Picture. Just as she is about to enter from stage right, a streaker cuts in front of her, runs naked across the stage. People shriek and cheer and howl when David Niven says something to the effect that there's a man making much ado about very little. When, somewhat shakily, Liz finally makes her entrance, she receives a standing ovation. As Michael and Tony stand, they button up their tuxedo jackets.

"Just remember *Cabaret*," I hiss into Michael's ear as we applaud. It won in all categories last year, but *The Godfather* won for Best Picture. Al Ruddy kept saying over and over, "You really had us worried there," and thanked Peter Bart and Bob Evans. Never mentioned Francis, the fool. Not the greatest public speaker. Not the greatest producer either.

Elizabeth Taylor is wearing a pastel sleeveless number. She has lost a considerable amount of weight. She is ample but still beautiful. She reads the nominees in her hushed, quasi-English voice. "And the winner is—oh, I'm so happy—*The Sting*."

I turn instinctively toward Michael and Tony, but they're already out of their seats and on their way to the stage. I toss my purse to Antoinette, per a prearrangement.

"See ya later," I say, and start to rise. Something is keeping me from getting out of my chair and it is strangling me at the same time. The pearls! They're caught on the arm of the chair. Michael has turned back. I'm ready to propel myself out of the chair and fuck the pearls, but he untangles me instantly. I'm pissed he's had to rescue me. I take a breath and reach out for him. The three of us walk up to the stage holding hands.

Liz steps to one side and puts the single award into my outstretched hands. I don't let go of it until it's wrested from me by an Academy official who says it has to be engraved. Her eyes really are violet. Tony steps up to the microphone and says something lame about being in the business for twelve years and having made all these friends and all this time in the business . . . He seems sullen, and his speech has no beginning and no end. His stepping away from the mike is the only signal that he is done, and the audience applauds pallidly.

Now it's my turn. I ease my way to the mike. I feel like I'm in a circus, walking on stilts. The lights seem very hot. I'm sweating. I can't see beyond the first three rows. Jack Lemmon and Walter Matthau are sitting next to each other in the first row. I address them. I fix a see-how-I'm-smiling grimace onto the lower half of my face.

"You can't imagine what a trip it is," I say, "for a nice Jewish girl from Great Neck to win an Academy Award and meet Elizabeth Taylor all in the same night."

Jack and Walter are laughing; so is the rest of the audience. I am enfolded into Liz's very famous cleavage. WHAT! A! RUSH! For somewhere between five and thirty seconds.

Michael does a nice wrap-up boogie about David Ward making it possible and George Roy Hill making it happen. Then he thanks me and Tony for bringing him into this business. We walk quickly into the wings, where Liza and George stand waiting.

"It still sage in the middle," Michael says to George. Liza kisses us. Liz teeters on very high heels right behind us; those amazing eyes vague somewhere in the middle distance.

"Has anyone seen my glass?" she whispers. No one has. She finds another. Beyond the darkness backstage is the Press Room, which emanates shafts of hot bright light. The group propels itself toward the light, moths toward the flame. Old Liz and old Liza know the bunch to stick with tonight. Most of the pictures in the papers the next day feature Liz and Liza, even though they aren't nominated for anything. Just now, Liza seems buzzed, Liz drunk, and I am getting sad.

Wait a second. Is this all there is? I wanna do it over. I feel cheated. Am I wrong to feel cheated? I feel like crying. I wanna go home. Take off my uncomfortable shoes. I wish the pearls had strangled me. I take a morose sip of Liz's drink and it makes my lips curl. E-e-e-u-u-uw . . . bourbon. The smell makes me pukey. The flashbulbs flash and the dumb questions commingle in the smoky air . . .

The portion of the evening that we spend at dinner at the Beverly Hilton passes in a blur. Lots of pats on the backs and people who ignored us a week before making sure to say howdy and congratulations. Hey, life's a trip . . . and then you get there.

.   .   .   .

Several days before, Frank Konigsberg, a heavy-duty agent in television at ICM, decides he's throwing us a Win Lose or Draw party. Frank has a house high on Miller Drive, where if you turn three hundred degrees your eyes are filled with both the Valley and La Cienega views. The city at night stretches around you, a land of light; from this high up it looks as if something is really going on down there. I wonder if attendance would be so high if we had lost.

We get out of the limo and walk toward the house and all Young Hollywood rushes us: Howard Rosenman ("You've given a lot of people hope"), Ron Bernstein ("Jewish girl from Great Neck—you'll go down in the annals of Oscardom"), Don Simpson ("I've got some good blow for you upstairs"), John Ptak

("J.P."), Andrea Eastman ("Big J!"), Paul Schrader (Unintelligible, spoken into armpit), Steven Spielberg, Peter Boyle, Michelle Phillips, Larry Gordon. Kisses, kisses, kisses. Behind them, hundreds of yet-to-bes fill the house.

Michelle is first out the door. Michelle is always first; it is her special gift. She dances around us jubilantly.

Once inside, Michael, Tony, and I quickly separate. Hey, it's the seventies. There's the party downstairs. Hi, howya doin', getcha' drink? Laughter. Bass line. Then there's the party upstairs. Guys. Drugs. Silence.

I'm upstairs in a jiff.

In all the fuss, I've heard Don's voice the most clearly. Need a hit. Simpson, Schrader, and Schrader's agent sit on the edge of the bed, passing around a gram bottle. In the half-light of the room, I can see coke lines forming around their mouths and under their cheeks. Why does that hardening always improve a man's looks, I wonder. And hurt mine.

They pass the bottle to me; I do two unsatisfying snorts per nostril. The coke is mediocre. Cut burns its way up my nose. I make a face. Generally, I don't like taking other people's drugs. For many reasons, not the least of which is you never know what you're getting. More important: with drugs, it's always better in the power equation if you give rather than receive. Particularly if you're a woman. Particularly with coke.

"I'm going downstairs," I blurt, and I'm out the door.

Antsy, I keep moving through and around people. I feel the incessant pounding of a heavy rock bass line coming from somewhere far away. Probably the next room. It syncopates with the throb of excitement around me. Now I'm being hugged and congratulated by Joan Didion and John Gregory Dunne. Joan wraps herself around me gracefully. In her profound childish whisper, sadly, "I'm so happy for you."

"Darling," John bellows.

They are drinking. I remember the first time I had dinner at their house. I'd let John Dunne mix my drinks. By the time the main course was served I was on my knees in the bathroom throwing up into the toilet. Jews shouldn't drink, I thought. Jews were not meant to drink. Drugs, money, sex, and dancing they could be good at, but rarely drinking. You had to learn that from childhood.

Since I was in their bathroom anyway, I checked their medicine cabinet. I always like to do that in a new house. Outside of my mother's, it was the most thrilling medicine cabinet I had ever seen. Ritalin, Librium, Miltown, Fioranol, Percodan . . . every upper, downer, and in-betweener of interest in the *PDR,* circa 1973.

"I got your letter this morning," I say to him as he hugs me warmly. He blushes. "I've got it in my purse," I lie. I move off toward the bass line.

"You don't really?" He's very pleased. He shouts after me but I'm out of verbal range. I turn, I nod, and I keep going . . .

.   .   .   .

Michael and Tony and I converge in the front hall of the house. What time is it?
I want to know. Three thirty, Michael says. He is the only one wearing a watch.

"Let's hit it!" we say simultaneously. We've been split for months and haven't
hung out much; tonight hasn't been a terrifically connecting experience, but here
it is. Another case of three-way mindlink. It has kept us going for longer than
we should stay. And here in this stranger's front hall, at a party that this stranger
is throwing for our victory, we experience that mindlink again.

"I'll just get my purse," I say, escaping the moment by running up the stairs.
Just one little hit for the road. Something to take away this sad little feeling. The
boys haven't moved from the edge of the bed.

"Anything left?"

"Sure," Don says coldly, and hands me a glassine package that must have held
an eighth at the beginning of the evening. The gram bottle has been retired, out
of stash, probably hours ago. I stick the fingernail of the pinky on my right hand
into the bag carefully.

It feels grainy. Like sand. I am just a speck of sand under the fingernail of a
larger being . . . This is not my favorite way to do coke. Maybe I just don't like
sticking my finger up my nose in front of people. I do a hasty two and two. Kiss
them in the general vicinity of their cheeks. Grab my purse. Leave.

Michael, Tony, and Antoinette are in the limo already. "Where did David
and Chris go?" I realize suddenly I haven't seen them for hours.

"Chris got pissed off because David was getting too much attention," Michael
says. "They left hours ago. Harry took them home."

Somewhere during the course of the evening, we've gotten on a first-name
basis with the limo driver, probably after we won. Why should the limo driver
be different from anyone else in Hollywood? When we drop the Bills off, we
hug and kiss and feel warm toward each other. Michael and I huddle together
in the backseat and Harry zooms up the Pacific Coast Highway. It is nearly five
ay-em. Dawn is coming on. We're hitting the beaches of Puerto Vallarta today.
This afternoon.

"Should we bother to sleep?" I ask.

"Nah. Let's pack and split."

"I'm not gonna take anything with me." Michael knows I mean no drugs.

"Good idea," he says. We'd had some end-of-a-long-night-doing-coke fights.
Nothing heavy, just enough to be scary. Ugly epithets exchanged. Perhaps a crystal piece or two thrown against a wall. A long day, here and there, of silent tears.

"Good idea," I repeat, trying it out. It doesn't sound too threatening. "Definitely using this time to clean up," I say. We'll be staying a week, per a plan we made together in happier times, not so long ago. I'll pass through my thirtieth birthday in five days, on foreign soil. I just hope I won't be deathly ill by then. I always get sick in Mexico.

I sit up. The sun creeps over the edge of the waves. It splashes the sea with an astonishing kaleidoscope of phosphorescent hues; an acid vision on the natch. Flashback to the first time I tried acid: I sat next to a pool for hours, completely enveloped in the changes on the surface of the water.

When we get home, we watch the sun come up, then fall asleep in our clothes. I awake with a start to the harsh persistent ringing of a phone. From its peremptory tone, I assume it is my mother. I pick up the phone anyway. Surprise!

"Well, well, how do you do," my mother-in-law, Sherry Phillips, chirps. Instinctively I turn to hand the phone to Michael, but I am alone in the bed. "Just a second," I say, covering the mouthpiece. "Michael," I holler, "your parents."

From somewhere down the hall in the living room, I hear him cooing to Kate. He picks up the other extension. Michael's parents tell us how proud they are and how excited they are and how cute we looked. Very supportive, everything one could ask for in parents. But I don't respect them, so their support doesn't count.

I take off my clothes and hang them up. I cream my face and wipe off last night's makeup. I scrutinize my face in the mirror. I look a hundred years old.

I swallow a diet pill and head out to the garage. I retrieve our one decent suitcase from a pile of stuff that we've shipped from New York City but never unpacked. Peter Boyle, who is renting Margot Kidder's and Jennifer Salt's house down the block, is walking slowly, deliberately, up our driveway. He looks like someone with a lot on his mind. When he sees me, he shoots me a reluctant smile. Wordlessly he takes the suitcase from me.

"Soooooo, whaddya think?" I ask as he lugs the suitcase down the hall to our bedroom. Sonya is making the bed. She smiles at me, something she does rarely. I guess she's proud. "I need some coffee," I say and point Peter toward the living room. Let's join Michael and Kate and leave Sonya to her chores.

Peter hugs Michael. Kate gurgles up at him.

"So, whaddya think?" Michael asks.

"I think that you should prepare yourself for a real education," Peter says seriously. "You're about to lose a lot of friends."

"Why?"

"Because people really like you best when you're struggling . . . when you're on the way up."

Michael and I are shocked into silence.

"The only thing they like better is if you're on the way down. That's the only way you have to go now."

"Hey, c'mon," Michael protests. "We're nowhere near where we plan to be."

"I'm just telling you the awful truth." Peter shrugs. "But, hey, what the hell do I know . . ."

The phone rings sharply. This time, no question, it's my mother. Both my parents are on the phone. They start out very excited. They liked the speeches. They want to know everything about the evening.

"I presume you wore the chicken feathers because you thought they were glamorous," my mother says sourly.

"What are you going to do for an encore?" my father asks.

Is this to be a stereophonic assault?

"Some women were talking about your speech in the elevator this morning," my mother adds, just for encouragement, "and decided you must be the daughter of someone in the business . . ." Hey, where's my congrats? Oh, I guess they forgot. And what about the L-word? It isn't mentioned, although the call is a long one. Not once . . .

For the next ten days, Michael and I try to reconcile in Puerto Vallarta. I sit in the sun too long and get a rash all over my body, necessitating a house call from a local doctor, who administers a shot of cortisone amidst a torrent of Spanish. I return with an arcane flu, which swells just about every major lymph node in my system, and spend the next six weeks in solemn retreat in my bed.

When it passes, I go back to work with a vengeance, ignoring Kate, ignoring Michael. Ignoring, most of all, myself. I do things that are harmful to my health. I drive too fast. I alter my consciousness with whatever is around, usually pot and coke, constantly. I openly tempt losers and bad guys and comedy writers.

Over the next couple of months, my relationship with Michael deteriorates beyond redemption and we separate.

July 29, 1974.

It is just two days before our eighth wedding anniversary.

Everything that rises must break up . . .

TITLE UP:

ROBERT STONE

Robert Stone is a novelist with some knowledge of Hollywood; his novels Hall of Mirrors *and* Dog Soldiers *were made into the films* WUSA *and* Who'll Stop the Rain? *In* Children of Light, *he set much of the action on a troubled Mexican film location, where a scene involving a character walking into the sea has inspired the filmmakers to consider what previous walking-into-the-sea movies they can steal from.*

from *Children of Light*

In a pink palazzo at the top of the hill, the Drogues and their womenfolk were whiling away the afternoon watching films in which people walked into the sea and disappeared forever. They had watched Bruce Dern in *Coming Home,* Joan Crawford in *Humoresque,* James Mason in the second *A Star Is Born* and Lee Verger in *The Awakening.* Now Fredric March and Janet Gaynor were on the out-sized screen before them. March stood clad in his bathrobe in the character of Norman Mayne.

"*Hey,*" he called to Janet Gaynor. "*Mind if I take just one more look?*"

Old Drogue picked up the remote-control panel and stopped the frame. His eyes were filled with tears.

"Listen to me," he told the others, "this guy was the greatest screen actor of all time. That line—the emotion under it—controlled—played exactly to movie scale. There was never anyone greater."

Joy McIntyre lay on some heaped cushions beside him, weeping unashamedly.

"Wellman was good," the younger Drogue said.

"The vulnerability," old Drogue said, "the gentleness, the class of the man. Never again a Fredric March. What a guy!" He let the film proceed and settled back with head on Joy's bare belly. "You see what I mean, sweetheart?" the old man asked his young friend. But Joy was too overcome to reply.

"Look at the nostrils on Gaynor," young Drogue said. "She acted with her nose."

"Do I have to remind you that she started before sound?"

"I love it," Patty Drogue said. *"Before sound."*

"She was ultra-feminine," old Drogue said.

The younger Drogue studied the images on the screen.

"Her face suggests a cunt," he said.

The old man sighed.

"I don't know why it does," young Drogue said. "It just does."

"You're a guttersnipe," Drogue senior said.

"Something about the woman's face, Dad. It makes a crude but obvious reference to her genitals."

"Some people are brought up in poverty," the old man said, "and they become cultivated people. Others grow up spoiled rotten with luxury and become guttersnipes."

"You look at her face," young Drogue declared, "and you think of her pussy." His brows were knotted in concentration. "Can that be the primal element in female sexual attraction? Can it explain Janet Gaynor?"

"People are surprised," Drogue senior said quietly, "when they find out you can get sex education lectures at the morgue. They're not in touch with the modern sensibility."

Joy was glaring sullenly at young Drogue. The old man shifted his position, the better to fondle her.

"What does he mean," Patty Drogue asked her husband, "sex education lectures at the morgue?"

"In San Francisco," young Drogue said absently. "The coroner explains about bondage. Pops got fixated on this."

On the screen, Fredric March's body double was wading toward the setting sun. This time it was Drogue junior who stopped the frame.

"This one was the best," his father said smugly. "Of all the walk-into-the-ocean movies this one was it."

"In the Mason and Judy Garland," his son told him, "the Cukor version, the scene's exactly the same. Frame for frame."

"The scene is conditioned by what's around it. The other one is a Judy Garland film. Entirely different thing."

Young Drogue went pensive.

"Well," he said, "with Judy Garland now, see, she . . ."

"Stop," his father said sternly. "I don't want to hear it. Whatever idiotic obscenities you were about to utter—keep them to yourself. I don't want to hear your sexual theories about Judy Garland. I want to go to my grave without hearing them."

"Some of us want to remember Judy the way she was," Joy McIntyre said primly.

"Who the fuck asked you?" young Drogue inquired.

Old Drogue kissed Joy on the thigh to soothe her.

"Ours is the best," the young director declared. "We took a great risk to honor the author's intentions. We had to reinvent a virtual chestnut because it was in the book."

"You're lucky you had a strong script," his father told him.

They watched Norman Maine's funeral and the end of the film.

"There was another Cukor version, right?" young Drogue asked. "Before Wellman's. It had a walk to the water, didn't it?"

"There was *What Price Hollywood?* by Cukor. It's a similar plot but it doesn't have anyone in the water."

"You sure?"

"Absolutely certain," the old man said.

JOHN WATERS

John Waters loves the movies, and more than any other director I can think of, he's a fan as well as a professional. He watches them, remembers them, savors them, and uses his status as a director to meet his heroes and heroines—sometimes casting such personal favorites as Tab Hunter, Troy Donahue, and Polly Bergen in his own films. In the opening chapter of his book Crackpot, *he provides a tour of Hollywood that includes stops far off the beaten path (Maureen's Problem Bras) and familiar sights seen in a new light (the Chinese Theater at 6:00 A.M., as Natalie Wood's footprints fill with water). This short essay suggests, in its own way, as much about the underside of Hollywood as anything I've ever read.*

"Tour of L.A."

Los Angeles is everything a great American city should be: rich, hilarious, of questionable taste and throbbing with fake glamour. I can't think of a better place to vacation—next to Baltimore, of course, where I live most of the time. Since I don't make my home in what the entertainment business considers a "real city" (L.A. or New York), I'm a perpetual tourist, and that's the best way to travel. Nobody gets used to you, you make new friends without having to hear anyone's everyday problems, and you jet back still feeling like a know-it-all.

Flying to L.A. is cheap. Make sure you get a window seat, so you can thrill to the horizon-to-horizon sprawl of this giant suburb and imagine how exciting it would be to see an earthquake while still airborne. In Sensurround yet.

There are millions of places to stay, either cheap or ridiculously opulent, but I recommend the Skyways Hotel (9250 Airport Boulevard), located directly under the landing pattern of every jumbo jet that deafeningly descends into LAX. "The guests complain, but we're used to it," confided the desk clerk on a recent visit.

Once you've checked into Skyways, change into something a little flashier than usual, then step outside your room and glance up at a plane that looks like it could decapitate you. If you're like me and think airplanes are sexy, you might want to plan a romantic picnic on nearby Pershing Drive. It's the closest you can humanly get to the end of the runway, where the giant 747s will scare the living bejesus out of you as they take off, inches over your head. There's even an airport lovers' lane (the 400 block of East Sandpiper Street), where dates with split eardrums cuddle in cars as the sound barrier breaks right before their eyes.

It's time now to rent a car, roll down the windows and prepare for your first big thrill: the freeways. They're so much fun they should charge admission. Never fret about zigzagging back and forth through six lanes of traffic at high speeds; it erases jet lag in a split second. Turn on the radio to AM—being mainstream is what L.A. is all about. If you hate the Hit Parade of Hell as much as I do, tune in to KRLA, an oldies station that plays *real* music, and listen for "Wild Thing," by the Troggs, which epitomizes everything you're about to see in Southern California.

You're now heading toward Hollywood, like any normal tourist. Breathe in that smog and feel lucky that only in L.A. will you glimpse a green sun or a brown moon. Forget the propaganda you've heard about clean air; demand oxygen you can *see* in all its glorious discoloration. Think of the lucky schoolchildren who get let out of class for smog alerts instead of blizzards. Picture them revving up their parents' car engines in their driveways before a big test the next day.

Turn off the Santa Monica Freeway at La Cienega and drive north. Never look at pedestrians; they're the sad faces of L.A., the ones who had their licenses revoked for driving while impaired. When you cross Beverly Boulevard, glance to the left and you'll see your first example of this city's fine architecture, the Tail O' the Pup, a hot-dog stand shaped exactly like what it sells. Turn left on Sunset Boulevard and take in all the flashy billboards created to stroke producers' egos. Be glad that Lady Bird Johnson lost her campaign to rid the nation's highways of these glittery monuments. Wouldn't you rather look at a giant cutout of Buddy Hackett than some dumb tree?

Proceed immediately to Trousdale Estates, the most nouveau of the nouveau riche neighborhoods. If anyone publishes a parody of *Architectural Digest,* this enclave should make the cover. It's true state-of-the-art bad taste, Southern California style. Every house looks like Trader Vic's. Now climb Hillcrest Drive to the top and shriek in amazement at Villa Rosa, Danny Thomas' garish estate, which boasts more security video cameras than the White House. Stop and gawk and wonder why he's so paranoid. Who on earth would want to assassinate Danny Thomas? It wouldn't even make the front page! Now detour to 590 Arkell Drive for the most outrageous sight of all—a house so overdecorated that it has curtains on the *outside.* Can wall-to-wall carpeting on the lawn be far behind?

.   .   .   .

When you get to Hollywood, you'll know it—it looks exactly the way you've always imagined, even if you've never seen a photograph. I always head straight for Hollywood Boulevard. Old fogies like Mickey Rooney are always dumping on this little boulevard of broken dreams, calling it a cesspool and demanding a cleanup. But they miss the point. Hollywood is supposed to be trashy, for Lord's sake. It helps to arrive around 6 A.M., so you can see the very small and oh-so-sick band of cultists who gather at Mann's Chinese Theatre (6925 Hollywood Boulevard) to witness Natalie Wood's footprints fill with water as the janitor hoses down the cement. Proceed up the street to the best newsstand in the world, the Universal News Agency (1655 North Las Palmas Avenue), and pick up *This Is Hollywood,* a guidebook that lists all the obvious tourist sights, like Diane Linkletter's suicide leap (8787 Shoreham Drive, sixth floor) and Kim Novak and Sammy Davis, Jr.'s love nest (780 Tortuoso Way). Further along the boulevard, you might encounter the legless, one-armed white guy who break-dances on the street for horrified families as they stroll up the Walk of Fame. Look around you and see all the real-life Angels (as in the film with the catch line "High-school honor student by day, Hollywood hooker by night") and the David Lee Roth impersonators. Marvel at the fact that Hollywood is the only town where everybody at least *thinks* they're cute.

Frederick's of Hollywood (6608 Hollywood Boulevard), that famous department store for closet hookers, is a must visit, not so much for the polyester imitations of their once-great line, but for a glimpse of their obscure CELEBRITY ROOM. There it was, at the top of the stairs, with a tacky star on the door and a twisted mannequin out front. "What celebrities go in there?" I asked a saleslady, so hard in appearance I'd swear she ate nails for breakfast. "Oh, you know, Liz Taylor," she said with a straight face. "Oh, sure," I thought, realizing I was dealing with a Pinocchio in stilettos. "Can I see the inside?" I pleaded. After much telephoning to various supervisors, I got a grouchy voice on the line that told me, "It's just a room." Finally, a manager, who could only be described as a dame, agreed to usher me in. "What celebrities come here?" I asked again. "None since I've worked here," she said, trying to position her body so I wouldn't see her use a credit card to jimmy open the lock. Finally inside, I felt like a fool. It was nothing more than a nondescript changing room that looked like it hadn't been used in years. Thanking her, I trotted back out to Hollywood Boulevard, feeling slightly more glamorous.

Since Liberace's museum is in Las Vegas, I recommend the next best thing: a visit to the Russ Meyer Museum (3121 Arrow Head Drive; by appointment only). If any director deserves to live so near the famed HOLLYWOOD sign, it's this great *auteur*. Revered for such movies as *Mudhoney, Common Law Cabin* and *Vixen,* featuring female stars with the biggest breasts in the world, Russ is now at work on his $1.5 million ten-hour swan song, *The Breast of Russ Meyer*. Five years in the making, with two more to go, Russ' movie is "an autobiographical film," he said, "with condensed versions of all my twenty-three films, with three ex-wives, five close girlfriends, army buddies and World War II, the most important part." I think he should rename it *Berlin Alexandertits.*

His museum includes one of the most incredible collections of movie memorabilia I've ever seen. Every wall is covered with astounding posters of all his movies. Volume after volume of leather-bound scrapbooks chronicle his thirty-year career. It's a virtual United Nations of Cleavage. Best yet is the "trophy room." There you'll find a display of memorial plaques, one for each film, listing titles and credits. Props from each set have been imbedded in the plaques. There's Kitten Natividad's douche bag from *Beneath the Valley of the Ultra Vixens,* a pair of biker sunglasses from *Motor Psycho,* even Tura Santana's famous black-leather glove from *Faster Pussycat! Kill! Kill!*

If you're lucky and a graduate student in Meyerology, the director might take you to the Other Ball (825 East Valley Boulevard, San Gabriel), an "exotic" dancing club where he discovered, and still looks for, buxom beauties. Since the liquor board apparently took away its alcohol license and one of the owners died, the club is not much fun anymore, but those supervixen types are still there and, for what it's worth, totally nude. As we exited, a guy passing by on a motorcycle yelled, "Pervert!" Now, I've been called a pervert before, but it's refreshing to be insulted for looking at nude women.

If you want to go farther "beneath the valley," stop by Maureen of Hollywood (1308 North Wilton Place), the costume designer for many of Russ' later opuses. It's hard to spot—the front window caved in "when the buiding settled"—but Maureen, a sweet and charming lady, is still there. Gone is her large sign, PROBLEM BRAS, indicating not mastectomy cases but undergarments for women whose "top wasn't consistent with their bottom." Or, as Russ puts it, "She likes to work with tits. She turns out really interesting things, but not in a tasteful way; she's strictly into sheer, bludgeoning exploitation. She's one of the last of the old Hollywood."

If you're looking for celebrities, the easiest one to find is Angelyne. She started her career by erecting giant billboards of herself in Hollywood (corner of Hollywood Boulevard and Highland Avenue), New York and London, displaying nothing but her likeness and a phone number. Dialing excitedly, I was thrilled that no one answered the first time—the ultimate in Hollywood attitude. Looking like a fifties glamour girl gone berserk, Angelyne drives around town in a hot-pink Corvette, wearing a matching, revealing outfit, blowing kisses to anyone who looks her way. She cheerfully responds to all comments, from "We love you, Angelyne!" to "Yo! Sit on my face!" Although she's making a record, she's currently famous for absolutely nothing.

Angelyne has everything it takes to become a star, but she has one fatal flaw: She has no sense of humor about herself. Every time she is queried about her past, she claims a "lapse of memory" and says her only heroine is "herself." When I asked if she identifies with the great Jayne Mansfield, she blasphemed, "Jayne went into the fourth dimension and copied me and did a lousy job." When she said, "I pride myself that I have more sex appeal with my clothes on than most girls have off," I wondered *who* would be attracted to this female female-impersonator. "I've got no competition" and "I'm very intelligent" were a few of her other humble remarks. Yes, Angelyne is a budding star and a vital part of the Hollywood community, but she desperately needs a new writer.

Of course, when you think about it, *everyone* in L.A. is a star. Idling in my car outside Charo's house (1801 Lexington Road, Beverly Hills), I spotted Charo's plumber, Leroy Bazzarone, pulling away in the company truck (John K. Keefe, Inc., Plumbing and Appliances, 9221 West Olympia Boulevard). Realizing he was more interesting in his own way than Charo, I called the company to get an interview, but I was juggled back and forth between the owner ("Is there any money in this?") and his son ("We're *very* busy!"). It dawned on me that Beverly Hills is the only community in the world where a plumber needs a press agent. After days of phone calls, it struck me that Charo's plumber was harder to meet than Charo *herself*.

Lana Turner's hairdresser, Eric Root (8804 Charleville Boulevard), was much more cooperative. I've been a fan of his ever since reading the *Daily Variety* account of Miss Turner's "rare public Hollywood appearance" at the Artistry in Cinema banquet of the National Film Society, where she "made a dramatic entrance on the arm of her young blond hairdresser." "I think she's an artiste," he told me, explaining that he and Miss Turner travel together but stay in "separate bedrooms, thank you." He does her hair once a week in the salon she had built in her penthouse. "She's got beautiful hair," he said. "I just changed her hairdo; I made it a little fuller. She likes it very close, precise. I softened it up for 'Night of 1000 Stars,' and it went over so well we're keeping it that way for a while." "Are there hairdresser wars?" I asked, wondering if beauticians try to steal celebrity clients from one another. "No," he sniffed, "when we go out together, we *don't* bump into *hairdressers*."

Much more elusive was Annette Funicello's garbageman. If you hang out all Wednesday night, the night she puts out her garbage (16102 Sandy Lane, Encino), you might spot him. His boss graciously declined to give out information, falsely assuming I wanted to look through Annette's cans. As I trembled with fear outside her house, looking over my shoulder for the ARMED SECURITY GUARD CONTROL that a posted notice on her lawn threatens you with, I sadly realized that I had missed the pickup and my chance to meet this mysterious trashman. Oh, well, maybe next trip.

Since visiting celebrity graves is an accepted tourist pastime in Los Angeles, I wanted to pay my last respects to the ultimate movie star, Francis the Talking Mule. Mr. Ed may be all the nostalgic rage these days, but Francis was the true original. Unfortunately, his final resting place is not listed in any guidebook, so the search for Francis had all the earmarks of a snipe hunt.

Most people I contacted laughed in my face. Even Universal's press agents came to a dead end. The Los Angeles SPCA Pet Memorial Park (5068 Old Scandia Lane) hadn't a clue ("But we have Hopalong Cassidy's horse"). The Pet Haven Cemetery-Crematory (18300 South Figueroa Street) had Jerry Lewis' and Ava Gardner's pets' graves, but explained that "a mule would be too large for a crematory." Wiping away a tear, I made a desperate, dreaded call to the California Rendering Company, "Buyer of Butcher Scraps, Fat, Bones" (4133 Bandini Boulevard), and was happy to learn that Francis hadn't ended up in this glue factory. Finally, through the grapevine, I located Donald O'Connor, Francis' on-screen costar. "Knowing the executives at Universal," he said, "they probably ate him. There was only one Francis, but he had a stand-in and three stunt mules. He was kept at the stables at Universal, and I heard he was forty-seven years old when he died. If you find Francis, let me know. We'll make another picture together."

Through the help of the Directors Guild, I found Francis' (*and* Mr. Ed's) great director, Arthur Lubin. Knowing that he was vowed to take the secret of how they made Francis talk with him to the grave, I didn't let on that Donald O'Connor had just spilled the beans. ("It didn't hurt Francis at all," Mr. O'Connor had told me. "They had two fish lines that went under the bridle, one to make him talk, the other to shut him up. There was a piece of lead in his mouth, and he'd try to spew it out. That's what made him move his mouth.") Mr. Lubin admitted that Mr. Ed was the smarter of his superstars ("Let's face it, a mule is dumb"), but relieved my anxiety by informing me that after Francis' career was all washed up ("We made five films; they thought that was enough"), the Humane Society placed him in a good home. Francis died on a nice ranch somewhere in Jerome, Arizona, a dignified star to the end.

. . . .

San Francisco may be known as the kook capital of the world, but isn't L.A. really more deserving of that much-coveted title? Think of the infamous crimes and colorful villains that have helped give this city its exciting reputation. Take a historical walk down Atrocity Lane and revisit some of the most infamous crime scenes of the century.

Start your day of touring madness by proceeding to Patty Hearst's SLA shoot-out scene (1466 East Fifty-fourth Street) in the heart of Watts. Gone is the charred rubble of the inferno where most of these media guerrillas met their death, but in its place is a spooky vacant lot that seems the perfect resting ground for the misguided rebels. The neighbors call it a "tombstone" and predict no one will ever build on this local battlefield. Across the street at 1447, Mr. Lafayette McAdory will show you his front door, still riddled with bullet holes, souvenirs of the shoot-out. Why hasn't he replaced it? It's "history," he said, waking from a nap on the couch in his garage. Another neighbor told me that the only people he sees snooping around are not tourists but cops, "to show the new ones where it happened." Patty Hearst may be a rehabilitated Republican now, but I wonder if she ever comes back and rides by, in the dead of night, shivering at the memory of what made her a household word.

Feel like going on a field trip? How about a visit to the Spahn Ranch (12000 Santa Susana Pass Road, Chatsworth), home of the most notorious villains of all time, the Charles Manson Family. There is nothing left, "not even a scrap," according to the new owner, but it's still worth the visit, if only to meditate. And if you use your imagination and look up into the mountains, you can still picture this demented Swiss Family Robinson, hiding out, plotting, about to make the cover of *Life* magazine. Make this trip soon, however, because even the grass won't be there much longer. Bulldozers are circling, about to eradicate the last trace of those "fires from hell." And what next? Tract homes? Spahn Acres? What about the pieces of ranch hand Shorty Shea's body, which were supposedly cut up and buried there? Will God-fearing, middle-class families discover a finger as they plant gardens in their new housing development?

Across the street, the Faith Evangelical Church is, ironically, under construction, and they are "quite well aware" of the situation. "We've had people who say there's a force of evil up there," a secretary told me over the phone. Even Gary Wiessner, the church business administrator, said, "The devil's still up there. I have felt his presence three times: at the Ethiopia-Somalia border, the Uganda border and at Spahn."

If you want to get really creepy, fast forward to 1985 and start following the McMartin School child-molestation case. It's the talk of L.A. The seven defendants, spanning three generations and charged with 115 counts of abuse and conspiracy, are despised by the public even more than the Manson Family in its heyday. An impartial jury is hard to imagine. The school itself (931 Manhattan Beach Boulevard), once very respectable, now sits like an obscene eyesore, vandalized by the community. The windows have been smashed, and the lawn dug up for evidence. Graffiti—RAY WILL DIE (defendant Raymond Buckey), RAY IS DEAD—echoes the city's lynch-mob attitude. What makes the scene especially macabre is the sight of children's rocking horses swaying in the breeze like props on the closed-down set of some horror flick.

The pretrial hearing (Judge Aviva K. Bobb's chambers, Municipal Court, Los Angeles Traffic Court, 1945 South Hill Street) is expected to last two years, and it's easy to get a seat. The McMartin defendants must be on hand every day, and they look nothing like the modern-day Frankenstein monsters the prosecutor would have you believe they are. Being open-minded, I had lunch with them. I have no idea if they're guilty or not, but they *do* present their innocence in a convincing way. Even Virginia McMartin, the seventy-seven-year-old matriarch of this clan, had a kind word or two. If you don't hold a cross up to them and scream, they will at least be friendly. After all, isn't lunch with the McMartin defendants more "drop dead" than, say, a lunch with Joan Collins?

Wondering how they could possibly feel, released on bail in their respective communities, I decided to do a little research. I attended a matinee of *The Care Bear Movie* by myself. The ticket seller gave me a funny look, maybe it was my sunglasses. The usher tore my ticket and snapped, "This is a children's movie, you know!" The theater was filled with harried mothers and their kids, many of whom were clutching Cabbage Patch dolls. I was the only adult male by myself and people actually moved away from me. I didn't dare make eye contact. Lasting only twenty minutes or so, I rushed from the theater, filled with anxiety, understanding a little better how Mrs. McMartin and her pals must feel every time they step out of the house.

If your vacation time is running out, there are still a few last-minute sights you may want to squeeze in. Try going to Venice Beach—the only place in Los Angeles that reminds me of the East Coast. Go directly to Muscle Beach (Ocean Front Walk between Eighteenth and Nineteenth avenues), but pay no attention to the pumping-iron showboats who exhibit themselves in a tiny cement arena surrounded by four tiers of tattered bleachers. Concentrate instead on their audience, and experience voyeurism of a new kind. Intently watching another voyeur as he voyeurs an exhibitionist is a thrill you probably won't get to experience at home.

Still feeling kinky? There's a downtown bar that will have to remain anonymous, but if what I heard is true, it sounds very *au courant*. Salvadoran sex changes are the main attraction, and in the spirit of LBJ pointing to his scar, these "girls" will show you their "operations" for $5.

As I finally boarded the plane back to Baltimore, I was so filled with the magic of L.A. I wanted to burst. Ignoring the stewardess' glare, I searched for an overhead compartment to store the "witch's-broom" (actually a dead palm) I found at Spahn Ranch. "You had to be there," I joked to a fellow passenger who quizzed me about my souvenir. During takeoff, I felt as if I might go insane from happiness over my wonderful vacation. Not wanting anyone to pop my bubble by speaking to me, I immediately began reading *Lesbian Nuns,* and that did the trick. No one attempted small talk. I had six blissful, silent hours remembering the heaven of being a tourist in L.A. I should have hijacked the plane and gone back.

APPENDIX

Sight & Sound
"The Greatest Films of All Time"

Every ten years, starting in 1952, the authoritative British film magazine *Sight and Sound* has polled an international cross section of cineasts and film critics, to determine the titles of the "ten greatest films of all time." Every such list is arbitrary, and many of the films that would be on the personal lists of typical moviegoers (*Gone with the Wind, Casablanca, Star Wars*) are scorned by the *S&S* voters.

Still, the lists provide a guide to the changing nature of cinematic reputations. In 1952, for example, Welles's *Citizen Kane* had been so little seen, especially outside the United States, that it didn't even make the list. By 1962 the film was securely in first place, where it has remained ever since.

Starting with the 1992 list, the magazine separated the votes of critics and directors. In all the previous lists it combined them.

What is the practical value of such a list? Younger film lovers sometimes want to know where to start in surveying the great films of the past. My advice is always: Start here.

THE 1992 LIST

Critic's Choices

1. *Citizen Kane,* Orson Welles
2. *La Règle du Jeu (The Rules of the Game),* Jean Renoir
3. *Tokyo Story,* Yasujiro Ozu
4. *Vertigo,* Alfred Hitchcock
5. *The Searchers,* John Ford

6. (tie) *L'Atalante*, Jean Vigo; *The Passion of Joan of Arc*, Carl Dreyer; *Pather Panchali*, Satyajit Ray; *Battleship Potemkin*, Sergei Eisenstein

10. *2001: A Space Odyssey*, Stanley Kubrick

Director's Choices

1. *Citizen Kane*, Orson Welles

2. (tie) *Raging Bull*, Martin Scorsese, and *8 1/2*, Federico Fellini

4. *La Strada*, Federico Fellini

5. *L'Atalante*, Jean Vigo

6. (tie) *Modern Times*, Charlie Chaplin; *The Godfather*, Francis Ford Coppola; *Vertigo*, Alfred Hitchcock

9. (tie) *Seven Samurai*, Akira Kurosawa; *The Passion of Joan of Arc*, Carl Dreyer; *Godfather II*, Francis Ford Coppola; *Rashomon*, Akira Kurosawa

THE 1982 LIST

1. *Citizen Kane*, Orson Welles

2. *La Règle du Jeu (The Rules of the Game)*, Jean Renoir

3. (tie) *Seven Samurai*, Akira Kurosawa; *Singin' in the Rain*, Stanley Donen and Gene Kelly

5. *8 1/2*, Federico Fellini

6. *Battleship Potemkin*, Sergei Eisenstein

7. (tie) *L'Avventura*, Michelangelo Antonioni; *The Magnificent Ambersons*, Orson Welles; *Vertigo*, Alfred Hitchcock

10. (tie) *The General*, Buster Keaton and Clyde Bruckman; *The Searchers*, John Ford

12. (tie) *2001: A Space Odyssey*, Stanley Kubrick; *Andrei Rublev*, Andrei Tarkovsky

14. (tie) *Greed*, Erich von Stroheim; *Jules et Jim*, François Truffaut; *The Third Man*, Carol Reed

THE 1972 LIST

1. *Citizen Kane*, Orson Welles

2. *La Règle du Jeu (The Rules of the Game)*, Jean Renoir

3. *Battleship Potemkin*, Sergei Eisenstein

4. *8 1/2*, Federico Fellini

5. (tie) *L'Avventura*, Michelangelo Antonioni; *Persona*, Ingmar Bergman

7. *The Passion of Joan of Arc*, Carl Dreyer

8. (tie) *The General*, Buster Keaton and Clyde Bruckman; *The Magnificent Ambersons*, Orson Welles

10. (tie) *Ugetsu Monogatari*, Kenji Mizoguchi; *Wild Strawberries*, Ingmar Bergman

THE 1962 LIST

1. *Citizen Kane*, Orson Welles

2. *L'Avventura*, Michelangelo Antonioni

3. *La Regle du Jeu (The Rules of the Game)*, Jean Renoir

4. (tie) *Greed*, Erich von Stroheim; *Ugetsu Monogatari*, Kenji Mizoguchi

6. (tie) *Battleship Potemkin*, Sergei Eisenstein; *The Bicycle Thief*, Vittorio de Sica; *Ivan the Terrible*, Sergei Eisenstein

9. *La Terra Trema*, Luchino Visconti

10. *L'Atalante*, Jean Vigo

THE 1952 LIST

1. *The Bicycle Thief*, Vittorio de Sica

2. (tie) *City Lights*, Charlie Chaplin; *The Gold Rush*, Charlie Chaplin

4. *Battleship Potemkin*, Sergei Eisenstein

5. (tie) *Louisiana Story*, Robert Flaherty; *Intolerance*, D. W. Griffith

7. (tie) *Greed*, Erich von Stroheim; *Le Jour Se Lève*, Marcel Carné; *Passion of Joan of Arc*, Carl Dreyer

10. (tie) *Brief Encounter*, David Lean; *Le Million*, René Clair; *Le Règle de Jeu (The Rules of the Game)*, Jean Renoir

ACKNOWLEDGMENTS

James Agee, excerpt from *A Death in the Family*. Copyright © 1957 by The James Agee Trust, renewed 1985 by Mia Agee. Reprinted with the permission of Grosset & Dunlap, Inc.

Woody Allen, "Snow White and the Seven Dwarfs" from *Playboy* (December 1969). Copyright © 1969 by Woody Allen. Reprinted with the permission of the author.

Nestor Almendros, "Matter of Photogenics" from *Projections: A Forum for Film Makers* (London: Faber and Faber, 1992). Copyright © 1992 by Nestor Almendros. Reprinted with the permission of the Estate of Nestor Almendros.

Kenneth Anger, excerpt from *Hollywood Babylon I* (New York: Straight Arrow Books, 1975). Copyright © 1975 by Kenneth Anger.

Sam Arkoff, excerpt from *Flying Through Hollywood by the Seat of My Pants*. Copyright © 1992 by Sam Arkoff. Reprinted with the permission of Citadel Press/Carol Publishing Group.

Lauren Bacall, excerpt from *By Myself*. Copyright © 1978 by Caprigo, Inc. Reprinted with the permission of Alfred A. Knopf, Inc.

Djuna Barnes, John Bunny interview from *Interviews*, edited with commentary by Douglas Messerli, pp. 119–124. Copyright © 1985 by Sun & Moon Press. Reprinted with the permission of the publisher.

André Bazin, "The Western; Or the American Film Par Excellence" from *What Is Cinema?, Volume II,* edited by Hugh Gray. Copyright © 1967 by The Regents of the University of California. Reprinted with the permission of University of California Press.

Robert Benchley, "Movie Boners" from *My Ten Years in a Quandary and How They Grew,* illustrated by Gluyas Williams. Copyright 1936 by Robert C. Benchley, renewed © 1964 by Gertrude Benchley. Reprinted with the permission of HarperCollins Publishers, Inc.

Ingmar Bergman, excerpt from *The Magic Lantern,* translated by Joan Tate. Copyright © 1987 by Ingmar Bergman. English translation copyright © 1988 by Joan Tate. Reprinted with the permission of Viking Penguin, a division of Penguin Books USA Inc.

Jeremy Bernstein excerpt from Jerome Agel, ed., *The Making of Kubrick's 2001* (New York: New American Library, 1970). Reprinted with the permission of the author.

Robert Bloch, "The Movie People" from *The Magazine of Fantasy and Science Fiction* (1969). Copyright © 1969 by Robert Bloch. Reprinted with the permission of the author's estate and the author's agent, Ricia Mainhardt, New York, New York.

Peter Bogdanovich, "Bogie in Excelsis" from *Esquire* (September 1964). Copyright © 1964 by Peter Bogdanovich. Reprinted with the permission of the author.

Joe Bonomo, excerpt from *The Strongman: A True Life Pictorial Autobiography of the Hercules of the Screen, Joe Bonomo* (New York: Bonomo Studios, 1968). Copyright © 1968 by Joe Bonomo.

Louise Brooks, excerpts from "Pabst and Lulu" from *Lulu in Hollywood.* Copyright © 1974, 1982 by Louise Brooks. Reprinted with the permission of Alfred A. Knopf, Inc.

Kevin Brownlow, excerpts from *The Parade's Gone By. . . .* Copyright © 1968 by Kevin Brownlow. Reprinted with the permission of Alfred A. Knopf, Inc.

Charles Bukowski, excerpt from *Hollywood.* Copyright © 1989 by Charles Bukowski. Reprinted with the permission of Black Sparrow Press.

Manny Farber, "Underground Films" from *Negative Space* (New York: Praeger, 1971). Copyright © 1971 by Manny Farber. Reprinted with the permission of the author.

Federico Fellini, excerpt from *Fellini on Fellini.* Copyright © 1976. Reprinted with the permission of Diogenes Verlag AG+ and Faber and Faber, Ltd.

F. Scott Fitzgerald, "Crazy Sunday" from *The Short Stories of F. Scott Fitzgerald.* Copyright 1932 by American Mercury, Inc., renewed © 1960 by Frances Scott Fitzgerald Smith. Reprinted with the permission of Scribner, a division of Simon & Schuster, Inc.

E. M. Forster, Prefatory Note from *Abinger Harvest.* Copyright 1936 and renewed © 1964 by Edward M. Forster. Reprinted with the permission of Harcourt Brace & Company, King's College, Cambridge, and The Society of Authors as the literary representatives of the E. M. Forster Estate.

Libby Gelman-Waxner, "Libby Noir" from *If You Ask Me.* Copyright © 1994 by Libby Gelman-Waxner. Reprinted with the permission of St. Martin's Press, Inc.

Brendan Gill, "Blue Notes" from *The New Yorker* (January 2, 1973). Copyright © 1973 by Brendan Gill. Reprinted with the permission of the author.

Interview with Buster Keaton by John Gillett and James Blue, from *Sight and Sound: A Fiftieth Anniversary Selection* (London: Faber and Faber, 1982). Copyright © 1982. Reprinted with the permission of *Sight and Sound,* British Film Institute.

Simon Gleave with Jason Forrest, "Frequently Asked Questions about Quentin Tarantino" (1996). Reprinted with the permission of Simon Gleave.

Graham Greene, "Memoirs of a Film Critic" from *The Graham Greene Film Reader: Reviews, Essays, Interviews, and Film Stories,* edited by David Parkinson. Copyright © 1993. Reprinted with the permission of Applause Theatre Books and International Creative Management.

Ben Hecht, excerpts from *A Child of the Century.* Copyright 1953 by Ben Hecht. Reprinted with the permission of the Estate of Ben Hecht.

Alfred Hitchcock, "My Own Methods" from *Sight and Sound: A Fiftieth Anniversary Selection* (London: Faber and Faber, 1982). Copyright © 1982. Reprinted with the permission of *Sight and Sound,* British Film Institute.

Bob Hope with Bob Thomas, excerpt from *The Road to Hollywood.* Copyright © 1977 by Bob Hope. Reprinted with the permission of Doubleday, a division of Bantam Doubleday Dell Publishing Group, Inc.

John Houseman, excerpt from *Run-through* (New York: Simon & Schuster, 1972). Copyright © 1972 by John Houseman. Reprinted with the permission of Joan Houseman and the Robert Lantz-Joy Harris Literary Agency, Inc.

John Huston, excerpt from *An Open Book.* Copyright © 1980 by John Huston. Reprinted with the permission of Alfred A. Knopf, Inc.

Christopher Isherwood, excerpt from *Prater Violet.* Copyright 1945 and renewed © 1973 by Christopher Isherwood. Reprinted with the permission of Farrar, Straus & Giroux, Inc.

Alva Johnstone, "The Wahoo Boy" from *Profiles from* The New Yorker (New York: Alfred A. Knopf, 1938). Originally published in *The New Yorker* (1934). Copyright 1934 by F-R Publishing Company.

Pauline Kael, "Tango" from *Reeling* (Boston: Little, Brown, 1976). Copyright © 1976 by Pauline Kael. Reprinted with the permission of Curtis Brown, Ltd.

Ryszard Kapuściński, excerpt from *Another Day in the Life.* Copyright © 1987, 1976 by Ryszard Kapuscinski. Reprinted with the permission of Harcourt Brace & Company.

Stanley Kauffmann, "Why I'm Not Bored" from *Before My Eyes: Film, Criticism & Comment* (New York: Harper & Row, 1980). Originally published in *The New Republic.* Copyright © 1974 by Stanley Kauffmann. Reprinted with the permission of Brandt & Brandt Literary Agents, Inc.

Klaus Kinski, excerpt from *Kinski Uncut,* translated by Joachim Neugroschel. Copyright © 1996 by Genevieve and Nanhoi Nakszynski. Reprinted with the permission of Viking Penguin, a division of Penguin Books USA Inc.

John Kobal, "Mae West" from *People Will Talk.* Copyright © 1986 by The Kobal Collection, Ltd. Reprinted with the permission of Alfred A. Knopf, Inc.

Howard Koch, excerpts from *As Time Goes By: Memoirs of a Writer* (New York: Harcourt Brace, 1979). Copyright © 1979 by Howard Koch. Reprinted with the permission of Anne Koch.

Akira Kurosawa, selections from *Something Like an Autobiography,* translated by Audie E. Bock. Copyright © 1982 by Akira Kurosawa. Reprinted with the permission of Alfred A. Knopf, Inc.

Spike Lee with Lisa Jones, excerpt from *Do the Right Thing.* Copyright © 1989 by Spike Lee. Reprinted with the permission of Simon & Schuster, Inc.

Janet Leigh with Christopher Nickens, excerpt from *Psycho: Behind the Scenes of the Classic Thriller.* Copyright © 1995 by Janet Leigh and Christopher Nickens. Reprinted with the permission of Harmony Books, a division of Crown Publishers, Inc.

Elmore Leonard, excerpt from *Get Shorty.* Copyright © 1990 by Elmore Leonard, Inc. Reprinted with the permission of Dell Books, a division of Bantam Doubleday Dell Publishing Group. Inc.

Oscar Levant, excerpts from *The Memoirs of an Amnesiac* (New York: G. P. Putnam's Sons, 1965). Copyright © 1965 by Oscar Levant. Reprinted with the permission of Gary N. DaSilva.

Dwight Macdonald, excerpt from *Dwight Macdonald on Movies.* Copyright © 1969 by Dwight Macdonald. Reprinted with the permission of Michael Macdonald.

Norman Mailer, "Tango, Last Tango." Copyright © 1982 by Norman Mailer. Reprinted with the permission of The Wylie Agency, Inc.

David Mamet, "The Tasks of a Director" from *Directing Film.* Copyright © 1991 by David Mamet. Reprinted with the permission of Viking Penguin, a division of Penguin Books USA Inc.

Groucho Marx, excerpts from *The Groucho Letters.* Copyright © 1967 by Groucho Marx. Reprinted with the permission of Simon & Schuster, Inc.

Terry McMillan, "The Wizard of Oz" from David Rosenberg, ed., *The Movie That Changed My Life* (New York: Viking Penguin, 1991). Copyright © 1991 by Terry McMillan. Reprinted with the permission of the author.

Anthony Quinn, "Neo-Realist Cowboys" from *One Man Tango*. Copyright ©
1995 by Anthony Quinn. Reprinted with the permission of HarperCollins Publishers, Inc.

Nicholas Ray, "James Dean: The Actor as a Young Man" from Susan Ray, ed.,
I Was Interrupted: Nicholas Ray on Making Movies. Copyright © 1993 by The Re-
gents of the University of California. Reprinted with the permission of Susan
Ray and the University of California Press.

Satyajit Ray, "A Long Time on the Little Road" from *Our Films, Their Films*. Copyright © 1976, 1994 by Orient Longman Limited (India) and Merchant-Ivory Productions, Inc. Reprinted with the permission of Hyperion.

Rex Reed, "Ava: Life in the Afternoon" from *Do You Sleep in the Nude* (New York:
New American Library, 1968). Copyright © 1968 by Rex Reed. Reprinted with
the permission of the author.

Jean Renoir, "D. W. Griffith" and "Le Regle du Jeu-1939" from *My Life and My
Films,* translated by Norman Denny. Copyright © 1974 by Jean Renoir. English
translation copyright © 1974 by Wm. Collins Sons & Co., Ltd., and Atheneum
Publishers, Inc. Reprinted with the permission of Scribner, a division of Simon
& Schuster, Inc.

Donald Ritchie, "Setsuko Hara" from *Japanese Film: Art and History*. Copyright ©
1982 by Princeton University Press. Reprinted with the permission of the publishers.

Jonathan Rosenbaum, "Rocky Horror Playtime vs. Shopping Mall Home" from
Moving Places: A Life at the Movies. Copyright © 1995 by The Regents of the University of California. Reprinted with the permission of the University of California Press.

Lillian Ross, excerpt from "Picture" from *Takes: Stories from* The Talk of the Town
(New York: Congdon & Weed, 1983). Originally appeared in *The New Yorker*.
Copyright © 1960 by The New Yorker Magazine, Inc. Reprinted with the per-
mission of the author.

Mike Royko, "Belushi's OK, But . . ." from *Like I Was Sayin'* (New York: E. P.
Dutton, 1984). Copyright © 1984 by Mike Royko. Reprinted with the permission of Sterling Lord Literistic, Inc.

Andrew Sarris, excerpt from *Confessions of a Cultist: On the Cinema 1955–1969* (New York: Simon & Schuster, 1970). Copyright © 1970 by Andrew Sarris. Reprinted with the permission of the author.

Delmore Schwartz, excerpt from *In Dreams Begin Responsibilities.* Copyright © 1961 by Delmore Schwartz. Reprinted with the permission of New Directions Publishing Corporation.

Martin Scorsese, excerpt from *Scorsese on Scorsese,* edited by David Thompson and Ian Christie. Copyright © 1990. Reprinted with the permission of Faber and Faber, Ltd.

Sight and Sound Best Movies of All Time Decade Polls. Reprinted with the permission of *Sight and Sound,* British Film Institute.

Susan Sontag, "The Imagination of Disaster" from *Against Interpretation.* Copyright © 1966 and renewed 1994 by Susan Sontag. Reprinted with the permission of Farrar, Straus & Giroux, Inc.

Robert Stone, "Of Light" (excerpt) from *Children of Light.* Copyright © 1985, 1986 by Robert Stone. Reprinted with the permission of Alfred A. Knopf, Inc.

Preston Sturges, excerpt from *Preston Sturges* by Anne and Tom Sturges. Copyright © 1990 by Anne Sturges. Reprinted with the permission of Simon & Schuster, Inc.

Andrei Tarkovsky, excerpt from *Sculpting in Time: Reflections on the Cinema,* translated by Kitty Hunter-Blair. Copyright © 1987 by Andrei Tarkovsky. Reprinted with the permission of Alfred A. Knopf, Inc.

Robert Lewis Taylor, excerpts from *W. C. Fields: His Follies and Fortunes* (New York: Signet, 1967). Copyright 1949, © 1967 by Robert Lewis Taylor.

David Thomson, "Norma Desmond" and "Rick Blaine" from *Suspects.* Copyright © 1985 by David Thomson. Reprinted with the permission of Alfred A. Knopf, Inc.

Michael Tolkin, excerpt from *The Player.* Copyright © 1988 by Michael Tolkin. Reprinted with the permission of Grove/Atlantic, Inc.

François Truffaut, "Orson Welles, Citizen Kane: The Fragile Giant" and "James Dean Is Dead" from *The Films in My Life,* translated by Leonard Mayhew. Copyright © 1975 by Flammarion. English translation copyright © 1978 by Simon & Schuster. Reprinted with the permission of Simon & Schuster, Inc.

Parker Tyler, "The Awful Fate of the Sex Goddess" from *The Meaning of Film.* Copyright © 1969 by Parker Tyler. Reprinted with the permission of Collier Associates.

Kenneth Tynan, excerpt from *Show People* (New York: Simon & Schuster, 1979). Copyright © 1979 by Kenneth Tynan. Reprinted with the permission of Roxane Tynan.

John Updike, "Suzie Creamcheese Speaks" from *Hugging the Shore.* Copyright © 1983 by John Updike. Reprinted with the permission of Alfred A. Knopf, Inc.

Gore Vidal, excerpt from *Hollywood.* Copyright © 1990 by Gore Vidal. Reprinted with the permission of Random House, Inc.

Gore Vidal, "Who Makes the Movies" from *The Second American Revolution and Other Essays (1976–1982).* Copyright © 1982 by Gore Vidal. Reprinted with the permission of Random House, Inc.

Andy Warhol and Pat Hackett, excerpt from *POPism: The Warhol 60's.* Copyright © 1980 by Andy Warhol. Reprinted with the the permission of Harcourt Brace & Company.

Robert Warshow, "The Gangster as Tragic Hero" from *The Immediate Experience* (New York: Atheneum Publishers, 1970). Copyright © 1962 by Joseph Goldberg. Reprinted with the permission of Paul Warshow.

John Waters, "John Waters' Tour of L. A." from *Crackpot: The Obsessions of John Waters* (New York: Macmillan Publishers, 1986). Copyright © 1986 by John Waters. Reprinted with the permission of Simon & Schuster, Inc.

Everett Weinberger, excerpts from *Wannabe.* Copyright © 1995 by Everett Weinberger. Reprinted with the permission of Citadel Press/Carol Publishing Group.

Nathanael West, excerpt from *Day of the Locust.* Copyright 1939 by the Estate of Nathanael West. Reprinted with the permission of New Directions Publishing Corporation.